European Product Liabilities

To our son,
Leo

European Product Liabilities

Second edition

Edited by:

Patrick Kelly
Partner, Solicitor, Laytons

Rebecca Attree
Solicitor, Attree & Co

Butterworths
London, Edinburgh, Dublin
1997

United Kingdom	Butterworths a Division of Reed Elsevier (UK) Ltd, Halsbury House, 35 Chancery Lane, LONDON WC2A 1EL and 4 Hill Street, EDINBURGH EH2 3JZ
Australia	Butterworths, SYDNEY, MELBOURNE, BRISBANE, ADELAIDE, PERTH, CANBERRA and HOBART
Canada	Butterworths Canada Ltd, TORONTO and VANCOUVER
Ireland	Butterworth (Ireland) Ltd, DUBLIN
Malaysia	Malayan Law Journal Sdn Bhd, KUALA LUMPUR
New Zealand	Butterworths of New Zealand Ltd, WELLINGTON and AUCKLAND
Singapore	Reed Elsevier (Singapore) Pte Ltd, SINGAPORE
South Africa	Butterworths Publishers (Pty) Ltd, DURBAN
USA	Michie, Charlottesville, VIRGINIA

A CIP Catalogue record for this book is available from the British Library.

ISBN 0 406 03256 4

Printed and bound in Great Britain by Butler & Tanner Ltd, Frome and London

Preface

Every year defective products cause millions of accidents resulting in personal injury and property damage in Europe. The liabilities arising from such accidents are a key concern to those involved in the manufacture and sale of products in Europe. The rights granted to consumers to enforce such liabilities reflect a trend of increased consumer protection in Europe which is to be welcomed. Indeed the consumer protection laws of EU countries have developed significantly over the last decade. Since the first edition, two important Directives have been issued, namely, the Product Safety Directive and the Unfair Contract Terms Directive. There have also been important developments in European case law which add further rights to consumers.

The need to know and understand the rights and liabilities established by these laws is a pre-requisite to the ability to export, manufacture and distribute consumer goods successfully. This book offers a practical guide to those laws, and the steps to be taken as a result of them. To achieve this, we have brought together contributions from leading practitioners in the field of consumer product liabilities in their respective jurisdictions. We are pleased to include contributions from Finland, Greece, Scotland and Northern Ireland in addition to those countries covered in the first edition. Each chapter has been updated and specifically refers to the national implementation of the Product Safety Directive and the Unfair Contract Terms Directive. In addition to the country specific sections, we have included chapters dealing with an overview of EC Product Liabilities Law, international considerations, risk management and insurance. There is also a 'bird's eye view' of European product liabilities for those seeking an executive summary. The law is stated as at June 1996.

We would like to thank each of the contributors without whom this book would not, of course, have been possible. We are also grateful to Elaine Gardiner, Stephen Macartney, Lynn Richards, Lorna Roberts and Nicola Warner of Laytons for their help in producing this book. Last but not least we are grateful to Butterworths for their support in publishing the second edition of this book.

Patrick Kelly, Laytons   October 1996
Rebecca Attree, Attree & Co

Contributors

Rebecca M Attree
Attree & Co
110 Cambridge Street
London SW1V 4QF
England
Tel: ++ 44 171 630 6019
Fax: ++ 44 171 630 8681

D Granger Brash
Alex Morison & Co WS, Solicitors
Erskine House
68 Queen Street
Edinburgh EH2 4NN
Scotland
Tel: ++ 131 226 6541
Fax: ++ 131 226 3156

Sonia Cortés
Bufete Mullerat & Roca
Avda Diagonal, 640 4°
08017 Barcelona
Spain
Tel: ++ 34 3 405 9300
Fax: ++ 34 3 405 9176

Muriel de Courreges
Salès Vincent & Associés
56 rue Notre Dame de Lorette
75009 Paris
France
Tel: ++ 33 1 42 80 63 73
Fax: ++ 33 1 42 66 58 95

Gabriele Dara
Studio Legale Morgante-Dara
Via Villa Sperlinga 5
90144 Palermo
Italy
Tel: ++ 39 91 30 34 79
Fax: ++ 39 91 62 53 172

Rene Diederich
Loesch & Wolter Avocats
11 Rue Goethe
BP 1107
L-1011 Luxembourg
Tel: ++ 352 48 11 48-1
Fax: ++ 352 49 49 44

Kaisa Fahllund
Heikki Haapeniemi Oy
POBox 232
Mannerheimintie 14B
00101 Helsinki
Finland
Tel: ++ 358 9 177 613
Fax: ++ 358 9 653 873

Hugh Garvey
LK Shields & Partners
39/40 Upper Mount Street
Dublin 2
Ireland
Tel: ++ 3531 661 0866
Fax: ++ 3531 661 0883

Patrick Kelly
Laytons
Carmelite
50 Victoria Embankment
Blackfriars
London EC4Y 0LS
England
Tel: ++ 44 171 842 8000
Fax: ++ 44 171 842 8080

Manuela von Kuelgelgen
Stibbe Simont Monahan Duhot
Rue Henri Wafelaerts 47-51 (box 1)
1060 Brussels
Belgium
Tel: ++ 32 2 533 5211
Fax: ++ 32 2 533 5212

Georg Lett
Lett & Co
Borgergade 111
DK – 1019 Copenhagen K
Denmark
Tel: ++ 45 33 12 00 66
Fax: ++ 45 33 12 12 66

Klaus-Ulrich Link
Lichtenstein, Körner & Partners
Heidehofstrasse 9
70184 Stuttgart 1
Federal Republic of Germany
Tel: ++ 49 7 4 11 89 79-0
Fax: ++ 49 7 11 4 81 57 7

Dr Peter Madl
Schönherr Barfuss Torggler &
Partners
Tuchlauben 13
(Eingang Kleeblattstrasse 4)
Postfach (POB) 41
A-1014 Vienna
Austria
Tel: ++ 43 1 534 370
Fax: ++ 43 1 533 2521

Wilhelm Matheson
Wiersholm, Mellbye & Bach
PO Box 400 Sentrum
0103 Oslo
Norway
Tel: ++ 47 22 400 600
Fax: ++ 47 22 410 600

David McFarland
Culber & Martin
Scottish Provident Buildings
7 Donegall Square West
Belfast BT1 6JB
Ireland
Tel: ++ 1232 325508
Fax: ++ 1232 438669

Ramon Mullerat
Bufete Mullerat & Roca
Avda Diagonal, 640 4°
08017 Barcelona
Spain
Tel: ++ 34 3 405 9300
Fax: ++ 34 3 405 9176

Jorge Santiago Neves
Santiago Neves & Associados
Av Eng° Duarte Pacheco,
Empreendimento das Amoreiras
Torre 2, 10° Piso
1070 Lisbon
Portugal
Tel: ++ 351 1 381 43 93
Fax: ++ 351 1 387 18 82

Gus J Papamichalopoulos
Kyriakides & Partners
6 Queen Sophia Avenue
106 74 Athens
Greece
Tel: ++ 30 1 7243 072
Fax: ++30 1 7250 670

Dr Thomas Sambuc
Lichtenstein, Körner & Partners
Heidehofstrasse 9
70184 Stuttgart 1
Federal Republic of Germany
Tel: ++ 49 7 4 11 89 79-0
Fax: ++ 49 7 11 4 81 57 7

Harri Salmi
Heikki Haapeniemi Oy
POBox 232
Mannerheimintie 14B
00101 Helsinki
Finland
Tel: ++ 358 9 177 613
Fax: ++ 358 9 653 873

Lucien Simont
Stibbe Simont Monahan Duhot
Rue Henri Wafelaerts 47-51 (box 1)
1060 Brussels
Belgium
Tel: ++ 32 2 533 5211
Fax: ++ 32 2 533 5212

Pernille Solling
Lett & Co
Borgergade 111
DK – 1019 Copenhagen K
Denmark
Tel: ++ 45 33 12 00 66
Fax: ++ 45 33 12 12 66

DA Thomas
Willis Corroon Limited
Willis Corroon House
Wood Street
Kingston-upon-Thames
Surrey KT1 1UG
England
Tel: ++ 44 181 787 6290
Fax: ++ 44 181 943 4297

Michael Thornton
Laytons
22 St John Street
Manchester M3 4EB
England
Tel: ++ 44 161 834 2100
Fax: ++ 44 161 834 6862

Lila Vassilaki
Kyriakides & Partners
6 Queen Sophia Avenue
10674 Athens
Greece
Tel: ++ 30 1 7243 072
Fax: ++ 30 1 7250 670

Christer Wagenius
Advokatfirman Wagenius & Partners
HB
Box 1393
251 13 Helsingborg
Sweden
Tel: ++ 46 42 19 96 60
Fax: ++ 46 42 13 00 62

Stan SH Wibbens
Rasker Duvekot & Wibbens
Herengracht 503
1017 BV Amsterdam
Netherlands
Tel: ++ 31 20 62 70 370
Fax: ++ 31 20 62 69 287

Contents

CHAPTER I

Overview of EC Product Liabilities Law

Patrick Kelly, Esq

Laytons
Carmelite
50 Victoria Embankment
Blackfriars, London
EC4Y 0LS

Tel: ++ 44 171 842 8000
Fax: ++ 44 171 842 8080

CHAPTER I

Overview of EC Product Liabilities Law

This chapter is divided into three sections. The first deals with some of the EC legislative framework which underlies issues dealt with by this book. It outlines the relevant articles of the Treaty of Rome as amended by the Single European Act and the Maastricht Treaty. It moves on to consider the contribution of EC case law to consumer protection and consumer law policy adopted by the European Community. Finally it very briefly reviews some of the legislative outcome of that policy.

The second section considers three particularly relevant Directives and one draft Directive:

1. Council Directive 85/374/EC on the approximation of the laws, regulations and administrative provisions of the member states concerning liability for defective products of 25 July 1985 ('the Product Liability Directive');
2. Council Directive 92/59/EEC on General Product Safety issued on 29 June 1992 ('the Product Safety Directive');
3. Council Directive (93/13/EEC) concerning Unfair Contract Terms ('the Unfair Contract Terms Directive'); and, finally
4. the draft Directive on consumer guarantees and after sales service as issued on 18 June 1996.

The third section of this chapter summarises rights and remedies created by Community law for consumers which are enforceable in national courts or before the European Court of Justice.

This legislative framework, (both at the level of the Treaty of Rome and the level of Council Directives as interpreted through the European Court of Justice with a growing body of case law), creates substantial new rights for consumers as well as additional liabilities for manufacturers and sellers of defective products.

The developments in case law may not always be so easy to understand at first sight, additionally it may be difficult to appreciate their practical significance to manufacturers, consumers and sellers. Nevertheless such decisions of the European Courts of Justice are becoming of greater importance as its decisions now permit businesses and consumers in each community country:

(a) to bring claims for damages against member states who fail to implement Directives; and
(b) in certain circumstances the right directly to enforce provisions of community law against others where such Community law has Direct Effect.

1   EC LAW BACKGROUND

1.1   Summary of relevant provisions of the Treaty of Rome (as amended)

1.1.1   Original position

The 1957 Treaty of Rome only made passing reference to consumer protection policy in the European Union as follows:

(a) In the preamble, which refers to an essential objective of the Community being 'the constant improvement of the living and working conditions of their peoples'.
(b) The above provision is referred to in article 2 as an objective of the Common Market being the promotion of 'harmonious development of economic activities, a continuous and balanced expansion, an increase in stability, an accelerated raising of the standards of living'.
(c) Article 39 which provides that one of the aims of the Common Agricultural Policy is to ensure that supplies reach consumers at reasonable prices;
(d) Article 85 which gives the Commission power to exempt certain agreements between undertakings subject to conditions (inter alia) that the consumer will 'receive a fair share of the resulting benefit'.
(e) Article 86 which deals with competition policy by prohibiting companies abusing dominant positions with the effect of 'limiting production, markets or technical development to the prejudice of consumers'.

1.1.2   Amendment to the Treaty of Rome by the Single European Act 1986

The introduction of article 100a into the Treaty by the Single European Act 1986 which came into force on 1 July 1987 changed the capacity of EC institutions to adopt consumer protection measures by permitting the Commission to make proposals on the internal market 'concerning health, safety, environmental protection and consumer protection' and the base of such protection would be a high level.

The Single European Act also gave more flexibility in the introduction of consumer policy by permitting the Council of Ministers to take certain decisions by qualified majority in relation to completion of the internal market, including those relating to consumer protection. Prior to this legislative amendment, unanimity had been required.

1.1.3   Amendments to the Treaty of Rome by the Treaty on European Union ('the Maastricht Treaty')

The Maastricht Treaty, which came into effect on 1 November 1993, amended article 3(s) of the Treaty of Rome to provide:

> that the activities of the Community shall include as provided in this Treaty and in accordance with the timetable set out herein:-
>
> ....(s) a contribution to the strengthening of consumer protection.

The Maastricht Treaty also provided that article 129a be amended to read as follows:

> 1. The Community shall contribute to the attainment of the high level of consumer protection through:

(a) measures adopted pursuant to article 100a in the context of the completion of the internal market;

(b) a specific action which supports and supplements the policy pursued by the Member States to promote the health, safety and economic interest for consumers and provide adequate information to consumers.

2. The Council acting in accordance with the procedure referred to in article 189b and after consulting the Economic and Social Committee shall adopt the specific action referred to in paragraph 1(b).

3. Action adopted pursuant to paragraph 2 shall not prevent any Member State from maintaining or introducing more stringent protective measures. Such measures must be compatible with this Treaty. The Commission shall be notified of them.

This provision gave power to the underlying provisions in the Treaty of Rome including article 3(a) (dealing with free movement of goods); article 3(f) (dealing with competition law), articles 30-36 (prohibiting quantitive restrictions on exports and imports) and articles 85 and 86 (dealing with rules on competition).

The amendments to the original Treaty of Rome therefore enabled much more significant steps to be taken within the European Union to bring about developments in consumer rights.

1.2 The contribution of EC case law to consumer protection

1.2.1 Three strands of cases

There are three strands of cases that are particularly important from the point of view of consumer protection. These are, first, cases interpreting articles 30-36 of the Treaty of Rome[1] and second, the case of *Alsthom v Sulzer*[2] recognising differences in national law and third, those dealing with interpretation of articles 85 and 86 on competition policy.

1.2.2 Cases involving articles 30-36

Articles 30-36 provide that quantitative restrictions on imports and exports shall be prohibited between member states. However, certain prohibitions or restrictions may be justified on grounds, inter alia, of public policy and the protection of health and life (including the health and life of consumers) and certain property rights.

Article 30 provides:

Quantitative restrictions and measures having equivalent effect shall, without prejudice to the following provisions, be prohibited between Member States...

Article 36 provides:

The provisions of articles 30-34 shall not preclude prohibitions or restrictions on imports, exports or goods in transit justified on grounds of public morality, public policy or public security. The protection of health and life of humans, animals or plants, the protection of national treasures possessing artistic, historic or archaeological value or the protection of industrial and commercial property. Such

---

1 For a detailed analysis of these cases, I would refer the reader to Peter Oliver *Free Movement of Goods in the European Community under Articles 30 to 36 of the Rome Treaty*, Sweet & Maxwell 1996.

2 Case 339/89 *Alsthom v Sulzer* [1979] ECR 120.

prohibitions or restrictions shall not, however, constitute a means of arbitrary discrimination as a disguised restriction on trade between Member States.

The most important cases pursuant to articles 30 to 36 of the Treaty of Rome in this area are those of *Cassis de Dijon*,[3] *Dassonville*[4] and *Keck and Mithouard*.[5] The *Cassis de Dijon* and *Dassonville* cases recognise that, while consumer protection is an implicit requirement of articles 30 and 36, national laws including consumer protection measures which are likely to hinder, directly or indirectly, actually or potentially intra community trade, amount to quantitive restrictions that are prohibited under article 30 of the EC Treaty. Thus, if a product is legitimately manufactured and sold in one member state, it must be given access to the market of other member states. However, member states may, if they wish, apply more restrictive conditions in relation to products made and sold in that same jurisdiction. The decision in the *Cassis de Dijon* case was underlined in its importance by the Commission issuing a Communication dealing with its consequences.[6]

In the *Dassonville* case it was therefore provided that consumer protection measures which are to be valid must meet the criteria of being:

(a) reasonable;
(b) necessary;
(c) equally applicable to domestic and imported products; and
(d) not constituting a disguised restriction on trade between member states.

The limit to the case law under articles 30 and 36 has been set by the *Keck and Mithouard* decision. The Court stated (inter alia):

> In 'Cassis de Dijon' it was held that, in the absence of harmonisation of legislation, measures of equivalent effect prohibited by article 30 included obstacles to the free movement of goods where they are the consequence of applying <u>rules that lay down requirements to be met by goods</u> (such requirements as to designation, form, size, weight, composition, presentation, labelling, packaging) to goods from other Member States where they are lawfully manufactured and marketed, even if those rules apply without distinction to all products unless their application can be justified by a public interest objective taking precedence over the free movement of Goods.

> However, contrary to what has been previously decided the application to products from other Member States of national provisions <u>restricting or prohibiting certain selling arrangements</u> is not such as to hinder directly or indirectly actually or potentially, trade between Member States within the meaning of the Dassonville judgment provided those provisions apply to all affected traders operating within the national territory and provided that they affect in the same manner in law and in fact the marketing of domestic products and those from other Member States.

> Where those conditions are fulfilled, the application of such rules to the sale of products from another Member State meeting the requirements laid down by that State is not by nature such as to prevent their access to the market or to impede access any more than it impedes the access of domestic products. Such rules therefore fall outside the scope of article 30 of the Treaty.

The important distinction being made is between rules on the one hand 'that lay down requirements to be met by goods' and 'selling arrangements' on the

3   Case 120/78 *Rewe-Zentral AG v Bundesmonopolverwaltung fur Branntwein* [1979] ECR 649.
4   Case 8/74, *Procureur du Roi v Dassonville* [1974] ECR 837.
5   C-267, 268/91 *Keck and Mithouard* [1993] ECR 6097.
6   [1980] OJ C256/2.

other hand. Although article 36 does not expressly provide that measures designed to enhance consumer protection are expressly within its ambit, it has been clear certainly since the *Cassis de Dijon* case that a measure otherwise falling foul of article 30 may be justified on grounds of consumer protection under article 36.

1.2.3 Alsthom v Sulzer

In a separate line of cases, probably the most significant decision of the European Court of Justice on national legislation relating to consumer rights and their differences in member states is *Alsthom v Sulzer*. While this case dealt with commercial disputes between businesses, the Court held that the national law provisions containing guarantee conditions which are more favourable to consumers in one country than another cannot be considered as contrary to Community law. The case indicated the disparity of national laws and how these can affect a company's competitive position within markets.

1.2.4 Competition law cases

The third line of cases influencing consumer rights and in particular those in relation to guarantees of consumer goods and after sales service have been those brought as a result of the competition law provisions of the Treaty of Rome.

This line of cases is very well described in the European Green Paper on guarantees for consumer goods and after sales service.[7] Community policy on producer guarantees has been based on competition law.

This policy was initially defined in 1977 in the Seventh Report on Competition Policy by the Commission.[8]

However, as the Green Paper concludes:[9]

...the contribution of community competition law to the development of the European Guarantee System and to consumer rights has some major limitations from a perspective of consumer protection, including:

(a) competition law merely obliges the producer who offers a guarantee to ensure that the guarantee will be honoured throughout the Community without regulating either the existence of the guarantee or its content, or the conditions invoking it;

(b) competition law concerns only business activities which come within the ambit of the law of concerted practices or dominant positions;

(c) competition law imposes certain obligations on firms; however, it does not create rights which the consumer can rely on ....; and

(d) competition law as such does not contribute either to harmonisation of guarantees or to the transparency necessary with a view to their application.

7   (COM 93) 509 at page 60.
8   The subsequent building blocks of the policy have included Commission Decision of 23/10/78 (Zanussi), OJ No L322 of 16/11/78, P36 and Commission Decision 10/12/84 (Ideal Standard), OJ No L20 of 24/1/85, P38; Hasselblad Judgment 21/2/84, Case 86/92, ECR 1984, P.883, ETA (Swatch) Judgment 10/12/85, Case 31/85, ECR85, P3933 and Commission Regulations Nos.123/85 of 12/12/84 (OJ No L 17 of 18/1/85) Distribution of Motor Vehicles and 4087/88 of 30/11/88, OJ No L359 of 28/12/88, P46 (Franchising Agreements).
9   At page 65.

It is against the legislative background set out above and the interpretation of that law by the European Court of Justice that the developments in consumer rights policy and the legislative fruits of such policy are considered below.[10]

1.3   Summary of EC Policy on Consumer Protection

1.3.1   Policy

The first significant development in consumer protection policy in the EC was the Consumer Protection and Information Programme adopted by the Council on 14 April 1975.

The Council of Ministers subsequently prepared an action plan and set out five fundamental consumer rights that should be promoted by the consumer policy:

(a) the right to protection of health and safety;
(b) the right to protection of economic interests;
(c) the right of redress;
(d) the right to information and education; and
(e) the right of representation.

This preliminary programme sowed the seeds, inter alia, for the Unfair Contract Terms Directive and the Product Liability Directive.

The second consumer programme was introduced in 1981[11] to follow on from the preliminary programme. This second programme was (inter alia) the birthplace of the Draft Directive on Guarantees for Consumer Goods.

The third programme[12] was launched in 1986 and amongst other things proposed the measures in relation to General Product Safety, as well as introducing a certain harmonisation in standards through what were known as 'new approach' Directives that set out basic principles with relevant Standards Authorities being empowered to specify detailed provisions.

These three consumer programmes were followed by two three-year Action Plans: one for 1990-1992[13] and the other for 1993-1995.[14] The Product Liability Directive having come to fruition in 1985 was followed by the adoption by the Council of the General Product Safety Directive in 1992 and further developments occurring with other product safety directives within specific areas.

The second three-year action plan started the process of implementing the General Product Safety Directive into national law by 1994 and, inter alia, produced the Green Paper on Guarantees for Consumer Goods and After Sales Service that has now resulted in a draft Directive on this subject.

---

10   The text of the first part of this Chapter is derived from a lecture I gave at the 13th annual Anti Trust Law Conference held by ESC Conferences in Cambridge in September 1995. For a much fuller and more authoritive accounts of the subject, I would refer the reader to Chapter II, The Development of EC Consumer Protection by Monique Goyens in *EC Consumer Safety* by Tony Ascombe and Ann Stoneham, Butterworths 1994 and to *EC Consumer Law*, Vivienne Kendall, Wyley Chancery 1994.
11   OJ C133 3.6.81 pl.
12   COM (85) 314 final of 27 June 1985.
13   OJ C294 22.11.89 pl and COM (90) 98 final of 3 May 1990.
14   COM (93) 378 final of 28 July 1993.

1.3.2 Legislative Outcome of EC Policy on Safety and Consumer Protection

The EC programme on consumer protection and safety has resulted in a formidable array of Directives and Regulations that have been implemented into the laws of member states with very considerable willingness. These are briefly and not exclusively summarised in the Table set out in Appendix 4 on page 631.

2 SUMMARY OF PRINCIPAL RELEVANT EC DIRECTIVES

2.1 The EC Product Liability Directive, 25 July 1985[15]

2.1.1 Council Directive 85/374/EC

This Directive on the approximation of the laws, regulations and administrative provisions of the member states concerning liability for defective products was issued on 25 July 1985. It was notified to the member states on 30 July 1985 and was to have been implemented in all the member states by 25 July 1988. By 1996 it had been implemented in all countries save France. As this book shows in each of the national chapters, the Directive has not been implemented identically in each member state. This section summarises and explains the principal provisions and implications of the Directive.

2.1.2 Objective

The Directive was issued to implement throughout the European Community a strict liability system to compensate consumers for death, personal injury or damage to personal property due to defects, industrial produce and movable products.

2.1.3 The system

The system to be implemented by the Directive introduced a fundamental change to the law relating to manufacturers' liability for defective products in many of the member states. Before the introduction of the Directive in the United Kingdom and Ireland, strict product liability was not available under national law to the consumer as a cause of action against the producer of products. In some other member states, an element of strict liability had been introduced where the burden of proof had been reversed in cases of claims in tort for defective products. The new system introduced by the Directive supplemented the then prevailing systems of consumer protection for defective products. It was designed to afford additional protection, co-existing with other consumer rights, whether based upon contract or tort law. Consumer rights which went beyond its scope were not precluded by the new law. Hence the national laws of member states may indeed in some cases continue to provide consumer rights whereby the producer of the product is strictly liable for defects without limit.

---

15 This section on the Product Liability Directive and section 3 on the enforcability of EC Law are both derived from the chapter on the EC Product Liability Directive by Andrew Turner which appeared in the first edition of this book.

The Directive therefore sought to introduce a system under which there were prescribed minimum consumer rights, upon which consumers throughout the European Community could rely and according to which producers would be responsible.

2.1.4   *The structure*

The Directive broadly divides into the following areas:

(a)   liability;
(b)   burden of proof;
(c)   defences;
(d)   compensation;
(e)   limitation;
(f)   implementation.

2.1.5   *Liability*

Article 1 provides that 'the producer' shall be liable for 'damage' caused by a 'defect' in his 'product'. This article sets out the basis upon which the Directive is formulated. It introduces the concept of liability without the need to prove fault. The obligation on a producer under article 1 arises solely from the fact of the supply of defective goods and there is no need for the consumer to prove more. The *fault basis of liability in tort does not* provide a consumer with a right of action against the manufacturer or supplier of defective products where:

(a)   there is no contractual link;
(b)   the consumer is unable to show that the manufacturer (or supplier) owed him an imposed legal duty to take care which was breached by the supply of the defective product; or
(c)   he is unable to prove that the manufacturer (or supplier) failed to comply with a particular consumer safety or health and safety at work law relating to the product.

The 'strict liability' approach extends the liability of manufacturers (and suppliers) to members of the public injured and who suffer loss through defective products 'without' the need to prove a contractual link, a duty of care and failure to take reasonable care or failure to comply with relevant legislation.

i   The producer   Under article 3, the producer means not only the manufacturer of a finished product but also the producer of any raw material or the manufacturer of a component part and includes any person who, by putting his name, trademark or other distinguishing feature on the product, presents himself as the producer.

Unless the person responsible for selling the product to the consumer is also its producer, he will not be primarily liable except in those limited circumstances discussed below, or under some other general principle of national law, for example in contract or tort.

Any person who imports into the European Economic Area a product for sale, hire, lease or any form of distribution in the course of his business shall be responsible as if he was its producer. This rule is fundamentally important: it ensures the consumer should have a right of action against a party in the European Economic Area, where the actual producer is not within the European Economic Area. However, on its true construction, the rule may enable an

importer to avoid liability provided the products brought into the European Economic Area are imported for use, as opposed to distribution.

If the producer cannot be identified, then each and every supplier is to be treated as if he was in fact the producer, except where he informs the claimant, within a reasonable time, of the producer's true identity or of the person who supplied the product to him. This rule is also to apply where an imported product does not indicate the importer's identity, even though the name of the producer is indicated.

The definition of 'producer' gives rise to a number of uncertainties: first, the liability of co-producers will be joint and several. The ability of the co-producer to obtain a contribution or indemnity from another co-producer will generally depend upon whether the applicable law allows for a right of contribution or recourse. In an international claim of this sort, the question of governing law will depend upon whether the right of contribution or indemnity is classified as a right in contract, tort or sui generis. Second, what constitutes a 'reasonable time' within which the identity of the next person in the chain of supply should be revealed, is unclear.

Finally, the Directive is unclear as to those details which must be given on a product (or its packaging) to identify the supplier, importer or producer; this will fall ultimately to be determined by national law which will often derive from specific EC product safety directives.

ii The damage For there to be a cause of action against a producer, damage must be caused by his product (article 1). Under article 9, 'damage' means:

(a) damage caused by death or by personal injury;
(b) damage to or destruction of any item of property other than the defective product itself within a minimum threshold of Ecu 500, provided that the item of property:
  (i) is of a type ordinarily intended for private use or consumption; and
  (ii) was used by the injured person mainly for his own private use or consumption.

Consequently, in an action for damaged property, the loss sustained must not be less than Ecu 500,000 and the property damaged must be goods for private use or consumption as opposed to business property, for example, damage caused to a company car would be excluded.

Article 9 states the definition of 'damage' is without prejudice to the national law relating to non-material damage. According to the Directive's recitals 'non-material damage' includes pain and suffering and such other non-material loss arising under the applicable national law. This may preclude actions for 'non-material damage' under the Directive if there is a restriction on claims brought under national law.

An alternative interpretation would be that claims for 'non-material damage' are permitted only where they may be brought under the relevant national law. On this basis, the Directive might provide a convenient route for claimants for defective products, such as the drug Thalidomide, to claim compensation for pain and suffering. Article 16.1 links the limits on maximum liability to damage resulting from death or personal injury. Whether claims of pain and suffering are included within those for death and physical injury is unclear from the Directive. It is not clear therefore whether member states have authority to limit the maximum compensation payable for pain and suffering. Limitations on liability are discussed in section 2.1.9 of this chapter.

iii   The product   Under article 2, 'product' means physical property and goods (viz movables), as opposed to land or rights in or in relation to real property (eg a house) and could include a whole product, part of another product or part of a fixture attached to a property (eg a light switch). Electricity is expressly included: primary agricultural products and game are excluded, even where they are incorporated into another product. (Article 15.1(a) allows member states to provide for 'products' to include primary agricultural products and game which would otherwise be excluded.)

Primary agricultural products are products grown in the soil, of stock farming or fisheries, but not those products which have undergone 'initial processing'. Determining at what point a prime agricultural product finishes being 'produce' and commences 'initial processing' may cause difficulty.

To illustrate this difficulty by way of an example, live cattle in a field are probably not yet 'a prime agricultural product', not having been slaughtered. They might, however, be 'defective' if the scientific link can be proved by virtue of having been given contaminated feedstuff during their life which could potentially cause a person eating them to suffer Creutzfeldt Jakobs Disease if on slaughtering them their spinal cord was not properly removed, as prescribed by slaughterhouse regulations. The cattle only finish being produced at their moment of death, at which time they become primary agricultural products. The potential defect contained in the product just described only becomes an actual defect at the time of initial processing in the slaughterhouse. Thus, any product liability claim that may arise will in this example lie against the slaughterhouse and not against the farmer.

iv   Defect   The definition of a defect is based on expectations of safety. It is not clear from the Directive if this expectation is objective or subjective. This is because a product is defined as defective when it does not provide the safety which a person is entitled to expect, taking all the circumstances into account, including:

(a) the presentation of the product;
(b) the use to which it could reasonably be expected that the product would be put; and
(c) the time when the product was put into circulation (article 6.1).

Thus, in the drafting of the Directive, it is not clear whether 'a person' is the person who is actually injured, who may be particularly sensitive or susceptible to injury or is a person judged by an objective standard being of ordinary sensitivity and susceptibility to injury.

The use to which the product could reasonably be expected to be put is likely to depend on its presentation and, for example, any instructions on the packaging. This is considered in further detail in chapter 2. The producer's responsibility may be further limited, or even removed, when, having regard to all the circumstances, it is concluded that the damage caused to the victim is both due to the defect in the product and also to the fault of the injured person or any person for whom the injured person is responsible (article 8.2). The effect is similar to contributory negligence.

The Directive is unclear as to the point in time when the product enters into circulation and therefore when a product first becomes defective. It does not specify whether this relates to the first sale of the product by the manufacturer or the date of subsequent sales by others in the chain of supply.

It is not even clear that the product is the specific product which caused damage, rather than the class of products to which it belongs.

Article 6.2 provides that a product will not be defective solely because a better product is subsequently put into circulation. Consequently, provided a dangerous product is believed to be safe on first circulation, it may be offered for sale to unknowing purchasers until the producer subsequently becomes aware of the risk. At such time the producer will become aware of the fact that a use to which a product could reasonably be expected to be put would be one that does not provide all the safety to which a person is entitled to expect. Whether under article 6.2 'circulation' occurs on sale from manufacturer to supplier or supplier to end-user is unclear.

2.1.6   *Burden of proof*

Article 4 provides that the 'injured person shall be required to prove the damage, the defect and the causal relationship between defect and damage'.

Article 4 is difficult to reconcile with article 7(b) (see below) under which a producer is not to be liable if he proves that, 'having regard to the circumstances, it is probable that the defect which caused the damage did not exist at the time when the product was put into circulation by him or that this defect came into being afterwards'. Article 7(b) implies that to avoid liability the producer has only to prove that he complied with the general duty of care which he might have been expected to perform in manufacturing and supplying products.

The producer might therefore be able to rely on Article 7(b) if he shows that he took reasonable steps to ensure that a defect in the product did not exist when the product was put into circulation by him. He could thereby show that the defect probably did not exist at that time.

Likewise, it is hard to reconcile article 4 with article 8.2, under which liability may be limited or removed altogether because the injured person was in some way jointly responsible with the defect for the damage caused (see section 2.1.5.iv above).

2.1.7   *Defences*

Article 7 provides the producer with six defences. The burden of proving the defences lies with the producer. The defences are as follows:

(a) *The producer did not put the product into circulation.* This would apply for example to equipment constructed for the producer's own use or to equipment in the course of manufacture.

(b) *Having regard to the circumstances, it is probable that the defect which caused the damage did not exist at the time when the product was put into circulation by the producer, or that this defect came into being afterwards.* This contradicts the fundamental principle of strict liability that there is no need to prove fault. It appears that the defence may be satisfied merely by the producer providing that he complied with the general standard of care (section 2.1.6 above), although this may not be easy some time after the product was produced unless appropriate procedure is undertaken during manufacture and adequate records of such testing are kept.

(c) *The product was neither manufactured by the producer for sale or any form of distribution for economic purpose nor manufactured or distributed by him in the*

course of his business. This is intended to take account of goods made as prototypes or supplied as gifts or 'good works' for charity.

(d) *The defect is caused by compliance of the product with mandatory regulations issued by public authorities.* Hence, compliance with voluntary standards would not provide a defence.

(e) *The state of scientific and technical knowledge at the time when the producer put the product in circulation was not such as to enable the existence of the defect to be discovered: this is known as 'the state of the art' defence.* Not only must the producer be ignorant of prevailing scientific and technical knowledge but there must be a universal lack of knowledge of the defect at that time. This therefore places a very high duty on producers who wish to rely on this defence; not only must they properly research the technical background to their product before they put it on the market but also during the life of the product and the time when they continue to put it into circulation they must remain aware of all scientific and technical developments that may affect its safety. It is unclear whether by virtue of the real producer succeeding with this defence, importers or other re-sellers would then be excused in the event that a defect becomes known subsequent to circulation, but prior to importation or resale.

The 'state of the art' defence does not as such require that upon subsequent discovery of a defect the product concerned should be recalled or that the public be notified, but other provisions of the Directive, such as article 6.1 may require that the product is discontinued. Other obligations under other laws in various countries, for example the English law of negligence or the provisions of the General Product Safety Directive, may request a recall or a notice to be given to the public of a defect when it is discovered.

Member states have a general discretion whether or not to incorporate this defence within their national legislation. Here, the Directive fails to address the conflict of laws which will arise where the sale of products occurs from a country excluding this defence to another country in which it is included; it does not indicate which law will apply. The ordinary international rules for determining applicable law are discussed in chapter XVII and will therefore have to be applied by the national court in which the action is commenced.

(f) *In case of a manufacturer of a component, it will be a defence that a defect is attributable to a design of the product in which the component has been fitted or to the instructions given by the manufacturer of the product.* Sub-contractors may therefore rely on product specification as a defence – and it appears that the knowledge of the sub-contractor of the defect would not prevent the defence applying.

2.1.8   Compensation

Rules for quantification of loss sustained by a victim of the defective product are not set out in the Directive. It simply sets out parameters within which national law must operate.

As discussed in section 2.1.5.ii above in an action for damage to property, the loss sustained must not be less than Ecu 500. It is not clear whether the first Ecu 500 of loss sustained would be recoverable and whether co-existing routes to compensation would have to be followed, for example insurance, contract or by fault-based proceedings in tort, for the balance (article 9). Indeed, the various member states interpreted this provision in different ways in their

implementing national laws. No upper parameter is set for a damages award, although member states may limit liability in this regard (see below).

Non-material damages, which include pain and suffering and may also include loss of enjoyment or loss of earning capacity, would appear to be subject to no such limits (see section 2.1.5.ii above).

In their implementing legislation, member states have the option to limit compensation for damage caused by death or personal injuries arising from a defect to not less than Ecu 70m. This limit applies whether a single product or to a class of products (article 16.1).

As mentioned above, the Directive fails to set out rules for dealing with the conflict of laws, therefore the ordinary rules of international law governing the applicable law would need to be followed. It is unfortunate that the point was not taken up since it is likely, where a discrepancy between national laws exists, that the victim will wish to assert his rights in the court of the country of the least limitations. For the producer, this adds uncertainty as to his liability from one member state to another. The potential for discrepancy means insurance policies need either to be geared to an unlimited basis of liability or carefully checked to ensure an appropriate level of cover representing a maximum limit for each member state in which the product may be circulated. The opportunity for member states to incorporate this limit within their legislation was presumably intended to give producers certainty as to their maximum liability.

2.1.9   Limitations

These broadly divide into three categories: time, liability and compensation. Compensation has been dealt with in section 2.1.8 above.

There are two principal rules governing the time permitted for bringing an action. Under article 10, the time period within which actions may be commenced is limited to the period of *three years* from the earlier of the following two dates:

(a) the day on which the plaintiff *became aware* of the damage, the defect and the identity of the producer;
(b) the date on which the plaintiff *should reasonably have become aware* of the damage, the defect and the identity of the producer.

This limitation period is, however, subject to national law regulating suspension or interruption of limitation periods generally. This means, for example, that in the UK where the victim is a minor, eg a person under eighteen years of age, the three year time limit may be suspended until the victim is no longer a minor. Once again, the uniformity of application which was a primary objective of the Directive has not been obtained.

An overall time limit is also imposed for bringing an action (article 11). Ten years after the date on which the producer put into circulation the *actual* product causing the damage, the right to institute proceedings against the producer is extinguished. This rule is mandatory and cannot be overridden by laws of member states regulating suspension. Hence, although a three year period can be suspended, such suspension will not be allowed if it would cause the ten year rule to be exceeded. However, the Directive fails to define at what point 'circulation' of the product occurs. If circulation were to occur when the manufacturer first sells the product to the supplier, then that could cause problems for the end user. The interval between the time of sale by the

manufacturer to the supplier and the time of sale by the supplier to the end user may exceed ten years. If that period was taken into account, then the time limit could run out before the end user had even purchased the product! It is likely that the widest possible interpretation will apply so that the time limit runs from circulation by the retail supplier on the basis that he is deemed also to be the producer (see section 2.1.5.i above). In turn, the supplier would then have a right of action under national law against the person from whom he purchased the product, and likewise up the chain.

The Directive provides that the producer's liability to an injured person may not be contractually limited or excluded.

2.1.10 Implementation

The Directive should have been implemented in the laws of every member state on or before 30 July 1988, applying to products put into circulation after the date on which the implementing legislation was effective. The Directive was introduced on time in less than one third of the member states, however, as at 1 May 1996 all countries with the exception of France had passed implementing legislation. Even where legislation has been passed, a number of member states, including the UK, have failed to implement the Directive correctly. Discrepancies in national law are discussed in subsequent chapters describing the law in each relevant country and highlighted in Appendix 2 to this book.

It is therefore important to consider the extent to which individuals are able to enforce the rights the Directive intended them to have. They may be prevented from doing so because of the non-existence or defective implementing legislation. This is considered later in section 3 of this chapter (see below).

2.1.11 Review

Under article 21, every five years the Commission shall present a report to the Council on the application of the Directive and, if necessary, shall submit appropriate proposals to it. The first such report has been prepared but has not recommended any significant change to the Directive.

2.2 The EC General Product Safety Directive of 29 June 1992

2.2.1 Introduction

The Council Directive (92/59/EC) on general product safety concerns the obligations on producers to place only safe products on the market, that is to say to comply with the Directive's general safety requirement. Distributors and others in the supply chain additionally should not supply products which do not comply with the general safety requirements of the Directive.

This Directive came into force in the European Union on 29 June 1992. The member states were required to implement national legislation by 29 June 1994. This section summarises and explains the principal provisions and implications of this Directive.

This Directive, while based on article 100a of the Treaty of Rome and being a measure to harmonise the laws of member states as part of the Single Market Programme, also has its origin as a consumer protection measure within the Commission's consumer programmes originating during the Commission's First Three Year Action Plan.

Prior to the introduction of the General Product Safety Directive, most EC safety law comprised a series of safety measures which concentrated on narrow sectors of products, such as toys, electrical equipment, construction products, machinery, personal protective equipment etc. Some of these vertical Directives that comprehensively cover all the safety aspects of certain classes of products include the New Approach Directives, eg toys, machinery, electro-magnetic compatablity etc.

The Product Safety Directive was designed to create general rules for product safety for all consumer products horizontally across the range of all such products, insofar as specific vertical safety Directives had not provided specific safety requirements for such products. The General Product Safety Directive was to apply to 'fill in the gaps' or to 'sweep up safety measures in those areas not already specifically covered'. This is a theoretically simple approach which in practice gives rise to considerable difficulty in deciding whether a particular product safety requirement falls to be dealt with only under one or more specific vertical Directives and/or under the horizontal General Product Safety Directive.

2.2.2 Objectives

The objectives of the Directive are harmonisation of national laws within the Community within a specific area; introduction of the general safety requirement in the manufacture of consumer products and the setting up of appropriate measures to enforce the general safety requirement, including the setting up of a system of rapid exchange of information in emergency situations in respect of the safety of products.

2.2.3 The system

The system to be introduced into the national laws of member states by this Directive is:

(1) the laying down of a manufacturing standard to apply where other standards have not otherwise been laid down by the EC. This is to ensure that products placed on the market are safe; and
(2) the setting up of local enforcement authorities in each country. These authorities have primary power to enforce the Directive as set out in national law.

In particular, each country, insofar as it did not already have such organisations, shall be obliged to give its relevant enforcement organisation appropriate power with a view, inter alia, to:

(a) organising appropriate checks on the safety properties of products, even after their being placed on the market as being safe, on an adequate scale, up to the final stage of use or consumption;
(b) requiring all necessary information from the parties concerned;
(c) taking samples of the product or product lines and subjecting them to safety checks;
(d) subjecting product marketing to prior conditions designed to ensure product safety and requiring that suitable warnings be affixed regarding the risks which the products may present;
(e) making arrangements to ensure that persons who might be exposed to a

risk from a product are informed in good time and in a suitable manner of the said risk by, inter alia, publications of special warnings;

(f) temporarily prohibiting, for the period required to carry out the various checks, anyone supplying, offering to supply or exhibiting a product or product batch, whenever there are precise and consistent indications that they are dangerous;

(g) prohibiting the placing on the market of a product or product batch which has proved dangerous and establishing the accompanying measures needed to ensure that the ban is complied with;

(h) organising the effective and immediate withdrawal of a dangerous product or product batch already on the market and, if necessary, its destruction under appropriate conditions (article 6).

Where a member state takes measures to restrict placing a product or product batch on the market or requires its withdrawal, the State must notify the Commission of the measures it has taken and reasons for doing so. This is not necessary when the measures taken are not local in effect and are just limited to the territory of the member state concerned or the restriction order was not made pursuant to other specific product safety laws. The Commission has power after consultation with the relevant member state to consider whether a measure taken by that member state was justified or not (article 7). Any such decision by the Commission would of course be subject to review by the Court of Justice.

Where a member state adopts or decides to adopt emergency measures to prevent, restrict or impose specific conditions on the possible marketing or use in its own territory of a product or product batch by reason of a serious or immediate risk presented by the product or product batch to the health and safety of consumers, that State shall inform the Commission provided the risks and effects are not limited to the territory of the relevant member state. The Commission, after checking such information, shall inform other member states through a procedure set out in the Directive. If the Commission believes that there is a serious and immediate risk from a product to the health and safety of consumers in various member states and:

(a) at least one member state has adopted measures to restrict the sale or marketing or is requiring withdrawal of the product;

(b) if there is a difference between the member states on how to deal with the risk in question;

(c) a member state requests the Commission to make a decision; and

(d) if the risk cannot be dealt with adequately under other procedures and can only be eliminated effectively by adopting notice throughout the Community,

the Commission can after a process of consultation with the member states set out in this Directive require the member states to take temporary measures concerning the affixing of relevant warnings, informing the public of risks, prohibiting the supply of the products, prohibiting relevant products on the market or organising withdrawal and, if necessary, destruction of the dangerous products (articles 8 and 9).

The Commission is assisted in its tasks in connection with this Directive by a committee on product safety emergencies and article 11 provides details for the operation of that Committee.

2.2.4 *Structure of liability under the Directive*

The Directive:

(a) applies to those persons who are known as 'producers or distributors who have dealings with products';
(b) aims to ensure 'safe' products and not 'dangerous' products are put on the market; and
(c) requires producers and distributors to observe various safety rules depending upon whether the General Product Safety Directive does or does not apply to the products in whole or in part.

Insofar as the General Product Safety Directive does apply to the products and distributors or producers fail to observe its provisions as introduced into national law, they will be liable to modify the product, provide warnings, information or even to withdraw the product from the market or cease its sale and may under relevant national implementing law otherwise be subject to sanctions.

2.2.5 *Liability*

i Producers and distributors   Under article 2 of the Directive, a 'producer' shall mean:

– the manufacturer of the product, when established in the Community, and any other person presenting itself as the manufacturer by affixing to the product its name, trademark or other distinctive mark, or the person who reconditions the product;
– the manufacturer's representative when the manufacturer is not established in the Community or, if there is no representative established in the Community, the importer of the product;
– other professionals in the supply chain insofar as their activities may affect the safety properties of a product placed on the market.

In essence, the definition of 'producer' is wide; indeed, it is wider than that of 'producers' under the Product Liability Directive.

In the Product Safety Directive 'distributors' shall mean 'any professional in the supply chain whose activity does not affect the safety properties of the product', thus this will include all franchisees, wholesalers, distributors, agents and others involved in bringing the product to the consumer.

ii Products   The definition of products, also set out in article 2, is widely drawn and, unlike the Product Liability Directive, deals with products in all stages of manufacture once any individual component has been supplied to another party. A product is defined as being 'any product intended for consumers or likely to be used by consumers, supplied whether for consideration or not in the course of the commercial activity and whether new, used or reconditioned. However, this Directive shall not apply to secondhand products supplied as antiques or as products to be repaired or reconditioned prior to being used, provided the supplier clearly informs the person to whom he supplies the products to that effect'. This final qualification in practice is likely to lead to difficulties as to whether adequate information has been given, either about the actual condition of the product or the full steps and techniques to be used in order to effect the appropriate repair. The fact that 'Products' in this Directive

are defined in relation to an intended use, viz use by consumers, means that, since many products are used and intended to be used on an everyday basis in both a business and consumer environment, manufacturers may have to satisfy different safety standards depending on whom they intend to buy and use their products.

iii '*Safe*' *Products and* '*Dangerous*' *Products*   The definition of 'safe products' is relatively pragmatic:

> ...any product which, under the normal or reasonably foreseeable conditions of use, including duration, does not present any risk or only the minimum risks compatible with the product's use, considered as acceptable and consistent with a high level of protection for the safety and health of persons taking into account the following points in particular:
>
> - the characteristics of the product, including its composition, packaging, instructions for assembly and maintenance;
> - the effect on other products where it is reasonably foreseeable that it will be used with other products;
> - the presentation of the product, the labelling, any instructions for its use and disposal and any other indications or information provided by the producer;
> - the categories of consumers at serious risk when using the product, in particular children.

The feasibility of obtaining higher levels of safety or the availability of other products presenting a lesser degree of risk shall not constitute grounds for considering a product to be 'unsafe' or 'dangerous'.

Likewise, the definition of 'dangerous product' shall mean 'any product which does not meet the definition of safe product' referred to immediately above.

When the definition of 'safe product' is compared with that of the definition of 'defect' in the Product Liability Directive, a different standard is seen to apply particularly in view of the reference in the Product Safety Directive to categories of consumer at particular risk in using the product. This makes the standard a potentially subjective one; this is to be contrasted with that of the Product Liability Directive, where products are to be made as safe as a person (rather than a particular category of person) is entitled to expect.

iv   Scope of the Directive's rules   The most difficult question raised by the Directive is the precise scope of the products covered by it. While it is theoretically simple that the products 'intended for consumers or likely to be used by consumers' that are covered by this Directive are those not otherwise covered by other Directives, this is difficult to ascertain in practice because of the wording of the recitals and article 1 of the Directive. The relevant provisions of the recitals are:

> ...whereas some Member States have adopted horizontal legislation on product safety, imposing, in particular, a general obligation on economic operators to market only safe products, whereas those legislations differ in the level of protection afforded to persons; whereas such disparities and the absence of horizontal legislation in other Member States are liable to create barriers to trade and distortions of competition within the internal market;
>
> ...whereas it is very difficult to adopt Community legislation for every product which exists or may be developed; whereas there is a need for a broadly based

legislative framework of a horizontal nature to deal with those products, and also to cover lacunae in existing or forthcoming specific legislation, in particular while ensuring a high level of protection of safety and health of persons as required by article 100(a)(3) of the Treaty;

...whereas it is therefore necessary to establish on a Community level a general safety requirement for any product placed on the market that is intended for consumers or likely to be used by consumers whereas certain secondhand goods should nevertheless be excluded by their nature'.

Article 1.2 of the Directive reads as follows:

The provisions of this Directive shall apply insofar as there are no specific provisions in rules of Community law governing the safety of the products concerned.

In particular, where specific rules of Community law contain provisions imposing safety requirements on the products which they govern, the provisions of articles 2 to 4 of this Directive shall not, in any event, apply to those products.

Where specific rules of Community law contain provisions governing only certain aspects of product safety or categories of risks for the products concerned, those are the provisions which shall apply to the products concerned with regard to the relevant safety aspects or risks.

Accordingly:

(a) the Directive applies to products (as defined) in respect of which safety obligations have not been wholly imposed by other Community safety laws;
(b) the corollary of this is that in respect of those products for which safety requirements have been imposed by other Community safety laws producers and distributors are free of the obligation to observe the general safety requirements set out in article 3;
(c) nevertheless the general enforcement obligations referred to in paragraph 2.2.3 do apply to 'products' as defined in the Directive in addition to any other provisions that may apply under other relevant Community Safety Laws; and
(d) although the third paragraph of article 1.2 is open to different interpretations, the provisions of the General Product Safety Directive are probably additional to those of other Community law safety provisions where such safety provisions do not wholly cover the relevant product.

In each case it is therefore necessary to read carefully not only the specific safety directive for a specific product, but also the General Product Safety Directive to ascertain where particular provisions are not in a specific safety directive but are in fact covered by the General Product Safety Directive.

2.2.6 Burden of proof

Since breaches of the General Product Safety Directive will presently be enforced by national authorities, the burden of proof will be the criminal standard applicable under the national law.

2.2.7 Defences

The Directive does not as such set out any particular defences that a defaulting producer or distributor may plead in the event of proceedings being brought against him for enforcement measures.

2.2.8   Enforcement and penalties

The prime enforcement action provided by this Directive is set out in article 6(d) to (h) whereby producers, distributors and others involved in the supply chain may have imposed upon them:

- requirements to affix warnings;
- requirements to inform consumers of risks by publication if necessary of special warnings;
- orders temporarily prohibiting them from supplying products or product batches;
- orders prohibiting the placing of a product or product batch on the market that is dangerous; and
- orders requiring organising withdrawal of the product from the market. In addition it may be necessary for further enforcement action by way of fines or, indeed, prison sentences to be imposed by the governments of member states.

Furthermore, where products are imported into the European Union customs officers additionally have power to suspend release of a product or batch of products that have a serious and immediate risk to health or safety or do not have appropriate safety warnings etc. attached to them as required by national legislation. Such powers of customs authorities stem from Council Regulation 339/93, 8 February 1993.

The powers of enforcement authorities in member states must be used in accordance with the degree of risk and conformity with the provisions of the Treaty of Rome and in particular with articles 30 and 36 thereof.

2.2.9   Implementation

The precise methods undertaken in each member state to implement the law may vary, as may the nature of sanctions, defences, fines etc. imposed on defaulting parties or even their directors, officers and employees.

Despite the fact that the implementation programme under the Directive should have been complied with by 29 June 1994 in all member states, this was not the case as is set out in the individual country chapters later in this book and summarised in Appendix 2.

One matter that has not been made clear is whether the General Product Safety Directive gives rise to any rights by consumers and others who may be harmed by defective products, to bring claims against producers, distributors and others in the supply chain. The recitals to the Directive and article 13 provide that the Directive should be without prejudice to the Product Liability Directive and it may be that the true meaning of the General Product Safety Directive is that it does not give any new civil law rights against manufacturers of defective products, such as those for breach of statutory duty or ancillary to a criminal prosecution. It will be interesting to see whether, when all the member states have completed their implementation of the General Product Safety Directive, the governments of any member states actually go so far as to expressly provide in their national implementing legislation that the general safety requirement of distributors and producers is not actionable. It may be that, since it is not clear that civil rights do not flow from the Directive, national governments are loath to introduce legislation expressly banning such rights as they might leave themselves open to a claim in damages by individuals relying

upon the decision in *Francovich v Italian Republic*[16] on the basis that the government failed to implement or correctly implement a Directive, thereby depriving the individual of the remedy that it otherwise would have had.

2.3   Directive on Unfair Terms in Consumer Contracts (93/13/EEC)

2.3.1   *The Directive and its implementation*

The Directive on Unfair Terms in Consumer Contracts was adopted by the Council of Ministers on 5 April 1993 and member states are required to implement its provisions into national law by 31 December 1994. The Directive was not implemented across the EU within the timescale originally envisaged as described in individual country chapters and Appendix 2.

2.3.2   *Application of the Directive*

The Directive applies to contracts (written or oral) concluded between a seller or supplier and a consumer (see section 2.3.4 below). However, it does not apply to a contract relating to (i) employment, (ii) rights of succession or under family law, (iii) the incorporation and organisation of companies or (iv) partnership agreements. The terms of contracts of insurance which define the insured risk and the insurers' liability are also excluded.

It would appear from the recitals that the Directive only applies to contracts for the supply of goods and services.

Contractual terms which reflect mandatory statutory provisions or principles of relevant international conventions are not subject to the Directive.

2.3.3   *The effect of the Directive*

The Directive provides that any unfair contractual term in a consumer contract which has not been individually negotiated shall be voidable. All written consumer contracts must be drafted in plain, intelligible writing.

2.3.4   *Consumer contract (article 2)*

A 'consumer' is defined as any natural person who, in contracts covered by the Directive, is acting for purposes which are outside his trade, business or profession; notably the definition excludes companies.

A 'seller or supplier' is defined as any natural or legal person who, in contracts covered by the Directive, is acting for purposes relating to his trade, business or profession. A seller or supplier may be either publicly or privately owned.

2.3.5   *'Unfair Term' (articles 3(1), 3(3) and 4(1))*

A term shall be regarded as 'unfair' if it causes a significant imbalance in the parties' contractual rights and obligations, to the detriment of the consumer. The onus of proof is on the consumer to show the term is unfair. In making the assessment consideration will be given to the nature of the goods or services, the circumstances of the contract, and the other terms of the contract or any associated contract. In the implementing law of certain countries such as the UK or Italy it will be possible for companies to consult an authority that oversees the application of the Directive, to see whether their standard terms and

16   [1992] IRLR 84.

conditions are fair. Further, this authority may request the Company to supply a copy of its standard terms in order to check that they are fair. That authority may then take steps to see that the law is implemented fairly and that sellers or suppliers observe the law.

Annexed to the Directive is an indicative and non-exhaustive list of terms which may be regarded as unfair. These include terms which exclude or limit liability for death or person injury, terms which enable the seller to terminate an indefinite contract without reasonable notice where there are no serious grounds, and terms which enable the seller to alter the contract terms unilaterally without a valid reason. These are set out in Appendix 8.

2.3.6   Individually negotiated term (article 3(2))

The Directive only applies to terms which have not been individually negotiated. It therefore principally applies to pre-formulated standard form contracts.

The fact that certain aspects of a term have been individually negotiated does not prevent the application of the Directive to the remainder of the contract, provided the contract is generally regarded as a pro forma.

The onus is on the seller or supplier to prove that a standard term has been individually negotiated.

2.3.7   Unfair terms voidable (article 6(1))

Any unfair terms contained in a contract governed by the Directive shall be voidable. The remainder of the contractual terms shall remain enforceable provided the contract can continue in existence without the unfair terms.

2.3.8   Applicable law (article 6(2))

If the contract has a close connection with a member state, a consumer may not lose the protection granted by the Directive by virtue of the law of a non-member state purporting to be the applicable law of the contract.

2.3.9   Prevention of unfair terms (article 7(1))

The Directive permits member states to choose how to deal with unfair terms, in particular whether to introduce criminal sanctions. It remains to be seen what steps member states will take in this regard.

2.3.10   Freedom to extend consumer protection (article 8)

The Directive permits member states to adopt or retain the most stringent provisions compatible with the Treaty of Rome in relation to unfair terms.

This effectively means that many of the existing domestic laws can remain in effect (such as the Unfair Contract Terms Act 1977 in England and Wales), supplemented by any new law introduced as a result of the Directive.

2.3.11   Competition law

The Commission has on occasions warned producers that their distribution agreements may be declared incompatible with competition law rules whenever the guarantees offered to consumers are not valid throughout the Community for products purchased in any member state.

Although the Directive does not directly entitle consumers to invoke guarantees, it may have a minor impact on the enforceability of guarantees. This is because contractual terms designed to reduce the scope of a guarantee provided to a consumer are often unfair. Among the examples of terms which may be unfair listed in the Annex to the Directive is any term which has the object or effect of inappropriately excluding or limiting the legal rights of the consumer vis-à-vis the seller or supplier or another party in the event of total or partial non-performance or inadequate performance by the seller or supplier of any of the contractual obligations ... (article 1.6 of the Annex).

Since in many member states the Directive supplements existing national law relating to unfair terms, it may be that even following its implementation certain terms of guarantees will be held valid in one member state but unfair and unenforceable in another. Such a position may be incompatible with competition law.

In view of article 6(2) of the Directive, it will not be possible for a manufacturer to seek to obtain a common position throughout the EU by applying the law of a non-member state to the guarantee.

2.4   Draft EC Directive on Guarantees for Consumer Goods

2.4.1   *Background*

This draft Directive was adopted by the Commission on 18 June 1996. It has its origins in the second Consumer Programme of 1981. In 1993 the Commission published its Green Paper on Guarantees for Consumer Goods and After Sales Service (COM 93) 509. The green paper was approved by an opinion of the European Parliament on 6 May 1994 proposing that a draft Directive be issued as soon as practicable.[17] The Draft Directive, however, is a substantially watered-down version of what was proposed in the Green Paper.

2.4.2   *General objectives*

The general objective of the draft Directive is the creation of a common minimum corpus of Community consumer law valid wherever consumer goods are purchased in the European Union. Under this proposed Directive, consumers will receive a two-year legal guarantee commencing on the date the goods are delivered to the consumer. This guarantee will be given by the seller of the goods. Furthermore, commercial guarantees voluntarily provided by manufacturers will be required to meet new minimum criteria and must be transparent in their operation and may not permit in any way any derogation of consumers' rights.

It will be observed that to a large extent the proposals set out in the draft directive run parallel to those applying to international sales of goods between businesses set out in the Vienna Convention 1980 on the International Sale of Goods.

2.4.3   *Article 1 – definitions*

In paragraph 2(b) 'consumer goods' are objectively defined as any goods excluding buildings and land normally intended for private use or consumption,

17   OJ No c 205, 25 July 1994, p 562.

whereas in article 2(a) 'consumer' is defined subjectively as 'a natural person who purchases a consumer good other than in the course of his trade, business or profession. Natural or legal persons purchasing consumer goods for purposes other than re-selling them or making them available to a third party for financial gain, shall be considered as consumers when the circumstances and nature of the transaction are such that they are indistinguishable from purchases normally made by consumers'. It is important to note that 'consumer goods' are not limited to consumer durable goods and may include perishable goods.

'Sellers' are defined in paragraph 2(c) of article 1 as natural or legal persons who sell consumer goods in the course of their trade, business or profession.

A final definition is the 'guarantee'. The 'guarantee' had been referred to in the Green Paper on the subject as the 'commercial guarantee'. It covers all commercial guarantees relating to the goods independently of the person offering it, as well as commercial guarantees offered against payment and extended warranties provided against payment over and above free guarantees.

2.4.4   Article 2 – conformity with the contract and delivery

This Article sets out the main principle of the draft Directive that goods supplied to Consumers must be in conformity with the contract. This principle runs parallel to the criteria set out in the Vienna Convention. The criteria for presuming whether the goods comply with the contract are as set out in paragraph 2 and include the need for the goods to comply with any description or any statement made in advertising or labelling or by any previous supplier in the same chain of contracts. The criteria also include what in the common law system would be called certain implied warranties of fitness for purpose and warranties of quality.

If the draft Directive is finalised and implemented, manufacturers may have to increase the quality of the instructions applying to the product to ensure that the product is correctly used and installed, as lack of conformity resulting from incorrect installation is considered as lack of conformity with the contract.

2.4.5   Article 3 – rights of the Consumer against a Seller

This article sets out the seller's liability for lack of conformity. The time at which goods are to conform with the contract is based on the provisions of article 36(1) of the Vienna Convention and it states that conformity of the goods with the contract should occur the moment the consumer receives the goods, thus it places the burden of risk in transport on the seller's shoulders. The article also provides a partial reversal of the normal burden of proof concerning the time of the existence of the lack of conformity in favour of the consumer and unless evidence to the contrary is produced, any lack of conformity arising within six months of delivery shall be presumed to have existed before delivery unless such presumption is incompatible with the nature of the goods.

The article sets out the remedies of the consumer against the seller when they are not in conformity with the contract. These rights are:

(a) to return the goods to the seller and to have the price paid reimbursed; or
(b) to have the goods replaced, if this is possible; or
(c) to have the goods repaired by the seller at his expense, if this is possible and provided that the repair will not entail an unreasonable cost for the seller; or

(d) to be paid a sum corresponding to the loss in value of the goods where appropriate expressed as a reduction in price.

The consumer may decide for himself which option to choose. However, if repair or replacement fails to bring them into conformity with the contract, the consumer may still exercise the other rights open to him, viz return and reimbursement or a price reduction. Additionally the consumer may be entitled to withhold payment until he obtains full satisfaction. However, if the goods lack conformity with the contract in a minor way, the consumer may not claim the remedies of price reduction or reimbursement as long as the seller can repair the goods in a reasonable time, but if this cannot be achieved, the price reduction remedy may be exercised. The consumer is only restricted in so exercising its rights, if the seller did not know and could not have been expected to know of the goods lack of conformity or the seller had no reason to believe the matter was of significant importance to the consumer while unaware of the lack of conformity.

2.4.6   Article 4 – obligations of the Consumer

If the consumer is to make a claim against a seller under article 3, the consumer must notify the seller of the lack of conformity of the goods with the contract within either a month of the consumer's detection of the lack of conformity, or one month from the date when the lack of conformity should have been detected. Notification in such a manner is an obligation of a consumer making such a claim in many of the EU countries already and is otherwise set out in article 39 of the Vienna Convention in respect of international sales of goods between businesses.

It is provided that, in parallel with business transactions under article 44 of the Vienna Convention, a consumer forfeits his rights if he does not give notice to the appropriate person within the one month deadline unless he has a reasonable excuse for not doing so.

2.4.7   Article 6 – deadlines

The draft Directive provides that the guarantee period shall be two years save that the right to have the price reimbursed or the goods replaced shall be valid for only one year from delivery. The time period is shorter than that provided in many jurisdictions, such as France, Belgium, England and Wales and Ireland. As mentioned above in relation to article 4, where the goods lack durability, claims for a reduction in the goods' value may be brought within a reasonable period depending on the circumstances, but shall not run for more than ten years from the date when the producer placed the actual goods on the market which do not conform with the contract. The article further provides for a guarantee period, which is generally two years. This limitation period runs for three years from the date the consumer has notified the supplier or manufacturer of the lack of conformity with the contract. Member states may permit longer limitation periods if they wish when implementing the Directive.

2.4.8   Article 8 – commercial guarantees

The draft Directive proposes a minimum standard for guarantees as defined in article 1 in that they must place the beneficiary of the guarantee in a more advantageous position than would result from the application of the legal

guarantee referred to in articles 1-4 of the draft Directive. The guarantee must be in writing stating the name and address of the guarantor, the persons to contact and how to make claims in a reasonably convenient way, the duration of the guarantee, the territorial coverage of the guarantee and a notice drawing the consumer's attention to the fact that they have other rights granted by law which are not affected by the guarantee.

2.4.9   Article 10 – binding nature

The consumer's rights may not be abrogated or waived under any circumstances, even if the consumer consents.

2.4.10   Conclusion

If this draft Directive is finalised and then implemented into national law, it will provide a useful harmonising provision in an otherwise unnecessarily complicated area of national law within the European Union.

3   ENFORCEABILITY OF EC LAW

3.1   Introduction

The issue of whether and to what extent Community law can create rights for and impose obligations upon individuals which are enforceable within national courts had been unclear but is now becoming more apparent as national courts and the European Court of Justice (ECJ) gradually give greater effect to Community law and clarify the doctrine of 'Direct Effect'.

3.2   Direct effect

Article 189 of the Treaty of Rome sets out the basic provisions for the applicability of Community law in national courts of member states and provides, inter alia:

> In order to carry out their task the Council and the Commission shall in accordance with the provisions of this Treaty make Regulations, issue Directives, take Decisions...
>
> A Regulation shall have general application. It shall be binding in its entirety and directly applicable in all Member States.
>
> A Directive shall be binding as to the result to be achieved, upon each Member State to which it is addressed, but shall leave to the national authorities the choice of form and methods.
>
> A Decision shall be binding in its entirety upon those to whom it is addressed.

Under article 164 the ECJ has the duty to interpret and apply the Treaty and under article 177 of the Treaty of Rome the ECJ has jurisdiction to give ratings on the interpretation of Community law that are referred to it by national courts.

The ECJ has developed the doctrine of Direct Effect concerning the direct applicability of Community law into national law.

The original leading case on the application and operation of Community law is *Van Gend En Loos*.[18] In that case, the European court held that:

> The Community constitutes a new legal order of international law for the benefit of which the States have limited their sovereign rights, albeit within limited fields, and subjects of which comprise not only Member States but also their nationals. Independently of the legislation of Member States, Community law therefore not only imposes obligations on individuals but is also intended to confer upon them rights which have become part of their legal heritage. Those rights arise not only where they are expressly granted by the the Treaty [of Rome], but also by reason of obligations which the Treaty [of Rome] imposes in a clearly defined way upon individuals, as well as upon the Member States and upon the institutions of the Community.

In that case the ECJ laid down the criteria to be applied in considering whether a provision of EU law had Direct Effect.

These included:

(a) the provision of Community law must not concern member states only if it is to confer individual rights
(b) the provision must be clear and precise
(c) it must be unconditional and not require a member state or the Community to have to adopt additional reasons in relation to it.

The European Court has rejected the view that obligations imposed by Directives can be invoked and enforced only by Community institutions or member states. If an obligation is 'by its legal nature, layout and wording capable of creating direct effects on the legal relations between the addressee of the measure and third parties' then the provision can be pleaded in national courts to enforce the right which flows from it. Hence, the measures must be clear and precise, expressed in unconditional terms and any transitional period ended.

3.3 Implementation of Directives

For legal certainty and clarity, member states are expected to legislate for national procedures to ensure compliance with legal rules mandated. It is not sufficient for Member States to implement a Directive only in part, or even substantially. A Directive must be implemented in *full* despite the fact that it may already be *directly effective*. In *Commission v Italy*[19] the European Court stated that the 'full and exact application of the provisions of a Directive' in the national legal system is required. There are no legal or political excuses which the European Court will accept for failure to implement a Directive correctly.

3.4 Vertical direct effect against a state

An individual affected by a failure of a state to implement a Directive correctly or in total may have legal rights to enforce it in the national courts.

The *effects doctrine* may give affected individuals rights against the national state at fault. To rely on the Directive against the national state it would be necessary to show the provision relied on is clear and precise, unconditional and capable of

18 Case 26/62 ECJ.
19 Cases 91 and 92/79 [1980] ECR 1099, para 6 and [1980] ECR, para 6.

operating without further action by the Community or the member state.

Whether or not a Directive has 'vertical' direct effect as between the Community and the member states *and* 'horizontal' direct effect imposing rights as between one individual (or company) and another is not entirely clear.

3.5   Horizontal direct effect

In *Marshall v Southampton and South West Hampshire Area Health Authority (Teaching)*[20] the ECJ ruled that, whilst Directives bind member states, they cannot be invoked against private individuals. In *Johnston v Chief Constable of the Royal Ulster Constabulary*[1] the European Court confirmed the position stating that Directives only create 'vertical direct effect'. However in the more recent case of *Brasserie du Pecheur SA v Germany*[2] the ECJ held not only that state liability arises in the event of directly effective treaty provisions but that a right to reparation is the necessary corollary of the direct effect of the provisions whose breach caused the damage sustained and as has been advanced by W Van Gerven.[3] There is no reason why liability should not arise also as a matter of Community law in the event of infringements by individuals of treaty provisions which like articles 85 and 86 of the Treaty impose specific obligations on individuals ie have horizontal direct effect. In *Faccini Dori v Recreb SRL*[4] the ECJ decided that, although directives may be relied upon by an individual against the State, the Community can only enact obligations for individuals with immediate effect where the Community has power to do so.

3.6   Horizontal indirect effect

An alternative doctrine may enable individuals to claim against each other on the basis of EC law. This is the Principle of Interpretation, otherwise known as the 'indirect' direct effects doctrine, which may be relied upon instead.

In *Von Colson*[5] the ECJ having concluded that under the Direct Effects doctrine a Directive could not create obligations upon which one individual could rely against another, the ECJ considered whether national courts were bound to interpret national law in accordance with a Directive. The courts stated:

> The Member State's obligation arising under a Directive to achieve the results envisaged by the Directive and their duty under article 5 of the Treaty [of Rome] to take all necessary measures, whether general or particular, to ensure the fulfilment of that obligation, is binding on all the authorities of Member States, including the matters within their jurisdiction, the [national] courts. It follows that in applying the national law and in particular the provisions of a national law specifically introduced in order to implement [the Directive] national courts are required to interpret their national law in the light of the wording and the purpose

---

20   Case 152/84 [1986] 1 CMLR 688.
1   Case 22/84 [1986] 3 CMLR 240.
2   Case C46/93 and C-48/93 [1996] ICEC 295 at 346.
3   [1996] ICLQ 607 at 530 'Bridging the Unbridgable: Community and National Tort Laws after *Francovich* and *Brasserie*'.
4   Case C91/92 [1995] 1 CMLR 665.
5   Case 14/83 [1984] ECR 1891.

of the Directive in order to achieve the result referred to in the third paragraph of Article 189 [of the Treaty of Rome].

This principle was followed in *Marleasing SA v La Commercial Internacional de Alimentacion SA*.[6] There, the ECJ found that insofar as Community law had not been implemented (before or after the Directive in question), national courts are bound to disapply national law or ignore its application insofar as this may be necessary to comply with European law when this is possible. This however has led in England to the national courts taking a restrictive line in construing matters.[7]

In *Factortame Ltd v Secretary of State for Transport*,[8] the European Court confirmed the approach in *Marleasing* and consolidated its position finding that various provisions of the Merchant Shipping Act were in breach of (inter alia) article 52 of the Treaty of Rome because they discriminate on the basis of nationality. The Court decided yet again that national law, in this case English law, must be interpreted in accordance with European Community law.

3.7 State liability for failure to implement Directives

In the most recent case on the subject, *Brasserie du Pecheur*,[9] the conditions for state liability for breaches of EU law were further considered. In particular, the three preconditions set out in the *Francovich*[10] case were held to be exclusive, namely:

(a) relevant provision of EU law must directly confer rights on individuals;
(b) the legal right must be breached by an act for which the State can be held responsible; and
(c) there must be a causal link between the breach and the harm suffered by the claimant.

This time the court held that liability cannot be incurred unless the institution 'manifestly and gravely' disregarded the limits on the exercise of its powers. Member states should only incur liability in comparable situations where they are acting in a field where they have a wide discretion comparable to that of the EU institutions in implementing the EU policies. Thus, where a state does have wide discretion as well as the conditions set out in the *Francovich*[11] decision, the claimant must demonstrate that the breach is sufficiently 'serious', bearing in mind the clarity and precision of the rule breached, the measure of discretion left to the state, whether the infringement and damage caused was intentional or involuntary; whether any error of law was excusable or inexcusable.

3.8 *Brasserie du Pecheur* and horizontal direct effect

It is uncertain whether the ECJ in the *Brasserie du Pecheur* case is moving towards a revival of the Community law action of horizontal direct effect to permit

6   Case 106/89, 13 November 1990 [1990] ECL 1-4135.
7   *Webb v Emo Air Cargo UK Ltd* [1994] QB 718.
8   No 3 (25th July 1991).
9   Cases C-46/93 and C-48/93 [1996] CEC 295.
10 [1992] IRLR 84.
11 Ibid.

individuals to bring cases against each other in Community law. The most recent case from ECJ of *El Corte Ingles v Rivera*[12] appears to confirm the previous decisions that directives do not have horizontal direct effect and even the amendment to the Treaty of Rome by the insertion of article 129a (see section 1.1.3 above) does not alter the existing case law.

4 CONCLUSION

There is now a sound bedrock in the European Union for the development of consumer law. A small section of this area of the Law is the subject of this book, namely the liability of manufacturers and suppliers to consumers for damage caused by defective products. The development of new legislation in this field is progressing with active policy programmes being put into place. This has created a solid framework of detailed legislation both at Community level and that of national law. An interesting example of this, is the draft directive on Guarantees for Consumer Goods, which, if finalised and implemented into national law, will give substantially enhanced remedies to consumers for defective products they buy and for the repair services that they receive from sellers and manufacturers. This in turn is likely to both increase the quality of consumers goods, and create changes in the way in which distribution systems are operated to cope with the enhanced quality of goods and services that manufactures and distributors will have to produce to customers. Increasingly, through the decisions of the ECJ and of national courts, the interests of consumers in the European Union are being enforced and new remedies are being developed such that it can now be said that consumer law within the European Union has become of age. There are still, however, many difficulties to overcome in producing an effective set of rules which can smoothly operate and be evenly enforced in an appropriate manner in this narrow area of manufacturers' and sellers' liability for defective products.

It will become evident from subsequent chapters that some of these difficulties arose from the harmonisation of product liability law, being impeded by member states' failure to implement the Product Liability Directive on time, consistently and in accordance with its terms. It is also clear that the effect of the General Product Safety Directive has also been impeded by member states' failure to implement that Directive on time.

While these difficulties have arisen, new remedies evolved in community law at the same time and whether directives were incorrectly or not fully implemented, individuals should nevertheless be able to derive the rights from those Directives discussed in this chapter. As has been set out, European case law now confirms that individuals may enforce those rights by relying on them in the national courts on the basis that national law, (eg implementing legislation, statute or common law) must be interpreted to give effect to the words and aims of the relevant Directive and claims in vertical direct effect can be made against member states failing to implement legislation. It will now be particularly interesting to see if the *Brasserie du Pecheur* case does again give rise to the doctrine of horizontal direct effect. If so, this may also lead to the possibility of individuals injured by defective goods bringing claims against

manufacturers not only under the provisions of the Product Liability Directive but also by bringing civil claims against manufacturers and suppliers for breach of statutory duty pursuant to the Product Safety Directive.

CHAPTER II

Austria

Dr Peter Madl

Schönherr Barfuss Torggler & Partners
Tuchlauben 13
(Eingang Kleeblattgasse 4)
Postfach (POB) 41
A-1014 Vienna
Austria

Tel: ++ 43 1 534 37-0
Fax: ++ 43 1 533 25 21

CHAPTER II

Austria

1 INTRODUCTION

1.1 Introduction to the legal system in Austria

Austria is a Federal Republic which consists of nine provinces. Legislation is divided between the Republic of Austria and the provinces. The Austrian Constitution stipulates that civil law, both regarding legislation and enforcement, is reserved to the Federal Republic of Austria. The provinces are involved in the creation of legislation insofar as the second chamber of the Austrian Parliament consists of representatives of the nine Provinces.

The lowest instance in the court system are the District Courts. The District Court is the competent court for general claims not exceeding ATS 100,000 and certain special claims without regard to the amount at stake (eg divorces, tenancy matters, land register matters). The next instance are the County Courts which are the competent courts for claims exceeding ATS 100,000 and for appeals against judgments given by the District Courts. If a County Court has given a judgment in the first instance, an appeal is decided by one of the four Appeal Courts. The third and final instance is the Austrian Supreme Court. Questions of fact can only be raised up to the second instance. The Austrian Supreme Court only rules on questions of law.

There are special procedures for commercial matters (in Vienna for example all commercial matters are concentrated at the Commercial Court of Vienna).

The judgment of the Court is given by a professional judge in the District Courts and the County Courts. In the County Courts the parties to a claim may request that in cases where a certain amount is at stake the judgment is given by a senate which consists of three judges. In commercial matters one of those judges is not a professional judge but a merchant who has been appointed as judge for a period of time. However, the right of the parties to request a senate to decide a case in the first instance is rarely used. Decisions in the courts of the second instance are made by a senate of three judges. The Austrian Supreme Court usually makes decisions in a senate of five judges, but has the possibility to decide in a larger senate in cases of important decisions.

There are certain minimum threshold amounts which must be decided upon in the first instance before an appeal to the second instance or the Austrian Supreme Court is admissible.

The parties deposit their pleadings in writing before the judge decides which evidence he wants to take. Usually the judge schedules a separate court hearing only with the attorneys of the involved parties to discuss and to decide upon which evidence will be heard. Witnesses are interrogated by the judge first and then both attorneys have the possibility to ask additional questions to the witness.

The judges are bound by the pleadings of the parties. If both parties state a fact as true, the judge must base his judgment on this fact. However, the judge is free to hear any witnesses and take any evidence he wants to.

1.2   Overview of the law relating to defective products in Austria

The law relating to damages for defective products as contained in the Austrian General Civil Code (ABGB) sections 1293 ff is based on the principle of liability for fault. The ABGB distinguishes between liability in tort and liability for breach of contract. In the latter case it is for the defending party to prove that he did not act culpably (ABGB section 1298). Further, he will be liable for any fault – as if it were his own fault – on the part of a person who participated in the performance of the duties of the defending party with the knowledge and intention of the defending party (ABGB section 1313a). In addition, the person who has caused the damage may be liable for pure financial loss.

If liability cannot be based on breach of contract, the plaintiff has to furnish proof of all the facts on which his claim is based, which includes proof of fault of the defending party. In tort, the defending party is only liable for a third party insofar as the third party is unfit or known to be dangerous (ABGB section 1315).

As there is usually no contract between the producer and the consumer, the stricter form of liability for breach of contract is, in principle, not applicable.

Contractual relations usually exist only between a consumer and a retailer. However, it will in most cases be possible for the retailer to prove that he carefully performed his duties (ie he properly controlled the product) and consequently cannot be charged with negligence. In response to this dilemma, legal theory and practice searched – before the adoption of the Product Liability Directive – for new solutions beyond the statutory basis.

The approach in Austria is based on the extension of contractual liability. The legal concept was that a contract may have protective effects for third parties. The end-user of a product is linked with the producer by a chain of contracts and, therefore, the producer owes duties of protection and care to him. A violation of these duties, therefore, constitutes a breach of contract to the end-user.[1]

The Directive was implemented in Austria by way of the Federal Act of 21 January 1988 on liability for a defective product (*Bundesgesetz vom 21.1.1988 über die Haftung für ein fehlerhaftes Produkt–Produkthaftungsgesetz*, BGBl 99/1988 [PHG]) and took effect on 1 July 1988. It was amended twice (BGBl 95/1993; BGBl 510/1994). The main reason for the enactment of the PHG was the realisation that the prior system of liability could not keep pace with the development of technical products.[2] The wish to keep up with the changes in EC law has – at least pursuant to the printed materials of the PHG – been of minor importance.

Liability based on the PHG is in addition to liability based on other Austrian legislation. The provisions of the Austrian Civil Code concerning warranty and

1   Compare Welser 'Das neue Produkthaftungsgesetz' WBl 1988, 165, 166 with further reference; Bydlinski in Klang *Kommentar zum Allgemeinen bürgerlichen Gesetzbuch* (2nd edn) vol IV/2, pp 180 ff.

2   Regierungsvorlage, 272 der Beilagen zu den Stenographischen Protokollen des Nationalrates XVII. GP (suggestion of the government, 272 of the enclosures to the shorthand protocols of the national assembly XVII legislation period).

damages as well as, for example, the provisions of Acts on pharmaceutical products and food are still valid and have to be observed.

Austria has implemented the EC Directive on product safety with the Product Safety Act 1994 which replaces the Product Safety Act 1984. Pursuant to this act, public authorities are entitled to take appropriate measures if a product cannot be used with the guarantee of safety for life and health which should be expected. Furthermore, there exists product safety legislation in Austria (eg for heating systems with gas).

With respect to guarantees given to consumers, the Austrian Consumer Protection Act (KSchG) provides that the legal provisions on warranty may not be changed by a contract, except that the seller may be entitled by contractual agreement to offer a repair or replacement instead of reduction in price. Therefore, any guarantee given by the seller to a consumer may not be less than the warranties provided for by law. As a manufacturer's guarantee is in addition to the warranties and/or guarantees of the seller, there are no restrictions with respect to the scope of a guarantee of the manufacturer.

2   PRE-CONTRACTUAL LIABILITY

2.1   Effect on the interpretation and extent of the obligations of the parties to a contract

Statements made during the negotiations and prior drafts of a later signed contract are one of the sources of interpretation of a contract. Such matters do not normally lead to any interpretation which is beyond the ordinary possible sense of the wording of the actual contract unless it can be proved that the parties to the contract did mean to use a certain clause in the contract in a sense which is beyond or even contrary to the understanding of the wording of the final contract.

2.2   Extent that non-disclosure of facts during negotiations may lead to liability

As soon as two persons come into contact to conclude a contract they have to comply with obligations to give information and to take care of the person and the other objects of legal protection of the other party. These obligations exist independently of the conclusion of a contract. In a contract for sale of goods, the parties are especially obliged to give information on the condition of the product in question. For example, it is necessary to tell a prospective customer if the product being sold does not fulfil the requirements of which he has informed the seller (eg the compatibility of a computer with a particular type of software) or if certain prerequisites are necessary (eg high voltage supply). The seller is also obliged to see to it that a prospective customer is not injured on retail premises (eg because of a banana peel or a slippery floor).

Pre-contractor's liability lies in contract. Therefore, any failure to comply with these obligations results in a liability which is based on the principles of liability in contract.[3] The seller could be held liable for the costs of a newly hired computer operator, the adaptation of a room for the computer and loss

---

3   Compare Koziol and Welser *Grundriß des bürgerlichen Rechts* (10th edn) vol I, p 206 with
    further reference.

of income if the computer sold is not able to fulfil the requirements of the customer which were known to the seller.

3   LIABILITY IN CONTRACT

3.1   Outline of contract law relevant to defective products in Austria

Many contracts in Austria are concluded on the basis of general terms and conditions. As with the other provisions of a contract, general terms and conditions are only valid upon mutual agreement of both parties. This agreement can be reached either expressly or impliedly. Therefore, it is enough if one party states before the conclusion of the contract that he is only willing to conclude the contract under his general terms and conditions and the other party nevertheless concludes the contract. For an implied agreement, it is necessary to make it clear to the customer that the producer is only willing to conclude under his general terms and conditions. In addition, the customer must at least have the possibility to see the contents of the general terms and conditions.[4]

Provisions in the general terms and conditions which are disadvantageous for the customer and which the customer would not normally expect are not deemed to be part of the contract (ABGB section 864a).

Even if general terms and conditions are incorporated into an agreement, it is still possible that certain provisions contrary to public policy will be void. These include the complete exclusion of a seller's warranty for new goods[5] and the exclusion of liability for stringent gross negligence.[6] Stringent gross negligence is defined as a fault which comes very near to intention and would never happen to an average attentive person in a similar situation.

The KSchG which applies to contracts concluded between a businessman (any person who enters into a contract in the course of his business) and a non-businessman, provides that certain provisions of the ABGB (especially warranty of quality and liability for damages) are mandatory.

3.2   Contractual warranties relating to the quality and safety of products

The seller must warrant that the product has the stipulated or customarily required characteristics (ABGB section 922). Depending on the defect, the buyer has the right either to have the defect corrected, the price reduced or the contract cancelled. In this respect it is irrelevant whether there is any fault on the part of the seller.

However, the right based on warranty does not constitute a claim for damages. Damage other than that to the product sold itself (eg personal injury or damage to other products) can only be recovered under the prerequisites of ABGB sections 1293 ff. The KSchG provides for that the seller may not exclude the legal rights of a consumer with respect to the warranties. The only exception is that the seller may contractually agree with the consumer that the consumer has no right to ask for a price reduction, as long as he has the possibility that

---

4   Compare Koziol and Welser, vol 1. p 110 with further reference.
5   Austrian Sup Ct in JB1 1970, 271.
6   Austrian Sup Ct in SZ 57/184; JB1 1986, 144.

the seller fulfils the warranty by repair or replacement of the product. With respect to damage claims, the KSchG provides that it is not allowed to exclude liability for intentional or grossly negligent acts of the seller or of any person for whom the seller is legally responsible.

3.3   Breach of contract for the supply of defective products

3.3.1   *Types of defect*

Constructural defects are defined as those where the construction, the design or the composition of the product are inadequate. In this case not only the individual item, but all products of the same series, are considered defective.

Instructional defects are those where the product itself is free from defects, but damage is caused by missing or faulty directions on use or installation, or insufficient warning against dangerous qualities of the product.

A manufacturing defect is a defect of one or more products of a correctly constructed series of products which is caused by the failure of a machine or a worker.[7]

The producer must check his product to see whether it has any – so far unknown – dangerous qualities. This is especially true for newly developed, mass-produced articles. In addition, the producer has – still as a contractual obligation – to follow the development of the state of the art and if a safer product is developed, he must adapt his product. The producer and, to a certain extent, the distributor, are obliged to warn either the users or the general public if they find a defect in the product. According to the prevailing opinion the producer is also obliged to recall defective products.[8]

3.3.2   *Causation*

A condition for the liability of the producer is that his act or omission has caused the damage. In the former case, the question to be determined is whether the damage would have occurred if the act had not happened. Where damage as the result of an omission is the issue, the question is whether the damage would equally have occurred as a result of reasonable behaviour ('conditio sine qua non').[9]

3.3.3   *Remoteness of loss and damage*

Further, the producer is only liable for damages if the cause of the damage is, according to its general nature, not completely inappropriate to bring about such a result and if this cause has not been just part of an extremely extraordinary chain of circumstances.[10]

A further restriction of liability is that a person is only liable for damage caused by the unlawful act or omission that should have been prevented by the infringed standards of conduct. This 'purpose of protection' is important for determining which heads of damages and whom is to be compensated.[11]

---

7   Austrian Sup Ct in JBL 1996, 188.
8   Welser *Produkthaftungsgesetz* (1988), annotation 33 to §5 with further reference.
9   Koziol and Welser vol I, pp 447 f with further reference.
10   Koziol and Welser vol I, pp 448 f with further reference.
11   Koziol and Welser vol I, pp 453 f.

Basically, only those persons whose absolute rights have been injured, who are protected by a specific rule of conduct or with whom contractual obligations existed which have not been complied with have the right to be compensated. The standard example given for these cases is the following: somebody destroys a power station and due to the lack of electrical power a third party suffers damage, eg frozen food is destroyed. According to the prevailing opinion the third party cannot claim damages from the person who destroyed the power station.[12]

3.4   Quantum of damage

Liability for damages includes medical expenses, loss of earnings and damages for pain and suffering. The highest amount of damages for pain and suffering ever awarded by an Austrian court amounted to ATS 1.2m (in the case at hand, medical malpractice had resulted in the victim vegetating below the level of an intelligent animal for the rest of his life).

Any claim for medical expenses is generally transferred by virtue of a legal provision (ASVG section 332) to the social security institutions so that it can no longer be claimed by the injured party. The claimants are then the social security institutions.

Loss of profit can in principle only be recovered in cases of gross negligence. According to commercial law loss of profit can also be recovered in case of minor negligence if one party to the contract is a businessman.[13]

Punitive or exemplary damages are not awarded under Austrian law.

3.5   Burden of proof

The plaintiff is required to prove the defectiveness of the product, the damage and the causal relationship between the two. The producer can avoid liability by proving that he took all necessary measures and therefore neither he nor any of the persons for whom he is responsible can be charged with negligence. The burden of proof for gross negligence lies with the injured person.[14]

3.6   Exclusion or limitation of liability

Under Austrian law liability may be excluded for damages which are caused by negligence provided that the negligent act or omission is not intentional.[15] Under the Austrian Act for Protection of Consumers liability can only be excluded for minor negligence.

In Austria, however, it is recognised that, consistent with the attempt to base liability of the producer on a chain of contracts (see section 1.2, above), a release from liability is permissible for product liability too.[16] If the producer has excluded liability for damage in his contract with the first dealer, it may

12   Austrian Sup Ct in SZ 49/96; SZ 50/34 and others.
13   Koziol and Welser vol I, p 459.
14   Austrian Sup Ct in SZ 43/80; JB1 1977, 648 and others; for other opinion see Koziol and Welser vol I, p 457 with further reference.
15   Koziol and Welser vol I, p 112 with further reference.
16   Austrian Sup Ct in SZ 51/169.

commonly be expected that he has also no intention to assume any duties of protection and care to the consumer. Consequently, it is possible largely to exclude liability for damages to the consumer by means of a simple clause in the first contract.

Directive 13/94 on Unfair Contract Terms has not been specifically implemented in Austrian law.

3.7 Limitation period

Claims for damages in contract are subject to a limitation period of three years. The limitation runs from the moment when the injured person had knowledge or ought reasonably to have had knowledge of the damage and the person liable for the damage.[17] Irrespective of this knowledge claims for damages become statute-barred after 30 years. The limitation period of 30 years also applies if the damage has been caused by an intentional criminal offence with a possible imprisonment of more than one year (ABGB section 1489).

Negotiations to reach a settlement cause a suspension of the statute of limitation. At the end of the suspension the remaining time begins to run.[18]

The limitation period is interrupted if the debtor acknowledges the claim or the injured person files a law suit. If the limitation period is interrupted, the time that ran before the interruption is disregarded. The whole time begins to run afresh after the interruption.[19]

3.8 Liability for third parties

The defendant is liable for any fault on the part of the person who participated in the performance of the duties of the defendant with the knowledge and intention of the defendant (ABGB section 1313a). However, the defendant is only liable for damage which has been caused by the performance of his duties. There is no liability of the defendant for damage which has been caused by the third person which happens to coincide with the performance of the contract (eg if the third person hits the plaintiff upon delivery of the product for personal reasons).[20]

4 LIABILITY IN TORT

4.1 Outline of the relevant tort law giving rise to liability for personal and property damage in Austria

The prerequisite for liability in tort is the violation of either an absolute right which is enforceable against everyone or a protective law,[1] such as, for example, the Austrian Road Traffic Regulations (StVO), the Act on Pharmaceutical Products (AMG) or the Food Act (LMG).

---

17 Schubert in Rummel *Kommentar zum Allgemeinen bürgerlichen Gesetzbuch* (2nd edn), annotation 3 ff to §1489 with further reference.
18 Koziol and Welser vol I, p 188 with further reference.
19 Koziol and Welser vol I, pp 188 ff with further reference.
20 Koziol and Welser vol I, pp 486 ff.
1   Koziol and Welser vol I, pp 450 ff with further reference.

Liability in tort may be concurrent with liability for breach of contract. The differences are that in tort the plaintiff must prove the fault of the defending party (ABGB section 1296 applies instead of section 1298), the defendant is only to a lesser extent liable for third persons (ABGB section 1315 applies instead of section 1313a) and that there is, as a rule, no liability for pure financial loss.

4.2   Causation and remoteness of loss and damage

The same principles as for liability for breach of contract apply (see sections 3.3.2 and 3.3.3, above). In addition, the relevant protective law must have intended to prevent damages such as the ones which occurred. For example, an employer is not liable if one of his employees is injured by a customer outside normal working hours. However, the employer would be liable if his employee suffers damage because he works too long hours.[2]

4.3   Quantum of damage

Pure financial loss can only be recovered if there is a protective law which intends to prevent those damages.[3]

Medical expenses, loss of income and damages for pain and suffering can be recovered on the same basis in tort as in contract.

4.4   Burden of proof

The plaintiff has to prove all the facts on which his claim is based. Unlike in a claim for breach of contract, in tort the plaintiff has also to prove that the defending party acted culpably.[4]

4.5   Exclusion of limitation of liability

Although the exclusion of liability in tort is not very practical, it is nevertheless possible with the same prerequisites as the exclusion of liability for breach of contract.

4.6   Limitation period

Pursuant to ABGB section 1489 the same provisions regarding the limitation period, the suspension and the interruption of limitation apply for claims in tort and contract.

4.7   Liability for third parties

A principal may be liable for the fault of a person he engages for the performance of any obligation whatsoever if the person is unfit or the principal knows that

---

2   Koziol and Welser vol I, p 453.
3   Koziol and Welser vol I, p 451.
4   Koziol and Welser vol I, pp 456 ff with further reference.

the person is dangerous (ABGB section 1315). A special duty of care owed by the principal to the injured person is no condition for the liability based on ABGB section 1315.[5]

A person is unfit in the sense of ABGB section 1315 if he is not fit for the activity he is engaged to do. In order for a person to be qualified as unfit, it is not enough that he makes a mistake. One can infer unfitness only from the commission of several mistakes or a single serious mistake.

The term 'dangerous' refers to the general human characteristic (eg the plumber who steals or the painter who starts a fire at the work place). The principal is liable for these persons only if the dangerous characteristic is known to him and the damage is caused by this dangerous characteristic.

The limited liability of the principal pursuant to ABGB section 1315 is expanded by certain specific provisions relating to dangerous items (eg section 10 of the Law on Pipelines and section 35 of the Law on Liability in the Field of Nuclear Energy). Based on these provisions, legal theory and practice generally impose a liability on the owners of dangerous items for the gross negligence of their personnel.[6]

5 LIABILITY FOR DEFECTIVE PRODUCTS ARISING FROM BOTH GENERAL LAW AND IMPLEMENTATION OF DIRECTIVE 85/324 ON PRODUCT LIABILITY IN AUSTRIA

5.1 Introduction

The PHG, which is based on the Directive, came into force on 1 July 1988. In the eight years since implementation, the Austrian Supreme Court has only decided relatively few cases based on the PHG. Therefore, the following is based mainly on legal theory.

5.2 Outline of provisions in Austria

5.2.1 Extent of liability

Pursuant to section 1 of the PHG, liability for damages arises if a defect of a product causes the death of a person, physical injury, harm to a person's health or damage to an item of material property (other than the product itself) which is not suffered by a businessman who uses the product predominantly for his business. The Austrian Supreme Court clarified that the producer of a part of a product is not liable if this defective part damages other parts of the product.[7]

Therefore, liability occurs in cases of personal injury and property damage other than to the product itself. Whether the buyer of a product has a remedy for a defect of the product itself depends on the provisions on warranty and damages in the General Civil Code (ABGB sections 922 ff and 1293 ff). According to the explanatory notes,[8] pure economic damages cannot be recovered under the PHG.

---

5 Koziol and Welser vol I, pp 486 f.
6 Koziol and Welser vol I, p 488 with further reference.
7 Austrian Sup Ct in ecolex 1994, 384.
8 Erläuterungen zur Regierungsvorlage, 272 der Beilagen zu den Stenographischen Protokollen des Nationalrates XVII. GP, p 8.

For example, profits which are lost due to a defective product must be recovered pursuant to the general rules of liability in contract and tort. However, since this restriction is not expressly stated in the text of the PHG, some[9] are of the opinion that – besides the repair cost – even pure economic damages can be recovered. In accordance with the intention of the PHG, this provision should be restrictively interpreted pursuant to the Directive, and damages only in respect of property damage, medical costs, loss of earnings and pain and suffering are recoverable.[10]

Only property damage exceeding ATS 7,900[11] can be recovered (PHG section 2). According to the text of the PHG this minimum shall be applied to each individual damaged item. This means, for example, that liability under the PHG will not arise if the damage to one item amounts to ATS 5,000 and the damage to another amounts to ATS 3,000.[12] However, the intention of the PHG demands that the PHG is applicable if the sum of the damages exceeds ATS 7,900.[13] Action for damages not exceeding ATS 7,900 can still be brought under the general rules of contract and tort.

5.2.2   Persons subject to liability

The producer, the importer and the dealer are all potentially liable under the PHG.

i Producer   The producer is the person who has manufactured and distributed the finished product, or a primary component, or a raw material thereof. If a component (eg the tyre of a car) is defective, the injured person may choose whether to sue the producer of the tyres or the producer of the car. A car with defective tyres is considered a defective car and as such the producer is not liable for the destruction of the car itself, but is liable for the injuries suffered by the driver (and bystanders). The producer of the defective tyre has not distributed it as an individual product distinct from the car itself, thus, he is not liable for the damage to the car itself but only for all damage for which the car producer is liable.[14]

According to the explanatory notes of the PHG the assembler may also be liable. This is incongruous with the Directive (which corresponds very closely to the Austrian PHG on this point).[15] In any event the definition of a producer does not cover the supplier of services. But the supplier of goods and services can be held liable under the PHG as a producer, importer, or dealer of the goods supplied.

Considerable problems of definition – whether a person is a producer or a dealer – arise in connection with the packing, transferring and mixing-up of products.

9 Fitz, Purtscheller and Reindl *Produkthaftung* (1988), annotation 21 to §1.
10 Compare Welser *Produkthaftungsgesetz*, annotation 7 to §1; Welser in WB1 1988, 168; Andréewitch 'Anmerkungen zum Produkthaftungsgesetz' ÖJZ 1988, 225, 227 ff.
11 Approximately the equivalent of Ecu 500 in 1985.
12 Welser in WB1 1988, 170.
13 Welser *Produkthaftungsgesetz*, annotation 2 to §2; Barchetti and Formanek *Das Österreichische Produkthaftungsgesetz* (1988) p 49.
14 Compare Austrian Sup Ct in ecolex 1994, 384; Welser *Produktgshaftungesetz*, annotation 5 to §1; other opinion; Fitz, Purtscheller and Reindl *Produkthaftung*, annotation 16 to §1; Schmidt-Salzer and Hollmann *Kommentar EG-Richtlinie Produkthaftung* (1986), annotation 28 to art 9.
15 Welser in WB1 1988, 171; Welser *Produkthaftungsgesetz*, annotation 5 to §3.

There is presumably no disagreement that a person transferring liquids from big to small containers or putting tea from a large into a small bag is not a producer under the PHG.[16] Indeed, the person who repacks has to be careful to avoid being liable as a quasi-producer. The dilution and refilling of liquid extracts is held to be the act of a producer, because the diluted, refilled liquid is essentially a new product.[17]

Is the physician who adds distilled water to a powdered medicine before giving it to the patient a producer under the PHG? It is thought not.[18] The theoretical difference between this act and the dilution of liquid extracts by a distributor is difficult to make.

ii Importer   The business entity that imports the product and distributes it on the market of the European Economic Area is referred to as an importer (PHG section 1.1.2).[19]

Until the Lugano Convention will enter into force in all EC and EFTA states and, therefore, the injured person can enforce a judgment of his home country in the country of the producer, section 17 PHG enlarges the definition of the importer. Import is also the import and distribution of a product from an EFTA state into the EC, from the EC into an EFTA state and from one ETA state into another EFTA state. This definition is partially reduced as the Lugano Convention enters into force between EC and EFTA states.[20]

The PHG also specifically addresses the liability of 're-importers'. Re-importers are business entities which re-import a product that has been manufactured in Austria and exported afterwards. Although this liability corresponds to the clear wording of the law, it is, according to some authors, nevertheless superfluous. The reason for the introduction of the liability of the importer was to provide the injured person with an Austrian or European Economic Area entity which can be held liable. In case of a re-import the national or European Economic Area producer can be held liable anyway and, therefore, it is not necessary to have a second liable person in Austria. However, it is an advantage for the injured person if the producer is insolvent and damages can, therefore, not be recovered from him, to have another liable person in Austria. Therefore, the courts will most probably not follow this opinion.[21]

iii Dealer   Every business entity which distributes a product is a dealer.
Pursuant to section 6 of the PHG, distribution is defined as the transfer of a product for the disposal or use of a third person based on whatever title.

5.2.3   Defective products

A party can be held liable only for defective products. The PHG contains more specific provisions defining product and defect.

i Product   Pursuant to section 4 of the PHG, a product is any movable, tangible goods. It also includes all forms of energy. Agricultural and forest

16   Welser *Produkthaftungsgesetz*, annotation 8 to §3.
17   Schmidt-Salzer and Hollman *Kommentar*, annotation 44 to art 3; other opinion Welser *Produkthaftungsgesetz*, annotation 8 to §3.
18   Welser *Produkthaftungsgesetz*, annotation 8 to §3; Welser in WB1 1988, 171.
19   Compare Preslmays, *Handbuch des Produkthastungsgezetzes* (1993), 20ff.
20   Compare Austrian Sup Ct in JBL 1995, 456.
21   Compare Welser in WB1 1988, 169.

products and game are exempted, as long as they have not initially been processed or are genetically engineered organisms.

ii Defect A product is defective if it is not as safe as can be expected considering all the circumstances. The PHG does not focus on the subjective expectations of the injured person, but considers only the general opinion of the average prospective user.[1]

Relevant circumstances under the PHG are: the presentation of a product, the use to which it can reasonably be expected to be put, and the time of distribution.

(a) According to the explanatory notes of the PHG[2] the presentation of the product includes advertising, labelling, packaging, enclosed written information and additional oral information given by a salesman. Insufficient information may render a product defective under special circumstances. On the other hand, adequate information may avoid the product being held to be defective.

A warning is sufficient only if it is clear, explicit and emphasised according to its degree of importance. If too many instructions are given, the average user may feel overwhelmed and thus the effect of each instruction may decrease.[3]

In this context, an important restriction must be made. The presentation must be made either by the liable person or at least with his knowledge.[4] The reference to oral information given by a salesman, which is stated in the explanatory notes of the PHG, is misleading in two respects. First, exaggerated information by the seller without the knowledge of the producer will not cause liability of the producer. Second, if oral information by a salesman was considered in determining liability, then subjective expectations rather than objective expectations would be focused on. This is against the intention of the PHG.

(b) Liability arises only in respect of the use of a product which can reasonably be expected. The term 'reasonable use' has a broader meaning than that determined by the nature of the product. Therefore, to some extent a party may be liable for the incorrect use and possibly even the misuse of a product. The distinction between a use which can reasonably be expected and a use which may not be reasonably expected is one of the most difficult problems in the application of the new law and must be resolved in each individual case.[5]

(c) A very important restriction of the term 'defect' results from the third requirement, which focuses on the time of distribution. This assures that products are not considered defective for the sole reason that a newer and a more technically advanced product is subsequently put in circulation. Since a product may be distributed several times in the distribution chain,

1 Compare Welser *Produkthaftungsgesetz*, annotation 3 to §5; Andréewitch in ÖJZ 1988, 228.
2 Regierungsvorlage, 272 der Beilagen zu den Stenographischen Protokollen des Nationalrates XVII. GP, to §5. Compare also Austrian Sup Ct in JBl 1993, 524 with annotation of Posch.
3 Compare Fitz, Purtscheller and Reindl *Produkthaftung*, annotation 10 to § 5; Welser *Produkthaftungsgesetz*, annotation 12 to §5.
4 Welser *Produkthaftungsgesetz*, annotation 13 to §5; Welser in WBl 1988, 172; Andréewitch in ÖJZ 1988, 228.
5 Compare Posch 'Produkthaftungsgesetz - Eine erste Analyse der Probleme' RdW 1988, 65, 69; Welser *Produkthaftungsgesetz*, annotation 14 to §5.

a change in the safety expectations during distribution will affect liability under the PHG.

If, after the first distribution of a safe product by the producer, but during later distribution of the product through the distribution chain, the level of safety expectations justifiably rises, the producer will not be liable because he had distributed a product which was considered safe at the time he put it into circulation.[6] Eventually, however, the importer and all other dealers who have distributed a defective product based on this higher level of safety expectation may be held liable.[7] Problems of recourse will be dealt with at a later time.

It is unclear whether ineffectiveness is a defect under the PHG. If, for example, a medicine is ineffective and the patient could have been cured by using another one, would this incur liability? It is assumed that such ineffectiveness is not covered by section 5 of the PHG.[8]

The effectiveness of a medicine can usually only be hoped for, not expected; even in the case of a correct prescription by a doctor and perfect quality of the product, the medicine may not help. The presentation of the product is important, especially the information enclosed with it by which an unrealistic expectation of effectiveness may be created or eliminated.

The same applies to other cases of product ineffectiveness. Generally, the question is whether the product is altogether inappropriate or whether the damage was caused by an operational difficulty or a malfunction of the product itself.[9]

5.2.4 Liability independent of fault

Liability under the PHG occurs regardless of fault. The proof that all conceivable measures have been taken is no defence. Under the PHG a party is liable, even if a single product shows dangerous defects, despite all possible care and control ('Ausreisser'). Development risk, however, is a good defence. If it is objectively impossible to recognise a defect as such under the state of science and technology at the time of distribution, liability will be excluded.[10]

5.2.5 Liability of producers and importers

The importer is liable in the same way as the producer for every defect of the product. This liability was implemented in order to spare an injured person litigation and/or execution of a judgment against a producer in a foreign country.[11]

The importer is now liable for every defect of the product, even if he has not caused the defect and even if the most diligent examination could not have revealed the defect.

---

6   Welser *Produkthaftungsgesetz*, annotation 17 to §5.
7   Fitz, Purtscheller and Reindl *Produkthaftung*, annotation 27 to §5; for other opinion regarding dealers see Welser *Produkthaftungsgesetz*, annotation 17 to §5.
8   Also Welser *Produkthaftungsgesetz*, annotation 20 ff to §5; Preslmayr, *Handbuch* , pp 71 ff;other opinion Fitz, Purtscheller and Reindl *Produkthaftung*, annotation 37 to §5; Musger, Zur Anwendbarkeit des PHG auf wirkungslose Produkte, WBl 1990, 289.
9   Welser *Produkthaftungsgesetz*, annotation 23 to §5.
10 Compare Welser *Produkthaftungsgesetz*, annotation 12 to §8; Fitz, Purtscheller and Reindl *Produkthaftung*, annotation 14 to §8; Austrian Sup Ct in JBl 1996, 188.
11 Regierungsvorlage, 272 der Beilagen zu den Stenographischen Protokollen des Nationalrates XVII. GP, to §1.

The producer or the importer can avoid liability by producing the following evidence:

(a) He did not distribute the product as a business person; thus, there is no liability for products stolen from the warehouse of the producer or importer respectively, or for products which cause damage while they are stored by the producer or importer.[12]

(b) The product was not defective at the time of distribution by the producer or importer. To avoid liability it is sufficient to prove that this was probable. There is no liability for the producer or importer if the defect was caused by incorrect storage by the dealer, and the producer or the importer respectively prove that this is probable.[13] In such a case the dealer is liable, as he was until the present legislation, unless he acted free of fault.

(c) By objective standards it was impossible according to the state of science and technology at the moment of distribution to discover the defect. In this case liability for the risk of development is excluded. The PHG states it is not necessary for the business person concerned to discover the defect if at the time of distribution nothing relevant was published anywhere in the world, which would have helped specialised scientists and technicians to recognise a particular characteristic of the product as defective.[14]

The time of distribution by the producer or importer is very relevant because the importer is responsible for and bears the risk of any technical developments during the period in which he stores the product.[15] This may be important especially as far as medicines are concerned: for years nobody knew that the medicines vital for haemophiliacs could transmit Aids, a virus at that time undiscovered. The Aids virus and its danger in some blood substitutes were only discovered after 1985. If an importer sells such a substitute after the discovery which he bought before the discovery, he – not the producer – will be liable regardless of whether he knew of the scientific discovery or not.

(d) The product is an agricultural or forest organism which was generically engineered by somebody different from the defendant.

(e) The criteria which constitute a defect are based on a mandatory provision of law or an official Directive. If regulations require that a bottle must have a thickness of 3 mm but safe handling requires 5 mm, there will be no liability if the bottle is 3 mm thick. However, there will be liability if the regulation requires only certain minimum standards. The producer or importer cannot avoid liability by complying with these minimum standards.

(f) Before the first revision of the PHG on 1 January 1994 also damages to property suffered by a businessman were covered by the PHG. In this case the defendant was allowed to prove that liability has been contractually excluded by direct agreement with the injured person. As opposed to liability under the ABGB (see section 3.6, above), it was no longer possible

---

12 Fitz, Purtscheller and Reindl *Produkthaftung*, annotation 6 to §7; Welser *Produkthaftungsgesetz*, annotation 6 to §7.

13 Welser *Produkthaftungsgesetz*, annotation 7 to §7; Taschner *Produkthaftung* (1986), annotation 10 to art 7; compare also Appeal Court Linz in ecolex 1994, 756.

14 Welser in WB1 1988, 174; Fitz, Purtscheller and Reindl *Produkthaftung*, annotation 14 to §8. Welser *Produkthaftungsgesetz*, annotation 12 to §8, wants to take into account unpublished discoveries too.

15 Compare Welser *Produkthaftungsgesetz*, annotation 13 to §8; Welser in WB1 1988, 174.

to exclude liability in the contract with the first dealer with the effect that a consumer cannot claim damages. Furthermore, an exclusion was only possible for damage to property suffered by a businessman under the KSchG. Liability for personal injuries as well as for damage to the property of a consumer cannot be excluded (KSchG section 9). As damages to property of a businessman predominately used in his business are no longer covered by the PHG, it is no longer possible to contractually exclude the liability under the PHG in advance (section 9).

5.2.6 Recourse

The person who has caused the damage shall bear the final liability.

Therefore, the importer has a claim against the producer provided that neither he nor one of his staff has caused the defect. This claim is even valid for a foreign middleman, if the producer cannot be confirmed. If the importer has partly caused the defect, the responsibility will be shared. This joint liability depends firstly on the fault and secondly on the causal relationship (section 12).

The producer of the finished product may have recourse against the producer of a defective part of the product. Also in this case joint liability will apply.

The recourse covers in any event the justified payment of compensation for loss. As a claim for payment of the costs of proceedings is not justified[16] this question should be clarified in the supply contract.

A change in the safety expectations or in the state of science and technology after the time of distribution by the producer and before the sale to the consumer means that the – currently – perfectly good product is considered defective and causes liability to the importer or dealer without giving him a right to have recourse under the PHG.[17] A possible claim could be based only on culpable violation of the duty of the producer to inspect the product or on an exemption clause covering this possibility.

Since the recourse is independent of a damage claim which has been passed by assignment by operation of law, the limitation period is 30 years.[18] According to this interpretation, the period of liability under PHG may be considerably longer than ten years, which is stated as being the absolute limitation period under the PHG.

According to the prevailing view in Austria,[19] Austrian law is applicable to a recourse against the foreign intermediary or producer, respectively.

5.2.7 Liability of the dealer

According to the PHG a subsidiary liability affects dealers, if for national products the producer, or for foreign products the importer, cannot be established. If the importer or the national producer is traceable, for example by an imprint on the product, then the dealer is not liable.[20]

---

16 Fitz, Purtscheller and Reindl *Produkthaftung*, annotation 10 to 12; Welser *Produkthaftungsgesetz*, annotation 15 to §12.

17 Welser *Produkthaftungsgesetz*, annotation 17 to §5 and annotation 13 to § 8.

18 Fitz, Purtscheller and Reindl *Produkthaftung*, annotation 4 to §13; Regierungsvorlage, 272 der Beilagen zu den Stenographischen Protokollen des Nationalrates XVII. GP, to §12; Welser in WBl 1988, 175; Welser *Produkthaftungsgesetz*, annotation 10 to §13.

19 Welser *Produkthaftungsgesetz*, annotation 5 to §12 with further reference.

20 Fitz, Purtscheller and Reindl *Produkthaftung*, annotation 42 to §1; Barchetti and Formanek *Produkthaftungsgesetz* p 41; Austrian Sup Ct in ecolex 1992, 843; other opinion Welser *Produkthaftungsgesetz*, annotation 21 to §1.

Even if there is liability, the dealer can avoid it if he informs the injured person, within a reasonable period of time, who the producer is or – for imported products – who the importer is, or – in any case – who his supplier is. The disclosure of a foreign producer or a foreign supplier does not exempt the dealer of his liability.

A period of time of one to two weeks is considered as reasonable.[1] The naming duty, according to this provision, includes not only providing the name, but also providing details of the particular purchase so that the injured person is able to produce evidence against the supplier that the defective product originates from him.[2]

The injured person will often succeed – for example, on the basis of an invoice – in proving that he has obtained the product from the dealer, although the product itself is no longer available. If the dealer has obtained the same kind of product from several producers and he can no longer establish by means of an invoice the producer of the defective product, the naming of all producers is enough to exempt the dealer from the liability. It is the injured person who must bear the risk that he cannot prove which producer has actually marketed the defective product.[3]

From this principle – that the dealer only has a duty to name his supplier – it follows that the injured person must bear the risk of insolvency of the producer or importer.[4]

In case the dealer does not name his supplier and becomes thereby liable, he may raise the same objections as those pertaining to the producer or the importer (see section 5.2.5, above). If he pays damages, then he can claim recourse against his suppliers, unless they exclude their liability by naming the domestic or foreign producer of the defective goods.

5.2.8   Burden of proof

As provided by the law before the PHG, the injured person has to prove that the product was defective, that he suffered a damage and that the defective product directly caused the damage. Furthermore, the injured person must also prove that the defendant produced or imported the defective product.[5]

Therefore, the injured person must also prove that the defendant and not a competitor was the real importer of the defective product. This has far-reaching practical consequences, for example, when there are several importers and if it cannot be established – for instance by the serial number – who really imported the defective product.[6]

The PHG reverses the general rules on the burden of proof in two cases. The producer or the importer must prove that he has not put the product on the market or that he did not act in the course of business in doing so. This

---

1   Erläuterung, 272 der Beilagen zu den Stenographischen Protokollen des Nationalrates XVII. GP, to §1; Austrian Sup Ct in ecolex 1992, 843 has allowed a longer period, but the plaintiff did not raise that argument because he based the claim on the assumption that the defendant is producer/importer; see also Austrian Sup Ct in JBl 1995, 592.
2   Compare Barchetti and Formanek *Produkthaftungsgesetz* p 43; Schmidt-Salzer and Hollmann *Kommentar*, annotation 330 to art 3.
3   Schmidt-Salzer and Hollmann *Kommentar*, annotation 329 to art 3.
4   Schmidt-Salzer and Hollmann *Kommentar*, annotation 335 to art 3.
5   Welser *Produkthaftungsgesetz*, annotation 1 to §7; Fitz, Purtscheller and Reindl *Produkthaftung*, annotation 1 to §7; compare also Appeal Court Linz in ecolex 1994,756.
6   Welser *Produkthaftungsgesetz*, annotation 4 to §7; Fitz, Purtscheller and Reindl *Produkthaftung*, annotation 53 to §1 and annotation 5 to §7.

shift of the burden of proof is not valid for other suppliers. Therefore, if a dealer faces a claim, the injured plaintiff must also prove that the defendant put the defective product on the market and acted thereby as a businessman.

Since it is assumed in favour of the injured person that a defective product was already defective when it had been put on the market by the defendant, the burden of proof on the defendant is relatively heavy.

5.3 Description of special or anomalous provisions in respect of product liability law in Austria

5.3.1 Quasi-producer

Anyone putting his name or his trademark on a product can be liable as if he were the producer. If the actual producer can be recognised from the product, the person additionally putting his trademark on the product will not be liable. If the trademark or name of the dealer is marked on the product, he will not be liable as a producer as long as his position as dealer is indicated clearly enough on the product. Anonymous products labelled only with the name of the dealer, without an explicit reference to his position as a mere dealer, will result in the liability of the dealer as a producer.[7]

The dealer, in order to avoid having the liability of a producer imputed to him, should make certain that the name of the producer is written on the package which is given to the consumer. An unambiguous indication of the dealer's position as dealer should also be made: eg 'distributed by X Company'.

5.3.2 Medical prescription

Who is the producer under the PHG when a pharmacist mixes a pharmaceutical preparation according to a physician's medical prescription? The physician has only contributed to the manufacturing process with his prescription (an immaterial contribution) and not with a movable, tangible good. Therefore, he can only be held liable for a wrong prescription under the rules heretofore in force. It is the pharmacist who should incur liability pursuant to the wording of the law. This is the opinion of most Austrian authors.[8] The opposite opinion – which is partly advanced by the Council Directive – is that a pharmacist is not liable as a producer, because he is only a small part of the production process. It is the physician who determines production: thus, if the physician is not liable as a producer, then a pharmacist who contributes only a small part to the production process should not be liable either.[9]

An argument for the opinion advanced by the Council Directive is that the physician is more likely to have been assigned to the patient than the pharmacist, who has coincidently been chosen by the patient. This case is comparable to a business entity manufacturing a product according to the specifications of a customer. In such a case, the prevailing opinion of Austrian authors[10] is that a businessman is liable – independent of fault – only for his

7 Welser *Produkthaftungsgesetz*, annotation 9 ff to §3; Welser in WB1 1988, 170.
8 Welser *Produkthaftungsgesetz*, annotation 3 to §4; Welser in WB1 1988, 171.
9 Schmidt-Salzer and Hollman *Kommentar*, annotation 14 to art 2; but compare Schmidt-Salzer and Hollmann *Kommentar*, annotation 67 to art 2.
10 Fitz, Purtscheller and Reindl *Produkthaftung*, annotation 14 to §3; for just a part of the opinion see Welser *Produkthaftungsgesetz*, annotation 18 to §3.

field of activity and the materials he used: for mistakes in the specification (submitted to him by the customer) he is as a rule only liable in case of fault.

5.3.3   Agricultural products

Agricultural and forest products and game are exempted from the PHG as long as they have not initially been processed or are generically engineered organisms.

Such initial processing triggers the liability of the producer – according to the definition. This vague legal term leaves room for confusion: the verdict on the question of initial processing will depend on the circumstances of the individual case. The destruction of natural development through harvesting, as well as later storage, is certainly not considered initial processing. The examples listed in the explanatory notes to the PHG avoid problem cases: sausages, canned vegetables, flour and wine are in any case products in the sense of the PHG.[11]

The following criteria are given to help in clarifying the distinction.[12] First, it depends in what condition a product – when properly used – must be to cause damage; this will normally be the case only after preparation. Second, it should be assessed whether preparation causes additional risks which do not already exist in nature. The production of frozen food, the sawing of trees into boards, or the production of sugar are 'processing' under the PHG. The packing for transport and debarking of trees are not 'processing' under the PHG.

Recently an analogous expansion of liability exemption for agricultural and forest products has been advanced.[13] Farmers and restaurants primarily working with such products should be liable only for risks additionally caused by their work, but not for already damaged products. An extension of this analogy for the processing of medical herbs would seem obvious, but such an extension cannot be agreed to in the case of agricultural undertakings larger than farms. The industrial processing of products must be subject to the more severe liability of the PHG.

5.3.4   Computer software

Problems arise especially in connection with software and hardware because 'product' is defined as a 'movable, tangible good'. Whether a person is liable for software defects under the PHG depends on whether software is a tangible good or not. Software itself is a mere intellectual achievement, and therefore, unlike hardware, its tangible substrate (eg magnetic tapes, discs) is intangible.

Consequently, it is generally considered[14] that a person is liable for damages only if the damage is caused by a defect in the hardware, but not in the software. The other less widely held view[15] is that since printed works are 'products' within the Directive the producer, the importer and the dealer are liable for mistakes with regard to the contents under the provisions of the PHG. For this reason, liability for defects of software under the PHG may arise.

11   Compare Posch in RdW 1988, 69; Welser *Produkthaftungsgesetz*, annotation 11 to §4.
12   Fitz, Purtscheller and Reindl *Produkthaftung*, annotation 21 to §4.
13   Koziol 'Zur Produkthaftung für landwirtschaftliche Erzeugnisse' RdW 1988, 154.
14   Welser *Produkthaftungsgesetz*, annotation 4 to §4; Welser in WB1 1988, 171; Andréewitch in ÖJZ 1988, 228; other opinion Fitz, Purtscheller and Reindl *Produkthaftung*, annotation 12 to §3.
15   Fitz, Purtscheller and Reindl *Produkthaftung*, annotation 12 to §3; Barchetti and Formanek *Produkthaftungsgesetz*, p 56.

5.3.5 Damage to property

Unlike the Directive, damage to property suffered by a businessman could also be recovered under the provisions of the PHG if the product was distributed before 1 January 1994. The liability was not limited to damage to the property of a consumer. However, liability for the property damages of a businessman could be excluded by direct agreement with the (later) injured person (section 9).

5.3.6 Precaution for coverage

Producers and importers – although not dealers – are obliged to take precautions for the settlement of damage claims under the PHG in a way and to an extent which is customary in fair business practice. This can be done, for example, by entering into an insurance agreement or in another suitable way, so that compensation claims based on the PHG can be met. According to the report of the parliamentary committee on Justice[16] this obligation can also be met by maintaining a sufficient balance sheet reserve or by obtaining cover from a sufficiently wealthy person, for instance from a foreign parent company. Since a balance sheet reserve is, however, only an asset on paper which does not constitute an actual coverage fund, this could possibly be considered as insufficient by the courts.[17] The indications concerning the sufficiently wealthy person are so imprecise (for instance, it is not clear whether the sufficient wealthiness must exist when the covering note is given or when the damage occurs) that practically the only way of fulfilling this provision would be always to enter into an insurance agreement.

The Act does not provide for direct liability of the managers and of the senior executive officers, contrary to some legal drafts. Only the firm or company is bound to provide for a coverage provision. Managers, members of the executive or the supervisory board, 'procurists' and other senior officers of a firm which have an authoritative influence are still liable within the limits set by the regulations on negligent bankruptcy. In civil law, a violation of the duty to provide a coverage provision makes the responsible person liable according to ABGB section 1311 for the losses of creditors which would not have been suffered in the case of a proper coverage provision.[18]

5.3.7 Transitional provisions

According to section 19 the PHG does not apply to damage caused by products which were marketed before its commencement date, namely 1 July 1988. The first revision applies only to products marketed after 1 January 1994. Even these transitional provisions contain several problems.

The wording of the PHG seems to focus on marketing by the liable entity.[19] Therefore, if the importer markets a product after 1 July 1988, which he has bought before this date from the producer, then the importer but not the producer is liable under the PHG. The same must be valid for a dealer. When

16 2. Bericht des Justizausschusses, 438 der Beilagen zu den Stenographischen Protokollen des Nationalrates XVII. GP (2nd report of the Committee for Juridical Matters).
17 Compare Fitz, Purtscheller and Reindl *Produkthaftung*, annotation 7 to §16.
18 Compare Karollus 'Zivil- und Strafrechtliches zur "Deckungsvorsorge" (§16 ProdHG)', RdW, 1988, 186; Roth 'Produkthaftung und Haftungsdurchgriff' GesRZ 1988, 119.
19 Fitz, Purtscheller and Reindl *Produkthaftung*, to §19; Posch in RdW 1988, 75; Posch 'Nochmals: Zur Übergangsbestimmung des Produkthaftungsgesetzes', RdW 1988, 378.

a dealer sells a defective, anonymous product after 1 July 1988 that he already had in stock before this date, he may be liable according to the PHG. He can still exempt himself from liability by naming his supplier, the national producer or the importer. However, according to this opinion these entities are not liable, since they marketed the product before 1 July 1988.

On the other hand, another opinion[20] is that marketing for the first time by the producer should be relevant, since the potentially liable entity could not adapt the already marketed goods to the stricter requirements of the PHG.

5.4   Optional provisions

Agricultural and forest products and game are not products under the definition of the PHG as long as they have not been initially processed.

The 'state of the art' defence is possible under the Austrian PHG.

The maximum amount for which a claim may be brought and which is optional pursuant to article 16 of the Directive does not apply in Austria.

---

20   Andréewitch 'Zur Übergangsbestimmung im Produkthaftungsgesetz' RdW 1988, 283; Welser *Produkthaftungsgesetz*, annotation 2 to §19.

CHAPTER III

Belgium

Lucien Simont Esq

Manuela von Kuegelgen

Stibbe Simont Monahan Duhot
Rue Henri Wafelaerts 47-51 (box 1)
1060 Brussels
Belgium

Tel: ++ 32 2 533 5211
Fax: ++ 32 2 533 5212

CHAPTER III

Belgium

1 INTRODUCTION

1.1 Introduction to the Belgian legal system[1]

Belgium is a Constitutional Monarchy. It has known fundamental constitutional reforms in the 1970s and 1980s and has been a federal state since 1993.

The Belgian state is headed by the King and includes, at federal level, an executive power vested in the King, who chooses his ministers; a legislative power exercised by the King; and a bicameral legislative body (the House of Representatives (*chambre des représentants*) and the Senate (*Sénat*)) with pre-eminency of the House of Representatives, and a judiciary power exercised by the courts and tribunals.

The Belgian state is divided in three regions (the Walloon Region, the Flemish Region and the Region of Brussels Capitale) and three communities (the French Community, the Flemish Community and the German-speaking Community), each having its own government and legislature. These federated entities have the power to enact legislative rules (called '*décrets*' except for Brussels where legislative rules are called '*ordonnances*') in their sphere of competencies, as defined by the Constitution and the special law on institutional reforms of 8 August 1980.

The Federal authority, for its part, has no competences other than those attributed to it by the Constitution or the laws on institutional reforms. Consumer protection matters remain an exclusive competence of this authority.

Judiciary power has not been affected by the constitutional reform. Courts and tribunals of the judiciary power have jurisdiction to hear all matters relating to civil subjective rights. Cases involving political rights may, for their part, be attributed to administrative courts. In this respect, the Council of State, is competent to void illegal or unconstitutional administrative acts.

On the other hand, the Court of Arbitration has the power to void *legislative* acts under certain restrictive conditions defined by the law.

The judiciary court system is pyramidal.

At the lowest level (county level), one finds Justices of Peace (*Justice de Paix*) and Police tribunals (*tribunaux de police*).

At district level, there are mainly four kinds of court:

(1) the court of first instance (*tribunal de première instance*), which comprises a civil and a criminal court and is a court of general jurisdiction;

---

1 This overview describes Belgian legal system in broad outline and is thus necessarily limited to certain main features of the system.

(2) the commercial court (*tribunal de commerce*), which is a court of special jurisdiction, and is mainly empowered to hear claims between traders or against a defendant who is a trader;

(3) the labour court (*tribunal du travail*), which is mainly empowered to hear matters relating to work relationships; and

(4) the juvenile court (*tribunal de la jeunesse*) which is part of the court of first instance and is competent to deal with juvenile matters.

The Presidents of the Courts mentioned under points 1, 2 and 3 above are empowered with specific competences. They are, inter alia, competent to order provisional measures in case of urgency.

At judicial area level, there are five Courts of Appeal (*cours d'appel*) divided into civil, commercial and criminal chambers. These courts are competent to reverse judgments delivered by the first instance courts. They also have specific competences in fiscal matters. There are also five Courts of Appeal for labour law (cours du travail).

Finally, there is one Supreme Court in Belgium. This court's first mission is to overrule courts' decisions which violate the law (in a broad sense). It has, in principle, no jurisdiction to review the *facts* of the cases it has to deal with, its competence being limited to *issues of law*. The Supreme Court has also specific competences listed in articles 609-615 of the Judicial Code.

Procedures before courts and tribunals are normally introduced by serving a writ of summons which must meet certain requirements enumerated in the Judicial Code. The procedure is generally adversarial subject to certain exceptions (for example in matters of extreme urgency). The arguments of the parties are developed in oral and written pleadings.

Judgments of first instance are generally subject to an appeal or, where delivered in the absence of one of the parties (*jugements par défaut*), to an opposition recourse. Moreover, a recourse before the Supreme Court may be filled in against judgments which are not subject to an appeal or an opposition. Finally, the Judicial Code organises 'extraordinary' recourses in certain circumstances (eg when a judgment is detrimental to a person who was not a party to the procedure).

1.2 Overview of the law relating to defective products in Belgium

Belgium has never adopted a comprehensive regulation on consumer protection, and product liability remains a multi-disciplinary law, involving elements of civil, commercial, economic, administrative and criminal law.

However, a 'Royal Commission of Study for Reform of Consumer Law' (CERDC) has elaborated a draft 'Code of Consumer Law' assembling the various regulations governing relations between professional and consumers and proposing several innovations in this field.

Consumer protection has undergone important developments since 1991.

First, the law implementing the Directive on Product Liability was enacted by the Belgian Parliament on 25 February 1991. This new regulation has, however, not caused a fundamental revision of the existing system since Belgian product liability law under the Civil Code was already comparable to the strict liability concept set out in the Directive.

Further, the Commercial Practices Act of 14 July 1971 was entirely revised by a law of 14 July 1991 on 'commercial practices and consumer information and protection' which came into force on 29 February 1992. Although this

law is judged to be unsatisfactory in several respects, it has achieved a global reform of the 1971 Act and fills in several lacunae of the former regulation. Moreover, and as its name suggests, the law – which codifies 'fair commercial practices' – aims at increasing consumer protection by enacting a set of mandatory rules applying to professionals in their relations with private customers.

The law increases consumer protection through stricter regulation of advertising and some types of sales. In addition, it expressly confirms certain rules and duties binding on professionals, which had been defined by case law. More particularly, it establishes a duty of information toward consumers and forbids the insertion in sale contracts of provisions defined as 'abusive'.

The law also provides a specific sanction where a 'seller'[2] is found guilty of an unfair commercial practice: a plaintiff may issue an action requiring the seller to cease the unlawful practice. This action may – under certain restrictive conditions – be brought by consumer groups and professional groups in order to protect the 'collective interests' they defend although, as a general rule, Belgian Court proceedings are only open to such groups if the group has itself suffered damage.

Finally, the Belgian Parliament has recently enacted a law relating to consumer safety (law of 9 February 1994, *Moniteur belge* 1 April 1994). The purpose of this law is, inter alia, to implement Directive No 92/59/EC of 29 June 1992. It establishes a general safety obligation and a duty of information binding on producers. It also provides various measures to ensure consumer safety and creates a 'Commission for Consumer Safety'.

Beside these new regulations, most civil and commercial claims remain dealt with under the provisions of the Civil Code relating to a seller's contractual liability and producer's liability in tort, which have been generally construed by case law so as to protect consumers.

Moreover, the 1964 Hague Convention introduced a Uniform Law for international sales of movable goods and provided a special set of rules applicable to seller's warranties and delivery obligations. This Uniform Law came into force in Belgium on 18 August 1972.

Belgian legislation also contains various special regulations concerning specific products, for example in the fields of foodstuffs, drugs and cosmetics. Special laws have also introduced strict liability for certain activities, eg nuclear production.

Professional and trade bodies have imposed their own codes of practice on members. Also, any trader may submit his products to the Belgian Quality Control and Informative Labelling Institute. Approval by the Institute entitles the producer to display a 'quality control' label on his product.

2 PRE-CONTRACTUAL LIABLITY

Pre-contractual negotiations are the steps taken before conclusion of the contract. They are not binding and, generally speaking, have no judifical effect, though their content is important for construction purposes, and they may give rise to a pre-contractual liability claim.

Where a contract is unclear or incomplete, the judge is obliged to construe its terms. In this view, he shall not only take into consideration the text of the

---

2 Defined in a broad sense which includes all persons exercising a commercial or industrial activity and selling products or services.

contract, but also possible outside elements capable of clarifying the parties' intentions. Pre-contractual negotiations are part of these elements and shall be especially useful if covered by written documents.

In other respects, pre-contractual negotiations are to be conducted in good faith. Each party is thus bound to provide his 'vis-à-vis' with all necessary information regarding the contract to be entered into.

If a party was induced to enter into the contract by reason of a substantial mistake (ie if the mistake relates to an essential point of the contract without which it would not have been concluded) he may void the agreement. This may be the case, for example, if the object sold has a hidden defect. In addition, if the defendant party has committed a *'culpa in contrahendo'* (ie a negligent pre-contractual misrepresentation), the plaintiff may claim compensation for the damage he has suffered. In this respect, non-disclosure of facts will often be regarded as a *'culpa in contrahendo'*. It can also be considered as a fraudulent misrepresentation. This will often be the case, insofar as professional sellers are concerned, considering the special duty of care imposed on them by the law and by case law (see below).

On the other hand, even if the contract is not voided, a party may, under certain circumstances, claim compensation if he has been the victim of a *'culpa in contrahendo'* during the negotiations.

The liability arising from a pre-contractual negligence or fraud lies in tort, though when 'pre-contracts' have been concluded, the pre-contractual liability is of a contractual nature.

3   CONTRACTUAL LIABILITY

3.1   Introduction

Besides the action based on a substantial mistake, there are two main types of recourse open to the purchaser who discovers a defect in the object sold:

(1) Articles 1609-1629 of the Civil Code oblige the seller to place in the buyer's control a product conforming to its description and specifications under the contract. Breach of this obligation may lead to the rescission of the sale and to damages (see 3.3 below).

(2) The seller is also obliged to ensure the purchaser due possession of the object sold (see Civil Code articles 1641–1649). With regard to this obligation, the seller will be liable to the purchaser if he furnishes a product which suffers from hidden defects detrimental or prejudicial to its normal use (article 1641). The purchaser may claim rescission of the contract or a reduction in the price. In addition, he will be entitled to additional compensation if the seller acted in 'bad faith', eg if he had knowledge of the defect and did not bring it to the purchaser's attention. In this way, Belgian courts have imposed stringent duties on professional sellers and manufacturers (see 3.2 below).

The scope of application of the aforesaid actions is uncertain and gives rise to much argument. What constitutes a defect giving rise to a breach of warranty or to an action based on a breach of the delivery obligation or based on a substantial mistake is often difficult to establish. The absence of a quality agreed between the parties may indeed also constitute a substantial mistake – since

such mistake must relate to a quality agreed under the contract – or to a hidden defect, especially a functional defect.[3]

3.2 Warranties relating to quality of goods and safety of goods

3.2.1 Definition and characteristics of the defect

Pursuant to article 1641 of the Civil Code, the seller is bound to warrant that the object sold is free from hidden defects which render it inappropriate for its intended use or which would restrict its application to the extent that the purchaser would not have bought it or would have paid a lesser price if he had had knowledge of the defect(s).

The purchaser discovering a hidden defect and suing the seller therefore does not need to prove fault on the latter's part.[4] He only has to establish that the object sold is affected by a *'vice rédhibitoire'*, a hidden and abnormal characteristic of the product which is unknown to the purchaser, which exists at the time of the sale, and the existence of which is seriously detrimental to the purpose for which the product was required (article 1641 of the Civil Code).[5] It is generally accepted that the defect renders the article sold unfit for its intended use when the article is improperly designed or manufactured, when it is incapable of fulfilling its function, or when the product endangers life, health or property.

For a long time it has not been clear whether a defect must be inherent in the object supplied or whether a functional defect can also give rise to a warranty under article 1641 of the Civil Code (a functional defect consists of a hidden characteristic which is not structural but which nonetheless renders the product unfit for its purpose). The Supreme Court of Belgium has decided that a hidden defect is a defect which renders the object unfit for the use to which the buyer intended to put it, even if it does not affect the object intrinsically.[6] It is still open to argument whether or not a functional defect meets the seller's obligation of delivery.[7] Nevertheless the existence of a functional defect in a product is likely to influence the nature of the remedies granted by the court.[8] In the case of an action based on a breach of the obligation of delivery, the court can require the seller to replace or repair the object sold, while in the case of an action based on a breach of warranty for hidden defects, such performance could not be imposed on the seller.

The use for which the product was intended must have been known by the seller. The seller is, however, deemed to know the normal use of the object sold[9] and any use he guaranteed in any advertising or in negotiating the

---

3 See L Simont 'La notion fonctionnelle de vice caché, un faux problème?' *Etudes en Hommage à René Dekkers* 1982 pp. 331-342

4 J L Fagnart *Product Liability* Brussels 1977, p 9, no 10; Supreme Court, 4 May 1939, Pas 1939, I, 225.

5 It is sometimes stated that the defect for which it is intended must be serious. In fact, the defect will always be serious if it seriously affects the purpose intended.

6 Supreme Court, 18 November 1971, Pas 1972, I, 258.

7 L Simont 'La notion fonctionnelle de vice caché: un faux problème?' *Etudes en hommage à René Dekkers* (1982) pp 331-342; L Simont, J De Gavre and P A Foriers 'Chronique de jurisprudence: Les contrats spéciaux' RCJB 1985, p 149.

8 J Van Ryn and J Heenen *Principes de droit commercial*, vol III, 1st edn, no 1717.

9 If the object is sought by the purchaser for a particular purpose which is not its normal use, he should inform the seller of such purpose, otherwise he will not be entitled to warranty if the object proves unfit for the use he intended.

contract.[10] In this respect, professional sellers must bear in mind that their advertising must comply with the Commercial Practices Act of 1991, which forbids advertising capable of inducing the public into mistaking the identity, nature, composition, origin, quality, availability, process and date of production of a product or its characteristics and effects on the environment, as well as its possible advantages or uses[11] and the results which may be expected therefrom.

The seller is not liable where the defect was known to the purchaser or was not hidden at the time of the sale. The seller's warranty of the object sold, whether express or implied, does indeed not extend to cover apparent defects where they could have been revealed by the purchaser's inspection on receipt of the goods.[12] The defect will nevertheless be considered to be apparent when it should have been discovered by a summary inspection (eg if the condition or the nature of the merchandise permitted an easy examination by the purchaser), when it is inherent to the nature of the object (eg a secondhand car could not be expected to perform as well as a new one), or when the seller has declared its existence at the time of the sale.[13]

The hidden nature of the defect will be taken into consideration by the courts as will the degree of specialist knowledge possessed by the purchaser. No particularly high level of scrutiny is to be expected from a private purchaser.[14] On the contrary, if the purchaser is a specialist or professional himself, courts will appraise this condition more severely.[15]

Finally, the defect must be present (at least potentially) at the time the object was acquired. If there is a dispute on this point, it is normally up to the purchaser to prove that the defect existed before title to the property passed.[16] This question will often require expert evidence.

3.2.2   Sanctions

Where the requirements of article 1641 of the Civil Code are fulfilled, the purchaser may bring an action claiming rescission of the contract (*action rédhibitoire*) or a reduction in the sale price (*action estimatoire*). The choice between both actions is left at the purchaser's discretion,[17] though this option shall be suppressed insofar as the buyer is not able to hand the product back in its original state.[18] Moreover, authors generally consider that where the buyer has claimed a reduction of the price, he may not claim the rescission of contract in the course of the same court proceedings.[19]

In other respects, the purchaser cannot claim the repair or replacement of the product, as this would constitute substantially different performance from

10   J Van Ryn and J Heenen, fn 6, above, 2nd edn, no 696.
11   J L Fagnart, note under Supreme Court, 28 February 1980, RCJB 1983, p 235.
12   Brussels, 24 January 1993, RW 1994-1994, p 820
13   P A Foriers 'Garantie et conformité dans le droit belge de la vente', *Les ventes internationales de marchandises*, Paris 1981, p 210.
14   T Bourgoignie 'La sécurité des consommateurs et l'introduction de la directive communautaire du 25 juillet 1985 sur la responsibilité du fait des produits défectueux' JT 1987, pp 357 ff.
15   J Limpens, *La Vente en droit belge*, p 72.
16   L Fredericq, *Traité de droit commercial belge*, vol III, p 169.
17   Court of Appeal Liege, 25 February 1991, R R D 1991, p 418.
18   L Simont, J De Gavre, P A Foriers, Chronique de jurisprudence, Les contrats speciaux, RCJB 1995, p 197.
19   H De Page, *Traité de droit civil*, vol IV, no 184; contra L Simont, J De Gavre, P A Foriers, op cit, p 199.

that in the original contract, and the seller for his part cannot offer such performance to escape from his liability. The court could, however, oblige the seller to refund the price of any equipment capable of remedying the defect.[20]

If the court finds that the defect is sufficiently serious, the plaintiff will succeed even though the seller acted in good faith, not knowing of the defect.

The obligation of the seller to warrant due possession is a 'warranty obligation' (*obligation de garantie*) the breach of which entitles the purchaser to compensation, within the limits outlined above, even if the seller has not been negligent.

Proceedings based on the seller's warranty obligations can also be brought against a remote vendor.[21] Sub-contractors therefore have a right of action against manufacturers, as set out in article 1615 of the Civil Code (the obligation of delivery includes the object of the sale and all its accessories). Sub-purchasers will, however, be dependent on the terms of the contract entered into by their own vendor and all defences (eg limitation, periods, contractual warranties, disclosure of the defect, etc) available to their vendor will be capable of being used against them.[1] Further, their action against the original vendor will be dismissed if the defect did not exist at the time of the first sale.[2]

Besides rescission of the contract or a reduction in the price, further compensation can be sought by the purchaser if the seller was aware of the defect and did not disclose it. In order to succeed in an action for damages in these circumstances the seller has to prove, besides the defect, the harm he has sustained and a causal link between the defect and the damage.[3] He should also give evidence of the fact that the seller actually knew of the defect's existence. On this point, the Belgian authorities have developed a special set of rules for professional sellers and manufacturers, which we will examine under section 3.4.

3.3 Breach of Contract for supply of defective products

The seller is obliged to deliver a product that conforms to the quantity and qualities set out in the contract, whether expressly or impliedly.

Breach of this obligation authorises the purchaser to claim:

(a) the rescission of the contract; or
(b) the binding execution thereof.

In each case, the purchaser may claim compensation for the damage he has suffered.

Such actions are, however, only available where the product has not been approved by the purchaser.[4]

Moreover, breach of the obligation of delivery gives rise in commercial sales to particular sanctions. In such a case, the purchaser is entitled to compensation

20   L Simont, J De Gavre, P.A. Foriers, cited at note 18 above.
21   H De Page, *Traité de droit civil belge*, vol IV, no 186.
1   L Simont, J De Gavre 'Examen de jurisprudence: Les contrats spéciaux' RCJB 1976, p 423.
2   T Bourgoignie 'Le traitement des produits défectueux en droit belge: pratique et perspectives' JT 1976, p 509.
3   J L Fagnart 'La responsabilité du fait des produits à l'approche du grand marché' DAOR 1990, 17 p 26, no 47.
4   H De Page, *Traité de droit civil belge*, vol IV, 3rd edn, No 113.

for the seller's default by buying other products from another seller at the full cost and expense of the first seller.[5] This 'replacement option' (*faculté de remplacement*) must, however, be exercised at the purchaser's own risk, as a court may decide that the breach was not sufficiently important to set the first contract aside. In such a case, the court might only permit a claim for a reduction of the price.[6]

3.4   Special duties binding professional sellers

3.4.1   Introduction

Professional sellers are bound, both at the time the sale is concluded and during its execution, to advise the purchaser of the defects and possible dangers of the product sold. Professional sellers also assume a duty of skill and of inspection of their products.

3.4.2   Duty of Skill

As a result of well established court decisions, professional sellers are presumed to be acting in 'bad faith', ie aware of the defects of their products, even if they did not actually know them in fact. The main consequence of such a presumption is to oblige the seller to compensate the purchaser for all losses he has suffered. Some authors consider that such presumption also limits the validity of exclusion and limitation clauses in contracts. Despite the case law, it is unnecessary to presume that professional sellers are acting 'in bad faith'[7] since it is their duty not only to deliver goods that are defect-free but also to be aware of the defects affecting their products.

The Supreme Court seems to have limited the presumption to the manufacturer of the product and the sellers specialised in that product line. Some authors however consider that the presumption applies to all professional sellers – provided they acted in the scope of their normal activity – but that the proof of their ignorance of the defect shall be higher if they are specialised.[8]

The duty of inspection and skill is indeed not absolute and the seller will escape liability if he can show that he could not have discovered the defect in the goods sold. This means that the presumption of bad faith is rebuttable, contrary to the jurisprudential rule in France.[9]

This statement has traditionally been upheld by the Belgian Supreme Court[10] although in two decisions delivered in 1977 and 1989 it was held that the seller is bound to pay compensation for defect in the goods sold unless he establishes 'the absolute undiscoverability of the defect'.[11] This Supreme Court decision has been construed as a reinforcement of the evidential requirement

5   J Van Ryn and J Heenen, *Principes de droit commercial*, vol III, n 1702.
6   See note 5 above.
7   P A Foriers, Chronique de jurisprudence: les contrats commerciaux, JCB 1987, pp 46, 47; P A Foriers, *la garantie du vendeur professionnel et la Cour de cassation: observations et réflexions* in *Les Obligations en droit français et en droit belge*, Journées d'Etudes de l'Université de Paris Saint-Maur et de la faculté de droit de l'ULB, Bruylant-Dalloz 1994, pp 181–185.
8   L Simont, J De Gavre, P A Foriers, Chronique de jurisprudence, Les contrats spéciaux, RCJB 1985, p 158; versus T Vansweevelt, Risques de développement in *Les assurances de l'entreprise*, Bruxelles, Bruylant 1993, pp 330-331.
9   P A Foriers, Garantie et conformité daus la vente, p 213 cited above at note 13.
10   Supreme Court, 4 Nov 1939, Pas 1939 I 223; Supreme Court 13 November 1959 Pas 1960 313; Supreme Court 6 October 1961, Pas 1962, I 152.
11   Supreme Court, 6 May 1977, Pas 1977, I, 907; Supreme Court 15 June 1989, Pas 1989, I, 1117.

that a seller must meet in order to escape his liability. The absolute undiscoverable character of the defect would compel the seller to prove that the current state of technical knowledge made the defect indiscernible.

Such absolute undiscoverability would thus be comparable to the 'development risks' defence set out in the Directive which is more stringent than a defence based on 'invincible ignorance'.

In a more recent decision, the Belgian Supreme Court has, however, again referred to the 'mere' undiscoverability of the defect,[12] confirming thereby that its former jurisprudence has not been overruled.

This decision is also interesting insofar as it decides that the undiscoverability is not subjective, i.e. dependent on the technical means and knowledge of the particular seller. Such character is to be appreciated objectively, namely that the defect is to be undiscoverable by any professional of the same speciality, placed in the same circumstances.[13]

3.4.3 Duty of information at the time of conclusion of the contract

The duty of information binding professional sellers does not arise from the Civil Code, but has been progressively established by Belgian case law. Moreover, it is now confirmed by article 30 of the new Fair Commercial Practice Act which provides that 'at least at the time of conclusion of the contract, the seller must, with good faith, provide the consumer with correct and useful information relating to the characteristics of the product or the service and to the conditions of the sale taking into account the need of information reasonably foreseeable or formulated by the customer'.[14]

In addition, article 7 of the consumer safety legislation of 9 February 1994 imposes on producers (as defined by article 1.3. of the law) a duty of information circumvented by the scope of their activity. Consumers must accordingly be provided with accurate information, enabling them to evaluate the risks of the product, when it is used in regular conditions or in a situation reasonably foreseeable by the producer. It is also to be noted that the level of safety to be met by any product will be evaluated by taking into account, inter alia, the presentation of the product, its labelling and the information given by the producer.[15]

Indeed, the duty of information rests upon the legitimate confidence of the private purchaser in the skill and statements of a professional seller and is conceived as a means to compensate for the inequality of knowledge of the product existing between buyer and seller. The seller is therefore obliged to draw the attention of the buyer to all substantial conditions of the agreement, ie to all elements which could have influenced the buyer to enter into the contract.[16]

12 Supreme Court 7 December 1990, Pas, 1991, I, 346.
13 See Vansweevelt, 'Risques de developpement', p 337 cited above at note 8.
14 With respect to the scope of this legal provision see Domont-Naert, 'L'information et la protection du consommateur dans la loi du 17 Juillet 1991 sur les pratiques du commerce et la protection et l'information du consommateur' in *Les pratiques du commerce et l'information et la protection du consommateur*, pp 118-120.
15 It should also be stressed that special negotiations require specific information to be given to the consumer (eg for foodstuffs, drugs, cosmetics). In other respects, article 498 of the Belgian Penal Code punishes false statements concerning the quality or the origin of the product sold as a criminal offence.
16 Note M Denève under Court of Appeal Brussels, 16 June 1970, ED 1973, p 154; Le Tourneau 'Conformité et garantie dans la vente d'objets mobiliers corporels' RTDC 1980, p 231.

Where a purchaser is not endowed with a particular skill, both the manufacturer and the seller have a special duty of information[17] imposed upon them, especially if they are in a specialised line of business. Such sellers and manufacturers are obliged to supply accurate advice on the possible uses and defects or dangers (as they are deemed to know them) of the product.[18] In this respect, inaccurate or unclear information or an over-optimistic presentation of the product will be regarded as a tort.

Accordingly, manufacturers and sellers would be well advised to include on the product itself, and/or on its packaging, precise and detailed instructions and warnings as to:

(a) the possible uses of the product (at least its normal uses);
(b) possible dangers that may arise from its use; and
(c) prohibited uses.

The more precise and accurate the instructions, the less rigorous the liability.

So far as more complex materials or products are concerned, such as computers or software, the seller must also supply information as to the potential applications of the product and its fitness for the purpose intended.[19] However, the seller is not absolutely bound to do this. He will only be held liable for breach of obligation if he has guaranteed a specific application of a complex product.[20]

The duty of information is, however, less stringent in practice than it initially appears. A minimal degree of skill is expected on the part of the consumer.[1] Further, the seller is not liable if the purchaser misuses the product or uses it for purposes outside its normal use and which the purchaser did not specify when he bought the product.[2] A professional purchaser is deemed to be aware of the dangers inherent in the purchased product and of its possible uses, provided the product is related to his business.[3]

According to these principles, the seller's duty of information has to be evaluated '*in concreto*', taking into account all relevant circumstances including among others the possible negligence of the purchaser and the content of instructions accompanying the product.[4] In addition, the Belgian courts are more flexible if the seller did not specialise in selling the kind of product that caused the harm.[5]

Sanctions relating to the duty of information are of three sorts:

(a) If the lack of information produces a justifiable and substantial mistake, the purchaser can sue the seller in order to have the contract declared void.[6]

17 J L Fagnart, note under Supreme Court, 28 February 1980, RCJB 1983, p 235.
18 Court of Appeal Brussels, 27 November 1963, JT 1964, p 75.
19 Dommering – Van Rongen L 'Produktaansprakelijkheid en software' *Computerr*, 1988, pp 227-232; *Le Droit des contrats informatiques*, Centre de recherches informatique en droit des facultés universitaires de Namur, 1983 p 137. J P Buyle, aspects contractuels relatifs l'information in *Le droit de l'informatique*, JB 1993 pp 213 ff esp pp 245-254.
20 Commercial Tribunal of Brussels, 18 February 1980, RGAR 1981, no 10274.
1 P A Foriers 'Garantie et conformité en droit belge de la vente' fn 13 above; Supreme Court, 29 March 1976, RGAR 1977, no 9772.
2 Commercial Tribunal of Verviers, 30 November 1983, Jur Liège 1984, p 228.
3 Civil Tribunal of Liège, 23 December 1955, RGAR 1956, no 5780; T Bourgoignie 'Le traitement des produits défectueux en droit belge: pratiques et perspectives' JT 1976, p 511.
4 J Ghestin, *Conformité et garantie dans la vente* (Paris, 1983) pp 22 ff.
5 H Cauvin 'La responsabilité aquilienne du vendeur professionnel de produits dangereux ou insatisfaisants' RGAR 1976, no 9628.
6 H De Page, *Traité de droit civil belge*, vol IV, no 171.

Further compensation will, however, not be awarded unless the seller is guilty of a '*culpa in contrahendo*' (see above).[7] This will often be the case where the seller or manufacturer was a specialist, as such people have a higher duty to give accurate information about their products.

(b) If the purchaser has been induced to enter into the contract because of a fraudulent misrepresentation (ie 'an intentionally false statement') the contract will be void and damages will be awarded to the purchaser (see above).[8] If the fraudulent misrepresentation had an effect only on a term of the contract (eg the price) the purchaser will only be entitled to claim damages, not the voiding of the agreement. Silence will not of itself constitute a negligent or fraudulent misrepresentation. However, where a party has a 'duty to speak', silence will be considered at least as negligent.[9]

(c) Finally, if the product appears to have hidden defects, or if the lack of information produces a product which is unfit for the purpose intended, an action can be brought under article 1641 ff of the Civil Code. The contract will thus be void or the price reduced and the seller will be obliged to compensate for losses or injuries sustained by the plaintiff.

As noted above, the Fair Commercial Practice Act of 1991 provides a specific sanction applicable where a seller fails to meet his obligations. This specific action – consisting of the ceasing of the unlawful conduct – could be brought by a consumer (or a group of consumers) if the lack of information or the misrepresentation attributable to a seller appears to be a practice exercised towards consumers in general.[10]

In addition, the law on consumer safety provides for criminal sanctions in case of a breach of the duty of information provided by article 7 of this regulation.

3.4.4 Duty of information during the execution of the contract

The seller's obligation to advise the buyer goes on after the contract has been entered into. This duty relates to the general principle of law of performance of contracts in good faith.

For example, the seller should inform the purchaser that the use he makes of the object sold is not consistent with its normal use.[11]

The purchaser, as victim of a breach of this obligation, may claim damages compensating him for the damage he has suffered.

3.4.5 Contractual guarantees

There is in Belgium no specific regulation relating to special guarantees given to a consumer. The content of such guarantees thus remain up to the parties. When giving these guarantees, professionals shall, however, take into account the requirements covered by special legislation such as the Commercial Practice Act and the law on consumer safety. On the other hand, special guarantees provided by a sale contract can neither replace nor reduce the legal warranty

---

7   P Van Ommeslaghe 'Examen de jurisprudence: Les obligations' RCJB 1986, p 147, no 60.
8   P Van Ommeslaghe, fn 7, above, at p 67, no 17.
9   J L Fagnart in RCJB 1983, cited above in fn 17 p 237; Court of Appeal Mons, 18 April 1978, Pas 1978, II, 71.
10 See J J Evrard, *Les pratiques du commerce, l'information et la protection du consommateur*, J T 1992, p 688.
11 See L Simont, J De Gavre, P A Foriers, *Chronique de jurisprudence, Les contrats spéciaux*, RCJB 1995, p 210 and the references cited.

contained in article 1641 ff of the Civil Code. More especially, the seller may not invoke these guarantees in order to avoid the rescission of the contract or the reduction of the price (see above).

The report drafted by the CERDC (see above) proposes, in this respect, to regulate the *form* of contractual guarantees given by the seller to the purchaser. Their terms would, for their part, remain entirely free provided they *supplement* the legal warranty.

3.5   Quantum of damages

As explained in more detail below, a plaintiff may recover either for 'patrimonial' or 'extra-patrimonial losses'. In theory, the remedy must cover the whole loss without limitation but Belgian courts usually allow very limited damages to compensate for 'moral harm', eg pain and suffering etc.

Patrimonial losses include personal injuries, such as physical injury, loss of income and loss of earning capacity. Capacity to earn will normally be evaluated on the basis of expert evidence. Patrimonial harm relates to material damage caused to business or private assets belonging to the victim. The damage to the product itself may also be compensated under contract. Compensation for damage to property extends to the replacement value of the object. Intangible losses including pure economic losses such as loss of profit, of trade or clientele, or business interruption, are also recoverable under Belgian law.

Extra-patrimonial losses relate to 'moral harm', ie non-physical loss or damage sustained by a victim or his relatives. There are numerous types of moral harm. Compensation could, for example, be claimed for 'aesthetic suffering', injury to reputation, grief suffered as a result of the death of a loved one, etc. As has already been noted, Belgian courts are usually reluctant to grant extended compensation for such losses.

The damage claimed must have occurred, or be certain to occur. Hypothetical damage is not actionable. Harm occurring later is recoverable provided its future occurrence is unquestionable.[12]

The measure of damages will be determined according to different criteria. The plaintiff must be restored to his former position and, to this end, the court must take into account all the circumstances of the case and evaluate the total damage suffered as at the date of judgment.[13] If the amount of damages cannot be assessed on the basis of precise and objective criteria, the court will proceed to estimate them '*ex aequo et bono*', ie what appears fair and reasonable.[14] As far as personal injuries are concerned, judicial expert evidence will often be required.

When considering which parties may be entitled to compensation, apart from the 'victim' and the victim's relatives (if they give evidence of their indirect moral or material harm),[15] insurers and employers may, to a certain extent, recover sums paid to the victim under an employment or insurance contract.

---

12   Supreme Court, 8 January 1974, Pas 1974, I, 474; R O Dalcq, Chronique de jurisprudence, la responsabilité délictuelle et quasi délictuelle, RCJB 1995, p 737.

13   Supreme Court, 22 June 1988, JT 1988, p 688; Supreme Court, 24 October 1990, Pas 1991, I, 205; Supreme Court, 2 May 1974, Pas 1974, I, 907; Supreme Court, 17 May 1978, Pas 1978, I, 1063.

14   However, the plaintiff shall not be entitled to compensation '*ex aequo et bono*' if such objective elements existed but he failed to produce them.

15   Relatives (descendants or children, for example) may only recover damages if they can demonstrate that their claim is based on tort. They may not start court proceedings in contract since there is no privity of contract.

3.6 Causation

According to well-established case law, the causal link between the 'primary fact' giving rise to liability and the damage is established when the plaintiff proves that but for the 'primary fact' (negligence, defect, etc) the damage would not have occurred. This principle applies in tort and in contract.

This theory, called the theory of 'equivalence of conditions' (*théorie de l'équivalence des conditions*) implies that where the damage occurred by reason of concurrent causes,[16] eg a defect and the negligence of a third party, the manufacturer or the seller and the third party will be liable for the whole damage[17] jointly and severally.[18] However, if the plaintiff has also been negligent, the defendant may invoke this in order to obtain an apportionment of the liability.[19]

As has been noted, compensation extends to all immediate and consequential losses. However, the plaintiff will not be able to recover for damage which is too remote or beyond the defendant's control.

3.7 General remarks concerning the burden of proof

Under Belgian law, it is normal for the plaintiff to establish the merits of his claim. The burden of proof, however, is reversed to a certain extent insofar as product liability is concerned, since case law almost presumes a producer's liability unless he proves an 'act of God'(*cas de force majeure*). Nevertheless, the plaintiff needs to give convincing evidence of the defect, the damage and the causal link between the defect and the damage. The proof of the causal link may also be arrived at by a process of eliminating inadequate causes of the damage.

3.8 Remoteness of loss and damage

Unlike the position where liability for a tort has been established, compensation for breach of contract is only available for foreseeable damage. This principle of foreseeability has, however, been much extended.[20] The whole damage suffered by the plaintiff must be compensated if the defendant is found to have intended the damage caused. Moreover, the possibility of damage occurring must be foreseeable, but not its extent.

---

16 That is to say, 'causes acting contemporaneously and together, causing injury which would not have resulted without either'.

17 Supreme Court, 18 June 1973, Pas 1973, I, 969; Supreme Court, 15 February 1978, Pas 1978, I, 694; Supreme Court, 28 September 1982, Pas 1983, I, 132; Supreme Court, 31 October 1984, Pas 1985, I, 292.

18 In this respect, Belgian courts distinguish joint and several liability from the so-called 'liability in solidum'. The latter applies to concurrent acts of negligence, the former to 'common' negligence or concurrent criminal offences. The differences between these two are, however, of minor importance.

19 Unlike the provisions of the Directive, the negligence of a third party for whom the plaintiff was liable (ie an employee) does not exonerate the producer's liability.

20 J Hayoit de Termicourt 'Dol et faute lourde en matière d'inexécution des contrats' JT 1957, p 601; Supreme Court, 23 February 1928, Pas 1928, I, 85.

3.9   Limitation and exclusion of contractual warranties

Generally speaking, contractual provisions restricting or excluding liability are valid unless:[1]

(a) they contravene mandatory regulations;
(b) they are so extensive in their scope that the seller's obligation is rendered ineffective; or
(c) they extend to cover intentional wrongs.

Contractual provisions contained in standard terms and conditions of sale (*conditions générales de vente*) are only valid if they are expressly approved by the party not seeking to impose such terms.

As far as liability under a sole contract is concerned, clauses limiting or excluding liability for hidden defects are valid unless the seller actually knew of a defect. It has been said that professional sellers by reason of their particular position are supposed to know of the defects affecting the products they sell or manufacture.

Following some authors, a second practical consequence of this presumption of knowledge of defects would be to avoid disclaimer of liability on the basis of contractual limitations. This opinion is very similar to that enacted by the law on product liability although, under Belgian law, manufacturers and sellers are allowed to invoke such contractual provisions provided they prove their complete ignorance of the defect, having taken all steps to check for the defect.

Under the law on Product Liability, contractual provisions aimed at restricting or excluding liability to the consumer are indeed void (see below). More generally, the Commercial Practice Act of 1991 forbids the insertion, in contracts concluded with a consumer,[2] of provisions which creates an obvious imbalance between the rights and obligations of the parties (see article 31 of the law).

The law also contains a list of provisions deemed to be abusive. Clauses modifying or suppressing the legal warranty for hidden defects or providing 'unreasonably short terms' to 'denounce a defect to the seller' are among others forbidden.

This new regulation further reduces the utility of provisions amending the legal warranty provided by articles 1641-1649 of the Civil Code.

However, some provisions remain useful in order to limit product liability.[3]

(a) Provisions defining the limitation period within which claims may be brought are valid if they are reasonable – that is to say, if they are not of such a nature that they would exonerate the seller from his liability.[4]
(b) Provisions disclosing the defects prevent further actions for damages or rescission of the contract.[5] Such clauses have to be precise: a vague or broad

---

1   L Cornelis 'Les clauses d'exonération de responsabilité couvrant la faute personnelle' RCJB 1982, pp 200 ff; Brussels Court of Appeal, 4 March 1988, JT 1988, 624. P Van Ommeslaghe, 'Des clauses limitatives ou exonétatoires de responsabilété en droit belge' in *Les obligations en droit francais et en droit belge*, Bruylant-Dalloz 1994, pp 181 ff.
2   Defined in the act as every person who acquires or uses a product or service exclusively for private purposes.
3   F Walschot 'De invloed van de E G Richtlijn produktaanprakelijkheid op de algemene contractvoorwaarden' TPR 1988, pp 763 ff and especially pp 782 ff.
4   P A Foriers, *La garantie du vendeur professionnel et la Cour de cassation*, fn7, p 68 above.
5   Supreme Court 25 May 1989, J T 1989, p 620.

reference to the 'possible' defects would be construed as a disguised restriction of liability.

(c) Clauses imposing special duties on the purchaser, such as periodic inspection and control, will also be advantageous for the producer, as a breach thereof eventually limits his liability if the damage was partially due to the purchaser's negligence. Besides, provisions defining uses and dangers of the product sold will restrict the producer's liability if the purchaser failed to comply with the warnings and instructions accompanying the product.

3.10 Limitation period

Court proceedings based on article 1641 ff of the Civil Code must be brought within a 'brief period' (article 1648 of the Civil Code).

The starting-point and duration of the 'brief period' is not set out in the Code and is left to the court's discretion. In practice it is likely to depend upon the nature of the defect, the type of product and local commercial customs and practices.[6]

The courts generally permit the brief period to be suspended during the negotiation of an out-of-court settlement, provided those negotiations are 'serious'.

The 'brief period' requirement is necessary to preserve evidence and to prevent the courts having to hear ill founded late claims. The lack of a unified limitation period is, however, a source of judicial uncertainty, as each court will assess the 'brief period' with more or less severity. The new law implementing the Directive has, however, not given rise to an amendment of article 1648 of the Civil Code.

3.11 Vicarious liability

The seller is liable to the buyer for negligence committed by his agents in the course of manufacturing or selling his products.[7]

The Supreme Court does not regard an agent as a party to the contract of sale in his own right. The 'agent of execution' (*agent d'exécution*) is not therefore contractually bound to the victim, and may not be sued in contract.[8]

The agent may thus only be liable in tort but only if the conditions for bringing an action in contract *and* tort are satisfied.[9]

When the negligence may be regarded as a criminal offence, the agent shall always be liable to the victim in tort.[10]

---

6 Supreme Court, 23 March 1984, RW 1984-1985, 127; M Fallon 'L'adaptation de la responsabilité du fait des produits la directive européenne du 25 juillet 1985' RGAR 1987, no 11245, p 7. Depending on such criteria, the limitation period will start to run from the discovery of the defect or from the date of delivery.
7 Supreme Court, 21 June 1979, JT 1979, p 675.
8 Supreme Court 7 December 1973 Pas 1974, I 397.
9 Supreme Court, 8 April 1983, RW 1983–1984, col 163; R O Dalcq and F Glansdorff 'Chronique de jurisprudence: La responsabilité' RCJB 1980, p 357.
10 Supreme Court, 26 October 1990, R C J B 1992, p.497 and note R O Dalcq 'Restrictions à l'immunité de responsabilité de l'agent d'exécution'.

3.12 Builder's liability

Since the Directive excludes immovable goods from its scope of application, only common rules of the Civil Code relating to building contracts will remain applicable to building contractors.[11]

Pursuant to article 1792 of the Civil Code, 'if a building is destroyed totally or partially by reason of a defect [whether apparent or hidden] in its construction, or the geology of its site, the architect and contractor will be responsible for the same for up to ten years'.

The defect referred to by this provision must significantly impair the building's strength and stability. The limitation period of ten years runs from the time approval of the building (*réception définitive*) was given by the owner (*maître de l'ouvrage*).[12]

Moreover, under a well-established line of authorities confirmed by a Supreme Court decision of 1985,[13] the contractor and architect are liable for minor hidden defects affecting the building. That is to say, defects which would not give rise to a breach of the provisions of article 1792 of the Civil Code discussed above. No precise limitation period has, however, emerged from the case law on this point.[14]

It has sometimes been judged that the brief period as referred to under article 1648 of the Civil Code was applicable to this claim.[15] Indeed, were the ordinary limitation period to be applicable, which is 30 years, the contractor would face greater exposure to a claim in respect of minor imperfections than to major defects.[16]

It has, however, been decided by the Supreme Court that article 1648 of the Code cannot be applied to a building contract.[17]

This does not mean, however, that the ordinary limitation period is applicable. The Supreme Court decision states that courts must decide in each case whether the claim was brought by the plaintiff 'in due time'.[18]

3.13 Guarantees concerning services

Since services are excluded from the law of 21 February 1991, the ordinary law of contract will continue to be applied to contracts for services. However, the rules which govern the provision of services are very similar to those applying to sale of goods. The professional contractor must, therefore, not only comply with the standards applicable in his field of activity and inform and advise his customers, but also anticipate and, where necessary, warn customers against any damage.[19]

---

11 Provided liability for hidden defects will be governed by articles 1641 ff of the Civil Code if the building was sold and provided strict liability will be applicable to the building's defective movable components.
12 Supreme Court, 4 March 1977, RW 1976-77, col 2413.
13 Supreme Court, 25 October 1985, Pas 1986, I, 226; P A Foriers 'La responsabilité de l'entrepreneur après réception: réflexions propos de l'arrêt de la Cour de cassation du 25 octobre 1986', ED 1988, pp 261 ff.
14 P A Foriers, fn 13, above, at p 267.
15 Civ Bruxelles 18 April 1989, J T 1989, p 733.
16 P A Foriers, fn 13, above.
17 Supreme Court, 15 September 1994, JT 1995, p 68.
18 G Baert, note under Supreme Court, 15 September 1994, R Cass 1995, p 29 ff.
19 See J P Buyle, *Chronique de jurisprudence d'informatique*, J T 1996, pp 208 and 210.

In addition, the Act of 9 February 1994 on Consumer Safety is applicable to services as well as to products. Contractors will thus assume all the obligations provided by this regulation and be bound by the measures and sanctions it provides (see section 5.2 below). The Supreme Court appears to consider that, insofar as the supply of services is accompanied by the delivery of goods, the rules of the guarantee for hidden defects will apply. In one case, a gas system had been installed in an 'injudicious' way. The Court considered that the fault in the way the delivered goods were installed constituted a hidden defect in the article, causing it to fall within the conditions of guarantee on the basis of article 1641 of the Civil Code.[20] We are, therefore, witnessing a growing convergence between legal guarantees which apply to sales, and those which apply to contracts for services.[1]

4. LIABILITY IN TORT

4.1 Introduction

Belgian tort liability is governed by the notion of fault. The theory of 'created risk' or 'profit risk'[2] has, indeed, never been generally adopted, although strict liability has occasionally been provided by specific regulations, eg in the field of nuclear exploitation.

So far as a producer's liability is concerned, the general rules set out in the Civil Code apply. A 'consumer' harmed by a defective product must establish negligence on the producer's part; in other words, a failure to meet the general duty of care or a breach of a legal obligation.

A consumer has no contractual recourse against a manufacturer or seller if he did not buy the product. Such a person stands in a weaker position than the purchaser, since liability does not arise from the mere fact that the product was defective and caused harm to the plaintiff.

A purchaser may, however, have an interest in bringing an action in tort, for example, if the 'brief period' provided by article 1648 has expired, or if the defect was apparent.[3] However, where a contract was entered into, conditions allowing an action in tort are very restrictive under the Belgian Supreme Court. In order for such a tort action to be successful, the breach of contract must be a failure to meet the general duty of care or constitute a criminal offence, and (provided the breach is not also a criminal offence) the damage suffered by the plaintiff must be distinct from the contractual damage thereby caused.[4] Such a requirement is, of course, very hard to establish. An action based on tort will thus often be dismissed if the parties to the action were also contracting parties.

20 Supreme Court, 6 May 1977, Pas 1977, I, p 907.
1   M Fallon 'La Cour de cassation et la responsabilité liée aux biens de consommation' RCJB 1979, p 171. The European Commission has now elaborated a draft directive on liability concerning services (see OJ 18.01.1991).
2   According to these theories, which have been developed in France, anyone who creates an activity generating risks or makes a profit out of such activity will be liable for all damages caused to third parties, even if no negligence can be proved on his part.
3   For a general comparison between contractual and tortious liability, R O Dalcq, *Traité de la responsabilité civile*, Brussels 1967, nos 32 and ff.
4   Supreme Court, 15 September 1977, RCJB 1978, p 428; R O Dalcq and F Glansdorff 'Chronique de jurisprudence: La responsabilité' RCJB 1980, p 359; Supreme Court, 21 June 1979, JT 1979, p 675; Supreme Court, 8 April 1983, RW 1983-1984, col 163; R O Dalcq 'Chronique de jurisprudence: La responsabilité extracontractuelle' RCJB 1976, p 30.

The provisions relating to extra-contractual liability are contained in articles 1382-1386 bis of the Civil Code. As far as product liability is concerned, (which in this context means liability in tort for defective products causing harm to a third party with whom the producer has no direct or indirect contractual relationship), articles 1382 and 1383 will be the main grounds for actions brought by 'consumers'. Under articles 1382 and 1383, any act causing injury compels the wrongdoer to pay compensation for injuries incurred whether by reason of a positive act or by negligence or lack of caution. This type of action is open to private consumers as well as to professionals so that material prejudice caused to professional assets are recoverable.

Article 1384 al 1 relating to the liability of a bailee for a defective product under his control will rarely apply to the producer, since the product is unlikely to be under his control when it causes the harm. The custodian, however, will have recourse against the producer if he is found liable in tort for the damage caused by the defect in the product. A producer will also be liable under article 1384 al 3 if the defective product was negligently made or the information negligently given by the producer's employees acting in the course of their duties.

4.2   Outline of tort law

The notion of negligence has been extended by case law to include a form of professional misconduct. As a general rule, manufacturers and suppliers owe the public a duty of care and diligence resting upon public reliance on the producer's skill.[5]

They must avoid manufacturing and marketing products which threaten life, health or property. This duty is now expressly provided by the law on consumer safety (see below). They should therefore be aware of technical and scientific progress within their field of activities and adapt the manufacture of their products accordingly. Failure to meet this duty will constitute negligence, even if a specific wrong is not established.[6] A producer's liability, however, is to be evaluated in the light of all the circumstances and depends upon the defendant's particular skills. The greater the degree of skill, the stricter the liability and the higher the duty of care. Consequently, a manufacturer carries a heavier obligation as he is responsible for the construction and design of the product. Suppliers, for their part, must avoid alterations of the product and ensure, for example, proper storage, but may not under current tort law be held liable for damage caused by a negligent manufacturer.

Manufacturers must comply with public safety regulations.[7] Breach of a legal obligation constitutes the most obvious case of tort. However, merely conforming to statutory regulations does not exclude a finding of fault, and will not discharge a manufacturer from his liability.[8] For example, even if a product is consistent with a standard embodied in a statute, it could be considered as defective and the manufacturer could be held liable, unless the

---

5   T Bourgoignie, JT 1976, p 511.
6   M Fallon, *Les accidents de la consommation et le droit*, Bruxelles 1982, p 84. T Vansweevelt, *Risques de developpements*, pp 341-342 fn 13, p 69 above.
7   R O Dalcq, in no 301, fn 3 above.
8   R O Dalcq 'Responsabilité quasi délictuelle et normes techniques et professionnelles' in *Le Droit des normes professionnelles et techniques* (Colloque Spa 1985) p 482; W Van Gerven 'Aanspraakelijkheid voor schade veroorzaakt door produkten' SEW 1970, p 271.

defect is the result of having complied with a mandatory regulation or public policy.

If a product is inherently or potentially dangerous, appropriate warnings must be given to the public.[9] The manufacturer must use all precautions available to reduce the risk of an accident. Moreover, he should comply with regulations applying to advertising, such as the Commercial Practice Act mentioned above and specific legislation in relation to particular products. Also, when the manufacturer discovers a defect in the product, he must take adequate steps to prevent the damage (eg he should give warnings and notices in the newspaper, recall the product, etc).

In this respect, the 1994 Act on Consumer Safety obliges producers, first to inform consumers of the risks of the product and second, to take appropriate measures including, if necessary, the recall of the products or services which are potentially dangerous. The producer is also obliged to inform the authorities of the fact that a product or service they commercialise does not meet the general safety obligation of article 1 of the law.

It follows from the above principles that manufacturers (and, to a certain extent, suppliers) owe a special duty of care and that their negligence is presumed.[10] Such principles are similar to those applying in contract.

4.3 Causation, remoteness of loss and damage, quantum of damage and burden of proof

The rules governing causation and burden of proof will also be the same in contract and tort. Damages will be evaluated in the same way in tort as in contract, although foreseeability of the damage is not a condition for compensation where a tort is concerned.

4.4 Exclusion or limitation of liability

Contrary to the principle applying in contract, producers will in general not be able to exclude or limit their liability to end users as no privity of contract will exist between themselves and plaintiffs.[11] Nevertheless, they will be discharged if they demonstrate either their diligent professional conduct, a fault of the plaintiff or the non-existence of the defect at the time the product was put onto the market.

4.5 Limitation period

Another difference between tort and contract lies in the limitation periods. In the case of an action in tort based on articles 1382 and 1383 of the Civil Code, the limitation period is theoretically 30 years after the plaintiff becomes aware

9   Court of Appeal Brussels, 10 December 1963, JT 1964, p 504.
10 M Faure and W Vanbuggenhout 'Produkt aanspraakelijkheid: de Europese richtliin, harmonisatie en consumenten bescherming' RW 1987-1988, part 1, no 3; Court of Appeal Brussels, 13 November 1987, Rev Liège 1987, p 1460. Court of Appeal Gent, 13 May 1988, RGDC 1990, p 219; versus T Vanweesvelt, *Risques de developpement*, fn 6 on p 78 above.
11 P Van Ommeslaghe, Les clauses limitatives ou exonératoires de responsabilite, p 22, cited at fn 1, p 74 above.

(or should have become aware) of the occurrence of the damage.[12] It is obvious, however, that an action brought, for example, 20 years after the damage occurred, will probably be dismissed for lack of evidence. If the negligence also constitutes a criminal offence, the civil action based on such offence was to be brought within a period of five years according to the Criminal Code.[13] In a recent decision, the Court of Arbitration has considered, however, that such limitation period breaches the article of the Constitution relating to the equality of Belgian citizens.[13a] Civil actions based on criminal offences shall thus normally be barred after 30 years.

4.6   Vicarious liability

As we have seen above, manufacturers and suppliers are liable for their employee's negligence. They may not disclaim this liability by proving they were vigilant in exercising their authority or in choosing their employees.[14] They will however be discharged of their liability if negligence was committed outside the course of the employee's duties.

Employers have a recourse against employees and may recover all damages paid on their behalf provided the employee is guilty of wilful misconduct, serious fault or of repetitive negligence (article 18 of the Employment Act of 3 July 1978).

Article 1385 of the Civil Code relates to the liability of a guardian for damages caused by animals under his control. A producer will rarely be the animal's guardian but an owner convicted on the basis of article 1385 could in certain circumstances exercise recourse against him.

5   LIABILITY FOR DEFECTIVE PRODUCTS ARISING FROM IMPLEMENTATION OF EC DIRECTIVE 85/374 ON PRODUCT LIABILITY

5.1   Introduction

The Belgian law implementing the Product Liability Directive was passed by Parliament on 25 February 1991 and published in the Belgian Official Gazette (*Moniteur belge*) of 22 March 1991. It came into force on 1 April 1991.

5.2   Outline of the provisions of Belgian product liability cover

The provisions of this law only apply to products put into circulation after this date. These provisions do not supersede common law. A victim may therefore have recourse against a producer on the basis of the rules relating to contractual and extracontractual liability.

Although the law offers substantial advantages for consumers – mainly by allowing compensation for damage even if the producer has not been negligent

---

12   The limitation period is, however, interrupted when the plaintiff serves a writ of summons on the defendant.
13   P Delvaux 'La prescription de l'action civile découlant d'une infraction, son point de départ et son avenir' RGAR 1982, no 10.504; Supreme Court, 28 October 1971, Pas 1972, p 201.
13a Court of Arbitration, 21 March 1995, MB 1995, p 8184.
14   Supreme Court, 26 October 1989, Pas 1990, I, p 241.

– the general law of contract and tort will continue to be useful for the consumer as a result of the limited field of application of the Directive.

Indeed, the new law places a primary liability on the manufacturer as defined by article 3 of the Law – the seller being only secondarily liable. Under the common law of contract, manufacturers and distributor vendors are liable on practically an equal foot.

Further, the purchaser will have no recourse other than that based on articles 1641 ff or 1382 ff of the Civil Code when the defective product is itself damaged or when property belonging to the purchaser and affected by the product's defect is for professional use.

Moreover, the definition of the defect is broader under common law than under the law on product liability since the former regards the product as defective if it is unsuitable for its normal use, whereas the latter is centred on defects regarding safety.

The notion of product is also more extensive under the general law since both agricultural products and game, which are excluded from the Belgian product liability law, are covered by the provisions of the Civil Code. This is also the case as far as defects in a building or to a certain extent defects in a product are concerned.

Finally, the notion of damage is broader under the Civil Code. Damage caused to professional property or to the product itself can be compensated. Further, actions can be brought under the Civil Code for minor injuries since there are no threshold amounts stated in the Code.

The law does not require compulsory insurance, although this would significantly increase consumer protection.

Finally, it is to be noted that an amendment to the draft law aimed at allowing consumer protection associations to bring actions on behalf of consumers has been dismissed by the Parliament. Common law will therefore continue to be applicable in this respect and such associations will only be allowed to sue a producer on the basis of the new law if they themselves sustained a damage covered by the law, which will in practice never be the case.

To the writer's knowledge, no decision based on the new law has been published at the time the present chapter was drafted.

5.3   Optional or anomalous provisions of the law

The Belgian legislator has not implemented any of the three options left to the discretion of member states by the Directive.

Primary agricultural products are thus not included in the scope of the regulation. Further, the producer may invoke the development risks defence. Finally, there is no limit on total liability. The text of the law thus appears to comply narrowly with the Directive.[15]

Article 14 provides that when the victim of damage covered by the law receives assistance from a social security system or an industrial accident or occupational compensation system, these payments will 'continue and take priority'. If the damage is not entirely compensated by one of these systems, the victim may claim additional compensation on the basis of the new law, provided an action is open against the liable party under general law.

---

15   For the reasons for not having implemented these options, see D Van De Gehuchte, *De aansprakelijkheid voor produkten*, Kluwer 1992, pp 6–9.

Moreover, damages obtainable pursuant to the law of 22 July 1985, relating to civil liability in the field of nuclear energy (see point 7.4 below), are excluded from the scope of the law by article 15.

Authors consider that these provisions could have effects inconsistent with the terms of the Directive.[16]

5.4   Differences between national law and the provisions of the Directive

Article 2 of the law defines the product as any tangible movable product which may be incorporated in another movable or in real estate or that has become 'real property by destination' ie movable product installed in real property for the purpose of being used for the latter's operation. This definition is more extensive than the one given by the Directive.

Further, it is to be noted that it covers software which is to be considered as a product.[17] Water, gas and electricity are also included in the scope of the law.

'Entry into circulation', which was not defined under the Directive, has been described by the law as being : 'the first action by which a producer gives effect to his intention to give to the product the use he intends to assign to it either by transferring it to a third party or by using it for the benefit of the same' (see article 6 of the law).

This notion of putting into circulation is of major importance under the law since it determines the calculation of limitation periods, fixes the moment at which the defect must exist, and allows the producer to dispute the imputation of the damage occurred.

The definition given by Belgian law was considered to be rather unclear by the Council of State in its preliminary advice on the draft law.[18] It has nevertheless been maintained. The authors of the law indeed believed that the concept of entry into circulation had to be explained in order to distinguish it from the concept of the placing of the product onto the market. Indeed a product could be placed thereon by a thief or a patent-infringer. The producer would in such a case not be liable for possible damage caused by the defect since he would not have had the intention of putting the product into circulation.[19]

The burden of proof of the defect, the damage and the causal link lies with the plaintiff. As a matter of fact, the plaintiff will also have to demonstrate that the defendant is a producer in the sense of the law or one of the persons he may sue under the provisions of the regulation and that the product and the damage are covered thereby.[20] The new system – although it is deemed to lighten the burden of evidence resting upon the plaintiff – is thus quite similar to the existing rules under contract and tort. To the opinion of authors it could moreover create new difficulties.[1]

---

16   See M Fallon, *La loi du 25 février 1991 relative la responsabilité du fait des produits défectueux*, J T 1991, p 467, n 10.

17   Travaux préparatoires, Rapport fait au nom de la Commission de la Justice par Monsieur Hermans, Doc Parl Ch, so 1989-1990 n 1262/5, p 5.

18   Avis du Conseil d'Etat relatif au projet de loi sur la responsabilité du fait des produits, Doc Parl Ch, so. 1989-1990 n 1262/1, p 32.

19   Travaux préparatoires, Exposé des motifs, Doc Parl Ch, so 1989-1990, n 1262/5.

20   See M. Fallon, p.470, fn 16 above.

 1   See M Fallon, p.469, fn 16 above; D. Van de Gehuchte, pp 36-37, *Aansprakelijkheid voor produkten*, fn 15, p 81 above; T Vansweevelt, pp 354-355, Risques de développement, fn 13, p 69 above.

The liability of several parties for the same damage will, under the new law, be joint and several. However this rule will not apply where several parties are judged liable for the same damage on different bases – some on the basis of the general law and others on the basis of the new law. In this case, the rules of Belgian law regarding liability explained in contract or in tort will apply.

The new law confirms that within the parameters of the rules governing this matter, the plaintiff may claim compensation for the moral harm he has sustained. It also provides that the rules regarding suspension and interruption of the limitation under the Civil Code will be applicable to the limitation periods provided by the new law.

5.5 Nature of the system implemented by the law of 25 February 1991

The system established by the law on product liability is theoretically an innovation in Belgian law since it introduces a strict liability of the producer of a defective product. However, it must be pointed out that Belgian case law has already contributed to the recognition of a 'quasi strict liability' of professional manufacturers and vendors.

Moreover it is open to argument whether or not the Directive (and thus the law of 21 February 1991) establishes a 'real' strict liability. The conduct of the producer shall indeed still intervene while appraising his liability under the new law, since such conduct shall be taken into account in order to determine the defect of the product.

Further, the notion of negligence remains present through the defences open to the producer . By proving that he has not put the product into circulation or by raising the development risks defence, the producer indeed establishes the absence of fault on his side.[2]

The strict liability imposed by law appears therefore to be still connected with common rules governing liability.

6 LIABILITY ARISING FROM GENERAL SAFETY LAW AND THE IMPLEMENTATION OF EC DIRECTIVE 92/59

6.1 Introduction and outline of implementation of Directive 92/59

The law of 9 February 1994 on consumer safety is the first global regulation adopted in Belgium on such matter. The initial draft was elaborated before the adoption by the EC Commission of the Directive 92/59. It has therefore been amended in order to comply with the terms of the Directive.

Belgian law has however a broader scope than the Product Safety Directive since it also covers services.

The law is centred on three main axes:

(1) a general safety obligation relating to products and services.
(2) a set of measures destined to ensure safety of products and to prevent or limit the risks and dangers they could reveal.
(3) the appointment of a Commission for consumer safety whose role is mainly to:

2　See T Vansweevelt, at p 356; fn 13, p 69 above.

(a) centralise information;
(b) ensure consultation between professionals and consumers; and
(c) inform the public.

Beside this regulation, specific laws on product safety have been enacted eg in the fields of toys, machinery and consumer health. A brief outline of these safety laws is given below.

6.2   The Product Safety Law of 9 February 1994 and anomalous provisions on the implementation of Directive 92/59/EC

6.2.1   *Scope of the law*

As stressed above, the law applies to both products and services.

Products are defined as any movable goods that are new, used or reconditioned, supplied in the field of a commercial activity, for free or subject to payment, and which are either destined to consumers or capable of being used by them or likely to affect a consumer's private life. Only antiques are excluded from the scope of the law although under the terms of the Directive, products which must be repaired or reconditioned before being used are also excluded therefrom.

A consumer is defined as any physical person who acquires or uses products or services for non professional use or who is likely to be affected in his private life by a product or service.

Services are described as any performance which constitutes a commercial act or an activity exercised by an artisan.

The law does not cover protection of workers or of the environment which are subject to specific regulations.

Finally, the law is of horizontal effect and thus only applies provided there exists no other specific regulation. However, in the case of an emergency, the measures it provides may be applied failing another procedure being organised by the specific regulation.

6.2.2   *General safety obligation and information duty*

According to the Directive the law provides a general safety obligation binding on producers as defined under the terms of article 1.3. This obligation does not, however, modify the strict liability set out in the law of 25 February 1991 nor the rules governing liability in general.

Pursuant to article 7 of the law, producers are also bound by a duty of information as set out in the Directive. The scope of this obligation is more extensive under Belgian law since producers also have to inform the authorities of the fact that their product does not comply with the general safety obligation (article 7 in fine).

6.3   Local optional provisions

6.3.1   *Measures aimed at preventing or controlling a danger*

The measures set out in the law are principally aimed at preventing or controlling dangers in products and services put onto the market. Any measure to be taken is therefore to be proportional to those dangers.

Broad powers have been granted in this respect to the executive power. Pursuant to article 4, the King may, on the one hand, determine the conditions under which products or services may be manufactured, imported, exported, transformed, sold, distributed or rented. He is also empowered to decide whether these products or services are to be recalled by producers. Before enacting such measures, the King is, however, obliged to consult the Commission for Consumer Safety.

Similar powers are granted to the Minister in charge of consumer matters whenever a significant danger occurs.

He may suspend the manufacturing, import, export and distribution of a product for a period not exceeding a year. In case of absolute necessity, he may even order that the product be destroyed. He may also command that accurate information be supplied to the public or that the product be recalled in order to be exchanged, repaired or refunded.

The producer must be consulted, if possible before, and in any case within the fifteen days after, the measure has been decided.

The Commission for Consumer Safety must also give an opinion.

Further, the Minister may address a warning to producers and require that their products be submitted to analyses whether in case of danger or if the characteristics of the product justify such measures. The product is deemed to be 'unsafe' when it has not been submitted to the analyses ordered by the authorities. This presumption is however rebuttable.

6.3.2   *The Commission for Consumer Safety*

The Commission created by the law is part of the 'Council for Consumer Matters'. Its aim is to deal with all questions relating to the safety of products and services and may issue opinions on these matters. The Commission must, moreover, centralise all information available on the potential risks of products and services.

In other respects, it has to ensure a dialogue between producers, distributors, consumers, authorities and specialised bodies.

Finally, the Commission may bring to the public's attention all information it judges necessary, provided the Minister has previously been informed and the producer or distributor heard (unless such hearing was impossible for emergency reasons).

All members of the Commission (which is composed of professionals, consumers, representatives of the authorities and experts) are bound by professional secrecy (criminal sanctions are provided in case of breach of this obligation). The law also provides a special procedure to avoid prejudicial disclosures of manufacturing secrets (see article 14 of the law).

In order to fulfil its tasks, the Commission may require to be provided with all documents it considers necessary or hear any person likely to supply it with useful information.

6.3.3   *Inspection*

The King appoints the agents in charge of monitoring the application of the law. These agents are invested with the power to enter all premises where necessary. They may also request to examine all documents useful to their inquiries and seize the documents which could constitute the proof of a breach of the law (see article 20).

The public prosecutor has, for his part, the right to seize products which infringe the law (see article 22). The agents mentioned above may also exercise this power.

6.3.4   Sanctions

Breaches of article 7 or measures ordered pursuant to articles 4 and 5 of the law give rise to a fine.

The judge may decide to confiscate the benefits obtained by such breaches and order publication of the judgment.

Corporations are vicariously liable for the fines and pecuniary sanctions levied against their agents or workers.

6.3.5   Extent to which Council Decisions EEC 84/133 and 89/45 have been implemented and are operative locally

Belgian National authorities do usually inform the EC Commission on the measures adopted in order to prevent dangers relating to a product. In addition, article 10 of the law on consumer safety provides that the King shall take adequate steps to inform the EC Commission on all measures taken in order to avoid or limit the commercialisation or use of products, considering a risk, grave and immediate, that such products may present for consumers' health.

6.4   Brief outline of specific regulations on product liability

6.4.1   The law of 29 June 1990 relating to Toy Safety

This law implements EC Directive 88/378 of 3 May 1988.

Pursuant to article 2, the King is in charge of determining the essential guarantees a toy has to meet in order to be put onto the market. In this respect, a Royal Decree of 9 March 1991, modified by a Royal Decree of 22 March 1993, provides that toys can only be put onto the market if they do not endanger consumer health or safety when they are used in normal conditions. The Decree also provides various health and safety requirements that a toy must meet. The toy which meets these requirements must bear the (EC) label affixed by the manufacturer.

If a toy, even bearing the 'EC' label, does endanger a consumer's or third parties' health or safety, the Minister in charge of Economic Matters may take all measures in order to stop or restrict distribution of the product on the market.

Officials are appointed by the King in order to monitor the application of the law and its Royal Decrees as well as of the measures ordered by the Minister. These officials may, among others measures:

(1) enter all premises, the access to which is necessary;
(2) take samples of a product;
(3) seize all documents useful to their purpose.

Fines amounting to BEF 500 to BEF 20,000 are applicable to any person who:

(1) fraudulently affixes the 'EC' label on a toy;
(2) affixes on a toy a label capable of causing confusion with the EC label;
(3) fails to comply with the Decrees enacted by the King or the Minister.

6.4.2   The law of 11 July 1961 relating to compulsory safety guarantees in respect of machinery

By virtue of the law of 11 July 1961, the King has the power to determine safety conditions which must be met in respect of machinery, machine parts, equipment, tools, apparatus and dangerous containers.

Several decrees have been adopted pursuant to the provisions of this law, in particular a Royal Decree of 23 May 1977 concerning machinery, apparatus and electric conduits. This decree requires products to be constructed in compliance with a 'code of practice' (*règle de l'art*). The product only satisfies this test where it fulfils certain European standards or provisions laid down by the countries in which it is manufactured. The product must display an adequate level of safety with regard to the user and his property. This condition is deemed to have been fulfilled provided that IBN (*Institute Belge de Normalisation*) or other standards offering the same quality level have been complied with.

In order to monitor compliance with executive orders, officials appointed by the King may visit companies, demand the production of documents such as accounts, take samples and draw up reports on any breaches. Moreover, they may take possession of equipment in the event of the breach being established.

The law provides for penal sanctions (albeit of minimal severity) for breach of royal decrees.

7   CIVIL LIABILITY FOR DEFECTIVE PRODUCTS ARISING FROM BREACH OF STATUTORY REGULATIONS DESIGNED TO PROTECT CONSUMERS AND/OR TO PROMOTE SAFETY

7.1   Introduction

Besides the laws of 1991 on Product Liability and the general safety regulation adopted in 1994 outlined above, legislative measures in favour of consumers have been limited to the adoption of specific legislation in the foodstuffs, cosmetics, household products and machinery sectors amongst others. These specific laws give the government extensive statutory powers for implementing the principles which these laws lay down. In practice, their application has, however, proved to be relatively ineffective.

Specific regulations sometimes provide a strict liability concept in the field of certain activities (see below).

Where standardisation is concerned, the IBN (*Institute Belge de Normalisation*) and CEB (*Comité Electrotechnique Belge*) have considerable power regarding the drafting of technical standards. These two institutions' membership is exclusively composed of professional federations. The standards which they prescribe can be accorded quasi-legislative force by royal decree. The IBN and the CEB also possess the power to register as Belgian standards which are defined on an international scale. Moreover, the trade marks BENOR and CEBEC, for which the IBN and CEB are holders, may be conferred to products which comply with the relevant Belgian standards.[3]

3   T Bourgoignie 'Réalité et spécificité du droit de la consommation' JT 1979, p 298.

Furthermore, it is compulsory for these trade marks to be affixed to certain products (compulsory fire extinguishers in cars and to some extent, toys (see article 4 of the law of 29 June 1990), for example).[4] The compliance of products with standards is not, however, a guarantee of non-liability and would not, for example, alter the position with regard to hidden defects or exempt the manufacturer from taking any other measures which are essential for ensuring the safety of his products.[5] It can be said, therefore, that compliance is a necessary requirement in respect of quality, but that it is not always sufficient. The general duty of care, which applies to professionals in particular, supersedes the obligations with regard to technical standards fixed by the law.[6]

7.2   The law of 24 January 1977 relating to consumer health protection (modified by the law of 22 March 1989 and 9 February 1994)

The industrial development of a continually expanding consumer society called for intervention on the part of the legislator regarding the quality of products in general consumption.

The law of 24 January 1977 appeared in this sector in the form of an 'outline law',[7] defining the objectives and requirements to be met, while leaving it to the government to determine the rules of application. Its field of application is relatively broad since it covers cosmetics, tobacco, detergents, foodstuffs and food additives.

These provisions deal with three main areas: prevention, inspection and sanctions.

7.2.1   Prevention

Intervention of the government in this field will take place at different levels:

(a) The King may lay down rules for or prohibit the manufacture, export or marketing of the foodstuffs and 'other products' referred to by the law. Legislative action in this context will mainly consist of determining the 'negative' composition of the product, that is to say, prescribing the substances (eg additives) which the product may not contain or which may only be present in limited quantities.

(b) The King may order the circulation of certain information to the consumer; thus, with regard to cosmetics, the royal decree of 10 May 1978 provides that the name of the manufacturer, the shelf life of the product and the instructions for use, must be affixed to the product, in indelible print using unambiguous and clearly visible terms.

(c) The King may also lay down regulations concerning advertising, ie any communication having the aim of promoting sales. Thus, the royal decree of 17 April 1990 prohibits the use in advertising of certain references relating to foodstuffs or the addition of information which is likely to

---

4   T Bourgoignie, cited in fn 3, p 87 above; H Cousy 'Les normes techniques en doctrine et en jurisprudence' in *Le droit des normes professionnelles et techniques* (Colloque Spa, 1985) p 402 and 407;

5   R O Dalcq 'Responsabilité quasi délictuelle et normes techniques et professionnelles' in fn 8, p 78 above.

6   R O Dalcq, fn 5 above.

7   Ie a law in which broad lines are laid down limiting the steps the government will be authorised to take by executive measures.

mislead the public with regard to the quality or the nature of the product. Also, tobacco advertising is governed by the decree of the French-speaking community of 2 December 1982. This decree aims to restrict, and prohibit advertising campaigns for tobacco.[8]

(d) Products pending import may, by virtue of a royal decree of 9 February 1981, be stopped at the border if they appear to be damaging or harmful or if a special regulation declares them to be harmful. Products will be inspected and samples taken if necessary. If permission to import is denied, the importer has two options: to agree to the destruction of the goods or to 're-export' them. If the product is 'judged' to be harmful in accordance with a special regulation, the importer may reprocess his goods in order to make them comply with the regulatory requirements.

(e) Finally, the King may set minimum hygiene conditions to be complied with in companies and at workplaces where foodstuffs are manufactured and in places where they are consumed.

7.2.2 Inspection

The authorities have the right to enter the premises where certain products destined for trade are manufactured or sold, in order to monitor the application of the law and royal decrees. They may also demand examination of commercial documents relating to these products and draw up a report on the official visit regarding the breaches which they have discovered. If a request for presentation of these documents is met with refusal or access to the site is denied, the manufacturers and traders will be liable to prosecution.

7.2.3 Sanctions

Breaches of the law or of these executive measures give rise to prison sentences and fines. These sentences are more severe for manufacturers and importers than for distributors.

In addition the 'damaging' or 'harmful' products (ie mainly products which are unsuitable for consumption or harmful to health) may be removed and destroyed. Should the manufacturer or the trader contest the harmful nature of his product, the products would be seized and samples be taken for analysis.

7.3 Human blood and blood by-products: Law of 5 July 1994

The law of 5 July 1994 provides specific rules regarding the taking, preparation, conservation and distribution of human blood and blood by-products. These acts may only be executed by firms determined by the King and authorised by the minister in charge of public health matters.

The law also prescribes specific requirements to be met in order to admit a person as a blood donor and the moralities of blood taking.

It is also to be noted that advertising relating to blood products or by-products is strictly forbidden.

Criminal fines are provided by article 22 of the law.

---

8   This decree has been partially amended by a royal decree of 10 April 1990. In other respects, it is to be noted that the Court of Arbitration has annuled article 13 of the decree which precisely aimed at prohibiting advertising for tobacco (C Arb, 5 February 1992, NB 1992, p 5297).

7.4   Pharmaceutical products and drugs: Royal Decree of 6 June 1960 (modified several times)

The manufacture, preparation, sale or import of pharmaceutical products are subject in Belgium to permission obtained in advance from the Minister for Health. This permission is only granted subject to various conditions being met.

The quality of the pharmaceutical product and its compliance with the laws and regulations on pharmaceutical products must be certified within each company by an 'industrial pharmacist'. Moreover, advertising for pharmaceutical products is strictly regulated by a royal decree of 9 July 1984 which, in particular, prohibits audio-visual advertising and certain claims about the products (eg promises of cures, the descriptions of symptoms of illnesses, etc).

7.5   Liability in the nuclear field: law of 22 July 1985

The law of 22 July 1985 implements the Paris Convention of 29 July 1960 in Belgian law and aims to 'achieve a coherent entity in matters of national and international legislation on civil liability in the field of nuclear energy'.[9]

The operator of a nuclear facility incurs strict liability towards third parties, based on the risk inherent in the operation of reactors and the use of fissionable materials. The liability is nevertheless limited to a ceiling of BEF 4 bn. In the event of there being several parties liable, liability shall be joint and several and cumulative, which means that each operator shall be bound to pay compensation equal to the maximum amount for which he is liable.

The operator is required to insure his liability. The risks of material damage sustained by the nuclear facility and the liability with regard to damage to property and bodily damage caused to the victims are insured by a group of insurers, SYBAN, each assuming a portion of the risks existing in Belgium.

Actions based on the law of 22 July 1985 shall be barred at the end of ten years from the date of the accident or at the end of three years from the date on which the victim became aware or should have become aware of the damage and/or of the identity of the liable party.

7.6   Liability arising from the distribution of electricity: law of 10 March 1925[10]

In Belgium the generation and distribution of electricity is a state monopoly. The local authorities and the associations of local authorities may generate, consume and distribute electricity within their territory. They may, moreover, grant an individual or a private company a concession for the distribution of electricity.

A special regime of liability follows from articles 17 and 18 of the law of 10 March 1925 which provides for operating companies to compensate owners for any damage which could result from using an electric grid. The question whether this liability is really a strict liability is, however, disputed.[11]

---

9   *Exposé des motifs de la loi du 22 juillet 1985*, Documents Parlementaires, Sénat, Session 1983-1984, nos 593/1 and 593/2.

10   This law has been modified, as far as the Wallon Region is concerned, by a '*décret*' of 29 November 1990.

11   *Répertoire pratique du droit belge*, Energie Electrique, Complément T IV, nos 158 ff.

7.7   Liability arising from toxic waste

Under articles 2 and 3 of the law of 22 July 1974, the dumping, sale or acquisition of toxic waste (ie waste dangerous to the environment and to living organisms and which is declared as such by a royal decree) in theory is forbidden unless specifically authorised. Conditions regarding the transporation, import and export of toxic waste are determined by the King. However the quantity of harmful substances which the waste (ie by-products of industrial, scientific or agricultural activity) must contain before it can be declared toxic is relatively high.[12]

Article 7 of the law introduces a system of strict liability which weighs heavily on the generator of toxic waste. The generator is obliged to have the waste destroyed, neutralised or eliminated at his own expense and remains liable to third parties for any damage occurring until it is disposed of, destroyed or neutralised, even if it is not under his control (for example, during transportation) and even if a third party is performing the destruction, neutralisation or disposal operation.

As far as the Brussels Region is concerned, the law of 1974 has been abrogated by an '*ordonnance*' of 7 March 1991. Articles 1 – defining the waste, 7 – cited above, 9 and 15 of the law remain in force however, pursuant to this '*ordonnance*'. In other respects it is noted that an environmenmtal permit is required to exploit or install a waste dump.

For the Flemish Region, the '*décret*' of 20 April 1994 abrogates the law of 1974 but keeps in force article 7 thereof.

Finally, with respect to the Wallon Region, various regulations have put in place a comprehensive regime of waste transport, storage, recycling, etc. Toxic waste is specifically governed by a decree of 9 April 1992. The law of 22 July has however not been abrogated by such regulation.

---

12   B Jadot, J P Hannequart, E Orban de Xivry, *Droit de l'environnement*, 1988, no 400.

CHAPTER IV

Denmark

Georg Lett, Advocate

Pernille Solling, Advocate

Lett & Co
Borgergade 111
DK – 1019 Copenhagen K
Denmark

Tel: ++ 45 33 12 00 66
Fax: ++ 45 33 12 12 66

CHAPTER IV

Denmark

1 INTRODUCTION

1.1 Introduction to the legal system in Denmark

The Danish Constitution was adopted by the Parliament in 1953 (Act No 169 of 5 June 1953). This Act provides that Denmark is a monarchy and that the legislative power is exercised by a Parliament of 175 members together with a king or queen. However, in reality the Danish queen has renounced her political influence and thus Denmark is a parliamentary democracy. The executive power is exercised by the government with the prime minister being head.

The Constitution provides that the legislative power normally cannot be exercised by supranational organs and thus international treaties are not a part of domestic Danish law unless they have been incorporated by repetition or reference in a Danish law. However, according to a special procedure provided in the Act of Constitution, Denmark became a member of the EC in 1972 and thus submits to Community law.

Danish law is, although influenced partly by Roman law and partly by Anglo Saxon law, not similar to either of these. The Danish court system is adversarial. The ordinary courts in Denmark are the Supreme Court (*Hojesteret*), the Eastern and Western High Court of Justice (*Ostre Landsret og Vestre Landsret*) and 82 city courts. These courts may decide on all matters, both criminal and civil. As a principal rule a case can be appealed to a higher court only once. Further courts are, for example, the Maritime and Commercial Court of Copenhagen (*Soog Handelsretten*), the Industrial Tribunal (*Arbejdsretten*) and the '*Rigsret*' which decides impeachments. The Danish constitution provides that ad hoc courts cannot be given judicical power.

1.2 Overview of the law relating to defective products in Denmark

The Sale of Goods Act of 1906 regulates the obligations between purchaser and seller in sales of movables. The committee that drafted the Act emphasised that a contract should not govern the right to compensation for damage caused by the product (*udkast til lov om kob* p 70). Since then courts have with few exceptions based product liability on the principles of the law of tort. The law of tort is not set out in any Act, but has developed over the centuries on a case by case basis. Claims for product liability were therefore until recently almost exclusively brought on the basis of jurisprudence. The implementation of the Directive on Product Liability in Act 371 of 7 June 1989 *om produktansvar* has of course modified this position. Further, a number of Acts deal with specific problems which also have an impact on product liability. For instance, the Act

on Liability in Tort (*Lov om erstatningsanvar*) deals in general with the amount of compensation to which an injured person is entitled, and compensation and indemnity from third parties if the tortfeasor is insured, and some other general questions relating to the law of tort.

There are also Acts on Liability for Nuclear Plants and Aviation, the Railway Liability Act and the Maritime Act which deal with product liability in specific areas.

Although the problems of product liability are not solved on the basis of contract law, the existence of a contract between the parties is not irrelevant. A contract between professional parties may of course regulate and limit the product liability itself and may be important when deciding whether the product is defective or not. It may, furthermore, stipulate the applicable law and jurisdiction. In addition, a possible obligation for the purchaser to check the product may be important when deciding whether there is any contributory negligence. However, it is totally immaterial whether the seller is in breach of contract or not: it is exclusively the law of tort that applies.

2   PRE-CONTRACTUAL LIABILITY

2.1   Effect on the interpretation and extent of the obligations of the parties to a contract

Misrepresentation during the marketing of the product such as failure to disclose relevant facts or change of circumstances or an untrue material statement of facts given during the marketing is of course of relevance when product liability is established.

2.2   Extent of non-disclosure of facts

The marketing of the product comprises all information given during the marketing, such as commercials, oral statements and instructions for use. The basic criterion of product liability is that the product is defective in the sense that it has qualities that under normal use could cause damage to things or persons. As 'normal use' may be defined by the information given during the marketing, misleading information in this material may give cause for product liability. This does not mean that any use of the product for example in a TV commercial can be considered as 'normal use', as the Danish courts tend to assume that people use their common sense. However, written or oral statements concerning the product should give correct information as to the use of the product. If the statements are true but relevant information is missing the consequences will be determined by assessing the facts such as the importance of the missing information and whether the injured party is private or professional. However, product liability probably requires a very low degree of negligence and thus non-disclosure of facts may easily give cause for product liability. Recent jurisprudence (U94 p 53H) has confirmed this.

2.3   Does pre-contractual liability lie in contract or tort?

In Denmark product liability is almost exclusively based on tort and the concept of pre-contractual liability is not usually connected with product liability.

3 LIABILITY IN CONTRACT

As stated above, Danish product liability law is almost exclusively based on tort. To the extent that the contract has any relevance, it will be mentioned in the appropriate place in this chapter.

The realm of contract law covers only damages that are not considered product damages. Some borderline problems are:

(a) The product's self-destruction is not governed by the rules of 'product liability'.
(b) The presence of a defective component in a complex product is more likely to render that product worthless as a whole than to result in actual damage. Consequently, any claim should be in contract rather than in tort.
(c) Denmark has implemented the UN Convention on Contracts for the International Sale of Goods (CISG). According to this Convention, product liability for damage of the purchaser's goods is based on the Convention, ie concrete law. It is an open question whether the injured can choose to make his claim on the basis of the product liability rules of tort.

The main difference between contract law and tort in relation to product liability is the limitation period for bringing claims. According to the Sale of Goods Act section 54 the limitation is one year from receipt (in CISG article 39(2), two years). Furthermore, the development risk defence is not available in contract.

However, if there is a contract between the injured and the tortfeasor the terms of this contract including contractual warranties relating to the quality or safety of goods will be of relevance when deciding whether the product is defective or not.

If a contractual warranty according to its wording or nature benefits not only the immediate buyer of the goods but any consumer, then such warranty may be relevant also when the injured has no contract with the tortfeasor.

Consumer guarantees are quite common in Danish commercial practice. However, according to the Act on Marketing, the term 'consumer guarantee' may only be used when the guarantee gives the consumers more favourable rights than the law establishes.

As to the Product Liability Act, it establishes that terms giving consumers less rights than those established in the Act are not valid.

The consumer's rights regarding after sale service is stipulated in the Sale of Goods Act and those provisions cannot be dispensed with by agreement between the parties. This act also establishes that terms that purport to give consumers less rights are not valid.

Denmark has implemented the EEC Directive No 13/93 on unfair contract terms in the Acts No 428 og 1098 of 1994. The provisions in these acts establish that unfair terms in contracts between a seller of goods on the one hand and the consumer of them on the other hand are not binding on the consumer.

4 LIABILITY IN TORT

4.1 Introduction

Since the implementation of the Directive, two sets of rules have been applicable to product liability. The Product Liability Act deals with product liability

involving personal injury and damage to consumer products. Insurance companies estimate that about 10% of the sums paid under product liability insurances are paid out for such damages. The remaining 90% of the sums paid out cover damages caused on non-consumer products, which we shall call 'professional products'.

4.2   Outline of relevant tort law giving rise to liability for personal and property damage in Denmark

Danish case law on product liability distinguishes between the liability of the manufacturer and the liability of the distributor.

4.2.1   *Liability of the manufacturer*

The liability of the manufacturer is based on the basic principles of tort according to which liability for damage requires negligence of the tortfeasor. This is, however, somewhat misleading, since the negligence in respect of product liability means a very low degree of fault which approaches the strict liability of the Directive.

The basic criterion is that the product is dangerous or defective in the sense that it has qualities that under normal use could cause damage to things or persons. It could have qualities it should not have, or it could lack qualities it should have.

The manufacturer is liable if the defect is due to negligence on his part. It could be negligence in design or manufacturing, or in providing adequate instructions for use.

Two defences are available. First, the development risk defence is based on the impossibility of having knowledge of the danger because of the absence of relevant scientific and technical knowledge at the time of marketing.

The other possible defence is system damage, ie damage caused by well-known but inevitable risks of the products. For example, the harmful effect of tobacco or alcohol. Another example is drugs which generally have good qualities, but have some well-known but undesirable side effects.

4.2.2   *Distributor*

If the manufacturer has delivered the product without defects to the distributor, the distributor can be held liable on the basis of negligence if he causes a defect to the product, either due to bad handling or negligence in the distribution, such as insufficient or wrong instructions or delivery of the wrong product (for example, poison instead of foodstuffs). The notion of negligence in this respect is probably also close to strict liability.

If the product delivered by the manufacturer to the distributor is defective the distributor will also be liable, but of course he will have a right of indemnity from the manufacturer. The injured party will have a free choice to hold either the manufacturer or the distributor, or both, liable in this situation. The liability of the distributor could be described as a kind of guarantee to the injured party for any claim against the manufacturer.

4.3   Causation

Liability presupposes that the defect has caused the damage. The question is, would the damage have happened if the defect had not been there?

If several causes have contributed to the damage there are in theory many possibilities, but courts tend to take a practical approach. If several liable causes have together effected the damage (such as the product being badly designed and the distributor issuing misleading warnings with it) the courts generally divide liability between them. If, on the other hand, some of the causes of the defect are non-liable (such as a drug bearing misleading warnings but stating certain side-effects clearly on the label), it is primarily a question of individual determination to what extent the loss has been caused by the defect and not by the non-liable cause (ie in this example, to what extent was the damage caused by following misleading labels rather than simply being the natural side effects common to most people who take the drug in question?).

4.4 Remoteness of loss and damage

Since the chain of causation is in principle endless it has been established in tort that liability will cease if the damage is too remote. Liability presupposes that the damage is a typical consequence of the act. It is, however, usually difficult to find practical examples where liability is excluded due to the remoteness of the damage. When it comes to product liability this is even more true, since a defendant may be held liable even for very remote damages. It is certainly not a condition of liability that the tortfeasor could have foreseen that the damage could occur. An example where the remoteness of the damage might exclude liability is product liability for transporters. If a raw material has been contaminated on board a ship, for instance by salt water during transportation, and later on causes damage to the final product in which it is incorporated due to this contamination, one might argue that this damage is so remote from the point of view of the transporter that he cannot be liable for product liability. As to the loss, it is generally accepted that the extraordinary size of the loss does not in any way exclude or reduce product liability (cf U82, p 1111H). This means that it is not possible to reduce the damages recoverable by maintaining that a defect in a small standard device caused damage to a very expensive and complicated plant in which the product was installed. Furthermore, the low price of the defective product does not exclude liability for far-reaching and expensive damage later in the chain of distribution.

4.5 Quantum of damage

The quantum of damage is assessed according to the general principles of tort.

4.5.1 *Personal injury*

The amount of compensation for personal injury is stipulated in the Act on Liability in Tort (*lovbekendtgorelse* 599 of 8 September 1986).

According to section 1, compensation for injury is paid for the following losses:

(a) loss of income;
(b) medical expenses;
(c) other losses;
(d) compensation for pain and suffering;
(e) compensation for invalidity (*varigt mén*);
(f) compensation for loss of the possibility to earn an income by working (*tab af arbejdsevne*).

i   Loss of income   Loss of income is a temporary compensation which is paid from the date of the injury until the injured person starts working again or, in the case of lasting invalidity, until his medical situation is stable. It is in principle the full income that the injured could be expected to have in the relevant period received net of taxes. Payments received duing the period, such as salary from the employer or social security benefits or insurance payments which are paid in order to compensate loss of income, are deducted from the compensation.

ii   Medical costs   The injured can claim compensation for medical costs. Due to the Danish social benefits system where hospital treatment is free of charge there are usually no substantial claims of this kind. With the introduction of private hospitals in Denmark the question could be raised whether the injured can choose to get medical care in such a hospital and recover the costs from the person liable. Considering that the injured has an obligation to mitigate his loss he will probably not in normal situations be able to do so.

iii   Other loss   This loss is thought of as a supplement to the medical costs and is primarily a compensation for future losses such as artificial limbs and other necessary equipment such as wheelchairs, future medicine, future transport costs, necessary changes in the home and the like. The estimated loss is capitalised and paid once and for all in a lump sum.

iv   Compensation for pain and suffering   This loss is usually paid out on the basis of a fixed amount per day from the date of the injury until the injured person can return to work, or his medical situation is stable. The daily payment is at present fixed to DKK 150 per day if the injured party is confined to bed and DKK 70 per day otherwise. If the claim exceeds DKK 22,000 these rates can be adjusted, in which case they are usually lessened. The absolute maximum is about DKK 50,000.

v   Compensation for invalidity   Compensation for invalidity is fixed at an amount calculated on the basis of an estimate of the degree of invalidity from a medical point of view, without regard to the consequences of the injured's business activity. The compensation for 100% invalidity is DKK 294,000 and, under special circumstances, DKK 353,000. If the injured person is only partially disabled he will get a proportion of this amount corresponding to the degree of invalidity. Invalidity under 5% is not compensated. If the injured is over 59 years old the compensation is reduced according to a special scale.

vi   Compensation for the loss of the ability to earn income   If the injured, after his medical condition has stabilised, has permanently lost the ability to earn his income by working, he is entitled to compensation. The estimation is based on the injured's capacity to provide income and is calculated in percentages of the total loss. No compensation is paid if the loss is less than 15%. The compensation is capitalised on the basis of the annual income. The capitalisation factor is 6. The maximum yearly income that can be compensated is DKK 514,500. The following example demonstrates the principles of the calculations. The annual income of the injured in the year preceding the injury was DKK 300,000. The loss of ability to provide income by his own work is estimated at 50%. The compensation is then:

DKK 300,000 x 6 x 50% = DKK 900,000

In any case where the income exceeds DKK 470,500 the calculation is based on DKK 470,500. The maximum compensation for 100% injury is accordingly:

DKK 514,500 x 6 x 100% = DKK 3,087,000

Special rules are stipulated for children and for people who have no working income.

vii Loss of breadwinner In case of the injured persons death it is decisive whether they are a breadwinner or not. If the injured is not a breadwinner only the funeral costs will be compensated under this head.

If the injured is a breadwinner further compensation shall be paid. A breadwinner may work at home. An unmarried couple is entitled to compensation for the loss of the breadwinner in the same way as a married couple. The compensation is 30% of the compensation that the injured person could have been expected to receive for loss of ability to earn income by working (ie head vi, above). The minimum is DKK 331,000 and the maximum DKK 926,100. If the deceased was over 55 years old the compensation is reduced on a sliding scale.

If the deceased was a breadwinner for children, the children are entitled to compensation amounting to what the deceased would be obliged to pay if he was divorced and did not have custody of the children. The amount is based on a monthly payment and varies according to the income and is payable until the child is 18 years old, or 24 years old if the child undertakes further education. The amount is capitalised when paid out as compensation for the loss of a breadwinner.

4.5.2 General remarks

Information concerning the degree of invalidation and the degree of loss of the ability to earn income by working is provided by a public authority (*Arbejdsskadestyrelsen*).

Another critical element in fixing compensation is the day when the medical situation of the injured became stable. Since the injured is entitled to full compensation of his actual income until this day, but only to the schematically calculated compensation for loss of possibility to earn income by working after this day, the determination of this day is of vital importance. In principle it is a medical criterion which reflects the moment when no further improvement in the recovery process can be expected and where the residual invalidity can be considered permanent. In practice the moment is determined with great difficulty. Usually the opinion of the public authority (*Arbejdsskadestyrelsen*) is considered decisive.

The amounts mentioned above are subject to modification in relation to inflation. They are fixed as at 1 April 1991. The level of compensation is fixed at the moment of the injury and accrues interest, at present at a rate of 14% per annum.

4.5.3 Damage to property

In principle compensation is assessed with reference to the individual loss of the injured. He must mitigate his loss if possible.

In the case of total damage the loss is usually equivalent to the repurchase price of the destroyed article, or if the thing cannot be repurchased the loss is the value of the article.

If the loss is partial the compensation is the repair cost. If the product is used in a professional context the injured canin addition claim the costs of hiring a substitute until the thing is repaired or replaced.

Consequential damages can in principle be claimed for damage to property but in practice the requirements of proof limit this. For example, if the damage has a consequence that a factory has to be closed for a period it is in principle possible to claim loss of profit. Only the direct loss will be compensated, based on a comparison with the turnover in the foregoing period. Claims for the more general loss of goodwill based on more theoretical calculations of the future development have not succeeded.

4.6   Burden of proof

In general, the burden of proof falls on the injured party, who must prove that there was a defect, that the defect caused the injury, and the size of the loss.

However, if the tortfeasor wishes to raise a defence of development risk or a system defect, the burden of proof rests on him. This is also the case if he wants to claim contributory negligence on the part of the plaintiff for his failure to mitigate his loss. These simple rules cover much more complex problems. Although the rules concerning burden of proof are fairly clear, the courts are free to assess the evidence submitted. From this has evolved a tendency to base rulings on assumptions. If, for instance, a defect is proven there is a tendency to assume that the defect caused the damage unless the opposite is proven. If, on the other hand, a product has been in use for a long time without problems and suddenly causes damage, there is a tendency to assume that the damage is caused by normal wear and tear or lack of maintenance, rather than by a defect.

The individual case must therefore be assessed on its merits and the clear-cut rules of burden of proof have their primary function in determining which of the parties has to provide the basic facts of the case. If the injured in a complex case has not obtained an expert's opinion on the product that he claims caused the damage, it is unlikely that a defect will be assumed.

4.7   Exclusion or limitation of liability

4.7.1   Warnings

Warnings are not considered as an exclusion or limitation of liability, but rather as a part of the product or instructions concerning its proper use, and when deciding whether a product is defective one must take into consideration the warnings supplied with or affixed to the product.

The necessity of warnings has to be considered from the consumer's point of view. It is not necessary to warn against unlikely types of misuse. If, however, the possibility of misuse is obvious or natural, a warning can be relevant. Warnings are not necessary if the danger is well known (for example, sharp razor blades). However, warnings are without legal relevance if the dangerous characteristic could be avoided by better design or more careful manufacturing. If the chain of a chain saw easily comes off due to bad design, it does not prevent liability that the chain saw is provided with a warning.

4.7.2   Limitations of liability in agreements

On the basis of the concept of freedom of contract it is possible under Danish law to limit product liability in a contract. Such clauses are valid except:

(a) if the clause restricts the liability unreasonably; or
(b) if the other party to the contract is not able to protect his interests.

The clauses are always interpreted in a restrictive way, so that the restriction of the liability does not go beyond the clear wording of the clause.

Clauses restricting liability phrased in general terms in a contract are not considered to encompass product liability. Several factors are relevant when deciding whether a clause restricting product liability is valid or not.

i The parties It now follows from the Product Liability Act that the seller cannot restrict product liability in a contract with a consumer (section 12). This is in accordance with article 12 of the Directive.

A special Danish rule has been inserted, concerning distributors who have sold the product but who are not manufacturers in the sense of article 3(1) of the Directive. Any other link in the chain of supply from the producer to the consumer (including manufacturers as defined in article 3(2) and (3) of the Directive) has a right of full indemnity from the manufacturer, if they have been held liable for product liability falling under the Act, and the manufacturer cannot limit such possibility by a contract with those parties (sections 11 and 12).

With regard to product liability falling under the Act, limitation of liability by contract is only possible between parties who are considered manufacturers in the terms of article 3(1) of the Directive (Product Liability Act, section 11).

With regard to product liability falling outside the Act the parties are in principle free to agree on limitations of product liability by contract.

ii Is the clause agreed between the parties? If the limitation clause is part of a written agreement it is presumed that it is duly agreed. If the written agreement contains a reference to general terms the clause restricting product liability is considered agreed if the general terms are standard documents well known in the trade or business, or if the general terms were incorporated in the agreement.

If the clause on limitation of product liability is printed on an order confirmation, or if it is printed on the invoice it is, according to recent legal writing, not considered to be agreed.

iii How the clause was agreed When considering whether the party in question could protect his interest, it must be taken into consideration whether the clause was negotiated or whether it was dictated in standard terms by the other party. If it was part of the standard terms of the other party it will be relevant whether that party informed the other party about the clause or in any other way drew his attention to the clause, eg by accentuation in the text.

iv Contents The main area in which clauses restricting product liability are used is consequential damage (loss of income and other damage that is not damage to persons or goods). For these losses the restriction on liability is generally accepted as valid. Furthermore, Danish standard terms on product liability encourage exclusion of liability for such losses (cf 9.4.3e). When it comes to damage to goods the possibility of restricting liability depends on whether the restriction is reasonable. On this basis it must be decided whether a total exclusion of liability is possible or whether liability can be restricted to a specified maximum, and if so, what maximum is reasonable. Clauses excluding liability for wilful or gross negligence will always be void.

If the injured party has discharged the burden of proof that the other party has caused the damage by negligence it is considered doubtful whether the clause can validly restrict the liability. The main area for the clauses restricting product liability is cases where negligence is not proved, and liability will be based on strict liability or presumptions of negligence.

4.8   Limitation period

The limitation period for bringing a claim for product liability in tort used to be five years, corresponding more or less to the three-year rule in the Directive, (ie a claim must be brought within three years of the discovery of the defect) and 20 year limitation corresponding more or less to the ten year limitation rule (ie the overall limit providing that a claim must be brought within ten years of the product being put into circulation) in the Directive. When implementing the Directive in Denmark it therefore had to be decided whether to continue with a double rule or to make a uniform limitation period for product liability falling within and outside the Directive. A solution in favour of a uniform rule was decided, and the final Act therefore contains a prescription rule for all product liability.

When implementing the rules of the Directive the Danish Act has, if anything, made things a little more complicated.

i   The three-year prescription rule of the Directive is implemented without modification   According to Danish law the limitation period can be suspended and interrupted according to the rules in the Act of 1908 on Prescription (Act 274 of 22 December 1908 *om foraeldelse af visse fordringer*). According to the Act the limitation period is interrupted if a law suit is initiated (complaint forwarded to the court), or if the claim is admitted by the defendant.

The limitation period is suspended if the injured person is either in excusable ignorance of his right to claim or of the domicile of the defendant and for this reason has been unable to bring the claim. Excusable ignorance in this context could be that an injured person is unaware of the fact that he will not recover his full working capacity.

As mentioned above, it is the clear intention of the Act that the three-year limitation period also limits product liability falling outside the Act. Some authors[1] claim, however, that the wording of the Act is too ambiguous to be interpreted in this way. If this is true, claims for product liability falling outside the Act can be made within five years from the date of damage.

ii   Ten-year limitation period   The claim is, furthermore, limited by the ten-year limitation period of the Directive, but only if the claim falls within the Directive. If the claim falls outside the Directive, the ten-year limitation rule is not applicable. If a claim falling under the Directive is prescribed according to the ten-year period but not according to the three-year period, it is still possible to raise the claim on the basis of the product liability rules based on jurisprudence (the same rules that are valid outside the Directive), if it is not prescribed according to the 20-year prescription rule (see below).

---

1   Dahl et al Juristen 90, p 168.

iii   Twenty-year limitation rule   According to Christian V's Danish law of 1683 5-14-4 a 20-year limitation period runs from the moment when the damage occurred. It is interrupted by any claim against the tortfeasor, for instance, a letter, with the consequence that a new 20-year period runs. It was earlier assumed that the 20-year limitation period could not be suspended. Recent jurisprudence (U89, p 1108H) has modified this. It is now doubtful whether the 20-year limitation rule has any practical bearing on product liability.

iv   Convention on International Sales of Goods   Denmark has ratified the Convention on International Sales of Goods (Act 733 7 December 1988 *om international kobelov*) which contains a limitation period for some kinds of product liability in article 39(2).

According to this rule there is a limitation period of two years from the day the goods were received by the purchaser. This limitation period also relates to damage caused by the goods to the purchaser's property (ie product liability). The more detailed rules in the Convention and the law implementing the Convention, however, are not discussed here.

4.9   Liability for third parties

Third party liability is based on Christian V's Danish law of 1683 3-19-2. According to this law a person or a company will be liable for damage caused by another person on the following conditions:

(a)   the acting person is in the service of the other party or specially authorised to act on his behalf;
(b)   the action is done in the course of the service and is naturally connected to that service;
(c)   the acting person would himself be liable;
(d)   the liability presupposes a certain possibility of control of the third party which excludes third party liability for independent contractors.

The rule is only necessary to explain the liability of the employer for product liability if one is basing the theory of product liability on the assumption of negligence. If the product liability of the employer is based on strict liability it is not necessary to presuppose negligence of the workers in order to impose liability on the employer.

In the present context it can be concluded that a manufacturer can be liable also for the actions of people who are not part of his staff, if they are acting on behalf of the manufacturer. If the design of the machinery is done outside the manufacturing premises, and if the design is inadequate and the product causes damage as a result, the manufacturer will be liable.

5   LIABILITY FOR DEFECTIVE PRODUCTS ARISING FROM BOTH GENERAL LAW AND IMPLEMENTATION OF THE EC DIRECTIVE 85/374 ON PRODUCT LIABILITY IN DENMARK.

5.1   Introduction

The liability for defective products in general law is described in section 4. The Directive has been implemented almost word for word with only a few amendments.

5.2 Summary

In section 1 the law defines its scope of application as being liability of the manufacturer and the distributor for damage caused by a defect in a product which is manufactured or delivered by them (product damage).

In section 2 'damage' is defined according to the terms of article 9 of the Directive.

In section 3 'product' is defined according to the terms of article 2 of the Directive. Denmark has elected to exclude raw agricultural products from the scope of the Act.

In section 4 'manufacturer' is defined according to the terms of article 3. Furthermore, the section defines 'distributor' as one who professionally markets the product without having manufactured it.

In section 5 a 'defect' is defined according to the terms of article 6 in the Directive.

In section 6 'strict liability' is defined according to article 1 of the Directive and the burden of proof is defined according to the terms of article 4 of the Directive.

In section 7 the defences are defined according to the terms of article 7 of the Directive.

In section 8 a damages threshold of DKK 4,000 is stipulated. This deduction shall be made even if the claim exceeds DKK 4,000. However, the injured can raise the claim for the first DKK 4,000 on the basis of the product liability rules set out in jurisprudence.

In section 9 of the rule the injured's contributory negligence is stipulated according to the terms of article 8 of the Directive. It is pointed out that the deduction according to section 8 shall be made in the total amount before deduction for contributory negligence.

In section 10 it is stipulated that the distributor is liable as guarantor for the product liability of the manufacturer in relation to the injured and in relation to subsequent businesses in the chain of distribution.

In section 11 it is stipulated that manufacturers may be liable jointly and severally according to the terms of article 5 of the Directive. Additionally, liability among several manufacturers, as defined in article 3(1) of the Directive, is shared between them if there is no agreement to that effect in relation to:

(a) the cause of the defect;
(b) the individual manufacturer's opportunity and capability of controlling the product;
(c) possible product liability insurances;
(d) other circumstances.

In section 11(3) it is stipulated that the distributor and the 'Producer', as defined in article 3(2) and (3) of the Directive, have the right of full indemnity against the real manufacturer. The indemnity can be reduced in cases of contributory negligence with the distributor.

In section 12 it is stipulated that liability cannot be excluded in relation to the injured according to the terms of article 12 of the Directive. Furthermore, it is stipulated that liability cannot be excluded in relation to anyone who subrogates in the injured's claim, which means that exclusion clauses between a manufacturer and a distributor are void. Manufacturers as defined in article 3(2) and (3) of the Directive are, in this context, considered as distributors.

Section 13 stipulates that the injured does not waive possible rights in other legislation as stipulated in article 13 of the Directive. Section 14 stipulates the rules on limitation of liability in time as explained in section 3.8, above.

In section 15 nuclear damage is excluded (cf article 14 of the Directive).

In section 15 the Minister of Justice is entitled to stipulate rules to implement international agreements on the choice of law in product liability cases. It is expected that the Hague Convention of 21 October 1972 on the law applicable to product liability will soon be implemented in Denmark.

In section 17 it is stipulated that the Act comes into force when published. It came into force on 10 June 1989.

It is stipulated that the law is not applicable to products marketed by the manufacturer before the Act came into force.

In section 18 it is stipulated that the law is not applicable on the Faroe Islands and in Greenland, but that it can come into force by special decree in these territories.

5.3   Description of optional or anomalous provisions in respect of product liability in Denmark

5.3.1   *Primary agricultural products and game*

Primary agricultural products and game are not governed by the Product Liability Act.

5.3.2   *Development risk defence*

The defence of development risk is made available for the manufacturer.

5.3.3   *Limitation on total liability*

Denmark has not introduced any limitation on total liability.

5.3.4   *Differences between national law and provisions of the Directive*

The differences are negligible and can be summarised as follows:

(a) Grounds for liability: The liability is strict in the Act, whereas earlier it was based on the concept of negligence. This difference is only formal since the law still presupposes a defect, and the presence of a defect will also imply liability according to the existing law of torts.

(b) Distribution of liability among several liable manufacturers: The rule is perhaps a modification compared to the earlier situation, but it is unlikely that there will be any drastic changes.

(c) Limitation in time: The limitation period has been reduced from five to three years, which must be considered as the most important change that has been brought about by the implementation of the Directive.

(d) Possibility of limiting liability in the relation between the manufacturer on the one hand and the distributor, importer and dealer on the other hand: The Act has excluded limitation of liability by contract between the manufacturer and distributor, importer and dealer, which is a restriction of the freedom of contract compared to the situation before the Act.

Apart from these points it is uncertain whether the act results in any changes to the Danish law on product liability. It may be that the defences introduced

by the Directive were not available to the same extent before the implementation of the Directive.

6   CRIMINAL LIABILITY FOR DEFECTIVE PRODUCTS ARISING FROM BOTH GENERAL LAW AND IMPLEMENTATION OF EC DIRECTIVE 92/59 ON PRODUCT SAFETY IN DENMARK

6.1   Introduction

Before the Directive on Product Safety was implemented, Denmark did not have any general laws on product safety. However, actions against dangerous merchandises were carried out under the provisions of the Act of Marketing. In addition a number of specific acts, the purpose of which is to maintain public health, stipulate rules sanctioned by fine.

6.2   Outline of implementation of Directive 92/59 EC in Denmark and date of implementation

The Directive 92/59 EC has been implemented in Denmark with the Act on Product Safety No 364 of 18 May 1994 which came into force on 15 June 1994.

6.3   Description of Anomolous Provisions on the implementation of EC Directive 92/59

Contrary to the Directive the Act does not only apply to products but also to real estate and to services rendered provided that the services are rendered in connection with a product, eg a component or a spare part. Moreover the aim of the Act is to protect all persons regardless of whether they are consumers or not and as a result it is stipulated that the Act applies to all products, except for products exchanged between private persons or products which are exclusively manufactured to be used in commercial production. Thus the definition in the Act is wider than in the Directive.

6.4   Description of local optional provisions

i   Nature of fines, prison sentences that may be imposed   In section 27 of the Act it is stipulated that the violation of the law is sanctioned by fine rather than imprisonment. No maximum amount for the fine is set and there is as yet no court practice on this subject.

ii   Name and description of the local regulatory authority   The local regulatory authority is according to section 17 in the Act *Forbrugerstyrelsen* (The Directorat of Consumers). *Forbrugerstyrelsen* is a public authority under the Ministry of Industry.

iii   Description of whether a product includes capital goods used by consumers eg lifts, escalators, aircrafts   As the law applies to all products with a few exceptions mentioned above a product includes capital goods used by the consumers.

iv Extent to which Council Decisions EEC 84/133 and 89/45 have been implemented and are operative locally. The Council Decisions EEC 84/133 and 89/45 are now a part of the system of notification established under the Act of Product Safety.

6.5 Brief overview of other significant Product Safety Law and the extent to which other EC Consumer Safety Directives have been implemented

Under the provisions of the Act on Marketing actions may be launched against dangerous products. Thus according to section 1 conducts which are contrary to good business practices are prohibited. The marketing of a dangerous product may well be a violation of this section. According to section 2 misleading statements which may influence the demand for or the offering of merchandises are prohibited. According to section 3 the seller should give an instruction which considering the nature of merchandise or the service is adequate. Violation of these clauses is not sanctioned as such, but the Consumers' Ombudsman can bring a case before the court, and the court can ban a possible marketing medium. A violation of the ban of the court is sanctioned by fine or imprisonment. However the Act on Marketing does not provide for a means of withdrawal.

Another significant product safety law is the Health and Safety at Work Act, which inter alia establishes rules on the designing of products, on warnings and on directions for use. The Act on Foodstuffs stipulates in section 12 that food that may be a danger to health may not be sold and the infringement is sanctioned by fine. Other important acts are mentioned in section 7.

The other EC Directives on consumer safety, eg the Directive on toys and the Directive on imitation of foodstuffs has to a great extent been implemented in Denmark with national laws. The Act on Product Safety establishes in section 25 due authority for the implementation of future EC Directives or decisions on consumer safety.

7 CIVIL LIABILITY FOR DEFECTIVE PRODUCTS BROUGHT ABOUT BY BREACH OF STATUTORY REGULATION DESIGNED TO PROTECT CONSUMERS AND/OR TO PROMOTE SAFETY

7.1 Outline of nature of protective regulations

A number of acts, the purpose of which is to maintain public health, stipulated rules concerning the production and distribution of certain products. Examples are the Health and Safety at Work Act, the Acts on Drugs, Chemicals and Foodstuffs, laws on the Protection of Plants and Animals in Agriculture, and Acts on Explosives, Fireworks, Electrical Devices, the Installation of Devices for Gas, Water and the Installation of Sewers, and Restaurants and Hotels.

7.2 Burden of proof

The general rule in Danish liability law is that the burden of proof lies on the injured party who must prove that the other is liable to pay compensation. However, the infringement of statutory regulations, the purpose of which is to

promote safety, may establish a presumption that the opponent is liable and thus reverse the burden of proof making it very hard for the opponent to avoid liability. For example has the Ministry of Work issued a number of specific regulations legalised by the Health and Safety at Work Act and a breach of these regulations are often successfully used in actions for damages. Some of these regulations are aimed at manufacturers and may thus be used in product liability actions.

7.3   Nature of liability, damage or criminal sanctions

Infringement of the rules in the acts mentioned above is usually sanctioned by fine. However a civil liability may often be imposed as mentioned in section 7.2 and thus these rules may be used in actions for damages.

CHAPTER V

Finland

Harri Salmi

Kaisa Fahllund

Heikki Haapaniemi Oy
PO Box 232
Mannerheimintie 14B
00101 Helsinki
Finland

Tel: ++ 358 9 177 613
Fax: ++ 358 9 653 873

CHAPTER V

Finland

1 INTRODUCTION

1.1 Introduction to the legal system in Finland

Finland has a statutory law system, according to which an act of Parliament is adopted when the Parliament approves a Government Bill for the act and the President of the Republic signs bringing the law into force.

According to the Constitution, the President of the Republic has the power to issue decrees on the implementation of acts. Also the State Council has the power, in certain cases specified by law, to issue statutes that are to be followed as legal norms. Furthermore, either a statute or a decree may empower a lower authority, such as a County Government or a Municipal Council, to enact by-laws binding on the local area administration in question.

The Finnish court system is based on independent courts which consist of two separate branches, the general courts and the administrative courts. Each of these two court organisations has three levels. The general courts are divided into the lower courts of general jurisdiction – the District Courts, the six Courts of Appeal and the Supreme Court.

1.2 Overview of the law relating to defective products in Finland

The substance of product liability and its evolution through legislation were widely debated in Finland in the 1960s and 1970s. Draft proposals for product liability law were presented as early as the 1970s, although the legislative work did not lead to legislative action, primarily due to the opposition from the business community. It was believed that strict product liability would cause considerable costs which would drastically weaken the position of Finnish industry in export markets. There was a will to postpone the reform until a future date and await the results from the initiatives going on within the EU (formerly EEC/EC) for regulating product liability. The legislative work in Finland started anew after the EU member states had reached an agreement on a product liability directive in 1985. The Finnish Product Liability Act was enacted in 1990 and adopted on 1 September 1991.

The concept of product liability existed, however, in Finland already before it became known by that term. Legal cases involving product liability can be found as early as the 1920s and 1930s. In spite of this, the opinion that product liability should be seen as a complex problem independent of the liability regulations governing transfer of movable property did not take root in Finland until the 1960s. Since then, seller's product liability in Finland has largely been regarded as negligent liability. For this reason it has become an unwritten rule

113

that product liability means negligent liability involving the seller as well as the importer and the manufacturer.

Debate on the principles of liability in product liability law gained new prominence in Finland in the 1970s at the same time as an extensive social discussion on consumer protection. Product liability based on negligence was criticised as the injured party often faced insurmountable problems in producing adequate evidence. Legal discussions concerning consumer rights created pressures on the legislation to develop the concept of product liability, and the first draft of Finnish consumer protection legislation included a chapter on product liability designed to impose strict liability on the manufacturer for damage caused by his product. This chapter was excluded, however, because of the heavy criticism from the business community.

The EC Product Liability Directive 1985 compelled the Community member states to adopt laws that harmonised with the Directive. Even though Finland at the time was not a member in the EC, it was considered necessary to recommence the legislative work. The new Product Liability Act adopted in 1991 was largely based on the EC Directive. The Act included some provisions conflicting with the Directive, and was subsequently amended in 1993 to harmonise more closely with the EC Directive.

The Finnish Product Liability Act is complemented by a separate Product Safety Act, adopted at the end of 1986. The Consumer Protection Act also includes a provision that marketing material that does not contain information necessary for consumers' health or financial safety will be improper. The Product Liability Act includes an express stipulation that the law does not restrict the right of the injured party to receive compensation pursuant to a contract, the Compensation Act, or some other law.

In case the seller has given any kind of guarantee to a consumer on the usability or quality of a product, the seller is responsible for all defects in the product during the guarantee period, even if the defect was found after the expiry of the guarantee period.

In case a contracting party is in breach of a statutory duty, the other party is entitled to receive compensation either pursuant to a specific act or the Compensation Act.

2   PRE-CONTRACTUAL LIABILITY

2.1   Effect on the interpretation and extent of the obligations of the parties to a contract

The most important contractual law in Finland is the law on legal transactions based on property rights (Legal Transactions Act). The Legal Transactions Act includes no explicit legal provisions regulating contract negotiations. Notwithstanding this, contract negotiations do not entirely lack a legal significance, although in Finland proposals presented during the negotiations are generally not held as being legally binding. In fact, manifestations of will during contract negotiations often clarify the objectives meant to be achieved by the contract and the issues on which the parties have wanted to agree. They may also perhaps clarify ambiguous formulations of the contract or shed light on matters verbally agreed upon. In that respect, contract negotiations are significant for the interpretation of the contract.

Contract negotiations are not permitted without having the ultimate objective of reaching an agreement. A party who engages in negotiations without a valid reason may be ordered to compensate the other party for the damage caused to him, for example on the grounds that the latter must do background research to the negotiations or travel to the meetings. A negotiating party who acts in bad faith may also otherwise be held liable to compensate for the losses of the other.

During the contract negotiations, the parties have not yet entered into a contractual relationship. Consequently, the Compensation Act can however be applied to compensation of damages between the parties. The Compensation Act determines that the party who intentionally or negligently causes damage to the other party, is liable to pay compensation. Pursuant to the Compensation Act, however, pure financial losses are not compensated in all circumstances, although participating in contract negotiations in bad faith could be seen as an extremely weighty reason that may incur the liability for compensation referred to in the Act.

2.2 Extent that non-disclosure of facts during negotiations may lead to liability

According to the Legal Transactions Act, a party who has been fraudulently induced to enter a legal transaction is not bound by it, provided that the other party to the transaction has induced it through fraudulent misrepresentation. First, fraudulent misrepresentation means presentation of a false circumstance. Second, it can also be done by distorting a fact. Sometimes withholding from the other party a fact significant for the signing of the contract may be deemed as fraudulent misrepresentation. It may also be done by presenting misleading information to the other party during the contract negotiations.

Compensation liability may be established on the basis of an invalid contract. Pursuant to the Compensation Act, compensation liability generally requires the existence of intention or negligence on the part of the injuring party. The recoverable damage is determined in accordance with the provisions of Chapter 5 of the Compensation Act. In other words, the injured party must be restored to the state where he would have been, had the invalid contract not been concluded. The anticipated gains resulting from the contract will thus not be recoverable.

2.3 Does pre-contractual liability lie in contract or tort?

Under Finnish contractual regulations, the contracting parties are bound by the pre-contract, provided that it specifies the contents of the contract in sufficient detail. Thus, a pre-contract that does not disclose the substance of the subsequent contract with sufficient detail is not legally binding. A pre-contract can also include a clause stating that the parties are not bound by it, provided that it is terminated within a specific time limit.

If the signing of the actual contract is refered to in the pre-contract but made subject to a subsequent expression of will by either contracting party, the pre-contract is not binding. Similarly, if the actual contract is subject to the fulfilment of certain preconditions, the pre-contract will not be binding, if the preconditions are not fulfilled.

If the pre-contract is binding, and one of the contracting parties does not voluntarily fulfil its conditions, the other contracting party can demand execution of the final contract, claim a settlement based on the pre-contract as well as damages, or alternatively accept damages only. However, the party violating the pre-contract is not liable for damages, if the pre-contract was not binding. An exception is damage caused by the fault of one contracting party. The fulfilment of the pre-contract can also be enforced by a conditional fine which the non-complying party is liable to pay to the other party. If the pre-contract is not binding a claim for negotiating in bad faith would be brought in tort and the Compensation Act would apply.

3   LIABILITY IN CONTRACT

3.1   Outline of contract law relevant to defective products in Finland

The Finnish Product Liability Act contains an explicit provision stipulating that the new Act does not restrict the right of the injured party to receive compensation pursuant to the contract. Thus, the Product Liability Act provides one more remedy for the injured party. Should the injured party so wish, he need not seek the support of the Product Liability Act, but continue to claim compensation based on the terms of a contract that is favourable to him, because the contractual product liability provisions remain valid and are not abolished by the Product Liability Act. In practice however, a claim that can be brought in product liability is rarely brought in contract law.

According to paragraph 2 of the Product Liability Act, damage caused to the product by the product itself is not within the scope of the Act. Also, damage caused to the product by its 'aggregate', namely the raw material and the components of the product, in addition to the material used in its manufacture, is not within the scope of the Act, provided that the aggregate was attached to the product before distribution. The reason for this delimitation is that damage caused to the actual product is generally covered by contractual liability, as the lack of safety in that case also implies a defect in the product, for example based on questions of liability relating to the sale of movable goods. In such circumstances, the injured party has the possibility of bringing a claim against the seller of the product for the damage under the contract.

Currently, Finnish contractual legislation is intended to exclude damages from the scope of contractual liability and to channel them as product liability claims. The Finnish Commercial Code was not meant to alter the established practice that liability for personal injuries is not determined on the basis of the compensation provisions of the Commercial Code. The provisions of the Commercial Code are intended to cover damage to other property with the exception of the object of the transaction only, provided that the use of the damaged property is directly related to the object of the transaction. However, the Product Liability Act also covers damage to property whose use is directly linked to the product provided that the damage to the product is not caused by the product itself or by its aggregate. In consequence, both the Commercial Code and the Product Liability Act overlap in this narrow area.

The same principles are applied to exclude product liability from the scope of contractual liability and the Consumer Protection Act. The Consumer Protection Act stipulates that if a product defect causes damage to property other than the object sold, the provisions of the Consumer Protection Act shall

not apply to the seller's compensation liability unless the damage concerns property whose use is directly linked to the merchandise that has been sold. If the seller pays compensation pursuant to this provision, the recipient's respective right to claim damages under the Product Liability Act transfers to the seller. The provisions of the Consumer Protection Act do not apply to compensation of personal injuries caused by the characteristics of the product.

According to the stipulations on consumer contracts for services included in the Consumer Protection Act, the party who has ordered the service is entitled to receive compensation for damage suffered due to an error of a service employee. The liability to pay damages includes the personal injuries and material damage suffered by the client with certain exceptions. This is because services cannot be covered by the same kind of product liability as the sale of movable goods. Product liability only covers the materials used for the service. If the material defect causes damage to property other than the object of the service, the compensation provisions of the Consumer Protection Act are not applicable to the supplier's compensation liability unless the use of the damaged property is directly linked to the object of the service.

Also, damage caused to the product because of its aggregate has been excluded from the Product Liability Act provided that the aggregate has been attached to the product before distribution. This restriction is based on the distinction between product liability and contractual liability and on the circumstance that the product liability basis is lacking if contractual liability provides sufficient compensation protection. If the damage appears in the product itself, it is generally covered by contractual liability, eg pursuant to a delivery contract or manufacturing contract.

The restriction concerning damage caused to the product by its aggregate is not applicable to raw materials; the restriction mainly applies to replaceable spare parts of the product.

3.2 Contractual warranties relating to quality of goods and safety of goods

In Finnish contractual law, the main rule has generally been based on negligent liability. This means that a business will only be liable if there has been negligence on its part. Some opinions, however, have been voiced in favour of manufacturer's and seller's strict guarantee liability for damage caused by the product. The manufacturer or seller who has assured, for example in a marking on the product packaging, in the instructions for use or in some other way, that the product is harmless in some respect, would always be held liable for the damage, if the assurance is false. Finnish legal literature has, however, taken a reserved attitude to so-called product liability guarantees.

3.2.1 *Commercial practice in giving consumer guarantees*

The practice of giving quality guarantees in conjunction with the sale of movable goods is quite common in Finland. These are either given as separate guarantees or included as special provisions in the contract, entitled 'Guarantee' or including the word 'guarantee' in their formulation. The normal practice for certain categories of goods is that the guarantee is given by a third party on behalf of the seller, for instance by the manufacturer, importer or other similar party.

Guarantee provisions are frequently included in many standard conditions of contract for sale of movable goods; in Finland, their significance and consequences are determined on the basis of the substance and interpretation of the conditions.

3.2.2   *Legal provisions regulating the form and content of legal guarantees*

The concept of a guarantee is mentioned in only one section of the Finnish Commercial Code. According to paragraph 21 of the Commercial Code, if the seller, by giving a guarantee or another comparable bond, has assumed responsibility for the fitness for use or other characteristics of the product for a given period of time and the deterioration happens in the period covered by the guarantee, the product is deemed to be defective. The underlay of the legislative work on the Commercial Code explicitly mentions that the provision is not meant to regulate the substance of the guarantee. Therefore, the legal consequences of a guarantee or other similar bond depend exclusively on the content and interpretation of the contractual terms.

The Commercial Code, paragraph 30, stipulates that if the product contains a defect not attributable to the buyer or to any factor relating to the buyer, he may request a rectification of the defect, a replacement product, or a price discount in accordance with the provisions of the Act, or cancel the transaction and also claim damages. He can also refrain from paying the purchase price.

Certain provisions on guarantees and their significance are also found in the Consumer Protection Act. The Consumer Protection Act, paragraph 15, stipulates that if the seller, by giving a guarantee or other similar bond, has assumed responsibility for the fitness for use or other characteristics of the product for a given period of time, the product is deemed to be defective provided that the product deteriorates to the extent referred to in the commitment. No liability for the defect exists, however, if the seller proves that the deterioration was due to an accident, wrong handling of the product or another factor attributable to the buyer. If the guarantee or other similar bond was given by another party in an earlier level in the distribution chain or on behalf of the seller and not by the seller, the product is also deemed to be defective under the aforementioned conditions. The seller is, however, not liable on the basis of a guarantee given by a party existing earlier in the distribution chain for a defect for which he would otherwise not be liable pursuant to the Consumer Protection Act, if the seller can prove that he has clearly informed the buyer of the matter before the transaction. A guarantee or other similar bond does not restrict the statutory liability for defects stipulated in the Consumer Protection Act.

3.3   Breach of contract for supply of defective products

Contractual violations involving defective products in Finland are primarily governed by the Finnish Commercial Code. Paragraph 21 of the Commercial Code stipulates that the defectiveness of the product is estimated on the basis of its characteristics at the time when the liability for risks transferred to the buyer. The seller is liable for the product defect existing at that time, even if it was only disclosed later. If the product deteriorates after the liability for risks has transferred to the buyer, the product is deemed to be defective if the deterioration is due to the seller's contractual breach. In other words, the party

who caused the defect intentionally or negligently is liable for the defect from the moment of its existence.

The point of time when the defect occurred can cause practical problems, because the reason for the defect may already exist at a given moment, although its consequences may only be revealed later. If the buyer can prove that the product was already defective at the time of the transfer of risks, he can also appeal to the existence of the defect, even if it is revealed only later.

The buyer cannot claim that a factor of which he can reasonably be assumed to have been aware at the time of the transaction is a defect. If the buyer, before the transaction, has inspected the product or without a valid reason neglected to observe the seller's request to do so, he cannot claim on the basis of a factor which he should have noticed during the inspection as being a defect, unless the seller has acted in a dishonorable and unworthy way. The buyer must inspect the product also at the time when it transfers in his possession or at least within a reasonable period of time thereafter. The buyer's opportunity to allege the existence of defect requires him to complain about it within a reasonable period of time after the defect was or should have been detected.

3.3.1 Types of defect

The Commercial Code defines product quality by stipulating that the type, quantity, quality, packaging and other properties of the product must be consistent with what can be deemed as agreed between the parties. If nothing else is deemed as agreed, the product shall:

(a) be suitable for the purpose for which such goods are generally used;
(b) be suitable for the special purpose for which the product was meant to be used, if the seller can be assumed to have been aware of that purpose at the time of the transaction, and if the buyer should have been reasonably assured of the seller's expertise and judgement;
(c) possess the same characteristics as those claimed by the seller by presenting a sample or a model; and
(d) be packed in a customary or other adequate way, if the packaging is necessary to preserve or protect the product.

If the product is not consistent with what is said above, it is defective. In other words, the provision also permits that the quality level specified in the contract to be lower than would otherwise have been the position in law by way of the above implied terms.

The product is defective also if it does not correspond to the information relating to its characteristics or use given by the seller when marketing the product or in some other way before the transaction and which can be assumed to have influenced the transaction. The same applies to a situation where some other party instead of the seller, for instance a party in an earlier level of the distribution chain or on behalf of the seller, while marketing the product before the transaction, gave information on the properties or use of the product which can be assumed to have influenced the transaction. Further, the product is not deemed defective in these circumstances if the seller was not and should not have been aware of such information. However, the provisions will not be applied if the information has been rectified in a clear and timely manner. In practice, the stipulation means that the information given by the seller before entering into the respective contract is integrated in the contract.

The Consumer Protection Act includes a general provision on product defectiveness, and its content is equivalent to the corresponding stipulation in

the Commercial Code. In addition, the Consumer Protection Act stipulates that the durability and other properties of the product must be consistent with what the consumer can generally and reasonably expect in the sale of such a product. The Consumer Protection Act also states that the product is defective if the buyer, at the time of the transaction, is not given the instructions necessary to install, assemble, use, service or store the product.

The buyer of the product has certain legal remedies at his disposal if the product is defective. First, both the Commercial Code and the Consumer Protection Act stipulate that the buyer has the right to request the seller to rectify the defect without any expense to the buyer, if it can be rectified without unreasonable costs or harm to the seller. The seller may deliver a replacement product instead of repairing the product. Under certain conditions, the buyer also has the right to request a new delivery. If the seller fails in his obligation to rectify the defect, the buyer is entitled to receive compensation for his reasonable costs spent in rectifying the defect.

3.3.2 Causation and remoteness of loss and damage

Pursuant to the Commercial Code, the buyer is entitled to receive compensation for damage suffered by him because of a defect in the product, unless the seller proves that the delivery of a safe product was prevented due to a legal stipulation. However, consequential damages are not compensated. The buyer retains his right to receive compensation, if the defect or damage is due to the seller's negligence or if the product at the time of the transaction differed from what the seller was expressly committed to deliver.

The Consumer Protection Act stipulates that the buyer is entitled to receive compensation for damage which he suffers because of a product defect. However, the seller is not liable for a consequential loss unless the defect or damage is due to his negligence, or the product at the time of the transaction differed from what the seller was expressly committed to deliver. A member of the buyer's family who suffers damage because of the defect has the same right as the buyer.

With regard to material damage, it is stipulated that if the defective product causes damage to property other than the sold product, the aforementioned regulations are not applicable to the seller's compensation liability unless the damage concerns property whose use is directly linked to the sold product. If the seller pays compensation on this basis, the recipient's possible respective right to claim damages pursuant to the Product Liability Act transfers to the seller. The provisions of the Consumer Protection Act are, however, not applied to compensate for personal injuries caused by the characteristics of the product.

The aforementioned regulations also apply to a situation where some party other than the seller has committed himself to rectify the product defect or otherwise assumed liability for the characteristics of the product.

The Consumer Protection Act also includes a provision on restriction of losses and conciliation of damages. It stipulates that the injured contracting party must take reasonable measures to restrict the extent of his loss. Failing this, he will have to bear the corresponding part of the loss.

3.4 Quantum of damage

The amount of damages is calculated primarily on the basis of the Compensation Act. The Compensation Act is based on the principle of full

compensation, meaning that the compensatable amount of damages must be sufficient to restore the injured party to the state where he would have been, had the damage not occurred.

The amount of damages payable for breach of contract can be reduced if it is unreasonable considering the reason of the breach, the opposing party's contributory negligence, the financial position of the contracting parties, the price of the product, and the possibilities of the injuring party to anticipate and prevent the damage, as well as other factors.

3.5   Burden of proof

The common practice in Finnish contractual law is to take presumed liability as the starting point. This principle implies that the party who fails to meet his contractual obligations must prove that he has observed due care, in order to be released from negligent liability. According to the legal arguments of the Commercial Code, this presumption of negligence has been intentionally abandoned taking the view that it belongs to the competence of the court to determine in each case who is the party with the burden of proof, and to consider the sufficiency of proof.

The general assumption under the Finnish Commercial Code is that the burden of proving the existence or absence of a defect in the product must fall on the party in whose possession the product is. This rule is, however, not without exceptions; there have also been opinions that the buyer must bear the burden of proving that the product is defective, if the product remains in the seller's possession because the buyer refuses to receive it, even if he should, or if the buyer neglects payment and the seller withholds the product as a result.

In addition, the provision of the Consumer Protection Act dealing with the time of the defect is formulated on the basis of burden of proof and stipulates that if the seller, by giving a guarantee or other similar bond, has assumed responsibility for the use or other properties of the product for a given period of time, the product is deemed to be defective if during that time it deteriorates as referred to in the bond. No liability for the defect exists, however, if the seller proves it likely that the deterioration was due to an accident, mishandling of the product or other factor attributable to the buyer.

3.6   Exclusion or limitation of liability

The freedom of contract relating to sale of movable goods prevailing in Finland has traditionally also embraced the freedom to agree that the buyer assumes the entire liability for the quality of the product. Notwithstanding this, Finnish legal literature has previously taken the view that the buyer is not bound by a clause excluding the seller's liability, if the seller has acted fraudulently. If the seller has known the defectiveness of the product and withheld his knowledge, he cannot appeal to the contractual clause to be released from liability. Both the Commercial Code and the Consumer Protection Act also seek to protect the consumer in situations where an exclusion clause would lead to an unreasonable outcome, even if the seller had acted fraudulently. Consequently, both the Commercial Code and the Consumer Protection Act contain a special provision regulating the *'tel quel'* (ie the product is sold 'as it is') conditions. The provision stipulates that if the product was sold 'as it is' or with a similar general reservation, it is nevertheless deemed as defective, if:

(a) the product is not consistent with the information given by the seller regarding its characteristics or use before the transaction and which can be assumed to have influenced the transaction;

(b) the seller has, before the transaction, failed to inform the buyer of any essential factor relating to the characteristics or use of the product, which he can be assumed to have known, and of which the buyer could reasonably expect to be informed, and if the failure can be assumed to have influenced the transaction; or

(c) the product is in an essentially worse condition than the buyer could reasonably expect, considering its price and other circumstances.

If the seller, in conjunction with a transaction governed by the Commercial Code, actually wishes also to be released from the quality liability described above, this must be disclosed in the contract with sufficient clarity. According to its legislative commentary, the Commercial Code can be disregarded by a contract also in this respect. Therefore, the contract can, for example, include a clause stating 'the buyer buys the product in its existing condition and may not appeal to the provisions of paragraphs 17, 18 and 19 of the Commercial Code'. However, a similar exclusion clause cannot be used in a consumer contract of sale.

3.7 Limitation period

The general limitation period stipulated in the Compensation Act is ten years. Compensation must be claimed within ten years of the date of the occurrence of the damage. There is, however, special compensation legislation in Finland which includes several provisions on an exceptionally short limitation period of the claim. The underlying reasons for this are the speedy settlement of matters and limitation of costs, particularly liability insurance costs.

3.8 Liability for third parties

Losses suffered by third parties are in Finland compensated only in exceptional circumstances. The relating provisions are included in the Compensation Act which is discussed in section 4.

4 LIABILITY IN TORT

4.1 Introduction

The Finnish Compensation Act and its established product liability provisions still form part of the currently valid law not abolished by the Product Liability Act. As is the case with contractual compensation liability, the Product Liability Act contains explicit provisions stipulating that the new Act does not restrict the right of the injured party to receive compensation pursuant to the Compensation Act.

The law which had been in force before the Product Liability Act still applies to all parties whose liability is not governed by the Act. Whereas for example pursuant to paragraph 6 of the Product Liability Act the seller's liability is merely vicarious and avoidable, provided that he can indicate another liable

party, the seller is in practice not liable pursuant to the Product Liability Act. Consequently, the seller's liability is still regarded as negligent liability discussed in paragraph 1.2 above.

Neither does the Product Liability Act apply to the liability of a business undertaking for property damage suffered by another business undertaking. Similarly, the liability of a business undertaking in relation to another business undertaking is traditional negligent liability.

The compensation rules based on the Compensation Act are relevant grounds for potential product liability primarily in situations where liability based on the Product Liability Act is lacking, for example because of an exclusion clause or expiration of the limitation period for the compensation claim.

However, even if the Product Liability Act is applicable, the injured party can appeal to the other compensation regulations discussed above to support his compensation claim, albeit that the compensation right based on the Product Liability Act is generally more extensive than that based on other stipulations, such as those relating to damages.

4.2   Outline of relevant tort law giving rise to liability for personal and property damage in Finland

The Finnish Compensation Act starts from the assumption that the party who either intentionally or negligently causes damage to another party is liable for compensation. Negligence is mostly due to carelessness. Guidance for determining whether the person has acted negligently is given in legislation. This is, however, not always practicable; consequently, the question of negligence must be determined depending on the kind of action that can be deemed as careful among the class of people where the person belongs. Liability is primarily established regardless of the extent of negligence which caused the damage.

The Finnish compensation law also recognises cases where compensation liability is based on objective, ie strict, liability. This mainly refers to liability of parties involved in generally hazardous activities, governed by special legislation.

4.3   Causation

Compensation in accordance with the Product Liability Act is determined partly on the basis of the Compensation Act. Its provisions on the types of recoverable damages include, inter alia, certain limitations on rights to compensation depending on the objects of damage. The Finnish compensation practice with regard to damages is to make a distinction between personal injuries, material damage and property damage. Property damage is recoverable only to a limited extent under the Compensation Act, ie only in circumstances where the damage was caused by crime or due to exercise of public authority, or if other weighty grounds exist. According to the arguments of the legislative work on the Product Liability Act, it does not apply to pure property damage. In fact, this type of damage is quite exceptional for product liability situations, although compensation may be possible for very significant reasons. On the other hand, if the property damage is related to personal injury or material damage, it is recoverable provided that the other preconditions of compensation liability are fulfilled.

Compensation for damages requires causation which means that the person is liable for compensation provided only that the damage is the consequence of his act or negligence. There must be a causal correlation between the behaviour of the injuring party and the damage. Basically, the act or negligence is deemed to be the cause of the damage provided that there would be no damage if the act or the negligence were to be removed from the chain of events resulting in the damage. The concept of causation which establishes liability has, however, been restricted to the extent that only those factors of the act or negligence are considered which, according to normal life experience, are likely to result in a similar damage. The compensation liability can also be removed or reduced by self-endangerment or consenting to the act which resulted in the damage.

4.4   Remoteness of loss and damage

As discussed above, the Finnish Compensation Act determines certain preconditions for recoverability of consequential financial loss and if they are lacking, no liability to pay damages exists. It should be noted, however, that the Compensation Act does not regulate contractual relationships where compensation of financial losses is the overriding rule. Similarly, stipulations of special laws disregard the Compensation Act, and financial losses are often compensated on the basis of such stipulations. For the liability to pay damages to be determined pursuant to the Compensation Act instead of special laws or a contractual right, it is required that the damage was caused by a punishable act or due to exercise of public authority, or that there are other weighty grounds for compensation.

4.5   Quantum of damage

The provision of the Compensation Act dealing with compensation of personal injuries stipulates that the party who has suffered bodily harm or other personal injury is entitled to receive compensation. Recoverable damages include costs of medical treatment and other costs, loss of earnings and livelihood, pain and suffering, as well as disability or other permanent harm caused by the injury. Other injury-related costs include travel costs and temporarily increased and permanently higher living expenses.

Material losses recoverable pursuant to the Compensation Act include repair costs of the object, other costs and value depreciation caused by the damage, or the value of the damaged or lost object. Also, reduced earnings and livelihood are compensated. Intangible losses are not compensated in conjunction with material damage.

The Finnish Compensation Act subscribes to the principle of full compensation, ie the compensation must be sufficient to restore the injured party to the financial state where he would have been had the damage not occurred. However, his position is not supposed to improve due to the damage; consequently, the benefit gained by the injured party because of the event is generally deducted from the compensation. One of the most significant exemptions to the principle of full compensation is, however, the regulations governing conciliation of compensation. The Compensation Act stipulates that compensation can be reasonably conciliated if the injured party has contributed to the damage or if another factor, non-related with the act which resulted in

the damage, has also been a reason for the damage. In product liability situations, negligence and carelessness can be manifested so that the user of the product neglects to study the using instructions for use sufficiently carefully or that the product is used in an unexpected or careless way, which together with the product lacking safety causes the damage.

Where there are several parties liable for compensation, the Compensation Act stipulates that they are jointly and severally liable for the damage suffered by the injured party. The amount of compensation is divided among the liable parties in a reasonable proportion, depending on the extent of guilt of each liable party, benefit gained from the event, and other relevant factors.

4.6 Burden of proof

The regulations on burden of proof in situations of statutory compensation liability start from the assumption that the injured party must be able to prove that he has suffered injury because of the acts of another party and that the preconditions of liability to pay damages discussed above are fulfilled. Failing this he will receive no compensation.

4.7 Exclusion of limitation of liability

The overriding principle of the Finnish Compensation Act is that statutory liability cannot be limited or removed. This is possible only in respect of liability based on a condition of contract. A contracting party cannot appeal against such condition, if he has caused the damage intentionally or by gross negligence.

The amount of compensation based on the principles for calculating damages can be disregarded in the verdict also for some other reasons. The reason can be a limitation expressed in money or stipulated in some other way by special legislation, the contributory negligence of the injured party or an external factor which contributed to the damage. Liability can also be reduced pursuant to conciliation provisions; the most important of these is discussed in section 4.5 above.

4.8 Limitation period

As stated above in section 3.7 the general limitation period in Finland is ten years. This general rule applies to liability in contract as well as liability in tort. Special acts contain provisions on shorter limitation periods.

According to the Compensation Act where the damage was caused by a criminal offence and the limitation period for that criminal offence is longer than the limitation period for the action for damages, the action for damages may be instituted during the longer limitation period.

The most fundamental reason for the present formulation of the limitation provision in the Product Liability Act is the EC Directive. The limitation provision of the Act is thereby harmonised with the corresponding regulations of the EC Directive.

The provision of the Product Liability Act on special limitation periods sets two time limits for instituting an action pursuant to the Act. The shorter three-year limit of action concerns information on the damage and the liable party. It provides that the action must be instituted within three years of the

date when the party claiming compensation was or should have been informed of the damage, of the inadequate safety of the product and of the party liable for compensation. The longer ten-year time limit refers to the launch of the product which caused the damage. The compensation action must be instituted within ten years at the latest of the date when the party liable for compensation launched the product.

The expiration of either period for action results in the running out of the limitation period. It is obvious, on the basis of the provisions on burden of proof in general Finnish civil law, that the party wishing to appeal that the limitation period has run out must also prove that this has happened.

The aforementioned limitation provisions only concern liability under the Product Liability Act, since the law does not restrict the right of the injured party to receive compensation on the basis of a contract or the Compensation Act. Even if the limitation period for liability based on the Product Liability Act has expired, the injured party can still institute a compensation action pursuant to the negligence provision of the general compensation laws. In fact, the limitation period of a claim based on the Compensation Act is, as a rule, longer than that of a claim based on the Product Liability Act. The Compensation Act requires that compensation must be claimed within ten years of the damage. In addition, the provisions only regulate the right of the injured party to receive compensation. By contrast, they do not govern the mutual relations between various liability subjects, eg importer and manufacturer.

With regard to the three-year rule, the relevant information referred to in the Act includes information about the disclosure of the defect, inadequate product safety and the liable party. In other words, the limitation period starts running only after the party who claims compensation has obtained sufficient information on all these factors.

The ten-year period starts from the time when the liable party launched the product which caused the damage. This limitation period is mandatory and is not influenced by the circumstance of whether the party claiming damage was informed of the damage. If the damage only occurs after the ten-year period, no compensation can be claimed for the damage pursuant to the Product Liability Act. Launching of the product refers explicitly to the product which caused the damage, not for instance to the beginning of marketing for a certain product lot or other similar event. If, on the other hand, the damage is the result of continued use of the same products, the period for instituting action starts from the time of launching the last product unit which contributed to the damage. Also this limitation period runs separately for each liability subject. This means that the period of action against the manufacturer is calculated from the date when he launched the product, and against the aggregate manufacturer from the date when he in turn launched the aggregate manufactured by him. On the other hand, the limitation period for the importer's and seller's liability expires later than the manufacturer's, depending on the respective time of launch.

As the Product Liability Act is compelling legislation, the right of the injured party to receive statutory compensation cannot be restricted by contracts signed before the damage. This does not, however, imply that the business undertakings in the product distribution chain could not mutually agree on the final division of product liability after one of them has been ordered to pay compensation for product damage to an injured party. It is also possible to agree on product liability based on some other law instead of the Product Liability Act.

4.9 Liability for third parties

Personal injuries of third parties are in Finland compensated only exceptionally.

Provisions on vicarious liability are included in the Compensation Act with respect to the relationship between employers and employees and public corporations and officials. There are no provisions on vicarious liability, for example of a principal for his agent or other party.

5 LIABILITY FOR DEFECTIVE PRODUCTS ARISING FROM BOTH GENERAL LAW AND IMPLEMENTATION OF EC DIRECTIVE 85/374 ON PRODUCT LIABILITY IN FINLAND

5.1 Introduction

As discussed in the previous paragraphs, the Finnish Product Liability Act was enacted in 1990 and adopted on 1 September 1991. Already at the enacting stage, the Product Liability Act was in all essential respects consistent with the EC Directive. However, the reason for adopting the Act was not the implementation of the EC Directive and consequently it contained certain dissimilarities. After Finland had signed the Treaty on the European Economic Area (EEA Treaty), the situation changed to the extent that the EEA Treaty required that the Finnish Product Liability Act should be harmonised with the Directive. As a result, the Finnish Product Liability Act was amended on 8 January 1993.

5.2 Outline of provisions in Finland

After the changes required by the EC Directive, the Finnish Product Liability Act governs compensation for damage caused to persons or to property meant for private use or consumption and used by the injured party primarily for such purpose. The changes caused by the EC Directive limited the scope of implementation to some extent. It was reduced in respect of products which are not actually meant for private use but which may nevertheless be used for such purpose. An example mentioned in the Government Bill for the amendment of the Product Liability Act is where a consumer buys for his domestic use a special tool or piece of equipment meant for production and requiring professional skill, he cannot receive compensation for the damage caused by the tool or equipment, for example by claiming that the instructions for use were so complex that an ordinary consumer could not understand them. Such tools and equipment are in fact not meant for private use.

'Product' means a movable object but not a building on the land of another party. The Act governs damage caused by a product even when the product is attached to another movable object or to real property. Consequently, a contractor who has built a house is not liable as manufacturer for the damage caused by defects in the construction. By contrast, if the damage to the building is due to the inadequate safety of a construction material or aggregate, the supplier in question may be liable for the damage pursuant to the Product Liability Act.

The original Product Liability Act had taken the view that whereas a product was assumed to be a movable object, energy, for example electricity,

could not be deemed as a product. The definition of product in article 2 of the EC Directive, however, also includes energy. As a result, the Finnish Product Liability Act was amended to include electricity in the scope of its regulations. This means that damage resulting from fluctuations of electrical voltage and frequency belong to the scope of the Act. On the other hand, damage due to power failure are not covered by the Act, because delayed delivery or failure to deliver a product are not deemed as product damages.

The scope of implementation of the Product Liability Act is not restricted to end products which are clearly consumer commodities by nature; also raw materials and product components can independently establish product liability referred to in the Act. This liability is, however, partly governed by special regulations based on the concept of 'aggregate'. As stated above, 'aggregate' refers to the raw material and component of the product as well as to the material used in its manufacture or production. The basic assumption is that if the damage was due to the lack of safety of the aggregate, the damage must be deemed to be caused by both the product and the aggregate (paragraphs 1.3 and 4).

Product Liability Act, paragraph 3, stipulates that compensation is payable for damage caused because the product was not as safe as could reasonably be expected. When assessing safety, the point of time when the product was launched, its anticipated use, marketing, instructions for use and other factors must be taken into consideration.

The previous Finnish Product Liability Act contained no provisions on the burden of proof relating to product damage. Consequently, the general principles of burden of proof were implemented. In order to harmonise the Finnish Product Liability Act with the EC Directive, a new provision on burden of proof was added to the Act in 1993. The provision stipulates that the injured party must prove the existence of damage, the insufficient safety of the product, as well as the causal correlation between the insufficient safety and the damage. The Directive does not, however, identify the preconditions of proof. As a result, the new provision of the Finnish Act is not meant to introduce a stricter proof than was required from the injured party already on the basis of general principles, but merely to clarify the prevailing situation.

The regulations on liable parties are intended to develop a system whereby liability is channelled as the burden of one single liable party. First, the manufacturer who manufactured or produced the product which caused the damage is liable for compensation. Second, the party who first imported the product into the European Economic Area is liable for compensation. Third, the party who imported the product for launch from an EFTA member state into the EU, from the EU into an EFTA member state, or from one EFTA member state into another, is liable for compensation. In addition, the party who marketed as his own the product which has caused damage, is liable for the damage provided that his name, brand or other visible symbol was indicated on the product. However, the Act includes an exemption to the EFTA rule, stipulating that the party who imports the product into Finland from a country which has adhered to the Lugano Convention is not liable as importer. The party claiming compensation is instead instructed to present his claim to the manufacturer or to the party who has imported the product to the area where the Lugano Convention is in force.

The Finnish Product Liability Act is based on a system where the liable parties referred to in the Act, ie manufacturer, importer and marketer, constitute the primary chain of liability. Each link is equally liable and cannot reject a

compensation claim by appealing to the compensation liability of another liable party. The Act further includes a provision indicating a sufficiently closely related liable party to the injured party in the event that the primary liable parties cannot be reached. In fact, paragraph 6 of the Act includes a provision stipulating that if the manufacturer or producer is not mentioned on the product, any party who has launched the product is liable in the same way as the manufacturer for the damage caused by the product, unless, within a reasonable time after receiving the compensation claim from the injured party or other request for information, he informs the injured party of the liable party or the party who offered the product for sale. For the party who launched the product to be released from liability it is sufficient that any one of the aforementioned liable parties is indicated on the product or its packaging. For instance the manufacturer's trademark on the product can be sufficiently informative to meet this requirement. However, a trademark alone may not always be sufficient, because the required information must be adequate to enable the injured party to present his compensation claim to the liable party.

5.3   Description of optional or anomalous provisions in respect of product liability law in Finland

5.3.1   Primary agricultural products and game

The implementation provision of the EC Directive excludes non-processed agricultural products and game from the scope of implementation of the Directive. Notwithstanding this, the member states are granted the explicit right to disregard the restriction in their national legislation on implementation of the EC Directive. Finland has made use of this possibility. The Product Liability Act therefore also covers damage caused by non-processed artificially reared fish products, game and non-processed piscicultural products. The group of people who as manufacturers could be liable for such products pursuant to the Product Liability Act is, however, exceptionally small. For a business undertaking to be liable as manufacturer pursuant to the Product Liability Act for damage caused by such products, his activity must be regarded as manufacture or production.

Since mere gathering of products from nature does not meet the criteria of manufacture or production, people who gather berries and mushrooms are not manufacturers referred to in the Product Liability Act solely because of such activity. Also hunting and fishing as such, as well as slaughtering of animals, are probably excluded from the concept of manufacture or production, while a stock farmer may be considered a producer. Product processing can readily bring the activity within the scope of manufacture or production.

5.3.2   Development risks defence

According to paragraph 7 of the Product Liability Act, if the lack of safety has occurred at the final assembly stage of the product, the manufacturer of the aggregate can avoid liability by proving that it was likely that the safety of the product manufactured by him did not have the defect which caused the damage at the time of the launch. According to the provision, the party who manufactured or produced the aggregate is not liable for compensation if he can prove that the lack of safety is due to the design of the product to which the aggregate has been attached, or to the instructions given by the manufacturer who ordered the product. When assessing the lack of safety, the anticipated

use of the product, among other things, must be taken into consideration; consequently, it may be necessary for the manufacturer of the aggregate to anticipate the use of his product as a component in various end products by giving adequate product information or by other arrangements, if he wishes to be released from liability.

5.3.3   *Limits on total liability*

The EC Directive determines that the right of the injured party to receive compensation for a product damage may not be restricted by appealing to the fact that compensation could be granted also on some other grounds. As a result, the Finnish Product Liability Act has been amended by abolishing the previously valid long list of restrictions of the scope of implementation. Therefore, the scope of implementation is currently restricted only to the extent that it does not cover:

(a) damage caused by the product to the product itself;
(b) damage caused by the 'aggregate' of the product; or
(c) damage referred to in the Nuclear Liability Act.

Damage caused to the product itself is generally within the scope of contractual liability, because such lack of safety also implies a defect in the product, eg on the basis of the liability regulations governing sale of movable goods. Also the restriction relating to damage caused to the product by the aggregate is based on the distinction between product liability and contractual liability and to the fact that the product liability ground is not present when contractual liability ensures sufficient compensation protection.

Compensation based on Product Liability Act are determined by implementing the Compensation Act when practicable, as discussed in section 4. The Product Liability Act further includes a compensation provision dealing with minimum quantum of liability, consistent with the EC Directive. The precise content of the Ecu 500 minimum claim in the EC Directive has been target for debate. Judged by the formulation of the introductory section of the Directive, the rule is intended to discourage claims involving small amounts. Consequently, the Finnish Product Liability Act includes a provision stipulating that damage of less than FIM 2,350 caused to property is not recoverable under the Act. The amount expressed in money can be adjusted by a statute, provided that the economic development and the capital market trend so require. The legislative materials for the Product Liability Act state that the provision should be interpreted so that no compensation liability will arise, if the damage is less than FIM 2,350. Should the damage be in excess of FIM 2,350, full compensation will be ordered. No maximum amount has been placed on damages recoverable.

5.3.4   *Difference between national law and provisions of the Directive*

The Finnish Product Liability Act does not apply to damage caused to a product by its 'aggregate', if the 'aggregate' was attached to the product before the product launch. This type of damage is not expressly excluded from the product liability norms of the EU Directive. When implementing its provision, however, this delimitation derives from the fact that damage to the actual product is excluded from the scope of implementation. The end product is in that case not regarded as property independent of the 'aggregate'.

The Product Liability Act also includes a provision stipulating that the party who has imported the product to Finland is liable to assist the injured party in translating the compensation claim into a foreign language. If assistance is not given, the importer must compensate the injured party for the necessary costs relating to the translation of the compensation claim. The assistance and liability to pay damages also concerns the subsequent launcher of the product, unless he indicates the identity of the importer at the request of the claiming party within a reasonable time.

6 CRIMINAL LIABILITY FOR DEFECTIVE PRODUCTS ARISING FROM BOTH GENERAL SAFETY LAW AND THE IMPLEMENTATION OF EU DIRECTIVE 92/59 ON PRODUCT SAFETY IN FINLAND

6.1 Introduction

For a considerable time, Finland lacked general product safety legislation. Public authorities could not address risks not belonging to the scope of the foodstuffs legislation or some other special laws. The Consumer Protection Act adopted at the end of the 1970s (20 January 1978, 1978/38) included, however, a marketing provision stipulating that marketing which does not contain information necessary for the health or financial safety of consumers must always be deemed as improper.

Finland has since also introduced the general Product Safety Act, adopted at the end of 1986 (12 December 1986, 1986/1914).

6.2 Outline of implementation of EC Directive 92/59 in Finland and date of implementation and description of anomalous provisions on the implementation of EC Directive 92/59

The first general Product Safety Act adopted in Finland in 1986 was from the outset compatible with the currently valid EC Directive. The Product Safety Act was last amended in 1993. The principal difference between the Finnish Product Safety Act and the EC Directive is that the Finnish Act is more detailed in some respects.

The Product Safety Act applies to consumer goods manufactured, marketed, sold or otherwise distributed or imported by a business undertaking, as well as to consumer services provided, marketed, sold or otherwise distributed by a business undertaking as part of its business. In addition to consumers, goods and services delivered by the business undertaking to schools, hospitals, etc, belong to the scope of the Act, provided that these distribute the goods or services for use by persons comparable to consumers.

The Product Safety Act is, however, not applied to consumer goods exported from or in transit through the country, unless they constitute a hazard in Finland. Neither is the Act applicable to consumer goods or services to the extent that prevention of their risks to health and property is expressly stipulated or governed in or by some other Act. For this reason pharmaceuticals and food products are not covered by the Product Safety Act.

The Product Safety Act, paragraph 3, includes an essential provision by way of a general clause. The provision stipulates that a business undertaking must observe due care as required by the circumstances to ensure that the

consumer commodity or service does not cause risk to the consumer's health or property. If the business undertaking learns about such possibility of risk, this must be immediately reported to the supervising authority. At the same time, he must also announce the measures which he has already undertaken due to the risk.

Risks to be considered include those relating to the normal use of the commodity. If it is used for some other purpose than originally intended, or against the instructions for use or other similar instructions, or without due care customary in similar circumstances, and this causes risk to health or property, the commodity is not necessarily deemed as hazardous. However, the fact that most consumers read instructions summarily and that often warnings and other instructions cannot be regarded as a sufficient safety measure especially in circumstances where the risk in question could be removed without unsurmountable problems or restricted by modifying the actual products, should be considered when assessing the hazardousness of a commodity. The product may be hazardous because of a defect or inadequacy in its structure or composition or because the product information given has been false, misleading or inadequate.

The authority which supervises compliance with the Product Safety Act and the relating regulations, orders and resolutions in Finland is the Consumer Administration. The task of the Ministry of Social Affairs and Health as the expert authority is to determine whether a consumer commodity should be held as hazardous to health. With regard to imported consumer goods, the Customs is the supervising authority. The supervising authorities exercise considerable power in questions of obtaining the necessary information. They can request a business undertaking to furnish the necessary information and present their books, correspondence and inventories for inspection. They also have the right of access to the premises of the business undertaking to perform inspections and they can also take the required samples of consumer goods. If necessary, they can request official assistance from the police to carry out their duties.

A prohibition issued pursuant to the Product Safety Act differs from a prohibition issued on the basis of the Consumer Protection Act, since the former can also be issued as a general prohibition concerning a certain consumer commodity, if necessary. A prohibition pursuant to the Consumer Protection Act is normally addressed to an individual business undertaking only. Pursuant to the Product Safety Act, the prohibition can concern any production or distribution process of the product, ie manufacture, marketing, sale and import of the product. The prohibition can concern the characteristics of a consumer commodity, as well as product information given on packaging of the product or in conjunction with other marketing. If the addressee of the prohibition is identified, the prohibition must be enforced by a conditional fine if not deemed inappropriate on special grounds. The conditional fine is ordered by the same authority who ordered the prohibition. If, on the other hand, the prohibition is general in nature, ie not addressed to anyone in particular, it cannot be enforced by a conditional fine. To ensure compliance with the prohibition it is, however, possible to order an additional prohibition against business undertakings which do not comply with the general prohibition.

If the aforementioned prohibitions are not deemed sufficient, the Consumer Administration or a customs' authority can order that the goods in the possession of the business undertaking must be destroyed, or if this is deemed inappropriate, order what action should be taken to dispose of the goods.

If the supervising authority has issued a prohibition or order to destroy the

goods or other similar action, he can also order the business undertaking to distribute information in an appropriate way of the prohibition or order, a risk relating to the commodity, service or their use and consumers' rights. However, the supervising authority can impose the information obligation only simultaneously with the prohibition.

6.3 Description of local optional provisions

The Product Safety Act also stipulates penal sanctions. A product safety crime exists when a party intentionally causes risk to consumers' health or property in his business by manufacturing, marketing, selling or otherwise distributing or importing hazardous consumer goods, and on the other hand in situations where a party neglects to observe a prohibition or order to destroy the commodity or other measures issued under the Product Safety Act. The penal consequence for the crime can be a fine or imprisonment of not more than three months. If the corresponding offence is due to gross negligence or carelessness, the party guilty of the offence must be sentenced to a fine for a product safety offence.

6.4 Brief overview of other significant product safety law and the extent to which other EC Consumer Safety Directives have been implemented

In addition to the Finnish Product Safety Act, the Foodstuffs Act includes an authority to issue a statute enabling the issuance of more detailed orders on the requirements for the safety of consumer goods. A great number of different statutes have been issued including ones on foodstuffs, detergents, cosmetics, etc. A statute can regulate or a State Council resolution can determine what kind of information concerning consumer commodities and consumer services is necessary for consumers, as well as on the minimum requirements of consumer commodities and services.

7 CIVIL LIABILITY FOR DEFECTIVE PRODUCTS BROUGHT ABOUT BY BREACH OF STATUTORY REGULATION DESIGNED TO PROTECT CONSUMERS AND/OR TO PROMOTE SAFETY

7.1 Outline of nature of protective regulations

As already discussed above, the Finnish Consumer Protection Act contains marketing provisions stipulating that practices which are indecent or otherwise improper from the perspective of consumers are not permitted. Marketing which does not include information necessary for the health and financial safety of consumers must always be deemed as improper.

7.2 Nature of liability, damage or criminal sanctions

The primary consequence for breach of the marketing provisions of the Consumer Protection Act is a prohibition based on market law. If necessary for consumer protection, the business undertaking can be prohibited from

continuing or renewing marketing which violates the Consumer Protection Act or other comparable marketing. The prohibition is enforced by a conditional fine, unless deemed as unnecessary for special reasons. When ordering the afore-mentioned prohibition, the Market Court can also order the business undertaking being the target of the prohibition to rectify the marketing activity within a set time limit.

Activities violating the Consumer Protection Act can also result in criminal liability. A party who in connection with professional marketing for goods or services gives untrue or misleading information significant from the perspective of the marketing target group can be sentenced to a fine or imprisonment of not more than one year for a marketing crime. Also a party who either intentionally or due to gross negligence violates the afore-mentioned provisions of the Consumer Protection Act can be sentenced to a fine for a consumer protection offence.

Compliance with the Consumer Protection Act is in Finland primarily supervised by the Consumer Ombudsman. The Consumer Protection Act contains no provisions on possible civil sanctions, eg damages for illegal marketing. It is possible, however, in certain circumstances to link a civil sanction to improper marketing on the basis of general contractual and compensation regulations. Practices violating the special provisions of the Consumer Protection Act are punishable, meaning that for instance a consumer who suffers damage not covered by a contractual relationship due to faulty marketing, could in principle claim damages pursuant to the Compensation Act, provided that the general prerequisites of damages are fulfilled.

7.3 Burden of proof

Violation of the general non-sanctionable provision of the Consumer Protection Act can result in damages only if the nature of the offence is such that extremely weighty grounds for awarding damages can be deemed to exist. In practice, it is virtually impossible for the consumer to prove that he has suffered concrete damage because of marketing activities not governed by a contractual relationship.

8 BIBLIOGRAPHY

Routamo, Eero:	Kaupan lait I, Helsinki 1990
Routamo, Eero and Hoppu, Esko:	Suomen vahingonkorvausoikeus, Vammala 1988
Saarnilehto, Ari:	Sopimusoikeuden perusteet, Helsinki 1991
Wilhelmsson, Thomas:	Suomen kuluttajansuojajärjestelmä, Helsinki, 1991
Wilhelmsson, Thomas and Rudanko, Matti:	Tuotevastuu, Helsinki 1991

CHAPTER VI

France

Ms Muriel de Courreges

Salès Vincent & Associés
56 rue Notre Dame de Lorette
75009 Paris
France

Tel: ++ 33 1 42 80 63 73

CHAPTER VI

France

1 INTRODUCTION

The French Constitution which inaugurated the Fifth French Republic in October 1958 was adopted under the aegis of General de Gaulle. It is generally considered that it instituted a semi-presidential system with a strong and two-headed executive (the President directly elected by the people and the Prime Minister appointed by the President and supported by a majority in Parliament) and a Parliament (*Assemblée Nationale* and *Sénat*) with reduced powers (eg the Government controls the Parliament's agenda). The President is deemed to be the 'guarantor' of the independence of the judicial authority.

The French court system is divided between judicial and administrative courts. The administrative courts are mostly in charge of disputes which involve public authorities (eg administrative acts and contracts). All civil and commercial disputes are generally heard before the judicial courts. The *Cour de Cassation* is the head of the judicial courts and harmonises the solutions adopted by lower courts for the interpretation of the law. The *Tribunal de Grande Instance*[1] and the *Tribunal de Commerce* have original jurisdiction over most civil and commercial disputes. The *Tribunal de Police* has jurisdiction over minor offences and breach of police regulations, the *Tribunal Correctionnel* has jurisdiction over offences and the *Cour d'Assises*, which is composed of a jury, has jurisdiction over crimes. Except for crimes where the only recourse is before the *Cour de Cassation*, appeals are taken before the *Cour d'Appel*. Civil and commercial procedures mostly pertain to an adversarial system. Criminal procedure, on the other hand, is rather inquisitorial.

France is a civil law country. The legal system is predominantly derived from statute law in the tradition of Roman law. French law was codified mostly during the French revolution. The codification work covered civil, criminal, commercial law as well as rules of civil and criminal procedure. These Codes which were adopted by other European countries in the nineteenth century are better known as the 'Napoleonic Codes'.

Until the recent introduction, in July 1993, of a new *Code de la Consommation*, most product liability law in France was governed by the articles of the Civil Code.

French product liability law has traditionally been based on the rules relating to a seller's liability for latent defects in article 1641 ff of the Civil Code. The courts have actively sought to extend this basic consumer protection. For example, they had developed sellers' and manufacturers' obligations to supply a product to conform with contractual provisions pursuant to article 1603 ff

---

1 Where the amount involved is less than FF 30,000, the *Tribunal d'Instance* has original jurisdiction over ordinary civil matters.

of the Civil Code, as well as the obligations to inform, advise and warn the purchaser of the conditions of use of the product and its potential dangers.

French law in this area has been marked by a multiplicity of grounds for product liability actions, and the complexity of the system as well as uncertainties in the rules have been the subject of criticism.

Legislation was introduced in the early eighties to confirm the manufacturer's obligation to supply safe products, which duty had been previously developed by the courts. This legislation which is aimed specifically at the provision of information to, and the protection of, the consumer and also at enhancing the safety of products to be introduced onto the market, gave specific powers to the administration to achieve these goals.

The Product Liability Directive was a welcome opportunity to harmonise and simplify the existing law in France relating to a manufacturer's liability for defective products. The French government presented on 23 May 1990, draft legislation to Parliament for the implementation of the Directive into French law.

However, this draft legislation, which was discussed at length before the Parliament in 1992 and was subject to multiple amendments, has not been adopted so far, and France was condemned by a Court of Justice decision on 13 January 1993 for lack of implementation of the Product Liability Directive. A new proposal (the 'Proposal'), which integrates previous discussions in the Parliament, was presented by a member of the Parliament on 13 July 1993. It has not yet been put on the agenda of the Parliament, and it is not known at the time of publishing (December 1996) when (and if) it will be discussed.

It seems likely that the Commission, which issued a new warning to the French government in January 1995 in respect of its failure to adopt the Product Liability Directive into French law, will initiate a new procedure pursuant to article 169 of the Treaty of Rome which may now result in the Court of Justice imposing fines for the delay.

In the meantime, French consumer law, that is to say most existing provisions dealing with product liability law, was codified (in July 1993) in the *Code de la Consommation*. The *Code de la Consommation* did not change existing law, it only put together all statute law relating to the protection of consumers. Decrees and regulations regarding general protection of consumers should be integrated at a later stage in a second part of the Code.

It should be noted that, compensating the delay in implementing the Product Liability Directive by law, at least vis-à-vis consumers, French courts have largely developed an autonomous safety obligation in a way to indemnify the plaintiff in a claim for a defective product unifying the remedies available in contract and in tort, and creating a general product liability for manufacturers.

2   PRE-CONTRACTUAL LIABILITY

2.1   Effect on the interpretation and extent of the obligations of the parties to a contract

If the purchaser has been mistaken as to the use and benefit he expects to enjoy from the product and would not have entered into the contract, (or would have entered into the contract on different terms), if he had been correctly and sufficiently informed, the contract will be declared void.[2]

---

2   Art 1110 of the Civil Code.

The contract will be declared void for lack of consent, on the grounds of mistake as to the substantive qualities of the product and its ability to perform in the expected manner.

Pursuant to article 1304 of the Civil Code, the purchaser can bring such action within five years after his mistake was discovered. The Courts have decided that the purchaser is not subject to the short limitation period imposed by article 1648 of the Civil Code, even though the mistake was the consequence of the hidden defect making the product improper for its intended use.[3] This solution is in line with the most recent case law.

Article L 111-1 of the *Code de la Consommation* now specifies that the vendor must provide the consumer with information which allows such consumer to know the main characteristics of the product before the transaction.

In addition, pursuant to special statutes specific information must be given in precontractual statements. Cars, for instance, are subject to specific requirements.

The seller's obligation varies according to the purchaser's capacity (acting in his professional capacity or for private use) and to the technicality of the product.[4]

2.2 Extent that non-disclosure of facts during negotiations may lead to liability

Where the seller has not wilfully misled the purchaser as to the substantive qualities of the product (ie characteristics essential/relevant to the consent of the purchaser), the latter will not be allowed damages but will be entitled to repayment of the price. Where on the contrary the seller has wilfully omitted to disclose information and misled the purchaser as to the substantive qualities of the product, the purchaser will be awarded damages to compensate for any loss of profits he may have suffered.[5]

2.3 Whether pre-contractual liability lies in contract or tort

As a matter of principle, a breach will be determined as either tortious or contractual (ie the victim will have a right of action in tort or contract but not both).

Traditionally, where the loss results from the failure of a party to perform his contractual obligations, the plaintiff must bring his action in contract. The sub-purchaser of the product (as well as the purchaser) must base his action against the manufacturer on contractual liability.[6]

However, where the loss does not result from the failure of a party to perform his contractual obligations, the plaintiff must base his action on tortious liability alone.

Although it may be difficult in practice to distinguish between contractual and precontractual obligations of the seller to inform the purchaser, the courts generally consider that the seller will be liable in tort if the statement was made (or should have been made) before the contract was entered into.[7]

3   *Cour de Cassation*, 1st Civil Chamber, 28 June 1988, DS 1989, p 450.
4   *Cour de Cassation*, Commercial Chamber, 3 November 1992, RJDA 8-9/93, no 685.
5   *Cour de Cassation*, 1st Civil Chamber, 4 October 1978, Bull Civ I, no 292.
6   *Cour de Cassation*, 1st Civil Chamber, 23 April 1985, Bull Civ no 125.
7   Paris, 22 April 1983, GP 83, 346.

3   LIABILITY IN CONTRACT

3.1   Outline of contract law relevant to defective products in France

Contractual liability for defective products has undergone many changes in the last few years, in an attempt of the courts to clarify existing law and also, as indicated above, due to the courts' willingness to reassert the liability of the seller for defective products and compensate for the delay in implementation for the Product Liability Directive by the French legislator.

For many years, liability of the seller for hidden defects pursuant to article 1641 ff of the Civil Code,[8] was the cause of action central to product liability law in France. It was the one most commonly used by a purchaser dissatisfied with a defective product to receive damages including generally all losses suffered caused by such defective product.

However, the courts have always been anxious to hold the seller liable to indemnify the purchaser where the defects are particularly serious, even though the conditions for liability for latent defects (especially the limitation period) were not met.

For this reason, they were deciding that given the obligation of the vendor to supply a product conforming to the purchasers' order or the contractual provisions pursuant to Civil Code articles 1603 ff [and 1184], the 'lack of conformity' of the product may consist in the seller's failure to supply a product which fulfils its normal purpose (*conforme à destination normale*), ie a non-defective product.[9] Such extensive interpretation of the Civil Code articles was criticised.

The courts now consider that defects which make the product unfit for its normal or intended purpose constitute the hidden defects defined by article 1641 ff of the Civil Code.[10] Save where the defect which makes the product unfit for its purpose also constitutes a breach of the obligation of the seller to supply a product in accordance with the specified terms agreed between the parties,[11] the purchaser can no longer bring an action to rescind the sale contract and claim damages based on article 1184 of the Civil Code for the non-performance by the seller of his obligation to deliver a product conforming to the purchaser's order or the contractual provisions. It seems that this more stringent application of the law only applies to economic damages to the goods.

The courts have on the other hand continuously developed a safety obligation and decide in the case of personal injury caused by a defective product that the seller is under the obligation to deliver products free of defect.[12] The purchaser of a defective product who has a contractual link with the manufacturer or with a prior seller, but who is not able to bring an action based on liability for hidden defects, may invoke a breach of an express or implied contractual term pursuant to article 1147 of the Civil Code.

8   Now also integrated in art L 211-1 of the *Code de la Consommation*.
9   *Cour de Cassation*, 1st Civil Chamber, 5 November 1985, Bull Civ I, no 287 and 14 February 1989, Bull Civ I, no 83.
10   *Cour de Cassation*, 3rd Civil Chamber, 27 March 1991, Cont Conc Cons, October 1991 no 198, 1st Civil Chamber, 5 May 1993, D 1993, p 506, 27 October 1993, Bull Civ I, no 305, 24 November 1993, Bull Civ I, no 347, 8 December 1993, D 1994, p 212 and Commercial Chamber, 26 April and 31 May 1994, Bull Civ IV, no 159 and no 199.
11   *Cour de Cassation*, 1st Civil Chamber, 16 June 1993, D 1994, 546.
12   *Cour de Cassation*, 1st Civil Chamber, 21 March 1962, Bull Civ I, no 174, 9 October 1974, Bull Civ I, no 262 and 22 November 1978, JCP 1979, II, 19139, 20 March 1989, D 1989, p 381, 11 June 1991, Bull civ I, no 201 and 27 January 1993, Bull Civ I, no 44.

As indicated in paragraph 2.3 above, the sub-purchaser of the product as well as the purchaser must base his action against the manufacturer on contractual liability.

The courts have for instance decided that the purchaser can bring an action founded on liability for latent defect, not only against the retailer that sold the product to him, but against any prior seller in the chain of supply, including the manufacturer.[13] The purchaser may also bring an action against the seller who sold the goods to him and the manufacturer, who will be held jointly liable.[14]

To bring such claims no intermediate purchaser should have had knowledge of the defect in the product.[15]

3.2   Contractual warranties relating to quality and safety of goods

A seller is, of course, entitled to give special warranties in respect of the products he sells.

The manufacturer may warrant the proper functioning of the product and freely undertake to replace parts in order to make the product suitable for its intended use or to replace the whole product. This free after-sales service is usually provided for a limited period and exceeds the seller's liability for latent defects as it also covers any imperfection in the product for which the purchaser is not responsible.

The vendor must inform the purchaser of any limitation of contractual liability and any special conditions of the sale or provision of services.[16] However, such information regarding the limitation of contractual liability is in fact irrelevant since, as indicated in paragraph 3.6 below, such limitation constitutes vis-à-vis a consumer an unfair contract term and is as such unenforceable. The professional who provides a contractual warranty is under a further obligation to specify clearly that he is still liable to the purchaser for all consequences of the hidden defects of the product sold.[17]

The notion of 'professional' was developed by the courts (in contrast with the notion of 'consumer') and has subsequently been used by the legislator. The 'professional' is any person acting in his professional capacity, in the course of his business. The consumer is generally defined as a person purchasing the goods for his private and not for any professional purpose. The obligations and the rights of a seller or a purchaser will often vary according to his 'professional' or 'non-professional' or 'consumer' status. Such distinction was adopted in the Product Liability Directive, which only applies to damage to items of property used by the injured person mainly for his private use or consumption as opposed to business or 'professional' use.

All information and warnings regarding products marketed in France including contractual warranties, conditions of use of the product etc, must be in French.[18]

13   *Cour de Cassation*, 1st Civil Chamber, 9 October 1979, Bull Civ I, no 241.
14   *Cour de Cassation*, Commercial Chamber, 15 May 1972, Bull Civ IV, no 144.
15   *Cour de Cassation*, 1st Civil Chamber, 13 May 1981, Bull Civ IV, no 182.
16   Art L 113-3 of the *Code de la Consommation*.
17   Decree no 78-464 of 24 March 1978, art 4.
18   Statute 94-665 of 4 August 1994, arts 2 and 23 and Decree 95-240 of 3 March 1995.

3.3   Breach of contract for supply of defective products

The courts have developed a general safety obligations autonomous from previous seller's liability for latent defect.

3.3.1   *Types of defect*

i   Latent defect   Pursuant to article 1641 of the Civil Code (which is now also integrated in article L 211-1 of the *Code de la Consommation*) the seller is liable in respect of hidden defects which render the product sold unsuitable for its intended use.

The seller will be liable, notwithstanding that the defect was only latent at the time of sale.[19]

The seller will be held liable even if he shows that he was not aware of, and could not himself have discovered, the defect in the product, and that he had exercised due care in the manufacture and design of his product.[20] A manufacturer who is found liable for hidden defects cannot rely on the development risk defence.

ii   Product unfit for its purpose due to a lack of sufficient information for the proper use of the product   The manufacturer may be held liable for damage resulting from a lack of adequate information being given on the condition of use of the product and precautions that must be taken as to use of the product, where the purchaser is subsequently deprived of the use and expected benefits arising therefrom, even though the characteristics are apparent.[1]

However, the professional purchaser may be deemed to be under an obligation to make proper enquiries.[2]

iii   Product potentially dangerous   Where the product is not necessarily defective but may prove to be dangerous in use, the professional purchaser, as well as the ordinary consumer, must be warned about the possible dangers of the product.

A lack of sufficient warning regarding the risks incidental to use of the product constitutes a breach on the part of the manufacturer.[3]

iv   Design or manufacturing defects which may create a danger for the person or for his possessions   The courts have found manufacturers who have put into circulation products which had design or manufacturing defects to be in breach of their contractual duties.[4] The seller and the manufacturer of a product, in fact, have an obligation to deliver products that are free of defects which may create a danger for the person/individual or for his possessions.[5]

---

19   *Cour de Cassation*, 3rd Civil Chamber, 6 November 1974, D 1975 IR 28.
20   *Cour de Cassation*, 3rd Civil Chamber, 28 November 1966, DS 1967, 99 and Commercial Chamber, 15 November 1971, DS 1972, 211.
1   *Cour de Cassation*, 1st Civil Chamber, 23 April 1985, Bull Civ I, no 125.
2   *Cour de Cassation*, 1st Civil Chamber, 26 November 1981, Bull Civ I, no 354.
3   *Cour de Cassation*, 3rd Civil Chamber, 28 March 1968, Bull Civ III, no 144 and 1st Civil Chamber, 14 December 1982, Bull Civ I, no 361.
4   *Cour de Cassation*, 1st Civil Chamber, 21 March 1962, Bull Civ I, no 174, 9 October 1974, Bull Civ I, no 262 and 22 November 1978, JCP 1979, II, 19139
5   *Cour de Cassation*, 1st Civil Chamber, 20 March 1989, D 1989, p 381, 11 June 1991, Bull Civ I, no 201 and 27 January 1993, Bull Civ I, no 44.

Such defect may also consist in a defect of one of the elements included in the product (for instance where the injury was caused by a design defect of the heating system of a mobile home and insufficient ventilation).[6]

The courts have also specified that the safety obligation consisted in the delivery of products which used in accordance with suppliers' specifications, do not normally present any danger for their users.[7]

3.3.2   Causation

In most product liability cases, the courts appoint an expert to determine whether the injury has been caused by the defective product.

The circumstances will sometimes clearly show that the damage resulted from the defective product (for instance, when burglars have been able to steal a large quantity of precious goods because of a hidden defect in a security system).[8]

The seller will also be liable when the damage is related to the defective product and would not have occurred without it, even though factors other than the hidden defect may have contributed to the damage.[9] Where the damage results partly from the action of a third party, the producer will in most cases be held jointly liable.

3.3.3   Remoteness of loss and damages

The damage suffered by the plaintiff which is the immediate and direct consequence of the defective product must be entirely repaired.[10]

It may, however, be difficult, in the case of commercial loss of profits to establish that the loss resulted directly from the use of the defective product in the business where, for instance, the purchaser argues that damage arising from such use has injured his reputation and has resulted in a loss of profits.[11]

3.4   Quantum of damage

3.4.1   Latent defect

Article 1644 of the Civil Code gives the purchaser a choice of two remedies. The first is for a reduction of the price proportional to the diminished value of the product (which is estimated by a court-appointed expert) and the other is the reimbursement of the price upon the return of the goods.

The courts have decided that the sub-purchaser (who may be entitled to obtain damages from the manufacturer) cannot seek to rescind the contract in situations where the purchase price in successive sales was significantly different.[12] Furthermore, only the seller to whom the goods are returned will have to repay the purchase price.[13]

---

6   *Cour de Cassation*, 1st Civil Chamber, 11 June 1991, Bull Civ I, no 201.
7   *Cour de Cassation*, 1st Civil Chamber, 22 January 1991, Bull Civ I, no 30.
8   *Cour de Cassation*, 1st Civil Chamber, 18 March 1986, Bull Civ I, no 75.
9   *Cour de Cassation*, 2nd Civil Chamber, 30 November 1988, unpublished no 87-15734.
10   Art 1151 of the Civil Code.
11   *Cour de Cassation*, Commercial Chamber, 17 October 1977, Bull Civ IV, no 233.
12   *Cour de Cassation*, Commercial Chamber, 27 January 1973, JCP 1973, II, 17445.
13   *Cour de Cassation*, Commercial Chamber, 17 May 1982, Bull Civ IV, no 182.

The Proposal adds to the Civil Code a new article 1644-1 according to which, where the sale was made by a professional seller, the purchaser may require, unless it is obviously unreasonable, (a) a reimbursement of the price on the return of the product, or (b) a reduction in the price, or (c) the repair of the product, or (d) the replacement of the product. The purchaser may not, however, seek reimbursement of the price or replacement of the product if he is unable, without legitimate reason, to return the product.

In addition, article 1645 of the Civil Code provides that the seller who knew about the defect in the product is liable not only to repay the purchase price but also to pay damages to the purchaser.

The courts in such cases have also set a different standard depending on the professional capacity of the seller. They have decided that professional sellers (which includes manufacturers) are presumed to know about the defects,[14] such presumption being irrebutable.

The damages payable in such a case include all losses suffered by the purchaser caused by the defective product, ie the diminished value of the products themselves, the cost of repair, loss of profits and personal injury or damage to other goods.

However, the liability of the manufacturer will be reduced where the plaintiff has used the product in abnormal conditions.

3.4.2   General contractual liability rules

As a matter of principle, damages directly caused by the contractual breach and, so long as it is not due to fraud, which have been or could have been foreseen at the time of contract, must be entirely repaired.[15] The courts have generally considered that the supply of a defective product constitutes gross negligence[16] which can be assimilated to fraud.

Damages will usually include compensation for personal injury and loss of profits or damage to other goods caused by the defective products.[17]

However, the manufacturer's liability may be reduced (or he may be exonerated) if he proves that the injury was due to an external cause, such as an Act of God, action of a third party or fault on the part of the plaintiff, eg when the plaintiff has used the product in abnormal conditions or ignored any warnings and advice given by the producer.

3.5   Burden of proof

3.5.1   Latent defect

The purchaser will have to prove the existence of the defect which has caused the damage. As indicated in paragraph 3.3 above, in most product liability cases, the courts appoint an expert to determine whether the injury has been caused by the defective product.

---

14   *Cour de Cassation*, 1st Civil Chamber, 19 January 1965, DS 1965, 389.
15   Art 1150 of the Civil Code.
16   *Cour de Cassation*, 1st Civil Chamber, 22 November 1978, JCP 1979, II, 19139.
17   *Cour de Cassation*, 1st Civil Chamber, 20 March 1989, D. 1989 p 381, 11 June 1991, Bull Civ I, no 201 and 27 January 1993, Bull Civ I, no 44.

The courts sometimes require that the plaintiff show the specific defect.[18] When the causes of the defect remain undetermined but external causes are unlikely the courts generally hold the manufacturer liable.[19]

The purchaser has to show that the defect existed prior to or, at the latest, at the time of the purchase.

It is often difficult for the purchaser to prove the existence of the defect at the time of sale and it will be necessary in most cases for the purchaser to have an expert appointed by the courts, who will investigate whether the defect existed at the time of the sale or whether the defect was due to the improper use or maintenance of the product by the purchaser, or to the operation of normal wear and tear upon the product. This means that where a product has been tested by the purchaser, or repaired by him, he will find it extremely difficult to prove that a defect existed prior to sale.

The courts, in deciding whether the defect existed prior to or at the time of the sale, will take into account all the facts and circumstances.

The Proposal adds a new article 1641-1 to the Civil Code which provides that any defect occurring within the period of a contractual warranty is presumed to have existed at the time of the sale unless the contrary can be established. In the absence of such a contractual warranty, the defect will be presumed to have existed at the time of delivery for a year commencing from the date of delivery. The Proposal thereby extends the reversal of the burden of proof operated by the Directive to liability for latent defects but only for one year. However, such presumption will not exist in sales between professionals (*professionnels*).

Once the existence of the defect (and possibly its cause) has been established, the court must be satisfied that the defect was hidden, especially where the seller claims that the defect could have been detected by the plaintiff.

The courts have set different standards depending on the professional status of the purchaser.

In the case of a consumer purchase, the court will be satisfied that the defect was hidden where the purchaser could not have discovered the defect upon preliminary inspection.[20] The behaviour of the plaintiff is taken into account to determine whether or not the defect was hidden.

Professionals, on the other hand, are presumed to go through an in-depth check of the product and the seller will not be liable for the defect where the purchaser who shares the same area of expertise as the seller had the capability to discover the defect.[1]

3.5.2   General safety obligation– design or manufacturing defects which may create a danger for a person or his goods

All the plaintiff will have to show is that the damage was caused by a defect which may create a danger for the person or for his possessions.[2]

---

18   *Cour de Cassation*, Commercial Chamber, 27 November 1984, GP 1985 1 pan 80.
19   *Cour de Cassation*, Commercial Chamber, 20 May 1986, unpublished no 84-17-675.
20   *Cour de Cassation*, Commercial Chamber, 11 May 1965, Bull Civ III, no. 306
 1   *Cour de Cassation*, Commercial Chamber, 8 December 1980, Bull Civ IV, no 415
 2   *Cour de Cassation*, 1st Civil Chamber, 21 March 1962, Bull Civ I, no 174 and 20 March 1989 D 1989, p 381 and 11 June 1991, D 1993, Som, p 241.

3.6 Exclusion or limitation of liability

When the liability arises out of a contractual breach, the clauses limiting or excluding liability have traditionally been deemed valid.

Provisions limiting or excluding liability are not, in any case, effective in limiting or excluding liability for damages for death or personal injury.

In addition, the courts decided that although article 1643 of the Civil Code provides that the seller may stipulate in the contract that he will not be liable for hidden defects of which he had no knowledge, clauses, whether limiting the duration of the liability, the types of defects or the nature of the damage for which the seller will be responsible, were invalid when a professional seller seeks to rely upon them against a consumer who brought an action based on liability for hidden defects, since the professional seller was presumed to know of the hidden defects in his product.

The solutions given by the courts for the liability for hidden defects had been confirmed by the legislator and extended to the general law of contract. Clauses excluding or limiting the liability of a professional for failing to perform his obligations are unenforceable against a non-professional or a consumer.[3]

The Unfair Contract Terms Directive which was implemented by Statute No 95/96 of 1 February 1995 (amending article L 132-1 of the *Code de la Consommation*) has not, in this respect, improved the protection of the consumer, already well protected by existing law. Article L 132-1 of the *Code de la Consommation* now specifies that clauses which have the object or the effect of causing a significant imbalance in the parties' rights and obligations to the detriment of the non-professional or the consumer, are unfair and as such void.

The courts have specified that these provisions should not apply to supply contracts directly linked to the purchaser's professional activity or for the needs of its business.[4] In the case of an action based on liability of the seller for hidden defects the courts traditionally found that a contractual exclusion clause was effective in contracts entered into between professionals, only when the seller could produce evidence to show that the purchaser had the same field of expertise as himself and therefore the technical capability to have discovered the defect at the time of the sale.[5] Surprisingly, this solution continues to apply for damages caused by a hidden defect.[5a]

3.7 Limitation period

3.7.1 *Latent defect*

Pursuant to article 1648 of the Civil Code (which has also been integrated in article L 211-1 of the *Code de la Consommation*), the purchaser of a product having a hidden defect must commence proceedings within a short period.

This limitation period runs from the time of discovery of the defect in the goods.[6] The acceptable length of such a period is left to the discretion of the

---

3 Statute 78-23 of 10 January 1978 for the protection and the information of consumers of products and services, Article 35, now art L 132-1 of the *Code de la Consommation* and Decree No 78-464 of 24 March 1978, art 2.

4 *Cour de Cassation*, 1st Civil Chamber, 4 January 1995 and 21 February 1995, Cont Conc Cons May 1995, p 5 and 3 January 1996, Dic Perm D Aff Com, Bull 424, p 909.

5 *Cour de Cassation*, 1st Civil Chamber, 20 December 1983, Bull Civ I, no 308.

5a *Cour de Cassation*, 1st Civil chamber, 20 February 1996, RTD Com, July-Sept 1996, p 514.

6 *Cour de Cassation*, Commercial Chamber, 22 November 1965, Bull Civ III, no 593.

courts which exercise it according to the circumstances and the nature of the defect. They may, for instance, take into account the fact that negotiations with a view to an amicable settlement have taken place and failed before court proceedings were commenced.[7] The short period therefore varies from one case to another, from a few weeks to over a year. Generally, proceedings brought within a few months from discovery of the defect fall within the time limit, but a period exceeding one year is often deemed too long. The fact that the purchaser is a foreigner domiciled abroad is one of the circumstances which may be taken into account by the courts.

Article 2244 of the Civil Code provides that the limitation period can be interrupted by interlocutory application (*action en référé*) (eg for the appointment of a judicial expert) and not necessarily an action on the merits.

The Proposal amends the limitation provisions currently set out in article 1648 of the Civil Code and provides that the purchaser's rights will expire where he has not informed the seller of the defect within a year from the time he has discovered or should have discovered the defect. However, this period of time may be modified amongst the professionals by trade usage or agreement.

The specific reference to the one-year period would have been a great improvement reducing the uncertainty linked to the application of the short period, in which proceedings must be brought. However, such impact is lessened by (a) the notion of when the defect should have been discovered, and (b) the reference to modification in respect of sales amongst professionals.

3.7.2 *General rules of contract liability*

The action based on general contractual liability for breach of the safety obligation is not subject to the brief limitation period provided under article 1648 of the Civil Code.[8] The limitation period is either:

(a) ten years starting from the day when the damage occurred, for an action initiated by a plaintiff who purchased the product for business purposes;[9] or

(b) thirty years for an action initiated by a plaintiff who purchased the product for private purposes.[10]

Accordingly, the action that a purchaser may have pursuant to this contractual warranty is not subject to the same rules as the liability for hidden defects and does not have to be initiated within the short limitation period required by article 1648 of the Civil Code.[11]

However, clauses providing for a shorter limitation period are valid when they are agreed between professionals in the same area of expertise.

3.8 Liability for third parties or for products used for the performance of a contractual obligation by a party contractually bound to a safety obligation

As a matter of principle one cannot be liable for third parties in contract.

7 *Cour de Cassation*, 1st Civil Chamber, 16 July 1987, D 1987, IR 182.
8 *Cour de Cassation*, 1st Civil Chamber, 11 June 1991, Bull Civ I, no. 201 and 27 January 1993, Bull Civ I, no 44.
9 Art 189 bis of the Commercial Code.
10 Art 2262 of the Civil Code.
11 *Cour de Cassation*, Commercial Chamber, 2 May 1990, JCP 1990, IV, 246.

In a comparable matter, the courts have recently decided that when a party to a contract is bound to a safety obligation, in this case a school for its schoolchildren, such party will be liable not only for damages caused by his personal wrongdoing but also for damages caused by products which it uses for the performance of a contractual obligation.[12]

4   LIABILITY IN TORT

4.1   Introduction

As indicated in paragraph 2.3 above, where the plaintiff in a product liability claim neither owns nor possesses the defective goods and has not at any time entered into a contract with either the manufacturer or any of the intermediate distributors or where the loss does not result from the failure of a party to perform his contractual obligations, the plaintiff must base his action on tortious liability alone.

As indicated in paragraph 1.2 above, the courts have been willing to provide the victims with sufficient protection regardless of the lack of contractual link with the manufacturer or a seller. They have developed the obligations of the manufacturer, from the articles of the Civil Code, imposing on the manufacturer similar obligations vis-à-vis contracting parties and third parties.

The courts have for instance developed a principle of strict liability from article 1384 paragraph 1 of the Civil Code which makes a person liable in respect of injury caused by products which a person has in his custody (*garde*).[13] They have steadily developed a general safety obligation on the manufacturer and more recently on the seller.

4.2   Outline of relevant tort law giving rise to liability for personal and property damage in France

The manufacturer can be held liable pursuant to article 1382 and 1383 of the Civil Code, which places liability on those who cause injury to others as a result of the tortious breach of article 1384, paragraph 1 of the Civil code (as indicated above) or also pursuant to article 1384, paragraph 5 of the Civil Code which makes an employer liable in respect of breaches caused by his employees acting in the course of their employment.

4.2.1   *Liability based on article 1384, paragraph 1 of the Civil Code*

In order to indemnify a plaintiff who has no direct contractual link with the seller or the manufacturer, the courts have developed the concept of custody of the structure of the product (*garde de la structure*) by which the manufacturer's liability continues after delivery of the product.[14] The manufacturer is deemed to be able to control the internal structure of the product and check whether the product could be used without danger, even though he no longer owns or possesses the product.[15] However, this concept of custody has been applied

---

12   *Cour de Cassation*, 1st Civil Chamber, 17 January 1995, D 1995, p 350.
13   *Cour de Cassation*, United Chambers, 13 February 1930, S 1930, 1-121.
14   *Cour de Cassation*, 1st Civil Chamber, 5 January 1956, D 1957, 261 and 2nd Civil Chamber, 5 June 1971, Bull Civ II, no 204.
15   *Cour de Cassation*, Civil Chamber, 12 November 1975, JCP 1976, Ed G, II, 18479.

only to products with inherent internal dynamic forces capable of becoming dangerous by exploding or imploding, such as, bottled gas, television sets, soft drink bottles, etc.[16]

Article 1386-18 of the Proposal states that, once the product is put into circulation, the manufacturer may no longer be held liable as 'custodian' of the product. This cause of action is regarded as unnecessary, especially in the light of the implementation of the Directive.

4.2.2 *Liability based on articles 1382 and 1383 of the Civil Code*

The breach may relate to design or manufacturing defects and also includes a situation where the manufacturer has failed to inform or warn the purchaser of the possible dangers of the product.

The courts have found manufacturers who have put into circulation defective products to be in breach of their tortious duties.[17]

In continuity with previous decisions and in consideration of the lack of implementation of the Product Liability Directive, the courts have asserted as a general principle the obligation of the manufacturer, and also of the professional seller, to deliver products free of any design or manufacturing defect which may create a danger for persons or goods, regardless of a contractual link between the plaintiff and the seller or the manufacturer of the defective product.[18]

Where the product is not necessarily defective but may prove to be dangerous in use, the professional purchaser, as well as the ordinary consumer, must be warned about the possible dangers of the product. A lack of sufficient warning regarding the risks incidental to use of the product constitutes a breach on the part of the manufacturer.[19]

4.3 Causation

The manufacturer may be exonerated or his liability may be reduced if he proves that the injury was due to an external cause, such as an Act of God, action of a third party or fault on the part of the plaintiff, eg when the plaintiff has used the product in abnormal conditions or ignored any warnings and advice given by the manufacturer.[20]

4.4 Remoteness of loss and damage: quantum of damage

In the same manner as for contractual liability, damages directly caused by a tortious breach must be entirely repaired.

As indicated in paragraph 3.3.3 above, it may, however, be difficult, in the case of commercial loss of profits, to establish that the loss resulted directly from the use of the defective product in the business.

16 *Cour de Cassation*, 2nd Civil Chamber, 5 June 1971, Bull Civ II, no 204.
17 *Cour de Cassation*, 1st Civil Chamber, 5 May 1964, Bull Civ I, no 234, 2nd Civil Chamber, 16 March 1966, Bull Civ II, no 350 and 1st Civil Chamber, 18 July 1972. Bull Civ I, no 189.
18 *Cour de Cassation*, 1st Civil Chamber, 17 January 1995, D 1995, p 350 to be compared with previous decisions, eg *Cour de Cassation*, 1st Civil Chamber, 26 April 1983, GP, 1984 I, compared with previous decisions, eg *Cour de Cassation*, 1st Civil Chamber, 26 April 1983, GP, 1984, I, 180.
19 *Cour de Cassation*, Criminal Chamber, 14 March 1974, GP 1974-1-417.
20 *Cour de Cassation*, 2nd Civil Chamber, 21 June 1962, Bull Civ II, no 537.

In practice, it should be noted that commercial courts are more inclined to repair economic loss than criminal courts.

4.5   Burden of proof

In principle, the plaintiff who bases a product liability action on articles 1382 and/or 1383 of the Civil Code must prove a tortious breach by the manufacturer. In the case of lack of sufficient warning regarding the potential dangers of the product, such proof will be easily produced.

In the case of damage caused by a design or manufacturing defect, the courts have ruled that all the plaintiff need show is that the product was defective (eg a design defect which presented in itself a risk of accident).[1]

Similarly, when the action was based on article 1384, paragraph 1, the plaintiff only had to show a causal relationship between the injury suffered and the product.

4.6   Exclusion or limitation of liability

Clauses limiting or excluding the liability of the manufacturer will be invalid in the case of an action based on tort.[2]

4.7   Limitation period

Pursuant to article 2270-1 of the Civil Code the limitation period for tort action is ten years as from when the damage occurred or the loss was further aggravated.

4.8   Liability for third parties

The manufacturer will also be liable for damage in respect of breaches caused by his employees acting in the course of employment, pursuant to article 1384, paragraph 5 of the Civil Code.

5   LIABILITY FOR DEFECTIVE PRODUCTS PROVIDED BY THE PROPOSAL FOR THE IMPLEMENTATION OF EC DIRECTIVE 85/374 ON PRODUCT LIABILITY IN FRANCE

5.1   Introduction

As indicated above, France was condemned on 13 January 1993 by the Court of Justice for failure to implement the Directive, and the courts have taken this lack of implementation into account to reassert and develop a general safety obligation on the manufacturer and the seller.

The information below is based on the last version of the Proposal, which integrates previous discussions in the Parliament but may of course be subject

1   *Cour de Cassation*, 1st Civil Chamber, 18 July 1972, Bull Civ I, no 189 and 17 January 1995, D 1995, p 350.
2   *Cour de Cassation*, 2nd Civil Chamber, 17 February 1955, D 1956, 17.

to future amendment by Parliament. However, as indicated above, it is not known when and if, the Proposal will be discussed.

The new rules would be inserted as a new Title IV bis of the third book of the Civil Code in between Title IV which relates to non-contractual liability and the Title V ff which regulate various types of contracts.

The new rules would apply to the products first put into circulation after the date of coming into force of the new statute, even where any such products were subject to prior contract.

5.2   Outline of provisions in France

Except for the provisions discussed in paragraph 5.3.4 below, the Proposal reproduces faithfully the provisions of the Directive.

5.3   Description of optional provisions in respect of product liability law in France

5.3.1   *Primary agricultural products and game: article 1386-3*

The new rules would apply to any movables including primary agricultural products (ie products of the soil, of stockfarming and of fisheries) and game.

The option to cover agricultural products is in line with traditional case law which has held producers to be liable for hidden defects of agricultural products.

5.3.2   *Development risks defence: article 1386-11(4)*

The French government strongly opposed this defence when the Directive was first drafted. The Proposal has finally adopted the development risks defence and does not take advantage of the derogation provision of article 15.1(b) of the Directive to maintain the existing law.

The defence was finally inserted into the Proposal in order to avoid creating a competitive disadvantage for French producers (mainly marketing their products in France), who could have been the only ones (together with Luxembourguese producers) to bear the cost of the development risk, as against the other EU producers.

As previously indicated, such a defence is not available under existing French law as a producer cannot avoid liability for latent defects, on the ground that he was not himself aware of the defect when he put the product into circulation, even where it was impossible for him to discover the defect.

It is likely, in the light of previous case law, that the French courts will be quite strict in assessing the state of scientific and technical knowledge required to enable the producer to discover the defect in the product. As indicated in paragraph 5.3.4 below, mere compliance with the 'state of the art' at the time at which the product was put into circulation is an insufficient reason for exonerating the producer from liability.

5.3.3   *Limits on total liability*

The Proposal does not limit the producer's total liability to Ecu 70m for damages resulting from death or personal injury and caused by identical items.

This solution is consistent with the existing French rules for product liability.

5.3.4   *Differences between national law and provisions of the Directive*

i   Damages: article 1386-2

(a) The new rules for product liability would apply to a wider type of damage than that stated in the Directive. Concerning the first category of damage, article 1386-2 of the Proposal refers to damage resulting from injury to the person. This would include not only damage resulting from death and personal injuries, but also non-material damage, such as pain and suffering.

   An injured person should therefore be able to recover in respect of a range of damage caused by a single product according to a single set of rules. This solution, although not prescribed by the Directive which finally left the question of recovery of non-material damages to national legislation, avoids unnecessary complication of proceedings.

(b) The new rules would apply to damage or to destruction of any item of property (other than the defective product itself) regardless of whether the type and/or use of the Product is private or professional. The Proposal has extended the field of application of the new rules to damage in respect of products of a professional nature or applied for professional use or consumption in order to simplify the rules governing the producers' liability. However, as indicated below, existing rules for product liability would remain applicable.

(c) The French version of the Directive differs from the English one as it refers not to a threshold for liability, but to a 'franchise', the effect of which, where damages are of an amount exceeding Ecu 500, renders the producer liable only for the excess balance. However, the Proposal for product liability would apply whatever the amount, whether it is below or above the threshold of Ecu 500.

It was also preferred to have a single set of rules to govern producers' liability. However, previous rules would be applicable whatever may be the amount of damage.

ii   Release of the product: article 1386-5   The Proposal specifies that a product is put into circulation when it is voluntarily released by the producer. It now also indicates that such a product can be put into circulation only once. Such provision would apparently reduce the limitation period in the case of a second release of the product (for instance, after a checking).

iii   Producers: articles 1386-6 and 1386-7   The Proposal specifies that producers who are held liable under the rules are those acting in their professional capacity.

   The Proposal also states that even where the producer or the importer of the product can be identified and the injured person is informed of his identity, the vendor, lessor or supplier of the product will be treated as a producer. The vendor, lessor or supplier, as the case may be, would then have a claim against the producer by the same rules as those applying to the plaintiff. He would have to commence proceedings within a year of proceedings being initiated against him.

   This solution is clearly more beneficial to the plaintiff than that provided by the Directive and confirms the existing French case law which holds the seller jointly liable with a producer for hidden defects and breach of safety.

iv   'State of the Art'; administrative approval; defences not available to the producer – article 1386-10   The Proposal specifies that the producer may be held liable even though the product was manufactured in compliance with the 'state of the art' or was the subject of an authorisation granted by an administrative body. This is consistent with existing case law.

If this provision is adopted, the courts will have to distinguish the notion of the 'state of the art' from the state of scientific or technical knowledge which could enable the defect's existence to come to light. This could cause some problems before the courts in the future as it might be presumed that the 'state of the art' should reflect the state of, if not scientific, at least technical, knowledge at the time when the product was put into circulation.

v   Fault of the victim: article 1386-12   The Proposal specifies that the use of the product in abnormal conditions that were not reasonably foreseeable by the producer constitutes a fault of the victim. This provision does not seem to contradict the Directive but seems unnecessary since the Proposal, in accordance with the provisions of the Directive, declares that a product is defective when such a product does not provide the safety which a person is entitled to expect and that in order to appreciate such safety all circumstances must be taken into account, including the use to which it could reasonably be expected that the product would be put.

Such provision is in line with existing French safety law, the provisions of which are discussed in paragraph 6.2 below.

The courts will have to apply the 'reasonable foreseeability' test to apply this provision which implies that at least some abnormal conditions of use can reasonably be expected by the producer.

vi   Cause exonerating the producer from his liability – appropriate measures to prevent damages: article 1386.14   This article states that the producer is liable within the conditions of Title IV bis if there is a defect in the product which appears within ten years from the date when the product was put into circulation and he has not taken all appropriate measures to prevent injurious consequences, including (a) making information available to the public, (b) recalling of the product for appraisal or (c) withdrawing the product.

This provision appears to be a ground of exoneration of the producer not expressly referred to in the Directive. Although, as indicated above, the Directive's definition of the defective product refers to the level of safety which a person is entitled to expect and may take into account the information given by the producer to the public, it seems that the producer could be exonerated under this defence even in circumstances where a person could reasonably expect the product to be safe. It may, however, be difficult to bring evidence (and to convince a judge) that the producer has taken all appropriate measures to prevent the injurious consequences caused by the defective product.

vii   Clauses limiting or excluding liability: article 1386-15   Clauses which purport to exclude or limit liability for defective products are prohibited and considered void. However, in contracts between professionals, provisions limiting or excluding liability of professionals in respect of damage to goods which are not used by the plaintiff mainly for his own private use or consumption, will be valid provided that they do not result from the abuse by the producer of economic strength which would confer an undue advantage.

This provision, which reflected existing statute law at the time of writing of the Proposal,[3] is not inconsistent with the Product Liability Directive which prohibits provisions limiting or exempting the producer's liability arising from the Directive, ie in respect of damage to goods used by the victim for his own private use or consumption.

viii   Breach of the producer: article 1386-16   Unless the producer has committed a breach, the rights of the victim under these rules are extinguished ten years after the product was put into circulation.

This means that after this ten year period, the existing general rules for determining the liability of the producer for contractual or tortious breach will continue to apply (so long as their limitation period has not already expired).

ix   Non-exclusive application of the new rules: article 1386-18   In accordance with the terms of the Directive the last version of the Proposal now states that the rules of Title IV bis shall not affect any rights which an injured person may have according to the rules of the law of contractual, non-contractual or special liability existing at the moment when the Directive is notified.

The producer remains liable for his own (contractual or tortious) breach and that of the persons for whom he is responsible (typically employees) and the articles of the Code relating to the liability for hidden defects are no longer excluded and may also apply simultaneously regardless of the type of damage (to the defective product itself but also, as previously decided by the courts, to damages caused to other goods and personal injury).

However, as indicated in paragraph 4.2.1 above, once the product has been put into circulation, the producer may no longer be held liable pursuant to Article 1384 as 'custodian' of the product, this cause of action being regarded as unnecessary in light of the implementation of the Directive.

The simultaneous application of articles governing hidden defects implies that in order to provide the producer with an effective development risk defence, the courts will have to abandon previous case law discussed in paragraph 3.3.1 above pursuant to which the seller or manufacturer is liable even if he shows that he could not have himself discovered the defect in the product.

6   CRIMINAL LIABILITY FOR DEFECTIVE PRODUCTS ARISING FROM BOTH GENERAL SAFETY LAW AND THE IMPLEMENTATION OF EC DIRECTIVE 92/59 ON PRODUCT SAFETY IN FRANCE

6.1   Introduction

In the case of accidents resulting in death or personal injury caused by a defective product, the manufacturer has traditionally been subject to criminal liability, for example, where he was guilty of gross negligence or non-compliance with regulations. For instance, the manufacturer of a dangerous product (and the seller when he is aware of the danger) who did not warn the purchaser of the product of its dangers, or who did not withdraw the product from sale when it had caused personal injuries, was subject to the criminal sanctions.[4]

---

3   Statute 78-23 of 10 January 1978 for the protection and the information of consumers of products and services, art 35.
4   Tribunal correctionnel de la Seine, 19 December 1957, S 1958, 137, *Cour de Cassation*, Criminal Chamber, 14 March 1974, GP 1974-1-417 and 27 May 1972, Bull Crim, no 174.

Breach of general safety obligation is now expressly mentioned in the newly revised Criminal Code effective since 1 March 1994.[5]

In addition, corporate entities are now subject to criminal sanctions for certain breaches including breach of a general safety obligation committed for their account by their agents/organs or representatives.[6] Such criminal liability does not exclude liability of the individuals who committed the breach.

The manager will usually be held responsible either for his personal acts and decisions or for his failure to organise production in a way to avoid breach by an employee. In the case of a *Société anonyme* managed by a Board of Directors, the chairman of the Board will be held responsible; in the case of a *Société Anonyme* managed by an Executive board, the members of the Board or its single executive director, as the case may be, will be held responsible.

In the case of a *Société à Responsabilité Limitée* or a *Société en Commandite par Actions*, the manager (*gérant*) will be liable.

Where several managers could be incriminated, the allocation of tasks may enable the courts to determine which person is actually responsible.

6.2   Outline of implementation of the Directive 92/59

Directive 92/59 has not been implemented in France by a specific statute. It is generally considered that existing French law is already in conformity with this Directive.

In Spring 1995 a working group at the Ministry of Justice considered whether the implementation of the Directive required that new legislation be adopted. However, the result of such work was not made public.

Pursuant to statute 83-660 of 21 July 1983 relating to consumer safety now integrated in article L 221-1 ff of the new *Code de la Consommation*, manufacturers are under an obligation to supply products which under normal conditions of use, or under conditions of use which could be reasonably expected by the manufacturer, provide a level of safety which a person can reasonably expect and will not injure the health of the individual.

It gives specific powers to the administration to regulate and prohibit the manufacture and distribution of products which do not satisfy safety requirements.[7]

The manufacturer, or the importer who is responsible for putting the product into circulation on French territory for the first time, must check that the product complies with the current mandatory regulations and when asked by inspectors from the administration must give proof of tests and controls carried out on the product.[8] The administration may also request manufacturers, importers or distributors to ensure that products already on the market conform to the safety rules.

When a product already on the market appears to be dangerous, or when the characteristics of a new product seem to justify such precaution, the administration may prescribe that professionals have their products checked by an authorised institution.[9]

---

5   Arts 221-6 and 222-19 of the Criminal Code.
6   Arts 121-2, 221-7 and 222-21 of the Criminal Code.
7   Arts L 221-2 ff of the *Code de la Consommation*.
8   Art L 212-1 of the *Code de la Consommation*.
9   Art L 221-7 of the *Code de la Consommation*.

The administration may also order the manufacturer to issue warnings to the public and make announcements as to particular precautions for use of the product.[10]

In case of serious or immediate danger, the administration may temporarily suspend the manufacture, importation or distribution of the product or require its modification, withdrawal or destruction.

6.3   Description of local optional provisions

6.3.1   *Nature of fines, prison sentences that may be imposed*

The level of fines and prison sentences that may be imposed vary according to the seriousness of the injuries and also the nature of the breach.

Sanctions that can be imposed on individuals in the case of death resulting from the breach of a safety obligation consist of imprisonment for up to three years, and fines of up to FF 300,000. These sanctions can be increased in case of voluntary breach of safety or care obligations imposed by law or regulations to give five years' imprisonment and a FF 500,000 fine.[11]

In the case of temporary disablement which lasts more than three months, sanctions consist of imprisonment for up to two years and a fine up to FF 200,000. These sanctions can be increased in the case of voluntary breach of safety or care obligation imposed by law or regulations to three years' imprisonment and a FF 300,000 fine.[12] In the case of temporary disablement which lasts less than three months, sanctions consist of imprisonment for up to one year and a fine of up to FF 100,000.[13]

The maximum fines on corporate entities are those that can be imposed on individuals multiplied by five.[14]

The corporate entity can be prohibited, either permanently or for a maximum period of five years, from exercising the type of business in the course of which the breach was committed. It can also be subject to judicial surveillance for a maximum period of five years. In the case of voluntary breach of safety or care obligations imposed by law or regulations the closing of the place of business where the breach was committed can be ordered, either as a permanent measure or for a maximum period of five years. The defective product can be confiscated and publicity measures can be ordered.[15]

In the case of exposing individuals to an immediate risk of death or permanent disability by a wilful breach of a specific safety or care obligation imposed by law or regulations, sanctions of up to one year's imprisonment and a FF 100,000 fine can now also be imposed (multiplied by five in the case of corporate liability).[16] These sanctions can therefore be pronounced even though no injury has actually occurred.

The manufacturer, importer or seller of a product can also be held liable vis-à-vis a party to a contract when it has wilfully deceived such party as to the substantial qualities of the product. Sanctions consist of imprisonment for up

10   Art L 221-5 of the *Code de la Consommation*.
11   Art 221-6 of the Criminal Code.
12   Art 222-19 of the Criminal Code.
13   Art 222-20 of the Criminal Code.
14   Art 131-38 of the Criminal Code.
15   Art 131-39 of the Criminal Code.
16   Art 223-1 of the Criminal Code.

to two years and a fine of up to FF 250,000. These sanctions can be multiplied by two when the breach made the use of the product dangerous to human (or animal's) health.[17] The courts find that a lack of sufficient check of conformity of the product with safety regulations constitutes such fraud.[18]

In addition, non-compliance with the administrative request or order will be subject to fines of a criminal nature,[19] publicity measures, withdrawal or destruction of the products and confiscation of profits arising from sale of the product.[20]

6.3.2   *Name and description of the local regulatory authority*

The French regulatory authority is the French government and especially the Minister in charge of *Consommation*. He is in fact active via his administration, ie the *Direction Générale de la Concurrence, de la Consommation et de la Répression des Fraudes* (better known under its initials *DGCCRF*).

The *Commission de la Sécurité des Consommateurs* is also central in the French safety system for the avoidance of accidents caused by unsafe products and services. It is composed of judges, sellers or suppliers, consumers and experts who are appointed for three years (renewable once) by the Minister in charge of *Consommation*. Its chairman is appointed for five years by the Government by decree adopted by the Council of Ministers.

The Commission can intervene at the request of any individual, corporate entity, courts, public authorities and *ex officio*.[1] It can obtain all information and consult any documents which it deems necessary to accomplish its task. Its chairman may hear all persons likely to provide information regarding a matter under investigation. Except in the case of an emergency, the Commission consults with the seller involved. It may make proposals and publicly release opinions in order to improve safety.[2]

Before issuing decrees, the Minister must consult the Commission.

6.3.3   *Description of whether a Product includes capital goods used by consumers eg lifts, escalators, aircraft*

The term 'product' does not apply to real estate, whether tangible real property or fixtures. Safety rules relating to lifts or garage doors have been enacted by special statutes.[3]

6.4   Brief overview of other significant Product Safety law

Specific labelling information requirements vary from one category of product to another (foodstuffs, cosmetics, pharmaceutical products, tobacco, dangerous products, seeds etc).

In the case of products comprising dangerous substances, various orders (*arrêtés*) laid down by the administration govern the various specifications

17   Arts 213-1 ff of the *Code de la Consommation*.
18   Paris, 11 January 1995, Cont Conc Cons, April 1995, no. 75.
19   Art 131-13 of the Criminal Code.
20   Art L 223-1 and L 223-2 of the *Code de la Consommation*.
 1   Art 224-3 of the *Code de la Consommation*.
 2   Art 224-1 of the *Code de la Consommation*.
 3   Arts L 125-1 and L 125-3 of the *Code de la Construction* (Statute 89-421 of 23 June 1989) and Decree 90-567 of 5 July 1990.

(colour, size, warning, symbols etc).[4] For instance, the word 'DANGEREUX' (dangerous) must be printed in very obvious black lettering on a green stripe. Non-compliance is subject to criminal sanction.

4   Labour Code, art L 231-6.

CHAPTER VII

Federal Republic of Germany

Klaus-Ulrich Link Esq

Dr Thomas Sambuc

Lichtenstein, Körner & Partners
Heidehofstrasse 9
70184 Stuttgart den
Federal Republic of Germany

Tel: ++ 49 7 11 4 89 79-0
Fax: ++ 49 7 11 4 81 57 7

CHAPTER VII

Federal Republic of Germany

1 INTRODUCTION

The administration of justice in the Federal Republic of Germany is organised in several divisions, namely Civil Courts, Criminal Courts, Labour Courts, Administrative Law Courts and Social Law Courts.

There are two levels of courts where civil litigation may be initiated. If the value in litigation is DM 10,000 or less, suit must be brought before the local court (*Amtsgericht*). The local courts must also be approached in special matters irrespective of the value in litigation, eg in landlord/tenant matters. Appeals against Judgments by the local courts can be made to the district courts (*Landgericht*). No further appeal is possible. If the value of the litigation is more than DM 10,000, the district courts are the Courts of First Instance. Appeals against their decisions can be made to the Court of Appeals, unless the amount determined by the district court judgment is less than DM 1,500. Appeals against Judgments by the Court of Appeals can in turn be made to the Federal Supreme Court (*Bundesgerichtshof* or 'BGH'), if the value of the dispute exceeds DM 60,000, or if the Court of Appeals has allowed a further appeal. The Federal Supreme Court may or may not hear a case brought before them, depending on their work load and the legal significance of the matter.

The Labour Law Courts, Social Law Courts and Administrative Law Courts also have two stages of appeal. Criminal law cases are brought before the local courts or the district courts, depending on the gravity of the crime or other offence. There are one or two stages of the appeal, again depending on the initial stage.

Normally product liability cases are dealt with by the civil courts. Only where a human life or health has been damaged negligently or wilfully by defective products, may there also be criminal prosecution.

If laws concerning product design and product safety are violated, there may also be criminal prosecution or administrative fines. In the latter case, the presumed offender may challenge the imposition of administrative fines in the Administrative Law Courts.

If the administration or a court disregard the basic rights of an individual or a company, the respective citizen or company may invoke the protection of his basic rights by the Federal Constitutional Court.

If the courts apply European law, or nationally implemented European law, the case may be brought before the European Court of Justice. This may apply particularly with regard to the EC Directive 85/374 on Product Liability, and similar directives.

Proceedings before the Civil and Labour Law Courts are adversarial, before the Criminal, Administrative Law and Social Law Courts they are inquisitorial.

161

Consequently, product liability cases are mostly governed by the adversarial system, since they are dealt with by the civil courts. The plaintiff must adduce the facts that give rise to his product liability claim against the producer, the distributor, or quasi-producer. According to 253 II No 2 of Code of Civil Procedure (*Zivilprozeßordnung* or 'ZPO'), the plaintiff must, inter alia, explain what his claim is, and what alleged facts he relies upon. In many cases, however, the plaintiff cannot know the detailed circumstances that may make the defendant liable. In such cases, the Federal Supreme Court has recently allowed the plaintiff to bring forward mere conjectures instead of facts, as long as they are not plainly whimsical or abusive.[1]

In general, a party must prove his factual allegations, if they are denied by the other party. The usual means of proof are witnesses, expert testimony and judicial inspection; under exceptional circumstances the parties may name themselves or the other party as a means of proof. In product liability cases expert testimony will often be necessary. It is for the court to decide whether an expert must be heard or not. However, where chemo-technical questions are at stake, the courts must always hear an expert and may not rely on their own knowledge.[2]

A party has only discharged his burden of proof when he has convinced the court of the truthfulness of his allegations. Convincing the court requires that there is a very high likelihood that the allegations are true. It is not necessary, however, that the court's conviction is free of any, even theoretical doubt.[3]

Only when all available means of proof have been used, and if the case is still not clear, the issue of burden of proof arises.

Product liability claims in Germany may be based either on contractual law or on the law of torts. Contractual law applies only between parties who have entered into some sort of privity of contract: claims based on the law of torts may be raised by anyone who has suffered injury or loss from a defective product.

Besides contractual liability proper, there is pre-contractual liability. Both give rise to claims based on representation of a specific quality, and breach of contract.

Non-contractual product liability differentiates between claims based on the law of torts, breach of protective laws, and the implementation of EC Directive 85/374 on product liability (*Produkthaftungsgesetz*).

German law has not yet enacted national legislation to implement Directive 92/59 EC on Product Safety.

The following expressions are used frequently in this chapter. The German has been added for clarification, since the more or less literal English translations sometimes have a different meaning within the Anglo-Saxon legal systems. Thus, the definitions and explanations are meant to explain only what a German lawyer would mean by the respective expressions.

(a) The *law of torts* deals with the non-contractual liability for damage based on fault.

(b) *No-fault liability* does not presuppose fault (defined under German law as

---

1   BGH in NJW.
2   BGH in NJW RR 1993, 792.
3   BGH in NJW RR 1994, 567.

intent or negligence) on the part of the liable person.

(c) *Product liability* (*Produkthaftung* or *Produzentenhaftung* – 'producer liability') is the liability of the producer, seller, supplier, or quasi-producer for consequential damage resulting from the use of a defective product.

(d) *Breach of contract* (positive *Vertragsverletzung*) is a fault-based violation of any contractual duty other than delay or inability/impossibility of performance.

(e) *Culpa in contrahendo* or *cic* is the violation of duties before or at the time of contracting.

(f) By *producer* we mean only the person who has actually produced the product (the Directive and the Act use this term in a broader sense which includes, in particular, persons who import products into the Community).

(g) *Seller* is anybody who has sold the product either for further processing or to the ultimate consumer.

(h) *Suppliers* are the producers of parts or components that are being used by the producer to make the finished product.

(i) *Quasi-producer* is a person who presents himself as a producer by affixing his name, trademark or other distinguishing feature.

(j) The *Product Liability Act* ('the Act') is the German Product Liability Act (*Produkthaftungsgesetz*) of 15 November 1989 which came into force on 1 January 1990. This Act implemented the Directive.

(k) *Protective laws* (*Schutzgesetze*) are laws designed to protect individuals from any kind of harm.

(l) The BGB is the German *Bürgerliches Gesetzbuch* or Civil Code of 1896.

(m) The *Directive* is the Council Directive of 25 July 1985 on the approximation of the laws, regulations and administrative provisions of the member states concerning liability for defective products.

(n) *Court decisions* are cited with their date, docket number and reference. German leading cases are generally given a name which is not derived from the parties but from the particular product or damage that the case deals with.

2   PRE-CONTRACTUAL LIABILITY

Pre-contractual ties oblige both parties to take more than average care of each others' interests. Even though they have not yet reached the state of contractual privity, they are already subject to a more intricate set of duties than strangers.

Violations of such pre-contractual duties are called *culpa in contrahendo*.[4]

This legal concept cannot be found in the BGB; it has been developed by the judiciary in a well-established case law.

Culpa in contrahendo does not play an important part in product liability, since losses and injuries are caused by defective products generally only after the product has been sold (and contractual privity has been established), and not during the pre-contractual stages. However, it may apply during the test phase of a product or when duties concerning proper instructions have been violated.

Culpa in contrahendo always presupposes fault.

---

4   Münchener Kommentar BGB, 3 e), d) annotation 32 before §275.

3   LIABILITY IN CONTRACT

Just like its tort counterpart, *contractual product liability* deals with the damage or injury someone has suffered as a *consequence* of a defect in a product. Such claims must be strictly distinguished from *warranty* claims, which concern the defective *product proper*.

In order to make the separation between the neighbouring areas of warranty and contractual product liability clear, set out below is an outline of warranty claims under German law.

3.1   Outline of warranty claims

Warranty claims are based on the fundamental idea that the buyer, who pays good money, should receive a good product in exchange, ie a product which is free from any defects and which can be fully used for the buyer's purposes. By contrast, product liability protects the buyer's and third party's interest not to incur injuries or losses except for the diminished value of the product proper. The integrity of protected legal interests (such as health, property or assets) must not be infringed upon by the (defective) product.[5] Since a warranty concerns only the product proper, it does not cover the consequential damage that typically gives rise to product liability claims.

In the case of a *sales* contract, the BGB gives the buyer a choice either to return the defective product in exchange for the price paid, or to reduce the sales price. The parties may also agree on having the defective product replaced, or on having it made fit for use by the seller. The buyer can only claim damages if he has been wilfully deceived by the seller, or if the product is lacking specific characteristics which have been the subject of an express representation by the seller.

The customer's legal rights are different, if he does not buy an already finished product, but if he engages in a *contract for work and services*, in which the contractor undertakes to bring about a particular result, eg to build a house or to repair a car. If the result of this work does not comply with the contractual requirements, the customer can require the contractor to make the product fit for use. Only if the contractor fails to do so may the customer ask for his money back, or reduce the agreed price, or claim damages (BGB, §635). Drawing a line between this claim for damages in the context of a contract for work and services, and a product liability claim based on the same defects, is difficult. The courts have made the following distinction: damages that can be claimed based on BGB, §635 have been limited to damage directly connected with the result of the work, whereas damage done to other objects as a consequence of the defective work can only be compensated if product liability applies. This distinction is not only of a theoretical nature, but it has extremely important practical consequences for the calculation of recoverable damages and for the scope of coverage by a product liability insurance.

For example, it is clear that insurance does not mean that the insurance company will have to perform the contract instead of the contractor. Still, both the warranty claim based on BGB, §635 and the product liability claim are rooted in the defect of the product.

---

5   Palandt, BGB, 55 ed, Produkthaftungsgesetz, §3 annotation 1.

If the defect in the product has not caused any consequential damage, the producer (in his capacity as *seller*) is obliged to remedy the defect, or to compensate damage done to the product proper. As long as further damage has not occurred, the customer's claims will be satisfied by the warranty.

If, however, the producer has made a car with defective brakes, and if this defect leads to an accident, in which the buyer of the car is injured and another car is written-off, we must distinguish between the following claims:

(a) The buyer has a warranty claim against the seller because of the defective brakes.
(b) The buyer will also want to be compensated for the injury he has suffered, and to be reimbursed for the payments he will have to make for writing-off the other car. These claims against the manufacturer stem from the consequences the defective brakes have had for other protected rights which can be clearly distinguished from the defective car itself. Therefore, these are *consequential* damages that can only be recovered under product liability. They do not relate to remedying the car's defects, and thus will fall under the cover of the product liability insurance.

After this digression into warranty, we will now turn to the actual subject of this chapter, namely, contractual product liability. The most important cases in which contractual product liability can be incurred are those involving the non-compliance with the seller's express representation that the product sold is of a specific quality, and breach of contract. Of lesser importance are *culpa in contrahendo* and promises of specific guarantees.

Even though the contractual product liability presupposes, as a general rule, contractual privity, third parties may also rely on it in exceptional cases.

3.2   Contractual warranties relating to guaranteed qualities of goods and safety of goods

The distinction between product liability and warranty is subject to an important exception in connection with the seller's representations concerning specific qualities of the product. The BGB refers to such representations only in connection with warranty claims, but they have gained increased importance in connection with product liability as well. This ambiguity is a consequence of the buyer of the defective product being able to choose between asking for his money back, or reducing the purchase price, or claiming damages (BGB, §463). These damages serve to compensate both for the product's defect and/or for consequential damages.

The buyer may raise these claims if:

(a) he has concluded a *sales contract* with the seller;
(b) the seller has made a *representation* that the product has specific qualities; and
(c) the product is actually *lacking* these qualities when handed over to the buyer.

This liability is particularly dangerous for the seller, because it does not presuppose fault.

The following points should be noted.

BGB, §463 applies to the usual sale of finished goods as well as to contracts for work and services, provided that the contractor does serial work to make a serial product. Thus, machines coming out of series manufacture are subject

to this strict liability. In particular, the seller's representation concerning performance specifications might trigger this strict liability.

The decisive prerequisite for this strict liability is the seller's representation of a specific quality.

There are three problems that require a detailed explanation. First, the seller's representation must have been agreed upon by the parties. The terms must be express, not implied (cf (a) below). However, even though the representation must be distinctly stated, it may be tacit (cf (b), below). Finally, since the parties often negotiate the product's qualities before the sale, it is necessary to single out those qualities that are the subject of the seller's representation from other qualities upon which the parties have agreed (cf (c), below).

(a) Products which are not the subject of a representation by the seller are, eg, advertisements or general product descriptions in the usual catalogues. Both serve to attract the customer's attention before the agreement has actually been concluded.

The position may be different when a catalogue contains specific assertions upon which the customer relies. In a case where a picture had been described in an auction catalogue in a detailed manner, and had been offered for sale for a very considerable price, the Court of Appeal held that this was a representation of the picture's authenticity. The Federal Supreme Court reversed this judgment and held that statements in an auction catalogue are not legally binding.[6]

(b) Under what circumstances can the representation of a specific quality be made tacitly? During the contract negotiations, the customer must make it clear that he attributes particular importance to the seller's statements, and the overall conduct of the seller – not necessarily his verbal statements – must be such that the buyer may assume that the seller is willing to guarantee the specific quality. The Federal Supreme Court established this prerequisite in a case where the buyer had submitted samples of wood to the seller in order to enable the latter to recommend an appropriate varnish. The court held that since the seller guaranteed the actual presence of the respective quality he thus declared his readiness to be responsible for all consequences that might follow from the actual lack of this quality. Of paramount importance is not the actual intention of the seller, but the impression his overall conduct, together with all the other circumstances of the case, make upon the buyer.[7]

(c) It is particularly difficult to distinguish the usual quality of a product, which is often the subject of discussions during the contract negotiations, from additional qualities being the subject of express representations. Again, the decisive criterion is the parties' consent that this quality is of particular importance for the buyer and that the seller accepts this (if only tacitly) and guarantees the quality.

Three groups of typical cases are of great practical importance:

(a) The seller's statements are considered a valid representation, if he realises that the quality in question is of particular importance for the buyer in regard to a *particular purpose or use* of the product.[8]

6   BGH in NJW 1980, 1619 – 'Gemälde'.
7   BGH in NJW 1972, 1706 – 'Kunstharzlack'.
8   BGH in WM 1971, 1121/1123 – 'Zucker'.

(b) It is not sufficient, if the sales contract refers to specific *industrial standards* (like DIN standards).[9]

(c) There is a tacit representation that the seller of a processed article has carried out the processing in accordance with the general custom of his trade.[10]

Examples from specific relevant areas of business are:

(a) *Construction business*: The water and acid resistance of an anhydrite mortar is considered a binding representation; the compliance of felt insulation with the pertinent DIN standard can be the subject of a binding representation, if this compliance is particularly important to the buyer; the fitness of glue for attaching plates to the ceiling can be considered guaranteed, if tests of this fitness have been made prior to the sale; the same applies to the fitness of a particular varnish to prevent the rotting of wood. On the other hand, the reference to an invitation to bid is not sufficient to assume that the absence of tensions in lighting domes has been represented; the elasticity of a specific construction material is the subject of a representation if the seller knows for what purpose the material will be used by the buyer; the usual pressure resistance of bricks normally is the subject of a tacit representation.

(b) *Computers*: So far, no court decisions have been published with respect to data processing equipment. The compliance with DIN software standards may be considered the subject of a binding representation, if the seller alleges such compliance *and* if the software is sold under an official quality or certification mark. Statements in performance specifications are per se not the subject of quality representations.

(c) *Foodstuffs*: The statement 'The goods are guaranteed for a period of 90 days after date of shipment' is a binding representation concerning the edible lifetime of the goods, also, that the foodstuffs are not contaminated; an indication of the place of origin of fruit may be a binding representation if this particular place has a reputation for the superior quality of fruit grown there; that wine has been bottled on the premises of the vineyard is a binding representation, as well as the absence of specific chemicals in wine.

(d) *Machines*: All of the following have been considered binding representations: the description of a truck as a 'long distance transporter'; the statement that a silo can be repeatedly assembled due to being screwable; the statement that a refrigerator produces clean air by maintaining a certain temperature; the statement that the seller guarantees for a machine providing certain heating functions; possibly also the statement that a product comes 'fresh from the factory'.

With respect to some specific products, the binding representations are required either by statutes dealing particularly with the product, or by the courts. For example, the seller of seeds is always considered to represent that his seed will produce the plant of the seed for which it is being sold; the seller of animal food is considered to represent that his food is free from adulteration.

Finally, whenever a sale is made by sample or on approval, the seller represents that the products will be as approved or comply with the sample (BGB, §494).

---

9 BGH in NJW 1981, 1501 – 'Gleichstrom-Nebenschlußmotoren'.
10 BGH in NJW 1988, 1018 – 'Garne'.

The question whether the particular quality was or was not present when the product was handed over to the buyer does not pose difficult legal problems; however, it will often be difficult to prove. The burden of proof for the absence of the represented quality is with the buyer.

3.3   Breach of contract for supply of defective products

Breach of contract (as defined in our introduction) is not dealt with (specifically) in the BGB. The German Civil Code deals only with two general forms of contract violations, namely with the inability of the debtor to perform at all (in the case of the seller, to hand over the object sold to the buyer), which is called *Unmöglichkeit*, and with delayed performance (*Verzug*). It became clear soon after the BGB was enacted, that these types of contract violation were not exhaustive and that the creditor (like, in the aforementioned case of a sale, the buyer) might have numerous other reasons for complaints against the other party, since a contract of any type normally entails a number of collateral duties towards the other party all of which might be violated. Such violations have traditionally been called *positive Vertragsverletzung*[11] which translates roughly as 'breach of contract'. In common with inability to perform or delay it applies to all types of contract (leases, hire of services, shipping contracts, etc) and is not limited to sales. Therefore, it falls into a category separate from, for example, warranty (which is a remedy given specifically to the buyer) and consequently claims based on warranty are not considered claims based on breach of contract in this context.

Again, the distinction between the purchaser's interest in receiving a product which is free from defects (covered by warranty), and his interest not to suffer harm or damage to his health or *other* property (as opposed to the purchased object) is essential. We are talking here only about breaches of contract that are rooted in the defect of the product, but which have led to detrimental consequences affecting legally protected interests other than the purchased product proper.

Therefore, the cases giving rise to claims for damages based on breach of contract are comparable to those based on tort. The typical contract cases and case categories that have emerged over the years from a large body of precedents are very similar to those in torts cases. There are only gradual differences in determining the required quality of the product and thus the existence of the defect: in tort law, the product requirements are standardised, whereas in breach of contract cases they must be determined with regard to the terms of the contract. Also, due to the privity of contract, the seller owes to the buyer stricter duties concerning product instruction than the producer owes to somebody that he is not contractually tied to. On the other hand, the difference between contractual and tortious liability is substantial with respect to the periods of limitation, defences and the recovery of damages for pure financial loss. Such pure financial loss is recoverable under breach of contract, but not under tort (cf section 5, below).

Since sales law is of particular importance to contractual product liability, we would like to exemplify breach of contract liability with sales cases. Wherever there are significant differences between sales and contracts for work and services, we will mention them as well.

11   Münchner Kommentar, annotation 95 before §275.

Any product liability based on breach of contract presupposes that the product is defective. BGB, §459 I says that there must be no defects in the product which diminish its value or its fitness to serve either typical purposes, or purposes which have been envisaged in the sales contract.

If specifications have been agreed upon contractually and are not being fulfilled, a product which would be fit for its usual purpose might be considered defective, and vice versa: a product which would not meet usual quality requirements might be fit for the specific purposes envisaged by the parties. For example:

(a) If a computer is sold which, based on the buyer's specification, must be able to solve very specific tasks, it will be considered defective if it cannot solve that task (for example, because its capacity is insufficient), even though the average buyer of this computer would be fully satisfied.

(b) If the parties have agreed to ship foodstuffs whose 'best before' date has already expired, these foodstuffs would not meet usual quality standards, but they will be considered free from defects, since this deviation has been agreed upon.

The liability for breach of contract is (unless the parties have stipulated otherwise) based on the violation of the same duties that the courts have imposed on the producer in tort, namely the duties to construct properly and manufacture new products and monitor the products that have already been distributed. For details and for the corresponding duties of sellers and suppliers see the section on tort below.

Instructions on use and maintenance of the product must be more specific, diligent and comprehensive within a contractual relationship than with respect to strangers. The seller will often be looked at by the buyer as the expert on whose advice he can rely. If this advice is wrong, the seller may be subject to contractual product liability, if the buyer suffers harm or damage as a consequence of being wrongly advised.[12] The instructional duties become more severe with the products becoming more complicated or sophisticated, for example, with respect to their operation and maintenance.[13] The requirements for proper instruction are particularly high with respect to electronic data processing equipment.

Contractual product liability is similar to tort product liability also in so far as there must be both a chain of causation between the contract violation and the damage, and fault (ie intent or negligence).

Since the law governing *contracts for work and services* already provides for a damages claim as part of the warranty system, there is only room for claims based on breach of contract for such consequential damages that are not covered by the warranty provision in BGB, §635. So far, the judiciary has failed to draw a clear line between damages recoverable under warranty on the one hand, and under breach of contract on the other. This failure is particularly deplorable since the periods of limitation differ widely between these two claims. If the period for bringing warranty claims (between six months and five years, depending on the kind of work and services) has elapsed, it is often hard to predict whether the plaintiff will be able to profit from the 30-year limitation that applies in the case of breach of contract.

---

12   BGH in NJW 1957, 746 – 'Chloridhaltiges Wasser'.
13   BGH in NJW 1983, 392 – 'Verzinkungsanlage'.

As a rule of thumb one can say that the chances of recovering consequential damages by relying on a warranty become less with increasing remoteness of damage, so that the plaintiff becomes more and more forced to rely on breach of contract the further away from the result of the contractor's work the damage occurs. Of course, this does not mean that the chance that his claim in contract will succeed increases with the remoteness of the damage. For example, the courts have granted damage based on breach of contract where fire damages had been caused by a ruptured oil tubing[14] or insufficient insulation,[15] or where soil and dirt had to be removed because a machine was improperly assembled.[16]

The contractor's duties to instruct and advise the customer properly are of particular importance with respect to contracts for work and services. The reason is the special expertise of the contractor who constructs or erects a machine, a house or an industrial plant. These duties are extremely severe, as can be exemplified by a decision by the Federal Supreme Court.[17] The object of this contract was the erection of a new type of heat generating plant which, as it turned out, was not per se defective in any way, but which did not completely comply with a contractual specification, namely 'securing' the generation of a certain heat supply with a certain amount of fuel. It turned out that the heat supply was not secured if an auxiliary machine were to fail. The court said that the contractor had been under an obligation to advise the customer of this danger, in particular, since he was offering a new type of heat generating plant. This duty comprises also aspects of economic efficiency.

Consequently, the contractor's risk of incurring liability for violating the duty to provide accurate information is considerable.

3.4   Quantum of damage

One important difference between product liability based on tort and that based on contract is that the latter does not presuppose that the damage has occurred as a consequence of bodily harm or physical damage; consequently, pure financial losses are recoverable under contractual product liability, but not under tort.

With respect to the claims dealt with in contract or pre-contract damages will be calculated as follows.

The basic principle for the calculation of damages is laid down in BGB, §249: the claimant must be put into the position he would be in, if the circumstances giving rise to his claim for damages had not occurred. What does this mean with respect to the various contractual claims?

Cases of *culpa in contrahendo* occur by definition before the conclusion of a contract. Consequently, the claimant is not yet entitled to the performance by his prospective contractual partner. Therefore, damages will not comprise the claimant's interest in the performance, but only his interest in the integrity of his vested rights.

In so far as damages can be claimed because *unwarranted representations* have been made with respect to the product's quality, the seller will have to put the buyer into a position he would have been in, if the product had in fact

14   BGHZ 58, 305.
15   BGH in NJW 1982, 2244.
16   BauR 1972, 127.
17   BGH in WM 1987, 1303 – 'Blockheizkraftwerk'.

had the represented qualities. In order to find out what position that would have been, one must examine in each case for what purpose the representation has been made. If it served only to secure the buyer's uninhibited use of the purchased product, he cannot claim consequential damages. Only if the representation was made to protect the buyer's interests beyond those in using the purchased product, may he be entitled to collect compensation for consequential damage.[18]

Thus, two questions must be answered:

(a) What specific qualities of the purchased product were the subject of the seller's representations?
(b) Is the damage in question covered by the representation's purpose and range?

Representations can also make damages recoverable that could normally not be recovered, eg those flowing from development risks which could not be foreseen at the relevant time.

In so far as damages for physical damage and injury are claimed based on *breach of contract*, they are calculated as in tort law (cf below).

If, however, there has been a *pure financial loss*, it can only be recovered under breach of contract, but not under tort. These are the cases where there has been no physical damage or injury, but where the claimant has been burdened, eg with losses of earnings or with claims from injured third parties. Of great practical importance are cases where defective products have been *processed*. If it turns out that the finished product cannot be properly used due to the defective component, the processor will want to be compensated for time, money, and/or other components having been wasted.[19]

A landmark case decided by the Federal Supreme Court[20] may serve as an illustration of the types of damages recoverable under breach of contract. Lifting gear which had been sold to an auto repair shop had broken down, because it had been defective. As a consequence of this breakdown, a car belonging to the shop owner was destroyed, and the repair shop could not be used for a lengthy period of time. Two sorts of damage must be distinguished:

(a) the destruction of the owner's car is a typical property damage, compensation for which is recoverable both under breach of contract and under tort.
(b) The impossibility of using the repair shop leads to pure financial loss, which is recoverable only under breach of contract. The same would apply if the destroyed car had not belonged to the owner but to another customer. In this case the owner would have been burdened by a compensation claim from this customer, without having himself suffered a tangible loss. Again, this pure financial loss would only be recoverable under breach of contract, not under tort.

In an economy where division of labour has greatly increased, such pure financial losses resulting from component replacements, work and investment made in vain, etc, can be considerable.

18 Staudinger, 12 ed; BGB, §463 annotation 37.
19 BGH in BB 1967, 433.
20 BGH in NJW 1983, 810 – 'Hebebühne'.

3.5   Burden of proof

The plaintiff, relying on *culpa in contrahendo* or breach of contract, bears the burden of proof with respect to the defect and the chain of causation between the defect and the damage (health, property, etc) on the one hand, and between the damage and the consequential financial loss on the other. He must also prove the amount of the damages he is claiming. The defendant must show and prove that he was not at fault. For details see section 3.6 below, on tort.

With respect to the liability for representations of quality there is a peculiarity which deserves attention. Until the product is handed over to the buyer, his claims are for the seller's performance. Therefore, the seller must show and prove that until this point in time the product complied with his representations. After the buyer has accepted the sales object, he will have to prove that the product did not comply with the seller's representation.[1]

3.6   Exclusion or limitation of liability

It is necessary to distinguish clearly between consumer contracts that have been made subject to the seller's general terms and conditions of sale (*Allgemeine Geschäftsbedingungen*), and specific contracts, where this is not the case. Depending on whether exclusions or restrictions of liability have been agreed upon in an individual agreement or in an agreement governed by general conditions, exclusions or restrictions of liability are subject to a more or less rigid legal control.

In cases where no general conditions have been agreed upon and no consumer is a party of the contract, this control is rather lenient. According to BGB, §276 II, one party cannot waive the other party's liability for intentional acts. Consequently, liabilities for all other wrongs can be waived. With respect to product liability, intention presupposes that the producer must be aware of his product's defects. It is not necessary that he intends the actual physical damage or injury to occur; it is, however sufficient that he forsees with some certainty that harm will occur and consents to this risk.

On 1 January 1995 the EC Unfair Contract Terms Directive No 13/93 came into effect. Article 3 III in connection with the annex to article 3 III (a) makes the exclusion and/or limitation of liability invalid, if the customer's rights will be infringed in relation to his life, his body or his health. Contrary to the German Act Concerning The Control of General Conditions, this directive is applicable to every contract, even individual ones, if a consumer is involved. However, the directive does not apply where the contents of a contract have been negotiated between the parties. Contract clauses stipulated only by one party are not considered 'negotiated'.

The relevance of the EC Unfair Contract Terms Directive No 13/93 will not be very significant in Germany, since the Act Concerning The Control of General Conditions already creates a high consumer protection level.

Of much greater practical importance are exclusions and limitations contained in general conditions. The concept of 'general conditions' is defined very broadly in §1 of the Act, Concerning General Conditions (*Gesetz zur Regelung des Rechts der Allgemeinen Geschäftsbedingungen – AGB-Gesetz*). It applies to all conditions that have been worded by one contract party for a

---

1   Baumgärtel, *Handbuch der Beweislast im Privatrecht*, vol 1, annotation 3, §463.

multitude of contracts. It does not matter whether the conditions have been attached to the contract document separately, or if they have become part of the contractual document proper.

Conditions are not considered 'general' if they have been negotiated individually between the parties (AGBG, §1 II). In order to discourage efforts to evade the protection granted by the AGBG, the judiciary applies severe standards when determining whether a clause has indeed been 'negotiated individually'.

A clause excluding or limiting liability will only be considered 'individually negotiated' if the seller can show a reasonable interest in such an exclusion or limitation, and if the customer had a real opportunity to exert influence upon the wording of the conditions, eg if he had been invited to make alternative proposals for the wording of the conditions.[2]

The authority of the judiciary to hold certain clauses invalid is greater when these clauses have been used in contracts with consumers than in contracts with business people. It is fair to say that with respect to consumers a limitation of liability in general conditions is in practice not admissible, even though the judiciary has not yet ruled so expressly.

It is equally clear that liability for *gross negligence* cannot be excluded in general conditions used in contracts with business people. The contrary has been assumed only in a case involving the ship-building industry, because in that industry such clauses are common. Therefore, among business people only liability for *(ordinary) negligence* can be excluded; however, the following should be observed:

(a) The clause should state expressly that *only* the liability for ordinary negligence (as opposed to gross negligence) is to be excluded. Without this restriction, the courts would attribute a sweeping meaning to this clause (including gross negligence) and consequently might invalidate the entire clause.

(b) A restriction of liability even for ordinary negligence will be held invalid if this restriction concerns contractual duties which are of the essence. The following duties have been held essential by the courts: in a contract for the finishing of textiles the duty to treat the textiles carefully; in contracts with computer sellers and installers the duty to provide for sufficient air-conditioning in the room where the computer is installed;[3] in a storage contract the duty to provide for a sufficiently low cooling temperature.[4]

(c) If representations have been made concerning certain qualities of a product, such representations can practically not be revoked in general conditions.

All this shows that the seller cannot be sure that the liability limitations in his general conditions will eventually be enforced by the courts.

3.7 Limitation periods

(a) Business people must examine the merchandise which they have received from the seller and must notify the seller of any defects without undue delay. Notice of hidden defects must be given after they have been discovered. If

---

2 Ulmer, Brandner, Hensen, AGBG, 6 ed, §1 annotation 51.
3 BGH in WM 1985, 522 – 'Klimaanlage'.
4 BGH in WM 1984, 477 – 'Kaltlagerung'.

a business person does not comply with this obligation, he loses his claims for damages (HGB, §377). This applies also to claims based on breach of contract.[5]

(b) The limitation periods differ widely depending on their legal ground:

  (i)   claims based on *culpa in contrahendo* are subject to a limitation period of 30 years;

  (ii) claims based on the absence of represented qualities or on breach of contract are subject to a limitation period of six months after delivery, provided that they are raised within a sales relationship;

  (iii) if breach of contract is relied upon within a contract for work and services, claims based on breach of contract become statute-barred only after 30 years.

3.8   Liability for third parties

Since we are dealing with contractual liability, the rights and liabilities are normally those of the contracting parties. However, it is not uncommon that third parties are involved as well, either on the side of the seller or on the side of the buyer.

Like all parties to any contract, the seller or contractor held liable for product liability is responsible for any fault of a person employed by him in the performance of his obligation (cf BGB, §278). 'Employment' is construed very broadly in this context, since it comprises not only employees, but also freelancers and independent contractors of whom the producer avails himself, eg of an advertising agency with respect to the proper wording of advertisements; of an architect with respect to planning and supervising construction; of a repair shop for the repair of a product.

The seller or contractor is liable for the acts of the person he employs to the same extent that he himself would be liable, if he were at fault himself.

A limitation of the liability for grossly negligent acts of the employed person is not permissible in General Conditions of Sale. This rule applies without exceptions to consumers; with respect to business people, the courts have held that such a limitation is permissible unless the limitation does not comply with the customs in the respective industry and concerns duties that are of the essence.[6]

A person who is not party to the contract may nevertheless claim damages from the seller or contractor based on contractual product liability, if the contract has been concluded for his benefit. This presupposes that it was clear to the seller/contractor that the third party deserved protection under the agreement and that the third party's interests might be infringed by a defect in the product. Contracts for the supply of goods are generally not considered to benefit third parties. Thus, the ultimate consumer does not benefit from the contractual duties the producer owes to the dealer.[7]

On the other hand, the purchaser's or the buyer's employees and the family of the customer in a contract for works and services have been considered protected as third parties. Not only the damage following from injury or property destruction is recoverable by the third party, but also pure financial

---

5   BGH in NJW 1988, 52.
6   Ulmer, Brandner, Hensen, op cit, §11 Nr 7 annotation 33.
7   BGH in BB 1989, 20.

losses. Therefore, the contractual protection granted to third parties is more effective than the protection arising in tort upon which third parties would normally have to rely.

4   LIABILITY IN TORT

4.1   Introduction

Unlike contractual product liability, which presupposes contractual privity between the parties, liability in tort can be relied upon by anyone. Most people who suffer injuries or damage from defective products are not contractually tied to the producer. Thus, in seeking redress for their losses they will normally rely on tortious liability.

Tort remains the most important ground for product liability, even after the no-fault Product Liability Act has come into force.

The central provision of the statutory tort law is BGB, §823, which reads:

> I.   Anyone who wilfully or negligently and without justification infringes upon the life, body, health, liberty, property or other right of another person is obliged to compensate the other person for the damage resulting from such infringement.
>
> II.   The same obligation is incurred by somebody who disregards a law that serves to protect another person. . . .

One paramount principle of the German tort product liability law becomes clear from the words of this provision: any liability presupposes that some specific right of the claimant has been infringed upon. Where this is not the case, no damages can be claimed. In particular, pure financial losses are not recoverable as a consequence of this principle.

4.2   Outline of tort law giving rise to product liability

Of the rights mentioned in BGB, §823 the following may become relevant with regard to product liability: life, body, health, property and, as examples of the 'other rights', possession and business operation.

(a)   *Life* has been violated if a human being has been killed. Life, as defined by the BGB, starts with birth.
(b)   Violations of *body* and *health* will mostly be the same, except in cases where mental health is impaired.

With regard to (b), if the health of an unborn child is damaged (eg by pharmaceuticals which the mother has taken during her pregnancy), the child may claim damages after birth.[8]

(c)   Of greatest importance are *property* violations. A considerable body of precedents deals with issues connected therewith.

The following have been considered *violations* of property: every damage, deformation, destruction or deprivation, every functional disturbance or interruption, pollution or contamination, even changes of the physical condition

---

8   BGH in NJW 1972, 1126.

or physical danger which prevents use (eg risk of explosion).[9] Property violation presupposes that the defective product has had an effect upon the claimant's property. In other words, the defective product itself does not qualify as protected property. Consequently, the courts have held until 1976 that the sale of a defective product does not constitute a violation of the property of that product, because that product was defective to begin with and the seller did not inflict damage upon it. This follows from the aforementioned principle that tort liability presupposes the infringement of some right. It also makes the drawing of a line between liability in tort and under warranty easier. Product liability in tort (like the one based on contract) does not serve to remedy the product's defects, but to remedy the damages that have flowed from such defects.

This distinction has been found clear, but unsatisfactory. Since a decision issued in 1976 and called *Floating Switch*,[10] the Federal Supreme Court has adopted a more discriminating view. The seller had supplied a cleaning installation. The entire installation caught fire and was destroyed because a small floating switch was defective. This switch had been part of the sales object, and if the sales object had been taken as a whole, there would have been no room for a product liability claim, since the sales object (taken as an entity) had been defective to begin with. However, since the function of the floating switch had been clearly defined within the entire installation, the court saw fit to distinguish between this small element and the remaining installation and held that the property in the latter had been damaged by the defective switch.

Since this landmark decision, the courts have continued to distinguish between the sales object in its entirety and defective parts thereof. In a case where a motor vehicle has been destroyed due to a defective tyre, the producer of the car was held liable for damaging that car. The same was held in a case where a defective accelerator had led to the destruction of the car of which it was part. Defective parts are considered as leading to a property violation of the entire product, if that defect can be clearly limited to that part, and if that defect has led to significant additional damage to the entire product.[11] This case law has been extended to include as a property violation also cases where a defective part has been connected to a part of good quality. A property violation has also been found where only the removal of a defective part has led to a destruction of the quality part.[12]

These rules are of particular importance in the *construction industry*. Whenever a defective part becomes indistinguishable within the entire product as a consequence of its being united, welded, glued, riveted, etc, into the new product, its function cannot be distinguished any more from that of the entire product, and consequently there is no room for the defective part inflicting property damage on the entire product. For example, when sand, which was unfit to be mixed with cement and chalk, was used to make rough-cast, that sand was not considered as having caused a property violation in the rough-cast. On the other hand, defective roofing was considered to have led to a violation of the property in the roof structure, after it had caused the latter to split.[13] A property violation is also assumed where normal use has been inhibited

9   Kullmann/Pfister KZA 1520, p 9/10.
10 BGH in NJW 1977, 379 – 'Schwimmschalter'.
11 BGH in NJW 1978, 2241 – 'Hinterreifen'; BGH in NJW 1983, 810 – 'Gaszug'; BGH in NJW 1985, 2420 – 'Kompressor'
12 BGH in NJW 1992, 1225.
13 BGH in NJW 1978, 1051 – 'Lotsand'; BGH in NJW 1985, 194 – 'Dachabdeckfolie'.

significantly by a defective product, eg in a case where a tube system has been affected by a cutting additive that was not smell and taste neutral.[14]

(d) Other rights protected by BGB, §823 I are the rights of *possession* and of *business operation*, but *not* financial assets per se. In other words, pure financial losses are not covered by BGB, §823 I.

In order to be held liable for the damage caused by his defective product, the producer's conduct must have been unlawful. He must have violated one (or several) of his duties, ie he must either have done something unlawful, or he must have failed or omitted to do something that he was expected to do under the law. Generally speaking, the producer is under an obligation to distribute only safe products. The distribution of defective and thus unsafe products is unlawful. Unlawful conduct is one of several presuppositions of a tort product liability claim which must be distinguished from the violation of a right and from fault.

The duties of the producer have been specified with respect to construction, fabrication, inspection, and follow-up product observation.

A product has a *construction* or *design* defect if its concept (as opposed to the tangible product itself) cannot result in the manufacture of a product which complies with the required safety standard.

Since there is not one single safety standard for every sort of product, proper construction must take into account usual use by an average owner. However, construction must also take into consideration that use of the product will often be made in unreasonable ways or for unreasonable purposes. Designers of a machine must safeguard against blunders or mistakes by the future machine operator; a handle must be designed to allow energetic transport of the object concerned. On the other hand, the producer need not take into consideration utterly unreasonable acts of the consumer, eg the use of glue, cleansing agents, or petrol for intoxicating or narcotic purposes.

In a recent decision, the Federal Supreme Court has imposed upon a producer the duty to examine whether ready-to-use-parts which he bought from another were fit for his purpose, even though he had no influence upon their construction.[15]

It goes without saying that all products that have to be officially approved must comply with the required approval standards. However, these official requirements will often constitute only minimum standards. In many cases the courts have held that products were wrongly designed even though they met the minimum standards. Compliance with official minimum standards does not relieve the producer of researching possible dangers himself and avoiding them in efficient, reasonable ways.[16] For example:

(a) If *asbestos* is used for making a product, its construction must ensure that the dangerous asbestos fibres are not set free in the form of cancer-generating dust.[17]

(b) *Baby toys* must be made without soluble poisonous substances, without sharp edges, and must avoid the possibility of body parts being squeezed in.

14   BGH in NJW 1994, 517.
15   BGH in NJW 1994, 3349.
16   BGH in NJW 1987, 1009; BGH in NJW 1987, 372.
17   Kullmann/Pfister KZa 1520, p 32.

(c) *Computer programs* that are part of larger equipment (eg a processor or CNC controlled machines) are always subject to product liability.[18] The integrated software must comply with the requirements for an effective control of the equipment or the machines.
(d) The safety standards for *motor vehicles* are a classic example for the legal requirements being only minimum standards. Compliance with them will often not be sufficient. For example, steering wheels are required to have a cushioned ring, a large rebounding surface, a rebound crasher behind the wheel and a steering column must be able to divert impact from an accident sideways.[19]
(e) Likewise, the Act Concerning Appliance Safety contains only minimum safety requirements for machines and technical installations. In addition, machines must be designed in a way which allows proper handling by the user without overstraining him with an over-sophisticated construction.[20]
(f) Medico-technical apparatus must be safeguarded against power failure (eg by installing a stand-by unit) and must have a specific warning device in case of improper functioning.

Manufacturing defects are those which occur during the manufacturing process. The manufacturing process must be organised in a way which allows products to be made to a consistent, flawless quality.

Raw materials and partially finished goods have to be selected carefully and must be checked for defects before using them in one's own manufacturing process.

Since manufacturing defects can often not be completely avoided, there must be a verifiable quality control. Depending on the risk involved in the event of a possible undetected flaw, quality control may be limited to random samples, or may include every single product. The latter applies in cases where undetected flaws involve health or even life risks, as in brakes, airplanes or medicinal-technical apparatus. When conducting random tests, the legally prescribed testing methods and the relevant DIN norms (like VDE, RAL, DIN 66051 and DIN 40080) must be observed.

Moreover, typical sources of defects in the production process must be identified and eliminated. If this is not possible, quality control must focus on these critical points.

Both the producer and the seller of a product must give the user proper *instructions*, if dangers cannot be ruled out even in a reasonable and foreseeable use of the product, or if harmful side effects may occur. This is so irrespective of whether or not the product has been constructed and made properly. Whether there are risks involved with the use of the product depends on the typical use by a typical user of average intelligence and proficiency.

If, however, the risk is such that it can easily be recognised and foreseen by the user, it is part of the risk generally involved with life. For such risks, the producer will not be held liable. For example, the producer of a blank cartridge pistol did not have to pay damages to a user of his product whose hearing capacity had been impaired by the noise usually connected with the operation of such a pistol.[1]

---

18   Bauer in PHI 1990, 39ff, 98.
19   Kullmann/Pfister KZA 1520, p 35.
20   BGH in VersR 1952, 357 – 'Rungenverschluß'.
 1   OLG Köln in VersR 1987, 573.

In a recent decision, the Federal Supreme Court has tightened the producer's *warning duties* further. In the past, he had only to warn of dangers that might originate from his own product. Since the so-called *Honda* decision[2] this warning duty applies also to accessories which have not been attached to the product by the producer but which might foreseeably be attached by the user. This decision deals with a motorcycle windshield spoiler, which had not been a standard feature of the motorcycle. Instead, it had been made by a company which was not related to Honda and which sold its products independently. At a certain speed, this windshield spoiler led to an instability of the motorcycle, which caused a serious accident. The defendant in this lawsuit was not the producer of the spoiler, but Honda. The court held Honda liable, because they had not appropriately warned the buyer of the motorcycle of the consequences that an additional windshield spoiler might have for the stability of motorcycle riding. The court stated that the producer of a motorcycle must not only safeguard the proper functioning of parts and accessories that are necessary to operate the motorcycle to begin with. The same applies to accessories the use and the attaching of which the motorcycle producer has made possible by providing drill holes, lugs, fixing devices, mountings, or the like.

If the producer must give a warning, the question is, how must this be done? The following basic rules apply:

(a) The warning must be easily understood. If the product is typically being used by a large number of people, the warning must take into account the intelligence and the capability of an average user. Normally it cannot be assumed that the product will only be used by experts.
(b) The warning must be clearly visible.
(c) The warning must not be limited to the usual instructions in an owner's manual, but must be emphasised.
(d) Warnings affixed to long-lived and durable goods must last as long as the product, and must remain visible and readable at any time.

Since 1990, there have been numerous law suits against producers of sweetened children's tea, in which the issue of proper warning of possible damages was at stake. These cases have become known as the 'Baby-Bottle-Syndrome' and 'Nursing-Bottle-Syndrome' cases. Sweetened children's tea had been sold in plastic bottles that could be sucked from with a mouthpiece which fitted with the child's jaw. Thus, the teeth were totally rinsed with the sweetened tea, the naturally protective saliva was washed away, and cavities were caused quickly. This 'Baby-Bottle-Syndrome' had been discussed among dentists since 1981. The advertising, however, had stressed that children liked the taste of this tea and that it was appropriate to use it as a 'Good-Night-Drink'.

Since sweetened children's tea had been known to cause cavities for many years, the sellers of this tea were held liable for damages.[3]

On this occasion, the courts made it clear that health warnings must not be mixed with directions concerning the dispensation.

In another decision, the Federal Supreme Court has required that the extent of the warning must take into consideration the most endangered user group. Consequently, the attention of consumers who do not read product instructions any more due to continuing use of the product has to be caught as well.[4]

2 BGH in WM 1987, 176.
3 BGH in NJW 1992, 560 – 'Kindertee I'.
4 BGH in NJW 1994, 932 – 'Kindertee II'.

On the other hand, consumers who had already been aware of the dangers, needed not be warned anymore.

Another decision dealt with a variation of the 'Baby-Bottle-Syndrome', the so-called 'Nursing-Bottle-Syndrome'. Here, carrot juice had been sold in bottles with a mouthpiece which again directed the juice behind the teeth, where the fruit sugar converted to acid and destroyed the protective layer of the dental enamel. Even though the court was not completely satisfied with the warnings, the producer was not held liable where he had applied a conspicuous warning ('**Important**') on the container.[5] The court seems hesitant to require a multitude of warnings, because then the important ones may be overlooked.

Finally, the producer must *follow up* on his product's performance in daily use by consumers and *observe* its performance. He must keep himself continuously informed about what consequences his product's use actually has.

In particular, he must think of instances where:

(a) an originally harmless product becomes dangerous by simultaneous use together with other products;
(b) new scientific research shows dangers that emanate from the product;
(c) practical experience during the daily use of the product shows flaws;
(d) it becomes apparent that buyers do not know how to use the product properly;
(e) new technology allows the elimination of product weaknesses.

In a case where between 0.5 and 1.0% of all products showed the same defect after they had been used, the producer was held liable because he had not bothered to eliminate the defect.[6]

The performance of mass products must be followed up and observed throughout the world.[7]

As the *Honda* decision shows, the producer must also observe dangers that arise from the combination of his products with those of other manufacturers.

If the product observation leads to the conclusion that the product is dangerous, the users must be notified of these dangers in an appropriate manner. Often, a *subsequent warning* will suffice, but in particularly grave instances a *recall* must be organised. Everyone who watches television or listens to the radio knows that such recalls take place quite often, particularly with respect to motor vehicles.

Since the costs of a recall are considerable and can be insured only in the automotive and aviation industry, it is of particular interest under what circumstances a recall will be required (and a subsequent warning will be considered insufficient). If the dangers connected with the use of the product cannot be averted by warning alone, *and* if there is considerable danger for the health or the lives of users, a recall will be necessary (but not necessarily if 'only' material goods are at stake).

Another criterion for the necessity of a recall is the possibility or impossibility of safeguarding the interests of third parties (as opposed to the user) by a mere warning. The car owner who has been notified of a brake problem may choose to ignore the problem, because he is willing to take the risk himself, but he endangers not only himself, but also innocent by-standers. Their interests must be taken into consideration by the producer as well.

---

5   BGH in NJW 1995, 1286.
6   LG Freiburg in Kullmann/Pfister KZA 7508/1.
7   BGH in NJW 1981, 1606 – 'Apfelschorf'.

4.3 Causation

Product liability presupposes two subsequent links of causation. First, a product defect must have led to the violation of one of the claimant's rights (section 4.2, paragraph 1), and this violation must have been the cause of the eventual financial loss for which compensation is sought.

If the violation of the claimant's right(s) would have occurred even if the product had not been defective, the defect was no cause of the violation. Also, the producer cannot be made responsible if the chain of causes that has led to the violation of the claimant's right is so extraordinary and unusual that it could not have been foreseen, even by a particularly experienced and careful person.[8]

Of greater practical importance is the question whether the eventual financial loss can be traced back to the violation of the claimant's right.

Again, the decisive criterion is whether an experienced and careful person could have foreseen that the particular infringement of the particular right of the claimant was apt to lead to the particular financial loss for which redress is sought.

This is considered *not* to be the case when:

(a) a car runs into a truck that has broken down due to brake failure, even though the truck has been properly guarded against the traffic;
(b) a defective product makes treatment by a doctor necessary, and the doctor commits grave malpractice;[9]
(c) a person contracts a flu infection in a hospital where he stays for the treatment of another disease, and dies from the 'flu.

4.4 Remoteness of loss and damage

Liability based on BGB, §823 I presupposes fault (intent or negligence). Negligence is disregard of due care. What care is due for a producer of goods has been described above (cf section 4.2, paragraph (2)(a)-(d), above). There are two degrees of negligence, namely, ordinary negligence and gross negligence. Whether the defendant is guilty of one or of the other, or even of intent, will affect the coverage of his liability by insurance.

An important question is, *who* must exercise what care at what point in time of the production or distribution process? Details are dealt with at p 177 above. Here we will deal only with the particulars connected with fault liability, as opposed to non-fault liability.

(a) The ground rule is that only the *producer* is responsible for the production, and that consequently he must have been at fault with respect to the presence of a defect.

This means for *suppliers* that only the supplier is responsible for the defective part he has made, unless the producer had an obvious opportunity to check the part upon receipt. For example, a motorcycle accident occurred because a steering part had miniscule cracks. This defect could have been detected only by a very sophisticated method, a so-called magnetic flooding. The magnetic flooding should have been carried out by the supplier of the steering part, since he was the expert in this field.

---

8   *Produkthaftungshandbuch*, 22, annotation 6.
9   BGH in NJW 1968, 247 – 'Schubstrebe'.

Consequently, a claim against the motorcycle manufacturer was dismissed.[10]

(b) The *seller* is not responsible for defects caused during the production. He is, however, responsible for his own selling organisation and the functions connected therewith. For example, he must advise the buyer that a product is not fit to serve the buyer's needs or purposes, and he must warn the buyer of incorrect and possibly dangerous applications of the product. The seller must be aware of the qualities of the goods he sells and the applicability of those qualities to his customers' requirements. Thus a pharmacist should not supply headache pills to a customer who needs pills for an upset stomach. The seller must not distribute goods that have perished or spoilt (particularly foodstuffs); nor may he sell dangerous substances to people who can obviously not handle them.

(c) *Distribution organisations*, which are directly connected to the producer, owe their customers a higher degree of instruction and information, since they are more expert with respect to the product's quality and specifications. Still, as long as such organisations are not identical to the producer company, they are not responsible for defects stemming from the production process.

However, *exclusive representatives* of a foreign producer must follow up on and observe their product's performance in the domestic territory.[11]

(d) Under *fault-based* product liability the *quasi-producer*, who presents himself as a producer by affixing his name or trademark to the product, is not considered as producer, but only as seller.[12]

(e) Nor is the *importer* treated like a producer. This applies particularly in cases where products from other EU countries have been imported, since the importer may rely on the fact that quality standards are applied in these countries that are comparable with domestic ones.[13] Imports from less developed countries need not be checked for construction or production defects unless the importer has reason to believe that the foreign producer may not have been capable of properly constructing or making the product (for example, if it is a sophisticated one, or requires special technology or skills which may not be present in the particular country of origin).

4.5   Quantum of damage

The general rule of compensation is that the claimant must be put into a (financial) situation that would have existed if the damaging event had not happened.

One must always bear in mind that the particular financial loss for which compensation is claimed must flow from the infringement of a protected right of the claimant. With respect to these particular rights, the following should be noted.

(a) *Property*: Either the damaged property must be fully repaired, or the loss of property value must be compensated financially. Furthermore, lost profits which would probably have been made if the damaged property

---

10   OLG Frankfurt in BB 1986, 1117 – 'Motorrad'.
11   Kullmann/Pfister KZA 1524, p 8 ff.
12   BGH in NJW 1980, 1219 – 'Klappfahrrad'.
13   *Münchner Kommentar*, BGB, §823 annotation 304.

could have been used, are to be compensated. But if *other* property, which is not physically affected by the damage, cannot be employed as a consequence of the damage done to one object, such losses would be considered purely financial, and consequently not recoverable under tort law. If an entire shop has to go out of business for some time because one machine was destroyed, the losses from this interruption are not totally recoverable, but only in so far as they are connected with the particular damaged machine.

(b) *Violations of life, body and health*: the statutory tort law provides for special regulations:

   (i) BGB, §842 says that if a person is injured the recoverable damages comprise also disadvantages flowing from the diminished capacity to make a living. If this capacity is permanently diminished or even destroyed, the injured person is entitled to a lump sum indemnification and/or periodical payments (cf BGB, §843).

  (ii) If a person is killed, a subsistence allowance must be paid to those who are entitled to maintenance.

An injured person is entitled to receive damages for *pain and suffering*. What amounts are fair and reasonable will be determined by the courts. The amounts that are awarded differ widely. Where no permanent disability is involved, the amounts will normally be below DM 10,000. If an eye or a limb is lost, damages up to DM 100,000 will be awarded. The maximum amount so far has been DM 350,000 in a case of paraplegia.

4.6 Burden of proof

The general rule in German law is that the plaintiff must prove all facts and circumstances on which his claim is based, including causation and fault. *This rule does not apply to product liability.* The courts have partially reversed this burden of proof in favour of the plaintiff. The burden of proof differs depending on which of the following facts is disputed:

(a) whether there has been a defect;
(b) whether the defect is rooted in the fabrication process;
(c) whether there has been a negligent or intentional disregard of due care, and whether this disregard has caused the defect;
(d) whether the defect has caused a violation of the claimant's right(s);
(e) whether the plaintiff's damage or injury has led to the financial loss for which compensation is being sought.[14]

The plaintiff must prove that the product was defective.

Generally, the plaintiff must also prove that the defective product was made by the defendant, and that the product was already defective when it left the producer's premises.

Practically speaking, the burden of proof with respect to the latter has been reversed by the Federal Supreme Court.[15] A bottle containing a carbonated beverage had exploded due to a crack in the bottle. It was unclear whether this crack had already been present when the bottle was filled, or whether it had

---

14 *Produkthaftungshandbuch*, vol 1, §30 annotation 19.
15 BGH in NJW 1988, 2611 ff – 'Mehrwegflasche II'; BGH in NJW 1995/2162 – 'Mehrwegflasche III'.

been caused during the subsequent distribution of the bottle from the beverage factory to the consumer. Since the bottle had been a reusable one, it seemed at least possible that the crack had been caused during previous use. The court imposed upon the maker of the beverage the burden of showing that the bottle had left his factory intact. This duty could in practice only be fulfilled by the quality control of every bottle, and the documentation and repetition of this check. Since this duty had not been met by the producer of the beverage, he was held liable even though it was impossible to establish that the bottle in question was already defective when it was shipped from his premises.

The burden of proof with respect to *fault* on the producer's side must be met by the plaintiff or by the defendant, depending on whether due care was (allegedly) disregarded, *within* or *without* the factory.

Everything concerning internal operations, ie whether the producer has exercised due care in the areas of construction and fabrication, must be proven by the producer. This means that he must *exonerate* himself from fault.

In practice, this exoneration almost never succeeds. On the other hand, the plaintiff must prove lack of care on the producer's side in the areas of instructions and follow-up product observation.[16]

The plaintiff also bears the burden of proof regarding both steps of causation, ie between the defendant's conduct and the infringement of the plaintiff's right(s), and between this infringement and the financial loss (cf section 4.3, above).

It is often difficult to determine exactly what financial loss has occurred. The amount must be proven by the plaintiff, but the Code of Civil Procedure in paragraph 287 enables the court to award damages based on estimation.

4.7   Exclusion or limitation of liability

Liability can only be excluded or limited within the framework of a contract. Therefore, it plays no significant part where product liability is based on torts.

However, where the producer (or another person responsible for the defect) is at the same time the seller of the defective product, the rules governing contractual product liability apply (cf section 3.6, above).

Recently, so-called 'quality protection agreements' have gained practical and legal importance. In such an agreement, the supplier not only undertakes to furnish the producer with goods which are free from any defects, but also to take upon himself all duties concerning quality control. The producer of the finished product (eg a car manufacturer) is indemnified from product liability regarding that particular part through a contractual right against his supplier. Especially in the automotive industry such agreements are of considerable importance for just-in-time deliveries (ie where the manufacturing process is run on the basis that minimum stock levels are held at all times).

Of course, such quality protection agreements shift the responsibility only internally between the supplier and the producer, and do not diminish the consumer's or user's rights vis-à-vis the producer.

16   BGH in NJW 1981, 104 – 'Derrosal I'.

Quality protection agreements are admissible when the supplier is able to ensure the safe and reliable performance of his duties. The range of these duties has to be stipulated specifically in the agreement.[17]

4.8 Limitation period

According to BGB, §852 claims for damages become statute-barred after three years counting from the day when the plaintiff became aware of the damage and of the liable person. The period does not run as long as negotiations take place between the parties. It continues to run if one of the parties refuses to continue the negotiations. Irrespective of the plaintiff's awareness of the damage and of the responsible person, the period of limitation is 30 years.

4.9 Liability for third parties

The law distinguishes between executive bodies of a company, and its employees, who in tort law terminology are called 'vicarious agents'.

BGB, §31 determines that culpable conduct of an executive body is considered conduct of the company. Therefore, whatever the management does is attributed directly to the company.

According to BGB, §831, the company is also liable for the conduct of the persons it employs in the pursuit of the company's activities. This concerns mainly workers and employees. However, the company can exonerate itself from liability for these persons if it shows that it has carefully selected and supervised them.

This possibility of exoneration comes into play particularly with respect to manufacturing and fabrication defects. The defendant company may raise the defence that it has carefully selected and supervised the entire production staff. However, the courts require the defendant to name the particular person who has been responsible for the product defect. This is extraordinarily difficult in the area of mass production. Even if the company could exonerate itself in this way, it might still be found guilty of a so-called 'organisational fault' if production has not been organised in a manner by which the occurrence of production defects could be avoided. In particular, quality control must be properly organised.

The 'Baby-Bottle-Syndrome' cases have raised the question whether one producer can be held liable for damages which another one has caused.

Under German law, where several wrong doers who have committed a tort jointly, each are responsible for the entire damage (BGB, §830, §840). In the 'Baby-Bottle-Syndrome' cases, the children had often drunk tea from different producers. The plaintiffs could not prove that the consumption of one producer's tea alone had caused cavities.

Since the courts were not satisfied that the respective contribution of each of the producer had caused the damage, and because they had not acted jointly, liability was denied.[18]

Thus, the German courts do not subscribe to a Market Share Liability, which has been established in California and in the Netherlands.

---

17 Kullmann/Pfister KZA 3250, pp 11ff.
18 BGH in NJW 1994, 1932.

5   LIABILITY FOR DEFECTIVE PRODUCTS ARISING FROM THE PRODUCT LIABILITY ACT (IMPLEMENTATION OF THE DIRECTIVE ON PRODUCT LIABILITY)

5.1   Introduction

The Product Liability Directive has been implemented in Germany with the Product Liability Act ('Act') of 15 December 1989. It was adjusted to the Trade Mark Act of 25 October 1994[19] and the Act concerning the jurisdiction and enforcement in civil and commercial law of 30 September 1994.[20] The Act came into force on 1 January 1990 (cf §19). According to §16, the Act will not be applied to products which have been distributed prior to 1 January 1990.

5.2   Outline of the provisions of the Act

The full wording of the Act can be found in *Bundesgesetzblatt* I 1989 S 2198. The most important concepts and provisions are the following.

Similar to the traditional product liability based on contract and torts, the law is based on the principle of *protected rights*. These are life, body and health, and things (and therefore property and possession): cf §1(1).

Under the Act, the defective product itself does not qualify as 'property' that can be infringed upon by the defect. As explained earlier, it is possible under fault-based product liability to recover compensation for damage caused to a complex product by a single, clearly distinguishable defective part. The Act requires expressly that *an object other* than the defective product itself must be damaged.

However, this does not affect cases where a *supplier* has provided a defective part, if this part damages the product into which it has been built.

The emphasis the Act gives to consumer protection has led to a restriction of liability for property infringement. Liability under the Act arises only if the damaged property is usually used privately and has also been used by the plaintiff mainly for private purposes (cf §1(1) second sentence). It is obvious that it will often be difficult to draw a line between private and business or professional use.

Property that is objectively normally used for business purposes is not protected by the Act. For example, it does not provide for compensation for damage done to an excavator, even if the owner of a construction business should have used its excavator for a private purpose during the weekend. If the damaged property does not typically belong in the private or the business sphere, it depends on whether its owner (*subjectively*) has used it predominantly for private or for business/professional purposes. The plaintiff who used his car for pleasure most of the time, and only makes occasional business trips, does not lose the protection provided by the Act. On the other hand, an attorney who uses his personal computer to work on his briefs will not be able to recover compensation under the Act for damage done to this computer.

The notion of 'product' is defined in §2 of the Act as a movable thing, including parts of other movable or immovable things. Electricity is expressly included among the products. Exempted, however, are primary agricultural

19   BGBl I 1994, 3081.
20   BGBl II 1994, 2658 und BGBl II 1994, 221.

products of the soil, of stock-farming, bee-keeping and fishery, unless they have been processed at least once.

By including parts of movable or immovable things in the 'products', the Act makes the liability of the supplier of parts possible.

The extension of product liability to movable things that are integrated into immovable things makes sure that the producer of defective construction material and the supplier of complete industrial plants are subject to product liability based on the Act. On the other hand, the no-fault liability does not concern immovable things that have been made from movable ones, eg the complete building as opposed to the bricks it was made from.

According to §3(1) of the Act, a product is *defective* if it does not provide the safety that can reasonably be expected considering all the circumstances. The producer must account for all uses of his product by the consumer that are not completely unusual or unreasonable. The required safety standard is the one that can be expected at the time when the product is being distributed.

As to the required product safety, we may refer to the treatment of general tortious liability, as far as *construction/design defects* and *manufacturing defects* are concerned. The factual and the legal treatment are the same. Section 3(1)(b) of the Act makes it clear that the producer must not only foresee that his product will be used for the purposes it is meant for, but also for purposes that can *reasonably be expected*. This coincides with judgments of Federal Supreme Court with respect to general tort law. For example, we have said that the inhalation of soluble substances contained in glue for the purpose of intoxication is too unreasonable to be taken into account by the producer.

The following is a rule of thumb:

> The more remote the plaintiff's use of the product was from the usual purposes of the product, the more it is for him to explain why in his opinion the producer should have accounted for the way in which he, the plaintiff, has actually made use of the product.[1]

The duties concerning proper *instructions* are referred to in §3(1)(a) of the Act by the notion of 'presentation of the product'. This notion extends the instructional duties that we have known heretofore. Until now, only cases of missing or insufficient warnings of dangers or harmful side effects were covered. In addition, 'presentation' means also descriptions of the product (for example, in advertising), of its qualities and its possible purposes.

Further, under the aspect of 'presentation' there can be liability for products having no effect at all. If a product is advertised as having certain beneficial effects (such as avoiding dangers normally connected with the use of such a product), it is being 'presented' as effective.

Product observation is not dealt with in the Act. Therefore, it provides no ground for action if the producer has not properly observed and followed up his product's performance in the marketplace.

When determining whether a product is defective, the time when the product was distributed is the relevant one (§3(1)(b)). It is clear from §3(2) that a product shall not be considered defective for the sole reason that subsequently an improved product was distributed. This applies only to design/constructional changes. The words 'for the sole reason' mean that improvements do not necessarily serve to eliminate defects. If improvements are made, this may or may not mean that the product had previously been defective.

---

1   Kullmann/Pfister, KZA, 3604, p 11.

The wording of §1(1), first sentence, 'if the defect of a product *leads to* the death of a person', means that there must be a causal relationship between defect and damage. The general rules explained above in the context of tortious liability apply. The number of relevant causes is restricted by the Act's requirement that the damage must be attributable to specific product risks. Thus, compensation cannot be claimed (in spite of a causal relationship between defect and damage) if risks other than those emanating from the product have materialised, eg if a product defect causes an injury that would not have been deadly, but the injured person dies in a traffic accident on his way to the hospital.

The liability based on the Act requires only an infringement of a protected right, and a causal relationship between the defect and this damage. Fault is not necessary. Unlike the classic tortious liability, the one based on the Act is *no-fault*.

This principle is modified in §6(1) of the Act in so far as the plaintiff is *contributorily negligent*. Thus, it is immaterial for the liability whether the producer was at fault, but contributory negligence on the part of the person who has suffered loss or injury is taken into consideration when it comes to determining the amount of damages to be paid.

Contributory negligence is dealt with generally in BGB, §254. According to this provision, the amount of damages payable to a contributorily negligent plaintiff is reciprocal to the degree to which he has contributed to causing the damage. Thus, operational mistakes or plain product abuse on the part of the user/consumer can be accounted for.

Section 1(2) and (3) of the Act deal with *exemptions from liability*.

(a) The producer is not liable if he has *not distributed* the product (§1(2)(1) of the Act). Distribution has taken place when the product has been put into the distribution channel in order to have it sold.

(b) Further, there is no liability if the product was *free from defects* at the time of distribution (§1(2)(2) of the Act). Consequently, the producer is not liable for damages caused by changes in the product that have been brought about by, eg, improper storage, contamination, or sabotage.

(c) Nor is the producer liable if the product was neither manufactured by him for sale or another form of distribution for economic purpose, nor manufactured or distributed by him in the course of his business (§1(2)(3) of the Act).

(d) According to §1(2)(4), the producer is also exempted from liability, if the *defect* is due to compliance of the product with *mandatory regulations* issued by the public authorities. Contrary to what the wording of this exemption suggests, its scope of applicability will be very narrow. It is a prerequisite that the regulation forces the producer to make or present his product in the specific way he has done, and in no other way. He is not exempted from liability if he has merely complied with certain standards prescribed by law (eg DIN norms, accident prevention regulations, etc).

(e) The exemption from liability in cases where *the defect could not be discovered based on the scientific and technical knowledge* at the time when the product was distributed (§1(2)(5) of the Act) will be construed narrowly. It does not matter whether the producer himself or someone else in the industry could have discovered the defect. This exemption can only be relied upon if the defect could not have been avoided even if the responsible person had been in possession of the entire available human knowledge.

(f) A parts supplier is not responsible for defects following from the design or

construction of the finished product that his part goes into; nor is he responsible for damages caused by the producer's instructions.

Section 4 of the Act introduces a significantly broadened concept of who is to be considered as a *producer*.

Consumer protection is further enhanced by §5, which allows the plaintiff to hold several injurers liable jointly and severally.

The kind and the amount of damages that can be awarded are largely the same under the Act (cf 5-11) and in tort). An important difference is that under the Act *no compensation for pain and suffering* can be claimed. Further, §10 provides for a maximum liability of DM 160m, and §11 for a threshold in the amount of DM 1,125 *in cases of property damage*. Producers may significantly profit from such retentions if they add up in cases of mass defects.

Section 1(4) expressly states that the *burden of proof* with respect to the defect, the damage and the chain of causation between the two is with the plaintiff. On the other hand, the producer must show and, if necessary, prove the presuppositions for an exclusion or a restriction of his liability. Since it is extremely difficult to prove that the product was free from defects at the time of its first distribution, circumstantial evidence will be admitted. Thus, the court will only ask whether, given all the circumstances of the case, the product could normally be expected to be free from defects. It need not fully convince itself that this was the case.

Section 14 outlaws any contractual exemptions from liability (§11). The *period of limitation* provided for in §12 of the Act is the same as the one in tort (three years), cf BGB, §852.

However, the injured parties' rights will be extinguished upon expiry of a ten-year period after the distribution of the product by the producer. Since there may be several 'producers' due to the broad definition in §4, their respective ten-year periods may not coincide. For example, the supplier will normally distribute his part earlier than the producer of the finished product.

Finally, §15(2) of the Act expressly states that the previously existing law of product liability continues to be in force. However, this does *not* apply to *drug manufacturers*, cf §15(1). Thus, drug manufacturers are privileged under the Act. Under §84 of the Drug Act, the producer is only liable for damages caused by consumption of his product which is in accordance with its purpose (and not, as provided for in §3(1)(b) of the Act, for damages caused by any means of consumption that could reasonably be expected). Also, the Drug Act 84 limits the liability to *medicinal information* printed on the leaflet included inside the package (cf §3(1)(a) of the Act).[2]

5.3 Liability of the various producers

Section 4 of the Act has led to a considerable increase in the number of people and businesses involved in the production and distribution process which may be held liable for product defects. The following points deserve attention.

The *designer* is not subject to liability under the Act, since he has not been listed as producer or similar responsible person in §4. Other than the producer's responsibility for the individual product, the designer's contribution is an intellectual one. It does not make a difference whether his ideas have materialised in drawings, descriptions, or the like.

2   Act of 24.08.1976 (BGB1, I S. 2445), last amended on 19.10.1994 (BGB1 1994, 3018).

Likewise, licensors or franchisors are not considered producers in the sense of the Act.

The supplier of component parts is also considered a producer in the sense of §4(1), first sentence of the Act. However, according to §1(3), the producer of a component part is not liable if his product has been free from defects, but was damaged when being built into the finished product, or if the component part was made according to the instructions of the producer. If, however, the supplier of the component part has recommended his product to be used in the finished product, or if he has recognised that his component part is not fit to function properly within the finished product, the defect is not only caused when the component part is being built into the finished product, but where the component part was defective to begin with.

According to §4(1), first sentence of the Act, the maker of *basic raw materials* is also responsible as a producer, but at the same time he is – like the supplier of component parts – privileged under §1(3).

The *producer of the finished product* is always liable. It is completely immaterial whether he makes the component parts himself, or buys them elsewhere. Therefore, *the assembler* is also considered as a producer of the finished product.

In the light of the very restricted liability of the seller, the distinction between a simple sales activity and assembling (which will lead to full liability) is of particular practical importance.

One does not become an assembler by simply adding protective devices or accessory parts to a finished product. On the other hand, someone who is putting the finished product together based on construction plans or other instructions, will be considered as an assembler. The same goes, eg, for those who do complete re-designs of motor vehicles (and not only improve their outer appearance). A producer is also a person who makes a new product by following instructions or prescriptions on how to combine the components or ingredients.

The liability of the so-called *quasi-producer* is of eminent practical importance. A quasi-producer is somebody who presents himself as a producer by affixing his name, trademark, or other distinguishing feature to the product. Thus, companies who avail themselves of cheap labour in less developed countries by having their products made there become liable. This applies particularly to mail order businesses, chain stores, etc.

By including all distinguishing features, more companies or individuals will fall under this provision than would be justified by the purpose of product liability. Therefore, it is of crucial importance to bear in mind that the trademark etc must lead to a *presentation as producer*. Many names or trademarks do not identify producers, but trade or sales organisations, or simply the owners of prestigious trademarks who have merchandised their trademark in a product field different from the one where the trademark has obtained its initial recognition. It is doubtful whether the consumer will be able to distinguish between traders', manufacturers', and merchandised trademarks.

According to §4(2) of the Act, the *importer* will be considered as a producer if he imports the merchandise into the European Union from an outside country. It is immaterial whether this merchandise consists of finished products, or of product parts.

Sellers (dealers) are considered as producers if the actual producer cannot be identified (cf §4(3) of the Act). The same applies to products imported into the EU from non-EU countries, if their importer cannot be established.

Individuals or companies who merely *install, purchase,* or *repair* products, are not considered producers, unless they fulfil the prerequisites of §4. Thus, a purchaser may be liable as producer if he buys products in a non-EU country and leases them within the EU; fitters or repairers may do work that qualifies them as assemblers.

Workers and employees are not subject to product liability under the Act.

A plaintiff in a product liability case may hold each company or individual liable that qualifies as producer or quasi-producer under § 4. They are liable jointly and severally. However, recourse may take place among them. For example, if one of the liable producers has completely indemnified the victim, he may be reimbursed for part or even all of his payment by one or several of the other liable producers. By attributing the share of responsibility, the law requires that the degree to which each one has contributed to the damage be taken into consideration.

The relations among jointly and severally liable debtors on the one hand, and the relations between them and the creditor on the other hand, are dealt with in detail in the Civil Code, §421 ff.

5.4   Description of optional or anomalous provisions in respect of product liability law in Germany

The German Parliament has availed itself of the discretion provided for in the Directive in favour of industry and agriculture.

Primary agricultural products and game are not covered by the Act (Directive, article 15(1)(a), Product Liability Act, second sentence).

A limitation of a producer's total liability has been provided for (Directive, article 16(1), Product Liability Act, §10). §10 of the Act provides for a maximum liability of DM 160m.

The Product Liability Act does not apply to medicinal drugs (§15).

The liability for development risks has been excluded (Directive, article 15(1)(b); Product Liability Act, §1 II No 5).

The Federal Supreme Court's first decision after the enactment of the Product Liability Act concerned the liability for development risks. In this case, it had not been technically possible to test every single product for flawlessness, or to record the test results. The court had to decide whether this falls under the development risk in the sense of §1 II No 5 of the Act (Article 7(e), Directive 85/234). The court ruled that the exclusion of liability for development risks covers only construction defects, but not defects attributable to individual production.[3]

5.5   Differences between national law and provisions of the Directive

5.5.1   *Comparison between the Act and law of torts*

Our treatment of product liability under the new Act above, and of product liability law as it existed before the Act (and continues to exist) has shown that the new Act does not cover all the areas that are covered by tort law. In the following areas, the traditional *fault-based tort law* will continue to play an important part:

3   BGH in NJW 1995, 2162.

(a) According to §1(1), second sentence of the Act, it gives rise to claims for property infringement only if the property was for private use or consumption and had in fact mainly been used privately. Thus, whenever the destruction or damage to property used for commercial or professional purposes is at stake, only tort law will apply.[4]

   Likewise, property damage caused to a compound machine or structure by an integrated part fulfilling a limited function, can only give rise to compensation claims under tort law, since §1(1), second sentence of the Act is applicable only to damage done to 'another object'.

(b) Defective agricultural products that have not yet undergone any processing can only give rise to a product liability claim under tort law,[5] since they are exempted from strict liability in §2 of the Act.

(c) Since the Act does not deal with claims based on missing or insufficient product observation, such claims must also be based on tort law.[6]

(d) By requiring a direct causation of damage or injury by risks emanating from the product, the Act excludes the compensation of damages that have been caused by the interference of other factors. Again, the plaintiff must in such cases rely on tort law.[7]

(e) The same goes for cases in which product defects could not be discovered based on the state of scientific and technical knowledge at the time of distribution.[8]

(f) Compensation for pain and suffering can only be claimed under tort law, since the Act does not deal with immaterial damages.[9] Immaterial damages means damages for pain and suffering (for non-pecuniary losses).

(g) Where the financial loss exceeds the maximum amount stated in §10 of the Act, the excess amount may be recoverable under tort law. Also, if the plaintiff wants to avoid the retention provided for in §11 of the Act, he must rely on tort law. Therefore, whenever more than DM 1,125 is claimed as property damage, the courts must examine whether this claim is justified under the Act or under tort law.

(h) If the product in question has been distributed more than ten years before the accident, tort law must be relied upon exclusively due to the time limit in §13.

(i) Where strict liability for defective drugs is excluded either under 15 of the Act or under the Drug Act, §84 (cf section 5.1, above), the plaintiff must again rely on tort law.

(j) All persons or companies involved in the production or distribution who cannot be held liable under the Act (designers, dealers, workers and employees) can only be held liable, if at all, under tort law.

5.5.2   *Comparison between the Act and contractual product liability*

(a) Pure financial losses can only be recovered under contractual product liability.[10]

---

4   Cf Ch F II 2.
5   Cf Ch F II 3 und C II 2 lit d.
6   Cf Ch F II 6 und C III Ziff.
7   Cf Ch F II 6 lit e und §1 Abs. 2 Ziff. 5 ProdHaftG.
8   Cf Ch C V 2.
9   Cf Ch A V 3.
10   Cf Ch A IV.

(b) Where the Act does not apply and where no fault can be found (thus excluding tort liability), the plaintiff may still rely on contractual liability in relation to missing qualities the existence of which have been represented by the seller.

(c) Also, where the producer has contractually agreed to furnish a product of a special quality which is supposed to meet more than the usual requirements, claims for not having met the superior standards can be based only on contractual product liability.[11]

6   CRIMINAL LIABILITY FOR DEFECTIVE PRODUCTS ARISING FROM GENERAL SAFETY LAW; IMPLEMENTATION OF EC DIRECTIVE 92/59 ON PRODUCT SAFETY

6.1   Introduction

There are a number of legal provisions concerning product safety. Often they are implementations of EC Directives. Based on the Council Resolution (EC Gazette No C 136 of 4 June 1985, p 1) a new concept in the area of technical harmonisation and standardisation has been developed.

The most important laws providing for special product liability are the Medicine Act (*Arzneimittelgesetz* – AMG),[12] the Food Act (*Lebensmittelund Bedarfsgegenständegesetz* – LMBG),[13] the Act Concerning Technical Tools And Appliances (*Gerätesicherheitsgesetz* – GSG),[14] Medicine Products Act (*Medizinproduktegesetz* – MPG)[15] and the Genetic Engineering ACT (*Gentechnikgesetz* – GenTG).[16] Some of these laws provide for criminal sanctions in case of offences.

6.2   Directive 92/59 EC on Product Safety

The Federal Government introduced a bill into parliament for an implementing Act (*Produktsicherheitsgesetz* – ProdSG, BR-Drucks, 457/95). The Federal Council (Upper Chamber) rejected this bill (BR-Drucks, 457/95), on the basis that the contents of this bill have already been dealt with in a number of special acts. The Federal Government, however, sustains its concept and introduced the bill into the *Bundestag* (Lower Chamber, cf BR-Drucks, 13/31/30 of 29 November 1995).

6.3   Description of anomalous provisions

The Federal Government was of the opinion that the Product Safety Directive 92/59 is inconsistent with article 100 of the EEC Treaty. However, in its decision of 9 August 1994, the European Court of Justice decided that the Commission has the power to issue legal measures concerning a specific

---

11   Cf Ch C VII.
12   BGBl I 1994, 3018 vom 19.10.1994.
13   BGBl I 1993, 1170 vom 8.7.1993; BGBl I 1994, 1963, 1983 vom 2.8.1994.
14   BGBl I 1992, 1794 vom 22.10.1992; BGBl I 1994, 1963/1987 vom 2.8.1994.
15   BGBl 1994, 1963 vom 22.10.1994.
16   BGBl 1993, 2067 vom 16.12.1993; BGBl I 1994, 1416, 1419 vom 24.6.1994.

product, or specific product categories, including individual measures concerning these products. Moreover, the commission may require a member state to issue preliminary measures concerning product safety.[17] Thus, article 9 of the Product Safety Directive 92/59 is consistent with EC law.

6.4   Description of local optional provisions

Since the Product Safety Directive has not yet been implemented, the national and local authorities, who will have the exclusive competence regarding this Directive 92/59 EC, have not yet been established.

6.5   Brief overview of significant product safety law and the extent to which other EC consumer Directives have been implemented

6.5.1   Medicine Act (Arzneimittelgesetz – AMG)

Medicine Law has been left largely to the member states. The proposals for a community medicine office, which should be competent for the admission and the control of medicines, have not yet been realised.

Objects of the German AMG are the orderly medicine supply to humans and animals, and medicine safety, particularly quality, effectiveness, and freedom from unknown side effects. The act regulates civil liability and penal sanctions.

The penal sanctions fall into the categories of crimes and mere offences. The latter provides for fines only, whereas crimes may also be punished by imprisonment. Severe violations of the AMG, eg the sale of medicines in spite of known or suspected adverse health effects, may be punished by imprisonment for up to three years. However, this presupposes an intentional violation; where there is only negligence, the wrongdoer can only be fined.

6.5.2   Medicine Products Act (Medizinproduktegesetz – MPG)

This act has come into force on 1 January 1995. During a transitory period until 14 June 1998, the producers may comply either with the new law, or with the old one (AMG, LMBG).

The MPG implements three EC-Directives, namely

(a) the Directive of 20 June 1990 (90/385/EEC)
(b) the Directive of 14 June 1995 (93/42 EEC)
(c) the amended Directive 93/68/EEC of 22 July 1993.

This act provides for basic requirements for medicinal-technical apparatus. The technical specifications have been established by the three European standardisation organisations CEN, CENELEC and ETSI in European norms. The products are labelled with 'CE'.

The act does not provide for any sanctions. However, there is a safety concept which regulates the internal risk management by security commissioners for medicinal products as well as the external risk management by the respective supervisory authorities.

17   European Court of Justice, decision of 9 August 1994 – RS C-359/92 (EuZW 1994, 627).

6.5.3 Food Act (Lebensmittelund Bedarfsgegenständegesetz – LMBG)

This act applies to all foodstuffs, additives, tobacco products, cosmetics, and objects of daily use. It regulates the design and contents of the products, as well as their labelling. There are civil law and criminal law sanctions. According to §51 et seq, offenders against the LMBG may be fined, or punished with up to three years of imprisonment, depending on the gravity of the offence.

6.5.4 Genetic Engineering Act (Gentechnikgesetz – GenTG)

This act protects life and health of humans, animals and plants, as well as the entire environment, and property of possible dangers arising from genetical manipulations and products thus made. It regulates the admission of genetic engineering and provides for civil and criminal liability. In severe cases, GenTG, §39 provides for imprisonment of up to one year, in other cases of wilful or negligent offences it provides for fines.

6.5.5 The Act Concerning Technical Tools And Appliances (Gerätesicherheitsgesetz – GSG)

This act applies to the distribution and exhibition of technical tools, as well as for the construction and the operation of plants that are subject to supervision. The aim of the act is to prevent the sale of technical tools and appliances that may be harmful to human life or health, even when used in compliance with the producer's instructions.

Offences may be punished according to GSG, §16, §17 with fines or imprisonment of up to one year, depending on the gravity of the offence.

The GSG concerns a number of EC Directives, eg the Machinery Directive (EC Gazette No L 183 of 29 June 1989) and the Directive Concerning Electro-Magnetic Compatibility (EC Gazette No C 44 of 19 February 1992) and thus leads to a respective harmonisation.

7 CIVIL LIABILITY FOR DEFECTIVE PRODUCTS BROUGHT ABOUT BY BREACH OF STATUTORY REGULATION DESIGNED TO PROTECT CONSUMERS AND/OR TO PROMOTE SAFETY

7.1 Outline of nature of protective regulation

BGB, §823 II says that anyone who disregards a law which serves to protect someone else must compensate the other person for the damage he has suffered as a consequence of such disregard. Thus, the plaintiff is spared one difficulty he faces if he relies on the first paragraph of §823, namely, to show the infringement of a particular right. Instead, he faces another difficulty; he must show that the particular law which the defendant has disregarded indeed served his (the plaintiff's) protection.

(1) What is a law in this context, and when does it serve the protection of the claimant?
  (a) 'Laws' are all Acts of Parliament (state or federal), statutory instrument (*Rechtsverordnungen*), EC law and sometimes even acts of administrative authorities.
  (b) In order to serve the protection of individuals, the law must order a certain conduct (to do something or to refrain from doing something)

which is meant to avert disadvantages for other individuals. This may also be the case if the law is for the protection of the public at large. However, if the law's requirements of conduct are too general, the individual may not fall into its protective scope. Laws which themselves provide for the payment of damages do not qualify as 'protective laws' in the sense of §823 II.

Classic protective laws are criminal laws.

(2) It may be difficult to determine the exact reach of the protective scope of a particular law. Sometimes it will reach further than the protection provided for individual rights in BGB, §823 I, sometimes it will fall short of this protection. For example, when certain requirements for the quality of animal food had been disregarded, the Animal Food Act was assumed to protect animal owners from the destruction of their livestock.[18] On the other hand, the Act Concerning Appliance Safety was not even considered to protect property.[19]

(3) Some of the most important protective laws will be dealt with in section 6, below.

A number of provisions in the Penal Code serve to protect life, health and property. These are protective laws in the sense of §823 II. Consequently, offences against criminal laws lead to double sanctions, namely penalties and damages. The responsible members of the management might be criminally convicted, particularly in cases of offences against bodily integrity and human life.

7.2   Burden of proof

Burden of proof is not shifted when it comes to the disregard of protective laws; instead, it remains entirely with the plaintiff.

7.3   Nature of liablity and damage

A number of laws contain special provisions related to product liability.

7.3.1   *Injuries caused by medicines*

A special product liability for defective medicines was introduced as a consequence of the infamous *Contagan* case, where unborn babies had been severely deformed by a soporific drug which their mothers had taken. This liability – like the EU product liability – is based on no-fault. However, a number of restrictions apply; cf §84 of the Medicine Act (*Arneimittelgesetz – AMG*):

(a) The damaging effect of the medicine must occur as a consequence of reasonable use of the drug. Liability is already excluded when larger quantities of the drug have been taken than was recommended. Therefore, the producer should always indicate the maximum dosage and the maximum treatment period.

(b) The adverse effect of medicine must exceed what is acceptable according to the state of the art in medicine. Consequently, insignificant side effects

18   BGH in VersR 1989, 91.
19   BGH in NJW 1977, 2120; Kullmann/Pfister KZA 3800, p 22.

cannot give raise to damage claims. A benefit/risk balance must be struck with respect to each particular drug. Serious side effects may be accepted in a medicine which is apt to treat life-threatening conditions. On the other hand, the benefit/risk balance does not allow the distribution of a drug against headaches that causes defects of vision.

(c) The Medicine Act does not give a ground for action, if a medicine has no effects at all.

(d) Liability may also be based on defects or mistakes in the legally required instructions for use. This applies also to the information on or within the packaging. The wording of instructions for use need not take into account the average user's medicinal knowledge, but may use scientific terminology. However, there must be clear warnings of the possible adverse effects of an overdose. The producer of an asthma spray was held liable, after a patient had suffered from an overdose of this spray, because there was no pertinent warning. The court said that there is a considerable danger of excessive use of drugs that are taken in situations where the patient may panic, like in the case of an asthma attack.[20]

(e) The person or company who offers and distributes the drug under their name in Germany is liable for product defects. Under the Medicine Act, §9 I, the importer is obliged to affix his name to the drugs he distributes. Consequently, the importer will generally be held liable instead of the foreign producer.

(f) the Medicine Act §88 provides for maximum amounts of liability. If a person is killed, the maximum amount is DM 500,000 and an annual pension of DM 30,000. If several people are killed, the maximum amount (irrespective of the number of people) is DM 200m and a total of annual pensions in the amount of DM 12m.

7.3.2 Food Act

The Food Act (Lebensmittelund Bedarfsgegenständegesetz – LMBG) is a protective law in the sense of BGB, §823 II. The Food Act prohibits the production and distribution of foodstuffs for humans which contain certain dangerous additives, pesticides, artificial hormones and other pharmacological substances, etc. as well as the distribution of foodstuffs that are spoilt or otherwise unfit for consumption, or labelled in a misleading manner.

These provisions serve to protect human health. Only illnesses that qualify as such under medicinal categories are considered as damage to health, but the illness need not be severe, eg, nausea is not considered a health impairment. The producer of the foodstuffs, as well as one who treats or processes them, and the seller to the ultimate consumer, may be liable, depending on at what point in the production and distribution chain the defect has occurred. In particular, retailers are under an obligation to examine foodstuffs about to be sold to check whether they comply with the various food laws.

7.3.3 The Act Concerning Technical Tools and Appliances

This Act is a protective law in the sense of BGB, §823 II. It protects the life and the health of the users of certain tools and appliances, both in the private and in the business spheres.

---

20   BGH decision of 24.01.1989, Az.: VI ZR 112/88.

The Act concerns technical tools, protective equipment, lighting, heating, cooling and air-conditioning appliances, household appliances, toys and sporting goods. Both the producer and the importer may be liable. The objective of the Act is to prevent defects that are contrary to industrial safety regulations and it requires warning instructions concerning dangers that can be prevented by proper installation of the tools or appliances. It also deals with the omission of furnishing the user with instructions for use. The *Bundesanstalt für Arbeitsschutz* (Federal Industrial Safety Agency) has issued a helpful guide for the wording of instructions for use.

CHAPTER VIII

Greece

Gus J Papamichalopoulos, Esq

Lila Vassilaki

Kyriakides & Partners
6 Queen Sophia Avenue
106 74 Athens
Greece

Tel: ++ 30 1 7243 072
Fax: ++ 30 1 7250 670

CHAPTER VIII

Greece

1 INTRODUCTION TO THE LEGAL SYSTEM IN GREECE

1.1 Introduction

The present Constitution was adopted by a specially empowered Parliament on 7 June 1975 and was amended on 6 March 1986. The main amendments to the Constitution consisted of transferring most of the presidential powers, except the ceremonial ones, to the Government and particularly to the Prime Minister.

The Constitution provides that Greece is a 'presidential parliamentary democracy' with the Prime Minister being head of the Government. The legislative power is exercised by a Parliament of 300-members and the President of the Republic. The executive power is exercised by the Government and the President of the Republic. The Government, however, is the main executive organ; any act of the President requires the countersignature of the competent Minister. In the field of public finance, important powers are exercised by the Parliament, which approves the annual budget, the general balance sheet of the State, as well as the public investment programme and levies taxes.

Article 28, paragraph 1 of the Constitution provides that the generally accepted rules of international law, as well as international treaties, constitute an integral part of domestic Greek law and shall prevail over any contrary provision as from the ratification by statute. Therefore, the generally accepted rules of international law and the international treaties ratified by Greece are placed between the Constitution and the acts of the Parliament.

Greek law follows the codified system and is substantially influenced by German civil law principles and French commercial and administrative law. Courts in Greece are divided into (i) civil, criminal and administrative courts, depending on their subject matter, and (ii) courts of first instance (small claims court, one-member and multi-member court of first instance) and (iii) courts of appeal, depending on the degree of jurisdiction.

The highest civil and criminal court is the Supreme Court (*Areios Pagos*), which decides final appeals on points of law, while the highest administrative courts are the Conseil d'Etat (*Symvoulio Epikratias*) and the Court of Auditors (*Elengtiko Synedrio*) to which the control of the public spending and the auditing of the accounts is entrusted. These comprise the other two Greek Supreme Courts.

Over and above the three permanent supreme courts, the Constitution provides for an ad hoc Constitutional court of limited jurisdiction and the Supreme Special Court (*Anotato Idiko Dikastirio*). The prerogatives of the Supreme Special Court include the review of constitutionality of an act of

Parliament in case of a conflict of interpretation or opinion arising between two of the other Supreme Courts.

The structure of the Greek Justice system includes three categories of Courts: Civil Courts, Administrative Courts and Criminal Courts, as follows:

CIVIL COURTS

i.   Supreme Court (*Arios Pagos*)
ii. Court of Appeal
iii. One member Court of First Instance/Three member Court of First Instance
iv. Magistrate Court

ADMINISTRATIVE COURTS

i.   Council of State
ii. Administrative Court of Appeals
iii. Administrative Court of First Instance

CRIMINAL COURTS

i.   Supreme Court (*Arios Pagos*)
ii. Mixed Court
iii. Court of Appeals
iv. Misdemeanor Court
v.   Petty Violation Court

1.2   Overview of the Law relating to Defective Products in Greece

Greek product liability law was based on the rules relating to a producer's or seller's liability for real and latent defects, as provided by the Greek Civil Code (article 513 ff). The Courts developed jurisprudence under which an action against a supplier or producer for damages caused by a defective product was accepted if the cause of action was based on the articles of the Greek Civil Code for contractual and tortious liability. Recently, special legislation has been promulgated for the protection of the consumer by implementing EU Directives 85/374 (Product Liability), 93/13 (Unfair Contract Terms) and 92/59 (Product Safety).

Law 1961/1991 re: 'Consumers Protection and other relevant provisions', as amended by Law 2000/1991 was applicable until the introduction of Law 2251/1994 re: 'Consumers Protection'. Law 2251/1994 gives the consumer the right to substantiate a claim either on the provisions of the Greek Civil Code for contractual and tortious liability, as well as by invoking the special liability established by the same law.

2   PRE-CONTRACTUAL LIABILITY

2.1   Effect on the interpretation and extent of the obligations of the parties to a contract

A general duty of good faith during the pre-contractual period is imposed by articles 197 and 198 of the Greek Civil Code (hereinafter 'the Code'). Article 197 of the Code provides that the parties must deal with each other according

to the dictates of good faith and business usage. According to article 198 of the Code, any damage caused in violation of this duty (*culpa contrahendo*) must be compensated for by the party at fault, even if the contract is not eventually concluded. The application of said articles by the Courts in relation to the liability arising from a defective product is rather limited due to the fact that the liability of the seller is established usually only after the delivery to the purchaser of the defective product.

According to the leading interpretation in this area, the provisions of article 543 et seq exclude the application of articles 197 and 198 of the Code, since the latter are general provisions of the Code[1] and therefore are superseded by the provisions of the Code dealing specifically with the liability arising from a defective product. *A contrario,*[2] Article 543 of the Code does not introduce a special liability for *culpa in contrahendo* and its application should not exclude the invocation of articles 197-198 of the Code. According to article 543 of the Code, the seller's liability is founded on the existence of a defective product and not on the lack of good faith during the pre-contractual period. The compensation provided for by article 543 of the Code is for the relief of the purchaser for any damage he has suffered due to the non-performance of the seller and not only for the damage caused from the breach of the fundamental principal of good faith during the pre-contractual period. Therefore, the application of article 198 of the Code must not be excluded when applying article 543 of the Code.[3]

2.2 Extent that non-disclosure of facts during negotiations may lead to liability

According to Article 536 of the Code, the seller can be held liable for real defects which were not known by the purchaser at the time of purchase. The same applies also for agreed specific qualities, the absence of which was not known by the purchaser at the time of purchase.

Article 537 of the Code provides that the seller cannot be held liable for actual defects, which the purchaser was not aware of at the time of purchase due to the purchaser's gross negligence except if the seller had represented the absence of a defect or had fraudulently hidden it from the purchaser.

2.3 Does pre-contractual liability lie in contract or tort?

Although pre-contractual liability lies in contract, claims in precontractual liability can be made in conjunction with claims in tort.

3 LIABILITY IN CONTRACT

3.1 Outline of contract law relevant to defective products

According to the general provisions of the Contract Law of the Code,[4] entering into a contract creates for both parties a duty to perform. The term 'perform'

1 See Balis, *General Principles of Civil Code*; Spiliopoulos, *Interpretation of the Civil Code*, arts 534-562; Gazis, *Interpretation of the Civil Code,* arts 335-348; Kambitsis, *Pre-contractual liability,* page 102; Koumantos, *Interpretation of the Civil Code-arts* 197-198.
2 See Zepos II, 3V3, page 82; Karasi, *Culpa in cotrahendo*, page 53 et seq.
3 See Georgiathi-Stathopoulo, *Interpretation by Article,*Vol III, page 134.
4 Arts 287 to 495 of the Code.

has a different meaning for each contracting party and extends not only to the obligation to perform or to refrain from performing as the case may be, but also to abstain from committing a tort, which creates a liability to compensate and substantiate a basis of unjust enrichment which again creates an obligation to make restitution.

Article 287 of the Code defines as 'obligation' (*enochi*) the relationship pursuant to which one party ('the debtor') is compelled to render performance to another ('the creditor'). The debtor is obliged to perform in good faith and to give consideration to business usage.

The Code deals with particular kinds of obligations which are most frequently encountered. Nevertheless, the parties are free to structure their contractual relationship differently, since the fundamental principle of freedom of contracts, as laid down in article 361 of the Code, allows other kinds of contracts as well.

One type of contract, which is regulated exhaustively by the Code (articles 513 to 573) is the contract of sale. In this contract the seller is bound to transfer ownership of the object, or, to transfer the right sold, and to deliver the object to the purchaser and the latter is obliged to pay the price agreed upon.

Article 514 of the Code provides that the seller is obliged to transfer the object free of any right enforceable by third parties. Rights enforceable by third parties are considered to be the real rights (ownership, *predial servitudes, personal servitudes*, mortgage and pledge), prenotation (title) rights, right of possession, confiscation rights, compulsory administration (ie receivership), restriction of sale in favour of certain persons.

Articles 534 to 562 of the Code regulate the *quasi* objective liability of the seller when the object of the sale is not transferred to the purchaser free from defects or when it lacks the represented qualities. The liability established under the said provisions varies in accordance with the following criteria: (a) whether the object of the sale is defined either by type or by class;[5] (b) whether the liability of the seller is based on the existence of a defect[6] or on the lack of the represented qualities[7] the purchaser and the seller have agreed upon; and (c) whether the seller has committed an offence.[8]

The application of the above criteria leads to the division of the seller's liability into two main categories: one based on the object of the sale (either defined by type or by class) and the second which is a graduated liability in each one of the two cases as follows:

(a) When the object is defined *by type:* (i) the liability of the seller for the existence of the defect arises on an objective basis;[9] (ii) the liability of the seller is upgraded however, where the lack of the represented qualities of the object of the sale existed prior to the sale being concluded. The purchaser in this case is more protected since the liability of the seller, which again is an objective liability, is enhanced; and (iii) the liability of the seller is also upgraded where the seller had knowledge of the existence of a defect or due to negligence he was not aware of its existence (subjective liability).

5 Arts 559 to 562 of the Code.
6 Art 534 of the Code.
7 Art 535 of the Code.
8 Art 543 sub-para 2, 544, 561 case (b) of the Code.
9 Art 543 in combination with art 536 of the Code.

(b) When the object is defined *by class*: (i) the liability of the seller for the existence of defects[10] and the lack of the represented qualities of the object[11] of the sale is on an objective basis and (ii) the liability of the seller is a subjective liability where the seller had knowledge of the lack of the represented qualities or the seller had fraudulently concealed a defect.[12]

The above mentioned provisions of the Code apply *mutatis mutandis* in the sale of defective components to a producer of a finished article. The purchaser can file an action based on liability in contract not only against the producer of a finished article but also against the supplier of the defective component of the article. Both defendants are liable in toto and may have recourse against each other if only one of them is held liable.

3.2 Legal provisions regulating the form and content of legal guarantees. Contractual warranties relating to quality and safety of goods and commercial practice in giving consumer guarantees

The Civil Code implies terms governing the quality of goods supplied. The Code requires that the goods are free from any defect and fit for their purpose and are of satisfactory quality. There is a strict liability for breach of those terms, as detailed in section 3.3 below.

According to the Code 'the seller shall be liable if the sold thing has real defects that substantially reduce its value or its use'. In addition 'the seller shall be liable if the supplied goods do not have the represented qualities'. The breach of these terms and conditions gives the right to the purchaser to claim damages or price reduction or to request the reverse of the sale transaction. However, there are restrictions to the seller's liability if the purchaser was aware of the defects or he ignored them by gross negligence.

The obligations considered above are imposed by law on sellers of goods. However, there are additional warranties given by manufacturers. Commercial warranties have become mandatory by Community law.

Law 2251/1994 re: 'Consumer Protection'[13,14] provides that the supplier is obliged in respect of each product sold to supply the consumer with specific instructions in the Greek language or by the use of internationally accepted signs for the safe use, maintenance, preservation and full use of the product, as well as information concerning the dangers arising from the use and maintenance of the product. The consumer is also entitled to be informed of the possible life expectancy of the product.

The supplier is obliged to supply the consumer with a written warranty in the Greek language or by the use of internationally accepted signs which must at least contain the tradename and business address of the supplier, details of the beneficiary of the warranty, the product covered by the warranty, the date

10 Art 559 of the Code.
11 Art 561 case (a) of the Code.
12 Art 561 case (b) of the Code
13 Law 2251/1994 implements EC Directives 85/374 re: General Product Safety (OJ No L 210/29) and 92/59 re: Approximation of the Laws, Regulations and Administrative provisions of the Member States concerning liability for defective products' (OJ No L 228/24).
14 Art 5, paras 1, 2, 3, 4, 5 and 6 are not implementing an EU Directive. The provisions reflect the spirit of the Green Bible re: Product Guarantees and Consumers service after the Sale (KOM (93) 509 dated 15 November 1993.

of validity and duration of the warranty. The warranty must be drafted in compliance with the concept of good faith and should not be limited by exemption clauses. The duration of said warranty must be reasonable in relation to the life of the product, especially as regards high technology products. The duration of the warranty must also be reasonable in relation to the period of time the product is anticipated to remain up to date with the technology, if such time period is shorter than the possible life of the product.

If a product defect arises during the validity of the warranty and the supplier refuses to repair the product or there is a significant delay in doing so, the consumer has the right to request either the replacement of the product with a new one or the cancellation of the sale. If the product or a component thereof is replaced, the guarantee of the product or the component is extended automatically. Any waiver from the protection provided by the Code is void.

The supplier of new products having a long term duration is obliged to provide to consumers a continuous technical service throughout their potential life for the repair and maintenance of the product. The same applies also as regards spare parts of the product.

3.3   Breach of contract for supply of defective products

The Code provides for three situations constituting a breach of contract triggering the application of the aforesaid provisions. The first situation is provided by article 514 of the Code (legal defect) (see section 3.1), the second situation is provided for by article 534 of the Code (real defect) and the third situation by article 535 of the Code (lack of represented qualities) (see section 3.1).

The distinction between the existence of a product's real defect from the lack of a product's represented quality is based on the importance of the defect which destroys or substantially reduces the value or use of the product.

The application of article 534 of the Code to this situation leads to the conclusion that the main characteristics of a real defect are: (a) that it is a defect in the product itself, a defect in relation to its characteristics, construction, etc. or its condition at the time when the liability was transferred to the purchaser; and (b) that this defect has a negative effect on the value or use of the product.[15]

Given that (i) the liability established by article 534 of the Code is for the protection and compensation of the purchaser; and (ii) said article is part of the framework regulating the abnormal construction of the contract where damage is caused by the defective product, it is clear that in order to verify whether the product has a defect or not, one must refer to the provisions of the contract per se. Only the interpretation of the contract can lead to a conclusion whether the purchaser intended to use the product within the terms of the so-called 'ordinary use' or if the purchaser desired a use beyond such use. If the latter case cannot be substantiated, then it must be accepted that the purchaser intended to use the product within the limits of the 'ordinary use'.[16]

---

15   Court Decision No 138/1978 of the Thessaloniki Court of Appeals, published Arm 32, 432; Spiliopoulos, ErmAK 534; Spiridaki-Peraki, art 534; Bostha, ArxN 15, 372.
16   Court Decision No 548/1970 of the One-Member Athens Court of First Instance, published Arm 25,171.

The seller cannot be held liable for real defects which were known by the purchaser at the time of purchase. The same applies in respect of claims brought by a purchaser who knew a product lacked the agreed specific qualities.[17]

A seller cannot be held liable for real defects, which the purchaser was unaware of at the time of purchase due to the purchaser's gross negligence, except if the seller had represented the absence of a defect or had fraudulently hidden it from the purchaser.[18] Both these provisions restrict the application of Article 534 of the Code. The seller has the right to raise an objection based on both Articles. In practice the objection based on article 536 of the Code is the primary one whereas the objection based on article 537 of the Code is second defence.[19]

The burden of proof lies with the seller who must prove to the court all the facts contained in the objections. The purchaser can either refute the allegations of the seller and prove otherwise or allege that the seller had represented the absence of the specific defect or that the seller knew the existence of the defect but had fraudulently hidden it. The seller has the burden of proof in this latter case.

Another distinction as regards the liability of the seller is in relation to the time at which the product is transferred (ie physical delivery) to the purchaser. In some instances the Courts have ruled that until the product has been delivered to the purchaser (whereupon the risk is transferred) the seller is protected by the general provisions of contract law regulating the non-performance.[20] The Supreme Court[1] in this case ruled that the special provisions of article 534 et seq of the Code, are applicable to the protection of the purchaser before the transfer of the product and the general provisions of the Code (ie articles 330, 335 et seq, 362 et seq, 374 of the Code) will not initially be applied. However, once the product is transferred to the purchaser the provisions of articles 534 of the Code are applicable.

Where the seller is liable for a real defect or lack of a represented quality, the purchaser is entitled to demand either the cancellation of the sale or a reduction in the price.[2] If at the time of the purchase there is an absence of a represented quality or there was a defect in the product and the seller had knowledge or ought to have had knowledge thereof, the purchaser may demand compensation[3] for non-performance instead of cancellation of the sale or a reduction in the price.[4] The seller also has the rights described above under article 543 of the Code, where the represented quality was absent at the conclusion of the sale or where the defect arose after the conclusion of the sale but before the physical delivery of the product.[5]

Where the product is described by class, the purchaser may demand cancellation of the sale or a reduction in the price instead of a replacement of the product with one free from defect.[6] Where the risk in relation to a product,

---

17   Art 536 of the Code.
18   Art 537 of the Code.
19   Court Decision No 192/1972 of the Piraeus One–Member Court of First Instance, published NoB 20, 537).
20   Art 374 et seq of the Code.
1   Court Decision No 518/1972, published NoB, 1319.
2   Art 540 of the Code.
3   See section 3.4 for the quantum of damages.
4   Art 543 of the Code.
5   Art 544 of the Code.
6   Art 559 of the Code.

which is defined by class, passes to the purchaser and the represented quality is absent, or the seller had fraudulently concealed a defect, the purchaser instead of demanding the cancellation of the sale or the reduction of the price or the delivery of another product, is entitled to compensation for the non-performance.[7]

3.4   Quantum of damages

The purchaser's right to compensation under article 543 of the Code is based on the liability of the seller, as defined in article 540 of the Code. In order to establish this liability, the product must have been delivered to the purchaser and the sale concluded, even if there was a failure of performance by the seller.[8] The compensation of article 543 of the Code is to cover every loss and damage of the purchaser as an immediate and direct consequence of the defect of the product or of the absence of the represented quality.[9] Therefore, the purchaser is entitled to demand both the restitution of the loss and the gains prevented, as well as any 'further damage' caused to the purchaser by the defect or due to the absence of the represented quality.[10] 'Further damage' is considered to be the damage the seller's property or health suffers due to the defect in the product or the absence of the represented specific quality.

As outlined above, the seller's liability is upgraded under article 543 of the Code when the absence of a represented quality or a real defect existed at the time of the sale, and, the seller at that time had knowledge, or, ought to have had knowledge of the existence of a real defect, or, the absence of represented quality. The purchaser in this case has the right to obtain redress for damages suffered due to the non-performance, instead of demanding the decrease in the price or the cancellation of the sale.

The purchaser is entitled to demand compensation to cover any loss the purchaser suffered due to the non-performance of the seller, since the purchaser is obliged to reject the seller's offer for a defective product and seek full compensation for damages as the sale was not concluded.[11]

As regards article 561 of the Code, the purchaser is entitled to compensation for the non-performance of the seller instead of demanding the cancellation of the sale or a reduction in the price or the delivery of another product, if the represented quality is absent when the product is physically delivered to the purchaser or the seller had fraudulently concealed a defect in a product, defined by class. As to the extent of the compensation (damages payable) the same provisions apply as above. Redress for pecuniary damages cannot be obtained in the context of an action in contract.

3.5   Burden of proof

The purchaser who brings an action based on the provisions of article 534 of the Code must present to the court the specific defects of the product[12] and

---

7   Art 561 of the Code.
8   Court Decision No 1703/1975 of the Athens Court of Appeal.
9   Supreme Court Nos 253/1961 and 971/1977, Court Decision No 319/1970 of the Athens Court of Appeal, Court Decision No 1353/1977 of the Thessaloniki Court of Appeal.
10   Court Decision No 496/1978 of the Athens Court of Appeal.
11   Court Decision No 1962/1970 of the Athens Court of Appeal.
12   Court Decision No 2328/1967 of the Athens Court of Appeal.

prove that they substantially affect the use and value of the product.[13] In case the purchaser brings an action based on the provision of article 535 of the Code, he must present to the court those qualities which were agreed upon and those which are absent.[14] The purchaser may allege that the product had a specific substantial defect or that it lacked the represented quality at the time when the risk was transferred to him (by way of physical delivery). Where a purchaser does not invoke the facts which substantiate the application of articles 534 or 535 of the Code, the action will be rejected as vague.[15] The purchaser's allegations must be invoked at the first hearing of the action so as to enable the court to order the necessary hearing of evidence by virtue of an interlocutory decision[16] and the burden of proof lies with the purchaser. The existence, or not of a real defect can be assigned by the parties to an expert arbitrator.[17] The amount claimed as further damages must also be proved.

3.6   Exclusion or limitation of liability

Article 2 of Law 2251/1994 re: 'Consumer Protection' implements EU Directive 93/13 dated 5 April 1993[18] re: 'Unfair terms in consumer contracts'. This article provides for thirty-one indicative cases of unfair terms out of which twenty-eight reflect the indicative list included in the Appendix of the Recommendation (76) 47 of the Ministers Committee of the Council of Europe dated November 16, 1976, regarding unfair terms in consumer contracts. The said recommendation is the most complete legal sample and the basis for the recent EU Directive.

The following terms, among others, are considered as unfair terms by Law 2251/1994:

(a) those which limit the undertaken contractual obligations and liabilities of the suppliers;[19]
(b) those which reserve to the supplier the right to consider whether his performance was according to the contract;[20]
(c) those which indicate that the product need not substantially meet its specifications or the special use that the consumer requires and the supplier has accepted;[1]
(d) those which limit the supplier's liability for hidden defects of the product;[2]
(e) those which exclude or substantially limit the supplier's liability;[3] and
(f) those which provide for the transfer to the producer of the seller's or importer's liability.[4]

Article 538 of the Code provides that an agreement which excludes or limits the liability is invalid where the seller had fraudulently hidden the real defect or concealed the lack of an important quality.

13 Court Decision No 95/1965 of the Crete Court of Appeal.
14 Court Decision No 2888/1977 of the Athens Court of Appeal.
15 Court Decision No 2328/1967 of the Athens Court of Appeal.
16 Court Decision No 2888/1977 of the Athens Court of Appeal.
17 Article 339 of the Civil Code Procedure.
18 OJ of the European Communities No L 95/29
19 Para 7, case (b) of art 2 of Law 2251/1994.
20 Para 7, case (g) of art 2 of Law 2251/1994.
 1 Para 7, case (i) of art 2 of Law 2251/1994.
 2 Para 7, case (l) of art 2 of Law 2251/1994.
 3 Para 7, case (m) of art 2 of Law 2251/1994.
 4 Para 7, case (n) of art 2 of Law 2251/1994.

In practice the exclusion or limitation of the seller's liability appears in the sale of industrial products and equipment. In such cases the seller uses a form of standard contract where the purchaser's right to demand a cancellation of the sale or a decrease in the price or the payment of compensation are in place of being the only available remedies that the seller will be obliged to either replace or repair the product.

3.7   Limitation period

Article 554 of the Code provides that a limitation period (a prescription) of six months applies to claims in respect of movable property based on the existence of a real defect or on the lack of a represented quality where the action claims the remedies of the cancellation of the sale, the decrease of the price or the payment of compensation.

Article 555 of the Code provides that the limitation period of six months runs from the date of delivery of the product. The date when the purchaser discovers the defect is not considered as a starting point of the limitation period.

A deviation from this short limitation period rule is provided for by article 556 of the Code where the seller guarantees that the product will have the represented qualities and will not have any defect for a certain time period. Such an agreement is subject to a different limitation period from the one provided for by article 554 of the Code. The interpretation of the Courts as regards article 556 of the Code, is that the parties cannot agree to a shorter limitation period than the one provided for by article 555 of the Code. This would be in violation of article 275 of the Code.[5] The parties may either postpone the starting point of the limitation period or extend the limitation period within which the purchaser is entitled to exercise his rights, up to the maximum limitation period of twenty years, as provided for by article 249 of the Code.[6]

Article 557 of the Code provides that the seller cannot benefit from the short limitation period provided for by articles 554-555 of the Code where he had fraudulently concealed the defect or the lack of a represented quality. In this case the limitation period for the purchaser is twenty years. This limitation period runs from the date of delivery of the product.[7]

The prerequisite of 'fraudulent concealment' in article 557 of the Code has been decided by the courts to occur only when the seller uses misleading means to hide the real condition or the lack of a quality from the purchaser. The fact the seller was aware of the product's condition and concealed this from the purchaser in order to induce the purchaser to enter into the agreement is not sufficient for the application of this article.[8] As to the time when the seller must have concealed the defect, it is accepted by the Courts that this may occur at any time from conclusion of the agreement up to the time of delivery of the product , in order to apply the provision of article 557 of the Code.

An exception to the time limitation within which the purchaser may exercise his rights, as specified in article 534 et seq of the Code, is provided by article

---

5   Art 275 of the Code: 'Any agreement excluding the application of prescription or defining a prescription of a shorter or longer period from the one provided for by law or in general encumbering or relieving the terms of prescription, is void'.

6   Supreme Court Decisions Nos 449/1970 and 97/1971.

7   Supreme Court Decision No 423/1961.

8   Court Decision No 195/1972 of the Thessaloniki Court of First Instance, Court Decision No 924/1975 of the Thessaloniki Court of Appeal, Court Decision No 1810/1969 of the Athens Court of Appeal.

558 of the Code. This article provides that the purchaser may exercise his rights which derive from a defect in a product or a lack of a represented quality, even if the time limitation has expired, provided he had informed the seller of the same by way of a written notice within the time limitation period.

The 'notice' as provided in article 558 of the Code must be specific. It must refer specifically to the defect or the lack of the represented quality and that the purchaser reserves his rights. In order to be binding upon the seller, the notice must be received by the seller within the time limitation period.

The purchaser may raise a counter-objection against the seller's notice based on article 554 of the Code[9] by invoking articles 557 and 558 of the Code which provide the legal basis for such counter-objection. The seller has the burden of proof of the real facts he invokes with the raised counter-objections. The seller against whom the counter-objection of fraudulent concealment of a defect is brought may defend his position by raising a further counter-objection based either on article 536 of the Code (ie that the purchaser had knowledge of the defect at the time of purchase) or on article 545 of the Code (ie that the seller had unreservedly received the product having knowledge of the defect or the absence of the promised quality).

3.8 Liability for third parties

Given that in contract the contractual liabilities are with the contracting parties, third parties may be involved either on the side of the seller or on the side of the purchaser. This can occur for example when the contracting parties use third persons (employees) in discharging their obligations. In this case the liability of a debtor (that is to say a person having an obligation to tender a performance to another) extends to the acts of the persons he uses for the discharge of his obligations.[10] A debtor is responsible for the fault of the person he employs in performing his obligations to the same extent that he himself would be liable, if he was at fault himself. As to the persons used by the contracting parties, they may be employees or independent contractors. The liability of an employee vis-à-vis the other contracting party can be limited in advance by an agreement. The limitation can include fraud or gross negligence. Such limitation is also valid for the employer's liability in tort. The limitation of the liability is void when the debtor's liability is excluded in advance for slight negligence and the creditor (that is to say the person to whom the obligation is owed) is an employee of the debtor.[11]

4 LIABILITY IN TORT

4.1 Introduction

Liability in tort is regulated by the Code[12] pursuant to which whosoever unlawfully and culpably causes damages to another person is obliged to make

9 Court Decision no. 1945/1976 of the Athens Pireaus Court, Court Decision no. 2500/1968 of the Thessaloniki Court of First Instance, Court Decision no. 80.1972 of the Pireaus One-Member Court of First Instance.

10 Art 334 of the Code.

11 Art 332 of the Code.

12 Arts 914-938 of the Code.

reparation for the damage caused. Liability in tort has been broadly interpreted by the courts. As such it applies in the relevant circumstances to both producers and suppliers of defective products. A claim in tort can be made in conjuction with the provisions of articles 543-544 or 561 of the Code relating to breach of contract. In both legal theory and in decided cases it is clear that the protection of life, health and property from damage caused by defective products is secured more effectively with the application of the provisions of article 914 et seq of the Code that deal with tort liability.

The liability in tort is primary, since the obligation to make reparation for damages suffered by the victim is founded directly on law, irrespective of whether there is a contractual relationship between the victim and the person held liable. On the contrary, the liability in contract is secondary, since it arises from the contractual relationship between the parties when, due to the non-performance, the other party suffers damages.

The following elements differentiate the liability in tort from the liability in contract. For example (i) in the case of liability in tort, reparations may cover non-pecuniary damage (damage to personality),[13] whereas in the case of liability in contract this recovery is not provided; (ii) slight negligence is sufficient to establish liability in tort, whereas in the case of liability in contract and particularly, in the sale of a defective product, the liability of the seller is *quasi objective;* (iii) the burden of proof in case of liability in tort lies with the victim, whereas in the case of liability in contract the burden of proof lies with the purchaser; (iv) the prescription of a claim based on liability in tort is five (5) years, whereas in the case of a claim based on liability in contract it is usually twenty (20) years, except in some cases where the prescription is six (6) months (for example in the case of article 555 of the Code); and (v) the establishment of liability in contract for third persons employed by the seller in assisting him to perform his obligations, does not require the existence of a dependant relationship between them, whereas in the case of liability in tort this is a prerequisite.

4.2   Outline of relevant tort law giving rise to liability for personal and property damage in Greece

Liability in tort is founded on the principal of culpability, which requires the fault or culpability (dolus or negligence) of the person who caused damage and for this reason is characterised as a subjective liability. Nevertheless, in some cases the liability in tort is a *quasi* objective liability.[14]

Besides the general principle of tort law, which is embodied in article 914 of the Code, a number of more detailed provisions regulate the consequences of specific tortious acts. Some of the provisions are applied to impose liability on producers or suppliers of defective products.

In this respect the following articles of the Code are noteworthy:

(a) article 922 of the Code, which regulates vicarious liability;[15]
(b) article 926 of the Code, which regulates the liability in tort if several persons unlawfully and culpably cause harm or several persons, together are

---

13   Art 932 of the Code.
14   Art 922 of the Code *re: Liability of employees,* Art 925 of the Code *re: Collapse of building,* Law/1911 *re: Liability arising from car accidents,* Law 551/1914 *re: Employer's liability arising from labour accidents.*
15   See section 4.9. below.

responsible for a particular harm. In this case they are all held jointly and severally liable. This article has been applied by the courts with reference to consumer protection. Thus, if two or more persons are liable for the same damage (manufacturer, importer or dealer), they shall be liable jointly and severally.[16]

(c) article 927 of the Code, provides that any one person who paid the whole amount of the damage is entitled to recourse against the others who are also liable in the case and the court will determine the extent that each is liable.

(d) articles 928 and 929 of the Code, which regulate issues of personal injury and death. In these cases, claims for compensation arise in favour of persons other than the victim and they can bring an action independently. Damages include medical expenses, funeral expenses, loss of maintenance or services.

4.3   Causation – remoteness of loss and damage

Liability in tort presupposes an unlawful or contravening *bonos mores* act or omission, which has been wilfully or negligently committed by a person resulting in damage to another person or their property.

The producer's liability for defective products in the area of tort law is based on the so-called 'trading obligations',[17] which are related to specific activities. For example, a trading obligation of a producer is the obligation to organise the production procedure having considered all safety measures. Such obligation covers all the production phases starting from the design of the product, the supply of raw material up to the time the product is put into circulation including the obligation to provide instructions for the safe use of the product. Such obligation remains in force even after the circulation of the product into the market and includes the obligation to recall dangerous products.[18]

Any violation of the trade obligations either by act and/or omission substantiates an unlawful act, as provided for by article 914 of the Code. In any event, a defective product in the modern and complicated production system is a result of a combination of acts and/or omissions, such as for an example, the use of defective raw material and a faulty inspection. An unlawful act is considered a violation of regulations to prevent dangers, as well as a deviation from the regulations of prudence and security, irrespective whether the result had caused damage or not.

4.4   Quantum of damage

The producer's liability is to compensate the consumer for the damage he has suffered from the use of a defective product. The compensation may cover the direct damage and any further damage the consumer has suffered from the risk of his life, health and body integrity, as well as for non material damages. The producer is also liable for loss of profits including accrued interest, if there is sufficient evidence of the claimed loss.

---

16   In conjuction with art 6, para 10 of Law 2251/1994 which implements art 5 of the EC Directive 85/374 re: General Product Safety (OJ No L 210/29).
17   See Gazi, *The non performance of a contract,* p 50 et seq.
18   See Pouliathi, *Product recall,* p 15 et seq.

4.5   Burden of proof

The consumer-victim has the burden of proof according to the letter of law. More specifically, the victim must prove:

(a) the existence of a harmful defect of the product;
(b) the damage he has suffered;
(c) the causal link between the product's defect and the damage.

The defendant-producer has to try to prove that the defect was not caused by a faulty product.

It is obvious that it is sometimes very difficult, if not impossible, for the consumer-victim to prove that the producer was in violation of his trading obligations and as a result the defective product has caused damage. As regards the hearing of evidence in a case of product liability, court decisions[19] have reversed the burden of proof as follows:

The consumer-victim must prove the existence of a harmful defect that arose in the product during the fabrication process. Once this is proved then the defendant-producer is considered to be in violation of his trade obligations and the burden of proof is reversed in favour of the victim.

4.6   Exclusion or limitation of liability

The provisions of the Code (articles 914 et seq) that regulate liability in tort are *jus cogens*. Accordingly clauses in a contract excluding or limiting the liability of the producer have no effect on an action based in tort.

4.7   Limitation period

According to article 937 of the Code the limitation period for an action in tort is five years from the day the injured party had knowledge of the damage and of the identity of the person liable for its cause subject to a maximum in all cases of twenty years from the commission of the act. In case the violation of the trade obligation is a criminal offence with a longer prescription period, such longer prescription prevails.

4.8   Liability for third parties

Article 922 of the Code introduces strict liability in the case of liability for employees. In this case a person who appoints another to perform is bound to make reparations to a third party for the damage his employee has caused by an unlawful and culpable act or omission in the course of his duties. Therefore, employers who are manufacturers are liable for the damage caused by their employees in the course of the employees' duties. The employers have recourse against such employees and may recover all the damage they have had to pay on behalf of the employees provided the employees have been guilty of wilful misconduct or of gross negligence.

19   Court Decision No 15/1989 of the Thessaloniki Multimember Court of First Instance, Court Decision No 930/1985 of the Thessaloniki Appeal Court.

5   LIABILITY FOR DEFECTIVE PRODUCTS ARISING FROM BOTH GENERAL LAW AND IMPLEMENTATION OF EC DIRECTIVE 85/374 ON PRODUCT LIABILITY IN GREECE

5.1   Introduction

EC Directive 85/374 was implemented in Greece by article 6 of Law 2251/ 1994 re: 'Consumer Protection'. Before the introduction of the Directive and in the absence of a specific legal framework, legal theory and decisions of the courts had based producer's and supplier's liability for defective products in contract and in tort. Initially, the Directive was introduced by a joint ministerial decision B.7535/1077/31.3.1988 with effect from 30 July 1988. The provisions of the ministerial decision were replaced when the Law 1961/1991 for the protection of the consumer and other provisions' was introduced. This reversed the producer's liability from a *quasi* objective to an objective liability, which was in violation of the Directive to an objective liability. The derogation from the liability imposed by the Directive became even greater with the introduction of article 26 of Law 2000/1991 re: 'Privatisation and other provisions for the upgrade of the competition rules', pursuant to which two categories of products (ie packaged goods and those sold in bulk) were excluded from the liability of the producer.

Greek law in this area was finally put on the current footing when on 16 November 1994, Law 2251/1994 implemented the Directive on product liability in full. Some provisions of the Directive were not included in Law 2251/ 1994, such as the relevant provision for the burden of proof, since these provisions are already available by the Greek legal system. Moreover, the definition of the term 'product' is based on the meaning of the term 'thing', as this is defined by the Code.

5.2   Outline of the provisions in Greece

According to paragraph 1 of article 6 of Law 2251/1994, a producer is liable for any damage caused by a defective product. The definition of 'producer' is provided in paragraph 2 of the same article and means the manufacturer of a finished product, the producer of any raw material or the manufacturer of a component part and any person who, by putting his name, trade mark or other distinguishing feature on the product presents himself as its producer. The Directive establishes in paragraph 3 of this article the same liability, as for the producer, for any person who imports a product for sale, hire, leasing or any form of distribution in the course of his business.

'Product'' is considered as any movable including those embodied as a component of another movable or immovable. The natural powers, especially electricity and heat, given that they are restricted within a specified area, are considered to be products pursuant to the definition included in the Code.

A product is considered 'defective' when it does not provide the safety which a person is entitled to expect, taking into account the presentation of the product, the use to which it could reasonably be expected that the product would be put and the time when the product was put into circulation. A product shall not be considered defective for the sole reason that a better product is

subsequently put into circulation. This definition of a defective product is identical to that provided in the Directive.

As to the term 'damages', paragraph 6 of the said article reproduces the text of the Directive. However, the option for a lower threshold was not exercised when implementing the Directive. The non-material damage is subject to compensation and the provisions of liability in tort are applicable in this case.

5.3   Optional provisions of the EC Directive

Article 6 of Law 2251/94 ignored the option provided in article 15(1) of the Directive, thus primary agricultural products and game are not included in the definition of the 'product'.

The 'state of scientific and technical knowledge' is not available as a defence.

As already mentioned above, Law 2251/1994 does not put a ceiling on the amount of damages that can be awarded and there is no minimum threshold imposed despite the option provided by article 16(1) of the Directive.

A limitation period of three years shall apply as regards proceedings for the recovery of damages. This limitation period shall begin to run from the day on which the plaintiff became aware or should reasonably have become aware of the damage, the defect and the identity of the producer. Upon expiry of a period of ten years from the date on which the producer put the product into circulation which caused the damage, the above right shall be extinguished.

As to the limitation of the producer's liability, a list of exemptions is included in paragraph 8 of said article, which are identical to those of the Directive. The same applies as the provisions concerning third party liability and contributory negligence.

According to Greek law the liability of the producer shall not be limited when the damage is caused cumulatively by both a defect in a product and by the act and/or omission of a third party, however it may be reduced or disallowed when the damage is caused both by a defect in the product and by the fault of the injured person or any person for whom the injured person is responsible.

Additionally, the Greek text provides that any agreement restricting or exempting the producer of his liability is void.

Article 4 of the Directive is not included in Law 2251/1994. According to this article the injured person shall be required to prove the damage, the defect and the causal relationship between defect and damage. However, this omission does not discharge the plaintiff-victim from the burden of proof since same is established by our national law.

6   CRIMINAL LIABILITY FOR DEFECTIVE PRODUCTS ARISING FROM BOTH GENERAL SAFETY LAW AND THE IMPLEMENTATION OF EC DIRECTIVE 92/59 ON PRODUCT SAFETY IN GREECE

6.1   Introduction

EC Directive 92/59 of 29 June 1992 on general product safety was implemented by article 7 of Law 2251/1994.

6.2 Outline of implementation of Directive 92/59 in Greece and date of implementation

Article 7 of Law 2251/1994 reflects identically the definition of a 'safe product', as well as the safety circumstances included in article 2(b) of the Directive. Thus, a 'safe product' 'shall mean' any product which, under normal or reasonably foreseeable conditions of use, including duration, does not present any risk or only the minimum risks compatible with the product's use, considered as acceptable and consistent with a high level of protection for the safety and health of persons, taking into account the following points in particular:

(a) the characteristics of the product, including its composition, packaging, instructions for assembly and maintenance;
(b) the effect on other products, where it is reasonably foreseeable that it will be used with other products;
(c) the presentation of the product, the labelling, any instructions for its use and disposal and any other indication or information provided by the producer; and
(d) the categories of consumers at serious risk when using the product, in particular children.

Paragraph 1 of this article provides that the suppliers are obliged to place only safe products on the market. Said provision introduces an obligation supplementary to that of article 6, paragraph 5 of the same Law which defines the term 'defective product' and at the same time constitutes an autonomous rule of law, since the infringement of the article under consideration constitutes an unlawful act and triggers the application of articles 281, 288 and 914 of the Code.

According to paragraph 3 of this article, the fact that there are other products presenting a lesser degree of risk on the market or that in the particular case higher levels of safety can be achieved does not constitute grounds as such for a product to be characterised as defective.

In any case the supplier is considered to have fulfilled his obligation for placing safe products on the market if such products meet the standards approved by the EU and the Greek law.

Finally, any pertinent authority may prohibit the disposal of a specific product if it entails serious and direct risk for the health and safety of the consumers. The withdrawal, the conditional disposal, as well as the lifting or taking of measures as regards the products is regulated by the Minister of Commerce or by any other pertinent Minister.

6.3 Description of anomalous provisions on the implementation of the EC Directive 92/59

Article 7 of Law 2251/1994 which implemented EC Directive 92/59, mentions only the term 'supplier' instead of the term 'producer' and 'distributor'.

Article 7, paragraph 4 of the Law contains a general provision according to which 'suppliers' are considered to have fulfilled their obligation of placing safe products on the market, if they comply with EU and national legislation, as well as with the standards enacted in favour of health and safety of the

consumers. The article does not implement the general safety requirement of the Directive, as regards the obligation of producers to provide consumers with the relevant information enabling them to assess the risks inherent in a product, where such risks are not obvious *prima facie* without adequate warnings and to take precautions against risks. However, the article provides for the withdrawing of the product in question from the market as a protective measure of the consumers.

6.4 Description of local optional provisions

Article 14 of Law 2251/1994 provides in general, that a fine may be imposed by the Ministry of Commerce amounting from 500,000 drachmae to 20 million drachmae for any infringement of the provisions of Law 2251/1994 by suppliers. In case of a second offence the fine is doubled. The Minister of Commerce following an opinion of the National Council of Consumers may order the enterprise or part of it to cease the operations for a period not exceeding one year in case of repetitive breaches.

The issues related to the compliance with directives, decisions, regulations and recommendations issued by the EU pertaining to consumption and protection of consumers are regulated by joint decisions of the Ministers of Commerce, National Economy, Justice and of any other pertinent Minister. By virtue of the above ministerial acts any supplementary measure for the application of the above may be taken.

The Ministry of Commerce is the basic regulatory authority as regards the protection of consumers and promotion of safety measures. Law 2251/1994 provides also for a new organ named 'National Consumer Council' (NCC). NCC is an opinion-rendering body attached to the Minister of Commerce. It consists of nineteen members, of which nine are appointed by Consumers Associations (CAs). The remaining members are appointed by various professional bodies or organisations. The main task of NCC is to submit its proposals to the Minister of Commerce for matters regarding the protection of consumers, promotion of consumers' interests, etc. Furthermore, NCC renders its opinion, albeit non-binding, for bills concerning or affecting consumer protection.

CAs having at least five hundred active members and registered with the Registry of CAs may file a class action against suppliers in order to protect consumers' interests claiming:

(i) prevention of any unlawful act or behaviour of a supplier, even before it takes place, as a preventive means of protection. Such act or behaviour may concern abusive contractual terms, prohibited outdoor sales, violation of the obligation of after sale services, production or importation or distribution of defective products etc;

(ii) compensation due to moral (non-pecuniary) harm. The amount to be paid is determined by the court on the basis of the particular facts of each case; if said claim is rejected by the court the defendant-supplier may counter-claim compensation from the CA and in person from its board members, both being held liable jointly and severally; and

(iii) injunctive relief to secure claims under paras (i) & (ii) until the issuance of a final court ruling.

As regards the issue of whether the term 'product', as defined by EC Directive 85/374 and implemented by Law 2251/1994, includes capital goods

which are not owned by the consumers but are used by them (eg escalators, elevators, etc), the interpretation of the relevant definition in Law 2251/1994 does not leave any grounds to establish its application to such goods. Case law has not as yet interpreted said definition so as to apply the special protection on capital goods of Law 2251/1994.

As regards EEC Council Decisions 84/133 and 89/45 these have not been implemented by our national law.

6.5   Other product safety laws

Besides Law 2251/1995, the 'Code for marketing and pricing of products' (*Agoranomikos Kodikas*) provides for the terms and conditions a product must meet in order to be placed in the market (ie packaging, labelling, etc). As an example, the label of the product must be in the Greek language and must reflect the ingredients of the product, the tradename of the producer, the origin of the product, the volume, the instructions for the proper and safe use and preservance of the product, the expiration date, etc. A joint liability of the producer and the importer is established in case the provisions regulating the above issues (labelling, etc) are violated.

Pharmaceutical products which may affect the health or safety of consumers are subject to registration with the National Drug Organisation (EOF in Greek). The procedure of registering a pharmaceutical product with EOF and obtaining the relevant approval before being put into circulation, consists in filing a petition which contains various information concerning the product, such as the trade name or trademark of the product, a description of the product's form, name of the petitioner, name of the manufacturer, the composition (ingredients) of the product, details of its labelling, the place of manufacture, samples of the product, etc. In case the product is imported from a non-EU country a certificate evidencing the appointment of an agent/representative of the producer in Greece is required. Such a certificate is not required if the product is imported from an EU member state.

As regards pharmaceutical products, the following EC Directives have been implemented by national law:

- 65/65, dated 26 January 1965;
- 75/318, dated 20 March 1975;
- 75/319, dated 20 May 1975;
- 78/25, dated 12 December 1977;
- 81/464, dated 24 June 1981;
- 83/570, dated 26 October 1983;
- 87/21, dared 22 December 1986;
- 89/341, dated 3 May 1989;
- 89/342, dated 25 May 25 1989;
- 91/507, dated 26 September 1991; and
- 93/39, dated 14 June 1993.

The Foods and Beverages Code (FBC) regulates the preparation, processing, marketing and approval of food products contributing to the consumer protection. The relevant Greek legislation follows European patterns and EU legislation implemented into the Greek legal order. FBC contains various provisions concerning the preparation, disposition, processing of foods, storage of foods, dietary foods, import and export of foods, labelling, advertising,

sampling, test of samples, chemical analysis etc. FBC devotes other chapters to packaging, additives, beverages and various generic food categories such as milk, fats and oil, meat, fish and seafood, cereals, coffee, tea, sweeteners, etc.

More specifically, the preparation and marketing of any kind of food whatsoever, requires the prior approval of the Supreme Chemical Council (AXS in Greek). In some cases the Supreme Hygiene Council (AYS in Greek) is involved in order to grant its approval as well.

FBC determines a number of food standards for various food categories concerning the basic and optional ingredients of a product, its analytical elements, as well as the manner of industrial or other processing, production, preservation and conservation of foods. The importance of the standards is focused on the principle that any product complying with such standards does not need a specific approval by AXS before being introduced in the market, in which cases such approval is deemed to be granted. Thus, any producer may place on the market food products complying with the standards, provided that he possesses the necessary means, premises and experience for such purpose. Nonetheless, AXS reserves the right to temporarily suspend or definitely rescind any such approval, if the producer does not have the necessary means, premises or experience for that purpose or the foods do not comply with the relevant standards or they are adulterated, etc.

7   CIVIL LIABILITY FOR DEFECTIVE PRODUCTS BROUGHT ABOUT BY BREACH OF STATUTORY REGULATION DESIGNED TO PROTECT CONSUMERS AND/OR TO PROMOTE SAFETY

As already mentioned in section 5 above, the basic legal framework for the protection of consumers for defective products is Law 2251/1994. Therefore, any violation of said Law triggers the application of its provisions, as well as the provisions of the Code. However, article 14 under title 'Transitional Provisions' of Law 2251/1994 mentions in paragraph 5, that if in a certain case of product liability the provisions of the Code offer the consumer greater protection than the provisions of the Law, then same must be applicable. An exception is made only as regards the provisions referring to prescription and exclusive term.

As the above provisions apply under Law 2251/1994 the mechanics of their implementation are as set out above.

CHAPTER IX

Ireland

Hugh Garvey Esq

L K Shields & Partners
39/40 Upper Mount Street
Dublin 2
Ireland

Tel: ++ 3531 661 0866
Fax: ++ 3531 661 0883

CHAPTER IX

Ireland

1 AN INTRODUCTION TO THE IRISH LEGAL SYSTEM

There are four main sources of law. The primary source is the 1937 Constitution, *Bunreacht na hEireann*. The second source is legislation, statute law, passed by those Parliaments which had jurisdiction over Ireland before 1922 as well as the *Oireachtas* (Parliament) which existed during the Irish Free State (1922-1936) and, finally, the *Oireachtas* which operates under the 1937 Constitution. The third source is common law, the rules developed by judges in decided cases both prior to and also since 1922. These rules are constantly being refined and further explained in cases which proceed through the courts. Judges play an important role in the manner in which existing laws, including common law rules, are applied in practice. Irish judges pay great attention to what has been decided in similar cases in the past including cases decided outside the jurisdiction. The deference to previous decisions is a central feature of a common law legal system and is known as the Doctrine of Precedent. This doctrine provides a guideline for a judge deciding a case today while not being strictly binding upon him. The fourth source of Irish law is the law which the European Union has generated which has become part of Irish law since Ireland joined the European Union in 1972.

When deciding cases, Irish judges are obliged to have regard to the provisions of the Irish Constitution to ensure that they are being adhered to. If a statutory provision is in conflict with any provision of the Constitution, the Constitution will prevail and the statutory provision shall be declared unconstitutional. Irish statute law takes precedence over decided cases and if there is a conflict between a statute and a decided case, the statute will prevail. If a provision of Irish statute law has resulted from Ireland's membership of the European Union, however, there is an express provision in the Constitution that if the enactment was necessary for Ireland to fulfil its obligations as a member of the European Union then it will not be declared invalid because it is inconsistent with a provision of the Constitution. The Constitution expressly provides in article 19.4.3 that 'no provision of the Constitution invalidates laws enacted, acts done or measures adopted by the State necessitated by the obligation of membership of the Communities or prevents laws enacted, acts done or measures adopted by the Communities, or institutions thereof, from having the force of law in the State'. Therefore, the Treaty of Rome and Directives, Regulations and other legislative enactments made thereunder take precedence over the provisions of the Constitution.

223

2   OVERVIEW OF THE LAW RELATING TO DEFECTIVE PRODUCTS IN IRELAND

Under Irish law there are a number of ways by which liability may be imposed on manufacturers of defective goods. Liability may arise by virtue of tort, contract or statute law and each will be considered in greater detail below. The following is a brief summary of the main principles involved.

2.1   Tort

Liability in tort for negligence in the manufacture of goods depends principally on the establishment of the following factors:

(a) that the manufacturer owed the injured party a duty of care when producing the goods;
(b) that the manufacturer failed in this duty of care; and
(c) that as a result of this failure the injured party suffered the injury of which he complains.

Perhaps the greatest difficulty for the injured party suing in negligence is to establish the existence of a duty of care in the particular circumstances. Further, in tort the question of whether economic loss is recoverable or not frequently arises. Tort also affords the manufacturer, in certain circumstances, the ability to exclude or reduce his liability to injured parties. The topic of exclusion of liability is dealt with in detail later in this chapter.

2.2   Contract

In addition to the terms which a manufacturer or retailer of goods and the consumer of such goods may agree in their contract, legislation also imposes certain conditions, such as merchantability and fitness for purpose. However, the manufacturer/retailer is restricted by statute in his ability to exclude many such terms. The establishment of liability under contract may be difficult because of the doctrine of privity of contract which means that for a party to have obligations or rights under a contract it is necessary for him to be a party to the contract. Thus, if the person injured by defective goods has no contractual relationship with the manufacturer or the retailer, contract law may not afford him a remedy.

2.3   Statute

Manufacturers may be liable in respect of defective products by virtue of statute law and statutory instruments. However the statutes or regulations concerned frequently cover a restricted range of products and the liability imposed by such statutes or statutory instruments is frequently criminal as opposed to civil. The issue of whether one can obtain civil compensation for breach of a statute or statutory instrument is discussed later in the chapter.

2.4   Product safety

The General Product Safety Directive EC 92/59 ('the Product Safety Directive') is intended to protect consumers against unsafe products. At the time of writing,

legislation has not been enacted to implement the Product Safety Directive into Irish Law.

2.5   Product liability

One statute, pursuant to whose provisions liability may arise, is the Liability for Defective Products Act, 1991 ('the 1991 Act') which became part of Irish Law on 16 December, 1991. The 1991 Act gives effect to the provisions of the Product Liability Directive EC 85/374 ('Directive 85/374'). The 1991 Act does not supplant any pre-existing tortuous, contractual or statutory remedies which may otherwise be available. The 1991 Act incorporates the text of Directive 85/374 as a Schedule to the 1991 Act.

As regards the derogations allowed by Directive 85/374 the following are to be noted:

(1) Directive 85/374 allowed member states to include primary agricultural products as being within the definition of 'products'. Ireland did not do so.
(2) The 1991 Act makes provision for the 'development risks' or 'state of the art' Defence (Directive 85/374 had given member states a discretion as to whether this Defence would be available in their respective jurisdictions).

2.6   Consumer guarantees

A guarantee is defined as meaning 'Any document, notice or other written statement, howsoever described, supplied by a manufacturer or other supplier, other than a retailer, in connection with the supply of any goods, and indicating that the manufacturer or other supplier will service, repair or otherwise deal with goods following purchase'.[1] Consumer guarantees normally arise in the context of a contractual relationship between the parties. Certain legal provisions relating to consumer guarantees are discussed later.

3   PRE-CONTRACTUAL LIABILITY

Being a common law jurisdiction Irish law does not encompass a doctrine of pre-contractual liability in the way that many civil law jurisdictions do.

It does, however, allow claims to be brought for misrepresentation.

3.1   Effect on the interpretation and extent of the obligations of the parties to a contract

As stated by Cheshire, Fifoot and Furmston:[2]

A representation is a statement of fact made by one party to the contract (the representor) to the other (the representee) which, while not forming a term of the contract, it is yet one of the reasons that induces the representee to enter into the contract. A misrepresentation is simply a representation that is untrue.

1   Section 15 of the Sale of Goods & Supply of Services Act, 1980.
2   At p 257.

A representation must be a statement of fact and not of intention, opinion or law. However, a statement of opinion may be a misrepresentation if it is an opinion not truly held or even if the representor had an opportunity to check its validity and the representee did not have such an opportunity.[3] An example of an opinion which was held not to be a representation is found in the case of *Bisset v Wilkinson*[4] where the defendant said that in his opinion land he was selling to the plaintiff would hold 2,000 sheep. The land had not previously been a sheep farm and the opinion, though wrong, was found to be honestly held and not a representation.

3.2   Extent that non-disclosure of facts during negotiations may lead to liability

For there to be a representation there must be a statement. However, silence, it has been held, may be a representation in the following circumstances:

(a) Where silence distorts a positive representation;
(b) Where the contract requires the utmost good faith (*uberrimae fides*), eg, insurance contracts; or
(c) Where the representation alleged is a case of silence or non-disclosure as opposed to a positive false disclosure, the question as to whether the contract is void depends on whether the representation related to a material fact of the contract. In the *Chariot Inns* case[5] the test was stated by Kenny J in the Supreme Court to be:

> It is not what the person seeking insurance regards as material, nor is it what the insurance company regards as material. It is a matter or circumstance which would reasonably influence the judgment of a prudent insurer in deciding whether he would take the risk and, if so, in determining the premium which he would demand.

A general duty of disclosure also exists where a fiduciary relationship exists between the parties.[6]

A false statement alone does not give rise to a cause of action. The statement must be one of the reasons the plaintiff entered into the contract. It follows that if the plaintiff did not allow the representation influence his decision to enter into the contract, no cause of action arises for the representation.[7]

Similarly, if the plaintiff was aware of the untruth of the representation at the time it was made he cannot subsequently seek to rely on it to found a cause of action.

There are three classes of representation and misrepresentation. These classes are relevant in determining what remedy attaches to the particular representation or misrepresentation at issue. A summary of the classes of misrepresentation is treated under the following heading.

3 *Esso Petroleum v Mardon* [1976] 2 WLR at 583.
4 [1927] AC 177.
5 *Chariot Inns Limited v Assicurazioni Generali SpA and Coyle Hamilton* [1981] 1 ILRM 173, SC.
6 *Dunbar v Tredennick* (1813) 2 Ball & B 304, Ch.
7 *Smith v Chadwick* (1884) 9 App Cas 187 and *Smith v Lynn* (1954) 85 ILTR at 57. In the latter case the court held that the plaintiff had not relied on the representation of the defendant but had relied on his own inspection of the premises.

3.3 Does pre-contractual liability lie in contract or in tort?

There are three classes of representation or misrepresentation.

3.3.1 Fraudulent misrepresentation

Fraudulent misrepresentation is where the representor makes a false statement which at the time he makes the representation he did not honestly believe to be true.[8]

3.3.2 Negligent misrepresentation

In *Derry v Peek*[9] the House of Lords ruled that an action would lie in the tort of deceit for a fraudulent misrepresentation but there is no liability in deceit for a false statement made carelessly and without reasonable grounds for believing it to be true. For liability to attach to a false statement there needs to be a contractual or a fiduciary relationship between the parties.

In *Hedley Byrne v Heller and Partners*[10] the House of Lords held that liability for negligent misstatements could arise in tort. In *Stafford v Keane Mahony Smith*[11] the requirements for liability to attach to a negligent statement were stated to be that:

> there must first of all be a person conveying the information or the representation relied upon; secondly there must be a person to whom that information is intended to be conveyed or to whom it might reasonably be expected that the information will be conveyed; thirdly, the person must act upon such information or representation to his detriment so as to show that he is entitled to damages.

3.3.3 Innocent misrepresentation

An innocent misrepresentation is a misrepresentation which is neither fraudulent nor negligent and gives the plaintiff limited redress.

Section 45(1) of the 1980 Act has created a statutory right of damages for a misrepresentation not made fraudulently, ie negligently or innocently. However, section 45(1) of the 1980 Act enables the representor to avoid liability if the representor believed and had reasonable grounds for believing the truth of the statement.

3.3.4 Incorporation of pre-contractual statements

Not every statement which precedes a contract will be held to form part of the contract. A pre-contractual statement having no contractual effect may be called a 'mere puff' or a mere representation. Such statements are treated as mere representations or puffs if the representation was not seriously meant and the other party ie the representee, should have realised this.

A pre-contractual statement may be held to be part of the ensuing contract if it falls under the category of 'warranty' although the formal use of the expression 'warrant' does not have to be used.[12]

---

8   *Carbin v Somerville* [1933] IR 227 SC and *Pearson v Dublin Corpn* [1907] 2 IR 27.
9   [1889] 14 App Cas at 337.
10 [1964] AC at 465.
11 [1980] ILRM at 53, HC.
12 *Scales v Scanlan* (1843) 6 Irish Law Reports at 367, Exchequer.

The view of the Irish Courts as to whether a pre-contractual statement is a mere representation, which is not incorporated into the contract, or a warranty which is, was expressed by Kenny J in *Bank of Ireland v Smith* [13] where he stated that modern cases showed a welcome tendency to 'regard a representation made in connection with the sale as being a warranty unless the person who made it can show that he was innocent of fault in connection with it'. The meaning of 'innocent of fault' in this regard is unclear but it is submitted that it should be taken as an expression of no more than an honestly held opinion.

It is accordingly a matter of construction as to whether a pre-contractual statement has been incorporated into a contract.

3.3.5   Statements, representations and the 1991 Act

The manner in which pre-contractual statements or representations may be relevant to the 1991 Act arises perhaps most directly from section 5 of the 1991 Act. This section sets out factors to be taken into account when determining whether a product is defective. It provides:

> For the purpose of this Act a product is defective if it fails to provide the safety which a person is entitled to expect, taking all the circumstances into account, including:
> (a) the presentation of the product;
> (b) the use to which it could reasonably be expected that the product would be put; and
> (c) the time when the product was put into circulation.

The relevance of a pre-contractual statement or representation is clear when consideration is given to section 5.1(b). The use to which one could reasonably expect that a product would be put may be dependant upon pre-contractual statements or representations. For example, where a purchaser is unsure whether a product will meet his needs and the vendor represents that the product will in fact meet his needs, such a representation may be treated as a pre-contractual statement. In circumstances such as these it would seem that the product could be held to be defective by virtue of section 5 if damage is caused while the product was being utilised in the manner which the vendor represented that it could be used. In summary, a representation will be incorporated into the contract if it:

(a) is a statement of fact made by one party to the contract;
(b) is made to the other party to the contract;
(c) is one of the reasons that induce the party to whom it is made to enter into the contract.

Section 46 of the 1980 Act is relevant where the vendor of goods attempts to restrict his liability to the purchaser in respect of a pre-contractual statement or representation. The section provides that where an agreement contains a provision attempting to exclude or restrict the liability of one party (usually the vendor of goods), for misrepresentations made by him before the contract was made, or where the contract contains a provision limiting a remedy available to another party to the contract by reason of such a misrepresentation, then the provision restricting the vendor's liability is not enforceable unless it is shown that it is fair and reasonable.

---

13   [1966] IR 646.

The term 'fair and reasonable' is defined in a Schedule to the 1980 Act by reference to the circumstances which were or ought reasonably to have been known or in the contemplation of the parties when the contract was made including the relative bargaining position of the parties, whether the purchaser had the option of entering into a similar contract with another vendor, but without the offending term, whether the purchaser knew or ought to have known of the existence of the term and whether the goods involved were manufactured, processed or adapted to the special order of the purchaser.

Therefore it is, at least in theory, possible to limit any liability which a party may have in respect of a misrepresentation. However, it should be noted that the 1980 Act restricts the vendor's ability to exclude liability for a misrepresentation which offends the conditions implied into the contract by section 10 of the 1980 Act.

4 LIABILITY IN CONTRACT

4.1 Outline of contract law relevant to defective products in Ireland

The law of contract in Ireland on the sale of goods is broadly covered by the terms of the 1980 Act. Prior to the 1980 Act this area was regulated by the 1893 Act. As we shall see the 1980 Act incorporates terms into contracts falling within its ambit in respect of matters such as the quality and safety of goods and sales by sample and/or description.

In addition, consumer rights have been bolstered by the Unfair Contract Terms Directive EC 13/93 ('Directive 13/93') which was enacted into Irish law by statutory instrument entitled the European Communities (Unfair Terms in Consumer Contracts) Regulations 1995 ('the 1995 Regulations'). The 1995 Regulations apply to contracts between a consumer and the seller of goods or the supplier of a service where the contract has not been individually negotiated between the parties.

Furthermore, as stated above, the 1991 Act does not alter the pre-existing position with regard to any liability whether in contract, tort or under statute.

4.2 Contractual warranties relating to quality of goods and safety of goods

In relation to the quality of goods the relevant provisions are contained in section 10 of the 1980 Act, whereas in relation to safety of goods there are provisions contained in numerous pieces of legislation including the Health, Safety and Welfare at Work Act 1989.

4.2.1 *Quality of goods*

Section 10 of the 1980 Act, which incorporates section 14 of the 1893 Act, states that there is no implied condition or warranty as to the quality or fitness for any particular purpose of goods supplied under a contract of sale. However, the section goes on to state that where the seller sells goods in the course of a business there is an implied condition that the goods supplied are of merchantable quality. This implied condition will not apply:

(a) to defects specifically drawn to the buyer's attention before the contract is made; or

(b) (if the buyer examines the goods before the contract is made), to defects which that examination ought to have revealed.

The section goes on to state that goods are of merchantable quality:

if they are as fit for the purpose or purposes for which goods of that kind are commonly bought and as durable as it is reasonable to expect having regard to any description applied to them, the price (if relevant) and all other relevant circumstances.

Where the seller sells goods in the course of a business and the buyer makes known (either expressly or impliedly) to the seller any particular purpose for which the goods are being bought then there is an implied condition that the goods supplied under the contract are reasonably fit for that purpose, whether or not that is a purpose for which such goods are commonly supplied. This implied term may be negatived where it can be shown that the buyer did not rely on or it was unreasonable for him to rely on the seller's skill or judgment in relation to the particular purpose. Furthermore, an implied condition or warranty as to quality or fitness for a particular purpose may be annexed to a contract of sale by usage.

Section 12 of the 1980 Act implies into contracts for the sale of goods a warranty that spare parts and an adequate after-sales service will be made available by the seller in such circumstances as are stated in an offer, description or advertisement by the seller on behalf of the manufacturer or on his own behalf and for such a period as is so stated or if no period is so stated for a reasonable period. The section allows the relevant Minister, by order, to state what constitutes a reasonable period. Any term of a contract exempting the seller from all or any of the provisions of section 12 is void.

Section 13 of the 1980 Act sets out conditions implied in every contract for the sale of motor vehicles. The section implies (except where the buyer is a person whose business it is to deal in motor vehicles) a condition that at the time of delivery of the vehicle it is free from any defect which would render it a danger to the public, including persons travelling in the vehicle. However, this condition is not to be implied if the seller and buyer have agreed that the vehicle is not intended for use in the condition in which it is delivered and a statement to that effect is signed by or on behalf of the seller and the buyer and given to the buyer before or on delivery and that the agreement between the buyer and the seller that the vehicle is not to be used in its condition when delivered is fair and reasonable. Other provisions relating to the quality of goods in section 13 of the 1893 Act are incorporated in the 1980 Act and provide that where goods are sold by description there is an implied condition that the goods shall correspond with the description. If goods are sold by example as well as by description it is not sufficient that the bulk of the goods correspond with the sample if they do not also correspond with the description. The section further states that there can be a sale by description notwithstanding the fact that the goods so sold, being exposed for sale, are selected by the buyer.

In relation to sales by sample section 15 of the 1893 Act (incorporated in the 1980 Act) states that in contracts for sale by sample three terms are implied:

(a) a condition that the bulk corresponds with the sample in quality; and
(b) a condition that the buyer shall have a reasonable opportunity of comparing the bulk with the sample; and
(c) a condition that the goods shall be free from any defect rendering them unmerchantable which would not be apparent on reasonable examination of the sample.

The ability to exclude some of these terms is discussed later in the chapter.[14]

i Advantages of contractual liability Although contractual liability may arise from negligence,[15] where a representor does not use reasonable care, it may also be strict, such as where there is a breach of a warranty as to quality or fitness of goods for a particular purpose. It was held in *Henry Kendall & Son Ltd v William Lillico & Sons*[16] that liability for breach of such a warranty would be imposed even where the defect was such that 'the utmost skill and judgment on the part of the seller' would not have detected it.

An advantage of contractual liability is that in certain circumstances not only may the contracting party reject the defective goods, he may also recover compensation for any damage flowing from their use. In addition, in contract the limitation period is greater than for some actions in tort. A further advantage is that the contracting party may be able to claim compensation in contract for purely financial loss. While this may also be recoverable in tort under the Hedley Byrne principle, there are, in tort, certain requirements to be overcome such as the existence of a 'special relationship' between the parties.

The major disadvantage of contractual liability arises from the doctrine of privity of contract which allows only those who are parties to the contract to sustain an action in contract. While the purchaser may claim against his immediate vendor, any person who used the goods without any contractual relationship with the vendor may have no remedy in contract for any defect which may cause him loss.

ii Implied terms in hire purchase contracts The implied statutory terms in a contract for the sale of goods apply to the vendor. In hire purchase contracts on the other hand the implied statutory terms apply to the owner. Sections 25-38 of the 1980 Act govern the terms implied in hire purchase contracts. These sections contain similar provisions in relation to title, letting by description, sample, etc as are implied in contracts for the sale of goods.

iii Conditions and warranties With regard to breach, not all terms of a contract are of the same importance. At common law all terms of a contract were independent. If two parties had entered into a contract with one another and one was in breach of a term of the contract, the other had to fulfil his side of the contract and sue for the loss which he suffered as a result of the breach by the other party. Later (Lord Mansfield in *Kingston v Preston*)[17] it was stated that there were three types of contractual covenants:

(a) dependent covenants, ie there was a condition precedent to the particular covenant arising at all;[18] and
(b) concurrent conditions, ie where the conditions applicable to the plaintiff and those applicable to the defendant had to be performed together and one party could not sue in respect of non-performance by the other unless he himself had or was willing to peform his conditions; and
(c) independent covenants, ie where the plaintiff could sue in respect of the non-performance of the defendant without reference to his own covenant.

14 See pp 236, 246.
15 See p 227 ff.
16 [1969] 2 AC 31.
17 (1773) 2 Doug 689.
18 *Re Application of Butler* [1970] IR 45, HC.

The difficulty in the interpretation of conditions in contracts and the importance of these conditions is recognised by section 11(2) of the 1893 Act (now part of section 10 of the 1980 Act) which states:

> whether a stipulation in a contract of sale is a condition, the breach of which may give rise to a right to treat the contract as repudiated, or a warranty, the breach of which may give rise to a claim for damages but not to a right to reject the goods and treat the contract as repudiated, depends in each case on the construction of the contract. A stipulation may be a condition, though called a warranty in the contract.

In deciding whether a term is a condition or a warranty Irish courts tend to look at the contract in the light of all the surrounding circumstances of the case and then to decide what the parties had intended the term of the contract to be.[19] It should be noted that many of the terms implied into contracts for the sale of goods under the 1980 Act (section 10) are deemed to be conditions. Therefore if the seller is in breach of any of these conditions the buyer may be entitled to repudiate the contract pursuant to the 1980 Act. It should also be noted that under section 11(1) of the 1893 Act (now incorporated in section 10 of the 1980 Act) the buyer is given the option of treating a breach of any condition imposed upon the seller as if it were a breach of warranty and seeking damages and not repudiation of the contract.

4.2.2   Safety of goods

The 1980 Act regulates, inter alia, the quality or fitness of goods. However, it may be argued that the effect in practice of section 10 of the 1980 Act, and specifically the implied condition therein as to the merchantable quality of goods supplied under contract, is to lay down a minimum safety standard which has to be met by all goods supplied under contracts covered by the 1980 Act. It could also be argued that the definition of merchantable quality, which requires the goods to be as fit for the purpose or purposes for which goods of that kind are commonly bought and as durable as it is reasonable to expect, in effect means that manufacturers should produce goods of a reasonable standard of safety as it is difficult to see how goods could comply with the definition of merchantable quality and yet be unsafe.

Where a party is injured by defective goods supplied under contract the normal course is to bring an action in negligence.[20] The safety of goods itself is not yet dealt with in any comprehensive manner in any legislation. This is perhaps due to the fact that there is such a wide variety of goods that the drafting of any legislation attempting to lay down minimum safety standards for each product would indeed be difficult.

Consumers expect that products which they purchase will live up to certain standards of safety. In most transactions the consumer will enter into a contractual relationship with the retailer of the product and not the manufacturer. Since the contract is normally with the retailer, it is the retailer who will normally bear the consequences of an action for breach of contract if the goods fail to meet the required standard of safety. In such circumstances the purchaser has the option of bringing an action in contract against the retailer or an action in tort against the manufacturer.

---

19   *Bensten & Son v Taylor* [1893] 2 QB 274.
20   See section 4.8, p 239 ff.

While the law of negligence in general terms imposes certain safety standards upon manufacturers, the legislature has not yet enacted a great deal of legislation dealing with safety standards required for specific products. The areas where the legislature has provided for minimum standards are areas where the products concerned affect public health. For example, legislation covers the sale of food and drugs,[1] the production of pharmaceuticals[2] and medical and health preparations.[3]

4.2.3 Commercial practice in giving consumer guarantees

Consumer guarantees by their nature vary from product to product. Indeed, it is generally open to the manufacturer, the supplier or retailer to decide whether or not a guarantee is granted. Furthermore the duration and scope of the guarantee (ie whether it covers the entire product or merely certain components) is also largely at the discretion of the guarantor.

That being said, the 1980 Act imposes certain statutory requirements as to the format and content of guarantees as outlined below.

4.2.4 Legal provisions regulating the form and content of legal guarantees

Sections 15 to 19 of the 1980 Act establish a quasi-contractual relationship between the purchaser and the manufacturer or intermediate supplier of goods, including an importer where such goods are supplied under a guarantee.

A guarantee is defined by the 1980 Act as meaning:

> Any document, notice or other written statement, howsoever described, supplied by a manufacturer or other supplier, other than a retailer, in connection with the supply of any goods and indicating that the manufacturer or other supplier will service, repair or otherwise deal with the goods following purchase.[4]

i Form and content of guarantees Section 16 of the 1980 Act imposes certain requirements as to the form and content of guarantees:

(1) A guarantee shall be clearly legible and shall refer only to specific goods or to one category of goods.
(2) A guarantee shall state clearly the name and address of the person supplying the guarantee.
(3) A guarantee shall state clearly the duration of the guarantee from the date of purchase but different periods may be stated for different components of any goods.
(4) A guarantee shall state clearly the procedure for presenting a claim under the guarantee which procedure shall not be more difficult than ordinary or normal commercial procedure.
(5) A guarantee shall state clearly what the manufacturer or other supplier undertakes to do in relation to the goods and what charges, if any, including the cost of carriage, the buyer must meet in relation to such undertaking.

Section 16 of the 1980 Act also provides that failure by a manufacturer or other supplier of goods to comply with the section is an offence for which

---

1 Sale of Food and Drugs Act 1875-1936 and Regulations thereunder.
2 Misuse of Drugs Act 1977.
3 Health Acts 1947 to 1970.
4 Section 15 of the 1980 Act.

criminal liability may be imposed. The 1980 Act also provides for the imposition of civil liability on a supplier, retailer or manufacturer under sections 17 to 19.

ii   Liability of seller under guarantee   Where the seller of goods delivers a guarantee to the buyer, irrespective of when or how it is delivered, the seller shall be liable to the buyer for the observance of the terms of the guarantee as if he were the guarantor, unless he expressly indicates the contrary to the buyer at the time of delivery.[5] Where however, the seller provides his own written undertaking to the buyer that he will service, repair or otherwise deal with the goods following purchase it is presumed, unless the contrary is proved, that the seller has not made himself liable to the buyer under the guarantee so delivered.[6] Furthermore section 17(4) provides that the liability of a seller to a buyer under this section is without prejudice to the rights conferred on the buyer under section 19.

iii   Exclusion of purchaser's rights under guarantee   Section 18 of the 1980 Act bolsters the rights of the purchaser by seeking to prevent the supplier, manufacturer or retailer from evading liability imposed upon him either by common law or by statute:
Section 18 provides:

(1)   Rights under a guarantee shall not in any way exclude or limit the rights of a buyer at common law or pursuant to statute and every provision in a guarantee which imposes obligations on the buyer which are additional to his obligations under the contract shall be void.

(2)   A provision in a guarantee which purports to make the guarantor or any person acting on his behalf the sole authority to decide whether goods are defective or whether the buyer is otherwise entitled to present a claim shall be void.[7]

iv   Rights of action under guarantee   Section 19 of the 1980 Act provides that the purchaser has a right of action against the manufacturer or other supplier who fails to observe any of the terms of the guarantee as if that manufacturer or supplier had sold the goods to the buyer and had committed a breach of warranty. In addition, the Court may order that the manufacturer or supplier take such steps as are necessary to observe the terms of the guarantee. Furthermore damages may be awarded as a result of a failure to observe the guarantee's terms.[8]

Guarantees can only be discussed in general terms due to their specific nature varying from product to product. However, it is clear that a consumer may maintain an action against a producer if the safety of a product is guaranteed and such a product transpires to be defective during the period of guarantee.

5   Section 17(1) of the 1980 Act.
6   Section 17(2) of the 1980 Act.
7   Section 18, sub-section 2 of the 1980 Act.
8   Section 19, sub-section 1 of the 1980 Act. In this sub-section the term buyer includes 'all persons who acquire title to the goods within the duration of the guarantee and, where the goods are imported, manufacturer includes the importer' thus it appears even the recipient of a present during the duration of the guarantee may maintain an action against a manufacturer or other supplier who fails to observe any of the terms of the guarantee.

4.3   Breach of contract for the supply of defective products

4.3.1   Types of defect

The types of defect which will be held to infringe section 14(2) of the 1893
Act (incorporated into section 10 of the 1980 Act) are those which render the
goods supplied of unmerchantable quality. This is so save where the defect has
been specifically drawn to the attention of the purchaser before the contract is
made or where the purchaser examines the goods before the contract is made
in which case the vendor will not be liable for any defects which the examination
ought to have revealed. Section 14(3) of the 1893 Act (incorporated into section
10 of the 1980 Act) states that goods are of merchantable quality:

> if they are as fit for the purpose or purposes for which goods of that kind are
> commonly bought and as durable as it is reasonable to expect having regard to
> any descriptions applied to them, the price (if relevant) and all other relevant
> circumstances.

The definition of merchantable quality would appear to exclude products
unmerchantable due purely to an aesthetic defect. This of course might not be
the case where the article bought was an aesthetic article and was sold as such.

4.3.2   Causation

Liability under the 1980 Act flows from a finding that the product does
not comply with the requirements of the Act. Once this is established the
purchaser becomes entitled to redress.

However, where the plaintiff alleges loss arising from a breach of contract
he must, as in tort, prove that there is a causal connection between the
defendant's breach of contract and his loss.[9] Much of what is stated on causation
in the section dealing with tort[10] is equally relevant. The courts have avoided
laying down any formal test for causation preferring to ascertain whether a
particular breach of contract is a sufficiently substantial cause of a particular
plaintiff's loss. As in tort the intervening acts of third parties and the plaintiff
himself are important in establishing if there is a causal connection.

4.3.3   Remoteness of loss and damage

The area of damages and breach of contract was fully considered in *Hadley v
Baxendale*.[11]

The loss which the plaintiff may recover for breach of contract is the loss
which was, at the time of the contract, a reasonably foreseeable consequence
of the breach. The knowledge of the parties at the time of the contract is
therefore important.

In *Heron II*[12] the House of Lords potentially widened the defendant's
liability by holding that the question was not whether the defendant should
have foreseen the damage but rather whether the probability of its occurrence
should have been within the reasonable contemplation of the parties at the time
the contract was made, having regard to their knowledge at that time.

---

9   *Sykes v Midland Bank Executor and Trustee Co Ltd* [1971] 1 QB 113.
10   See section 5.3, p 242 ff.
11   (1854) 9 Exch 341.
12   [1969] 1 AC 350.

In *Lee and Donoghue v Rowan*[13] a farmer had to destroy his crops when a drying shed which he was having erected was not completed in accordance with the contract. Though this damage was held not recoverable, as it was not within the reasonable contemplation of the defendant, the plaintiff was allowed the estimated costs of putting his crops into storage, including transport costs. It should also be noted that as in tort the plaintiff is under an obligation to mitigate his damages.[14]

4.4   Quantum of damage

Under section 51(3) of the 1893 Act, where the seller fails to deliver goods which are readily available in the market-place, the buyer can go to the market, purchase the goods and the measure of damages is the difference between the price he paid for the goods in the market and that which he contracted to pay upon delivery.

Where there has been late delivery of goods the loss is measured as the fall in the value of the goods from the date of delivery in the contract to the date of actual delivery.[15]

4.5   The burden of proof

The degree of proof required in civil proceedings, including contract and tort, is the balance of probabilities.[16]

4.6   Exclusion and limitation of liability

It is proposed to treat the above with regard to:

(a) the provisions of the 1980 Act; and
(b) the provisions of the 1995 Regulations.

4.6.1   The 1980 Act

There is an inherent conflict contained in sections 11 and 22 of the 1980 Act which deal with the exclusion of liability. Section 11(4) states that:

> it shall be an offence for a person in the course of a business to furnish to a buyer goods bearing, or goods in a container bearing, or any document including any statement, irrespective of its legal effect, which sets out, limits or describes rights conferred on a buyer or liabilities to the buyer in relation to goods acquired by him or any statement likely to be taken as such a statement, unless that statement is accompanied by a clear and conspicuous declaration that the contractual rights which the buyer enjoys by virtue of sections 12, 13, 14 and 15 of the Act of 1893 are in no way prejudiced by the relevant statement.

---

13   17 November 1981, HC, unrep, Costello J.
14   *Bord Iascaigh Mhara v Scallan* (8 May 1973 unrep), HC, Pringle J).
15   *Heron II* [1969] 1 AC 350.
16   *Millar v Minister of Pensions* [1947] 2 All ER 372 at 373-374 per Denning J: 'If the evidence is such that the tribunal can say: 'We think it more probable than not', the burden is discharged but if the probabilities are equal it is not'; and *Cooper v Slade* (1858) 6 HL Cas 746 at 772.

On the other hand, section 22 of the 1980 Act states that whereas a party cannot contract out of or exclude section 12 of the 1893 Act, which relates to the seller's title to sell the goods in question, under any circumstances, a party may in certain circumstances exclude the provisions of sections 13 to 15 of the 1893 Act (now incorporated into section 10 of the 1980 Act) relating to sales by description, sample and implied terms as to quality of goods.

These terms may be contracted out of where the buyer of the goods does not deal as a consumer[17] and where the exclusion is fair and reasonable.[18]

Thus, the inconsistency is apparent. While a party may contract out of terms implied under sections 13-15 of the 1893 Act (now incorporated into section 10 of the 1980 Act) so long as the exclusion is fair and reasonable and the buyer does not deal as a consumer, if a party makes any statement to the effect that it is contracting out of sections 13 to 15 a criminal offence is committed under section 11(4).

Further, according to section 22 of the 1980 Act (incorporating section 55(1) of the 1893 Act):

> subject to the subsequent provisions of this section, where any right, duty or liability would arise under a contract of sale of goods by implication of law, it may be negatived or varied by express agreement, or by the course of dealing between the parties, or by usage if the usage is such as to bind both parties to the contract.

Thus, it is difficult to envisage a case where a party could in accordance with the above section exclude the implied conditions contained in sections 13 to 15 in accordance with section 22 of the 1980 Act without the use of a statement as defined in section 11 and incur the subsequent criminal liability attaching thereto.

The same inconsistency is apparent in sections 30 and 31 in relation to the hire purchase of goods and the exclusion of implied conditions broadly similar to those contained in sections 12-15.

4.6.2   The 1995 Regulations

The 1995 Regulations were brought into effect by ministerial regulation rather than by an Act of the *Oireachtas*. As a result, it has been argued that the rights and remedies offered by the 1995 Regulations have not obtained the exposure or public scrutiny that legislation of this importance warrants.

The 1995 Regulations apply to contracts between a consumer and a vendor of goods or supplier of services where the terms of the contract have not been individually negotiated. There is a presumption that a term has not been individually negotiated with the onus lying upon the vendor or supplier to show that it was. By their terms the 1995 Regulations apply to all such contracts concluded after 31 December 1994. Any term in such contracts which is unfair is not binding upon the consumer.[19] The remainder of the contract is binding to the extent to which the unfair term can be severed. If the unfair term cannot be severed eg if it represents the main body of the contract, then the contract as a whole is unenforceable. The 1995 Regulations do not apply to all contractual terms but to those contained in standard form contracts entered into between a consumer and a seller of goods or a supplier of services.

---

17   Dealing as a consumer is defined in s 3 of the 1980 Act.
18   See p 229.
19   Regulation 6.

Contracts relating to immovable property have not been excluded from the scope of the 1995 Regulations. Regulation 3(2) provides that a contractual term falling within the scope of the 1995 Regulations shall be regarded as unfair if 'contrary to the requirement of good faith, it causes a significant imbalance in the parties' rights and obligations under the contract to the detriment of the consumer'. In assessing what is regarded as unfair the 1995 Regulations identify certain factors for consideration, for example the nature of the goods or services, the circumstances surrounding the conclusion of the contract, the other terms of the contract or any other contract on which it is dependent. Each term of the contract will be assessed on its own merits. In addition, in assessing whether 'good faith' exists, other factors are considered, including the strength of the bargaining position of the parties and whether the consumer has received any inducement to agree to the term of the contract.

The 1995 Regulations contain a non-exhaustive list of terms which may be regarded as being unfair, including, for instance, terms which have the object or effect of:

(a) irrevocably binding the consumer to terms with which he had no real opportunity of becoming acquainted before the conclusion of the contract;
(b) enabling the vendor or supplier to alter the terms of the contract unilaterally without a valid reason which is specified in the contract;
(c) giving the vendor or supplier the possibility of transferring his rights and obligations under the contract, where this may serve to reduce the guarantees for the consumer without the latter's agreement;
(d) requiring any consumer who fails to fulfil his obligation to pay a disproportionately high sum in compensation;
(e) automatically extending a contract of fixed duration without the express consent of the consumer.

Furthermore it is incumbent on the vendor or supplier to ensure that the terms of the contract, where the contract is in writing, are drafted in plain, intelligible language. If it is not written in plain, intelligible language the contract may be rendered void. If a term is found to be unfair it will not be binding on the consumer.[20] However if the remainder of the contract is 'capable of continuing in existence without the unfair term' the balance of the contract will not be affected.

4.7 Limitation period

An action based on a simple contract,[1] must be brought within six years from the date on which the cause of action accrued, which normally is the date of the breach. The contract terms may determine the date on which the cause of action accrued. However, as in tort,[2] where there is an action for damages for breach of a duty and the damages claimed include damages in respect of personal injuries, a party has three years to bring the action from the date the cause of action accrued.[3]

20   Regulation 6(1).
1   Section 11(1)(a) of the 1957 Act.
2   Section 11(2)(b) of the 1957 Act.
3   In the case of a deceased defendant a two-year limitation period applies: Civil Liability Act 1961, s 9. A period of three years after attaining majority may apply in certain circumstances to an infant.

Where a person using a motor vehicle with the consent of the buyer suffers loss as a result of a breach by the seller of the implied condition inserted by the 1980 Act[4] he may bring an action against the seller in respect of the breach as if he were the buyer. In such cases a two-year limitation period applies.[5]

An action brought upon an instrument under seal upon the expiration of twelve years from the date on which the cause of action accrued will be statute-barred.[6]

The cause of action accrues on the date on which the breach occurred and not on the date when damage is suffered. Accordingly it will be necessary to consider the terms of the contract to establish the date of its breach.[7]

In an action for breach of condition or warranty against a vendor of goods the date of accrual of the cause of action is the time the goods are delivered and not the date on which the breach is discovered.[8]

4.8   Liability for third parties: vicarious liability

Liability is most frequently sought to be excluded in respect of employees or agents. The conditions and warranties implied by the 1980 Act cannot be excluded, save as indicated earlier.

Another obstacle to excluding liability in respect of third parties is the doctrine of privity of contract.[9] In *Scruttons Ltd v Midland Silicones Ltd*[10] the court was of the opinion that notwithstanding lack of privity the liability in respect of third parties (in that case stevedores) may be excluded in certain circumstances, namely:

(a) if the contract makes it clear that the stevedores are to be protected by the provisions in it which limit liability;
(b) if the contract clearly provides that as well as contracting on his own behalf the carrier also contracts as agent for the stevedores in relation to these provisions; and
(c) that the carrier has the stevedores' authority to contract on his behalf as agent; and
(d) that difficulties about consideration moving from the stevedores are overcome.

5   LIABILITY IN TORT

5.1   Introduction

The Courts formerly were reluctant to impose liability in tort on a manufacturer of goods in respect of persons injured by those goods unless privity of contract between the parties was shown to exist. To this general reluctance, there were some exceptions, such as that a supplier of goods was under a duty to refrain from deceit.[11] There was also a recognised duty to give a warning when there

---

4   1980 Act, s 13.
5   Section 13(8) amends s 11(2) of the 1951 Act.
6   1957 Act, s 11(5)(a).
7   *Morgan v Park Developments Ltd* [1983] ILRM 156.
8   *Lynn v Bamber* [1930] 2 KB 72.
9   See pp 224, 231.
10   [1962] AC 446.
11   *Langridge v Levy* (1837) 2 M & W 519.

was an awareness of a defect or danger.[12] Liability was also recognised in respect of goods which were inherently dangerous.[13]

5.2   Outline of relevant tort law giving rise to liability for personal and property damage in Ireland

Liability for the negligent manufacture and supply of defective goods in Ireland was developed in broadly the same manner as English law following the decision of *Donoghue v Stevenson*[14] and the 'neighbour' formula enunciated by Lord Atkin therein, namely:

> the rule that you are to love your neighbour becomes in law you must not injure your neighbour; and the lawyer's question, who is my neighbour? receives a restricted reply. You must take reasonable care to avoid acts or omissions which you can reasonably foresee would be liable to injure your neighbour. Who, then in law, is my neighbour? The answer seems to be persons who are so closely and directly affected by my act that I ought reasonably to have them in contemplation as being so affected when I am directing my mind to the acts or omissions which are called in question.

This principle was applied in England by cases such as *Home Office v Dorset Yacht Co Ltd*[15] and *Anns v Merton London Borough Council.*[16] In the latter case Lord Wilberforce restated the 'neighbour' formula previously enunciated by Lord Atkin stating that in order to determine whether a duty of care exists in any particular situation, two questions fall to be determined:

> First one has to ask whether, as between the alleged wrongdoer and the person who has suffered damage, there is a sufficient relationship of proximity or neighbourhood such that, in the reasonable contemplation of the former, carelessness on his part may be likely to cause damage to the latter, in which case a prima facie duty of care arises. Secondly, if the first question is answered affirmatively, it is necessary to consider whether there are any considerations which ought to negative, or to reduce or limit the scope of, the duty or the class of person to whom it is owed or the damages to which a breach of it may give rise.

Lord Wilberforce's position was criticised. In *Governors of the Peabody Donation Fund v Sir Lindsay Parkinson & Co Ltd*[17] Lord Keith favoured the position that a court, in determining whether or not a particular defendant was under a duty of care, should consider whether it was 'just and reasonable' to impose such a duty. In *Leigh and Sillivan Ltd v Aliakmon Shipping Co Ltd*[18] Lord Brandon also criticised Lord Wilberforce's approach and considered that Lord Wilberforce could not have intended to provide a universally applicable test of the existence and scope of a duty of care in the law of negligence. Lord

---

12   *Heaven v Pender* (1883) 11 QBD 503 at 517 and *Farrant v Barnes* (1862) 11 CB (NS) 553.
13   *Longmeid v Holliday* (1851) 6 Ex 761 at 767, *O'Gorman v O'Gorman* (1903) 2 IR 573; see also the unreported judgment of Walsh J in *O'Sullivan v Noonan* (28 July 1972) SC (89/103/109 – 1970).
14   [1932] AC 562.
15   [1970] AC 1004.
16   [1978] AC 728.
17   [1985] AC 210.
18   [1986] AC 785 at 815.

Wilberforce was dealing with a novel type of factual situation which was not analogous to any factual situations in which such a duty had already been held to exist.

The Supreme Court in *Ward v McMaster*[19] followed Lord Wilberforce's restatement in *Anns v Merton London Borough Council*. In Ireland, since its exposition by Lord Atkin in *Donoghue v Stevenson* and its subsequent restatement by Lord Wilberforce in *Anns v Merton London Borough Council*, the 'neighbour' formula or proximity principle continues to be the cornerstone of the law of negligence,[20] despite its recent apparent demise in England. Previously, landlords could not be made liable in negligence in respect of defects existing in premises which they let.[1] The court in *Siney v Dublin Corpn* stated that in the light of recent developments this could no longer be so. O'Higgins CJ made strong obiter dicta statements that 'in these circumstances I can see no basis for suggesting that the principle of *Donoghue v Stevenson* should not apply'. The circumstances referred to by the Chief Justice were that the defendants were providing statutory housing, remained privy to the design of the dwellings, supervised the construction and inspected the completed flat before accepting it from the builders. The Chief Justice appeared to be of the view that as the defendant should have had the plaintiff in its contemplation when making its inspection of the premises, and made the inspection accordingly, it could be liable in negligence for having failed to do so. A further case in this line of authority is *Purtill v Athlone UDC*.[2] The defendants owned and controlled an abattoir in which the method of slaughter was a humane killer; a pistol-like instrument and detonators were kept on the premises to facilitate its use. Some children had been allowed on to the abattoir on previous occasions and had taken detonators which they exploded off the premises. On one of these occasions a young boy was severely injured when a detonator exploded in his hand. The plaintiff argued that the defendants had been negligent and should have foreseen that the detonators were a cause of allurement to the boys. The defendants argued that the boys were trespassers and therefore the only duty of care they owed was a duty not to set traps for them. However, Walsh J stated that 'the liability, if established, is therefore one which arose by virtue of the proximity of the parties and it would be the same wherever the parties might find themselves, provided their proximity to each other was the same'.

Walsh J considered that the first question to be considered was that of the proximity of the parties. The duty, he stated 'is based upon the duty that one man has to those in proximity to him to take reasonable care that they are not injured by his acts. What amounts to sufficient care must vary necessarily with circumstances, the nature of the danger and the age and knowledge of the person likely to be injured'.

Further cases which accepted and relied on the 'neighbour principle' are *McNamara v ESB*,[3] *McMahon v Ireland*[4] and *Ward v McMaster*.[5] The 'neighbour' formula would appear to apply also to cases of damage to property.[6]

---

19   10 May 1988, SC.
20   *Siney v Dublin Corpn* [1980] IR 400.
 1   *Robbins v Jones* 15 CB (NS) 240.
 2   [1968] IR 205.
 3   [1975] IR 1.
 4   [1988] ILRM 610.
 5   10 May 1988 SC..
 6   *Frank Lynch v Liam Hetherton* [1990] ILRM 857.

5.3   Causation

5.3.1   Factual causation

Factual causation means that if the defendant did not in fact cause the plaintiff's injury, other than on grounds of vicarious liability, then he cannot be liable for such injury. If he did in fact cause the plaintiff's injury then he may be liable. Various qualifying adjectives have been attached to the word 'cause' to determine whether the consequence is too remote. Adjectives such as effective, real or substantial have been used by the courts at various stages. Therefore if the defendant's action was not the substantive or the real or effective cause of the plaintiff's injury the defendant will not be made liable.

The 'but for' test is frequently relied on by the courts in determining factual causation. The courts look at the possible causes of the plaintiff's injury and ask the question: 'but for' the act of the defendant, would the plaintiff have suffered the injury?[7] This test rules out events which were not factual causes of the plaintiff's injury and leaves the remaining causes to be scrutinised to establish whether they were the legal causes of the plaintiff's injury.

5.3.2   Legal causation

Once it is established that the act was factually the cause of the plaintiff's injury it must then be established that the act was legally the cause of the plaintiff's injury.[8] An important question in determining whether the defendant will be made liable for the plaintiff's injury is whether there was a '*novus actus interveniens*', an act which occurs between the defendant's act and the plaintiff's injury caused by the plaintiff himself or by some third party. For the *novus actus interveniens* to absolve the defendant of liability for his action it must be of such substance as to break the causal connection between the defendant's act and the plaintiff's injury.[9]

Since *Crowley v AIB*[10] it appears that for the intervening act to break the causal connection it must be a reckless or intentional act on behalf of the plaintiff or a third party and not an act which is merely foreseeable by the defendant. This principle is illustrated in *Conole v Redbank Oyster Co*[11] where the defendant's captain put to sea in a boat which he knew to be unseaworthy and was sued for causing loss of life following the capsizing of the boat. The defendant sought to join the manufacturers as co-defendants but was held not entitled to do so as the manufacturers' negligence was not the cause of the accident. The court held that the defendant's decision to put to sea in a boat which it knew to be unseaworthy was a reckless act and as such was sufficient to act as a *novus actus interveniens* and thus discharge the manufacturers' liability. Recklessness in this regard is equated with gross carelessness and does not require the perpetrator of the act to appreciate the risk he is taking.[12]

---

7   *Kenny v O'Rourke* [1972] IR 339, *Meehan v Reid and Murphy* (5 March 1985, unrep), HC, Murphy J, *Hanrahan v Merck Sharpe and Dohme (Irl) Ltd* [1989] ILRM 629.
8   *Burke v John Paul & Co Ltd* [1967] IR 277, *Connolly v South of Ireland Asphalt Co* [1977] IR 99.
9   *Power v Bedford Motor* [1959] IR 391.
10   [1988] ILRM 225.
11   [1976] IR 191.
12   *Donovan v Landys Ltd* [1963] IR 441 at 461 462.

5.4 Remoteness of loss and damage

Re Polemis and Furness Withy & Co Ltd[13] laid down the strict test that if any reasonable person would foresee that an act such as that in issue would cause damage then the actor would be liable for all damage which was directly traceable to the act in question. However, the fairness of the test of reasonable foreseeability to establish liability and then to use a different test of direct consequences to establish the parameters of such liability was questioned in the case of *Overseas Tank Ship (UK) Ltd v Morts Dock & Engineering Co Ltd (The Wagon Mound, No 1)*[14] which held that the question of liability and the extent of liability were not two questions but one and that the test of reasonable forseeability should be the only test to be used when deciding the question of liability. The test of reasonable foreseeability, as expounded in *The Wagon Mound, No 1*, in relation to remoteness of damage, has been followed in Ireland.[15]

5.5 Quantum of damage

Damages in Irish Law fall under five separate headings;[16]

i Nominal damages Where the plaintiff's legal right has been infringed but the plaintiff has suffered no real damage, the award which he is given will be of a nominal amount only.

ii Contemptuous damages Where the plaintiff's right to damages is based on a mere technicality but for which he would not be entitled to damages, the court may go against the general rule and may award the plaintiff damages but may award costs against him.

iii Special and general damages General damages are those which it is is said are assumed to flow from the act complained of whereas special damages are those (beyond the general damage) which result from the particular circumstances of the case and ought to be set out by the plaintiff in his pleadings.

iv Restitutio in integrum and compensation Where possible the plaintiff should be placed in the same position as if the tort had not occurred but this is not always possible and where this is so damages are awarded according to what is deemed to be 'fair'.

v Exemplary damages There has always existed a controversy as to whether a court should award exemplary or punitive damages over and above normal damages where there was a 'wanton' interference with the plaintiff's rights.[17]

In *Rookes v Barnard*[18] the court's ability, in limited circumstances, to award such exemplary damages was accepted. In that case the court held that exemplary damages could be awarded in three categories of case:

13 [1921] 3 KB 560, CA.
14 [1961] AC 388, PC.
15 *Condon v CIE* (16 November 1984), HC, Barrington J, and *Egan v Sisk* [1986] ILRM 283.
16 McMahon and Binchy, p 769.
17 *Loudon v Ryder* [1953] 2 QB 202.
18 [1964] AC 1129.

(a) where there was 'oppressive, arbitrary or unconstitutional action by the servants of the government';
(b) where 'the defendant's conduct has been calculated by him to make a profit for himself which may well exceed the compensation payable to the plaintiff'; and
(c) where such damages were 'expressly authorised by statute'.

However, even if the plaintiff's claim fell within one of these three classes the court's power to award exemplary damages was to be used with restraint and the party's means, normally irrelevant in calculating damages, would be relevant in calculating exemplary damages.

The classes set forth in *Rookes v Barnard* have received much criticism as being arbitrary and ambiguous. The decisions of the High Court in this jurisdiction show two schools of thought in relation to the award of exemplary damages, some judgments favouring *Rookes v Barnard* and its consequent limitations and other judgments disapproving of it.[19]

Some judges have used, as a basis for an award of exemplary damages, sections 7(2) and 14(4) of the 1961 Act. An example in this regard is the judgment of Hamilton P in *Kennedy v Ireland*[20] where he stated that it was 'quite clear from a consideration of the Civil Liability Act 1961 and in particular sections 7(2) and 14(4) thereof that Irish law recognises a distinction as between "punitive damages" and "exemplary damages"'.

However, a judgment taken from the other school of thought is Barron J in *Conway v Ireland*[1] where he stated that 'The exemplary damages should be measured in an amount to meet the wrongdoing rather than to benefit the wronged'.

5.5.1   Damages for personal injury

In contrast to other EU jurisdictions, Irish courts may only make lump sum awards in respect of personal injury as distinct from instalment awards. Since 1988 juries have been abolished in personal injury actions but the quantum of damages does not appear to have fallen substantially.

The factors to be taken into consideration when calculating damages for personal injury were set out by Walsh J in *Long v O'Brien & Cronin Ltd*:[2]

> It is the duty of the plaintiff to adduce evidence sufficient to go to the jury when he sets out to establish that the result of his injuries will be to cause him pecuniary loss in the future . . . Not merely is the former earning capacity of the plaintiff relevant but so also is the present physical condition, his prospective physical condition, the state of the labour market, the particular trade or skill which he has and the prospects for exercising it in the future having regard to the diminution of his capacity to do so resulting from the injuries he has sustained.

The plaintiff may also be awarded damages for pain and suffering and loss of expectation of life, though in regard to damages for pain and suffering the Supreme Court in *Sinnott v Quinnsworth Ltd*[3] has stated that there should, in

---

19   Judgments against *Rookes v Barnard*: *Dillon v Dunnes Stores* (20 December 1968, unrep), (SC), *McDonald v Galvin* (23 February 1976, unrep), HC, McWilliams J. Decisions for *Rookes v Barnard*: *Whelan v Madigan* [1978] ILRM 136, *Kearney v Minister for Justice* [1986] IR 116.
20   [1988] ILRM 472.
 1   2 November 1988, HC, Barron J.
 2   24 March 1972, unrep, SC.
 3   [1984] ILRM 523.

most cases, effectively be a ceiling of IR £150,000 for general damages and this guideline has been adopted in subsequent cases.[4] With regard to damages for loss of expectation of life, section 7(2) of the 1961 Act provides that where a cause of action for personal injury passes to the estate of a deceased plaintiff, damages are not to be awarded under this heading to his estate. It was recognised by the House of Lords that damages may be awarded under the heading of loss of expectation of life,[5] and it was stated:

> A man has a legal right that his life should not be shortened by the tortious act of another. His normal expectancy of life is a thing of temporal value, so that its impairment is something for which damages should be given. However, the courts have been inclined to award moderate amounts in respect of damages under this heading.[6]

5.5.2 *Damages for injury to property*

Henchy J[7] has stated that relevant factors in deciding on damages for injury to property are:

> the nature of the property, the plaintiff's relation to it, the nature of the wrongful act causing the damage, the conduct of the parties subsequent to the wrongful act, and the pecuniary, economic or other relevant implications or consequences of reinstatement damages as compared with diminished-value damages.

5.6   Burden of proof

The general rule is that the person alleging negligence must prove it on the balance of probabilities. This general rule is subject to the principle of *res ipsa loquitur*, discussed below. The plaintiff's evidence must 'pass beyond the region of pure conjecture into that of legal interference'.[8] Where the negligence alleged consists of an omission rather than a commission it has been held that it is sufficient for the plaintiff to prove, not that the omitted act, had it been committed, would have prevented his injury, but that the omission materially increased the risk of the harm occurring'[9] O'Dalaigh CJ stated:

> all that is required for a plaintiff to succeed is to establish facts from which an inference of negligence on the part of the defendant may reasonably be inferred … it is a mistake to think that because an event is unseen its cause cannot be reasonably inferred.[10]

5.6.1 *Res ipsa loquitur*

It would be an impossible task in some cases for the plaintiff to prove negligence as frequently the defendant is the only person with knowledge of how the act or omission occurred. In such cases the doctrine of *res ipsa loquitur* may assist the plaintiff:

---

4   *Griffiths v Van Raaj* [1985] ILRM 582.
5   In *Rose v Ford* [1937] AC 826.
6   See judgment of O'Dalaigh J in *McMorrow v Knott* (21 December 1959, unrep), SC.
7   *Munnelly v Falcon Ltd* [1978] IR 387 at 400.
8   Salmond and Heuston.
9   *McGhee v National Coal Board* [1973] 1 WLR 1.
10   *Gahan v Engineering Products Ltd* [1971] IR 30 at 32.

Where the thing is shown to be under the management of the defendant or his servants, and the accident is such as in the ordinary course of things does not happen if those who have the mangement use proper care, it affords reasonable evidence, in the absence of explanation by the defendant, that the accident arose from want of care.[11]

From this statement the conditions required to invoke the doctrine are:

(a) that the thing was under the mangement of the defendant or his servants; and
(b) that the accident would not occur in the normal course of events if proper care had been used.

Some courts have held that for a thing to be under the required degree of management the thing must be under the actual management of the defendant while others have held this to include former possession.

The procedural effect of this doctrine is uncertain. One view is that once the doctrine applies the plaintiff has established a case. Another view is that the defendant has the burden of proving that the accident was not in fact due to his negligence. In cases where the courts are willing to draw an inference of negligence the burden of proof shifts to the manufacturer who is then obliged to prove that he is not at fault. The manufacturer may frequently be faced with a difficulty in discharging this onus of proof. In *Mills v Coca-Cola Bottling Co (Dublin) Ltd*,[12] it was held that evidence of a specific nature must be produced if the producers of mass manufactured products are to succeed in rebutting inferences of negligence. Evidence of general care is not enough. Even if a manufacturer demonstrates that he has a high standard of quality control in his factory the courts may then say to him that an employee must have been guilty of negligence, in which case vicarious liability will attach to the manufacturer.[13]

5.7   Exclusion or limitation of liability

Section 22 of the 1980 Act provides that any attempt to exclude the conditions implied in consumer contracts by section 10 of the 1980 Act is void. Where the contract is not a consumer contract the exclusion must be shown to be fair and reasonable (other than the implied condition in section 12 of the 1893 Act) in accordance with the Schedule to the 1980 Act.

An exclusion clause has to be incorporated into the contract.[14] Generally, an exclusion clause will only be binding if notice of it is given before the contract is concluded. Once it is established that an exclusion clause has in fact been incorporated into the contract the clause must then be construed and this can give rise to certain difficulties. There is the difficulty of the clarity of the exclusion clause and the rule that where the clause is capable of more than one interpretation it will be construed against the party who seeks to rely on it.[15] Another difficulty is in determining the nature of the liability the clause is

11   *Scott v London & St Katherine Docks Co* (1865) 3 H & C 596 at 601. See *Hanrahan v Merck, Sharp & Dohme (Ireland) Ltd* 1989 ILRM 629.
12   8 May 1984, unrep, HC.
13   *Hill v James Crowe (Cases) Ltd* [1978] 1 All ER 812.
14   *Parker v South East Railway* [1877] 2 CPD 416.
15   *Sproule v Triumph Cycle Co* [1927] NI 83, NICA.

attempting to exclude. The cases show that the courts' inclination is to give the clause a narrow scope of application where possible.[16]

Where a party desires to exclude liability for negligence this may be done where the clause shows a clear intention to exclude liability for negligence and covers whose negligence is to be excluded.[17]

The final issue is whether one can have an exclusion clause which attempts to protect the proferens from any liability in the event of his not performing the contract at all, and not just an exclusion of liability for performing the contract badly. Where a party is attempting to exclude liability for a loss resulting from a fundamental breach of contract the exclusion clause must be specific and even if it is so the standing of such an exclusion clause is doubtful.[18]

5.8   Limitation period

The relevant legislation is the 1957 Act as amended by the Statute of Limitations (Amendment) Act 1991. Recent cases show a trend by defendants in certain circumstances to invoke the terms of the Constitution to attempt to avoid the statutory period of limitation in cases where it should apply.

Generally a party has six years to commence an action in tort from the date on which the cause of action accrued.

However, the appropriate period[19] for an action claiming damages for, inter alia, negligence on the part of the defendant where the plaintiff is claiming damages for personal injuries to any person, is three years.[20]

When the tort alleged is actionable per se, such as in libel, the limitation period runs from the date on which the wrong was committed even though actual damage may not result for some time. Where the tort requires proof of actual damage then 'the traditional view is that time begins to run from the date on which the damage occurs'.[1]

In relation to the accrual of a cause of action a distinction was formerly drawn between injury to the person and injury to property. In relation to property, Carroll J held in *Morgan v Park Developments Ltd*[2] that the cause of action did not accrue until such damage had been discoverable by the plaintiff.

In a recent decision[3] Finlay CJ of the Supreme Court stated that he 'must disagree with Carroll J in the conclusion reached by her in *Morgan v Park Developments*'.[4] Finlay CJ went on to hold that 'the time . . . commenced to run at the time when a provable personal injury, capable of attracting compensation, occurred to the plaintiff which was the completion of the tort alleged to be committed against her'.[5]

An important decision in this area was that of *O'Domhnaill v Merrick*[6] which was summarised by Finlay CJ in *Toal v Duignan*[7] as being that:

16   *Ronan v Midland Railway Co* (1883) 14 LR (IR) 157, QBD.
17   *Canada Steamship Lines v R* [1952] AC 192 at 208.
18   *Clayton Love v B & I Steampacket Co* (1970) 104 ILTR 157; *Photo Production Ltd v Securicor Transport* [1980] AC 827.
19   1957 Act, s 11(2)(b).
20   Statute of Limitations (Amendment) Act 1991, s 3.
1   Brady and Kerr, p 42.
2   [1983] ILRM 156.
3   [1990] ILRM 403.
4   [1983] ILRM 156.
5   [1990] ILRM 411.
6   [1984] IR 151.
7   27 November 1987, SC, at 279-286.

where there is a clear and patent unfairness in asking a defendant to defend a case after a very long lapse of time between the acts complained of and the trial, then if that defendant has not himself contributed to the delay, irrespective of whether the plaintiff has contributed to it or not, the court may as a matter of justice have to dismiss the action.

It is important to note the new discoverability rule in section 7 of the 1991 Act. This states that an action for the recovery of damages shall not be brought after the expiration of three years from the date on which the cause of action accrued or the date (if later) on which the plaintiff became aware, or should reasonably have become aware, of the damage, the defect and the identity of the producer.

The 1991 Act provides that the time of the accrual of a cause of action, and the expiry of the limitation period, depend upon the injured person having a reasonable opportunity of becoming aware of the damage which he has suffered.

5.9   Liability for third parties

5.9.1   *Vicarious liability in tort*

In product liability the primary question is under what circumstances a producer can be made liable for the torts of his employees? The courts have devised a number of tests to determine who are 'employees'.

The first was the 'control test'. This provided that where the employer had a degree of control over an employee in respect of the manner in which his work was to be done then the relationship of employer/employee existed and vicarious liability could be imposed upon the employer.[8] Other relevant factors are the methods of paying the employee and whether the tools used in the course of his employment are those of the employer or the employee.

Other tests favoured by the courts in deciding whether a particular person is an employee are the 'organisation' or 'integration' test, the 'mixed factor' test and the 'business on his own' test.

The 'integration' test looks to whether the work of the employee is integral or incidental to the employer's business.[9] To be deemed an employee the work done must be an integral part of the business of the employer. The 'mixed factor' test looks at all the circumstances of the employment including factors such as the keeping of accounts, the ability to delegate and the designation in the service contract.[10]

The 'business on his own' test looks at all the above factors together with the opportunities which the employee has to make profits on his own account.[11] If the person has a reasonable opportunity to control his own level of profit it is likely he will be held to be an independent contractor. Once it has been established that a particular person is an employee the liability of the employee for the torts of that person will depend upon whether the tort was committed in the course of the employment of the employee.[12] A wrongful act is done in the course of employment if:

---

8   *Moynihan v Moynihan* [1975] IR 192, *Lynch v Palgrave Murphy* [1964] IR 150.
9   *Stevenson, Jordan and Harrison Ltd v Macdonald* [1952] TLR 101.
10   *Ready Mixed Concrete (South East) Ltd v Minister of Pensions* [1968] 2 QB 497.
11   *Market Investigations Ltd v Minister of Social Security* [1969] 2 QB 173.
12   *Poland v Parr (John) & Sons* [1927] 1 KB 236.

(a) it is a wrongful act authorised by the employer; or
(b) it is a wrongful and unauthorised mode of doing some act authorised by the employer.

Clearly most liability arises under (b), above. Where the wrongful act of the employee is one which the employer has expressly warned him not to do, this factor will be taken into account.[13]

Whether a person is an employee is important because in tort there is a general rule that a person is not vicariously liable for the acts of his independent contractors[14] subject to cases where work involving strict liability or work of an inherently dangerous nature is involved.[15] It has been stated[16] that the reason an employer is liable in some cases for the torts of his independent contractor is not because he is liable for the contractor's breach of duty but rather the liability is imposed as the employer himself is liable for a breach of his own duty: the duty to choose a contractor who is reasonably competent to do the proposed work and to give reasonable instructions and reasonably oversee the work of the independent contractor.[17]

The employer is not liable for the collateral negligence of his independent contractor. This is illustrated in *Padbury v Holliday and Greenwood Ltd*[18] where the contractor's tool fell from a window ledge and injured a passer-by. The ultimate employers were held not liable for this collateral negligence on the part of their independent contractor.

6 LIABILITY FOR DEFECTIVE PRODUCTS ARISING FROM BOTH GENERAL LAW AND IMPLEMENTATION OF EC DIRECTIVE 85/374 ON PRODUCT LIABILITY IN IRELAND

6.1 Introduction

The 1991 Act was brought into force by the Minister for Industry and Commerce on 16 December, 1991 to give effect to the provisions of Directive 85/374 EC ('Directive 85/374') dated 25 July, 1985.

The belated implementation of Directive 85/374 raises the question as to whether the State could be liable for its failure to bring this Directive into force within the time specified for its implementation. In light of the *Francovich*[19] case, an injured plaintiff who had failed in an action at common law might be able to bring an action against the Irish Government if the individual could establish that had Directive 85/374 been implemented within the specified time he or she would have recovered damages for injury or damage caused by a defective product.

Furthermore, the European Court of Justice, under the doctrine of direct effect, has permitted individuals to rely upon the terms of a directive even where the member state has failed to implement the directive within the allotted time.[20]

---

13 *Strong v McAuley, McIlroy & Co Ltd* 63 ILTR 39.
14 McMahon and Binchy, p 761; Salmond and Heuston, p 544.
15 *Boylan v Northern Bank Ltd and James Corcoran Ltd* (21 July 1977, unrep), HC Costello J.
16 *Daniel v Rickett, Cockerell & Co Ltd* [1938] 2 KB 322.
17 *Sumner v William Henderson & Sons Ltd* [1964] 1 QB 450.
18 (1912) 28 TLR 494.
19 *Francovich v Italy, Bonifaci v Italy* (Joint Cases, C-6 and C-9/1990), 1991 ECR I 537.
20 Cases 41/74 *Van Duyn v Home Office* [1974] ECR 1337, [1975] 1 CMLR.

Thus, it remains to be seen whether a prospective litigant will seek to rely on Directive 85/374 to seek compensation in respect of damage or injury sustained as a result of a defective product which occurred between 30 July 1988 and 16 December 1991.

6.2   Outline of provisions in Ireland

Directive 85/374 had the objective of approximating (as opposed to harmonising, a more complex objective) the laws of member states with regard to liability for defective products. It could be said that this aspiration was blunted somewhat by the discretion it afforded to the member states as to the inclusion/exclusion of certain provisions and defences.

The 1991 Act does not supplant pre-existing tortious, contractual or statutory remedies.[1] The remedies and liabilities contained in the 1991 Act are in addition to any remedies and/or liabilities existing prior to its implementation. As a result, the laws of the member states are far from approximated as certain member states have multi-tiered systems of liability.

The 1991 Act incorporates the text of Directive 85/374 in a Schedule to the 1991 Act. In addition, the 1991 Act must be construed in a manner consistent with Directive 85/374. The 1991 Act seeks to provide the injured consumer with a remedy against the producer supplementary to pre-existing tortious, contractual and statutory remedies. Accordingly, what the 1991 Act deems to be 'product'[2] and what comes under the rubric of 'producer'[3] are integral concepts both for the purpose of Directive 85/374 and for the 1991 Act.

Directive 85/374 offered member states a certain amount of freedom in the manner of its implementation. It allowed member states to derogate from certain provisions. For example member states could exclude primary agricultural products from falling within the definition of 'products'. In light of the fact that agriculture constitutes approximately one sixth of Ireland's Gross National Product it is perhaps unsurprising that Ireland availed of this exclusion.

Furthermore the 1991 Act allows producers to avail of the 'development risks' or 'state of the art defence' (Directive 85/374 had given member states a discretion as to whether producers could rely on this defence in their respective jurisdictions).

In treating the provisions of the 1991 Act it is proposed to focus on certain key questions, namely:

(a) Who is a producer?
(b) What is a product?
(c) When is a product defective?
(d) Who is liable, and for what?

6.2.1   *Who is a producer?*

Section 2(1) of the 1991 Act states that:

> the producer shall be liable in tort for damage caused wholly or partly by a defect in his product.

---

1   Section 11.
2   Section 1(1).
3   Section 2(2).

The question immediately arises as to who is a producer for the purposes of the 1991 Act. This question is answered by section 2(2). This section defines the term producer widely including:

(i) the manufacturer or producer of a finished product, or
(ii) the manufacturer or producer of any raw material or the manufacturer, or producer of a component part of a product, or
(iii) in the case of products of the soil, of stock-farming and of fisheries and game, which have undergone initial processing, the person who carried out such initial processing, or
(iv) any person who, by putting his name, trade mark or any other distinguishing feature on the product or using his name or any such mark or feature in relation to the product, has held himself out to be the producer of the product, or
(v) any person who has imported the product into a member state from a place outside the European Communities in order, in the course of any business of his, to supply it to another, or
(vi) the supplier of a product who may, in certain circumstances be liable as the producer of the product where the producer of the product cannot be identified.

6.2.2   What is a product?

The 1991 Act defines product as meaning:

All movables with the exception of primary agricultural products which have not undergone initial processing, and includes
(a) movables even though incorporated into another product or into an immovable, whether by virtue of being a component part or raw material or otherwise,
(b) electricity where damage is caused as a result of a failure in the process of generation of electricity.

Most immovables compromise the incorporation of a number of movables. Accordingly, the 1991 Act may apply where an immovable is damaged as a result of the incorporation into it of a defective movable. It is to be noted however, that immovable or real property is excluded from the provisions of the 1991 Act.

6.2.3   When is a product defective?

Pursuant to the terms of the 1991 Act, a product is defective if it fails, taking all the circumstances into account, to provide the safety which a person is entitled to expect.[4] Accordingly to fall within the ambit of the 1991 Act the product must not only be defective, it must also be unsafe. The circumstances relevant to determining whether a product is defective are identical to those set down in Directive 85/374 and include:

(a) the product's presentation,
(b) the use to which it could reasonably be expected that the product would be put, and
(c) the time when the product was put into circulation.

---

4   Section 5(1).

In addition, the 1991 Act[5] mirrors Directive 85/374 in providing that a product shall not be considered defective for the sole reason that a better product is subsequently put into circulation.

It remains to be seen whether the Irish Courts will judge the concept the 'safety which a person is entitled to expect' objectively (ie from the point of view of the reasonable consumer) or subjectively (from the point of the view of the injured consumer). That being said, it is clear that the list given is non-exhaustive in that other factors such as warnings, instructions for use and the general labelling of the particular product may all be considered in determining whether a particular product is defective.

6.2.4   *Who is liable and for what?*

The producer is liable in tort for damage caused wholly or partly by a defect in his product. Damage is defined by the 1991 Act[6] as:

(a) death or personal injury; or
(b) loss of damage to, or destruction of, any item of property other than the defective product itself.

This is subject to the proviso that the item of property:

(i) is of a type ordinarily intended for private use or consumption; and
(ii) was used by the injured person mainly for his own private use or consumption.

The producer is liable to the injured person who is the person who has suffered damage caused wholly or partly by a defect in the product. If the injured party has died the producer may be liable to the injured person's personal representatives or dependants as defined by law.

The injured person must suffer damage in excess of IR£350[7] before he can avail of the provisions of the 1991 Act. This figure excludes the value of damage suffered to the defective product itself. There is no upper ceiling on the producer's potential liability under the 1991 Act.

6.3   Optional or anomalous provisions in respect of product liability law

6.3.1   *Primary agricultural products and game*

Member states had the option of including primary agricultural products and game within the definition of product in their implementing legislation. Ireland did not do so. The producer of such goods still remains open to liability in tort, contract or under statute. If however, such goods are processed (within the meaning of the 1991 Act) they fall within the 1991 Act's strict liability regime. If processed, it is the initial processor who may be regarded as the producer or manufacturer.

6.3.2   *Development risks*

The 1991 Act identifies several defences available to the producer.[8] The so-called 'development risks' defence is to be found in section 6(e). It provides

---

5   Section 5(2).
6   Section 1(1).
7   Section 3(1).
8   Section 6.

that a producer shall not be liable under the terms of the 1991 Act if he proves 'that the state of scientific and technical knowledge at the time when he put the product into circulation was not such as to enable the existence of the defect to be discovered'.

Directive 85/374 permitted member states to derogate from the 'development risks' defence and to provide that the producer would be liable even where he proved that the 'state of the art' at the time he put the product into circulation was not such as to enable the existence of the defect be discovered. Under the provisions of the 1991 Act if a producer can prove that the product was manufactured in accordance with the 'state of the art' and that the 'state of the art' would not have uncovered the existence of the defect he may escape liability. Producers should be aware that this defence may not be open to them in respect of products exported throughout the European Union.

6.3.3 Limits on total liability

The 1991 Act provides that the producer is liable for damage caused wholly or partly by a defect in his product.[9] That being said, not all damage that may be sustained falls within the remit of the 1991 Act.

Section 1(i) of the 1991 Act defines damage as:

- damage or personal injury; or
- loss of, damage to, or destruction of, any item of property other than the defective product itself.

However, it is also provided that the damaged property is firstly required to have been of a type ordinarily intended for private use or consumption and secondly the property is required to have been used by the injured person primarily for his own private use or consumption.

The 1991 Act excludes the recovery of damages for the loss of, damage to, or destruction of the defective product itself. Furthermore, in order to bring a claim under the 1991 Act, damage (excluding the value of any damage to the defective product) is required to exceed IR £350.[10] Where damage exceeds that amount only the excess is recoverable. It is arguable that whilst this threshold seeks to obviate small product liability claims, it is potentially incompatible with article 9 of Directive 85/374. Indeed if one looks to the equivalent English legislation implementing Directive 85/374, the Consumer Protection Act 1987, it can be seen that article 9 was construed as allowing full recovery in all cases where the qualifying threshold of STG £375 (the Sterling equivalent of Ecu 500) was attained.

There is no ceiling on the maximum damages recoverable for injury or damage sustained as a result of a defective product.

7 CRIMINAL LIABILITY FOR DEFECTIVE PRODUCTS ARISING FROM BOTH GENERAL SAFETY LAW AND THE IMPLEMENTATION OF EC DIRECTIVE 92/59 ON PRODUCT SAFETY

The Product Safety Directive obliges member states to establish authorities to ensure that all products on sale comply with the required EU safety standards.

9   Section 2(1).
10   Section 3(1).

In short, it seeks to prevent unsafe products being put on the market. The Product Safety Directive was due to have been implemented by 29 June 1994. As yet, no domestic measures have been taken to implement it in Ireland. It has been said however, that without adequate funding and legislation to implement the Product Safety Directive it may be somewhat redundant due to the standard and lack of facilities for testing products in Ireland.

The Irish Director of Consumer Affairs has stated that 'It is vital that Ireland is not seen as a place of weak enforcement of this Directive':

> It is in the interests of industry to ensure that strong resources are put in place to make sure that this does not happen, as Ireland could then become a dumping ground for unsafe goods and if cheaper products are available, consumers will buy them safe or not.

At the time of writing, a statutory instrument is being drafted which, when passed, is intended to implement the Product Safety Directive.

It will be interesting to see whether the Statutory Instrument provides for any anomalous provisions, independent of the Product Safety Directive, ie covering the nature of criminal sanctions to be prescribed – the nature of fines and/or prison sentences which may be imposed and the scope of the statutory instrument. It will also be interesting to see whether the definition of 'product' in the proposed statutory instrument includes capital goods as well as consumer goods.

8   CIVIL LIABILITY FOR DEFECTIVE PRODUCTS BROUGHT ABOUT BY BREACH OF STATUTORY REGULATIONS DESIGNED TO PROTECT CONSUMERS AND/OR TO PROMOTE SAFETY

8.1   Outline of nature of protective Regulations

Certain consumer protection in Ireland is provided by Acts of the *Oireachtas* containing a framework under which Regulations are issued to control or regulate a range of product types. For example, production and manufacture of drugs and medicines is controlled by regulations which the Minister is enabled to implement under the provisions of the Misuse of Drugs Act 1977, as amended, and the Health Acts 1947 to 1970.

The manufacture of products is controlled in Ireland by the Government standards agency, Forbairt (formerly EOLAS) through which Regulations have been laid down under the Industrial Research and Standards Act 1961 which governs the standards to be met by such items as electrical appliances and children's night clothes.

The packaging of products is controlled by the Packaged Goods (Quantity Control) Act 1980 which enables the appropriate Minister to make Regulations, inter alia, to apply to packages generally or to packages of a particular class or description. Where the Act is expressed to apply to certain packages, it enables inspectors appointed in accordance with the Act to carry out certain tests to ensure that the quantity of goods contained in the containers is as stated.

A final example is the Safety, Health and Welfare at Work Act 1989 which imposes a general duty upon 'any person who designs, manufactures, imports or supplies any article for use at work' to ensure that such is, so far as is reasonably practicable, safe and without risk to health when used by a person at a place of work and a corresponding duty upon persons who design or construct places of work. The Act also imposes upon employers and employees

a duty in relation to their health and safety at work and establishes the National Authority for Occupational Safety and Health giving powers of inspection and enforcement.

8.2 Burden of proof

The burden of proof is different for civil and criminal proceedings. Where it is sought to impose criminal liability for the breach of a statutory regulation the burden of proof is the test of 'beyond reasonable doubt'. Where it is sought to impose civil liability for breach of a statutory regulation and obtain damages, the 'balance of probabilities' is the test.

8.3 Nature of liability

The liability imposed under Acts of the *Oireachtas* and related Regulations is, for the most part, criminal pursuant to the offences and penalties established under the relevant Acts. The question whether civil liability may flow from the breach of a statutory duty is complex and unsettled. The courts appear to ask the following two questions:

(a) Does the Act expressly allow a civil remedy? If the Act does so, the courts will respect this but if the Act does not, then the courts ask the second question which is:
(b) Is the Act for the benefit of the public as a whole or a specific class or section of the public?

Only where the courts hold that the Act was passed to benefit a specific section of the public are they likely to award damages for breach of duty imposed by the Act.[11]

Even where the court holds that damages should be available for a breach of statutory duty the plaintiff still must establish that he is one of the persons within the class of persons that the Act was designed to protect and that he has suffered loss. Further, the court must then decide whether it should award a large or a nominal amount of damages. In determining the level of damages the courts seem open to two views. Under both views the courts look to the nature of the penalty provided by the Act. One view is that if the penalty is low or if there is none at all, damages should also be low.[12] The other view is that where the penalty contained in the Act is low then damages should be high.[13]

9 DEFINITION AND CLASSIFICATION OF TERMS

The following abbreviations are used throughout this chapter.

1995 Regulations	European Communities (Unfair Contract Terms in Consumer Contracts) Regulations 1995
1991 Act	Liability for Defective Products Act 1991

11 *Reilly v Moore* [1935] NI 196; *O'Callaghan v Minister for Posts and Telegraphs* 81 ILTR 162.
12 *Representative Church Body v Dublin Board of Assistance* [1948] IR 287.
13 *Hughes v Dundalk Harbour Comrs* [1923] IR 38.

The Product Safety Directive	The General Product Safety Directive 92/59 EC
1980 Act	Sale of Goods and Supply of Services Act 1980
1893 Act	Sale of Goods Act 1893
1957 Act	Statute of Limitations 1957
1961 Act	Civil Liability Act 1961 (as amended)
1963 Act	Companies Act 1963 (as amended)
Cheshire, Fifoot and Furmston	Cheshire, Fifoot and Furmston *Law of Contract* (11th edn)
WLR	Weekly Law Reports
AC	Appeal Cases
ILRM	Irish Law Reports Monthly
ILTR	Irish Law Times Reports
SC	Supreme Court
unrep	Unreported judgment
IR	Irish Reports
Ir LR	Irish Law Reports
HC	High Court
DC	District Court
QB	Queen's Bench
Exch	Exchequer Division
All ER	All England Reports
KB	King's Bench
McMahon and Binchy	McMahon & Binchy *Irish Law of Torts* (2nd edn)
Salmond and Heuston	Salmond & Heuston *Law of Torts* (19th edn)
NICA	Northern Ireland Court of Appeal
QBD	Queen's Bench Division
Lloyds Rep	Lloyd's Reports
Brady and Kerr	Brady and Kerr *The Limitation of Actions in the Republic of Ireland* (1st edn)
TLR	Times Law Reports
JISLL	The Journal of the Irish Society for Labour Law
NI	Northern Ireland
M & W	Meeson & Wellsby's English Exchequer Reports
Ball & B	Ball & Beatty, IR
CBNS	English Common Bench Reports, New Series by John Scott
Doug	Douglas English King's Bench Reports
HL	Cas House of Lords Cases, English
the Constitution	Bunreacht na hEireann 1937.

CHAPTER X

Italy

Gabriele Dara

Studio Legale Morgante-Dara
Via Villa Sperlinga 5
90144 Palermo
Italy

Tel: ++ 39 91 30 34 79
Fax: ++ 39 91 62 53 172

CHAPTER X

Italy

1 INTRODUCTION

1.1 Introduction to the Italian legal system

Like virtually all civil law systems, the Italian legal system is chiefly based on a code which should, at least in theory, provide a comprehensive system of laws. The Civil Code ('the Code') presently in force was enacted in 1942 and was intended to regulate family, succession, property, contract, company, labour and tort law. Bankruptcy law is regulated by statutes enacted in 1942 and, for large companies, by statutes dating from the late 1970s. The structure of the Code has, however, been substantially altered by a number of statutes that have either amended it or, whilst not substituting the basic definitions contained in the Code, have introduced sweeping changes in the discipline of the area of law concerned. This is particularly true of family law,[1] of landlord and tenant law, which is now almost entirely regulated outside the Code,[2] of company law, where the code has been amended to implement some, but not all, of the EC Directives on the matter, and of labour law.

The judicial system used to be based on a five-tier structure of courts of which the lower three are alternatives, depending on various circumstances, of which more will be said below. The lowest court – *Conciliatore* – had jurisdiction over claims where the amount does not exceed the sum of Lire 750,000.[3] The *Pretura* exercised appellate review of the judgments rendered by the *Conciliatore*. It also had jurisdiction over claims where the amount involved did not exceed the sum of Lire 5 million[4] and exclusive jurisdiction on certain other matters, amongst which the most relevant being the power to grant interlocutory injunctions, irrespective of the amount claimed or involved. The next higher ranking court – *Tribunale* – exercised appellate review on the *Pretura*'s decisions and acts as court of first instance in all other cases. The *Tribunale*'s judgments can be appealed to the *Corte d'Appello*. It is possible to appeal to the *Corte di Cassazione* against the decisions of the *Corte d'Appello*, the *Tribunale*, or the *Pretura* (if the last two are sitting as appellate courts) but only on questions of law.

The system outlined above has been amended with effect from 1 May 1995. However, all cases pending to such date shall be decided under the previous

---

1 The 1970 Divorce Law and the 1975 Family Law Reform Law have radically altered Italian succession rules.
2 See Law 392/78 and Law 115/85.
3 Approximately £350.
4 Approximately £2,300.

rules of procedure. The new system has not changed the basic five tier structure outlined above although it has modified rules of jurisdiction. The three lowest courts are:

(a) The *Guidice di Pace* which has jurisdiction over claims where the amount does not exceed the sum of Lire 5 million (approximately £2,000) and which do not concern real estate. It also has jurisdiction over claims for damages deriving from accidents between cars, motorbikes and boats provided always the claim does not exceed the sum of Lire 30 million (approximately £12,000);

(b) The *Pretura* which has jurisdiction over claims which do not exceed the sum of Lire 50 million (approximately £20,000). The *Pretura* also has exclusive jurisdiction over disputes concerning the renting of real property irrespective of the value of the claim. Contrary to the previous rules of procedure, the power to grant interlocutory injunctions now rests with the court which has jurisdiction to adjudicate the merits of the case.

(c) The *Tribunale* exercise appellate review over the judgments rendered by the *Guidice di Pace* and the *Pretura* and acts as a court of first instance in all other cases. It also has exclusive jurisdiction in matters concerning family law and company law. The appeal system has not been changed.

As said before, the jurisdiction of the courts of first instance is determined by the cause of action and the amounts claimed. However, given that the judicial system is not centralised – that is to say there are a few hundred *Pretura* and *Conciliatore* and over 100 *Tribunale* – the venue is decided on a number of criteria which depend largely on the cause of action and take into account, eg, the place of conclusion or of performance of the contract, the domicile of the debtor or defendant etc – all of which are regulated by the Code of Civil Procedure.

The Brussels Convention of 27 September 1968 on Jurisdiction and the Enforcement of Judgments in Civil and Commercial Matters was given effect in Italy by Law 804 of 21 June 1971.

Disputes can also be solved by way of arbitration provided always that the arbitration clause is valid under Italian law (see articles 800-831 of the Code of Civil Procedure) and that the arbitrators' decision is validated on matters of form by the *Pretura* of the place where enforcement is sought.

It also has to be borne in mind that, subject to the limitations mentioned above in relation to appeals to the *Corte di Cassazione*,[5] there is an absolute right to appeal – that is, once certain formal requirements have been satisfied, there is no need to obtain leave to appeal.

The system briefly outlined above refers to the resolution of civil disputes. Criminal matters and tax matters are adjudicated under a slightly different system. The decision of any other administrative body can be challenged, although not on its merits unless the decision is patently unreasonable, before the *Tribunale Amministrativo Regionale* and, on appeal, before the *Consiglio di Stato*, the decision of which is final.

During the course of the proceedings before any of the aforementioned courts, if the constitutional validity of any provision invoked is challenged and if the judge thinks it appropriate, the matter can be brought before the *Corte Costituzionale* whose decision upon the constitutional validity of the challenged provision is final.

---

5   Always with the possibility of appealing to the *Corte di Cassazione*.

If the *Corte Costituzionale* finds that any provision is unconstitutional in its spirit or its effect, such provision is declared void with immediate effect. Whatever the decision of the *Corte Costituzionale*, the case is then remanded to the appropriate court

1.2 Overview of the law relating to defective products in Italy

The liability for defective products in Italy is now regulated by Decree 224 of 24 May 1988 ('the Decree') which implemented the Directive. However, it is appropriate, before entering into a detailed examination of the Decree, to recall the general principles of Italian law on contractual and tortious liability for defective products. This is in view of the fact that the Decree does not exclude or limit any other cause of action, be it in tort or in contract, that the damaged party may have according to the law in force. Also, the Decree expressly refers to some provisions of the Code in connection with the determination of the quantum of damages. Furthermore, certain other provisions of the Decree, such as those regulating causation and remoteness of damage, should be construed in the light of the existing law.

1.3 Definition and classification of terms

The Decree uses terminology which is similar to that used in the Directive and the same as that used by Italian courts in implementing existing law. The more widely used terms are:

(a) Parties:
   (i) 'Producer'. The term is used in preference to manufacturer and includes the manufacturer of the whole product or of a part and the producer of a commodity incorporated therein;
   (ii) 'Supplier'. The term is used in the Decree and is intended to refer to wholesalers, retailers and the importer(s) of the product in the EU. The Decree further specifies that the definition includes lessors or any other person that imports the product for hire or any other form of distribution. The Decree also holds responsible for the damage caused by a defective product all those persons that put their name or trademark or other distinguishing feature on the product or on its packaging (Decree, article 3(3)(4));
   (iii) 'Injured party'. The party that suffers injury or loss caused by the defective product and can claim compensation. Such party is generally referred to as 'the consumer' or 'the user'. As the Decree establishes a liability in tort, the injured party need not be the purchaser of the product but could also be a third party.
(b) 'Object'. A product is defined as any movable even if incorporated in a building. The definition expressly includes electricity. Agricultural and fish products are excluded provided always that they have not undergone any 'transformation'.

   'Transformation' is defined as 'a treatment that modifies the characteristics [of the product] or adds any substance'. Packaging and any other treatment of agricultural or fish products that make controls by the consumer difficult, or give rise to reliance as to the product's safety, are considered to be 'transformation' (Decree, article 2(3)).

(c) 'Damage' means:
  (i)   damages resulting from death or personal injury;
  (ii) damages to things but not to the product provided that such things were normally used by the injured party;
  (iii) consequential damages according to remedies available under general tort law.
       Compensation for pain and suffering is recoverable under strictly limited circumstances (see below).
(d) 'Defective product'. The Decree uses the term as opposed to 'defect'.
(e) 'Contributory negligence'. The negligence of the consumer or of the third party which contributes in whole or in part – eg failure to follow instructions or misuse of the product – to the damage. It may exclude liability or reduce it proportionally.

2   PRE-CONTRACTUAL LIABILITY

The Code does not expressly provide for liability for pre-contractual statements short of actual fraud. However, article 1337 of the Code, which imposes a general duty of good faith during the pre-contractual period, has been construed as imposing a duty on each party not to cause unreasonable or detrimental reliance by the other party on the fact of conclusion of the contract. Damages are limited to expenses suffered in reliance by one party on the other and losses consequential to foregone opportunities. There are no precedents of court decisions concerning defective products and article 1337 of the Code.

3   LIABILITY IN CONTRACT

Under the general principles of Italian contract law, a contract is legally binding if it is entered into by parties of sufficient legal capacity and has as its object the exchange of any item of economic value between the parties or otherwise the regulation of any other matter of economic value.

The Code regulates a number of contracts (eg of sale, loan, barter etc) but parties are free to enter into other kinds of contracts provided always that their structure and objectives do not conflict with the general principles of law or public policy.

3.1   Outline of contract law relevant to defective products in Italy

The bases of the liability of the seller for defects of the product sold are set out in articles 1497-1495 of the Code.

3.2   Guarantees

3.2.1   Contractual warranties relating to the quality of goods and safety of goods

Apart from the statutory warranty outlined above, the seller, particularly in the case of machinery, may choose to insert a contractual warranty that the product will perform its function. Such a guarantee may be invoked by the purchaser under the following conditions.

- only 'defects' which it was impossible to identify at the moment of purchase are covered;
- the guarantee period must be stipulated in the contract, otherwise the guarantee is void unless commercial usage provides for an implied warranty. The burden of proof of the existence of the implied warranty is on the purchaser;
- the purchaser must prove only the bad functioning of the product as well as the existence of a guarantee of good functioning;
- by contrast, the vendor is not bound by the guarantee if he proves that the bad functioning depends on a cause which materialised after the contract or is the result of abnormal use by the purchaser.
- on pain of forfeiting his rights, the purchaser must notify the vendor of the defect within 30 days of discovering it; the time limit for bringing the action is six months from the date of discovery;
- the purchaser may choose between replacement of the product and its repair;
- the vendor, under the terms of the Civil Code itself, may not repudiate liability for damages.

The specific rules on the commercial guarantee govern only the relationship between the seller and the purchaser. All other guarantees offered by third parties to purchasers are governed by the common law.

3.2.2 Commercial practice in giving consumer guarantees

The Civil Code contains provisions relating to the guarantee offered by the seller or imposed on it by custom.

3.2.3 Legal provisions relating to the form and content of legal guarantees

The legal guarantees are set out in articles 1490 to 1496 of the Civil Code (principally being a guarantee against latent defects) and Article 1497 of the Civil Code (a mandatory guarantee against quality defects). Case law has also established an obligation on the part of the seller to deliver the goods. For the guarantee against latent defects to operate, the defect must have existed prior to the sale and prevent the normal use of the item or considerably diminish its value.

Such warranty can, however, be excluded by agreement but any such agreement would be invalid if the seller has, in bad faith, hidden the existence of defects (Code, article 1490(2)). The warranty is also excluded if at the time of the contract the buyer knew of the defects or if the defects were clearly noticeable, unless in the latter case the seller had expressly stated that the product did not have any defects (Code, article 1491).

The guarantee against quality defects operates when qualities promised or qualities which are essential for the use of an item are absent, provided the quality defect exceeds normal tolerance limits.

The legal guarantees are enforceable only as between sellers and purchasers. The remedies afforded to the consumer pursuant to the guarantee are reduction in the price of the product or payment of damages, if the vendor acted in bad faith. There is a presumption of bad faith, which the vendor may rebut by proving his ignorance without fault of the defect.

The purchaser must notify the seller within eight days of discovery of the defect, and must bring the action within one year from delivery of the product.

3.3   Breach of contract for supply of defective products

In the case of supply of a defective product, where the statutory warranty has not been properly excluded, the buyer has the choice between:

(a) the termination of the contract and reimbursement of the price;
(b) a reduction of the price paid proportional to the extent of the defect (Code, article 1492).

The defects that give rise to such actions are those that make the product completely impossible to use for its normal purpose or otherwise unfit for use – although it could theoretically be possible to use it.

In the case of breach of a contractual warranty (of the type outlined above in section 3.1) the warranty usually contains an undertaking from the seller to repair or substitute the defective product in whole or in part. In the absence of such an undertaking, the buyer would be entitled to any of the other remedies described above.

3.4   Quantum of damages

In both the cases outlined above (breach of statutory or contractual warranty) the buyer can obtain redress for damages suffered. In both cases the quantum of damage is determined on the basis of the general rule concerning contract damage: the award should put the aggrieved party in the position where it would have been had the contract been properly performed.[6] Accordingly, the seller will be liable for the actual losses suffered by the buyer and any consequential loss of profit so long as they are the 'immediate and direct consequence' of the breach (Code, article 1223). The concept of 'immediate and direct consequence' has been construed to include all those losses that are 'normal consequences of the breach'[7] but does not include unforeseeable damages unless the breach was a result of a wilful or grossly negligent act of the seller (Code, article 1225).

It is worth noting that the definition has been applied in a flexible way so as to include, eg the damage caused to the commercial reputation of a buyer who had unknowingly resold defective products.[8] Contrary to the case where a fixed sum of money is due, the sum awarded, which will refer to the value of the currency at the time of the breach, can be revalued to take into account inflation. The sum awarded can also be reduced in proportion to the contributory negligence of the buyer (Code, article 1227(1)).

The redress of non-financial damages is regulated by article 2059 of the Code.[9] It is widely held that redress for non-financial damages cannot be obtained in the context of an action in contract. However, as courts have allowed the possibility of pursuing redress for damages suffered by means of concurrent actions both in tort and in contract, it is always possible to recover damages for non-financial losses. Finally, it should be noted that the buyer has a duty to mitigate the consequences of the breach, but such duty does not extend to include the duty to make good the loss (Code, article 1227(2)).

6   See *Corte di Cassazione* ('Cass') 15 April 1980, No 2458 in *Massimario Giurisprudenza Italiana*, 1980.
7   See Cass 19 July 1982, No 4263 in *Giurisprudenza Italiana*, 1983 1,1,424.
8   Cass 1512/1969.
9   Of which further in section 4.3 below.

3.5   Burden of proof

In the case of an action in contract, the purchaser of defective products must prove:

(a) the existence of a contract;
(b) the defect; and
(c) the monetary value of any damage suffered.

The seller can avoid liability if he proves that:

(a) (i)   the breach depends on a fact for which he cannot be held liable. The fact must be such that the correct performance of the contract is made impossible and not merely more difficult or expensive;
    (ii) the buyer knew of the defect at the time of sale; and
    (iii) the damage was entirely caused by the contributory negligence of the buyer – that is, the loss would not have occurred but for the act or omission of the buyer; or
(b) there was a valid clause of exclusion or limitation of liability in the contract between the parties.

3.6   Exclusion or limitation of liability

As stated in section 3.1 of this chapter, the seller can insert in the contract a clause to the effect of excluding or limiting the liability for damages caused by a defective product. Such clause could not be invoked in an action in tort brought by the buyer or a third party. To be effective the clause has to satisfy a formal requirement which consists in its specific approval by the buyer. The requirement is, in practice, satisfied by drafting a specific clause approving limitation or exclusion of the liability which bears a separate signature of the buyer (Code, article 1341(2)). The clause may completely exclude the liability of the seller or limit it to a certain amount – as in the case of liquidated damages. Despite its formal validity, however, a limitation or exclusion clause cannot be invoked when the loss arose from a wilful or grossly negligent breach of the contract (Code, article 1229(1)) or where the seller has wilfully failed to disclose the existence of any defect (Code, article 1490(2)).

The Unfair Contract Terms Directive was implemented into Italian law by the insertion of article 1469*bis* into the fourth book of the Civil Code in February 1996. This created a substantive control of exclusion and limitation clauses, in addition to the pre-existing formal control. It is generally considered that the formal requirement of article 1341(2) will be residual and applicable only to those contracts which are not concluded between a business and a consumer.

3.7   Limitation period

An action based on the statutory warranty must be commenced within one year of delivery provided always that the seller was notified of the defect within eight days of its discovery (Code, article 1495). In the case of a contractual warranty, the action must be commenced within six months of the discovery of the defect provided always that the seller was notified of the defect within 30 days of the discovery of the defect (Code, article 1512).

3.8   Liability of third parties: vicarious liability

A seller is liable to third parties under the general principles of tort law. The seller is not liable when an intervening action or omission of a third party occurs, if such act or omission is by itself apt to cause the damage. The seller is liable also if the damage was caused by the act or omission of any subject which is outside his organisation and of which he has availed himself in order to perform the contract (Code, article 1228).

4   LIABILITY IN TORT

4.1   Introduction

The general principle of tort law is embodied in article 2043 of the Code which states that 'any event caused by fault negligence or wilful misconduct binds its author to indemnify any damage deriving therefrom'.

4.2   Outline of relevant tort law giving rise to liability for personal and property damage in Italy

Together with the above mentioned article, the Code provides a number of more detailed provisions regulating the consequences of particular tortious acts, all of which have been used by the courts to impose liability on producers or suppliers of defective products. In this respect, the most relevant provisions are:

(a) article 2050 which holds that whoever carries out an activity that, because of its nature or the means used is potentially 'dangerous', is liable for any damage caused by a defective product unless he proves that 'all the appropriate measures to avoid the loss had been taken' (Code, article 2050);
(b) article 2051 which holds liable a bailee for damage caused by things in his possession. This article has been used to establish the liability of suppliers in cases where it was not possible to sue the producer.[10]

4.3   Causation, remoteness of loss and damage

The Code, article 1223, which regulates the principle of causation for actions in contract, can also be applied to actions in tort. All that is required therefore is that the damage caused be the 'immediate and direct consequence' of the tortious act. In addition, the Code does not limit the recoverable damages to those that were foreseeable at the time of the event but includes any unforeseeable damages. Liability is, however, excluded or reduced in the case of contributory negligence (Code, article 1227). Courts have applied this provision in cases where the consumer had not followed the instructions or the warnings for the use of the product.[11] Finally, the courts have held jointly

---

10   *Corte d'Appello* of Rome, 8 October 1986 in *Foro Italiano*, 1987 1, 1590.
11   Cass 6 February 1978 No 595 in *Foro Italiano*, 1979, 1, 422.

and severally liable in tort both the producer of a single part of a product and the assembler. The rationale given by the courts is that the producer is at fault for having manufactured a defective product whilst the assembler is negligent for not having properly inspected the part and therefore having failed to detect the defect.[12]

4.4 Quantum of damages

Damages in tort should restore the aggrieved party to the position where it was before the tortious act. Damages should cover not only the expenses incurred and the losses suffered, but also loss of earnings and other consequential losses suffered as a result of the tortious act.

As for moral damages – that is, all those losses that do not have a prima facie economic value – article 2059 states that they can only be recovered if the tortious act is criminal.

The article, however, has been construed by the courts as having a rather narrow scope. It has in fact been held that its provisions intend to cover only the so-called 'subjective moral damages' – that is, only those damages to which no economic value can be attributed, such as pain and suffering. On the other hand, the redress of other kinds of damages which do not have an immediate economic value, such as damages to health or reputation, have been recognised as being outside the scope of article 2059[13] and can therefore be compensated even if the tortious act is not relevant with respect to criminal law.

4.5 Burden of proof

In an action in tort, the plaintiff has to prove:

(a) an act or omission on the part of the defendant;
(b) its unlawfulness;
(c) negligence (the degree of which may vary);
(d) damage; and
(e) a causal link between the act or omission and the damage.

In practice, however, particularly in the case of actions in tort for damage caused by defective products, the courts have practically reversed the burden of proof in relation to the proof of negligence. In a leading case decided in 1964, the *Corte di Cassazione* held that the proof of the negligence of the producer

---

12 Cass 13 March 1980 No 1696 in *Giustizia Civile*, 1980, 1, 1914.
13 A leading case on the matter is the judgment of the *Corte Costituzionale* of 14 July 1986 Mo 184 in *Foro Italiano*, 1986, 1, 2053 which clearly stated the principle that damage to health is regulated by article 2043 of the Code and not by article 2059. Courts have interpreted the judgment of the *Corte Costituzionale* as giving rise to two separate claims for damages. On the one hand a claim for the damage to the health of the person injured by the tortious act; on the other a claim by the relatives and dependants of the injured party deriving from the loss of support and from the pain and suffering that the sufferings or the death of the injured party may have caused to the claimant. The second prong of the latter claim, however, can be brought pursuant to article 2059, where the tortious act was relevant with respect to criminal law (see Cass 6 October 1994 No 8177 and *Corte Costituzionale* 27 October 1994 No 372).

was in the fact that the product was defective.[14] In other cases, the courts have applied article 2050 of the Code which places on the producer engaged in activities defined as dangerous the burden of proving that he had adopted all the appropriate measures to avoid the damage – a burden of proof which in most cases has been impossible to discharge. The courts have, for example, qualified as dangerous the sale of children's balloons filled with helium,[15] the sale of bottled gas[16] and the manufacture of pharmaceutical products which were based on or contained human blood.[17]

4.6   Exclusion or limitation of liability

Article 1229 of the Code has been applied to causes of action in tort. Therefore clauses that exclude or limit liability of the producer have been held to be invalid in the case of gross negligence or wilful misconduct. In general, however, as most actions in tort are brought by and against parties amongst which there is no contractual relationship (eg the producer of soft drinks and the ultimate consumer) it is unlikely that such problems may arise.

4.7   Limitation period

The limitation period for an action in tort is five years (Code, article 2947) from the day of the tortious action, or the day when the damage occurred if later. If the tortious act qualifies as a crime, then the limitation period is the same as the one for the commencement of the criminal proceedings (Code, article 2947(3)). If the crime is pardoned or a final judgment given on the matter, the limitation period runs from the date of the pardon or of the final judgment.

4.8   Liability for third parties

Vicarious liability is established by article 2049 of the Code which holds employers liable for damage caused by their servants and employees if the tort was committed in the course of their employment. The rule has been held to encompass the liability of the state for acts of civil servants. As in the case of contractual liability, liability is excluded if an intervening act or omission of a third party occurs, provided always that such act or omission by itself is apt to cause the damage.

---

14   See Cass 25 May 1964 No 1270 in *Foro Italiano*, 1965, 1, 2098. In that case, the plaintiff had eaten some biscuits which were unfit for human consumption. The court held that the mere fact that the biscuits had deteriorated was sufficient proof of the negligence of the producer. See also Cass 28 October 1980 No 5795 in *Repertorio Foro Italiano* 1981.
15   *Pretura* of Genoa 15 February 1974 in *Repertorio Foro Italiano*, 1974.
16   Cass 13 January 1981 No 294 in *Foro Italiano*, 1981, 1, 1326.
17   Cass 15 July 1987 No 6241 in *Foro Italiano*, 1988, 1, 144 and again Cass 20 July 1993 No 8069.

5   LIABILITY FOR DEFECTIVE PRODUCTS ARISING FROM NATIONAL LAW IN ITALY: IMPLEMENTATION OF EC DIRECTIVE 85/374 ON PRODUCT LIABILITY

5.1   Introduction

The implementation of the Directive by means of the Decree has introduced some relevant modifications to the pre-Directive position with regard to liability for defective products.

Whilst the Directive and the Decree are consistent with the general principles of Italian tort law, the new legislation has introduced material changes in a number of areas, such as the identity of the defendants, the burden of proof, the quantum of damages, the limitation period and the defences that the producer can raise.

5.2   Outline of the provisions in Italy

The basic principle introduced by the Decree is that the producer is liable for the damages caused by the defects of his product as a consequence of the mere fact of having put it into circulation.

We shall now examine in more detail the most relevant provisions of the Decree.

5.2.1   Defendants

The provisions of the Decree differ from those of the Directive with respect to the release from liability of the supplier upon disclosure of the identity of the producer or of the importer. According to the Decree, the consumer must ask the seller in writing to disclose the name of the producer or importer. The supplier has a term of three months from the date of the request to disclose the identity of the producer or of the importer. The request must contain information on the product and the date and the place of purchase and can be made before commencing the proceedings. If the injured party fails to ask the seller to disclose the name of the producer or importer, the supplier can disclose it within three months of commencement of the proceedings. The supplier may also at the first hearing ask the court to grant a further three-month term within which the seller may disclose the name of the producer. The disclosure of the name of the producer or the importer will mean that the producer or importer will be joined in the case as defendant pursuant to article 106 of the Italian Code of Civil Procedure.

The effect of the application of article 106, however, is not immediately to release the supplier. The scope of article 106 is to prevent related causes of action from being decided in different proceedings, but it does not go so far as to release any of the parties involved.

The Decree does not provide for cases in which the producer does not appear in court or is outside the reach of the jurisdiction.

In the light of the general scope of the Decree – that is, to ensure the protection of the consumer – it could be argued that, if the producer cannot be brought before the court, the liability should be borne entirely by the supplier.

5.2.2   *Defective product*

The Decree, unlike the Directive, specifies that a product is to be considered defective when it does not provide the same degree of safety as that 'normally offered by any other product of the same series' (Decree, article 5(3)). On the other hand, whilst article 6(2) of the Directive does not allow a product to be considered defective 'for the sole reason that a better product is subsequently put into circulation', the Decree seems to expand such exception. In fact, the corresponding provision refers to a 'better product that has, at any time, been put into circulation' (Decree, article 5(2)). The wording of the Decree seems, however, to be consistent with the principle, stated in article 6 of the Directive and article 5 of the Decree, that a product is defective when it does not provide the level of safety which a person is entitled to expect – this is different from the level of safety which it is technically possible to obtain.

5.2.3   *Damages*

The Decree does not put a ceiling on the amount of damages that can be awarded thus exercising the option granted by article 17(1) of the Directive. The Decree also states that the recovery of damages to property is limited by a lower threshold of Lire 750,000.

In the first case decided by an Italian court after the implementation of the Directive, the *Tribunale* of Monza[18] has awarded to a consumer Lire 7.5 million (approximately £3,000) as damages for the personal injuries suffered as a result of a fall from a defective mountain bike.

Apart from the historical fact that this case was the first to be decided in Italy under the Directive, the most important feature remains that the damage redressed by the Court was the personal injury suffered by the plaintiff which did not include the cost of the mountain bike itself

This is consistent with the provision of the Directive which limits the redress to the personal damages suffered and does not cover the damages to the product.

5.2.4   *Defences*

Article 6 of the Decree contains a list of exclusions of producers' liability which mainly reflect the provisions of the Directive. There are, however, some differences.

Whilst article 7(b) of the Directive excludes the liability of the producer if the latter proves that 'it is probable that the defect did not exist at the time when the product was put into circulation by him or that the defect came into being afterwards', article 6(b) of the Decree requires that 'the defect did not exist at the time when the product was put into circulation by [the producer]'. The difference would appear to be substantial. However, in article 8(2) the Decree seems to reintroduce the wording of the Directive when it states that, in order to exclude the liability pursuant to article 6, 'it is sufficient to prove that, in the circumstances, it is probable that the defect did not yet exist at the time when the product was put into circulation'. It would therefore appear that, albeit in a rather contorted way, the Decree substantially adheres to the wording of the Directive in connection with the exclusion of liability as stated by the latter in article 7(b).

---

18   *Tribunale* of Monza, 20 July 1993 in *Foro Italiano*, 1994 I, 251

The second part of the provision of article 6(b) of the Directive is excluded from the Decree which would bring into play any defect that came into being after the product was put into circulation.

Article 6(d) of the Decree (which reproduces the corresponding provision of the Directive) is consistent with a general principle of Italian law according to which no one can be held liable for the detrimental consequences of his act or omission if such act or omission were due to compliance with an existing law or regulation.

It is, however, worth noting that such provision could contradict article 6(e) which excludes the liability of the producer if it is proved that the defect could not have been discovered taking into consideration the existing 'state of the art'.

In fact, it is not uncommon that laws and regulations are not regularly updated to take into account any change in scientific and technological knowledge and therefore it could well happen that a product, though it would formally satisfy the conditions laid down by paragraph (d), would be considered defective and give rise to liability under paragraph (e). Although courts have not yet been called to decide on the issue, it is possible that they will allow a defence under paragraph (d) to stand only if the producer can prove that existing laws or regulations compelled him to manufacture the product in only one possible way.

Article 6(e) of the Decree adopts a wording which is not altogether the same as that of article 7(e) of the Directive. In fact, whilst the latter excludes liability when 'the state of scientific and technical knowledge at the time when he [the producer] put the product into circulation was not such as to enable the existence of the defect to be discovered', the former refers to the fact that scientific and technical knowledge did 'not yet allow the product to be considered as defective'. The different wording seems to introduce a 'subjective' element in the appraisal of the state of scientific and technical knowledge and such an approach would appear to be in contrast with the more objective one that is suggested by the wording of the Directive.

Finally, it should be noted that the Decree has accepted the broad principle contained in article 7(e) of the Directive – even if in a slightly different wording, and possibly in an even softer form – rejecting the stricter option provided by article 15(1)(b) of the same.

5.2.5 *Extinction of the right to compensation*

The Directive provides that the right to obtain compensation should be extinguished within ten years of the date when the defective product was put into circulation. Such extinction would be avoided only if the injured party commenced proceedings against the producer. In the Decree, the extinction of the right is avoided not only by the commencing of proceedings – if the case is not then abandoned – but also by the admission of the party which is liable or the presentation of a statement of claim in the liquidation of the producer or any other liable party (Decree, article 14(1)(2)). Article 14(3) of the Decree also states that any such act mentioned before, which would avoid the extinction of the right, would have effect only with regard to the liability of the party (defendant) concerned.

5.3 Optional provisions in the EC Directive

The Directive allowed for a number of optional provisions to be inserted in the national implementing laws.

5.3.1   *Agricultural produce*

With respect to agricultural produce, the Decree has implemented the Directive in its main formulation, rejecting the option provided in article 15(1) of the Directive – that is, choosing not to include 'primary agricultural products and game' in the definition of a product. In this respect, it is appropriate to recall that the Decree also contains an elaborate description of what is a 'primary agricultural product which has undergone initial processing' (see above in section 1.3 of this chapter).

5.3.2   *'State of the art' defence*

The Decree includes 'the state of the art' defence – albeit in a slightly different wording (see section 5.2.4 of this chapter).

5.3.3   *Limitation of the total liability for damage*

The Directive gave the option of limiting the total liability for damages caused by identical products and resulting in death or personal injuries. The Decree does not contain any such limitation.

5.3.4   *Differences between national law and the provisions of the Directive*

i   Notion of 'product put into circulation'   The Decree, unlike the Directive, specifies when a product is considered as 'put into circulation'. Article 7 of the Decree states that a product is to be considered as put into circulation when:

(a) it is delivered to the purchaser or the user, or an employee or agent of the former, even if such delivery is made for the sole purpose of testing or otherwise inspecting the product (Decree, article 7(1));
(b) the product is not delivered directly to the purchaser or user but is delivered to a carrier or forwarding agent for delivery (Decree, article 8(2));
(c) in the case of forced sale, the debtor has not specifically indicated the defect to the bailiff at the time of the attachment or within 15 days of the attachment by lodging in court appropriate notice or by notifying the creditor (Decree, article 7(3)).

ii   Third party liability   The Decree does not reproduce article 8(1) of the Directive which states that the liability of the producer is not excluded by the contributory act or omission of a third party. The absence of such provision reinforces the liability of the producer, but it would not seem to prejudice its right of contribution against a third party.

iii   Contributory negligence   Article 8(2) of the Directive provides for reduction or exclusion of the liability of the producer in the case of contributory negligence on the part of the consumer. In the corresponding provision of the Decree (article 10) it is stated that contributory negligence should be evaluated in the light of article 1227 of the Code. Also, the said article 10 provides for exclusion of the liability of the producer in the case of there being a willing assumption of the risk – as in the case of a consumer who, although not acting negligently in using the product, had knowledge of the defect and had nevertheless willingly exposed himself to the risk of damage (Decree, article 10(2)). Finally, article 10(3) of the Decree states that, to the limited extent of the compensation for damage to property, the contributory negligence of whoever is in possession

of the defective product is to be construed as contributory negligence of the injured party.

6 CRIMINAL LIABILITY FOR DEFECTIVE PRODUCTS ARISING FROM BOTH GENERAL SAFETY LAW AND THE IMPLEMENTATION OF EC DIRECTIVE 92/59 EC ON PRODUCT SAFETY

6.1 Introduction

The criminal liability introduced by the decree implementing Directive 92/59 into Italian law is imposed for breach of the obligation not to put into circulation defective products or the failure to supply information to the Italian Ministry of Trade.

Such penalties include prison terms of up to one year or a fine between Lire 5 million and Lire 30 million.

The decree further specifies that these provisions do not limit the application of the appropriate sanctions where the act performed also constitutes a different crime (see also section 6.5 below).

6.2 Implementation of Directive 92/59

Directive 92/59EC was implemented into Italian law by Decree No 115 of 17 March 1995.

6.3 Description of anomolous provisions

No anomalous provisions appear to have been inserted in the Italian decree.

6.4 Local optional provisions

A producer who has introduced a defective product to the market may be imprisoned for up to one year or fined between Lire 5 million and Lire 30 million (approx £2,500 – £15,000). A producer who fails to adduce information requested of it by the relevant regulatory authority is liable to be fined between Lire 1 million and Lire 6 million (approx £500 – £3,000).

Enforcement of the provisions of the Directive is vested in the various ministries, as appropriate, such as the ministry of trade, commerce and craft, of health, of work and social security, of finance and of transport.

A 'product', as defined in article 2, may include capital goods used by consumers, since it is not specifically excluded.

6.5 Other safety laws

Examples of other safety laws are Law 547 of 1955, which lays out the necessary precautions to ensure safety at work, and Decree 927 of 1981, which imposes a duty of placing a health warning on the packaging of dangerous substances. Another interesting example is provided by Law 592 of 1967 and the Decree of 15 September 1972 which discipline the manufacturing and importing of

medicines based on or containing human blood. Specifically, Law 592 prescribes that any medicine should, before being distributed, be approved by the Ministry of Health. Such approval, however, was held not to exclude the liability of the manufacturer for damage suffered by consumers.[19]

The Decree of 15 September 1972 states that in the case of imported medicines the importer can also be held liable for damages. A general duty of information on medicines is imposed upon the National Health Service (*Servizio Sanitario Nazionale*) by Law 833 of 1978 but any failure to do so does not seem to result in liability on the part of the Health Service.

Finally, it is worth noting that the manufacture, distribution or importation of defective medicines gives rise, in certain cases, to criminal liability pursuant to articles 443 and 452 of the Italian Penal Code.

7   CIVIL LIABILITY FOR DEFECTIVE PRODUCTS BROUGHT ABOUT BY BREACH OF STATUTORY REGULATION DESIGNED TO PROTECT CONSUMERS AND/OR TO PROMOTE SAFETY

The Italian legal system provides a number of statutory regulations that are designed to promote safety and/or protect consumers, examples of which are given in section 6 above.

In general, however, all the above-mentioned regulations, whilst envisaging different forms of criminal liability for the case of non-compliance, do not provide any specific provision for the redress of damage caused to third parties. This is consistent with the widely held opinion that the principles of tort law contained in the Code are applicable to any case of tortious liability.

---

19   Cass 15 July 1987 no 6241 in *Foro Italiano*, 1988, 1, 144, and again Cass 20 July 1993 No 8069.

CHAPTER XI

Luxembourg

Rene Diederich, Esq

Loesch & Wolter Avocats
11 Rue Goethe
BP 1107
L-1011 Luxembourg

Tel: ++ 352 48 11 48-1
Fax: ++ 352 49 49 44

CHAPTER XI

Luxembourg

1 INTRODUCTION TO THE LEGAL SYSTEM IN LUXEMBOURG

1.1 Introduction

The Grand-Duchy of Luxembourg is an independent sovereign State, organized as a Constitutional Monarchy headed by a Hereditary Grand-Duke who exercises his powers in accordance with the Constitution. The first constitution was established in 1841 but today's constitution dates back to 1868 and has been amended several times since then. The political system is that of a Parliamentary Democracy.

1.2 Civil Court System

As far as the legal system is concerned, the *Tribunal d'Arrondissement* which is divided into specialised sections has full and common jurisdiction. There are furthermore several courts having special jurisdictions in matters such as, for example, administrative law, labour law or social security law.

Claims involving compensation for property damages or for personal injuries may be entered not only in the civil courts but also in the criminal courts when the damage or the injury is chargeable to a fault committed by a person who is prosecuted for it. In that case, the court will not only punish the prosecuted (fine, prison, etc) but also indemnify the victim if the latter acts as a *partie civile*.

Litigation regarding property damage and personal injury may therefore be heard in every court according to circumstances.

The general court system – save for exceptions falling outside the scope of this study – can be summarised as follows:

(a) Litigation in civil or commercial matters valued in excess of LUF 400,000 (except those which must be brought before the *Tribunal du Travail*) must be brought before the *Tribunal d'Arrondissement*. As from 1 December 1996 (pursuant to the law of 11 August 1996) claims in civil and commercial matters valued below LUF 400,000 must be brought before the *Justice de Paix*. The *Tribunal d'Arrondissement* also hears appeals from decisions of the *Justice de Paix* (allowed when the original claim is in excess of LUF 30,000). Litigation in employment matters must be brought before the *Tribune du Travail*.

(b) Litigation concerning facts subject to criminal prosecutions are heard, as a rule, without consideration of the amount of the civil claim. The court used will depend upon the type of the offence (when the offence is a contravention, it is heard by the *Tribunal de Police*; when it is a *délit* it is

277

heard by the *Tribunal Correctionnel* and when it is a *crime* it is heard by the *Chambre Criminelle*). The *Tribunal Correctionnel* deals with the appeal of a judgment rendered by the *Tribunal de Police*.

(c) Litigation arising out of administrative decisions of the State and other public authorities are brought, either directly, or after unsuccessful complaint to the competent Minister, before the Litigation Committee of the *Conseil d'Etat*.

1.3   Fees related to litigation

The losing party normally bears the legal costs which include the bailiff's fees, expert's fees and other costs, but not the fees or expenses of the lawyers of the winning party. The sharing of costs may however be decided by the court if the winning party did not obtain everything he claimed. Each party has to bear the fees of its own counsel.

However, if the court is of the opinion that it is inequitable that a party has to pay certain costs, ie lawyers' fees other than those already included in legal costs, the judge may order the other party to pay such sum.

1.4   Arbitration

Any dispute relating to a contract may be resolved by arbitration, if the contract so provides or the parties agree.

Disputes relating to the legal status and the capacity of a person, matrimonial relations, divorce and separation, as well as matters relating to the incapacity and the absence of persons are excluded from arbitration.

Luxembourg is a party to various international agreements in respect of international commercial arbitration.

As far as recognition and enforcement of foreign arbitral awards are concerned, the application for enforcement has to be filed with the Presiding Judge of the *Tribunal d'Arrondissement*.

2   OVERVIEW OF THE LAW RELATING TO DEFECTIVE PRODUCTS IN LUXEMBOURG

Prior to the implementation of the Directive in Luxembourg law, the product liability rules were mainly based on the provisions embodied in articles 1641-1649 of the Luxembourg Civil Code dealing with the liability for latent defects in products under sales contracts.

French and Belgian case law which a Luxembourg Court having to decide on the question will consider, has developed in many types of contracts an ancillary safety obligation, based upon the above mentioned articles of the Civil Code, which is binding upon professional sellers, pursuant to which the seller is liable under the sales contract for accidents caused to the purchaser by a product which has been sold. Therefore this safety warranty of the seller resembles the warranty of the seller for hidden defects.

As explained below, liability in contract can only be relied upon if a contractual relationship exists between the parties whereas liability in tort may be invoked in the absence of any contractual relationship between the parties involved. Therefore only third parties, ie persons who are not parties to or

beneficiaries of a contract, may sue the manufacturer of a defective product on the basis of liability in tort.

As to the Law on Defective Products which does not prejudice the rights of the plaintiff to claim compensation for the damage suffered on the basis of liability in contract or in tort, this Law supplements, rather than amends, the existing provisions of Luxembourg law governing the liability of the seller or manufacturer for defective products.

3 PRE-CONTRACTUAL LIABILITY

3.1 Effect on the interpretation and extent of the obligations of the parties to a contract

The Luxembourg Civil Code does not expressly address pre-contractual negotiations and the legal regime applicable to such negotiations has therefore mainly been developed in the case law. In the course of contract negotiations, parties often enter into some form of pre-contractual agreement. It is important to note that the qualification given by the parties to their pre-contractual agreement will not be decisive in determining whether and to what extent such an agreement is binding. The courts will instead consider the contents of the agreement and the intention of the parties in order to determine whether or not it is binding.

However, as far as the obligations of the seller in a sale contract are concerned, the Civil Code expressly provides that they must be precisely defined.

Indeed article 1602 of the Civil Code provides that the seller is bound to explain to the purchaser clearly what his obligations will be under the sales contract. An obscure or ambiguous agreement will be construed against the seller.

The liability of the seller under this provision of the Civil Code is a contractual one.

3.2 Extent that non-disclosure of facts during negotiations may lead to liability

Although the Luxembourg Civil Code does not contain any specific provisions with respect to a duty of information which could be binding upon the parties prior to the conclusion of a contract, Luxembourg case law provides that professional sellers are bound to inform their potential customers of the advantages and dangers of a contemplated measure or action and of any circumstances which might influence the other party to enter into an agreement.

The professional seller has to give full information to his potential customers so they may decide whether or not to buy the product with full knowledge of the facts. The professional seller does not however have to act as the adviser of his potential customer.

3.3 Does pre-contractual liability lie in contract or tort?

Under the *culpa in contrahendo* theory, the failure of a negotiating party to comply with its duty of information is to be interpreted on the basis of the

principles of tort law (article 1382 et seq of the Civil Code). Consequently, a party availing itself of the *culpa in contrahendo* theory must prove that the other party failed to comply with its duty of information, that he suffered injury, and that a causal relationship exists between the injury and such failure.

4   LIABILITY IN CONTRACT

4.1   Outline of contract law relevant to defective products in Luxembourg

Prior to the implementation of the Directive and as in France and Belgium, the product liability rules in Luxembourg were mainly based on the provisions contained in articles 1641–1649 of the Luxembourg Civil Code dealing with the liability for latent defects in products under sales contracts.

The Luxembourg courts have traditionally and repeatedly expressed the view that the provisions of articles 1641–1649 of the Civil Code can be applied to sales contracts as general principles of law. Similar rules have also been applied by the Luxembourg courts to other kinds of contracts as, for instance, building contracts, lease contracts etc.

The courts developed the seller's and the manufacturer's obligations under these kinds of contracts to supply a product which had to conform with the provisions of the contract. A number of ancillary obligations were also developed by the courts which were imposed on the seller and the manufacturer, in particular the obligation to inform, advise and warn the purchaser of the conditions of use of the product and its potential dangers.

4.2   Contractual warranties relating to quality of goods and safety of goods

According to article 1603 of the Civil Code the seller has two main obligations under a sales contract, the first is to deliver the product, meaning that the seller has to place within the actual control of the purchaser a product which conforms to the object sold, and the second is to warrant the object sold.

The warranty to be given by a seller under a sale contract is twofold: first, the seller has to ensure that the purchaser has peaceful and 'untroubled possession' of the object sold and, secondly the seller must give a warranty to the purchaser against the hidden defects in the object sold or redhibitory defects. The breach of the obligation to deliver the product may lead to the rescission of the sale contract and may entitle the purchaser to claim further damages, unless the purchaser accepted the object acquired.

The warranty as to the peaceful and untroubled possession of the product which has been sold is mandatory and perpetual. The seller is bound to this warranty unless he can give evidence that the non-performance of his obligation under the sale contract is due to an external cause.

A breach of this warranty may lead to the reimbursement of the price paid by the purchaser and the payment of further damages, as the case may be.

Although the Civil Code does not contain any specific provision imposing a warranty on the seller for the safety of the products sold by him, Belgian jurisprudence has developed in many types of contracts an ancillary safety obligation which is binding upon professional sellers.

Numerous court decisions have admitted that the seller is liable under the sales contract for accidents caused to the purchaser by a product which has been sold.

To a certain extent, this warranty of the seller relating to the safety of the products sold and the warranty of the vendor for hidden defects may merge into one another.

However, this may not be completely true and the warranty deriving from the safety obligation may complete the effects of the warranty for hidden defects. A seller may, indeed, be held liable to the purchaser on the basis of this safety obligation without the necessity for the purchaser to give evidence that the hidden defect has caused the damage.

4.3   Commercial practice in giving consumer guarantees and legal provisions regulating the form and content of legal guarantees

There are no specific legal provisions regulating commercial guarantees. The commercial guarantees depend on the type of product sold and on the commercial policy of the manufacturer (commercial guarantees are for instance frequent in the car trade).

The Law of 25 August 1983 on Consumer Protection provides, however, that descriptions of the main features and characteristics of a product or of a service provided in written form and in advertisements, as well as any kind of warranty offered, are deemed to be part of the contract relating to the product or to the service, even though the information or publicity originates from the manufacturer, the holder or the operator of the trademark, or any other professional person at a prior stage in the supply chain to the seller or the supplier of the product or services concerned.

4.4   Breach of contract for supply of defective products

4.4.1   *Types of defect*

Article 1641 of the Civil Code provides that the seller is bound to give a warranty for hidden defects in the product sold which render the product unsuitable for its intended use or which restricts that use to such a degree that the purchaser would not have bought it or would have paid a lesser price had he known of the defects.

According to article 1642 of the Civil Code the seller is not bound to give a warranty for visible defects which could have been detected by the purchaser himself.

The purchaser discovering a latent defect may sue the seller if:

(i)   the product under consideration cannot be used for the purpose for which it has normally been designed; and
(ii) the defect is latent or hidden, which means that the purchaser was not able to notice it at the moment of the purchase; and
(iii) the defect existed prior to the purchase; and
(iv) the defect is within the product itself.

It is generally admitted that a defect is deemed to be latent if it was not reasonably possible to discover it at the very moment when the purchaser took possession of the product and the existence of the defect could not be revealed

by any circumstance. For a purchaser having no technical knowledge, the defect is deemed to be hidden if only a qualified technician could have detected it. The defect is, however, deemed to have been visible if a normally skilled person could have discovered it by an elementary but not superficial examination.

Subject to the above-mentioned conditions, the seller will be liable for any hidden defect which has been discovered.

However, the Civil Code makes a distinction with respect to the extent of liability incurred between a seller who was unaware of the defect in the product and who, as a consequence, acted in good faith, and a seller who knew of the defect in the product at the very moment of the sale and who therefore acted in bad faith.

Whereas the seller who has acted in good faith may, on the one hand, have to repay the price of the defective product and reimburse the purchaser for the costs of the sale and may, also, be entitled to take advantage of a provision of the contract limiting his liability, the seller who has or is deemed to have acted in bad faith will have to repay the price and he will also be bound to compensate the purchaser against any and all damages suffered by the purchaser.

It is also important to mention in this context that the seller having, or deemed to have, acted in bad faith may not avail himself of any provision of the contract limiting his liability.

Pursuant to well-established law, professional sellers are presumed to have knowledge of all hidden defects and the professional seller therefore has the same liability as a seller having acted in bad faith. This rule applies equally to manufacturers, suppliers and retailers.

Luxembourg jurisprudence considers that this presumption is irrebutable and the professional seller (or the manufacturer) may not escape his liability by pleading that it was technically impossible to discover the defect or to avoid the appearance of the defect.

Indeed the Luxembourg courts have decided that, as a professional, the seller is liable for the quality of the product used, even though he did not know of the defect or the characteristics of the product. The 'development risks' defence is therefore not available under Luxembourg contract law.

Where the requirements of article 1641 of the Civil Code are fulfilled, the purchaser may either sue the seller in order to have the contract rescinded ('redhibitory action'), or he may sue the seller in order to obtain a reduction of the sale price ('estimatory action').

The Luxembourg courts have also admitted that apart from these two actions the purchaser can also claim from the seller other types of performances such as the replacement of the product or the repair of the defect. The court will not order a seller to repair a product where the repair is impossible or if the repair will run up costs which are out of all proportion to the value of the object which has been sold.

The purchaser may only sue the seller on the basis of the redhibitory action if the object sold is absolutely unusable for the purpose for which it is intended. If, however, the defects may easily be repaired and the repairing of the object does not deprive the purchaser of the use of the object for a long period, the purchaser may only make a claim for the repair of the product.

It should be noted that the warranty for hidden defects is transferred together with the product if it is sold several times. The ultimate purchaser may bring a direct action based on this warranty for latent defects against a remote seller or even against the manufacturer.

The manufacturer and the successive sellers will be held jointly and severally liable towards the ultimate purchaser, save that in this chain only the persons who sold the product after the hidden defects came to existence will be liable.

Besides rescission of the sale or reduction of the price, further compensation as indicated above can be sought by the purchaser if the seller acted in bad faith.

4.4.2 *Causation*

According to article 1150 of the Civil Code contractual compensation is only due for foreseeable damages, that is to say, for damage which was or could be foreseen when the contract was concluded. This principle does not apply however if the non-performance of the contractual obligation is a consequence of fraud or wilful misrepresentation.

In this respect, it is important to make a distinction between the nature and the extent of the damage, on the one hand, and the monetary equivalent which has to be paid in order to compensate this damage on the other hand.

The seller will, of course, only be held liable for a foreseeable damage which is a consequence of the non-performance by the seller of a contractual obligation.

Compensation for all other kinds of damage may only be sought against the seller on the basis of a liability in tort even though the defendant and the plaintiff are contractually bound.

As a consequence, the seller will have to compensate the purchaser for any foreseeable damage resulting from the non-performance by the seller of any of his contractual obligations and it will be for the seller to prove that certain damage claimed by the purchaser was not foreseeable at the moment of the conclusion of the contract.

It follows that, in this context of the liability in contract, the main question to be solved will not be the question of the causation but the question of the foreseeability of a certain damage.

4.5 Remoteness of loss and damage

The plaintiff will only be compensated for an immediate and direct damage meaning that the plaintiff will have to give evidence of a direct relationship between the breach of contract and the damage.

The damage suffered by the victim must be actual. The plaintiff may not be compensated for a potential damage.

As far as the parties who may claim compensation are concerned besides the victim itself and the relatives of the victim (if they can give evidence of their indirect material or immaterial loss and if they can demonstrate that their claim is based on negligence), legal insurers for injuries to workers, property insurers and employers may, to a certain extent, recover sums paid to the plaintiff whether under an employment agreement or under an insurance contract.

4.6 Quantum of damage

As indicated here above contractual compensation is only due for the foreseeable damage.

Even in the latter case, the amount of damages which will have to be paid to the plaintiff may only be in compensation for the damage suffered (*damnum emergens*) by the person entitled to performance of the contractual obligation and of the profit of which such person has been deprived (*lucrum cessans*), that is to say, for all those damages which can be seen as an immediate and direct consequence of the non-performance of the contractual obligation.

It is indeed a general rule under Luxembourg law that a plaintiff has to be compensated for the entire damage he has suffered, no more and no less.

As far as the principle of foreseeability is concerned, it has been ruled that the damage must be foreseeable only as to its possibility not as to its amount.

The plaintiff may recover either for material or immaterial losses.

These damages include all losses suffered by the purchaser of a defective product either to his property or to his person such as physical harm, loss of income and of ability or earning capacity.

Immaterial losses which may be claimed include moral and aesthetic sufferings including pain and suffering.

Pursuant to article 1152 of the Civil Code if the agreement stipulates that the party failing to perform its obligation under the contract has to pay a specific sum of money to the other party in order to compensate for the damage suffered by the party, it will not be possible to allocate to the recipient of the contractual obligation either a greater or a lesser sum of money.

The Law of 15 May 1987 has introduced a second paragraph to this article 1152 of the Civil Code. This paragraph provides that the court may reduce or increase the agreed penalty if this penalty obviously appears to be excessive or ridiculous. This legal provision contained in paragraph 2 of article 1152 is a mandatory provision of Luxembourg law.

4.7   Burden of proof

Under Luxembourg law, the onus is normally on the plaintiff to establish the merits of his claim.

The burden of proof, however, is reversed to a certain extent insofar as product liability is concerned, since the law almost presumes the manufacturer's liability unless the seller proves an 'act of God' (*cas de force majeure*).

4.8   Exclusion or limitation of liability

Generally speaking, provisions contained in a contract limiting or excluding the liability of one of the contracting parties are deemed to be valid unless they are expressly excluded by mandatory legal provisions or they cover fraud or wilful misconduct.

It should also be noted, in this context, that according to article 1135-1 of the Luxembourg Civil Code a clause in a contract which includes a limitation of the liability of the person who has prepared the pre-established terms and conditions (ie normally the seller) has to be accepted by a special signature of the other contracting party.

Provisions limiting the seller's liability in respect of either his delivery obligation or his obligations with respect to the conformity of the product sold have traditionally been deemed valid.

However, as the professional seller is presumed to know the defect latent in his product, where such clauses limit the duration of the liability, the types of defect or the kind of damage for which the seller will be responsible, are considered to be invalid.

In the case of contracts entered into between professionals, the seller may produce evidence to show that the purchaser had the same kind of professional skill and expertise as himself and therefore had the technical knowledge and capability to discover the defect at the time of the sale. In this event, a contractual provision excluding or limiting the liability of the seller would be effective.

According to article 1645 of the Civil Code, if the purchaser is a non-professional end-consumer a contractual provision limiting or excluding the liability of the seller is considered to be null and void.

It should be noted that the Unfair Contract Terms Directive has not yet been implemented in Luxembourg. A draft law is under discussion and will modify the current article 1135 -1 of the Civil Code and certain provisions of the Law of 25 August 1983 on the Consumer Protection and of the Law of 16 July 1987 on Sale from Door-to-Door, Itinerant Trading and the Display of Goods.

4.9   Limitation period

Pursuant to article 1648 of the Civil Code, in respect of the appearance of latent defects, the purchaser must declare the hidden defect to the seller within a short period from the time when the purchaser discovered or should have discovered the hidden defect.

Article 1648 gives no clear-cut definition of this short period. The acceptable length of such period will therefore be left to the discretionary power of the courts, which will come to a decision taking into consideration the circumstances of a given case and the kind of defect.

The purchaser loses his right to sue the seller after the expiry of a period of one year starting on the date the purchaser disclosed the latent defect to the seller, in the event the purchaser was not in a position to start the proceedings due to a fraud committed by the seller.

This limitation period may be suspended by negotiations with a view to an amicable settlement between the seller and the purchaser and may also be interrupted by summary proceedings or by any other judicial means with respect to the latent defect.

A new limitation period of one year will then start at the moment when the seller notifies the purchaser by registered mail that he has decided to break off negotiations or at the moment when the purchaser has been informed at the end of the judicial proceedings initiated in order to establish the alleged latent defect.

After the expiry of this further period of one year, the purchaser will no longer have the right to protection in respect of the latent defect, even by way of defence or counterclaim to an action by the seller. However, according to article 1648(5) of the Civil Code, the purchaser, who has not yet paid the price of the product and who has complained of the latent defect within the short period mentioned above, has the right to put it to the seller, as a defence to a claim for the payment of the price and a counterclaim in order to obtain a reduction of the price or compensation for further damages.

An action for lack of conformity of the product sold to specification or to the provisions of the sale contract is not subject to the limitation period provided under article 1648 of the Civil Code.

In accordance with the general rules of liability in contract, the limitation period is either:

(a) ten years for actions taken against a manufacturer or professional seller; or
(b) thirty years for actions taken against a private seller.

However, clauses contained in a contract providing for a shorter limitation period are valid

(a) if they are agreed between professionals having the same kind of expertise and
(b) to the extent that the shorter limitation period provided for leaves a sufficient and reasonable period of time for the plaintiff to initiate proceedings in order to enforce his rights.

4.10   Liability for third parties

The Civil Code does not embody any provision of a general nature which provides for liability in contract for third parties. For certain types of contract, however, legal provisions state that the debtor of the contractual obligation(s) will be held liable if a person who substituted him failed to perform his contractual obligation(s) or performs his obligations improperly. Such provisions exist for instance in respect of lease contracts, contracts for transport of goods, and contracts for work.

Except for the specific types of contract referred to above, there is no published Luxembourg case law on the question of a general principle of liability in contract for third parties. A Luxembourg court having to decide on that question would, given the similarity between Luxembourg and French law, turn to French case law existing on the same question.

According to leading French case law, the principal debtor will be held liable for misperformance or failure to perform by his substitute when the following conditions are met:

(i)   the principal debtor must be personally liable for the execution of the obligation performed by the substituted debtor;
(ii) the principal debtor must voluntarily have delegated the performance of the contractual obligation to the substituted debtor; and
(iii) the principal creditor may not have discharged the principal debtor of any liability in the performance of the contractual obligation by the substituted debtor.

Leading French case law recognises that if these conditions are met, the principal debtor will automatically be held liable for misperformance or non-performance of the contractual obligation by its substitute without the plaintiff having to establish the existence of a negligent act or omission by the principal debtor. However, there is no uniform case law as to whether the plaintiff also has to establish the existence of a negligent act or omission by the substituted debtor.

5 LIABILITY IN TORT

5.1 Introduction

Provisions relating to extra-contractual liability are contained in articles 1382-1386 of the Civil Code.

As a rule, the victim of damage is not free to choose between liability in contract and liability in tort in order to recover in respect of the damage suffered. Under Luxembourg law, the liability in contract and the liability in tort are both mutually exclusive. Where there has been a contractual relationship between the person who is held liable and the plaintiff, the plaintiff should start proceedings against the responsible person on the basis of the contract, even though this rule is not a mandatory one. This means that normally only third persons may sue the manufacturer of a defective product on the basis of liability in tort. Third persons are defined as being all those who are not parties to or beneficiaries of a contract.

The manufacturer of a defective product may be held liable in tort either on the grounds of articles 1382 and 1383 of the Civil Code, which provide for the liability of those who cause injury to others as a result of a tortious breach or negligence, or on the grounds of article 1384(1) of the Civil Code, which provides that a person may be held liable for an injury caused by a product or an object which he has in his custody (*garde*).

5.2 Outline of relevant tort law giving rise to liability for personal and property damage in Luxembourg

5.2.1 *Liability in tort based on articles 1382 and 1383 of the Civil Code*

The principle embodied in articles 1382 and 1383 of the Civil Code is that anyone who through his/her negligence injures another person is liable for this injury. Article 1382 of the Civil Code applies this principle to negligent acts whereas article 1383 of the Civil Code applies it to negligent omissions.

The plaintiff harmed by a defective product must establish fault or negligence on the manufacturer's part. This fault or negligence may relate to design or manufacturing defects and also includes the failure of the manufacturer to inform or warn consumers of the possible dangers of the product.

The French courts have been very liberal and have considered that a manufacturer has, in fact, an obligation to deliver products free of defects and to know all the possible defects of his products. This means that the mere fact that the manufacturer has carried out quality control procedures and the necessary checks to ensure the maximum safety of his products will not necessarily exclude him from liability.

This also means that the plaintiff will only have to give evidence that the product under consideration was defective. To date, the Luxembourg courts have not reached similar judgments. However, as the Luxembourg courts tend to follow the jurisprudence of the French courts in such matters, it can be expected that in a similar situation the Luxembourg courts will adopt the same kind of solution.

5.2.2   *Liability in tort based on the Civil Code article 1384(1)*

The Luxembourg courts have developed from article 1384(1) a principle of strict liability in respect of injury caused by products which a person has in his custody (*garde*). In most cases, this person is the legal owner of the product.

Article 1384(1) of the Civil Code applies generally to all kinds of products, whether dangerous or not, whether defective or not. For instance, electricity is considered in this respect as being a 'product'.

Article 1384(1) of the Civil Code relates to the rules of evidence which have been developed: a person is not only held liable for products in his custody, but also for damage caused by the products.

The following distinctions have been made:

(a) If there has been no physical contact between the inanimate product and the injured party, the injured party has to give evidence:
   (i) of the intervention of the product in causing the damage; and
   (ii) the abnormal character of the inanimate product.

   Possible defences are: evidence either of the interference of the injured party or of a third party, or of the occurrence of an extraneous cause (as, for example, *force majeure*).

   However, the defence of interference of a third party is only possible provided that such interference has the characteristics of a '*cas de force majeure*'. In order for an event to be considered as being a '*cas de force majeure*', it has to be unforseeable, irrefutable (incontrovertible) and extraneous to the injured party.

(b) If there has been contact between an inanimate product and the injured party, the injured party has to give evidence of the abnormal character of the product, ie of the abnormal position, installation or behaviour of the said product.

   Possible defences are: evidence of the passive role of the product, or of an extraneous cause.

(c) If the product was in movement and there has been no contact between the product and the injured party, the injured party will have to give evidence:
   (i) of the intervention of the product in the occurrence of the damage; and
   (ii) that the movement of the product is the cause of the damage.

   Possible defences are: evidence either of the interference of the injured party or of a third party, or of an extraneous cause.

(d) If the product was moving and came into contact with the injured party, it is presumed that the injured party has given evidence of the existence of the causal link between the damage and the accident.

   Possible defences are: evidence of the passive role of the product, or the intervention of a third person or the injured party.

In order to indemnify a plaintiff who has no direct contractual link with the seller or the manufacturer, the courts have developed the concept of custody of the structure of the product (*garde de la structure*) by which the manufacturer's or the manufacturer's liability continues after delivery of the product.

The manufacturer is deemed to be able to control the internal structure of the product and check whether the product could be used without danger, even though he no longer owns or possesses the product. This concept of custody

has been applied only to products with inherent internal dynamic forces capable of becoming dangerous by exploding or imploding, such as bottled gas, television sets, soft drink bottles, etc.

The plaintiff will only have to show a causal relationship between the damage suffered and the product.

The 'custodian' of the product may exonerate himself in proving that the damage was due to an external cause, such as a mistake committed by the plaintiff. His liability will be reduced if he shows that the plaintiff has contributed to the damage.

5.3 Causation

Where tort liability is based on articles 1382 and 1383 of the Civil Code, the plaintiff must establish in order to be compensated for the damage suffered the existence of the following three elements:

(i) a negligent act or omission;
(ii) the damage which he has suffered; and
(iii) a causal relationship between the negligent act or omission and the damage.

Where tort liability is based on articles 1384(1) of the Civil Code, the plaintiff must establish:

(i) the intervention of the product in causing the damage or the abnormal character of the product according to the distinctions drawn above;
(ii) the damage which he has suffered; and
(iii) a causal relationship between (i) and the damage.

In case of a custody of the structure of the product (*garde de la structure*) as described above the plaintiff will only have to show a causal relationship between the damage suffered and the product.

5.4 Remoteness of loss and damage

The plaintiff but also the plaintiff's relatives may claim compensation if they can give evidence of their indirect material or immaterial loss.

As for liability in contract, the damage suffered by the plaintiff must be actual. The plaintiff may not be compensated for a potential damage.

5.5 Quantum of damage

According to Luxembourg law, the damage has to be:

(i) lawful (ie not contrary to public order);
(ii) certain;
(iii) direct; and
(iv) personal (ie this covers also the damage suffered by the plaintiff's relatives which it is deemed by law to be a personal damage)

The amount of damages which will have to be paid to the plaintiff for liability in tort is determined along the same principles as those applied in

respect of liability in contract save for the distinction between foreseeable and unforeseeable damage which does not apply to liability in tort.

The general rule under Luxembourg law that a plaintiff has to be compensated for the entire damage he suffered, no more no less, is also true in respect of liability in contract. The plaintiff will thus be compensated for the damage suffered (*damnum emergens*) and for the profit of which the plaintiff has been deprived (*lucrum cessans*).

As in liability in tort the plaintiff may recover either for material or immaterial losses. These damages include all losses suffered by the purchaser of a defective product either to his property or to his person, such as physical harm, loss of income and of ability or earning capacity.

Immaterial losses which may be claimed include moral and aesthetic sufferings, including pain and suffering.

5.6   Burden of proof

The onus is normally on the plaintiff to establish the merits of his claim.

However, as in liability in tort, the burden of proof is reversed to a certain extent insofar as product liability is concerned since with the development of the concept of custody of the structure of the product (*garde de la structure*), the plaintiff only has to show a causal relationship between the damage suffered and the product.

5.7   Exclusion or limitation of liability

Contractual clauses excluding or limiting the liability of the manufacturer have no effect on an action based on tort liability.

5.8   Limitation period

The limitation period for an action in tort is the general limitation period of 30 years from the date the damage occurred.

5.9   Liability for third parties

In accordance with article 1384(3) of the Civil Code, employers who may be manufacturers are liable for the damage caused by their employees in the course of the employees' duties.

They may disclaim this liability by proving that they were vigilant in exercising their authority or in choosing their employees.

They are also discharged if the fault or negligence occurred outside the scope of the employees' functions.

In any case, employers have recourse against such employees and may recover all the damages they have had to pay on behalf of the employees provided the employees can be found guilty of wilful misconduct or of gross negligence (article 47 of the Law of 24 May 1989 on employment contracts).

6   LIABILITY FOR DEFECTIVE PRODUCTS ARISING FROM BOTH GENERAL LAW AND IMPLEMENTATION OF EC DIRECTIVE 85/374 ON PRODUCT LIABILITY IN LUXEMBOURG

6.1   Introduction

The Directive was implemented in Luxembourg by a law of 21 April 1989, regarding the liability deriving from defective products (the 'Law on Defective Products').

In accordance with article 8 of the Law on Defective Products, the legal provisions implementing the Directive do not prejudice the rights of the plaintiff to claim compensation for the damage suffered on the basis of the 'common' law of contractual or extra-contractual liability or on the basis of any other specific laws on liability.

This means that the Law on Defective Products supplements, rather than amends, the provisions of Luxembourg law governing the liability in contract or the liability in tort of the seller or the manufacturer of the defective product or of any other professional contractor.

It goes without saying, however, that this choice of the Luxembourg legislator presents a number of difficulties and it is foreseeable that the co-existence of the general rules of liability in contract and liability in tort with respect to defective products and the specific rules contained in the Law on Defective Products will give rise to conflict.

6.2   Outline of provisions in Luxembourg.

The basic principle of the Law on Defective Products is contained in article 1, which is worded as follows: 'The manufacturer is liable for the damage which has been caused by a defect of his product.'

(a) Article 2.2 gives a more explicit definition of 'the producer' as being the producer of a final product, the producer of a raw material or the producer of a component, as well as any person presenting himself as the producer in affixing to the product his name and trademark, or another distinguishing sign. For all products which have been manufactured in a non-EC country, the importing person or entity is considered, for the purpose of this law, as 'the producer'.

If, however, it is not possible to identify the producer of the product, each and every supplier is deemed to be the producer save if he can indicate the identity of the producer or of his own supplier to the plaintiff within a reasonable time. The same applies with respect to a product which has been imported from a non-EC country, if this product does not indicate the identity of the importer, even though the name of the producer is indicated on the product.

(b) Article 2.1 of the Law on Defective Products defines the product as any movable product even if it is incorporated in another item of movable or immovable property. The same article specifies that the term 'product' also includes electricity.

As a consequence of this definition of the product, it is important to stress that the Law on Defective Products does not apply to immovable or to intangible products.

(c) A product is defective if it does not offer the safety which could reasonably be expected with regard to all the circumstances and in particular with regard to:

(i)   the presentation of the product;

(ii) the use of the product which one could reasonably expect;

(iii) the time of putting the product into circulation.

The law specifies that a product may not be regarded as being a defective product by the mere fact that subsequently a more sophisticated product has been put into circulation.

(d) The damage which will be taken into consideration is defined as each and every type of damage save:

(i)   damage deriving from nuclear accidents;

(ii) damage caused to the defective product itself;

(iii) damage caused to a product or the destruction of a product where this product:

  -   is of a kind which is not normally aimed at private use or consumption; and

  -   has not been used by the plaintiff mainly for private use or consumption.

As a consequence, it appears from the foregoing that the main purpose of the Law on Defective Products is to grant protection to private end-consumers.

On the basis of the Law on Defective Products, the plaintiff may seek compensation of the entire corporal damage he has suffered without any restriction and of damage to his property with a deduction of an amount of approximately LUF 22,500.

Pursuant to article 3 of the Law on Defective Products, the plaintiff will have to prove the damage, the defect of the product and the causal link between this defect and the damage.

The producer will not be held liable in accordance with the Law on Defective Products if he succeeds in establishing:

(a) that he did not put the product under consideration into circulation;

(b) that, with regard to the circumstances of the matter, it would be admitted that:

(i)   the defect that caused the damage did not exist at the very moment when the product was put into circulation by him; or

(ii) that the defect appeared at a later stage;

(c) that the product has neither been manufactured for sale or for any other means of distribution with an aim to profit on the part of the producer nor has it been manufactured or distributed within the parameters of the producer's professional activity;

(d) that the defect is due to the conformity of the product to mandatory rules established by the authorities; and

(e) where the person qualifying as the producer is the producer of a component, that the defect is attributable to the conception of the final product of which the product under consideration is only a component, or is attributable to the instructions which have been provided by the producer of the final product.

If the damage has been caused jointly by a defect of the product and by the mistake of the plaintiff or of a person under his responsibility, the producer will only be held liable to the extent the defect of the product has contributed to the damage.

The producer may not, however, be relieved totally from his liability if he establishes that the damage has been caused jointly by a defect of the product and by the intervention of a third party.

According to article 5(3) of the Law on Defective Products, the liability of the producer in accordance with the provisions of this law may not be restricted or excluded by a contractual clause.

The Law on Defective Products does not require the existence of a contractual relationship between the plaintiff and the producer.

The liability of the producer will only pass through the existence of a contractual relationship between the producer and some other person. Putting a product into circulation can therefore be seen as putting it on the market through a contract transferring its ownership.

Finally, if, on the basis of the provisions of the Law on Defective Products, several persons are liable for the same damage, they will be held liable jointly and severally according to article 6 of the Law on Defective Products.

Article 7 of the Law on Defective Products provides for the following *limitation periods*:

(a) an action for compensation on the basis of the Law on Defective Products has to be started within three years from the date when the plaintiff has or should have discovered the damage, the defect and the identity of the producer (this limitation period may be suspended or interrupted in accordance with the general rules contained in the Civil Code);

(b) the right of the plaintiff to obtain compensation under the Law on Defective Products will expire at the end of a period of ten years from the date on which the producer put into circulation the defective product which caused the damage, except if during this period the plaintiff has started court proceedings against the producer.

6.3 Description of optional or anomalous provisions in respect of product liability in Luxembourg

6.3.1 Primary agricultural products and game

Luxembourg has incorporated in its national legislation the option of the Directive to provide for 'products' to include primary agricultural products and game. Under Luxembourg law liability for agricultural products and game are not dealt with separately.

6.3.2 Development risk defence

Luxembourg has not incorporated the 'state of art' defence (development risk defence) according to which the liability of the producer may be excluded if the state of scientific and technical knowledge at the time when the producer put the product into circulation was not such as to enable the existence of the defect to be discovered.

6.3.3 Limits on total liability

Luxembourg has not incorporated in its national legislation the option to limit the compensation for damage caused by death and personal injuries arising

from a defect. The plaintiff is entitled, under the Law on Defective Products, to seek compensation of the entire corporal damage he has suffered without any restriction and of damage to his property with a deduction of an amount of approximately LUF 22,500.

6.3.4   *Differences between national law and provisions of the Directive*

In accordance with article 8 of the Law on Defective Products, the provisions of this law do not prejudice the rights of the plaintiff to claim compensation for the damages suffered on the basis of the common law of contractual or extra-contractual liability or on the basis of any other specific laws on liability. It seems therefore obvious that the provisions of the Law on Defective Products will give rise to a certain number of difficulties.

(a) On the one hand, it is clear that all matters other than those related to the safety of a product will only be subject to the rules governing liability in contract or liability in tort. As has been explained above, certain products do not qualify as products as defined by the Law on Defective Products and the rules laid down by the Law on Defective Products do not apply to damage caused by a product which has not been put into circulation. The main purpose of the Law on Defective Products appears to be the protection of the private end-consumer against the defects of a product which is intended for private use or private consumption.

(b) On the other hand, it appears also that the provisions of the Law on Defective Products will only constitute a part of the more general rules governing liability for defective products.

However, there may be situations where compensation for damage caused by a defective product may not be possible pursuant to the general or the specific provisions contained in the Civil Code and a plaintiff might, therefore, sue the producer on the basis of the Law on Defective Products.

(c) Finally, it is not yet clear whether and to what extent it will be possible to take advantage of both the provisions contained in the Civil Code relating to liability in contract and liability in tort for latent defects and the provisions contained in the Law on Defective Products.

(d) As the rules and principles governing liability in contract and liability in tort are highly developed in Luxembourg, it is possible that the provisions contained in the Law on Defective Products will be of only limited practical interest and impact. In any case, it seems for the time being premature to make final statements in this respect.

7   CRIMINAL LIABILITY FOR DEFECTIVE PRODUCTS ARISING FROM BOTH GENERAL SAFETY LAW AND THE IMPLEMENTATION OF EC DIRECTIVE 92/59 ON PRODUCT SAFETY IN LUXEMBOURG

This Directive has not yet been implemented in Luxembourg. At the time of writing no draft implementing law has been promulgated.

Under Luxembourg law, in the case of an accident resulting in death or personal injury caused by a defective product, the manufacturer may be subject to criminal liability, for instance, if he is found guilty of gross negligence or non-compliance with regulations.

The manufacturer of a dangerous product (and consequently also the seller who is aware of the danger) who does not warn the purchaser of the product's dangers or who does not withdraw the product from the market when it has caused personal injury, may be subject to criminal sanction.

In this respect it should, however, be stressed that only individuals are liable to criminal sanction.

The managers of a firm may be held liable either for their personal acts and decisions or for their failure to organise manufacture in such a way as to avoid a breach by an employee.

8   CIVIL LIABILITY FOR DEFECTIVE PRODUCTS BROUGHT ABOUT BY BREACH OF STATUTORY REGULATION DESIGNED TO PROTECT CONSUMERS AND/OR TO PROMOTE SAFETY

The Luxembourg legislature has adopted a series of specific regulations in the field of, amongst others, foodstuffs, cosmetics, drugs and medicines, environment, consumer protection etc.

We do not purport to be exhaustive in describing these various specific regulations, we will only briefly summarise some of these provisions and highlight their main features.

8.1   Law of 25 August 1983 on Consumer Protection

Pursuant to article 1 of the Law of 25 August 1983, a clause or clauses contained in a contract entered into between a professional supplier of consumer goods, whether durable or not, or a professional supplier of services and a private end-consumer, which will unevenly balance the contract to the prejudice of the consumer, is considered to be excessive and as such is presumed to be null and void.

The Law of 1983 lists clauses which in particular are to be considered as being excessive. These include clauses:

(a) excluding or limiting the legal warranty for hidden defects;
(b) increasing the amount of the claim of the professional supplier in the event of possible court proceedings;
(c) prohibiting the consumer from suspending the whole or part of the payment of amounts due to the professional supplier if the latter does not fulfil his obligations under the contract; in particular, and according to article 2 of the Law of 25 August 1983, clauses excluding or limiting the legal warranty for hidden defects;
(d) authorising the professional supplier of products or services to amend or to terminate unilaterally the contract without any specific and valid reason stipulated in the contract;
(e) authorising the professional supplier of products or services to determine unilaterally whether or not the products or the services are to be considered as conforming to the contract;
(f) excluding the right of the consumer to terminate the contract if the product has not been delivered or the service has not been rendered within the time promised or within a reasonable or a customary time if no period has been specified;

(g) authorising the professional supplier to determine unilaterally and without any valid and specified (in the contract) reason the date of performance of his obligation;

(h) providing that the products may not correspond to specifications for the consumer or to the sample or to the use which has been specified by the consumer and accepted by the supplier or to their normal use, if no specification has been given;

(i) extending the duration of the contract for more than one year if the consumer does not terminate the contract at a given date;

(j) providing that the price will be determined at the moment of delivery or at the moment of successive deliveries or authorising the professional supplier to increase the price, even with regard to objective criteria, if the consumer does not at the same time have the right to terminate the agreement if it appears that the final price will be excessive for the consumer compared to the price which could be expected by the consumer at the conclusion of the contract;

(k) forcing the consumer to submit his complaints to the supplier within a period which appears to be unreasonably short;

(l) excluding the right of the consumer to terminate the agreement if the supplier is under the obligation to repair the product and he does not comply with this obligation within a reasonable time;

(m) excluding the right of the consumer to sue the supplier in the normal jurisdiction;

(n) authorising the supplier to substitute for the product or the service promised in the contract a different product or service, save if this has been specified in the contract and been formally and explicitly accepted by the consumer;

(o) placing on the consumer the burden of proof which normally has to be borne by the supplier;

(p) forbidding the consumer to set off his obligation to pay against the obligations of the supplier;

(q) imposing on the consumer a minimum consumption obligation in a contract providing for the delivery of gas, electricity or fuel;

(r) which, in relation to the liability of the professional supplier, who commits himself to accomplish a specified work on a product sent to him for that purpose, exclude or limit his obligation to take care of the product which has been remitted to him and to return this product to the consumer after the completion of the work;

(s) pursuant to which the consumer waives his rights to file a claim against the repairer of the product or against the person having done work on this product, on the basis of the legal warranty of the professional seller with respect to the work which has been accomplished by him and the new spare parts supplied by him;

(t) pursuant to which a private end-consumer consents to a transfer of the supplier's claim to a third person and gives a waiver with respect to the rights and defences which he could assert the third party.

Notwithstanding any clause providing to the contrary, the provisions of the Luxembourg Law of 25 August 1983 apply to sales contracts and to contracts for the supply of services entered into between professionals, whether established in Luxembourg or not, and private end-consumers having their normal residence in Luxembourg:

(a) if the conclusion of the contract has been preceded in Luxembourg by a specific proposal or by the advertisement, and if the consumer has accomplished in Luxembourg all the requisite acts for the conclusion of the contract; or
(b) if the contracting party, being a consumer or his representative, has received the order in Luxembourg; or
(c) if the contract qualifies as a sale of products and if the consumer, being resident in Luxembourg, has travelled to a foreign country and has placed the order in this foreign country, subject to the condition that the journey has been organised by the seller with the purpose of inciting the consumer to enter into a sales agreement.

If the parties to the contract did not specifically designate the applicable law, the agreement will be governed by Luxembourg law if the consumer has his normal residence in Luxembourg and if the contract has been concluded in the circumstances described above under 3(a) to (c), above.

However, these provisions do not apply:

(a) to transportation contracts; and
(b) to contracts for the supply of services if the services to the consumer are to be rendered exclusively in a country other than the country of the consumer's normal residence.

The provisions do, however, apply to those contracts offering a global price for combined services of transport and accommodation, i.e. package tour holidays.

The professional supplier who has been successfully sued in proceedings initiated by a private end-consumer, where the application of a clause or of a combination of clauses has been declared excessive and null and void by a final judgment, may be sentenced to a fine between LUF 3,000 and 100,000.

According to article 11 of the Law of 25 August 1983, descriptions of the main features and characteristics of a product or of a service provided in written form and in advertisements, as well as any kind of warranty offered, are deemed to be part of the contract relating to the product or to the service, even though the information or publicity originates from the manufacturer, the holder or the operator of the trademark, or any other professional person at a prior stage in the supply chain to the seller or the supplier of the product or services concerned.

If the product or the service does not conform to the description provided, the consumer is entitled to ask for the rescission of the agreement or a reduction of the price.

8.2 Law of 25 September 1953 relating to the Reorganisation of the Control of Foodstuffs, Drinks and Common Products, as amended.

By virtue of this law, the manufacturing, preparation, transformation, trade and distribution of all kinds of foodstuffs, drinks or drugs used by men and animals, all kinds of consumer products and clothes, cosmetic products etc are submitted to control by the Luxembourg authorities in the interests of public health.

In pursuance of the provisions contained in the Law of 25 September 1953, a certain number of decrees have been adopted, including the following:

(a) the decree of 8 April 1991 concerning products which, appearing to be other than they are, endanger the health or safety of consumers (this decree implements EC Council Directive 87/357 of 25 June 1987)
(b) the decree of 30 July 1994 concerning cosmetic products (which implements EC Council Directive 76/768 of 27 July 1976 as amended)

8.3   Specific regulations relating to pharmaceutical products and drugs

The manufacture, preparation, import and sale of pharmaceutical products are subject in Luxembourg to authorisation obtained in advance from the Ministry of Health.

On the one hand, the manufacturer or the importing body needs to obtain a licence and on the other hand, each product needs to be approved separately by the Ministry of Health.

The manufacture of medicines has to be done under the effective control of a responsible pharmacist, who has been approved by the Ministry of Health. The entity, having obtained an authorisation to import medicines into Luxembourg, has to entrust either a pharmacist or an approved laboratory with the control of the conformity to specifications of each and every portion of medicine imported. This condition is, however, not applicable if medicines are imported from another member state of the EU.

The manufacturing or the importing entity must also comply with a series of conditions in order to ensure that the authorised operations are made under irreproachable conditions regarding employees, premises and equipment.

An information sheet has to be enclosed with every medicine which is distributed in Luxembourg which has to state the counter-indications, the side effects and the kind of precautions the recipients of the medicines need to take. However, there is no formal requirement to appoint a specific person in Luxembourg or elsewhere to report to the Ministry of Health on the recipients' medical reactions.

Although the development risk defence is not permissible under Luxembourg law, the possibility cannot be excluded that the Luxembourg courts might follow French jurisprudence with respect to damage caused by pharmaceutical products and might consequently admit that a manufacturer may not be held liable for damage caused by a pharmaceutical product if it was the only one to enable a certain kind of medical treatment.

8.4   Liability in the nuclear field

The Paris Convention of 29 July 1960, as well as all subsequent international treaties and conventions regarding liability in the nuclear field, have not yet been ratified by the Grand Duchy of Luxembourg.

8.5   Liability arising from certain industrial activities

A Grand-ducal Decree of 10 April 1987 has implemented EC Directive 82/501/EEC of 24 June 1982, as amended by Directive 87/216/EEC of 19 March 1987 relating to the risks of major accidents deriving from certain industrial activities.

The Grand-ducal Decree gives a list of activities which make use of one or several dangerous substances and which present a risk of major accident.

According to article 3 of the Grand-ducal Decree of 10 April 1987, a manufacturer is under an obligation to take all the requisite actions in order to avoid major accidents and in order to limit the possible consequences of such accidents for persons and the environment. The manufacturer must at any time be in a position to show that he has determined the existing risks of major accidents, that he has taken all the appropriate safety measures and informed, trained and equipped all persons working on the site to ensure their safety.

The manufacturer is also under an obligation to inform the authorities immediately of any major accident and he must communicate to the authorities all the circumstances of the accident and the dangerous substances which have been used. He must also give the authorities any information which might be of help in evaluating the significance of the accident and its effect on people and the environment.

8.6   Liability arising from the Law of 11 March 1981 on the control of the placing on the market and the use of certain dangerous substances and preparations, as amended

Under Article 2 of the Law of 11 March 1981 ('the Law'), the substances and dangerous preparations listed in the Annex of the Law may only be produced, placed on the market or used pursuant to the conditions set forth in the Law. These limitations do not apply to the production, the placing on the market or the utilisation of these products for purposes of research or development or analysis.

Infringement of the Law is subject to criminal fines ranging from LUF 2,501 to LUF 5 million and to imprisonment between eight days to one month or to one of these fines only.

Associations organised under the Law of 11 August 1982 concerning the protection of nature and natural resources may exercise the rights of a *'partie civile'* in respect of facts constituting an infringement to the Law and causing a direct or indirect prejudice to the collective interests which they defend.

CHAPTER XII

Netherlands

S S H Wibbens, Esq

Rasker Duvekot & Wibbens
Herengracht 503
1017 BV Amsterdam
Netherlands

Tel: ++ 31 20 62 70 370
Fax: ++ 31 20 62 69 287

CHAPTER XII

Netherlands

1 INTRODUCTION

The introduction of new legislation on product liability in the kingdom of the Netherlands took place just before a comprehensive renewal and restructuring of the Civil Code, which has transformed it into an up-to-date system relevant to the modern world.

The Dutch Civil Code was based directly on the French Civil Code, which was introduced into this country by Napoleon Bonaparte's brother Louis Napoleon. It is a long way, however, from there to the introduction of the new legal rules which will henceforth govern the general area of the law of property and of obligations; these came into effect in the Netherlands on 1 January 1992. These new rules contain a separate section dealing with product liability based on the provisions of the Directive.

1.1 Overview of legal provisions relating to defective products in the Netherlands

As in most other European states, the law and practice relating to defective products is dealt with through the law of contract, tort and product safety, together with industrial self-regulation schemes and the criminal law.

In Book VI of the Civil Code, which deals with rules concerning contracts, the compensation rules are found in the section concerning the consequences of the non-fulfilment of a contract. Further, Book VII of the Civil Code contains a separate title dedicated to purchase and exchange, in which title specific provisions stipulate the consequences of the non-fulfilment of obligations by the selling party in relation to either the consumer or the professional buyer.

Section 9 of the more general Book VI contains provisions concerning the consequences of the non-fulfilment of obligations, while title 3 of the same book deals inter alia with product liability and sets out the rules for the non-fulfilment of the other legal obligations. Article 6:162 of title 3 describes tort as 'an infraction of a right as well as an act or omission contradictory to any legal stipulation or which is proper in accordance with the unwritten law in social life, unless there are grounds for justification'. As mentioned above, section 3 of this title of Book VI deals with product liability in articles 6:185 to 6:193.

One of the innovations in the Civil Code is that compensation law is dealt with in one single section of this code. The rules set out in articles 6:95 to 6:110 relate to both obligations for compensation from the law and to accountable shortcoming in the case of contracts. Only insurance contracts, penal contracts and so-called security or guarantee contracts fall outside the scope of this section.

The compensation claimed may be used on both an accountable default and an illegal act. As a result of this, it is also possible for the contracting party, if he succeeds in proving negligence or fault resulting in damage on the part of the seller, to invoke the rules relating to tort liability, which are contained in article 6:162 of the Civil Code. In this case, an obligation also comes into being, but instead of arising from a contract, it arises as a legal obligation directly from the Civil Code. It is as a direct result of a long-running series of cases before the Supreme Court (*Hoge Raad*), that the aforementioned system of damage compensation became also available to those persons who have not had a direct contractual relationship with the manufacturer or seller. The implications of this system are dealt with later in this chapter in section 3 below.

Since 1935, the Dutch Government has caused a number of laws to be adopted for the purpose of protecting the consumer, the most relevant of which is the Goods Act 1935. This provides a mechanism enabling the Government on a legal basis to adopt general executive measures in order to ensure that all products meet certain standards of health and safety and, under the provisions of the 1935 law, regulations governing cosmetics, toys and many other specific products have been brought into effect.

The Goods Act places obligations on both manufacturers and suppliers to take the necessary preventative measures and imposes criminal sanctions for breach of such obligations through the Law Relating to Economic Offences (*Wet Economische Delicten*). As this law now stands, traders in dangerous products can be required to issue appropriate warnings to the public and, where the authorities issue the warnings, in the event of their failing to comply with this obligation, traders can be required to bear the cost. The legal system of the Netherlands also includes specific laws concerning the safety of persons in various other situations.

A system of self-regulation applies to quite a large degree in the trade and industry of the Netherlands, the establishment of the Travel Industry Guarantee Fund by those involved in that particular line of business being a case in point. Many other sectoral arrangements have come into being as a result of pressure exercised with varying degrees of flexibility by the authorities, such as the system of self-regulation which applies in the advertising of cigarettes and of alcoholic beverages, and arrangements which constitute a natural corollary to certain rules contained in the Goods Act, such as the product-recall system.

Provisions can be found in the Penal Code concerning:

(a) the distribution of products which are harmful as a result of their defects; and
(b) the knowledge of such defects by those involved.

Article 174 of the Penal Code lays down penalties ranging from a maximum of 15 years' imprisonment to relatively high fines in respect of the person who sells, offers for sale, supplies or distributes goods in the knowledge that these are harmful to human life or health, and who fails to draw attention to their harmful nature. The criminal intent and guilt on the part of the person concerned must be proved by the public prosecutor.

Article 175 of the Penal Code lays down penalties for the person who is to blame for selling or supplying or distributing faulty products which are harmful to human life or health without the buyer and/or the recipient being aware of these harmful effects. Since this offence is related mainly to criminal negligence, the penalties reflect this, ie imprisonment or custody of a maximum of six

months or moderate fines. In the case of both types of offence, the penalty is increased where the person affected dies as a result. This criminal negligence is expressed in more general terms in articles 307 and 308 of the Penal Code. Article 307 provides that the person through whose fault the death of another person has occurred shall be punishable by imprisonment for a maximum period of nine months. Serious injury sustained through the fault of another person is punishable by imprisonment of that person for a maximum of six months.

2   PRE-CONTRACTUAL LIABILITY

The conclusion of a contract is normally preceded by a certain period in which negotiations take place. For the vast majority of purchases made by consumers, negotiations are confined to the unilateral announcement of an offer, whereupon the other party makes his acceptance coincide with the conclusion of the contract. Dutch case law accepts that the statements and the conduct of the parties during this pre-contract stage can be relevant to the relationship between the parties, regardless of whether the contract is eventually concluded or not. Thus it is possible to establish, in the light of these (mutual) statements, whether or not there actually exists a particular obligation between the parties. It is also possible for the terms of a contract between the parties to be analysed by a judge in the light of the statements which were made and the events which occurred during the pre-contract stage.

The Dutch courts have held that the negotiating parties have to deal with each other in a reasonable and fair manner, so that the negotiating parties are governed by the rule that the negotiating parties must conduct themselves in a manner which is compatible with their mutual legitimate interests.

Given the history of the importance attached in the Netherlands to the pre-contract stage, it is appropriate that the question of liability for certain statements made or information given at the time of offering goods for sale should be governed by the law of obligations. The reason for this is that even though the basis for liability laid down by the Directive remains article 6:185 of the Civil Code, an action for damages arising from certain statements can also be based on the breach of pre-contractual relations between the parties.

3   LIABILITY IN CONTRACT

3.1   Outline of contract law, relevant to defective products in the Netherlands

Contrary to the old Civil Code, in which Book 4 contained provisions about a 'wide variety of day-to-day transactions' the new Civil Code contains a more diffused regulation. This diffusion results from the layout used in the new Civil Code, in which Book 3 deals with law of property, Book 8 with the business laws, Book 6 with the general section of the law of obligations, Book 7 with specific contracts and Book 8 with transport resources and traffic, whereby a more systematic layout has been obtained.

In order to prevent any confusion in the terminology used, several definitions have to be dealt with first.

Article 6:1 of the Civil Code states that obligations may only result from the law. This distinguishes obligations from other commitments that may arise out of unwritten rules.

'Obligations' is the umbrella term used for Book 6 of the Civil Code and includes among others: illegal acts, contracts, unwarranted payment, business representation and unjust enrichment.

A contract is a legal dealing, in which one or more parties enter into an obligation with one or more other parties (article 6:213). The general rules for contracts are included in Book 6. In addition, Book 7 contains provisions about specific contracts such as purchase, exchange, order, contracting etc.

With respect to the fulfilment of obligations, Articles 6:27 and 6:28 provide that the debtor is obliged to supply an individual item, the 'specific purchase', in respect of which he has a general duty or is obliged respectively up to the point of supply to supply a certain item of the type of goods, 'the generic purchase', which may not be of less than good average quality.

The rule of hidden defects as it was incorporated in article 1527 of the old Civil Code is not adopted in the code in view of the fact that this provision had been marked out as being old-fashioned.

When an item supplied does not comply with the contract, we speak of breach and the debtor should be given a reasonable time, in which he can still comply with what was agreed (article 6:81 et seq). If there is no compliance within this period, the debtor is considered to be in breach and he is obliged under article 7:74 et seq to compensate the damage suffered by the creditor because of this, unless the breach cannot be attributed to the debtor (6:75; *force majeure*). It is not necessary to distinguish any more between the specific and generic purchase since the provisions of article 6:74 et seq apply to both types of items. Where there is a question of default in the fulfilment of a reciprocal contract by a party, the other party has the option of suspending his obligations under article 6:262, the so-called '*exceptio non adempleti contractus*'. Article 6:265 provides that each breach of a party in the fulfilment of his obligation authorises the other party to dissolve the contract in whole or in part unless, considering the degree of shortcoming, this is unjustified. In the case where dissolution follows, the defaulting party is obliged to compensate this damage (article 6:277 of the Civil Code).

Article 6:173 imposes a risk liability on the owner of a good which is defective. 'Defective' means 'if it does not satisfy the requirements which may be placed on the item in the given circumstances', as a result of which the item could cause particular danger to individuals.

The owner may only escape liability under the provisions of articles 6:162 et seq if the damage would not have occurred if he had known about the danger at the time the defect arose.

This means that the owner is not liable where the defect arose through the fault of the injured party, or where the owner had insufficient time to take any precautionary measures after the creation of the defect and the occurrence of the damage. The burden of proof rests on the owner.

As far as purchase is concerned, article 7:9 of the Civil Code provides that the seller is obliged to transfer ownership of and supply the item sold with appurtenances.

In the case where the product obtained does not comply with the contract the buyer may, under article 7:21 of the Civil Code, demand delivery of missing items, repair of the item supplied or replacement of the item supplied.

The buyer must, however, inform the seller of a defect he has discovered, or should have discovered, within an appropriate time of discovering this (article 7:23 of the Civil Code).

If in the case of a consumer purchase the item supplied does not satisfy expectations, the buyer is entitled, according to article 7:24 of the Civil Code, to damages compensation under the provisions of article 6:74 et seq of the Civil Code in addition to the remedies stated in article 7:21.

The provisions in Book 7 concerning purchase apply correspondingly to exchange contracts (article 7:50 of the Civil Code).

If the defect in a product results from product liability incorporated in articles 6:185-193, the owner or the purchaser in article 6:173 and 7:24 of the Civil Code is partly exempted from the liability resulting from the product liability.

Moreover, it is not relevant to the different provisions whether the defect affects the entire item or only a part of it; in all cases there is a question of breach of the obligation. This results from article 5:14 of the Civil Code which provides: 'a component which forms part of a main item is considered to be bound to that main item in such a way that it forms a whole with it'.

Finally, reference should be made to articles 6:175 et seq of the Civil Code in which the liability for the use of dangerous substances is regulated, and to articles 8:620 - 627, 8:1030-1037, 8:1210-1220 and 8:1670-1680 in which the transport of dangerous substances on board seagoing vessels, inland water vessels, vehicles and railway stock respectively is regulated. These provisions incorporate a risk liability for the owners of the means of transport.

3.2 Contractual warranties relating to quality of goods and safety of goods

3.2.1 *Commercial warranties*

As has already been stated, the person who supplies a certain individual item has a general duty of care for this item. Substantiation of the care depends on the circumstances of the case, including the content and extent of the obligation and custom.

Depending on the specific type of item, the item supplied may not be less than good average quality, which is usually market quality.

If an item does not satisfy the stated requirements, the supplier may be held in breach for the failure to satisfy what was agreed and the purchaser may claim compensation.

In addition to these general provisions, Book 6 of the Civil Code also contains more specific provisions that influence the quality and safety of goods.

Article 6:214 of the Civil Code provides that a contract, in which one of the parties deals as a company or in a professional capacity, is subject not only to legal provisions but also to standard regulations if such a regulation applies to the branch of business concerned. This standard regulation will apply unless the parties agree otherwise. No use has yet been made of the standard regulations option.

One of the most important provisions for contractual 'warranties' in Book 6 of the Civil Code is section 6.5.3: the general conditions. General conditions are understood to include (article 6:231 of the Civil Code): 'one or more written stipulations drawn up with the objective of being incorporated in a number of

contracts, with the exception of stipulations indicating the core of performance.'

The party declaring these general conditions should make them available to the other party. This is not satisfied if it is simply stated in any way whatsoever (headed paper, order forms) that the conditions apply.

In principle, there is no limitation for the incorporation of stipulations in the conditions. In general, conditions are included for delivery, payment, exoneration clauses, applicable law etc.

Conditions may be removed if they can be deemed objectionable to the opposite party. What should be understood by this depends on the nature and content of the contract, the method of its origination and the mutual interests of the parties (article 6:233 of the Civil Code). The definitions of reasonableness and fairness from article 6:248 likewise play a part here.

Where the other party is a natural person not dealing as a business or in a professional capacity, articles 6:236 and 6:237 of the Civil Code list the stipulations presumed to be reasonably objectionable ('the grey list').

Article 6:236 incorporates stipulations under a-g that limit the rights of the opposite party or the obligations of the user as being reasonably objectionable. An opposite party may therefore not be limited in his right to dissolution (under b) or his right to suspension (under c). Article 6:237 ff presumes unreasonable a stipulation in which the user of the conditions or a third party is released from a part of the legal obligation to compensation, ie an exclusion clause.

In addition to clause 6:27 of the Civil Code concerning general conditions, article 7:17 of the Civil Code provides in the contract of sale that a supplied item must comply with the contract (the conformity requirement), which means that the item must have the properties that the buyer could expect based on the contract. Some of the factors that play a role here are: the nature of the item, the price level, the type of shop, the purchasing conditions and the sales person's information.

A further factor is whether the properties involved are required for normal use or for special use provided for in the contract.

If an item does not comply with the conformity requirement, there is a question of non-fulfilment of the obligation and the special consequences of non-fulfilment by the seller arising from article 7:20 et seq of the Civil Code, as well as the general provisions of article 6:74 et seq of the Civil Code applying.

It is important for consumers that article 7:17 of the Civil Code is regarded as a mandatory law (article 7:16 of the Civil Code). This means that any limitation or exclusion in guarantee certificates may be negated. It is not the willingness of the sales person that determines the content and duration of the guarantee, but rather the justified expectations of the buyer based on price, advertising and the way the item operates in daily life.

In articles 6:194-6:196, reference is made to the use of misleading advertising. Misleading statements about properties of an item of merchandise or a service or about the scope, content and duration of guarantee made by a person pursuing a business or profession are considered to be tortious and may lead to compensation of damage suffered.

3.2.2   *Commercial practice in giving commercial guarantees*

Commercial Guarantees are given by manufacturers and sellers of products in different ways but subject to complaints by consumers.

3.2.3   Legal provisions concerning the form and content of commercial guarantees

Vendors' commercial guarantees may not limit consumer rights, however manufacturers may to some extent limit consumer rights so far as it is not unreasonable to do so (see article 7:16 of the Civil Code).

Commercial guarantees are subject to controls on misleading advertising concerning its terms and conditions (see articles 6:194-6:196 of the Civil Code).

3.3   Breach of contract for supply of defective products

The seller's duty to provide the relevant guarantees extends to both legal and actual defects in the product sold. Thus, the seller must indemnify the purchaser of the product in relation to third parties who claim to have certain rights or claims on the product or on part of it.[1] It is possible as a matter of contract for the seller to exclude this guarantee of good title. However, the seller remains liable for any claims by third parties which result directly from his own previous acts or omissions.

The supply of a defective product is generally treated in Dutch law as constituting a form of unsatisfactory performance, since a seller who fails to fulfil his obligations (within any agreed time limit) infringes the buyer's rights and has consequently unsatisfactorily performed the contract. In principle, the seller of a defective product is automatically held to be in default. An order requiring the proper performance of the agreement is unnecessary in such cases. The fact that the seller is in default opens the way for payment of compensation.

Each shortfall in the performance of an obligation compels the seller to compensate the purchaser for the damage incurred as a result – unless the shortfall cannot be ascribed to the seller, as is the case with an event of *force majeure*.

The seller may invoke the doctrine of *force majeure* if a shortfall in the performance of the contract arose which was not his fault and for which he is not liable. It is perfectly possible for the manufacturer or seller of industrially mass-produced goods (ie 'unascertained' goods) to replace the product which has not been properly supplied and therefore fulfil his obligations. It is clear that, as one writer puts it:

> ...a defendant cannot rely upon *force majeure* in cases where, as a result of the agreement concluded between parties, he is held liable for the occurrence of the event which prevents performance. This is the case, for example, where the seller of a product warrants the absence of a certain harmful property and it appears, subsequent to delivery, that the product supplied actually does possess that harmful property.[2]

Where a purchaser incurs costs in preventing damage arising from a defective product, he can claim this in addition to claiming a replacement product. Also, where it is impossible for the supplier to replace the product, the purchaser will have a claim in damages. If replacing the article is completely impossible, any damage suffered can be compensated or, if no damage has been incurred, the agreement can be rescinded. If the latter occurs, the sale price must be reimbursed to the consumer.

---

1   Supreme Court, 29/1/1971, NJ 1971, 221. Supreme Court, 10/5/1963, NJ 1963, 288: folding machines.
2   Hartkamp, *Asser-Rutten I*, p 264.

In summary, depending on the circumstances of the case, the purchaser of a defective product has a choice between various possibilities:

(a) he may apply to the courts for

    (i)   the performance of the obligation by repair;
    (ii) compensation by way of replacement for unsatisfactory performance; or
    (iii) both performance and payment of additional compensation;

(b) he may apply to the court for the rescission of the sale on grounds of unsatisfactory performance plus compensation.

The rules in the Civil Code on the subject of compensation in cases of unsatisfactory performance are the same as those which apply in the case of tort liability.

3.4   Damages for breach of contract

The term 'damage' is understood as meaning the disadvantage which the purchaser suffers from the unsatisfactory performance of a defective product. The principle adopted in assessing damage is that the purchaser should be put back as closely as possible into the state he would have been in if the damage-causing event had not occurred. The damage for which the seller has to indemnify the purchaser will include material damage and any other disadvantage to the extent that the law makes provision for such compensation. As well as in destruction, damage and business loss (ie reduced competitiveness), unsatisfactory performance may also result in immaterial damage. The person affected must, in the present state of the law, be compensated for such damage within certain limits. These limits are not closely defined and are open to judicial interpretation.

Material damage includes both losses which the disadvantaged person has actually suffered and loss of earnings. In addition, compensation may also be obtained in respect of any reasonable expenses incurred in attempting to prevent or restrict the damage which has occurred precisely as a result of the event on which liability is based. Reasonable expenses incurred in establishing damage and liability or in obtaining a settlement out of court, as well as costs lost by the product being defective, must also be compensated.

The extent of the loss to be compensated is established by a valuation carried out by the court. The court will compare the situation resulting from the defect with that which would have prevailed if the product had not been defective.

The Dutch system of compensation is very precise and it has been said that literally every penny and/or item of damage suffered must be stated and proved. Such items of compensation are calculated on the basis of invoices, declared expenses and costs of repair, as well as generally accepted flat rates in relation to current market value, as is the case with cars. In view of the difficulties inherent in calculating earnings or expected earnings, the lawyers and the injured plaintiff will be at the mercy of the damage assessment by the court, which will determine the amounts *ex aequo et bono*. This compensation can be spread over many years by means of payment by instalments on the part of the defendant or his insurer.

3.5 Burden of proof

When it comes to allocating the burden of proof, the general principle is applied that the person who alleges damage must prove it in its entirety. As a result, the plaintiff must, in the case of unsatisfactory performance, make sure that all the elements of the damage are attributable to the defect, and at the same time he must, if he brings an action for compensation, state and prove the damage in question. These elements include the extent of the damage and the defective nature of the product, in addition to which the so-called 'causal link' between the damage and the defect will need to be proved by the plaintiff. In most cases, unsatisfactory performance consisting of a failure to supply within the agreed time limit, or of partial supply, will be relatively easy to prove, whereas damage resulting from unsatisfactory performance will be more difficult to prove. Further, the purchaser, whether he is a consumer or not, may experience considerable difficulties in proving the causal link between the defect and the damage. As will be discussed later, the draftsmen of the Directive have made an individual consumer's task easier on this point. Moreover, this process of easing the burden of proof on the part of the consumer had already started in the shape of a series of judgments in the Dutch courts which had, incidentally, been developed in the context of statutory liability under article 1401 of the Civil Code.

3.6 Exclusion or limitation of liability

In the context of the attribution of the damage to the person who supplied the defective product or who performed the contract in an unsatisfactory manner, a doctrine based on the degree to which the consequences were reasonably foreseeable was invariably applied by the Supreme Court in cases of unsatisfactory performance from 1927-1970. Gradually, this theory was replaced by a more modern doctrine under which the person who unsatisfactorily performs the contract is liable for the damage caused if this damage, taking into account the circumstances of each particular case, could be reasonably attributed to him. This theory of attribution sought to give the courts the necessary degree of freedom to judge each case on its merits when determining liability and the extent of the damage to be compensated.

Having discussed above the general trends as they appear in cases where the parties made no agreement amongst themselves concerning unsatisfactory performance and the resultant damage, it is necessary to take a closer look at the world of business, where the parties involved frequently agree not to invoke unsatisfactory performance or to claim the resulting compensation.

The principle of freedom of contract leaves all traders free to exclude their own liability. Such an exclusion or limitation of liability requires the consent of both parties and, in the absence of such consent being given, the non-mandatory provisions of the Civil Code will apply.

The businessman obviously tries to limit or completely exclude the implications of any damage caused by his products whether they arise in contract or tort. Nevertheless, such exclusion or limitation of liability requires the consent of the other party, and it is precisely on this point that the present-day manufacturer can be faced with problems. Such exclusions must be clearly worded, and in practice usually arise by means of a written notice, either on

the packaging itself or on an insert. If the exclusion clause is to be enforced, this clause must be addressed in a very precise manner to the purchaser, as a result of which the latter may be deemed to have given his consent. It is precisely in this area of so-called standard terms and conditions that there exists a conflict between the interests of the producer and those of the consumer. It has been remarked that:

> ...it hardly appears to be an exaggeration to state that it is precisely the clauses limiting liability, as they regularly appear in standard terms and conditions, which have resulted in the standard terms and conditions being regarded as a problem area. Moreover, the proposed new Civil Code contains provisions in relation to consumer purchases which represent a real danger for such unilateral exclusions or limitations.[3]

In the meantime the Supreme Court has ruled that the exclusion of the guarantee against any hidden defects is not valid in respect of defects which were known to the seller.[4] More recently, the court gave a ruling which went even further[5] which concerned a defect not known to the seller, but one of which he should have been aware in view of his expert knowledge. In that case, in spite of the existence of an exclusion clause, the seller was held to be liable by the Supreme Court.

3.7   Limitation period

Under the principle of freedom of contract, it is possible to exclude or limit liability for claims brought within a shorter period of time than that prescribed as the limitation period in the Civil Code.

The judicial concept of legal prescription of an obligation arising from a contract or from the law is specifically regulated in the Civil Code. The general period of negative prescription after which proceedings cannot be brought used to be 30 years. In the new version of the Civil Code, this period is reduced to 20 years. The prescription period begins at the time when the claim becomes defined or with effect from the day following that on which the event triggering the start of the prescription period took place.

More especially with regard to product liability, article 6:191 of the new law states that a legal claim in respect of product liability may not be brought after the expiry of three years. This expiry date does not depend on the attitude of the parties, but is a statutory limit which is mandatory in law. In view of the short period of product liability, it appears reasonable that this period only begins as of the moment when the victim gains or is able to gain a clear understanding of the damage and the identity of the producer responsible. The term 'producer' should be understood to have the widest possible meaning. After the passing of this three-year limit, an injured party can still invoke the tort liability for several more years.

Especially in the new Civil Code, a large number of specific rules exist relating to limitation of actions, particularly under consumer legislation. Furthermore, claimants have a number of means at their disposal of interrupting a period of limitation once it has started, such as writing a warning, serving a

---

3   Van Empel, *Produktaansprakelijkheid*, p 40.
4   Supreme Court, 26/5/1950, NJ 1951, 18.
5   Supreme Court, 7/5/1982, NJ 1983, 509.

writ or taking legal proceedings. Acknowledgment of fault by the defendant also interrupts the period of limitation. Where the exercise of a certain right is not subject to a compulsory legal expiry date as is the case in articles 6:185 ff of the Civil Code, the producer can contractually specify in his standard conditions or elsewhere that this right must be exercised within a certain period, or else it will expire.

Lastly, it is important to mention here that under article 6:191 the right of an injured party to lodge a complaint lapses after ten years from the day following the day that the defective product was brought into circulation.

3.8 Liabilities for third parties and vicarious liability

In principle a defendant is liable for any breach of contract or for any tort caused by sub-contractors, employees and agents that he has used to perform his contract. If the defendant has excluded his liability in contract, he cannot be held liable for the breach of contract of one of his helpers, collaborators and/or employees.

In the case of a breach of contract, the party not in breach can claim the loss and damage he has suffered from the party in breach and can also require him to perform the contract in accordance with its terms. The circumstances in which the party that has committed the breach can hold a third party liable will depend on the type of contract between these two parties. Exclusions of liability between the first two parties in the form of a *force majeure* clause are very common but do not always take into account the non-performance of a third party. Trading companies may often use conditions of purchase in which they preserve the right to attribute responsibility and liability for defects to their suppliers, in case they themselves are summoned to perform and find themselves in a position where they cannot do so as a result of a breach of contract by their suppliers. The liability of a third party may be important where non-performance of an obligation goes together with an obligation arising from the law, eg in the case of a reckless fault by a subordinate or a third party engaged to execute a contract. Where an employee or a contract carrier recklessly damages products in transit to a retailer, the supplier can be held liable for deficient supply (non-performance) and the executing employee or carrier can be personally liable for negligence (tort). If the supplier has excluded his liability for non-performance in the contract, the employee or carrier can be held liable. To avoid such an unsatisfactory outcome for the consumer, the new Civil Code contains rules which prevent such exclusion of liability.

Where liability is based principally on non-performance, a defence that the third party has caused the non-performance seems reasonable. In section 4.8, below, we shall see that in other circumstances the relevant employee or third party contractor can be held liable.

4 LIABILITY IN TORT

4.1 Introduction

The new product liability legislation has been implemented in section 3 of title 3 of book 6 of the Civil Code, and is therefore close to the other articles which provide for compensation to be paid in specific situations.

4.2   Outline of relevant tort law giving rise to liability for personal and property damage

The meaning of the term 'unfair deed' has been greatly expanded through jurisprudential developments in the twentieth century. The well-known *Lindenbaum v Cohen* judgment of the Supreme Court in 1919 defined an 'unfair deed' as:

> Any act or negligence, that either infringes another's right, or is in contravention of the perpetrator's legal duty or goes against good custom or against the carefulness that should be observed in society with regard to other persons or goods.

As demonstrated above, the growth of product liability is part of this broad trend, and concepts such as 'conflict with normal legal duty' and 'misuse of rights' also form part of the trend.

The new article 6:162 reads:

> He, who commits to another an unfair deed, which can be attributed to him, has the obligation to compensate for the damages that the other suffers as a result thereof.

Article 6:162.3 continues that an unfair deed can be attributed to him, if it can be deemed his fault or its cause is found in a circumstance that he can be held accountable for in accordance with the law or the common opinion.

4.3   Causation and remoteness of loss and damage

The principles applying to causation in contract cases apply equally in tort cases. Therefore, the defendant has to compensate the damage resulting from his breach of contract or tort, which means that between the tort and the damage the causal connection has to be proved by the plaintiff. The theory of 'adequate causation' is also important here (see section 2.7, above).

During the 1970s this theory of adequate causation in tort liability was removed from its dominant position and replaced by the ruling that the person who commits a tortious act is liable for the damage caused by that act, so long as the damage can be logically attributed to the tortfeasor. As can be expected, there is a multitude of case law on this topic.

Historically the Dutch courts have held that even where the damage has been caused by an extremely dangerous product, all the elements of the tort, including fault, have to be established in full by the injured party and proved. In modern product liability cases though, the judges have decided that the producer's liability is almost strict.

In the famous *Ford* case, a production fault in the steering mechanism of a car was established and Ford was held liable for all the consequences arising from such defect. The production error by Ford was such as to be contrary to the degree of 'carefulness, that should be observed in society'. Also instruction faults or errors, non-deliberate as they may be, are by now regarded as elements that make a producer and/or the vendor strictly liable.

4.4   Quantum of damage

The basic principles for the assessment of damages in tort cases are the same as apply in contract cases and have been described in sections 2.5 and 2.6,

above. When injuries or death occur, the statutory tort rules of article 6:162 of the Civil Code automatically apply and bring about an obligation for the party causing the damage to pay compensation.

Torts resulting in personal injury give rise to an obligation to pay compensation for the transport of the injured person, medical and surgical assistance, medicines, hospital expenses, damage to clothing, loss of future income, physiotherapy treatment etc. Immaterial damages can be claimed by an injured person to compensate pain, mental suffering, fear and loss of enjoyment of life.

Torts resulting in death give rise to an entitlement to the direct relatives, such as parents, spouse and children, insofar as they depend on the deceased for income. In the Netherlands, such relatives are not entitled to compensation for immaterial damages, which remain attributable only to the injured person himself.

In the case of damage to property belonging to a person who was not contracting with the party causing the damage, the tort rules of the Civil Code also apply. This damage, including loss of income, is compensated through the rules of contract law on the non-performance of an obligation (see section 2.5, above).

The leading principle in Dutch tort law is that the court should award damages of a sufficient measure to put the injured party back in the position that he would have been in, so far as possible, had the injury or loss not occurred. Again, the assessment of the extent of the damage is to be estimated by the court. The damage not only includes the actual damage, but also future loss and damage.

4.5   Burden of proof

As we have seen above, the general principle remains that the injured party has to provide the proof of all the elements of tort as set out in article 6:162 of the Civil Code. During recent years a gradual shift of the burden of proof in product liability cases has come about in case law, notably concerning the element of fault. Further, in the Netherlands it remains accepted that consumers of industrial products have to prove that the cause of damage was in the product itself.

4.6   Exclusion or limitation of liability

As in many other countries, it is possible in the Netherlands to contract so as to exclude liability in tort. There are certain non-excludable elements such as gross neglect or malicious intention and criminal intention. Considering that much liability in tort arises between parties who have not entered into contracts, this point remains rather academic.

For the manufacturer, however, it is of the greatest importance to protect his interest by introducing as many exclusions as possible into his contract and/ or conditions of sale. Many manufacturers try to exclude carelessness and neglect of employees and other collaborators through the use of guarantee documents, although these are frequently ineffective if the provisions of the guarantee contradict a supplier's statutory obligations to a consumer.

A widely known technique for the exclusion of liability is for a manufacturer to point out in writing on the product or its packaging that a particular use of

the product concerned may be dangerous and that the user must take precautionary measures. The validity of such warnings will depend on the nature, skill and experience of the user and the means of giving the warning.

In one case a manufacturer of roof insulation material was held liable for damage resulting from his incomplete instructions. Further, it was held that the manufacturer has a duty to inform his distributors of revisions of the instructions for use, where they are up-dated as a result of new information.[6]

4.7   Limitation period

The new Civil Code provides that from 1 January 1992 the limitation period in tort claims is reduced to 20 years.

Pursuant to paragraph 2004 of the Civil Code the provisions regarding the limitation period, its suspension and interruption apply in the same way for tort as for breaches of contract. Paragraph 6:185 of the Civil Code provide that in product liability cases a limitation period for making claims of three years will apply and such limitation period will run from the moment when the injured person knew or ought reasonably to have known of the damage, the defect and the person(s) liable in this respect.

4.8   Liabilities for third parties

A principal is liable for the fault of any person he uses to perform any of his obligations if such person is unfit or the principal knows that the person might be reckless in certain conditions.

Further, legal theory and practice generally impose a liability on the owners of dangerous installations, products or heavy equipment for the gross neglect or carelessness of their personnel.

5   SPECIAL LIABILITIES ARISING IN RESPECT OF PARTICULAR PRODUCTS

Most of the above-mentioned Acts take the safety of the human being and, in a broader sense, the environment into consideration. In order to protect the consumer, laws such as the Goods Act force producers to fulfil many requirements as to the quantity and quality of products as well as diverse labelling requirements in respect of the composition and quality of products. In case such requirements are not met, the import, trade and transport of such products can be forbidden, while in the case of gross neglect the public prosecutor's office can take the producer to court to have the producer sentenced to pay a fine, have his licence withdrawn and/ or the condemnatory judgment publicised. When the non-fulfilment of vital requirements causes injury, the public prosecutor can institute proceedings under the general Penal Code, which provides for more severe punishments and higher fines (see section 1.1, above). It is important to mention here the Act on Nuclear Energy and the Act on Waste Disposal, which emphasise the safety of human beings, flora and fauna and the environment,

---

6   The Hague Court, 7/12/1979, NJ 1981, 670.

much more than the consumer as such. It is beyond the scope of this book to describe these and the many other environmental laws in detail.

6 LIABILITY FOR DEFECTIVE PRODUCTS ARISING FROM NATIONAL LAW IN THE NETHERLANDS

6.1 Outline of provisions in the Netherlands

The adaptation of Dutch legislation to the requirements of the Directive was formulated in a Bill that was submitted to Parliament on 11 September 1986 (no 19636). This Bill was accepted in amended form after lengthy discussions on 20 March 1990. It passed into law with effect from 1 November 1990. Bill 19636 has thus taken its place in amending article 1407 of the Civil Code which will be renumbered 6:185-6:193 of the Civil Code.

The law does not contain any interpretation of concepts in cases where the Directive does not itself give an explanation or does not expressly leave the interpretation to Dutch legislation. According to the legislators, interpretation is reserved for the European Court of Justice.

The articles of the Civil Code are summarised below.

6.1.1 Article 6:185

The producer is liable for the damages caused by a defect in his product, unless:

(a) he did not bring the product into circulation;
(b) he can show that the defect that caused the damage did not exist at the time he brought the product into circulation or the defect arose later;
(c) the product was not manufactured for sale or for any other form of distribution having a commercial objective, nor was it manufactured or distributed in the normal course of trade;
(d) the defect arose as a consequence of the producer making the product conform with compulsory government regulations;
(e) given the state of scientific and technical knowledge at the time of bringing the product into circulation, it was impossible to discover the existence of the defect; and
(f) in the case of a manufacturer of a component, the defect is attributable to the design of the product of which the component forms a part.

The producer's liability may be reduced or eliminated if the damage is caused both by a defect in the product and by the fault of the aggrieved party or a person for whom the latter is responsible.

The liability of the producer is not reduced where the damage is caused both by a defect in the product and by the action of a third party.

6.1.2 Article 6:186

A product is defective where it does not offer the safety that one might expect, taking into consideration:

(a) the presentation of the product;
(b) a reasonable expectation of its use; and
(c) the time at which the product was brought into circulation.

A product is not to be regarded as defective simply because a better product is subsequently brought into circulation.

6.1.3   Article 6:897

The term:

(a) 'product' means any movable property including electricity, with the exception of agricultural products and game;
(b) 'pgricultural products' means products of the soil, of stock-breeding and of fisheries, with the exception of products which have undergone initial preparation or processing;
(c) 'producer' means the manufacturer of the finished product, as shall be the producer of a raw material or the manufacturer of a component, or anyone presenting himself as the producer by affixing his name, his trademark or some other distinguishing sign on the product.

Without prejudice to the liability of the producer, anyone importing a product into the EC in order to sell it or lease it out or to supply it in some other way, is regarded as the producer; his liability is the same as that of a producer.

Where it is not possible to determine the identity of the producer, any supplier of the product shall be regarded as the producer, unless he is able within a reasonable time to inform the aggrieved party of the identity of the producer or of the party who has supplied him with the product. In the case of a product imported into the EC, if it is not possible to ascertain the identity of the importer into the EC of that product, any supplier shall likewise be regarded as the producer, unless he is able within a reasonble time to inform the aggrieved party of the identity of the importer into the EC or of a supplier who has supplied him with the product.

6.1.4   Article 6:188

The aggrieved party must prove the damage, the defect and the causal connection between the defect and the damage.

6.1.5   Article 6:189

In the event that, by virtue of article 6:185, different persons are responsible for the same damage, each of them is responsible for the whole.

6.1.6   Article 6:190

The liability referred to in article 6:185 exists for damage due to death or physical injury and damage caused by the product to another object which is normally intended for use or consumption in the private sphere and is chiefly used as such, with the proviso that the damages must amount to at least Hfl 1,263.85.

6.1.7   Article 6:191

The limitation period for making claims is three years; this period starts to run on the day when the aggrieved party becomes aware of the damage, the defect and the identity of the producer. The right to damage compensation lapses ten years after the start of the day following the day on which the producer brought the object which caused the damage into circulation. The same applies

to the right of a third party jointly responsible for the damage to seek redress against the producer.

6.1.8   Article 6:192

The liability of a producer towards an aggrieved party cannot be excluded or limited. If a third party who does not use the product in the exercise of a profession or business is also liable to the aggrieved party, the duty of redress of the producer against the third party cannot be limited or excluded.

6.1.9   Article 6:193

The aggrieved party is entitled to damage compensation from the producer without prejudice to any other rights or claims.

The right to damage compensation from the producer cannot be subrogated, except where the benefit paid by the insurer relates to the liability of the insured party, and another party is jointly liable by virtue of this article. Nor can a party for whom redress or subrogation is ruled out by the first and second paragraphs obtain the rights referred to in the second paragraph according to an agreement or have these rights exercised on his behalf by the entitled party in his name.

Finally, the implementing law of articles 6:185 ff contains a second article which states, in so many words, that the liability of producers in respect of products brought into circulation before such law came into effect is regulated by the law that was in effect at that time.

6.2   Description of special or anomalous provisions in respect of product liability law in the Netherlands

6.2.1   Agricultural products

Agricultural products as defined in article 6:187 and which have not undergone an initial preparation or processing, fall outside the product liability regulations, such as glasshouse products, vegetables and typical Dutch products such as herrings - not kippers!

6.2.2   Computer software

It has been held that software is to be seen as a product and as such falling within the scope of the new regulations. The view is widespread that software should be seen as information as such, and therefore as a service and consequently cannot fall within the scope of the new regulations. On the other hand, software is easily brought within the scope of the new regulations if it is closely connected with the PC-board or any kind of component that carries software in it. It seems that in the making of the new product liability regulations, the complexity of software was not clearly considered.

The European Commission recently answered a question put in the European Parliament expressing its view that software is to be considered a product in the sense of the Directive.[7]

---

7   Pub EC 8/5/1990, no C 114, 142.

6.2.3   *Buildings and the liabilities of the constructors thereof*

In the Netherlands a specific provision was enacted in the tort section of the Civil Code.[8] As can be seen, the legislators chose to make the owner of the building directly liable; this of course does not prevent the owner starting an action against the builder or decorator of the building for defects brought about by their activities. Such a guarantee procedure may be based on product liability in the future, namely in claims against the manufacturer of a defective component that has become part of an immovable property, eg sash windows, spiral staircases and revolving doors as well as joists and rafters.

So far as buildings and engineering works constructed prior to the adoption of the amendments to article 6:185 are concerned the old tort rules will continue to apply in the situation, where no specific cause of the defect in the construction can be found.

6.2.4   *Equipment*

Defects of a product liability nature could fall within the scope of the Act on Dangerous Equipment of 1952. This Act prohibits the possession, delivery and exhibition of dangerous equipment and the like, which has not been approved and marked with a sign of approval by the appropriate authorities. This Act further provides a basis for regulations concerning the production, import and use of dangerous equipment. For instance, the import has to be notified to the proper authorities. In respect of equipment such as lifts, baling machines and grinding machines, specific control methods and safety requirements are required by this Act.

6.3 Optional provisions in the Directive

The Directive enables divergent national rulings on certain optional points. We set out below the options chosen by the Netherlands listed by articles of the Directive.

6.3.1   *Article 2*

In the Netherlands, the option to include agricultural produce and game was not taken up, so agricultural produce and game were excluded from the definition of a product in Dutch law. This was contrary to a considerable volume of advice given to the Government.

6.3.2   *Article 5*

Where, as a result of this part of the Directive, different persons are liable for the same damage, each of them is severally liable, without prejudice to the terms of the national law regarding redress. The redress rules are contained in article 6:190 of the Civil Code.

6.3.3   *Article 7(e)*

The option not to adopt the 'state of the art' defence has not been taken up by the Dutch. This defence has been incorporated by the Dutch Government into

---

8   Arts 6:173 ff of the Civil Code.

the proposed article 6:185 of the Civil Code. Therefore where the producer can prove that on the basis of scientific and technical knowledge at the time when the product was brought into circulation it was impossible to discover the existence of the defect, he cannot be held liable. Moreover, the word 'impossible' indicates that heavy demands are made in terms of the furnishing of proof.

6.3.4   Article 8

Without prejudice to Dutch legal provisions regarding the right of redress, the liability of the producer is not reduced where the damage was caused both by the defect in the product and by the action of a third party, where this party uses the product as a private person. But this does not apply to traders and professional persons.

Where national law concedes the validity and scope of an agreement sharing liability between the various producers or links in the chain of production and distribution, they are free to proceed with such an agreement. Liability exclusions are valid, as these may be used by suppliers of components.

6.3.5   Article 9

Compensation arrangements are left to the national legislators. The amount of financial compensation for pain, suffering and reduced enjoyment of life is very difficult to determine under Dutch law. The normal practice here is to fall back on precedents. Every three years, a fairly complete review is given in the monthly journal *Verkeersrecht* (Traffic Law) published by the General Dutch Motorists' Association (ANWB).

6.3.6   Article 10

The first paragraph of this article states that a claim for damage compensation is excluded after three years. It will be necessary on the basis of applicable national legislation to see whether there can be any question of suspending or interrupting the limitation period, as detailed in article 6:191 of the Civil Code.

6.3.7   Article 13

The rights which the aggrieved party can derive from national legal rules are left unimpaired insofar as these go beyond the Directive in terms of the protection afforded. The producer must therefore continue to take account of the rules which apply in the Netherlands.

These are specified in article 6:193, which states that without prejudice to articles 6:185 ff, all the other national rights and claims to damages remain available to the injured party. According to circumstances, claims may be made for: damage to the defective product itself; damage to other products in a public environment such as offices, factories, etc and damage of a value lower than Ecu 500. Therefore the new legislation does not affect the existing possibility of claiming damages based on contract liability or tort liability, both with limitation periods of 20 years.

It is possible for business parties to contract to share the relation to the burden of product liability. It is also possible to insert a clause providing for liquidated damages for product liability.

6.3.8   Article 16

This article leaves it for each member state to determine the maximum amount to which the liability of the producer for damages resulting from death or physical injury caused by identical articles exhibiting the defect should be limited. In the Netherlands there is no upper limit. The Parliament was of the opinion that a reasonable elaboration of article 16(1) will lead to a system of apportionment. This will result in all timely claims being divided proportionally.

7   LIABILITY FOR DEFECTIVE PRODUCTS BROUGHT ABOUT BY BREACH OF STATUTORY REGULATION DESIGNED TO PROTECT CONSUMERS AND/OR TO PROMOTE SAFETY

7.1   Outline of protective regulations

The Netherlands have for a long time adopted administrative regulations to control the socio-economic activities of producers and specify requirements that must be adhered to by different industrial groups such as meat producers, farmers, toy producers and electricity suppliers. The most important Act amongst this legislation is the Goods Act 1935. An important paragraph of this Act is paragraph 14 which gives a clear-cut authorisation to the Dutch Cabinet to designate 'General Decrees' in which very specific requirements for the quality, design and safety of certain products may be laid down. These decrees also contain rules on the marking and description of food and drinks as well as non-food products, in the interest of the public health or for reasons of fair trading. Nowadays, many of these decrees are greatly influenced by EC regulations.

Together with this very general Goods Act there exists a variety of protective regulations, including the Act on Butchers Inspection, the Act on Agricultural Quality, the Electricity Act and environmental laws such as the Act on Chemical Disposals, the Act on Insecticides and Pesticides, the Act on Dangerous Materials and the Act on Air Pollution. In view of the multitude of these laws it is important to take into account that the Netherlands, after Hong Kong and Monaco, is one of the most densely populated countries in the world.

The enforcement of this socio-economic legislation is mainly in the hands of diverse administrative bodies, such as the Inspectorate for Public Health. These inspectorates work in regional areas with inspectors in order to avoid the sale, consumption and use of goods which are dangerous for public health or are of poor quality and/or composition. The import and transit of dangerous products can be officially forbidden on the same grounds.

The system of public health inspectors and diverse local inspection laboratories is designed to control and detect breaches of statutory regulations. The Goods Act sets out very specific regulations concerning the taking of samples, including a rule that at the request of the producer or supplier a duplicate sample must be taken by the inspector and given to the producer or supplier. Also on the basis of the quality of such a specimen, the head of the local laboratory can take the decision to request the local public prosecutor to commence criminal proceedings.

The public prosecutor will base his prosecution on the Economic Offences Act (*Wet Economische Delicten* – WED). All breaches of the decrees concerning the denomination, quality and requirements of products, or their import and transit are deemed offences. This means that they are not considered criminal misdemeanours. This important penal distinction means that the defendants, whether they are persons or legal entities, cannot be punished with imprisonment (in the latter case, of their directors) for more than six months or a fine higher than that of the so-called third category – a sum of Hfl 10,000 – or these two punishments combined. Only on rare occasions is the judge entitled to award a higher fine.

In addition to these punishments other socio-economic forms of redress for the situation may be ordered by the judge, such as the payment of the amount of money that the offender has gained as a result of his breach of the decree. Another measure is to place the enterprise of the defendant under administration. A much more apt measure is that the defendant can be sentenced to perform that which he has unlawfully neglected, nullifying that which has been unlawfully performed, and such action as will remedy the situation, all at the expense of the defendant, unless the judge rules otherwise.

Gradually, some ministerial or cabinet Decrees are being replaced by self-regulatory measures introduced by trade and industry bodies. This gives manufacturers and retailers the benefit of the possibility of a maximum say in the establishment of the decrees and measures. As a result of European unification, some important decrees made under the Goods Act are products of Community harmonisation, such as the General Indication Decree and the Quantity Indication Decree.

Exceptionally precise regulations operate in relation to the production and sale of medicines in the Law on Medical Supplies where, logically, the consumer is more protected than under other law. Other laws in this field are the Law on Serums and Vaccines, the Opium Law and also the Law on Human Blood.

7.2   Burden of proof

Since breaches of these statutory regulations on consumer safety generally fall under the scope of the Economic Offences Act, the basic rules and stipulations of the penal law system apply. Therefore the public prosecutor's office will have to construct the case and provide proof of all the elements of the offence on which it bases its claims against the defendant producer or trader.

In the Dutch penal system it is possible for victims or injured persons to join in the procedure by putting themselves forward as the aggrieved person. The penal judge can award the victim an amount of money, which has to be paid by the defendant where he is found guilty and sentenced. The maximum sum that can be awarded to the injured person has been reset to higher amounts recently.

The possibility of joining in criminal proceedings is therefore mostly used by the injured party's lawyers, who automatically receive all the documents concerning the criminal case and with the help thereof can construct their own civil case before the civil court against the same defendants. It is important to keep in mind that in the latter case, the injured's lawyer will have officially to withdraw his claim in the penal case; for once a defendant has been sentenced to pay the maximum penal sum, it is no longer possible to file a civil suit against him.

7.3   Nature of liability, damages or criminal sanctions

The liability of a manufacturer who fails to comply with the regulations or requirements imposed under the various administrative measures on the basis of the Goods Act or other socio-economic laws is in essence no different from liability for tort. Certainly a civil judge having to deal with a civil claim is more likely to assume that accountability and blame lie with the defaulting manufacturer. In addition to the above, the manufacturer can be criminally charged with this offence and suffer penalties, including the withdrawal of a licence. With the introduction of articles 6:185 ff of the Civil Code and the reversal of the burden of proof, an injured party in future is likely to refrain from a civil suit in a penal case as described above, whereas earlier he would have tended to make his own civil claim with reference to the possible penal judgment on the basis of the Economic Offences Act.

CHAPTER XIII

Norway

Wilhelm Matheson, Esq

Wiersholm, Mellbye & Bech
PO Box 400 Sentrum
0103 Oslo 1
Norway

Tel: ++ 47 22 400 600
Fax: ++ 47 22 410 600

CHAPTER XIII

Norway

1 INTRODUCTION

1.1 Introduction to the legal system in Norway

Norway is a monarchy and the legislative power is exercised by Parliament.

Accordingly, Norway is a parliamentary democracy. The executive power is exercised by the government with the prime minister being head. Norwegian law is partially created by statute but some significant parts are regulated by common law or jurisprudence; however treaty obligations have no direct effect without corresponding implementation in national legislation, if so required. The Norwegian court system is adversarial.

1.2 Overview of the law relating to defective products in Norway

In Norway, liability for defective products is governed by three areas of law: the Product Liability Act, the Purchases Act and the common law. These three areas of law are not mutually exclusive and overlap in some instances of their application.

The Norwegian Product Liability Act (*Produktansvarsloven*) was passed in 1988 (Act 104 of 23 December 1988, governing product liability) ('PLA') and came into force in 1989. The PLA regulates questions of liability for damage caused by defects in general products and medicines sold or made available for distribution after its coming into force. Norway is not a member of the European Union. However, when the PLA was adopted in 1988, the EC-Directive 85/374 EEC on Product Liability served as a 'model law'. Later, in 1992, when Norway became a party to the European Economic Agreement (EEA), the said Directive became formally binding. This led to certain amendments of the PLA.

The Purchases Act (*Kjøpsloven*) (Act 27 of 13 May 1988, governing the sale of goods) ('PA') also regulates a vendor's liability for any items he may sell. The provisions of the PA governing liability for damage caused by defective products can be applied to only a limited extent in cases where the product damages the environment.

Product liability is not a new concept in Norwegian Law. Liability for damage caused by defective products derived from the early so-called common law relating to damages. Producers, wholesalers and retailers of products can be made liable for any injurious characteristics the product may have which result from negligence or a breach of duty imposed on manufacturers to check the product is free from defects prior to distribution. The common law is still of importance in fields which are not regulated by the PLA.

1.3   Definition and classification of terms

In general usage, the term 'product liability' is defined as the rules regulating a producer's, retailer's or other party's (eg importer's) liability for damage resulting from a defective product he has put into circulation. This liability is, however, regarded as different from the liability for defects regulated by legislation governing purchases. The latter liability exists, for example, if a new washing machine fails to start when turned on, having been satisfactorily delivered and installed. If, however, the clothes in a washing machine are torn to shreds by a defect in the machine, a claim for damage to the clothes will be covered by the product liability law. The boundary between the two types of liability can sometimes be difficult to define. In Norwegian law, product liability is generally understood to apply to movable property and not to real estate. It does, however, apply to building and construction materials incorporated into land and buildings.

2   PRE-CONTRACTUAL LIABILITY

2.1   Effect on the interpretation and extent of the obligations of the parties to a contract

Acts, behaviour and representations of one party prior to entering into a contract can have an effect on the subsequent interpretation of that contract by a court.

2.2   Extent that non-disclosure of facts during negotiations may lead to liability

According to the PA, the vendor can be held liable for damages vis-à-vis the purchaser if the sales item does not correspond to the conditions of delivery, correspondence, contract negotiations and other preconditions upon which the agreement is based (cf PA, section 17).

The vendor can also be liable if the goods, their characteristics or their use do not correspond to the statements which the vendor made in his publicity materials or elsewhere which can be assumed to have exerted an influence on the purchaser (cf PA section 18). Such statements do not have to be in writing. However, in order for the statements to provide a basis for liability, they must take a concrete form and be proved adequately. Many of the statements given in conjunction with the marketing of a product will be so general and vague that it will be difficult to use them as a basis for claiming liability for damages.

2.3   Whether pre-contractual liability may lie in contract or tort

Such liability may lie in contract. It should, however, not be disregarded that such liability may also lie in tort.

3 LIABILITY IN CONTRACT

3.1 Outline of contract law relevant to defective products in Norway

As already mentioned, the PLA is the key Act governing liability for compensation as a result of damage caused by products. This applies regardless of whether a contract exists between the parties or not. Where a contractual relationship exists, however, limited product liability can be claimed against the vendor pursuant to the PA. Contractual liability deriving from the PA is supplemental and in some cases an alternative to, a liability deriving from the PLA.

Apart from the PLA, generally only the PA is relevant in relation to contractual claims for product liability. Provisions of the PLA will be dealt with in greater detail under section 6 below. The following paragraphs will therefore concentrate on the provisions of the PA.

The PA primarily deals with claims for damage to and defects in the product itself.

The PA has limited scope for application where damage is caused to items other than the product itself. For example, the PA cannot be applied where a defective product has caused personal injury. Further, damage to property which affects the item's environment generally lies outside the scope of the PA.

There will, however, be a small area which is covered by both the PLA and the PA. Provisions of the PA governing liability can be applied if damage is caused to items which have a close physical or functional relationship with the product. For example, if clothes are damaged by a defective washing machine, a claim can be made against the vendor to replace these. Furthermore, the damage must be of an extent which could be reasonably predicted at the time of the sales agreement. Where a sale of a defective product is made to a consumer, the consumer can also claim under section 84 of the PA against the producer, the wholesaler, the distributor and other parties providing a link in the sales chain.

Such a claim is made upon the basis of a right to take over the seller's recourse/claim for reimbursement against any person or business who was at a prior stage in the distribution chain. The injured person is entitled to make his claim directly to the party at the prior stage in the distribution chain provided the seller could have made a claim for reimbursement from the party at the prior stage in the distribution chain. None of the businesses in the distribution chain can exclude their liability to the consumer for any claims made against it in contract law. In practice, the only way a producer can reduce his liability for such claims is for him to claim an indemnity from someone higher up the distribution chain. In this instance the two sets of regulations supplement each other – but the injured party will only be entitled to receive compensation once. This being the case, the possibilities for applying the PA to matters of product liability are very limited in practice. This limitation must be borne in mind quite clearly when reading the following explanations of the provisions of the PA governing damages.

3.2 Contractual warranties relating to the quality of goods and safety of goods

Section 40(3)(b) of the PA regulates instances in which the vendor has guaranteed the product's quality or safety characteristics for a warranty period.

The Act stipulates in this respect that the purchaser can claim damages in all instances if, at the time of the agreement, the products differed from the description of them given by the vendor. The question of whether such warranty exists on the part of the vendor must be determined through an interpretation of the sales agreement. If an expression such as 'guarantee' or 'assurance' is used, this would tend to indicate that a warranty exists as defined by the Act. The vendor's warranty or guarantee must normally refer to specific concrete characteristics of the product if the warranty or guarantee is to be enforced as a contractual liability.

3.3   Breach of contract for supply of defective products

The purchaser's right to claim damages in the event of defects is regulated by section 40 of the PA. This provision imposes a strict liability for defects. However, the strict liability does not apply if the purchaser proves that the failure was due to circumstances beyond his control. This liability relates solely to direct losses. Damages for indirect losses can only be claimed according to general liability (cf PA, section 67(2); see below). Alternatively, it is possible to claim that the damage has resulted from the fact that the goods did not possess the claimed characteristics (cf PA, section 40(3); see section 5, below).

3.4   Quantum of damage

Section 67 of the PA lays down the main provisions for the scope of the damages. The provisions are constructed on the principle that the injured party is to be compensated fully for losses and expenses attributable to the breach of contract. Only those actual losses which could reasonably have been foreseen as the possible consequence of the breach of contract can be claimed.

3.5   Burden of proof

In a claim for damages, the general provisions governing the burden of proof are applied (cf section 4.6, below).

3.6   Exclusion on limitation of liability

The application of the PA is obligatory where consumers are involved. Where a businessman is supplying goods to a consumer he cannot supply them on terms and conditions which exclude the supplier's liability under the Act. Businesses when dealing together, however, can freely conclude agreements deviating from the provisions of the Act and excluding the seller's liability under the Act. The provisions of the EC Directive on Unfair Contract Terms are effectively included within the provisions of the Act on Marketing and Contract Terms and Conditions of 16 June 1972.

3.7   Limitation period

According to section 32 of the PA, the purchaser loses his right to put forward a contractual claim relating to a defect if he does not submit a complaint to

the vendor within a reasonable time after he has discovered, or ought to have discovered it. The question of what is understood by 'reasonable time' depends, among other things, on who the purchaser is. A quicker reaction is required from businesses than from private consumers.

The Act also lays down an absolute deadline for complaints of two years from the date on which the goods were actually handed to the purchaser (cf section 32-2(1)). The vendor incurs no liability if defects are not revealed or complaints are not made until after this period has expired. The vendor may extend the limitation period through his guarantee.

4 LIABILITY IN TORT

4.1 Introduction

Liability in tort arises from a mixture of statute law under the PLA and common law.

4.2 Outline of relevant tort law giving rise to liability for personal injury and property damage in Norway

4.2.1 Product Liability Act

As mentioned above in sections 1 and 2 and also in section 6 below, the PLA applies both within and outside contractual relationships. Provided the relationship is between businesses the Act does not cover damage to goods belonging to the business undertakings, which are covered by the common law of damages (see below) or contractual liability. The PLA always applies in respect of personal injuries, however.

4.2.2 Common law relating to damages

The common law relating to damages has developed over a long period of time. This law provides that a vendor, producer etc is liable for damage caused by a product he has put into the distribution chain. The liability can derive from negligence.

Negligence can relate to either the manufacture or distribution of the product, whether in the form of the choice of raw materials, the design, the production or inadequate information given to the user regarding dangerous aspects of the product. The key question is whether the producer, vendor, etc is at fault for the damage which has occurred and whether this could have been prevented by alternative action. In certain instances, the producer can also be liable for the product's injurious characteristics on the basis of strict liability, ie liability regardless of fault. Liability of this kind may be applicable if the product involves an extraordinary or continuous risk that it will cause damage and, from an evaluation of the risk, it is natural to place liability with the producer who produced a product involving an extraordinary or continuous risk or the part thereof which caused such an extraordinary or continuous risk to arise.

In principle, there are no limits to which a party can be held liable regardless of fault. However, in practice the injured person will claim against the principal producer who actually put the product into circulation (or the vendor if he acted

negligently when selling the product and this negligence has a causal link to the damage). The parties referred to above will claim reimbursement on an indemnity basis from the relevant party in the chain who is actually liable. In cases of the producers'/vendors' insolvency etc the claimant may have a relevant interest in bringing the claim against, for example, the manufacturer of the defective component.

The PLA in many ways incorporates an unwritten basis for claiming damages. The injured party does not have the right to raise a claim for damages in addition to, or as an alternative to, the liability deriving from the provisions of the PLA. As already stated, the PLA cannot be applied to commercial damage which does not involve personal injury. Such instances are fully covered by the existing jurisprudence.

4.3   Causation

Norwegian law governing damages is built on what is known as the causation principle. The need to establish a causal relationship between the action leading to the damage and the damage itself is structured on common law and a long period of legal practice. Furthermore, a logical causal relationship will be sufficiently substantiated if it can be shown to exist on the balance of probabilities.

The question as to what can be legally regarded as the cause of damage can be problematic where there are several proven causal relationships. If the damage is the result of several causes, each one will normally be regarded as the cause of the damage. In some instances, however, it may be natural to differentiate between significant and completely insignificant aspects of the causal picture and to make the main cause of the damage the reason for the liability.

4.4   Remoteness of loss and damage

The loss must be reasonable for it to justify a claim for damages. In other words, a producer is not liable for the consequences of a defect in a product if these could not be envisaged. This applies irrespective of whether the liability derives from the PLA or from jurisprudence. Norwegian law has no written provisions regarding reasonableness. The provisions derive from general principles of law (judicial rulings) governing damages.

If the relationship between the product defect and the concrete damage/loss which has arisen is too remote, the result can be either reduced liability or no liability for the producer, vendor etc.

4.5   Quantum of damages

The rules for calculating the quantum of damages in claims under the PLA are the same as generally apply in Norwegian law regarding damages: the injured party is entitled to claim compensation for the entire financial loss he has suffered under the Norwegian Compensation for Damages Act (cf Act 26 of 13 June 1969 sections 3-1 and 4-2 governing compensation for damages). In addition, certain non-financial damage can be recovered, including damages for personal injury. These assessment principles apply regardless of the basis for damages; see, amongst others, PLA, section 2-5.

If the claimant as a consequence of the damage, in addition to all financial losses, suffers permanent disablement, pain and suffering, he may receive compensation for his suffering, eg inability to sleep well or to enjoy his usual hobbies.

In the event of personal injury, the occupational damage/disability is of decisive importance for determining the magnitude of the damages.

The consequential losses resulting from product damage (eg loss of income in the event of suspension of production) is covered only to the extent that the consequential loss is reasonable and can be compensated in accordance with the general rules of the law governing damages.

With regard to section 5-2 of the Compensation for Damages Act, liability for damages can be alleviated if the court, taking account of the extent of the damage, the financial capacity of the party responsible, insurance policies and the opportunities to take out insurance, the apportionment of blame and other relevant matters, finds the burden of liability weighs unreasonably heavily on the party responsible. The same applies when, in special cases, it is reasonable for the injured party to bear the damage either wholly or in part.

4.6 Burden of proof

The Compensation for Damages Act does not include any provisions relating to the burden of proof. In principle, the injured party must prove fault and the causal relationship between the product's damaging characteristics and the damage itself. The injured party must also prove the losses to be compensated. The proof required may depend to some extent on the position of the parties. Stricter requirements regarding the provision of evidence or counter-evidence can be made on a producer than on a general consumer as regards a product's characteristics etc.

As regards who must prove that the loss is not too remote, it is incorrect to talk about a 'burden of proof'. The Norwegian system is that the defendant alleges the claim is too remote and the defendant opposes such an application. The court in its discretion decides whether, according to the relevant situation, it will rule on the question of remoteness or not.

4.7 Exclusion or limitation of liability

Agreements which restrict or limit liability of any person who may be held liable for a claim relating to a defective product under the provisions of the PLA are invalid (cf section 2-6). In practice it is difficult for a manufacturer to limit his liability to an end-user in respect of a product liability claim as he mainly sells direct to the end-user and cannot get the consumer to agree to limit his liability. Beyond the scope of the Act, agreements which waive liabilities can (in theory) be set aside in accordance with section 36 of the Contract Act (Act 14 of 31 May 1918 on Contracts) relating to the prohibition of unreasonable business terms and conditions.

4.8 Limitation period

The provisions of the Act of Limitation of 18 May 1979, No 18, apply to questions of product liability ensuing from common law. The provisions on a

limitation period for liability under the PLA are covered by specific provisions in the PLA (cf.section 2-7 and section 5.2.9 below).

The limitation period for claims under the common law and the PLA is normally three years from the time the injured party learned of the damage and the party responsible (cf Act of Limitation section 9(1)). This first rule is subject to an overriding rule that liability is statute-barred ten years from the day the damage occurred, ie from the time the damage manifests itself, even if the injured party is not aware of this (Act of Limitation section 9(2)). A similar limitation period is provided for liability under the PLA, cf section 5.2.9 below.

The limitation period for claims under the common law is subject to a further rule that in no circumstances can a claim be brought more than 20 years after the date of the damaging act was committed or seized. If the damage has not occurred within this period, the right to claim damages is lost even if the damage manifests itself at a later date.

However, no limitation period applies if the damage results from a commercial activity and if at the date of the damaging act the producer knew or ought to have known that it could endanger life or represent a serious danger to health.

4.9   Liability for third parties

In certain circumstances, intervention from a third party may result in the producer being relieved of liability. For example, this may occur where damage is attributable to a third party being negligent in performing modifications to a product.

The producer can also be held jointly liable with a third party, depending upon the other party's 'contribution' to the damage. The issue here is one of joint causation of damage. The principal rule in such cases is that the producer and the third party are held jointly and severally liable for the damage (Compensation for Damages Act, section 5-3).

It is important to appreciate that 'third party' here refers to persons who are not defined as 'sub-producers' within the terms of the PLA. A sub-producer and a principal producer are treated as jointly and severally liable vis-à-vis the injured party. This does not apply if the sub-producer can prove that the safety defect of the sub-product is attributable to a planning design or specification by the principal producer and that the sub-producer cannot be blamed for having followed instructions.

5   LIABILITY FOR DEFECTIVE PRODUCTS ARISING FROM NATIONAL LAW IN NORWAY: HARMONISATION OF THE DIRECTIVE WITH NORWEGIAN LAW

5.1   Introduction

As mentioned above, Norway is not a member of the European Union but the Directive became binding on Norway when Norway became a member of the EEA. This led to certain amendments to the PLA.

The PLA lays down rules aimed primarily at protecting the consumer. Damage to property resulting from business enterprises falls outside the scope of the Act. Commercial damage which does not involve personal injury continues to be covered by jurisprudence relating to damages and by contractual agreements between the parties involved.

5.2 Outline of provisions in Norway

5.2.1 The products covered by the Act

The PLA covers all types of goods and movables, whether they are raw materials or finished goods, sub-products or main products (cf PLA, section 1-2(1)). Indeed, the Act can only be applied where products which fall within the scope of the Act are manufactured or distributed as a link in the commercial chain, starting with the initial manufacturers and ending with the consumer (PLA, section 1-1).

The term 'products' also includes those items incorporated into other movables or into real estate (eg machine parts, electrical components, concrete, supporting structures). Waste from the production process is also covered if it is distributed as a link in the commercial chain where, for instance, the waste from one manufacturing process may be used as a raw material in another production process. Water, gas, oil etc are also included in the term 'product' – not only where these are supplied in packaged quantities, but also when supplied via pipeline.

However, the term 'product' excludes real estate from the scope of the Act. This means that, among other things, building and construction contracts are not automatically included in the provisions of the Act. It must be noted, however, that the Act applies to building and construction materials which are incorporated into real estate. It is therefore necessary to resort to jurisprudence/contractual provisions to determine liability for building and construction work.

The term 'product' also encompasses electricity (PLA, section 1-2).

5.2.2 Which producers are liable?

The Act does not restrict liability to producers as such, but extends to importers and, to a certain degree, vendors.

As regards goods produced in Norway, the principal liability for defective products is borne by the manufacturer (cf PLA, section 1-3(1, a)). Parties other than the manufacturer can be held liable if the party concerned presents the product as his own by attaching his name or trademark etc to it (PLA, section 1-3(1, b)). Agents bear a secondary product liability if the producer is unknown (PLA, section 1-3(1, c)).

In the case of goods produced abroad, product liability will always be borne by the importer (PLA, section 1-3(1, e)). Secondary product liability also applies to agents of importers of products if the actual importer is unknown (PLA, section 1-3(1, f)).

5.2.3 Basis for liability

Section 2-1 of the PLA sets out a special basis for liability. According to this provision, the party responsible for the product is liable to pay damages if the product does not provide the safety which a user or the general public could reasonably expect. In assessing the safety which can be expected, consideration must be taken of all aspects related to the product, such as its presentation, marketing and envisaged use. The Act defines the absence of the safety which a user could reasonably expect as a safety defect.

The basis for liability introduced by the PLA is new in Norwegian law. The point of focus is no longer the circumstances relating to the producer but rather the product itself. The question of what the producer could have done

differently to prevent the injurious characteristic is no longer posed. Instead, the Act concentrates solely on whether the product provided the safety the user could have reasonably expected of it for the envisaged area of application. It is important here to understand that it is not the user's concrete safety expectations which are decisive. In other words, if the subjective safety expectations exceed what are otherwise generally expected, the producer cannot be held liable, ie an objective safety standard applies. The safety standard implies, for example, that one can expect a child's toy not to react explosively when brought into contact with a naked flame. On the other hand, however, one cannot expect vehicles, for example, to be completely safe from accident. A special problem arises in conjunction with the safety standard in cases where safety equipment (eg smoke detectors, emergency radio beacons, inflatable life rafts, etc) fails to work. Such failure would represent a safety defect of crucial importance. There is nevertheless a problem in recovering damages since there must always be a causal relationship between the failure and the damage which occurs. It is, for example, not certain that a drowning accident could have been prevented in the event of a shipwreck if the emergency radio beacon had worked and a rescue operation could therefore have been mounted. However, the causal relationship is much more apparent where, for example, a life raft fails to inflate as expected or a fire extinguishing system fails.

The safety standard means that development faults fall within the scope of product liability. Norwegian law makes no exceptions in this regard. A development fault is present if, on the basis of known and optimal technological know-how and scientific knowledge, there was, at the time of production, no way of foreseeing the defective characteristic resulting in the damage. The producer is not freed of liability even if, on the basis of known technology, he has done all he can to optimise the product.

5.2.4   *The circumstance triggering liability*

According to section 2-2(1) of the PLA the circumstance triggering liability is the actual act of distributing the product. Distribution here is also taken to include providing samples of goods and transferring the product to shipping agents.

5.2.5   *The damages covered*

The Act encompasses personal injury and damage to property determined for private use or consumption, provided the property was in fact used or consumed privately by the injured party (PLA, section 2-3(1)). As mentioned earlier, however, damage to property occurring between business enterprises does not fall within the scope of the Act. For damage to property covered by the Act, an own risk (*de minimis* level) amounting to NOK 4.000 applies (PLA, section 2-3 (3)).

5.2.6   *Exemption from liability due to the kind of damage*

Damage caused to the product itself is exempted from product liability (cf PLA, section 2-3(1, a)). Compensation for damage of this type must be claimed under the PA or contractual agreements.

Furthermore, all damage which a sub-product causes to a main product before the latter is distributed to a user will be exempted from liability (cf PLA,

section 2-3(2, b)). On the other hand, all damage to the main product occurring after the user himself (possibly with specialist assistance) has incorporated the sub-product causing the damage will be covered.

As already outlined above, liability for damage to property is limited to property determined for private use or consumption, provided the property was in fact used or consumed privately by the injured party. Liability for damage to property occurring between business enterprises must be resolved through the provisions of the common law on damages and contractual agreements.

5.2.7   Exemptions from liability due to delineations to other regulations governing damages

Section 1-5 of the PLA exempts damage covered by the following Acts or resulting in the following situations:

(a) Act Governing Third Party Liability for Motor Vehicles;
(b) Act Governing Road-Freight Agreements;
(c) damage to property caused by railways;
(d) damage to property caused by a boat, ship, hovercraft or aircraft, or by permanent or mobile equipment on the Norwegian continental shelf;
(e) third party liability in the field of nuclear energy;
(f) Petroleum Act.

If, for example, a motor vehicle causes damage due to a safety defect, the injured party must claim damages through the Act Governing Third Party Liability for Motor Vehicles and not through the PLA. If circumstances exist for claiming damages, the insurance company covering this liability can, however, make an indemnity claim from the motor vehicle manufacturer at common law.

5.2.8   Exemption from liability

According to section 2-6 of the PLA, agreements which restrict or limit liability under the PLA are void.

5.2.9   Limitation period

PLA, section 2-7 contains particular provision on limitation period for liability questions covered by the Act. The provision complies with article 10 of the Directive.

The limitation period for claims under the PLA is normally three years from the time the injured party learned of the damage and the party responsible (PLA, section 2-7 (1)). The liability is finally statute-barred ten years from the day the product was put into circulation (PLA, section 2-7 (2)).

The limitation provisions in the PLA differ slightly from the provisions that apply to damages not covered by the PLA, cf section 4.8 above. However, the PLA does not prevent the injured party from claiming damages pursuant to common law (PLA, section 1-1 (2)). In such an event, the liability will expire according to the provisions in the general Act of Limitation of 18 May 1979 no 18. If the producer at the date of the damaging act (eg the date he put the product on the market) knew or ought to have known that it could endanger life or represent a serious danger to health, his liability may (also) be attributed to common law where no limitation period applies.

5.3   Description of optional or anomalous provisions in respect of product liability law in Norway

5.3.1   *Agricultural produce*

Agricultural produce constitutes a 'product' within the terms of the PLA and is subject to the same liability regulations as every other product.

5.3.2   *Computer software*

Product liability within the terms of the Act is limited to material products only. The Act does not encompass computer software.

5.3.3   *Optional provisions in the EC Directive*

The Norwegian PLA encompasses both agricultural produce and development faults. Furthermore, with the exception of the limitations which apply for liability relating to damage to private property and to drugs and medicines, no other restrictions have been laid down as regards the maximum damages recoverable. The Norwegian Act has therefore chosen the most severe options laid down by the Directive.

6   CRIMINAL LIABILITY FOR DEFECTIVE PRODUCTS ARISING FROM BOTH GENERAL SAFETY LAW AND THE IMPLEMENTATION OF EC DIRECTIVE 92/59 EC ON PRODUCT SAFETY IN NORWAY

6.1   Introduction

Norwegian consumer protection legislation is well developed and in some cases exceeds current EC requirements.

6.2   Outline of implementation of Directive 92/59 EC in Norway

The Act of 11 June 1976 governing product supervision (*Lov om produktkontroll*) mentioned in more detailed in section 7 below is generally considered to comply with the provisions of the General Product Safety Directive. It is, however, more far-reaching in its effect as it covers every product throughout the whole of the manufacturing process.

6.3   Description of local optional provisions

Violation of the Product Supervision Act is punishable by fines or imprisonment of up to three months.

6.4   Brief overview of other significant product safety law

If the distribution of a dangerous product results in personal injury, this is (in theory) punishable as a violation of the provisions of the General Civil Penal Code relating to bodily harm caused through negligence. This can be punished by fines or imprisonment of up to three years.

7 CIVIL LIABILITY FOR DEFECTIVE PRODUCTS ARISING FROM BREACH OF STATUTORY REGULATION DESIGNED TO PROTECT CONSUMERS AND/OR TO PROMOTE SAFETY

7.1 Outline of nature of protective regulations

Act 79 of 11 June 1976, governing product supervision (*Lov om produktkontroll*) has the object of preventing the manufacture of products causing damage to health or environmental pollution. According to section 3 of the Act, a producer, importer, vendor, etc of a product which can damage health, etc is obliged to exercise caution and pursue measures directed at preventing and restricting such damage. These parties undertake to obtain the knowledge necessary to assess whether the product can have effects which are damaging to health.

According to section 4 of the Act, the Government is empowered to adopt measures relating to how a product is to be manufactured, marketed, distributed, identified, used or handled, etc. It is also empowered to adopt measures covering the composition of a product or prohibiting a product from being manufactured, marketed, distributed or used.

Official identification standards have been laid down for, eg, power saws, motor mowers, detergents and certain chemicals. Certain standards also apply for child-proof packaging.

In addition to the above, Norway has adopted a number of international product standards (eg SENELEC). The regulations for approved electrical products are particularly prominent in this respect.

7.2 Burden of proof

The Product Supervision Act does not include provision for any claims for damages to be made by anyone who suffers loss as a result of any producer, importer etc being in breach of its provisions. As discussed below, the failure of a manufacturer or importer etc to produce or sell products that conform to the requirements of the Product Supervision Act may result in claims under contract product liability law or under common law being more likely to succeed, as well as criminal sanctions. Nor does the Act contain any provisions relating to the burden of proof of liability which can be attributed in the event of a breach of the Act. The burden of proof relating to actions for damages is subject to the same regulations as other claims for damages (cf section 4.6 above).

7.3 Nature of liability and damages

Official approval or compliance with product standards in accordance with the Product Supervision Act or international standards can be a key issue for determining liability in claims based in contract law under the PLA or pursuant to the terms of the common law on damages. The general principle adopted is that official approval does not free the producer from liability. The producer is subject to independent liability for defective products which is separate from any such approval.

Where production is performed in compliance with officially defined production standards, the producer is relieved of liability only if the standard is mandatory and provides the producer with no possibility of deviating from

the principal standard. Insofar as deviation is permissible, the producer bears independent liability for deviations he undertakes.

7.4   Special liabilities in respect of particular products

7.4.1   Radioactive products

Damage and injury caused by radioactivity (radioactive substances) are covered by special legal provisions providing for strict liability, obligatory insurance for product liability involving very high coverage and channelling of liability towards the operator of the nuclear plant, cf Act 28 of 12 May 1972. The Act implements the Paris Convention on Third Party Liability in the Field of Nuclear Energy of 29 July 1960 with subsequent amendments.

7.4.2   Drugs and medicines

As stated in the introduction, the PLA contains special provisions governing liability for drugs and medicines. This liability also extends to substances which are tested in medical experiments on humans as part of the process of developing drugs.

The party which is liable according to these special provisions is not the producer of the drugs or medicines, but the underwriters of insurance policies. As laid down by the Act, it is compulsory for manufacturers of the drugs in question to take out insurance policies. Liability for damage to health caused by drugs and medicines is thus channelled to a special insurance arrangement which is directly liable to the injured parties.

This arrangement is based on an obligatory insurance which must be taken out for all medicines sold in Norway. A special association for liability in the field of drugs and medicines known as the Association of Liable Medicine Producers (*Legemiddelansvarsforeningen*) is responsible for ensuring that the obligatory insurance is taken out.

The PLA imposes strict liability for damage to health caused by drugs and medicines (cf section 3-3(1)). It is sufficient to demonstrate that damage to health has occurred and that a causal relationship exists between the consumption of the product and the damage to health.

The section on drugs and medicines includes various exceptions from liability. These include instances where the course of the illness can be attributed to the person's own state of health. Limitations are also laid down as to the maximum indemnities which can be paid out under the insurance per year/per illness. According to section 3-6 of the Act, the total volume of damages relating to this section must not exceed NOK 80m for illnesses ascertained in the same calendar year. The total compensation for serial damage to health resulting from the same substance in one or more drugs or medicines is further limited to NOK 100m. If the indemnity sums laid down in the Act are insufficient to cover the losses of everyone entitled to damages, the level of these damages is reduced in accordance with section 3-7 of the Act.

CHAPTER XIV

Portugal

Jorge Santiago Neves, Esq

Santiago Neves & Associados
Av Eng° Duarte Pacheco, Empreendimento das Amoreiras
Torre 2, 10° Piso
1070 Lisbon
Portugal

Tel: ++ 351 1 381 43 93
Fax: ++ 351 1 387 18 82

CHAPTER XIV

Portugal

1 INTRODUCTION

1.1 Introduction to the Portuguese legal system

The Portuguese legal system can be characterised as a civil law jurisdiction of Roman and Germanic tradition, which in recent years was profoundly marked by the sweeping changes of democratisation brought about by the Revolution of 1974. As with other civil law jurisdictions since the eighteenth century, the most important rules which govern the organisation and functioning of society have been compiled and consolidated as codes. The Portuguese Civil Code which is of particular importance to liability for defective products was adopted in 1966, substituting the previous Civil Code which had been approved in 1867. Whereas the 1867 Code had been strongly influenced by the landmark French Civil Code of 1804, the 1966 Code reflects the impact on Portuguese legal thinking of the German Civil Code of 1900 – with its more technical and detailed approach – and the manner in which it was adopted as the model for the Italian Civil Code of 1942. In 1977, following the adoption of the post-Revolution Constitution of 1976, the Civil Code was brought into line with the rights and freedoms enshrined in the new Constitution.

Civil procedure, on the other hand, has evolved little since the adoption of the present Code of Civil Procedure in 1961, and it is generally recognised that the arrival of a new code, introducing a simpler and more expedited procedure is long overdue. In its present form civil procedure can be said to represent a balance between the individual initiative, or adversarial, and the inquisitorial approaches. Prior to the establishment of the dictatorship in 1926 (which was to last until 1974) the system was clearly adversarial, in keeping with the liberal doctrines of the period, and the judge's role was quite passive. With the changes introduced from 1926 onwards judges were attributed greater control over civil procedure, although, on a positive note, greater oral intervention by the parties was also allowed. Given the interventionist attitude of judges in western European judicial systems in recent years, it is unlikely that the expected reform of civil procedure will reduce the role of judges in Portuguese civil actions, so that the present balanced approach can be expected to continue.

Civil (as opposed to *criminal*) liability is usually classified as contractual or non-contractual. In Portuguese law contractual liability is something of a misnomer since it is not limited to contractual performance, but covers the breach of any obligation to perform, be it as a result of a contract, a unilateral obligation, eg a public promise, or an obligation established by law, eg the obligation to negotiate a contract in accordance with the rules of good faith. Non-contractual liability or, more precisely, liability for illicit acts (which for

the purposes of this chapter, we shall later refer to as liability in tort) refers to the breach of a duty of care or abstention (ie. causing damage by violating the rights of others or breaching a rule of law designed to protect the interests of others). In keeping with the trend of many civil jurisdictions, the present Civil Code has brought these two forms of liability closer together, in recognition of the fact that the traditional distinction between them is not justified in terms of practice or logic, as many of the rules for one form of liability apply to the other. Indeed the rules governing the obligation to repair damage resulting from the two forms of liability are exactly the same. For these reasons, the Portuguese Civil Code divides civil liability into three areas: non-contractual liability, articles 483 ff; contractual liability, articles 798 ff and the obligation to repair damage irrespective of its nature, articles 562 ff. A particular category of non-contractual liability, and one which is of special interest to product liability, is no-fault liability, which the Portuguese Civil Code deals with in articles 499 ff. Articles referred to in this chapter, where not otherwise identified, are those of the Portuguese Civil Code. All translations of the provisions of Portuguese law used in this chapter are the author's own.

In section 3 below we shall cover contractual liability, and in section 4 we shall look at liability in tort. The rules on the obligation to repair damage irrespective of their nature (article 562 ff) govern both forms of liability, in particular as to the quantum and payment of damages, and the fault of the injured party, and so shall be analysed concurrently with contractual and tortious liability. No-fault liability, to which many of the rules for tortious liability apply, will be dealt with in section 5. In section 6 we shall consider the liability which arises for producers who breach statutory regulations designed to protect consumers and promote safety.

In the analysis which follows our references will be largely statutory rather than judicial, as can be expected when analysing the law of a civil law system such as that which exists in Portugal. Some references will, however, be made to the rulings of the higher courts (ie. appeal courts and Supreme Court) where these help to clarify a point of law or give useful indications as to its practical application. These rulings are identified by their date and the law report in which they appear – *Boletim do Ministério da Justiça* ('BMJ') or *Colectânea de Jurisprudência* ('CJ'), followed by the identification of the volume number in the case of the BMJ, year and number of volume in the case of the CJ, and the page number.

1.2   Overview of the law relating to defective products in Portugal

Until the enactment of Decree Law 383/89 (henceforth referred to as 'DL 383/89') implementing the Product Liability Directive ('the Directive'), there was no product liability law as such in Portugal. It is, however, possible to find various pieces of legislation dealing with matters related to liability resulting from defective products other than DL 383/89, the most important being the Portuguese Constitution, the Consumer Protection Law and the Civil Code (governing liability in contract and tort). The Consumer Protection Law and the Civil Code will be dealt with in detail in the remainder of this chapter, so it is worth reflecting here only on the Constitutional provisions mentioned.

Article 60(1) of the Portuguese Constitution establishes the general principle that 'All consumers are entitled to [a reasonable degree of] quality of

goods and services consumed, to training and information, to the protection of their health, safety and economic interests and to the recovery of damages'.

This rather vague statement gives no indication of what can be expected in terms of 'quality' of goods and services, and is of no use in determining whether the consumer is entitled to the recovery of damages according to the usual rules of contract or tort, or whether, failing these, he can rely on no-fault liability. There is also no indication as to whom the consumer can expect to recover his damages from – the manufacturer, the distributor or even the State as guarantor of the consumer's constitutional rights.

In short, this express constitutional principle appears to be of little practical use. In a more positive vein, however, it may be said that this constitutional reference to consumer rights inspired the Consumer Protection Law of 1981 but, as we shall see further on, this Law produced no substantial change to the rules consumers could already rely on, namely those included in the Civil Code.

Before proceeding with our analysis of the Consumer Protection Law and the relevant provisions of the Civil Code, we should bear in mind that these are limited in their scope to establishing and protecting a person's right to purchase products which are not defective or unsuitable for their stated purpose, and his right to redress if they are. The introduction of legislation which created a general no-fault liability for damage caused by a defect in a product was a substantial innovation in Portuguese law, and one which was, no doubt, overdue.

2   PRE-CONTRACTUAL LIABILITY

2.1   Effect on the interpretation and extent of the obligations of the parties to a contract and extent that non-disclosure of facts during negotiations may lead to liability

In what is basically an adaptation of the Italian Civil Code's article 1337, the Portuguese Civil Code's article 227(1) states that 'Whosoever negotiates with another person with a view to concluding a contract shall, both in its preliminaries and in its formation, proceed in accordance with the rules of good faith, failing which he shall be liable for any damages he causes to the other party'.

The important point to retain is that there is a general rule of bargaining in good faith, so that a liability is created for the party who:

(a) by his deeds or by ignoring a duty to inform, leads another party into believing that a contract will be concluded when that is not, in fact, the intention, or;
(b) leads the other party into concluding an invalid contract.

Once this liability exists there is an obligation to repair the damage arising, such damage is subject to the rules common to contractual and tortious liability, as mentioned above, concerning the quantum and payment of damages and the fault of the injured party.

This is the extent of pre-contractual liability in Portuguese law, which means that only so-called 'negative damages' may be claimed, ie damages which would not have arisen if negotiations had not taken place, or if an invalid contract had not been concluded. So-called 'positive damages', ie for breach

of contractual obligations per se, may only be claimed on the basis of the contract which is eventually concluded. However, to understand the circumstances in which pre-contractual liability will arise, it is necessary to consider briefly the general rules in Portuguese law concerning misrepresentation and its effect both on the determination of the boundaries of pre-contractual good faith, as well as on the validity of contracts, generally. The matter of misrepresentation in Portuguese law is a complex and detailed one, so we shall consider only the position relevant to liability for pre-contractual statements.

A party making misrepresentations, or deliberately dissembling the opposite party's error, will incur liability, and the party who has been thus misled will be entitled to annul the resultant acts (article 254(1)). If, on the other hand, the misleading statement is of a 'non-serious' nature, then the creation of a liability will depend on the circumstances in which the statement is made. In effect, article 245 states that:

(1) A non-serious statement made in the belief that the lack of serious intention is understood, does not produce any effects;

(2) If, however, the statement is made in circumstances which lead the party receiving the statement into justifiably accepting the seriousness of the statement, he will have a right to compensation for damage incurred.

It is important to note that the non-serious statement referred to in both paragraphs of the aforementioned article is made in the belief that the other party is aware of the non-serious nature of the statement, and in both cases the party making the statement has no intention to mislead. This is an essential distinction between this form of misrepresentation and the other form mentioned, ie that which is intentionally misleading. Only when the non-serious statement is made in circumstances which justify the other party's belief that it is serious, will liability for damages arise, whereas, as mentioned previously, when the statement is intentionally misleading, and influences the acts of the party receiving the statement, these acts may be annulled (article 254(1)) and give rise to liability.

In recognition, however, of the complex nature of human relationships and social intercourse, the law tolerates misleading statements which may be considered 'legitimate according to [society's] dominant concepts' and accepts the dissembling of another party's errors when there is no obligation to elucidate either in law, in contract or in accordance with society's dominant concepts (article 253(2)). In other words, the law draws the line between a form of deception which it is prepared to tolerate, the so-called *dolus bonus* (which will neither give rise to liability nor produce voidable acts) and *dolus malus* (which will produce such effects, pursuant to article 254(1), as mentioned above). Although it is not difficult to grasp the logic behind this distinction, it does raise practical difficulties, particularly as judicial rulings on the topic are rather scant. It is clear that a dishwasher advertised as 'the best on the market', when the manufacturer is aware it occupies a more modest position in the dishwasher league, will be a case of *dolus bonus,* whereas if a retailer sells a used dishwasher claiming that it is brand new, this will be a case of *dolus malus,* but a lot may lie in between.

2.2   Whether pre-contractual liability lies in contract or tort

Given the limited scope of pre-contractual liability, on the one hand, and, on the other, the previously mentioned tendency for the boundary separating

contractual and tortious liability to disappear, the question of whether pre-contractual liability in Portuguese law lies in contract or in tort, can be considered as largely academic. The predominant doctrine, however, is that pre-contractual liability lies in contract because, as was explained earlier, contractual liability covers all cases of breach of an obligation to perform, and not solely obligations arising from a contract per se. In practical terms, though, once pre-contractual liability has been established, the rules governing the obligation to repair damages are those of articles 562 ff, which apply to both contractual and tortious liability. The only respect in which pre-contractual liability follows the same rules as those of tort is in the case of the limitation period applicable, which is that of tortious liability, ie three years, rather than the twenty which applies in contract.

3 LIABILITY IN CONTRACT

3.1 Introduction and outline of contract law relevant to defective products in Portugal

As in most other Western European legal systems the principle of privity of contract (identified in Portuguese law as the 'principle of relativity') limits the effects of a contract to its respective parties. The only recognised exceptions to this principle are those contracts concluded expressly for the benefit of a third party, or contracts where one of the parties is later to be substituted by a third party (and it is arguable whether the latter is truly an exception). Various attempts have been made over the years to import foreign doctrines, such as the French '*action directe*', or the American 'implied warranties', to establish a contractual relationship between the producer and the consumer, but these have been rejected. Liability in contract is therefore only possible as between the parties to the contract, eg, in the distribution chain, between a manufacturer and his distributor, or between a vendor and a purchaser.

3.2 Contractual warranties relating to the 'proper functioning' of goods

The Portuguese Civil Code establishes that the vendor makes a promise to the purchaser that the goods sold will 'function properly', so long as such a warranty has been agreed to by the parties or is usual in the circumstances of the sale (this will always be the case if the sale occurs through the usual retail channels, but it is unlikely to be the case if one neighbour sells his used television set to another). This warranty creates an obligation for the vendor, irrespective of any fault on his part, to repair the goods sold or to substitute them when such substitution is necessary, and the goods are of such a nature as to make the substitution possible (article 921 of the Portuguese Civil Code, in turn based on article 1512 of the Italian Civil Code).

When the warranty period has not been established contractually or cannot be determined in accordance with custom, it is legally fixed as six months after the delivery of the product, although within this period, the failure of the product to 'function properly' must be notified to the vendor within 30 days of the purchaser's knowledge of the defect arising. An action at law for satisfaction of the warranty must be brought within the period mentioned for notification

of the vendor, or within six months of the date on which the notification was made to the vendor of the failure of the product to function properly.

The warranty covers only the 'proper functioning' of the goods sold, so that the warranty will not apply if the goods are used improperly. A further limitation to the warranty results from a 1984 ruling by the Portuguese Supreme Court when, in interpreting article 921, it stated that it resulted from the clauses of the contract in question that only manufacturing defects are covered by the warranty, and not defects which may result from imperfect conception of the goods' design (4.10.1984, BMJ, 340-364).

The limitations of warranties of proper functioning of goods are, however, mitigated by the general understanding that they do not exclude the purchaser's rights based on breach of the relevant sale of goods contract which is described in section 3.3 below.

3.3   Breach of contract for supply of defective products

3.3.1   Types of defect

The law recognises a limited number of defects in products which give rise to breach of contract (article 913):

(a) a defect which devalues the product;
(b) a defect which prevents the product from fulfilling the purpose for which it is sold;
(c) the non-existence of characteristics specified by the vendor; and
(d) the non-existence of characteristics necessary for the fulfilment of the purpose for which the product is sold.

Where such defects arise, certain rules must be satisfied before it can be concluded that a breach of contract has occurred. Namely, it will be necessary that the purchaser has acquired the defective product mistakenly believing it not to be defective, or has been misled by the vendor into believing that the product is not defective. For the purchaser's error regarding the defect of the product to be relevant, the defect must be one which the vendor should or could have recognised as essential to the purchaser's decision to buy.

Once the defect has been detected, various outcomes are possible:

(a) the purchaser may opt for rescission of the contract;
(b) the vendor may, of his own initiative, repair the defect so that it is no longer possible for the purchaser to rescind the contract, unless he has already suffered damage as a result of the defect, or has already brought an action at law to rescind the contract;
(c) the purchaser may demand that the vendor pay damages, although the extent of such a right will depend on:
    (i)   whether the purchase was made because the vendor deliberately misled the purchaser as to the characteristics of the product, in which case the purchaser is entitled to damages; or
    (ii) whether the purchase was made because the purchaser was mistaken in assessing the characteristics of the product, in which case, the purchaser will not be entitled to damages if the vendor through no fault of his own was unaware of the product's defect;
(d) the purchaser may demand that the defect be repaired, or that, where this is not possible, the product be substituted, if it is of such a nature as to

make substitution possible, but this will no longer be the case if the vendor, through no fault of his own, was unaware of the product's defect (in which case the purchaser may only exercise his right to rescind the contract, and liability for damages will not occur);

(e) given the circumstances, the vendor may prove that, if the purchaser had not been mistaken or misled, he would still have acquired the product, but at a lower price, in which case the purchaser will only be entitled to a reduction of the purchase price, although this will not affect his right to recover damages (cf. (c), above).

3.3.2   Causation

As was mentioned in the introduction to this chapter, the Portuguese Civil Code deals with the obligation to repair damage irrespective of its nature, consequently such rules apply to both contractual and tortious liability. We shall, therefore, analyse the various aspects of damage, namely causation, remoteness of loss, and quantum, bearing in mind that the same rules apply to tortious liability which will be dealt with in section 4.

The obligation to pay damages does not cover all and any form of damage directly or indirectly resulting from the event giving rise to the liability. Of the various doctrines which have attempted to establish the limit of damages to those actually caused by an event, the Portuguese Civil Code opted for the doctrine of 'adequate causation' according to which the obligation to repair damages will only exist in relation to the damages that the injured party would probably not have suffered if such an event had not occurred (article 563). The Civil Code thus bases causation on the idea of the probability of the damage. Given that the Civil Code expresses the matter in terms of 'probabilities' it has become the topic for much academic debate, and since this gives rise essentially to questions of fact, the matter has been largely left to the first instance courts to decide, with often conflicting results. It is, nevertheless, possible to state that the doctrine adopted, when applied in practice, means that the cause of damage is an act which, in abstract terms, is sufficient to have produced the damage.

3.3.3   Remoteness of loss

If an act actually caused the damage, but would not in the usual course of events in everyday life have been expected to have caused such damage, then no causal link is established, eg if a person is highly susceptible to shock and dies of a heart attack on witnessing the explosion of his television set, the explosion of the television set cannot be considered as adequate cause of his death. On the other hand, it is important to take into account the knowledge of the agent of the action, eg if, in the above example, the explosion of the television set was provoked by the victim's wife, who was fully aware of his susceptibility, then the explosion would be an adequate cause of death.

3.3.4   Quantum of damage

Article 562 establishes the general rule that the obligation to pay damages implies the reconstitution of the situation which would have existed if the event which created the liability for damages had not occurred. This covers not only the damage actually caused, but also the benefits lost as a result of such damage, and, where these are foreseeable, it is also possible to recover losses which will be incurred in the future as a result of the breach of contract (article 564).

The law establishes that reparation should bring about the 'natural restoration' of the situation which existed before the damage occurred, and only when this is not possible or insufficient to redress fully the damage, or proves itself excessively burdensome for the liable party, should the damage be redressed in money (article 566(1)). In accordance with the general principles of contractual freedom, however, the parties may agree differently, eg to redress the damage in money even when 'natural restoration' would have been possible.

The quantum of damages to be paid by the person causing the damage may, however, be reduced or disallowed entirely, if the damage has also been caused or aggravated by the fault of the injured person (article 570(1)). In such cases, if the liability is based on a presumption of fault (ie in certain cases of tortious liability (see section 4.6 below) then, notwithstanding any rule to the contrary, it shall be disallowed entirely (article 570(2)).

3.4   Burden of proof

The general rule regarding the burden of proof is that whoever claims a right must prove the facts giving rise to such a right (article 342(1)). However, in the case of breach of contract it is for the party whose obligation it is to perform to prove that the breach or defective performance is not that party's fault (article 799(1)), although the burden of proof regarding the existence of breach or defective performance shall, in accordance with the general rules above, rest on the party claiming breach or defective performance.

3.5   Exclusion or limitation of liability

Article 809 stipulates that any clause excluding contractual liability is null and void. This does not exclude the possibility of waiving a right to damages once this right has come about as a result of breach of contract, but it does categorically preclude the possibility of waiving such a right before the breach has occurred. The only exception to this rule is in the case of vicarious liability (section 3.7 below).

Limitation of liability is not clearly forbidden by the law, nor is it clearly permitted. However, based on general rules of law, in particular those of contractual freedom, and on the fact that article 602 allows a debtor to agree with his creditor that only a certain part of his property may guarantee a debt, which is in effect a limitation of liability, the Portuguese Supreme Court (in its ruling of 2 July 1981, BMJ, 309-319) and leading academics generally accept that limitation clauses in contracts are valid so long as they do not:

(a) conflict with public welfare;
(b) limit liability to a negligible or insufficient sum, so as to amount, in fact, to an exclusion of liability; and
(c) cover cases of serious fault or intentional breach by the liable party.

These rules on the exclusion or limitation of liability are reinforced by the statutory restrictions resulting from Decree-Law 446/85 of 26 October (henceforth DL 446/85) which governs the use of 'general contractual clauses' or contracts with standard clauses, of which the current text is the result of alterations introduced by Decree-Law 220/95 of 31 August, which implemented EC Directive 93/13 of 5 April 1993 on 'abusive clauses' in contracts between

consumers and professionals (whom, for our purpose, we shall refer to as vendors and producers). In this instance, and given the express provisions of the Directive, namely article 8, the Portuguese legislator decided to make only minor changes to previous law, to the extent necessary to accommodate the Directive, and took the opportunity also to make the changes necessary to bring national law into line with the Rome Convention on Contractual Obligations of 16 June 1980, which Portugal had in the meantime adhered to as a result of the Funchal Convention of 18 May 1992. To compare the situation in the Directive and that resulting from DL 446/85, we should first identify the 'abusive clauses' listed in the Annex to the Directive which might, directly or indirectly, exclude or limit a vendor or producer's contractual or tortious liability, these being (to use the lettering for these clauses as they appear in the Annex):

(a) clauses which exclude or limit liability in the case of death or injury to consumers;

(b) clauses which exclude or limit liability in the case of non-performance or defective performance of contractual obligations;

(i) clauses which declare the consumer's acceptance of clauses of which he could not have been apprised before concluding the contract;

(j) clauses which allow the vendor or producer unilaterally and unjustifiably to alter the terms of the contract;

(k) clauses which authorise the vendor or producer to alter unilaterally the characteristics of the product;

(m) clauses which establish the right of the vendor or producer to decide whether the product is in conformity with contractual stipulations, or confer upon him the exclusive right to interpret the clauses of the contract;

(p) clauses which allow the vendor or producer to transfer his contractual position to a third party in such a manner as to weaken the position of the consumer, without the latter's consent;

(q) clauses which create unfair restrictions on the consumer's right to bring judicial actions and to use the means of proof at his disposal.

With one exception – clauses foreseen in (k), which are omitted altogether – all of the above clauses, which in the Directive are described only as clauses which 'might be considered as abusive' (article 3(3)), insofar as they may be contrary to principles of good faith, appear in DL 446/85 as 'forbidden clauses', and as such shall be treated as null and void. It must, however, be pointed out that DL 446/85 distinguishes between 'absolutely forbidden' and 'relatively forbidden' clauses, the criterion for the distinction being that 'relatively forbidden' clauses have to be viewed in the context of their respective contracts, taking into account, presumably, such factors as the degree to which the contract is the result of real negotiation between the parties.

Where the clauses listed above are defined as 'absolutely forbidden' clauses it is possible to agree with the observation contained in the preamble to DL 446/85 which describes Portuguese legislation as stricter and more far-reaching than the Directive. This is not entirely true, however, if we take into account the omission in DL 446/85 of clause (k) of the Directive, and if we further consider that clauses (j) and, to a certain extent (b), of the Annex to the Directive, are only classified as relatively forbidden clauses. It may be argued that since the Directive only describes these clauses as 'potentially' abusive, their inclusion in DL 446/85 as 'relatively forbidden' satisfies the implementation requirement of the Directive. This argument is perhaps

acceptable in what concerns clause (j), which may be considered as less essential to the preservation of a consumer's rights, unless, of course, the alteration of the contract consists in an outright exclusion or limitation of liability, although this would clash with the prohibition of clause (b). The argument does not appear valid, however, when applied to the partial inclusion of clause (b) amongst the 'relatively forbidden' clauses in DL 446/85.

As explained above, clause (b) refers to the exclusion or limitation of liability in the case of non-performance or defective performance of the producer or vendor's obligations, and there can be no doubt that such a clause represents the very essence of the type of abusive clauses which the EC Council intended to stamp out by adopting the Directive. In DL 446/85, article 18 (c) classifies as 'absolutely forbidden' the exclusion or limitation of contractual liability for non-performance, delay in performance or defective performance of obligations which are intentional or the result of gross negligence, whereas article 22(g) classifies as only 'relatively forbidden' clauses which 'unjustifiably' exclude rules (ie not only contractual, but also legal) relative to defective performance or to time limits concerning the exercise of rights resulting from defective performance. The distinction thus made by DL 446/85 between contractual liability resulting from an intentional act or one of gross negligence (where exclusion or limitation is absolutely forbidden) and liability in other cases (where exclusion is relatively forbidden, if unjustifiable) is entirely unsatisfactory for the following reasons:

(a) The exclusion or limitation of contractual and tortious liability, irrespective of the sort of act which gives rise to it, in consumer-producer/vendor relationships was precisely what the Directive sought to prohibit;
(b) The distinction made in articles 18(c) and 22(g) is based on criteria (intention and gross negligence on the one hand, non-serious negligence or absence of fault on the other) which do not correspond to those in use in the Portuguese Civil Code in the field of contractual liability and warranties in sales contracts. This creates unnecessary complexity and confusion, in what is already a legal minefield (cf 3.2 and 3.3 above);
(c) The combined effect of articles 18(c) and 22(g) of DL 446/85 is a serious erosion of the protection afforded to the consumer, in that it is possible to include clauses in a consumer-producer/vendor contract which:
   (i) limit, but do not exclude, warranties or contractual liability arising from breach of contract and the respective periods for the consumer to exercise his rights resulting therefrom, where there is absence of fault or non-serious negligence on the part of the producer/vendor;
   (ii) 'justifiably' (note, the law does not explain this concept) exclude warranties or contractual liability and respective periods for the consumer to exercise his rights, in the conditions mentioned above.

These arguments notwithstanding, article 22(g) cannot be classified as a clear breach of Directive 93/13, particularly because, as mentioned previously, the 'abusive clauses' listed in the Annex therein are merely indicative of clauses 'which may be considered abusive'. In matters covered by the product liability directive (Directive 85/374, cf. Section 5, below), however, any contractual limitation of liability clashes with the express prohibition of article 10 of the implementing national statute, ie DL 383/89, and is consequently inadmissible, because, in accordance with Portuguese rules of construction, a specialised statute, or one of more limited scope, such as DL 383/89, prevails over a general statute, ie in this case DL 446/85.

3.6   Limitation period

Liability in contract is subject to the general limitation period of Portuguese Civil Law, which is 20 years from when the damage occurred (article 309), although within this period, it is necessary to take into consideration shorter periods which might apply for bringing an action for the rescission of the contract, for damages or for substitution or repairing of goods, thus:

(a) If the purchaser chooses to exercise his contractual warranty relating to the proper functioning of the product, and wishes to sue the vendor for substitution of the product or to have it repaired, he must within a period of six months of the date of delivery, notify the vendor within 30 days of his becoming aware of the defect having arisen, and an action at law for satisfaction of the warranty must be brought within this period of notification of the vendor, or within six months of the date on which the notification was made to the vendor of the failure of the product to function properly (article 921(3) and (4));

(b) If the purchaser chooses to exercise his rights resulting from the vendor's breach of the sales contract (cf section 3.3 above):

   (i) If the breach was not deliberate, the purchaser must notify the vendor of the defect or inappropriate qualities of the goods within six months of delivery of the goods, and within thirty days of his becoming aware of the defect or of the goods' inappropriate qualities (article 916). To rescind the contract or to sue for damages or to demand that the defect be repaired or the product substituted, the purchaser will have to bring the action within the period established for the notification of the vendor, or, if he has notified the vendor, within six months of such notification (article 917). When the object of the sales contract is an immovable, the purchaser must notify the vendor within one year of detecting the defect, and within five years of purchase (article 916(3)). If the vendor has been notified of the defect, these periods will be extended so long as the sales contract has not been executed (article 287(2)), eg if delivery has not been made, or if an ancillary obligation is still to be fulfilled, in which case the action may be brought within the general limitation period of twenty years.

   (ii) If, on the other hand, the vendor deliberately misled the purchaser concerning the defect or the characteristics of the product, the purchaser is not under an obligation to notify the vendor, and may bring an action against the vendor up to one year of his becoming aware that the vendor deliberately misled him as to the quality or characteristics of the product (article 287(1)), although, again, this will be subject to the general limitation period of twenty years.

(c) If the breach of contract does not fall within the forms of breach especially foreseen for sales contracts regarding defects in the product or lack of appropriate characteristics, then the general limitation period of twenty years will apply. This is the case where the breach of contract consists of a defect which is not intrinsic to the product but rather to the way in which its use has been defined, eg through marketing or instructions.

In the case of 'commercial' sales contracts, ie, generally speaking, a sale concluded between merchants for the purpose of resale, the purchaser must notify the vendor within eight days if he is not satisfied with the product sold (article 471 of the Portuguese Commercial Code).

Given the longer limitation period for contractual liability of twenty years, albeit with the restrictions referred to above, and given the shorter period of three years for tortious liability (cf section 4.8 below), although without the aforementioned restrictions, one point of controversy which arises is the situation which may occur when liability results from both contract and tort (eg damage arising from the supply of a defective gas canister which subsequently explodes). In such cases the law does not prescribe any criteria for determining the limitation period which prevails. Different rulings of the Portuguese Supreme Court have gone in opposite directions, but the Appeal courts have quite consistently viewed such situations as essentially cases of contractual liability, and a priori subject to the longer limitation period of 20 years (eg Lisbon Court of Appeals, ruling of 25 June 1985, CJ, 1985, 3-173), although most authors conclude that such a solution is only acceptable in cases where the restrictions mentioned above on the limitation period do not apply; if they do, then it is reasonable that an injured party should be able to avail itself of the relatively longer limitation period of tortious liability to seek damages based on tort.

3.7   Vicarious liability

A party to a contract shall be liable for the acts of his legal representatives or of the persons he engages in performing his contractual obligations, in the same way as if such acts were carried out by that party (article 800(1)). The only concession made by the law to limit such liability is the possibility of its being limited or excluded by prior agreement of the parties to the contract, so long as this is not contrary to mandatory rules (article 800(2)). It has, however, for some time been the view of the courts that this exclusion of liability is limited to cases where contracts are actually negotiated by the parties, and does not extend to standard agreements where one party is limited to accepting the clauses drafted by the other (ruling of 11 May 1981 of the Appeals Court of Coimbra, CJ 1982, 3-90). This position is reinforced by DL 446/85 (cf section 3.5 above), of which article 18(f) expressly and 'absolutely' prohibits the exclusion or limitation of liability (contractual or tortious) for the acts of representatives, or 'auxiliaries' who have acted with intention or gross negligence. From this one can draw the conclusion that it is possible to exclude or limit liability if it arises from the act of a representative who was not grossly negligent or who was not at fault, particularly as no provision is made in DL 445/85 for such situations in the case of vicarious liability. This once again represents a serious erosion of consumer protection, contrary, in our view, to the aims of Directive 93/13, and subject to the same criticism levelled against the treatment in DL 446/85 of direct liability (cf section 3.5 above), although given the judicial precedents mentioned above, a clause which excludes or limits liability resulting from the acts of representatives, when representatives are neither grossly negligent nor at fault, shall only be valid in the case of contracts which have been the object of negotiation between the parties.

4   LIABILITY IN TORT

4.1   Introduction

Tortious liability arises when the law creates an obligation for one person to redress the damage suffered by another resulting from an illicit act for which

the first person is responsible. The illicit acts giving rise to such an obligation are classified as intentional or arising from mere fault. Intentional acts are those carried out in the knowledge that they will produce a damaging result, whereas those in the second category, mere fault, are the result of negligence or lack of care on the part of the person responsible. The Portuguese Civil Code establishes some practical consequences based on this distinction, which are considered later.

The general principle governing tortious liability is to be found in article 483(1) which states that 'whoever, intentionally, or through mere fault, illicitly violates the rights of another person or breaches any rule of law designed to protect the interests of other persons shall be under an obligation to compensate the injured person for the damage arising from such violation or breach'. In article 483(2) it is added that no-fault liability for damages will only arise in those cases expressly foreseen in the law.

The rule of 483(1) presupposes tortious liability will only arise where there is a voluntary act on the part of the agent and there is a link of causation between the act and the resulting damage. The fact that the injured party may only claim damages if the act was intentional or arose through 'mere fault', ie negligence, distinguishes this form of liability from that introduced by DL 383/89 in implementation of the Product Liability Directive.

4.2 Liability in tort

4.2.1 Voluntary acts

Only acts which represent voluntary human conduct may give rise to tortious liability. This excludes cases of *force majeure* and of fortuitous circumstances (lightning, floods, etc). The conduct in question may consist either in committing an act which violates a duty not to interfere with another person's rights or an omission which causes damage. Omissions are dealt with in article 486 which states that 'omissions give rise to liability for damage when, without prejudice to other requirements of the law, an obligation to carry out the omitted act existed in law or covenant'. Taking into account the general requirement of causation, this means that omissions will only be relevant where there was a legally binding obligation to commit the omitted act and, if it had been carried out, it would, at least probably, have avoided the damage.

One particular form of omission relevant to product liability is that foreseen in article 485(2), where a liability is established for those cases where there is a legal obligation to 'counsel, make recommendations or inform and the agent has proceeded with negligence or the intention to cause harm, or when the agent's action is punishable by [criminal] law'. In certain cases the law does establish an obligation to inform, eg instructions which must accompany pharmaceutical products, labelling of food products, etc. Unfortunately, no judicial precedent of note has been developed around this rule and given the practical difficulties of proving intent or negligence, it can be expected that persons suffering injury as a result of such an omission will prefer to base their claim on the no-fault liability created by DL 383/89.

4.2.2 Illicit acts

As stated above, an act is illicit when it involves the violation of the rights of another person or the breach of a rule of law designed to protect the interests

of others (article 483(1)). The rights in question are considered by Portuguese legal doctrine to include, generally, all personal rights (the rights to physical and moral integrity, ie right to life, to physical well-being and health, to freedom, honour, good name and reputation, sometimes referred to as 'absolute rights') and property rights. As to rules of law designed to protect the interests of other persons, these are to be found in laws relating to specific matters, such as laws regulating the production and sale of, and information concerning, toys (DL 237/92 of 27 October), foodstuffs (DL 170/92 of 8 August) and pharmaceutical products (DL 72/91 of 8 February), which are dealt with in section 6.5 below.

Liability for certain acts may be precluded. Generally speaking, such liability will be precluded when a right is exercised in a regular and acceptable manner or in fulfilling a duty. Apart from these two situations, the law deals with special cases of justification for acts which might otherwise give rise to a liability:

(a) *direct action* (article 336): the use of force to protect certain rights;
(b) *legitimate defence* (article 337): acts designed to fend off aggression;
(c) *necessity* (article 339): destruction or damage to a third party's property in order to remove the danger of a more serious form of damage or injury;
(d) *consent of the injured party* (article 340): generally, an act which violates the rights of another party is lawful if that other party consents, unless such consent is contrary to a prohibition of law or custom.

4.2.3   Intent and mere fault

Tortious liability, as a rule, presupposes some sort of intent or psychological connection between the act giving rise to the damage and the agent, and it is only in the limited cases of no-fault liability that a simple material connection will suffice. The psychological connection may be classified as *intent* or *mere fault* in producing the damaging act.

In Portuguese legal doctrine intent is classified as:

(a) direct;
(b) indirect or necessary; or
(c) eventual.

In the case of *direct intent* the agent acts with the intention of producing the illicit result, eg he deliberately sets fire to another person's property. When the intent is *indirect* or *necessary* the agent's objective is not to cause the illicit act, but he is aware that it is likely to result as a consequence of the course of action he has chosen, eg a manufacturer of fire-resistant suits uses inferior materials to reduce production costs after tests have proved that such materials will not tolerate temperatures over x degrees which are likely to occur in the case of chemically fuelled fires. *Eventual intent* occurs when the agent foresees the possibility of an illicit result but acts in the hope that it will not occur, eg a boiler is manufactured to withstand x pressure, it being possible, but unlikely, that it may, for its intended purposes, have to withstand greater pressure.

In practice it may be difficult to draw a line between these different forms of intent. However, the object in creating these distinctions is not to extract different legal consequences from them, but rather to extend the concept of intent to cover all situations other than mere fault or negligence, which may produce different consequences for the liable party, in other words, these distinctions help to define the boundaries between *intent* and *negligence*.

Mere fault or *negligence* will arise through a lack of diligence which can be expected of the agent, and as a result of which he does not foresee the occurrence of an illicit act, eg a manufacturer of foodstuffs, through lack of verification, uses ingredients which are past their prime and, on being consumed, these foodstuffs produce effects of ill health for consumers.

4.3   Causation

As stated previously, article 483(1) obliges the party responsible for the illicit act to repair 'the damage arising from violation of the rights of a third party or breach of any rule of law designed to protect a third party's interests'. This clearly means that the defendant is only liable for the damage caused by the illicit act and only to the extent that it has been produced by the illicit act. To establish causation the Civil Code then relies on the general rules provided in article 563, which follow the doctrine of 'adequate causation' and have already been discussed under contractual liability (see section 3.3.2 above).

4.4   Remoteness of loss and damage

Again, as regards remoteness of loss and damage, the rules applicable are those we have already considered under contractual liability, and represent a corollary to the doctrine of 'adequate causation' which underpins the legal treatment of this issue (cf section 3.3.3 above).

4.5   Quantum of damage

In the case of both intent and mere fault the obligation will arise for the agent to redress the damage caused (article 483(1)). However, in the case of mere fault it is possible that the agent may only have to partially redress the damage caused, and this will depend on the degree of fault of the party responsible, the economic situation of both the agent and the injured party, and other circumstances pertinent to the matter (article 494). Further, in certain very particular cases, the obligation to repair damages will only arise when the agent has acted with intent, these cases being:

(a)   articles 814(1) and 815(1), whereby, when a creditor, without justification, does not accept the fulfilment of an obligation or does not carry out the acts, which on his part are necessary for the fulfilment of the obligation, the debtor of that obligation (of which, note, despite the creditor's act, he has not been relieved) may only be liable for non-performance if he, the debtor, in turn acts with intent, and

(b)   article 1681(1), which refers to liabilities arising between spouses in situations where one of them is responsible for administering joint property, or the property of the other spouse.

Damage covers damage to both property and persons. Damage to property occurs when property is destroyed or when the person in possession of property is deprived of its use. Personal damage is a more abstract notion which refers to a negative effect on a person's moral or spiritual state, eg the physical pain suffered as a result of an injury or the suffering caused by the death of a relative.

As regards personal damage, the Civil Code states that in fixing compensation the courts must take into account personal damage which, because of its gravity, deserves the protection of the law (article 496(1)). This allows the courts a certain degree of discretion so that they will not be obliged to consider all claims, although they will always consider claims for physical injury and serious offences to a person's honour.

In calculating the quantum of damages the same rules apply as those discussed above in connection with contractual liability (section 3.3.4 above), although special rules apply in the case of personal damage. For personal damage the sum of compensation shall be established on an equitable basis and taking into account the degree of fault of the defendant, his economic situation and that of the injured party, as well as the circumstances of the case (article 496(3)). In the case of death, not only the suffering of the victim, but also the suffering of his surviving close relatives (wife and descendants, or in cases where these do not exist, parents and other ascendants, or, failing these, siblings or nephews) shall be taken into account (article 496(3)). Apart from redress for the suffering inflicted in the case of death or personal injury, both the injured party and his dependants shall have a right to compensation for loss of earnings resulting from the death or injury. It should be stated, however, that Portuguese courts are notorious for awarding extremely low sums of compensation for death and personal injury, except in cases where it can be shown that the injured party was prevented from earning substantial sums through death or injury. It is possible that the courts are influenced by the very low legal limits applicable to the special case of no-fault liability for accidents caused by vehicles (see section 4.9.2 below), so it is hoped that the much higher limits introduced by the Product Liability Directive will change this attitude. Whatever the reason, and even taking into account Portugal's relatively low standard of living, there can be no doubt that awards of 500,000 Escudos for loss of life, which are not uncommon, fall far short of granting suitable compensation.

4.6   Burden of proof

The burden of proof of the fault of the defendant (be it through intent or mere fault, as discussed above), lies with the injured party, except where the law establishes a presumption to the contrary (article 587(1)) (as explained in the next paragraph). The fault itself is to be assessed in the light of the diligence of a good '*paterfamilias*', taking into account the circumstances of the case (article 487(2)). In other words, it is usually for the injured party to prove that the defendant was at fault in causing the damage, in the sense that he did not act diligently and reasonably in the circumstances of the case.

The law does, however, foresee a number of situations where the defendant is presumed to be at fault, unless he is able to prove otherwise. For example, if damage is caused by incapacitated persons, those responsible for their care shall be liable, unless they prove that they satisfied their duty of vigilance, or that the damage would have occurred even if they had fulfilled such a duty (article 491). The same rule is decreed in article 492 for those who own or possess buildings or other forms of construction, which cause damage as a result of collapse arising from a defect in construction or conservation. One further instance of legal presumption of fault of the defendant occurs where damage

is caused by a movable or fixed object, or animal, which is in a person's possession and which he has a duty to invigilate, in which case that person must prove that there was no fault on his part, or that the damage would have occurred even if he had been exempt from fault (article 493(1)). An extension of this situation, and one of great practical significance, is the presumption of fault for those who cause damage when carrying out an activity which is considered dangerous by its very nature or as a result of the means used in such activity. In this instance the defendant is under an obligation to pay damages for harm caused except where he can prove that he undertook every precaution that could be expected in the circumstances with the object of avoiding the damage (article 493(2)). This rule has led to a large number of decisions by the Appeals and Supreme Courts, particularly with regard to the definition of 'dangerous activities', which have been held to include such situations as the storage of inflammable materials, the use of explosives in quarrying and even the transport of cotton (given the possibility of spontaneous combustion).

4.7 Exclusion or limitation of liability

The rules which apply to the exclusion or limitation of contractual liability (cf section 3.5 above) apply equally to liability in tort.

4.8 Limitation period

Article 498(1) establishes a limitation period of three years commencing on the date on which the injured party became aware of his right to compensation (if the three years are to be counted from a date after the act, however, it is for the injured party to prove that he was not aware of his right to compensation until that date), as well as a maximum limitation period of 20 years from the time when the damage occurred, irrespective of the injured party's knowledge of his right to compensation. If, however, a longer limitation period is established for the same illicit act in criminal law, then, in accordance with accepted doctrine and judicial precedent, that will be the period applicable to the tort (eg five years in the case of homicide through negligence: Portuguese Criminal Code, article 118(1)(c)). As to the limitation period in situations which give rise to both liability in contract and in tort, these have been referred to in section 3.6 above.

4.9 No-fault liability

In Portuguese law liability is contractual or tortious, and in the latter case it always presupposes the existence of intent or mere fault. The only exceptions to this rule are clearly laid down in law, and the implementation of the Product Liability Directive adds one more such exception to the list. Of those in existence before the Directive, because of the light they may shed on product liability, it is worth considering the following cases of no-fault liability: vicarious liability, accidents caused by road vehicles and damage caused by electrical or gas installations. Except where the law provides otherwise, the rules of tortious liability analysed above apply to cases of no-fault liability (article 499).

4.9.1   Liability for third parties

This is dealt with in the Civil Code as a specific case of no-fault liability whereby 'whoever charges another person with the commission of an act shall be liable, irrespective of any fault, for damages caused by that person, so long as that person is also liable' (article 500(1)). The rules of tortious liability analysed above apply (article 499). Such liability shall, however, only occur in cases where the person carrying out the act, the agent, is in some way subordinated to, or dependent on, the person commissioning the act, the commissioner, and the act giving rise to the liability was carried out in the course of the functions assigned to that agent.

Once the commissioner has redressed the damage he shall have a right of recourse against the agent, except to the extent that the commissioner is also at fault, either through the choice of agent, through the instructions given or through defective control of the agent's activity. In such cases, depending on the degree of fault of the two parties, the commissioner may have no right of recourse, or may have a right of recourse to only a part of the compensation he has satisfied.

4.9.2   Accidents caused by road vehicles

The cases of civil liability most frequently decided in Portuguese courts are those connected with motor vehicle accidents, and it is useful that where intent or mere fault cannot be proven it is possible to fall back on the no-fault liability foreseen in article 503 for those who, in their own interest, have effective control over, or use of, a road vehicle of any sort. Such liability may only be excluded when the accident has been caused by the injured party, by a third party, or is the result of *force majeure* unrelated to the functioning of the vehicle (article 505).

The maximum limits for such liability are established in article 508 as:

(a) 4 million Escudos in the case of death or injury of one person;
(b) 4 million Escudos per person, in the case of death or injury of more than one person, up to a maximum of 12 million Escudos;
(c) three times the amounts stated in (a) and (b), ie 12 million Escudos or 36 million Escudos in the case of accidents caused by vehicles used in public transport (ie to passengers);
(d) ten times the amounts stated in (a) and (b), ie 40 million Escudos or 120 million Escudos in the case of accidents caused by trains;
(e) 2, 6 or 20 million Escudos for damage to property, depending, respectively, on whether the accident is caused by a road vehicle generally, or by a vehicle used in public transport or a train.

4.9.3   Damage caused by electrical or gas installations

In this particular case of no-fault liability, those responsible for the production, storage, transport and distribution of gas or electricity are liable for damage caused by these forms of energy, unless the installations used are in accordance with the technical rules applicable and in a perfect state of repair (article 509(1)). Before DL 383/89 liability was excluded in the case of *force majeure* which covered all exterior causes unrelated to the functioning or use of the installations (article 509(2)), and damage caused by utensils which use gas or electrical energy (article 509(3)). Although these exclusions have not been expressly revoked, the adoption of DL 383/89 has made them clearly inapplicable.

5 LIABILITY FOR DEFECTIVE PRODUCTS ARISING FROM IMPLEMENTATION OF EC DIRECTIVE 85/374 ON PRODUCT LIABILITY IN PORTUGAL

5.1 Introduction

Directive 85/374 was published in the Official Journal of 25 July 1985, which was some months before Portugal's accession to the European Community on 1 January 1986. Article 19 of the Directive required that member states should bring into force national measures for the implementation of the Directive not later than three years from the date of notification. Given the principle of *acquis communautaire*, embodied in article 2 of the Treaty of Accession of Portugal and Spain, and according to which new member states are bound by Community law in the same way as existing member states, Portugal should have implemented the Directive within the prescribed period. In fact, the Directive was only implemented on 6 November 1989.

Despite the delay, it can be said that the Decree Law which finally implemented the Directive is an almost faithful reproduction of the latter's provisions, with one important exception in relation to the maximum limit of liability prescribed therein (see section 5.2).

5.2 Outline of Decree Law 383/89

Article 1 of the Decree Law establishes that the producer is liable, irrespective of intent or mere fault, for damage caused by defects in his products. The producer is defined in article 2 in a manner which includes both the definition of 'producer' in article 3(1) of the Directive (ie the manufacturer of a finished product, of a component part or of any raw material, and any person who represents himself as a producer by placing his name, trademark or other distinguishing feature on the product) and of the importer and supplier of the product as provided for in article 3(1) and 3(2) of the Directive.

The 'product' is defined in article 3 in the exact terms used in article 2 of the Directive, save that no mention is made of electricity, but the accepted view in Portuguese law, taking into account the definition of movables and immovables given in articles 204 and 205 of the Portuguese Civil Code, is that electricity is classified as a movable object, so such a specific inclusion in DL 383/89 would have been superfluous.

The definition of defect is provided for in article 4 and reproduces the definition in article 7 of the Directive. The same is true of article 5 which reproduces verbatim the list of cases of exclusion of liability foreseen in article 7 of the Directive,

The rule of joint and several liability is established in article 6(1). In articles 6(2) and 6(3) it is stated that in apportioning liability between the jointly and severally liable parties, it shall be necessary to take into account the circumstances of the case, in particular, the risk created by each liable party, the gravity of fault with which the party may have acted and the party's contribution to the damage. In cases of doubt, the liability shall be apportioned equally between the parties.

Pursuant to article 7(2) the liability of the producer shall not be reduced when the damage is also caused by the intervention in any way of a third party

(this must be presumed to include omissions, if article 8(1) of the Directive is taken into account), without prejudice to the rules of article 6(2) and 6(3), described above, on the apportioning of liability.

The definition of damage in article 8 is the same as that contained in article 9 of the Directive, namely damage resulting from death or personal injury, and damage to property, other than to the defective product itself.

The remaining articles of DL 383/89 (articles 10-15) transcribe almost literally the Directive's provisions on the prohibition of the producer's exemption or limitation of liability (Directive, article 12); limitation period (Directive, article 10(1)); extinction of the rights conferred on the injured person (Directive, article 11); the safeguarding of rights of the injured person conferred by national rules on contractual and non-contractual liability (Directive, article 13); the exclusion of nuclear accidents covered by international conventions (Directive, article 14) and the non-application of the Directive to products put into circulation before the entry into force of DL 383/89 (Directive, article 17).

5.3   Description of optional or anomalous provisions in respect of product liability in Portugal

The definition of 'product' excludes primary agricultural products, ie no use is made of the possibility of derogation provided for in article 15(1)(a) of the Directive allowing member states to include agricultural products and game.

The 'state of the art' defence of article 7(e) of the Directive is included, in other words, no use has been made of the possibility of derogation provided for in article 15(1)(e) of the Directive.

The lower threshold of Ecu 500 provided for in article 9 of the Directive appears as 70,000 Escudos in article 8(2), and a maximum limit for damage is defined in article 9(1) as 10,000 million Escudos. It appears from the amounts of the lower threshold and maximum limit that the Portuguese legislator had some difficulty in informing himself of the exchange rate for the Ecu. Article 18(1) of the Directive provides that the equivalent in national currency of the amounts stated in the Directive in Ecu 'shall initially be calculated at the rate obtaining on the date of adoption of this Directive'. On 11 November 1989, the day on which DL 383/89 came into force, the Ecu was quoted, in round figures, at 175 Escudos. At this rate the lower threshold of Ecu 500 would have been 87,500 Escudos and the maximum limit of Ecu 70 million foreseen in article 16(1) of the Directive would have been 12,250 million Escudos, ie more than 20 per cent higher than the limit established in DL 383/89. A party seeking damages under DL 383/89 which exceeded the 10,000 million Escudos limit might attempt to overcome such a limitation by invoking the *Von Colson* principle (Case 14/83 *Von Colson and Kamman v Land Nordrhein-Wesfalen* [1984] ECR 1981, ECJ, according to which courts of a member state are obliged to interpret national legislation passed to implement an EC Directive so as to give effect to it), but it is possible that the courts would consider such an attempt as more than simply a matter of construction of the law, and rather as an effort to establish (horizontal) direct effect for a Directive, ie invoking the rules of a Directive to create rights and obligations between private parties, something which the European Court of Justice has never accepted (eg Case 152/84 *Marshall v Southampton & West Hampshire Area Health Authority (Teaching)* [1986] 1 CMLR 688).

Article 7(1) provides that the liability of the producer may be reduced or disallowed when, taking into account all the circumstances, the damage has also been caused by the fault of the injured person, but this has not been drafted also to include 'any person for whom the injured person is responsible'. The reason for this omission on the part of the Portuguese legislator probably lies in the fact that he deemed the inclusion of persons for whom the injured person is responsible as superfluous in the light of the rule of article 491 of the Portuguese Civil Code. This article states that those responsible for the care of others are responsible for the damage they cause to third parties, so that the damage caused by a person the injured person is responsible for would be the same as damage caused by the injured person himself and consequently any reference in DL 383/89 to persons for whom the injured person is responsible would be unnecessary. The flaw in this logic, however, is the caveat provided for in article 491, which excludes the liability of the caretaker if he can prove that he fulfilled his duty of care or vigilance, or that the damage would have occurred even if such a duty had been fulfilled. Such a caveat definitely falls outside the scope of the Directive and, in keeping with the *Von Colson* principle must be considered inapplicable.

5.4 Comparison of the effects of Decree Law 383/89 with the previous position in contract and tort

As can be concluded from the preceding analysis, DL 383/89 represents a major improvement for the consumer who has suffered damage resulting from a defective product, as compared with his situation before the adoption of the law. On the one hand, he can overcome the limitations of contract law which restrict the effect of contracts to the parties who conclude them, on the other hand, he no longer has to face the sometimes formidable hurdle of proving the intent or mere fault of the party who caused the damage.

The need for such protection of the consumer has been recognised in a number of western countries, indeed the topic had been the subject of debate in Portugal for some time, and it was disappointing that the legislator did not choose to introduce no-fault product liability when the Consumer Protection Law (section 6 below) was adopted.

The other side of the coin is that Portuguese manufacturers and insurers are now faced with potential liabilities which are beyond the means of many of them to satisfy. If the Consumer Protection Law of 1981 had included no-fault product liability with lower maximum limits, more suitable to Portuguese economic conditions, then manufacturers and insurers may have had some time to adapt and develop experience in risk management. As it is, most companies in Portugal are quite unprepared for the levels of liability foreseen in DL 383/ 89, although it must be said that even if the Directive had not been implemented in Portugal, Portuguese economic agents would still be subject to the product liability created therein whenever they exported their products to another member state which had implemented the Directive, and with Portugal's ratification of the Brussels Convention on Jurisdiction and the Enforcement of Judgments in Civil and Commercial Matters (which came into force on 1 July 1992), it would always be a relatively simple matter to enforce, in Portuguese courts, the judgments on claims brought before the courts of other member states. As a final note it should be mentioned that thus far no judicial decision has been published concerning DL 383/89, so that we must look to

the judicial experience of other members of the European Union to obtain answers to some of the questions raised in this section.

6   CRIMINAL LIABILITY FOR DEFECTIVE PRODUCTS ARISING FROM BOTH GENERAL SAFETY LAW AND THE IMPLEMENTATION OF EC DIRECTIVE 92/59 ON PRODUCT SAFETY IN PORTUGAL

6.1   Introduction

The Consumer Protection Law, Law 29/81 of 22 August ('the Law') was published with the intention of satisfying the constitutional requirements of consumer protection (Portuguese Constitution, article 60(1)). It has proved, on its own, at least, to be little more than an enunciation of principles to be fleshed out by legislation which has been subsequently adopted, particularly following Portugal's accession to the EEC. The most important principles stated in the law are those which establish the right of consumers to protection against risk of damage to their interests; the effective reparation of individual or collective damage and the active participation of consumer organisations in the legal and administrative definition of consumer rights and interests (article 3). It is in the context of the first of these principles that various laws have been adopted in the field of safety of products and services, the most important being DL 213/87 of 28 May and DL 311/95 of 20 November, the latter of which implemented Directive 92/59 of 29 June on product safety and partially revoked DL 213/87.

DL 213/87 was one of the few important pieces of legislation to have been adopted solely to regulate the Consumer Protection Law without a prior EEC Directive, however the paucity of its definitions has limited its practical application. In its brief text, it devoted two articles to the prohibition of the supply of both products and services which might cause danger to the physical safety and health of consumers when used in normal or foreseeable conditions, which should be taken into account by producers, importers and suppliers of services, without providing any definitions for the concepts used in this prohibition. The rest of its text (fourteen elliptic articles in all) was devoted to the creation of a Commission for Safety in Services and Products, and the definition of fines and other penalties for breach of the law.

Depending on the gravity of the offence (to be determined pursuant to the usual rules applicable to fines, to be considered in section 6.4 below), a producer, importer or supplier of goods or services who, intentionally or negligently, endangered the physical safety or health of consumers, was subject to a fine of up to five million Escudos, and the goods causing the risk might be impounded, or the provision of the services in question subject to a prohibition. The application of the fine and other sanctions described was the responsibility of the Commission for the Application of Fines in Economic Matters, and its decisions subject to judicial review. This did not exclude the application of, and, indeed, would be substituted by, the more severe penalties of the Portuguese Criminal Code when the conduct of the economic agent constitutes a crime punished therein (section 6.6 below).

With the enactment of DL 311/95, DL 213/87 was revoked with the exception of the rules concerning the safe provision of services, which continue to apply. This produces the somewhat anomalous situation whereby what had

until now been governed by a common set of rules, ie safety for both products and services, is now the object of two sets of rules, one much more elaborate and precise, dealing with products, the other vague, dealing, paradoxically, with the inherently more complex issue of safety in services. The incoherence of this approach is further illustrated by the fact that the sanctions applicable under DL 311/95, which now apply to products (section 6.4 below), are of a more severe nature than those foreseen under DL 213/87, described above and which continue to apply to services, namely because DL 311/95 establishes a higher upper limit for applicable fines, and punishes not only intentional or negligent acts, but also *attempts* to provide unsafe products.

6.2   Outline of Decree Law 311/95

DL 311/95 was published on 20 November, 1995, and came into force five days later, more than a year after the date established for implementation of Directive 92/59. The declared objective of DL 311/95 is to implement Directive 92/59 (article 1), and it can be stated that overall this objective has been achieved successfully, for although the Decree-Law tinkers with the sequence in which the rules are laid out in the Directive, the fundamental provisions of the latter – in what concerns the definitions of 'products', 'safe products', 'producers' and 'distributors' and the basic tenet that a producer shall only place safe products on the market, as well as the ancillary obligations thereby of the producer and distributor – are laid down in very similar terms in articles 2, 3 and 4 of the Decree Law. The definition of product in the Decree Law, however, explicitly excludes immovable objects (article 2(1)(a)), whereas the Directive does not distinguish between movables and immovables. Pursuant to article 204 of the Civil Code, which defines immovables in Portuguese law, this exclusion is, in principle, extensive to movables which are an integral part of an immovable, eg doors, escalators and elevators. It is, however, the opinion of this author that within the scope of the Decree Law such movables which later become an integral part of an immovable, because they are placed on the market by a producer in a *movable* state, ie prior to their integration, will create a liability for that producer if they do not conform to the safety requirements of the Decree Law.

The remaining salient features of the Decree Law consist of article 5, which establishes the presumption that products of which the characteristics correspond to those established in laws or regulations shall be considered safe, although this shall not prevent the appropriate authorities from adopting measures they may consider necessary to restrict the commercialisation of the product or to withdraw the product from the market if, notwithstanding such conformity, the product is considered to be dangerous to the health or safety of consumers, and articles 6 to 11 which are devoted to the creation and functions of a Safety Commission to oversee the safety of products placed on the market, to be supported logistically and administratively by the Institute of the Consumer (article 16), whereas the powers to control the conformity of products with the stipulations of the Decree Law, and apply fines where appropriate are attributed to the General Inspectorate of Economic Activities (article 13). Article 12 establishes the fines applicable to breaches of the rules of product safety, and article 14 creates the obligation for producers to cover the costs of withdrawal and destruction of unsafe products.

6.3　Description of anomalous provisions in Decree Law 311/95

As mentioned previously the Decree Law follows the Directive closely, so that few anomalies exist in its implementation, and those which do exist do not affect the attainment of the objectives of the Directive. The most serious discrepancy lies in the omission of the part of the definition of a 'safe product' contained in the Directive which states that a product shall not be considered unsafe or dangerous simply because a greater degree of safety may be achievable or because of the existence of other products with a lower risk factor. This aspect of the definition in the Directive is clearly an important hermeneutic tool in limiting the extent of the producer's obligations under the Directive, and pursuant to the *Von Colson* principle (section 5.3 above) should be considered as implicitly incorporated in the Decree Law's definition of 'safe product'.

The other discrepancies of any relevance consist of:

(a) the omission of the definition of a 'dangerous product' contained in the Directive, of which the inclusion in the Directive might, in any case, be considered superfluous, given that a producer will not satisfy his obligations under the Directive if the product in question is anything but 'safe';

(b) the inclusion in the Decree Law of a definition of 'normal or reasonably foreseeable use', which is undoubtedly tautological given that the concept in question is described by combining in article 2(e) of the Decree Law various terms included in the criteria listed in article 2(b) of the Directive, to define 'safe products', and which are reproduced in article 2(b) of the Decree Law.

6.4　Description of optional provisions in Decree Law 311/95

To oversee and coordinate product safety at a national level article 6 creates a Safety Commission composed of a variable number of members (variable because it includes representatives of a number of ministries which may vary, depending on the government's cabinet arrangements) who represent different state bodies and consumer, industrial and commercial organisations, including experts in the field of product safety. The Commission is responsible for deciding whether products placed on the market are of a dangerous nature and ensuring the observance of the general obligation of product safety, as well as for making proposals to the minister responsible for consumer protection for the adoption of measures aimed at improving product safety (article 7). In this capacity the Commission may make recommendations to producers so that these may eliminate risks to consumers caused by their products, and for this purpose the Commission may also issue public warnings regarding the use of unsafe products (article 10). To carry out its functions the Commission has the power to request of any public body that it carry out the acts the Commission may deem necessary, and it further has the power to demand of any company or grouping of companies that it provide any information or documentation the Commission may consider necessary (article 8).

When the measures adopted by the Commission involve products which are part of intra-Community trade, then such measures shall be notified either to the Consumer Institute or to the Institute for the Protection of Agro-Foodstuff Production, who, in turn, will immediately notify the European Commission of these measures, in accordance with article 8 of Directive 92/59 (article 11). The exact procedures and mechanisms for these regulations

are yet to be regulated, as this is the first time that Portuguese legislation addresses the issue of notifying the European Commission of measures adopted in the field of product safety, since no internal laws were ever adopted to implement Council Decisions 84/113 and 89/45 (on the rapid exchange of information on dangers arising from the use of consumer products).

The enforcement of the rules contained in DL 311/95 and of the measures adopted within its ambit is the work of the General Inspectorate of Economic Activities (article 13). The breach of the obligations established for producers and distributors in articles 3 (article 3(1) and 3(2) of the Directive) and 4 (article 3(3) of the Directive), respectively, will make these liable for fines ranging from 10,000 Escudos to 500,000 Escudos for physical persons and 50,000 Escudos to 6 million Escudos for bodies corporate (article 12(1)), and jurisdiction for the application of such fines is attributed to the Commission for the Application of Fines in Economic Matters (article 13(1)). Both negligent breaches and attempts to breach the rules mentioned will make a producer or distributor subject to the fines described. DL 311/95 further establishes that apart from the fines foreseen therein a producer or distributor may be subject to the 'accessory sanctions laid down in general law'. The law in question is DL 244/95 of 14 September, and the ancillary rules contained therein, and applicable to DL 311/95, greatly amplify the paltry sanctions which at first glance appear to be the limit of producers' and distributors' liability.

To establish the exact fine applicable within the minimum and maximum amounts laid down in DL 311/95, account shall be taken of the 'seriousness of the infraction, the degree of guilt, the economic situation of the infractor and the economic benefit [resulting from] the infraction' (article 18(1) of DL 244/95). However, if the party responsible for an infraction has obtained an economic benefit in excess of the maximum fine payable, and it is not possible to eliminate such benefit through ancillary sanctions, then the maximum fine shall be increased by up to one third (article 18(2)). As to the ancillary sanctions, a wide range of these are available to the sanctioning body, and those applicable to the infraction established in DL 311/95 are:

(a) loss of objects belonging to the guilty party, ie the dangerous products in question;
(b) prohibition of future professional or economic activity, for a maximum period of two years, which depend on an authorisation from a public body, eg activities dependent upon a manufacturing licence;
(c) prohibition of taking part in public tenders for the supply of goods, for a maximum period of two years;
(d) closure of establishments or facilities dependent upon authorisation by a public body, for a maximum period of two years.

6.5 Other significant product safety law

The Consumer Protection Law, mentioned previously, prescribes, amongst other actions, the regulation of the sale of an extensive list of products of particular importance to the protection of the health and safety of users, such as pre-packaged foodstuffs, cosmetics and detergents, toys, textiles and pharmaceutical products. In fact, as mentioned previously, it was only following Portugal's accession to the European Community in 1986 that such regulation came about as the result of the adoption of various laws in implementation of EC Directives on consumer protection. These are too numerous to describe

in an analysis of this scope, but to illustrate this matter it is worth mentioning DL 170/92 of 8 August, which implemented various Directives on the labelling, presentation and advertising of food products (Directives 79/112/EEC, 86/197/EEC, 87/250/EEC, 89/395/EEC, 89/396/EEC, 91/72/EEC, 91/238/EEC); DL 72/91 of 8 February, which implemented a total of ten Directives concerning pharmaceutical products and DL 237/92 of 27 October, which implemented Directive 88/378/EEC concerning safety of toys.

6.6   Criminal liability

Portuguese law establishes a distinction between *administrative infractions*, ie breaches of laws enforced by administrative bodies, such as DL 311/95, which are subject only to fines, and *crimes,* which are considered more serious offences, subject to both fines and/or prison sentences. A particular category of crimes which may create a liability for producers are what the Portuguese Criminal Code designates as 'crimes of common danger', ie crimes which, generally speaking, create a risk for the safety and well-being of others, and include risks resulting from arson; the importation of arms and explosives; the breach of rules of construction; pollution; the corruption of food substances or medicines and the spread of contagious disease. Conduct which falls within the scope of these last three crimes may very well create a criminal liability for a producer who does not proceed with due care:

(a) *pollution* (Criminal Code, articles 279 and 280): pollution of air, water or soil which exceeds prescribed limits will make the defendant subject to a prison term of up to three years or a fine of up to sixty million Escudos, for intentional conduct, or up to one year or the same fine, in the case of negligence; when such pollution imperils the physical integrity or property of substantial value of others, the prison terms applicable will be from one to eight years when both the conduct and the creation of the danger are intentional, and up to five years when the conduct is intentional and the creation of the danger is the result of negligence;

(b) *corruption of food substances or medicines* (Criminal Code, article 282): 'corruption' is defined in very wide terms to include any undue alteration, including the reduction of nutritional or therapeutic value of foods or medicines, by anyone involved in the production, packaging, transport or treatment of these, or any alteration caused by inappropriate storage, or any sale taking place after the sell-by date, by anyone involved in the commercialisation of such products. Such conduct, when it imperils the life or physical integrity of others, shall be subject to a prison term of one to eight years. However, if the conduct is intentional, but the risk is the result of negligence, the prison term applicable will be five years, and if the conduct itself is negligent the prison term may not exceed three years;

(c) *spread of contagious diseases* (Criminal Code, article 283): the spread of contagious disease in such a manner that it may jeopardise the life or physical integrity of others is punishable in exactly the same manner as described above for the corruption of food substances and medicines.

The essence of the crimes discussed above is the creation of a risk to life, physical integrity or property. Conduct which is actually prejudicial to the life, physical integrity or property of others will be classified as distinct crimes, eg

homicide, physical harm to others or destruction of property, the punishment of which, depending on the circumstances, may substitute or be concurrent with the punishment of crimes of common danger. A topical example is the situation which might arise from the sale of aids-contaminated blood, which may give rise both to the crimes of spread of contagious disease and negligent homicide.

7 CIVIL LIABILITY FOR DEFECTIVE PRODUCTS BROUGHT ABOUT BY BREACH OF STATUTORY REGULATIONS DESIGNED TO PROTECT CONSUMERS AND/OR TO PROMOTE SAFETY

The Consumer Protection Law did not develop any particular form of producer liability, and limited itself to stating that the consumer has a right to 'the reparation of damage [to his interests] which has been caused by defective goods or services, or defective post-sales service, or, in general, breach of the contract of supply' (article 7(e)). The Law is silent as to the manner in which such reparation is to be obtained, which means that it leaves both the consumer and producer in exactly the same position they were in before the adoption of the Law, in terms of civil liability, ie claims and defences must be based on the rules of contractual or tortious liability, or on the no-fault liability resulting from DL 383/89, as described above. The different laws adopted in regulating the Consumer Protection Law, and discussed in the preceding section have in no way altered this position. The same can be stated regarding the subject of burden of proof, which has remained unaltered, the rules applicable being those described previously in sections 3.4 and 4.6. As regards the related issue of whether compliance with statutory rules governing product quality may be used as a defence by the producer, the rule applicable is that contained in DL 383/89, article 5(d), which corresponds to article 7(d) of the product liability directive, according to which the producer shall not be liable if he proves that the defect in his product is due to compliance with mandatory regulations. In accordance with Portuguese rules of construction, this rule shall apply, by analogy, to other cases of producer liability.

8 FURTHER READING

Cordeiro, A Menezes — *Direito das Obrigações* (Associação Académica da Faculdade de Direito de Lisboa, 1994).

Costa, MJ Almeida — *Direito das Obrigações* (Coimbra Editora, 6th edn 1994).

Lima, P & Varela, A — *Código Civil Anotado* (Coimbra Editora, Vol I, 4th edn, and Vol II, 3rd edn, 1986).

Neto, A and Martins, H — *Código Civil Anotado* (Livraria Petrony, 7th edn, 1990).

Neto, A — *Notas Práticas ao Código das Sociedades Comerciais* (Livraria Petrony, 1989).

Rodrigues, JVC — *A Responsabilidade Civil do Produtor Face a Terceiros* (Associação Académica da Faculdade de Direito de Lisboa, 1990).

Silva, J Calvão — *Responsabilidade Civil do Produtor* (Almedina, 1990).

Telles, I Galvão   *Direito das Obrigações* (Coimbra Editora, 6th edn, 1989).

Varela, A   *Das Obrigações em Geral* (Almedina) Vol I (8th edn, 1994) and Vol II (6th edn, 1995).

CHAPTER XV

Spain

Mr Ramon Mullerat

Mrs Sonia Cortés

Bufete Mullerat & Roca
Avda Diagonal, 640 4º
08017 Barcelona
Spain

Tel: ++ 34 3 405 9300
Fax: ++ 34 3 405 9176

CHAPTER XV

Spain

1 INTRODUCTION

1.1 Introduction to the legal system in Spain

The Spanish Central Parliament has basic jurisdiction on consumer protection policy, but most Spanish Regional Parliaments have jurisdiction to develop any legislation enacted on such a basis (eg Catalan Act 1/1990 of 8 January).

As provided in article 149.1.13 of the Spanish Constitution, the Spanish Central Legislature has exclusive jurisdiction to set forth the basis and co-ordination of the economy's general planning, which includes consumer protection policy. However, most Regional Parliaments have exclusive jurisdiction to develop the legislation enacted by the Central Parliament, by approving Regional Acts and Regulations within the scope of such national basic legislation, since most Autonomous Regions have included such a jurisdiction in their Statutes of Autonomy. The Constitutional Court shall decide whenever there is a conflict of jurisdiction between Central and Regional legislative bodies.

The Spanish system is adversarial. There are four main jurisdictions: (i) civil jurisdiction; (ii) criminal jurisdiction; (iii) administrative jurisdiction ('*contencioso-administrativa*') which is competent to deal with acts issued by the public authorities and (iv) the labour jurisdiction which is competent to deal with any labour issues.

General legislation is approved by Parliament (Central or Regional) and is called 'act' ('*ley*'). Acts approved by the Central Parliament may be organic if they affect fundamental rights or regular acts in all other cases. In cases of urgency, royal legislative acts may be issued by Parliament or royal decree acts may be issued by the Central government and ratified by Parliament. The legislation developing the described provisions have a lower rank and is approved by the government or other administrative bodies (royal decree, decree, order, etc.). Autonomous regions have similar rules regarding their regional legislation.

1.2 Overview of the law relating to defective products in Spain

As with most civil law systems, Spanish legislation used not to contain provisions expressly dealing with civil liability for defective products. For a long time, the legal basis for product liability had to be found in several provisions enacted in the nineteenth century: the Commercial Code (1885) and the Civil Code (1889). These provisions contained two main hurdles as regards bringing a claim for product liability, namely (a) the principle of privity of contract, which prevented a victim who was not a party to a contract (eg a bystander) from

375

obtaining a contractual remedy, and (b) the need for the plaintiff to prove that there was fault or negligence by the seller.

Product liability law was thus not properly developed and the courts failed to provide case law that could create a modern system in this field. One of the reasons for this lack of evolution in civil liability must be found in the fact that in most cases where a defective product has caused injuries, the plaintiff generally institutes criminal proceedings which may be more efficient since the judge has a more active part ('ex officio') and his judgment also covers civil damages.

More recently, the General Act on Defence of Consumers and Users 26/84 approved on 19 July 1984 ('GAC') introduced the principles of the producer's liability for damage caused by his product to consumers and users as a consequence of his negligent behaviour, and strict liability (regardless of the existence of negligence) for certain categories of products. Even if incomplete and technically deficient, the GAC provided the basis for future legislation on the matter and thus represented an undeniable development in this field, with the resulting increased risk of exposure to product liability claims for producers, suppliers and others.

EC Directive 85/374 on Product Liability was implemented in Spain with much delay by Act 22/1994 of 6 July 1994 on civil liability for damages caused by defective products ('the Act').

EC Directive 92/59 on Product Safety has been implemented in Spain by Royal Decree 44/1996 of 19 January, which entered into force on 13 March 1996.

2 PRE-CONTRACTUAL LIABILITY

Article 1450 of the Civil Code provides that the purchase and sale is valid between the purchaser and the vendor if they consent on the goods and the price even if neither of them has been delivered. Under article 1451 of the Civil Code the promise of purchase and sale, where the parties have agreed on the object and on its price, enables each party to request the other party to comply with its obligations.

Any statement made before the contract is agreed that may be the basis on which a party enters into the agreement is deemed representation. Spanish contract law makes few particular references to pre-contractual misrepresentations and the case law is somewhat contradictory.[1] Among the few judgments on this matter we should highlight the judgment of the Supreme Court dated May 16, 1988 where a bank was sentenced to pay a compensation for damages to its employee for unjustified termination of negotiations ('*culpa in contrahendo*') regarding his displacement to the bank's office in Miami. Indeed, given that the parties had almost reached an agreement, the employee sold both his cars and his wife applied for a sabbatical year, decisions which caused economic damage to the employee given which the bank had to compensate. Although the bank's liability in this case was considered to be liability in tort,[2] judgment of 30 October 1988 (only few months later) deemed

---

1 Supreme Court judgment of 12 December 1976; 30 October 1984; 13 December 1984; 16 May 1988; 30 October 1988.
2 Civil Code, art 1902.

that liability was contractual[3] as so did an older judgment dated 12 December 1976.

However, misrepresentation is rather deemed an element affecting the parties' consent to the agreement,[4] ie dolus or error. When misunderstanding leads to a mistake regarding the object or the substance of the agreement or any essential conditions that formed the basis of the consent, the party that suffered error may request that the agreement is annulled[5] in which case the parties should return the object and price of the agreement, with interests and any income. If there is an absolute mistake, there is no agreement at all for lack of consent and thus the agreement is null and void. On the contrary, if misunderstanding is irrelevant the contract will be valid. Any mistakes affecting the figures of the agreement entitles the parties to ask for a correction thereof. The question of whether a mistake is relevant or not depends on several issues, including whether the party who suffers it was negligent or should have been aware of it (eg if he was a professional or an expert in such field) and is clarified on a case-by-case basis. In principle, relevant mistakes are exceptional and are those which could not be avoided by acting with regular diligence. In a judgment dated 9 October 1981, the court declared that there was no question of annulling the agreement when the painting was found not to have been painted by the famous painter Sorolla, because the purchaser was an antique dealer and it was the practice in such business not to do so in such cases.[6] Judgment of 4 January 1982 declares that the mistake is relevant given that the party who suffered, the purchaser, was not an expert in such field whereas the vendor was indeed an expert.

Where one of the parties has maliciously (dolus) hidden essential information regarding the agreement or has cheated or deceited the other party with false information,[7] the other party may challenge the validity of the agreement if the misrepresentation is serious, ie it affects an essential part of the agreement which formed the basis of its consent.[8] On the contrary, 'incidental dolus' (does not affect elements of the agreement which were not essential for the other party to accept) does not entail that the agreement is annuled but only entitles the party who suffered it to obtain a compensation for damages. In judgment of 26 October 1981 the sale purchase agreement for the acquisition of all the shares in a company which owned a land was declared null and void because it had maliciously not been disclosed that such land was of public domain and the decision to acquire the shares was based precisely on the ownership of the land.

GAC, article 10 provides that all clauses, conditions or stipulations which in a general manner are applied to the offer, promotion or sale of products or services to consumers, shall fulfil the following requirements:

(a) Concrete, clear and simple wording which is easily understood should be used and references to other texts or documents that are not provided should be avoided. The contract shall make express reference to such documents.

(b) A receipt, voucher, copy of the transaction or budget must be delivered to the consumer unless expressly waived.

---

3   Civil Code, art 1101.
4   'Vicios del consentimiento'.
5   Civil Code, art 1266.
6   Similar judgments are those of 28 February 1974 (antique dealer) and 18 April 1978 (builder).
7   Civil Code, art 1269.
8   Civil Code, art 1270.

(c) Good faith and fair balance of the consideration including the avoidance of a number of unfair trade practices listed in the GAC, eg omitting the rate of interest applied when payment is deferred, including abusive clauses that place the consumer in a blatantly disadvantageous situation or abusive credit conditions, unfairly limiting liability, etc.

3   LIABILITY IN CONTRACT

3.1   Outline of contract law relevant to defective products in Spain

Spanish law has traditionally been based on privity of contract (*relatividad de los contratos*), in the sense that only the parties to a contract may reciprocally claim enforcement of its clauses, since as provided by article 1257 of the Civil Code, 'contracts only entail effects for the parties who execute them'.

To be legally valid, contracts require the consent of the parties (who must have sufficient legal capacity), an object and a consideration.[9]

The vendor is liable to the purchaser for the product's latent defects (*saneamiento por vicios ocultos*),[10] if the product is not fit for its purpose (to the extent such purpose was obvious or clearly stated by the purchaser) or when its usefulness is reduced to such an extent that if the purchaser would have known, he would not have acquired the product or would have paid less for it.

Conversely, the vendor is not liable for any disclosed defects, nor for those which the purchaser could have ascertained upon inspection. If the purchaser is an expert in the field a higher degree of knowledge is expected, since the vendor will not be liable for undisclosed defects that the purchaser could have easily spotted due to his profession or job.

On that basis, the vendor may be found liable for any defects in the product he did not disclose to the purchaser. It is no defence for the supplier to state that the defect was due to the manufacturer's fault if the vendor could have noticed the defect if he had acted with sufficient diligence.

A specific liability is provided for building constructors and architects in case of collapse (*ruina*) of a building due to construction or engineering defects.[11] This liability may never be contractually excluded by the parties (*jus cogens*). The action to claim damages expires after a term of ten years after the completion of the construction or fifteen years if the damage is due to the constructors' breach of the contract. There is an overwhelming amount of case law on this matter as a result of the construction boom which has occurred in Spain in the last thirty years. The courts have set up a complete system of construction liability based on the provisions of the Civil Code. A draft bill on construction contemplating liability has been discussed in the last years but has not yet been passed.

3.2   Contractual warranties relating to quality and safety of goods

Under Spanish law the general principle of freedom of the parties to agree is only subject to compliance with the law, morality and public order (article 1255

---

9   Civil Code, art 1261.
10   Civil Code, art 1484 and Commercial Code, arts 336.2 and 342.
11   Civil Code, art 1591.

of the Civil Code). The vendor's liability for the latent defects can be the object of different agreements by the parties as long as the vendor is not aware of the existence of such defects (article 1485 of the Civil Code). However, the parties to a contract frequently agree on certain warranties provided by the vendor to the purchaser.

The parties to a consumer contract may, in principle, agree on the covenants they deem appropriate. However, there are certain rules with which they should comply and may not be excluded. According to GAC, article 3.1, no products launched on the market may entail risks for the consumer's health or safety, except for those usually or statutorily accepted in normal and foreseeable conditions of use.

The scope of legal guarantee for consumer products in general is limited. There are some regulations developing the GAC regarding products in certain sectors,[12] which regulate in more detail the term and the scope of legal guarantee. Breach of legal guarantee will entitle consumer to the repair or replacement of the good, the option to terminate the agreement with reimbursement of expenses or to reduction of the purchase price or even to payment of damages if the vendor acted in bad faith.

3.3 Breach of contract for supply of defective products

Under the traditional codes (Civil Code and Code of Commerce) when the vendor supplies a defective product, the purchaser has the right to choose between either (a) terminating the contract (returning the product and collecting the purchase price), with reimbursement of the expenses incurred as part of the remedy of termination, or (b) having the purchase price proportionally reduced according to expert judgment.[13]

If the vendor knew of the hidden defects, the purchaser will have not only the rights described above, but also the right to claim damages if he chooses to rescind the contract. If the transaction is deemed to be commercial (ie when the parties are acting within the sphere of their respective businesses), the purchaser shall have the right to receive damages in any case, even when the vendor was not aware of the defect.

The types of defect are those which render the product unfit for its use or which diminish its value to such extent that the purchaser would have paid a lower price if he had been aware of the defect.

The damages to be compensated are those having a cause-effect relationship, which the plaintiff has to evidence. Damages cover expenses incurred, personal injuries, moral damages, etc (see section 3.4) so long as the plaintiff can sufficiently evidence them. The level of evidence demanded by Spanish courts is generally very high. As regards remoteness of loss and damage, it should be noted that Spanish judges tend to grant only a compensation for direct damages.

---

12   Royal Decree of 10 January 1986 for motor vehicle repairs, Royal Decree of 29 January 1990 for repairs of household appliances, Royal Decree of 8 March 1991 regarding durable goods, all providing six months' legal guarantee.

13   Civil Code, art 1486.

3.4   Quantum of damage

The behaviour of the vendor must be taken into account:

(a) If he acted in good faith (ie was not aware of the defect and acted diligently), the purchaser may either terminate the contract and claim the expenses incurred or reduce the purchase price in proportion to the gravity of the defect.[14] Compensation shall cover loss of the purchased object and any expenses and damages incurred. If loss of the product is due to *force majeure* (unforeseeable or incontrollable cause), the vendor will also be liable for damages and interest.
(b) If he acted in bad faith (ie if he was aware of the defects and did not disclose them to the purchaser) the latter shall have the same choice as in the above paragraph, but he shall be entitled to damages if he chooses termination of the contract.[15]

Compensation for damages includes the value of the actual damage and any loss of profits, even if they were not foreseeable at the time of the agreement. As stated above, evidence should be provided of the defect of the product, the damage and the causal relationship, ie the link between the defect and the resulting damage. Further, a claim to obtain compensation should contain sufficient elements in order to quantify damages (including loss of profits).

Damages for personal injury are generally calculated on the basis of a particular amount per day the victim has not been able to work, in addition to any moral and physical damage or costs incurred (eg medical expenses) etc. Resultant personal damages (eg scars) are also calculated on the basis of a system of points according to the seriousness of the damage and the effect on the person; points are then given a value. Courts are free to follow this system, but it is often used as a guideline.

There are no punitive damages under Spanish law.

3.5   Burden of proof

In principle, the burden of proof is on the purchaser, who as plaintiff has to prove the existence of the contract between the parties, the defect of the purchased product, the fact that it makes the product useless for its purpose, the damage caused and the causal relationship, according to the rule that the burden of proof of the contractual obligations rests with the party claiming their fulfilment.[16] However, in civil cases the courts have frequently accepted the shifting of the burden of proof from the plaintiff to the defendant (see section 4.6 below).

3.6   Exclusion or limitation of liability

The level of diligence to be employed for the obligations arising out of a contract can be agreed by the parties.[17]

---

14   Civil Code, art 1488.
15   Civil Code, art 1486.
16   Civil Code, art 1214.
17   Civil Code, art 1104.

In a standard contract the parties may exclude the liability of the supplier as long as this agreement is not contrary to law, morality or public order.[18] This agreed exclusion of liability shall be effective as long as the vendor was not aware of the defects in the products.[19] However, if the agreement is considered to be a consumer contract, it falls within the GAC and thus no absolute exclusion of liability may be agreed to.[20] The Act also declares that exclusion or limitation of liability is null and void.

At the time of writing, the Unfair Contract Terms Directive No 13/93 EC has not yet been implemented into Spanish law.

3.7 Limitation period

Under Spanish contract law personal actions in general must be commenced within 15 years of the date when the action could be exercised[1] (when the plaintiff became aware of the damage, when the damage became apparent, when the plaintiff was able to obtain the necessary evidence in certain cases, etc.). Actions for claims relating to defective products have a time limit of six months, starting from the date of delivery of the product.[2] If the transaction is subject to commercial law (the parties are traders acting in the scope of their business), actions for defective products have a time limit of 30 days[3] or four days when furnished in packages.[4]

3.8 Liability for third parties

Spanish law provides reference to certain particular cases of liability involving third parties in tort. The employer or manager is liable for damage caused by his employees within the scope of their jobs; parents and tutors are liable for damage caused by children under their responsibility and the state is liable in some cases for the acts or omissions of civil servants, except whey they can prove that they acted with the required diligence to avoid the damage.[5] The Act of 7 January 1991 amended the former Criminal Code (article 22) and Civil Code, articles 1903 and 1904 which declared the liability of teachers with respect to their pupils, and declared instead the liability of owners of schools for the damage caused by the pupils as minors under the control of the teachers. The new Criminal Code (see section 6.2 below) declares that parents and tutors are only subsidiarily responsible for civil liability incurred by the persons over 18 they are responsible for and who live with them if such parents or tutors have acted negligently (article 120). Civil liability also applies subsidiarily for the State and the employer under the new Criminal Code (articles 120.3, 120.4 and 121).

The law also provides for liability of owners of machines that expel polluting fumes, owners of land whose trees fall and cause damages, owners of buildings

---

18 Civil Code, art 1255.
19 Civil Code, art 1485.
20 GAC, art 10.c.6.
1 Civil Code, arts 1964 and 1969.
2 Civil Code, art 1490.
3 Commercial Code, art 342.
4 Commercial Code, art 336.
5 Civil Code, art 1903

which fall, etc. In the case of buildings, the architect of the builder shall be liable if damage is caused due to a construction defect.[6]

The intervention of a third party may avoid liability of the vendor whenever the intervention can be considered to have been of such a degree that the link between the defect of the product and the damage caused is broken.

3.9   Conclusion

The provisions described above regarding contractual liability under traditional Spanish law entail major disadvantages for the consumer injured by a defective product, for example:

(a) if a person suffers injury caused by a defective product, he can only claim against the vendor (generally the retailer) who sold him the product and not against the wholesaler, the distributor or the producer, since he holds no contractual relationship with them;

(b) if the transaction is not a commercial one, the purchaser will only have the right to receive damages if he can prove that the vendor was aware of the defects and he did not reveal them to the purchaser. This rule is based on the principle of subjective or fault liability, which in terms of contractual obligations is established in article 1101 of the Civil Code in the sense that a party shall be deemed liable for damages whenever he has acted negligently (*'negligencia'* or *'culpa'*). On this basis, proper redress of the damage can only be obtained by the person injured by a defective product if he can furnish proof that the producer acted negligently in the manufacture of the defective product;

(c) the burden of proof is on the plaintiff (purchaser) and not on the defendant (vendor), so the purchaser must provide any required evidence;

(d) the purchaser fails to obtain damages if the vendor becomes insolvent. Indeed, in the case of insolvency, the creditor holds the same right which is not extinguished by this reason and is thus added to the claims of creditors in the liquidation of the vendor. However, in practical terms he shall seldom receive any compensation;

(e) the above-mentioned rights only protect the purchaser but not his relatives, friends or any bystanders who (unless they are heirs of a deceased purchaser) have no action against the vendor for liability in contract (privity of contract);

(f) the action of the purchaser to claim his rights expires six months after delivery of the object of the agreement for the sale and purchase. Furthermore, whenever the contract is deemed to be commercial, the Commercial Code reduces this term to 30 or to four days depending on the situation.

4   LIABILITY IN TORT

4.1   Introduction

Extra-contractual liability (liability in tort) is based on a general provision of the Civil Code pursuant to which 'whomsoever causes damage to another person by an act or omission and with negligence or fault is liable for the damage

---

6   Civil Code, arts 1908 and 1909

caused'.[7] This provision is broad enough to grant protection to any injured person who suffers damage by any kind of tort.

The courts have constantly repeated that the following requirements are necessary for the existence of extra-contractual liability:

(a) action or omission;
(b) unlawfulness;
(c) negligence;
(d) damage; and
(e) causal link between the act or omission and the damage.

It should be borne in mind that Spanish law as within the case law tradition does not provide different 'torts' as is the case in the common law countries (negligence, nuisance, etc). The above broadly worded provision based on the Roman law principle '*alterum non laedere*', however, includes any such situation.

4.2 Outline of the law of tort giving rise to liability for personal and property damage

Spanish law is traditionally founded on subjective or fault-based liability in the sense that such liability only arises when the tortfeasor has acted negligently or with dolus (malicious intent). According to the traditional system if a manufacturer is not aware of the defect in a product and acted diligently enough to avoid any such defect, he shall not be liable in tort for damage caused by the product.

This principle, summarised in the expression 'no liability without fault' (*no hay responsabilidad sin culpa*) has been confirmed by a large number of court judgments. Besides proving the existence of an unlawful act or omission, the damage caused and the causal relationship between the act or omission and the damage, the consumer must give sufficient evidence that the manufacturer acted negligently when manufacturing the product, which is a very heavy burden of proof.

Prior to the GAC, the Spanish courts developed the relevant case law so as to mitigate this harsh situation for the consumer by introducing certain elements of a strict liability system (not essentially depending on the behaviour of the defendant) and inversing the burden of the proof although the principle of subjective liability was never completely set aside.

4.3 Causation

For there to be liability in tort, the damage caused must be a direct result of the negligent action of the producer (supplier, importer, etc). Such causal relationship (*nexo causal*) is examined on a case-by-case basis using certain criteria such as reasonable consequence, sufficiency of cause to give rise to the damage etc. For instance, a judgment of the Supreme Court of 30 December 1981 found a company supplying electric power liable for the death of a person due to electrocution as a result of the lowering of certain overhead electricity cables.

---

7   Civil Code, art 1902.

4.4   Remoteness of loss and damage

No liability shall be found whenever the relationship between loss and damage on the one hand and the negligent act or omission on the other is too remote. In this sense, any element that is considered to break the causal relationship exempts the defendant from liability, whenever it is unforeseeable or inevitable. The case law has not defined unforeseeability, and thus has found liability in cases where a child threw a firecracker at a girl causing her to become blind,[8] and also where a company left chemical material near a river bank polluting nearby cultivated land when the river rose.

The following may be causes allowing exclusion of liability: *force majeure* (eg earthquake),[9] intervention of a third party (eg the supplier introduces essential amendments to the design of a product which entail a substantial degree of risk, thus excluding the liability of the manufacturer if he was not to blame as well) or negligence of the victim (eg a pedestrian suddenly walks onto the road without checking whether any cars are coming and in a way that the driver could never have foreseen, or avoided, even having acted diligently).

Economic loss is recoverable, subject to sufficient evidence of the cause-effect relationship, and including loss profits and damage effectively caused.

4.5   Quantum of damage

Damages in tort cover all damages directly caused by the negligent act and those that may be deemed to have been caused by the act, but not those that are too remote. In particular, they include the replacement of the product, damage effectively caused and an amount for compensation for damage to property and other prejudices and non-physical damage (*pretium doloris*) including pain and suffering, reputation, etc. They cover not only the damage (*damnum emergens*) but also lost profits (*lucrum cessans*) if there is sufficient evidence of the loss. In general, Spanish case law provides for a lump sum to be paid for all the heads of damage. The Court of Appeal of Girona recently awarded compensation of 40m pesetas to an unfortunate child who lost both legs in an incident involving a cultivator. There are no punitive damages under Spanish law.

Some criteria had been drawn up mainly by insurance companies to calculate compensation for settlements in damages caused in motor accidents. These criteria were also often used by judges as guidelines to calculate compensations not only in motor accidents, but also in other cases of liability for personal injuries. The recent Act on the Regulation and Supervision of Private Insurance[10] has provided the legal criteria to calculate compensations in motor accidents.[11] These criteria which follow a system of points are now mandatory for compensations in motor accidents and it is to be expected that they will also be used by courts as guidelines to calculate compensations involved in other cases of personal injuries.

8   Judgment of the Supreme Court of 4 May 1984.
9   Which is contemplated by Civil Code, art 1105: 'nobody is liable for such events which cannot be foreseen or which, if foreseen, were unavoidable'.
10   30/1995 of 8 November.
11   The criteria are provided as an annex to the Act on Civil Liability and Insurance on Circulation of Motor Vehicles approved by Decree 632/1988 of 21 March.

4.6   Burden of proof

According to the letter of the law, the victim must establish the main elements of the action (unlawful act or omission, damage, link between act or omission and damage and negligence of the defendant). However, Spanish case law has in practice altered this situation by introducing a presumption of negligence by the defendant, thus inverting the burden of proof. Important case law concerning extra-contractual liability has been based upon a presumption of negligence of the person causing the damage, such presumption being susceptible to being overturned by means of conclusive evidence (*juris tantum presumption*).[12]

4.7   Exclusion of limitation of liability

Liability arising in tort may not be restricted.[13]

4.8   Limitation period

A claim for damages in tort must be brought within one year from the moment the plaintiff was aware of the damage.[14]

However, whenever the plaintiff's fault qualifies as a crime, the victim's claim in civil liability may be brought within 15 years of the time when the plaintiff was aware of the damage.[15]

4.9   Liability for third parties

Spanish law provides reference to certain particular cases of liability involving third parties in tort. The employer or manager is liable for damage caused by his employees within the scope of their jobs; parents, teachers and tutors are liable for damage caused by children under their responsibility and the State is liable in some cases for the acts or omissions of civil servants, except when they can prove that they acted with the required diligence to avoid the damage (article 1903 of the Civil Code). The Act of 7 January 1991 amended article 22 of the Criminal Code and articles 1903 and 1904 of the Civil Code which declared the liability of teachers with respect to their pupils, and declares instead the liability of owners of schools for the damage caused by the pupils as minors under the control of the teachers.

The law provides for liability of owners of machines that expel polluting fumes, owners of land whose trees fall and cause damage, owners of buildings which fall etc. In the case of buildings, the architect or the builder shall be liable if damage is caused due to a construction defect.[16]

---

12   Judgments of the Supreme Court of 22 June 1931, 10 July 1943, 23 December 1952, 24 March 1953, 14 May 1963, 20 October 1963, 11 March 1971, 9 March 1974, 20 December 1982, etc.
13   Civil Code, art 1255.
14   Civil Code, art 1968.2
15   Criminal Code, art 117 and Civil Code, art 1964, Judgment of the Supreme Court of 1 April 1990.
16   Civil Code, arts 1908 and 1909.

4.10   Implications for producers and defendants

Generally, the requirements to be fulfilled by a consumer in order to sue a producer or a supplier for liability in tort are difficult to comply with. However, Spanish case law mitigated the situation in the following ways:

(a) reversal of burden of proof, as described in section 3.6 above;
(b) relaxation of the requirement of proving the facts ('principle of expansion'), whereby the courts have sometimes accepted weak evidence in order to protect the weaker party;[17]
(c) requirement of a higher degree of diligence, in the sense that some judgments have been based on the fact that the defendant should have acted with a higher level of diligence according to the nature of the obligations and the circumstances of persons, time and place as provided in article 1104 of the Civil Code for contractual liability;[18]
(d) relaxation of the requirement of unlawful behaviour (*antijuridicidad*), since it has been found in certain cases that even lawful behaviour causing damage may give rise to compensation whenever the defendant has not acted with sufficient diligence;[19]
(e) non-acceptance of the justification that regulatory provisions have been complied with, since it has been found that such a defence is not enough to relieve a person from liability.[20] A judgment of the Supreme Court of 20 December 1982 held in a case concerning a manufacturing business whose easily flammable products were set on fire, that mere compliance with regulations was not sufficient to relieve from liability when the duty to foresee and thus avoid the foreseeable and avoidable damages had failed, thus showing insufficient care;
(f) acceptance of liability for the creation of risks, close to strict liability, in the sense that whoever develops a business activity that involves risks for others is liable for any damages arising therefrom.[1]

The same judgment of the Supreme Court of 20 December 1982 declared that 'even if originally based on fault-based liability, the case law has developed extracontractual liability towards strict liability, although the moral or psychological factor and the evaluation of the subject's behaviour have not been completely disregarded'. This new approach has been due to the increase in dangerous activities and is based on the principle that those who obtain the profit from a dangerous activity are liable for the compensation for damages resulting therefrom. This trend is based on the general principle[2] that the provisions are to be interpreted within the scope of the social sphere in which they operate.

The evolution referred to relates to liability in tort in general and not only to product liability. Decisions on product liability have been very scarce. A judgment of the Supreme Court on 14 November 1984 declared that liability

---

17 Judgment of the Supreme Court of 5 April 1963.
18 Judgments of the Supreme Court of 14 February 1974, 14 April 1962, 9 April 1963, 28 June 1974, 10 October 1975, 22 October 1977, etc.
19 Judgments of the Supreme Court of 14 February 1944, 23 February 1950, 23 December 1952, 24 March 1953, 30 June 1959, 14 March 1963, 28 June 1974, etc.
20 Judgments of the Supreme Court of 14 May 1963, 30 October 1963, etc.
 1 Judgments of the Supreme Court of 30 October 1963, 15 June 1967, 25 October 1973, etc.
 2 Civil Code, art 3.1.

of the producer for damages caused to consumers and users by the product he manufactured should either be based on a negligent manufacturing of a defective product launched on the market[3] or on the failure to provide the required specific information and instructions for the use of the product and warning on the dangers involved therefrom.[4] In spite of the efforts of the courts, there has been no decisive case law for product liability in Spain as in some other countries like the USA or Germany. As indicated earlier, plaintiffs prefer on many occasions to bring actions in the criminal courts instead of the civil courts. The reason is that the criminal jurisdiction is often more effective and cheaper. Furthermore, the criminal courts have a more important role in the proceedings since they act *ex officio*, enabling them to consider any necessary evidence (in civil procedures they can only consider evidence put forward by the parties). The criminal judgments also cover any civil damages. This was the situation in a case for compensation of the effects of a toxic oil ('*aceite de colza*'), which caused more than one hundred deaths and hundreds of serious injuries. This is the reason why case law in civil product liability has not expanded sufficiently.

5   LIABILITY FOR DEFECTIVE PRODUCTS ARISING FROM BOTH GENERAL LAW AND IMPLEMENTATION OF EC DIRECTIVE 85/374 ON PRODUCT LIABILITY IN SPAIN

5.1   Introduction

The process leading to the final approval of the Act of 6 July 1994, implementing the Directive was long and implementation was done well after the time limit provided in the Directive.

5.1.1   *Evolution towards implementation of the EC Directive 85/374*

Spanish law slowly evolved towards a concept of liability based on the risk rather than the fault of the producer, thus gradually introducing into Spanish law the principle of strict liability.

There had been several legislative developments in the field of strict liability before the Act was approved, namely:

i.   *Motor vehicles*   The Act of 21 December 1962 laid down that: 'The motor vehicle driver who, as a consequence of traffic, causes damage to persons or property, shall be obliged to compensate the damage caused, unless it is evidenced that the event was due solely to fault or negligence on the part of the injured person or to *force majeure* . . .' (article 1).

ii.   *Air navigation*   The Act of 21 July 1960 introduced strict liability for a carrier for damage involving death or injuries suffered by the passengers and involving the destruction of merchandise and luggage (article 116), as well as for damage to persons or property on the land surface caused by aeroplanes (article 119).

---

3   Judgments of the Supreme Court of 26 March 1982 and 29 March 1983.
4   Judgment of the Supreme Court of 20 October 1983.

iii. Nuclear energy   Under the Paris Convention of 1960 and the Spanish Act of 29 June 1964 and its Regulations of 22 July 1967, a company running a plant which produces or deals with radioactive materials is strictly liable for the damage it may cause.

iv. Hunting   Under the Hunting Act of 4 April 1979 and its Regulations of 25 March 1971, the hunter shall compensate for the damage caused by the hunting activity, except for that due to *force majeure* or to the negligence of the injured person.

The legal basis for the protection of consumers is set forth in the Spanish Constitution approved on 27 December 1978, which provides that 'the public bodies shall guarantee the defence of consumers and users by protecting their safety, health and lawful economic interests through efficient procedures' (article 51.1).

Subsequently there were three main legislative precedents leading to the approval of the General Act in the Defence of Consumers and Users (GAC).

(a) The Basque Consumer Statute (Basque Act of 18 November 1981) represented an important advance in the field of product liability, though the Constitutional Court declared that the legal provisions regarding product liability were unconstitutional on the grounds of the lack of determination of some essential elements (Judgment of 30 November 1982).

(b) On 7 November 1988 Spain ratified The Hague Convention on the Law Applicable to Product Liability dated 2 October 1973.

(c) The Catalan Consumer Statute 1/1983 of 18 February 1983.

The General Act for the Defence of Consumers and Users of 19 July 1984 (GAC) provided a system of product liability to protect consumers. However approach was hesitant and confused and was far from bringing a clear and coherent system of liability without fault (strict liability) and from offering technical solutions close to those provided for by the Council of Europe Convention of 27 January 1977 and by the Directive. In many aspects the GAC went beyond simple protection in the field of product liability but in others it revealed important shortcomings.

Although the GAC was approved on 19 July 1984 when the proposal for the Directive was very advanced, the GAC did not follow the general principles of the draft Directive. The GAC was an incoherent and technically defective system of product liability. However, it represented a step forward as regards the protection of consumers since it overcame the difficulties stemming from:

(a) subjective liability, by introducing specific cases where liability is found even when no negligence has been involved and disregarding the fact that the producer acted diligently; and

(b) privity of contracts, by granting consumers direct action against the manufacturer, importer, supplier, etc.

5.2   Outline of provisions in Spain

The Directive was implemented by Act 22/1994 of 6 July ('the Act'). It took several years to be approved due to technical difficulties and opinions. There

were several alternative methods by which the Directive could have been implemented in Spanish legislation:

(a) modification of the liability system of the Civil and Commercial Codes; or
(b) modification of the GAC (directly or through regulations); or
(c) enactment of a specific act for product liability.

Finally, option (c) was selected and by approving the Act, the part of the GAC dealing with this field was superseded (articles 23-28 were revoked).

The Act follows the Directive very closely. It is thus based on strict liability ('*responsabilidad objetiva*') and is applicable not only to consumers (unlike the GAC), but to any kind of persons (consumer or not) who is damaged by defective products.

5.2.1   Legal concept of product

For the purposes of the Act, 'product' means all movable goods, even if incorporated into another movable or immovable good, with the exception of primary agricultural and stock-farming products and game and fish which have not undergone initial processing (article 2). In addition, 'product' includes electricity. Unlike the Directive, the Act also includes gas. The Act excludes real estate from its scope. On the basis of international conventions, nuclear accidents are also not covered by the Act (article 10).

The Act will not be applicable to products put into circulation before its entry into force (Transitory Provision).

5.2.2   Legal concept of defective product

In the same sense as the Directive (article 6), the Act defines a 'defective product' as one which does not provide the safety which one can legitimately expect, taking all circumstances into account and particularly the presentation of the product, its reasonably foreseeable use and the time when the product was put into circulation (article 3.1). A product shall not be considered defective for the sole reason that an improved product of the same type is put into circulation after the original product is put into circulation (article 3.2).

The Act (article 3.3) adds a new rule regarding defective products which is not contained in the Directive. According to this rule, in any case, a product shall be deemed as defective if it does not offer the safety which is normally offered by other units of the same series (article 3).

5.2.3   Legal concept of producer and importer

The term 'manufacturer' is the same as that provided in the Directive and includes the following (article 4.1):

(a) the manufacturer of a finished product;
(b) the manufacturer of any integrated part of a finished product;
(c) one who produces a raw material; or
(d) any person who presents himself to the public as its manufacturer, putting his name, trademark or any other distinctive sign on the product or on the package, envelope or any other element of protection or presentation. The Act is more specific and broader than the Directive as regards where a sign identifying an importer can be placed so as to treat him as a producer.

The importer is the person who in the scope of its business imports the product in the European Union for its sale, lease, leasing or otherwise (article 4.2).

If the manufacturer or the importer cannot be identified, each supplier of the product shall be deemed to be a manufacturer/importer, unless he informs the injured person within a period that the Act fixes in three months (the Directive does not fix the term) of the identity of the manufacturer or of the person who supplied him with the product (article 4.3).

The Act introduces a new case of liability for the supplier acting in bad faith, ie. a supplier will be liable as if he was the manufacturer or importer when he supplies the product knowing of the existence of the defect. In such a situation, a supplier may have recourse to the manufacturer or to the importer (Additional Provision).

5.2.4   Proof

Like the Directive (article 4), an injured party seeking compensation for damages is required to prove the defect, the damage and the causal relationship between the two (article 5). Liability is strict, without the need to prove any fault.

5.2.5   Manufacturer's defences

The Act (article 6) substantially reproduces the manufacturer's defences listed in article 7 of the Directive, namely the following:

(a) he did not put the product ito circulation;
(b) having regard to the circumstances, it is probable that the defect which caused the damage did not exist at the time when the product was put into circulation by him or that this defect came into being afterwards;
(c) the product was neither manufactured by him for sale or any form of distribution for economic purpose nor manufactured or distributed by him in the course of his business;
(d) the defect is due to compliance of the product with mandatory regulations;
(e) the state of scientific and technical knowledge at the time when he put the product into circulation was not such as to enable the existence of the defect to be discovered;
(f) in the case of a manufacturer of a component, that the defect is attributable to the design of the product in which the component has been fitted or to the instructions given by the manfuacturer of the product.

As regards defence (d), the Act does not provide that mandatory regulations are those issued by the public authorities, as provided by article 7(d) of the Directive. Therefore, the Act may give way to a broader defence to the manufacturer, since regulations not specifically issued by the public authorities could also be grounds of defence, eg safety rules approved by the industrial sectorial bodies, eg AENOR.

The Act makes an original partial use of the derogation provided for in article 15.1(b) of the Directive, concerning defence (e) above relating to technological risks, and provides that the manufacturer or the importer of medical products, food and food products aimed at human consumption shall not be able to invoke this exemption from liability (article 6.3).

5.2.6   *Joint and several liability*

Persons liable for the same damage under the Act shall be jointly and severally liable (article 7), in accordance with the Directive (article 5). Therefore, the injured person can choose to sue any of them (ie the most solvent party) or all of them. They will all be liable to the injured person for the total amount of the compensation and the person who pays has an action against the other persons liable for reimbursement of their part of liability.

5.2.7   *Fault of third parties and of injured persons*

In accordance with the Directive (article 8), the manufacturer's or importer's liability shall not be reduced when the damage is caused both by a defect in the product and by the intervention of a third party, although they have recourse against such third party to claim a portion of such compensation (article 8). Conversely, when the damage is caused both by a defect in the product and by the fault of the injured person or any person for whom the injured person is responsible, the manufacturer's liability may be reduced or eliminated (article 9).

5.2.8   *Scope of the protection*

Following the Directive (article 9), the Act covers death and personal injuries as well as damage to any item other than the defective product itself, provided that the damaged item is objectively intended for private use or consumption and was used by the injured person mainly for his own private use or consumption (article 10). All other damages, including pain and suffering ('*daños morales*'), may be covered according to general civil legislation. The Act does not apply to injury or damage arising from nuclear accidents and covered by international conventions ratified by the member states.

5.2.9   *Limitation period and expiration of liability*

The limitation period for any legal action derived from the Act is three years. However, the Act differs from the Directive in defining the moment when such period starts. Indeed, while in the Directive (article 10.1) such term begins to run from the day on which the injured person knows or should have known about the damage, the defect and the producer, in the Act (article 12.1) it begins to run from the day on which the plaintiff suffered the injury or damage 'given the defect of the product or the damage that such defect produced', as long as the person liable is known.

   The claim of the person who has paid the compensation for damages against other persons who are also liable has a time limit of one year from the date the compensation was paid. The Directive does not consider this issue.

   As provided by the Directive (article 11), liability pursuant to the Act shall be extinguished upon the expiry of a period of ten years from the date on which the manufacturer put the product into circulation (the actual product which caused the damage) unless the injured person has in the meantime instituted proceedings against the manufacturer (article 13).

5.2.10   *Contractual and non-contractual liability*

Legal actions under the Act (article 15) do not affect any rights that the injured person may have according to the law of contractual (see section 3 above) or

non-contractual liability (see section 4 above) of the manufacturer, importer or any other person.

5.3   Optional provisions

The three main options granted by the Directive to member states by way of derogation of the Directive's provisions were solved as follows by Spain.

5.3.1   *Primary agricultural products and game*

The Act excludes primary agricultural and stock-farming products and fish which have not undergone initial processing and game from the application of the Act (article 2). Therefore a farmer who causes damage by polluting a natural product (eg fruit) would not be liable under this strict objective legislation, but under the general system of tort.

5.3.2   *Development risk defence*

The Act provides that the development risk can be used as grounds for a defence by producers. However, the Act has made partial use of the derogation provided for in article 15.1(b) of the Directive for specific producers, ie the defence is not available to producers of medical products, food stuff and food products aimed at human consumption (article 6.3). As regards the distinction between food stuff (*alimentos*) and food products (*productos alimentarios*), the former are nutritive or dietetic products, whereas the latter are products merely suitable for human consumption.

5.3.3   *Limits on total amount of damages*

The Act (article 11) provides a higher maximum limit of liability than that provided in the Directive (article 16) for death and personal injuries caused by identical items with the same defect, ie 10,500 million pesetas (approximately US$ 86 million) as opposed to Ecu 70 million provided in the Directive.

Claims for a compensation covering damages other than death or personal injury should be for at least 65,000 pesetas (approx US$520) in the sense that claims under such minimum amount are not acceptable. Such limit is not applicable to claims when the damages that have been caused are death or personal injury.

5.4   Comparison of the effects of product liability law with the previous position in contract and tort

The main feature of product liability law in Spain after approval of the Act is the overcoming of two main legal obstacles faced in contract and tort under the Civil Code and the Commercial Code, namely:

(a) privity of contract which prevented the injured person from suing others except the party which whom he had contracted and his heirs; and

(b) the difficulty faced by the plaintiff in proving that the defendant has acted negligently (subjective fault).

These hurdles had been partially overcome by the GAC. Indeed, the GAC provided for the liability of the producer and the importer (besides that of the

supplier) for damage caused by the product and it was their responsibility to prove that they acted without negligence by proving that they complied with all the legal requirements and acted with the required diligence.[5]

The main innovations that implementation of the Directive by the Act entails in relation to the current system provided in the GAC is as follows:

(a) the Act protects any person who suffers death, injuries or damage to property and not only consumers as in the GAC;

(b) the Act imposes strict liability (instead of the GAC system which is based upon liability with fault with some exceptions);

(c) the definition of products that may entail liability according to the Act is narrower than that provided by the GAC which covers immovables and agricultural products;

(d) the Act provides a subsidiary system to identify the liable party in the chain of supply by enabling the supplier to avoid liability if he informs the consumer of the identity of his own supplier, whereas the GAC, which gives no definition of producer, provides for the joint liability of all persons in the chain of supply (producer, importer and supplier);

(e) the Act defines the concept of defect and provides grounds of defence related to it (article 7) which are not currently contemplated in the legislation in force;

(f) the Act is also precise as regards damage. The GAC made no precise reference to damage and thus was broader. The Act provides a similar definition to that of the Directive, thus limiting damage to death, personal injury, property and possibly non-material damage shall depend upon the national criteria;

(g) as regards grounds for defence, the Act provides a list of defences available to the producer thus enabling manufacturers of products requiring a warranty of safety, listed in GAC article 28, to avoid liability in certain cases, which were not available under the GAC;

(g) the implementation of the Act causes a reduction or exclusion of the producer's liability to occur not only when damage is due to the exclusive fault of the consumer or of the persons for whom he is responsible as was the case in the GAC, but also when damage is caused by both the consumer's fault and a defect in the product;

(h) the introduction into Spanish law of the time limitations laid down in the Directive (three years to institute proceedings and ten years for rights conferred upon the injured person) represents a considerable change to the provisions in legislation that enable Spanish consumers to bring an action against a producer.

6   CRIMINAL LIABILITY FOR DEFECTIVE PRODUCTS ARISING FROM BOTH GENERAL SAFETY LAW AND THE IMPLEMENTATION OF EC DIRECTIVE 92/59 ON PRODUCT SAFETY IN SPAIN

6.1   Implementation of EC Directive 92/59 EC on Product Safety

EC Directive 92/59 EC on Product Safety has been implemented in Spain by Royal Decree 44/1996 of 19 January, that entered into force on 13 March 1996 ('SD').

---

5   GAC, art 26.

This Decree is not applicable to products that are subject to a more specific legislation based on European Community law. It is not applicable either to used products, to antiquities or to products that need to be repaired or refurbished before being used as long as the supplier has warned thereof to the person he supplies the product to (article 1).

SD defines product as any product addressed at consumers or that may be used by a consumer, which is supplied for free or for consideration on the basis of a business and which is either new, used or refurbished (article 2.1). A product is safe when in standard and reasonably forseeable conditions of use including its term, it does not entail any risk or only minimal risks which are compatible with the use of the products and which are acceptable taking into account the high level of protection to consumers' safety and security of persons and taking into account its characteristics, effects of its use, presentation, labelling, instructions of use, consumers it is addressed to (particularly when addressed at children), etc (article 2.2).

A product is not insecure or dangerous only because a safer product has been launched into the market.

The definition of producer is very similar to that provided in the legislation for product liability described in this chapter (article 2.4), ie producer, importer into the EU and other subjects in the chain of distribution inasmuch as their activities may affect the product's safety.

The SD provides producers' general obligation to take any appropriate measures to keep consumers informed of the risks related to the products they market and if any of their products create a risk, they should take the necessary measures to put an end to such risk, including the recall of the product. Warnings do not exclude the obligations provided in this provision (article 3.1).

Distributors are also subject to the obligation not to supply products when they are aware or should have been aware taking into account the information they have and their professional knowledge that such products are not safe enough (article 3.2).

Safety of a product is estimated taking into account the EU and Spanish mandatory rules of safety, non mandatory legislation, European and Spanish technical specifications and subsequently the rules of good conduct in the specific sector, as well as the situation of practice and technique and the safety that consumers are entitled to expect (article 4).

SD regulates which are the public bodies competent in the field of product safety and the procedures to achieve the required transfer of information and the coordination of measures to be taken, particularly between national and autonomous bodies. A Technical Commission for the General Safety of Products is set up. The public bodies competent to enforce safety regulations have the power to:

(a) carry out general controls on safety of products;
(b) demand all the required information from the parties involved;
(c) collect samples of the products;
(d) impose preliminary conditions to market a product so that it is safe and impose the obligation to attach warning labels and notices;
(e) ensure that persons exposed to risks are made aware thereof, including through the publication of the necessary notices;
(f) temporarily forbid the supply of products suspected to be dangerous until the necessary studies are carried out to ensure the required level of safety;
(g) forbid the market of a product that has proved to be dangerous and take the necessary measures to ensure enforcement of this prohibition;

(h) efficiently and immediately organise the recall of dangerous products and
(i) if necessary, destroy dangerous products (article 6.1).

Any resolutions taken by the authorities that may involve a restriction to
the marketing of a product should be taken through a specific procedure that
includes the right of the parties involved to make any comments or defences in
that respect (article 9).

6.2   Criminal law

The case of toxic oil (see section 4.10 above) entailed the insertion in the
Criminal Code of a number of provisions of frauds related to food products. A
new Criminal Code was approved by Act 10/1995 of 23 November (CmC)
and entered into force on 24 May 1996.

The main offences provided in CmC regarding product liability are the
following:

(a) the unauthorised production of products that are dangerous for health or
chemical products that may cause alarm or the distribution thereof;[6]
(b) the dispatching or distribution of the products referred to in (a) with the
required authorisation but in breach of the relevant formalities;[7]
(c) the issue or dispatching of damaged or out of date drugs or drugs that do
not comply with the technical requirements regarding composition, stability
and efficiency or that have been replaced by other products, when public
health is endangered;[8]
(d) the alteration of a drug to the extent that its therapeutical efficiency is barred
and public health is endangered; the production of products or substances
simulating they have beneficial benefits when it endangers public health
and advertising of such products;[9]
(e) the offer by a producer, distributor or trader of food products that do not
comply with the law as regards their time limit and composition to the
extent they place consumers at risk; the production and sale of damaging
food products and beverages; the production of unauthorised products that
are harmful for health; the hiding or stealing for the purpose of their sale
or acquisition of items addressed at being disinfected or destroyed;[10]
(f) the addition of unauthorised additives or other substances to food products
or beverages when they may endanger health;[11]
(g) the pollution of water or other food products or substances for
consumption.[12]

It should be noted that most of these offences do not require a result
(damage) and thus they provide for strict liability, ie the mere carrying out of
the action described in the CmC is a criminal offence and thus gives raise to
criminal liability. The penalties for these offences include imprisonment and
closure of business besides civil liability.

---

6   Criminal Code, art 359.
7   Criminal Code, art 360.
8   Criminal Code, art 361.
9   Criminal Code, art 362.
10 Criminal Code, art 363.
11 Criminal Code, art 364.
12 Criminal Code, art 365.

Given that criminal proceedings are far more intimidating and flexible than civil ones, claims tend to be instituted before a criminal court when the action may constitute a criminal offence. Criminal court judgments may also decide on civil liability compensations arising from criminal offences. However, given that Spanish criminal courts tend to grant lower damages than those granted by civil courts, the claim for compensation of damages is often instituted at a later stage before the civil courts.

7   CIVIL LIABILITY FOR DEFECTIVE PRODUCTS BROUGHT ABOUT BY BREACH OF STATUTORY REGULATION DESIGNED TO PROTECT CONSUMERS AND TO PROMOTE SAFETY

The Spanish Constitution provides consumers' right to safety and health (articles 51 and 43). The GAC developes this general rule by providing in article 3.1 the general obligation that all products launched into the market and addressed at consumers or that are expected to be used by them should be safe.

Producers of unsafe products are liable for the damages caused by their products as provided in Act 22/1994 of 6 July described earlier in this chapter (section 5.2). The production or distribution of a defective product for breach of statutory regulations is also subject to fines, criminal sanctions in certain cases and to closure of business.

Infringements of the SD and other safety regulations are considered infringements of health statutory regulations and at the same time infringement of consumer law.

The fines for infringement of safety regulations is subject to the fines provided in Chapter VI of the General Act for Health (Act 14/1986 of 25 April), which provides for sanctions of up to 100 million pesetas (approx US $820,000) and closure of business (article 36).

The fines for infringement of consumer law are provided in Royal Decree 1945/1983 of 22 June 1983, which regulates infringements and sanctions in relation to consumer protection and the production of primary agricultural products (including products of stock-farming) for human consumption and use (foodstuff, drugs, beverages, woollen clothes, etc). This regulation, which was not superseded by the GAC nor the Act, was meant to merge with and update the piecemeal provisions in this area and it also provides a maximum fine of 100 million pesetas and the possibility of closure of business (article 7).

Infringements related to these issues are classified as follows:

(a) Health infringements: Non-compliance with regulations regarding the manufacturing and quality of particular products; acts or omissions creating risk or damage to consumers' health; non-compliance with regulations regarding pollution; the promotion or sale of foodstuffs containing non-authorised additives; the manufacturing, supply or sale of foodstuffs with misleading presentation regarding its health or nutritional characteristics; the distribution, supply or sale of foodstuffs containing toxic substances etc.

(b) Consumer protection infringements: Selling, supplying or manufacturing products fraudulent as to quality, weight etc, or with misleading labels; selling at higher prices than those legally authorised and other acts of unfair competition etc.

(c) Infringements to regulations regarding the protection of the quality of agricultural and farming foodstuffs: The sale of products without the

required authorisation; the ownership of machines not having the required authorisation; fraud in quality, weight etc of such products; sale of counterfeited products etc.

Serious sanctions are imposed on any participants for infringements of the above-mentioned provisions and wide powers are granted to the authorities in order to carry out inquiries. Sanctions are subject to a time limit of five years from the date of infringement.

CHAPTER XVI

Sweden

Christer Wagenius, Esq

Advokatfirman Wagenius & Partners HB
Box 1393
251 13 Helsingborg
Sweden

Tel: ++ 46 42 19 96 60
Fax: ++ 46 42 13 00 62

CHAPTER XVI

Sweden

1 INTRODUCTION

1.1 Introduction to the legal system in Sweden

On 1 January 1995 Sweden became a member of the EU. Most of the Directives have already been implemented into Swedish National Law. The Lugano Convention, which is parallel to the Brussels Convention but includes EFTA countries as well, also forms a part of the Swedish legal system of today. Therefore, the legal situation in Sweden, complying with the EU Regulations and Directives, should be rather similar to that of other member states of EU.

The Swedish Judiciary traditionally consists of a general three instance court system, with 97 District Courts, 6 Courts of Appeal and the Supreme Court. There are also General Administrative Courts with three instances. There is no special court for commercial matters. Therefore, arbitration is often used in major commercial disputes.

1.2 Overview of the law relating to defective products in Sweden

1.2.1 Definitions

When discussing liability for defective products in Sweden, a distinction must be made between product liability and contractual liability.

The term *product liability*, as normally defined in Sweden, means liability – irrespective of negligence and contract – arising from:

(a) either personal injury caused by a product; or
(b) property damage caused by a product to other items.

In this chapter the term *product liability* is used in this sense.

On the other hand the normal *contractual liability* of the seller towards the buyer regarding defects in goods sold is not regarded as product liability unless it involves consequential damage to persons or to property other than the product itself.

The contractual liability under the Swedish Sale of Goods Acts as described below is largely restricted to matters arising between the seller and the buyer regarding the *goods as such*. In this chapter the term 'goods' instead of 'product' will be used when referring to contractual liability.

Owing to the range of this subject, only a brief summary of Swedish legislation can be provided in this chapter. Therefore, the survey must not be regarded as a full and comprehensive statement of Swedish law regarding defective products.

1.2.2   Product liability

The first Swedish Product Liability Law (*Produktansvarslagen*) entered into force on 1 January 1993. Before that, product liability was mainly based on the principle of *negligence*, the degree of fault needed for negligence however over the years becoming very low, closing the gap to *strict liability*.

A translation of the Swedish Product Liability Law appears as Appendix 10.

Product liability in Sweden is also based on certain provisions in the Consumer Sale of Goods Act (*Konsumentköplagen*) and the Consumer Service Act (*Konsumenttjänstlagen*) as well as on specific laws, mainly regarding various dangerous activities. The said Consumer Acts are applicable when professionals as part of their business activity sell goods or services to consumers; that is to say, goods mainly intended for consumers' private use.

There is also a Product Safety Law (*Produktsäkerhetslag*) which has been in force since mid-1989 aimed at preventing personal and property damage being caused by unsafe products and services. This law enables the authorities to act against the suppliers of products and services which are deemed unsafe. It is not a law establishing product liability for the suppliers of the said products and services.

1.2.3   Contractual liability

The Swedish Sale of Goods Act and Consumer Sale of Goods Act are both now in force, from 1 January 1991. The Consumer Service Act is from mid-1986 but has been modified in 1988 and 1990. A translation of the Sale of Goods Act appears as Appendix 11.

2   PRE-CONTRACTUAL LIABILITY

2.1   Effect on the interpretation and extent of obligations

Pre-contractual statements will normally have effect on the interpretation and extent of the obligations of the parties to a contract. The general principles of the Swedish Contract Act (*Avtalslagen*) regarding the interpretation of negotiations and agreements and the consequences thereof, form the basis for such a legal point of view. The Sale of Goods Act, the Consumer Sale of Goods Act and the Consumer Service Act contain specific provisions in this respect (see section 3.1.4 below).

2.2   Non-disclosure

Correspondingly, also non-disclosure of relevant facts during negotiations may lead to liability, eg under section 19:2 of the Sale of Goods Act, section 16 of the Consumer Sale of Goods Act and section 11 of the Consumer Service Act.

2.3   Liability in contract or tort

The pre-contractual liability lies in contract, especially regarding matters falling under the Sale of Goods Act. However, as those provisions of the Consumer Sale of Goods Act and the Consumer Service Act, which are safeguarding the

interest of the consumer, are mandatory, the extent of the pre-contractual liability under these acts are similar to liability in tort.

3   LIABILITY IN CONTRACT

3.1   Outline of contract law relevant to defective products in Sweden

3.1.1   Introduction

As mentioned earlier, the Swedish Sale of Goods Acts are largely restricted to matters arising between buyer and seller concerning the goods as such. Liability of the manufacturer in a more general sense, as product liability, is left for other legislation, mainly for the Product Liability Law. However, the Acts specially related to *consumers* contain provisions extending the liability beyond the goods sold or services rendered (see section 3.1.2 below).

Regarding the *international sale of goods* it should be observed that Sweden has adopted articles 1-13 and 25-88 of the UN Convention of 11 April 1980 on Contracts for the International Sale of Goods; with the exception of sales where both seller and buyer have their place of business in Sweden, Denmark, Norway, Finland or Iceland. The question of applicable law regarding the international sale of goods is dealt with in a Swedish law from 1964. If the parties have not agreed upon a governing law, the law of the country where the seller receives the order from the buyer will normally apply.

3.1.2   Product liability under contract law

The Sale of Goods Act does not contain any provisions regarding product liability as defined above, ie liability for personal injury or damage to property other than the goods. On the contrary, in section 67 it is expressly stated *that damages under the Act do not comprise compensation for loss due to damage to anything else than the goods sold* (see Appendix 11).

The Consumer Sale of Goods Act contains, however, a provision of product liability similar to that contained in the Consumer Service Act, see next paragraph, namely that *the liability of the seller also extends to damage caused by the product to other property, provided that the property damaged is intended for personal use and belongs to the purchaser or a member of his household.* The reasons for extending the seller's liability when the buyer is a consumer are mainly the following: It is natural for the consumer to claim compensation for all the damage (eg not only for the malfunctioning deep-freeze as such but also for any stored products damaged therein), the damage is usually compensated by a small sum (the damage is restricted to items for personal use by household members), and the liability of the seller is also limited to what falls under his power of control (see section 3.4.2 below).

Under the Consumer Service Act anyone who is commercially rendering services to consumers will be liable for damage caused by faults therein not only to the object of the service but also to *any other goods owned by the consumer or by a member of his household.*

3.1.3   Liability for the goods as such under contract law

Under Swedish contract law goods sold (as well as services provided) are required to be defect free and the liability of the seller (or the provider of the service) is closely related to the type of defect.

In order not to be defective the goods/services should – as further specified in section 3.3, below – primarily be in conformity with what is expressly stated or implied in the contract. But they can also be regarded as defective under a broader interpretation, eg if they vary from what could reasonably be expected by the buyer.

As further specified in sections 3.3.4–3.3.6, below, the consequences of liability involve the right for the buyer to have the goods/services remedied, to get a reduction in price or to cancel the contract and claim damages. He may also withhold his payment for the goods or services (to a certain extent).

3.1.4   Pre-contractual liability

Concerning a seller's/provider's pre-contractual liability for statements and representations made, it can generally be said that such statements and representations still apply under the contract if they can be deemed to have had an influence on the buyer's/consumer's decision. Misrepresentations in this respect are regarded as defects in the goods sold or the services rendered. The consequences of such defects are the same as of other defects in the goods (see sections 3.3.4–3.3.6, below).

In the Sale of Goods Act these principles are laid down in sections 18 and 19 and similar provisions are found in sections 16 and 19 of the Consumer Sale of Goods Act as well as in sections 10 and 11 of the Consumer Service Act.

3.2   Contractual warranties

Liability for defects according to the Sales of Goods Act and the Consumer Sale of Goods Act requires that the defect existed *at the time of delivery*, that a claim is made without delay and normally within a maximum two years from delivery.

However, it is very common that the seller/manufacturer gives a specific warranty regarding goods sold. There are no legal provisions limiting such warranties and they vary depending on the goods concerned, general market conditions and actual competition. Such a warranty normally stipulates that any defect discovered within a certain time after the delivery – eg six months, a year or more – will be remedied by the seller, irrespective of whether the defect can be shown to have existed at the time of delivery or not. Under such circumstances a consumer may actually have two possibilities to claim a remedy of a defect, namely the mandatory maximum two year guarantee period under the Consumer Sale of Goods Act, to be used if the defect can be deemed to have existed already upon delivery, but also the specific warranty period which may have been granted by the seller/manufacturer regarding the goods in question.

3.3   Breach of contract for supply of defective products

3.3.1   Sale of Goods Act

In order not to be defective, the goods must conform to the contract between the seller and the buyer in respect of:

(a) character;
(b) quantity;

(c) quality;
(d) other properties; and
(e) packaging.

Unless otherwise provided for in the contract, the goods shall also be suitable for their normal or intended use. Furthermore, the goods shall have those properties which the seller may have referred to by showing a sample or model, and they shall also be properly packaged if packaging is needed to keep or protect them. Finally, if the goods vary from what could reasonably be expected by the buyer, they may also be regarded as defective.

3.3.2 Consumer Sale of Goods Act

In order not to be defective under the terms of the Act, the goods must first comply with the corresponding requirements as under the Sale of Goods Act.

Furthermore, necessary instructions regarding:

(a) assembly;
(b) use;
(c) storage; and
(d) handling

must be delivered with the goods.

If the seller has omitted to inform the buyer of circumstances regarding the goods which the buyer could reasonably have expected to be informed of, and if this omission can be assumed to have had an influence on the purchase, the goods may also be regarded as defective.

Under this Act the goods are expressly regarded as defective due to *safety* reasons:

(a) if they are sold despite a prohibition due to safety reasons (eg a prohibition declared by the authorities under the Product Safety Law); or
(b) if their use clearly endangers life or health.

3.3.3 Consumer Service Act

Under the Consumer Service Act a service is defective if:

(a) the result is not in conformity with what the consumer had reason to expect regarding professional skill and due respect for the consumer's interests;
(b) the result is not in conformity with regulations mainly aiming at the service being safe; or
(c) the service has been performed despite prohibitions due to safety reasons.

3.3.4 Remedies under the Sale of Goods Act

In case of a defect in the delivered goods the buyer is entitled to:

(a) remedy of the defect; or
(b) delivery of a replacement without defects; or
(c) reduction of the price; or
(d) cancellation of the delivery; and
(e) damages.

The buyer may also withhold payment by way of set off (in order to bring some pressure on the seller to remedy etc).

The buyer has the right to demand that the seller shall remedy the defect without any cost to the buyer, if this can be made without unreasonable cost or inconvenience for the seller. The seller is free to replace the goods instead, if he so prefers.

The buyer has the right to demand a replacement delivery of the goods if the breach of contract is of substantial importance to him and the seller was or should have been aware of this. (This is not applicable if a new delivery would mean an unreasonable burden on the seller.)

The buyer may demand a price reduction, if remedy of the defect or replacement delivery is not an issue or not fulfilled within a reasonable time. The buyer may cancel the delivery if the breach of contract is of great enough importance to him and the seller was aware or should have been aware of this.

3.3.5   *Remedies under the Consumer Sale of Goods Act*

In case of defect in the delivered product, the consumer is, in a similar way to buyers under the Sale of Goods Act, entitled to:

(a) remedy of the defect; or
(b) delivery of a replacement without defects; or
(c) reduction of the price; or
(d) cancellation of the delivery; and
(e) damages.

The consumer may also withhold payment by way of set off.

In detail the provisions regarding these alternatives for consumers are somewhat different from those referred to regarding the Sale of Goods Act, mainly because they put the consumer in a better position than other buyers. For example, the consumer may cancel the contract if the defect is of great enough importance to him; there is no requirement of the seller's awareness of this importance.

3.3.6   *Remedies under the Consumer Service Act*

If the service is defective, and such defect is not due to acts or omissions by the consumer, the consumer is entitled to:

(a) have the defect remedied; or
(b) have a reduction of price; or
(c) cancel the contract; and
(d) claim damages.

The consumer may also withhold payment corresponding to what is needed to safeguard his claim.

3.4   Quantum of damage

3.4.1   *Sale of Goods Act*

The buyer is entitled to damages due to any defect in the goods unless the seller proves that the defect is caused by a circumstance outside his control and which he could not reasonably have expected, avoided or overcome. Thus, the scope of 'seller's control' plays an important role in this legislation, forming a basic principle for liability.

Damages for breach of contract comprise compensation for expenses, difference in price and loss of profits as well as other direct or indirect losses due to the breach of contract. Certain indirect losses, eg loss of production, loss of contract, are however not compensated in the circumstances described in the paragraph above.

The buyer is, however, always entitled to compensation if the defect is due to the seller's *negligence* or if the product differs from what the seller *expressly promised*.

Damages according to this Act do not include compensation for loss or damage caused to goods other than the goods sold.

The buyer is obliged to minimise his losses.

Furthermore, if the damages in the circumstances are deemed by the Court to be unreasonably high, they can be lowered.

3.4.2 Consumer Sale of Goods Act

The consumer is entitled to damages in respect of any defect in the goods except where the seller is able to prove that the defect is caused by circumstances outside of his control which he could not reasonably have expected, avoided or overcome.

The consumer is always entitled to compensation if the goods differ from what the seller expressly promised. Damages comprise compensation for expenses, loss of income and difference in price as well as other losses due to the delay or the defect.

Damages according to this Act do not comprise compensation for loss caused to other goods, with the exception of damage to such other goods that belong to the buyer or a member of his household and are intended mainly for private use.

3.4.3 Consumer Service Act

The consumer is entitled to compensation for loss caused to the consumer due to a defect in services rendered unless the provider of the service proves that the loss is not caused by his or his representative's negligence.

3.5 Burden of proof

Following general principles of law, the burden of proof rests with the party referring to the respective circumstance in his favour.

Accordingly, the burden of proof regarding:

(a) the existence of a defect rests with the buyer/consumer;
(b) the excuse for a defect rests with the seller/provider;
(c) the extent of loss due to a defect rests with the buyer/consumer.

If a price has not been agreed, the burden of proof whether a price is reasonable or not rests with the seller/provider (at least towards a consumer).

3.6 Exclusion or limitation of liability

The Consumer Sale of Goods Act and the Consumer Service Act are mandatory to the benefit of the consumer, and thus the contract may not limit the liability

of the seller laid down in these Acts but might very well extend the same.

Furthermore, Sweden has implemented the Unfair Contract Terms Directive No 13/93 EC in a new Consumer Contract Terms Act (*Lagen om avtalsvillkor i konsumentförhållanden*) which entered into force 1 January 1995.

The liabilities under the Sale of Goods Act may however freely be altered by contract. In fact, section 3 of the said Act expressly stipulates the contractual freedom of the parties (see Appendix 11).

3.7   Limitation period

The buyer/consumer must complain within a *reasonable time* after discovering the defect. If he fails to complain within *two years* from receiving the goods or services he loses his right to complain unless otherwise stipulated in the contract. Under certain circumstances (eg gross negligence) the limitation period will be extended.

3.8   Liability for third parties

Regarding damages due to defective goods/services, the seller/provider is in principle liable for his representatives/subsuppliers/subcontracters as for himself (Sale of Goods Act, sections 40 and 27; Consumer Sale of Goods Act, section 30; Consumer Service Act, section 31).

4   LIABILITY IN TORT

4.1   Introduction

As pointed out earlier in this chapter, the Swedish Product Liability Law (*Produktansvarslagen*) entered into force on 1 January 1993.

Nevertheless, the Swedish Tort Liability Act (*Skadeståndslagen*) and some special laws, mainly regarding various dangerous activities, are still also of importance regarding liability in tort.

4.2   Outline of relevant tort law

4.2.1   Tort Liability Act

Liability under the Tort Liability Act is based on *negligence* (*culpa*). However, under court practice, the degree of fault required for the establishment of 'negligence' has been diminished increasingly over the years.

In a decision by the Supreme Court (NJA 1986, s 712) the manufacturer of a safety device for a crane was held responsible for a defect in the safety device (part of which was provided by a sub-contractor) causing damage to property (the crane turned over due to overload). The Supreme Court argued that the safety device was an important item and that *insufficient control* must have been exercised either by the manufacturer or by his subcontractor.

In another case (NJA 1989, s 389) the Supreme Court clearly acknowledged strict liability. A schoolteacher was granted compensation for personal damage caused by food served to her at school, although the Court expressly recognised that no negligence could be shown.

Nowadays, the Product Liability Law in force since 1993 would also be applicable. However, the Tort Liability Act is still of importance, especially for damage not covered by the Product Liability Law, eg damage to property not intended for personal use.

4.2.2 Special laws

Strict liability for damage caused can be found in laws regarding certain dangerous activities, namely;

(a) Nuclear Liability Law (*Atomansvarighetslagen*);
(b) Environmental Liability Law (*Miljöskadelagen*);
(c) Railroad Traffic Law (*Järnvägstrafiklagen*);
(d) Air Traffic Law (*Luftfartslagen*);
(e) Electrical Power Plant Law (*Elanläggningslagen*)
(f) Maritime Act (*Sjölagen*);

4.2.3 Insurance coverage

The provisions regarding product liability which can be found in the special laws referred to above are not giving the full picture of how product liability issues are in reality currently dealt with in Sweden. Various insurance arrangements also play an important role regarding compensation for personal damage and injury to property.

Liability under the Motor Traffic Damage Law (*Trafikskadelagen*) is connected to a mandatory insurance coverage. For personal injury or damage to property occurring due to a motor vehicle accident in Sweden, compensation shall be paid out under the mandatory traffic insurance for the vehicle concerned. (If no insurance has been taken out for the vehicle in question, compensation will nevertheless be paid out – based on joint responsibility amongst all the insurance companies.) The insurance company paying may claim compensation from the person actually causing the accident only if it was caused wilfully or by gross negligence.

For personal injury there is basic coverage under social security provisions, namely under the Law of General Insurance (*Lagen om allmän försäkring*). This insurance is mandatory and automatic, covering in principle everybody domiciled in Sweden. Regardless of the cause for a personal injury, compensation will be paid out under the insurance (mainly for medical care and for loss of income).

It is very common for insurance coverage offered by the general insurance to be increased by various Group Insurance Systems offered to employees etc.

Furthermore, there is a Occupational Injury Insurance (*Arbetsskadeförsäkring*) financed by social security contributions and covering all those gainfully employed. Compensation is paid out for occupational injury and disease (mainly for medical care and loss of income). The coverage is increased by the Security Insurance for Work Connected Injuries (*Trygghetsförsäkringen vid arbetsskada*) which is based on an agreed strict liability for the employer in respect of the employee's occupational injury and is an arrangement agreed between trade unions and employers' associations in collective agreements. This insurance is underwritten by a consortium of Swedish insurance companies. As mentioned, the insurance covers a strict liability; the employee is compensated even if no negligence of the employer can be shown.

On 1 January 1997 a Maltreatment Liability Law (*Patientskadelagen*) will entre into force. Liability under this law will follow whenever the maltreatment is the most probable cause of the injury. There will not, however, be any liability for unavoidable consequences of necessary treatment in very serious cases, nor for consequences due to the use of pharmaceutical products unless prescribed or provided contrary to the current regulations therefor. A mandatory insurance will cover the liability to pay damages for maltreatment under the law.

Finally, there is the Pharmaceutical Injuries Insurance (*Läkemedels-försäkringen*) covering the liability of producers or importers of pharmaceutical products for injuries caused by their products.

5 IMPLEMENTATION OF EC DIRECTIVE 85/374 ON PRODUCT LIABILITY IN SWEDEN

5.1 Introduction

The Swedish Product Liability Law which entered into force on 1 January 1993 implements the Directive.

5.2 Outline of the provisions of the Product Liability Law

The Swedish Product Liability Law closely follows the Directive. There are, however, some differences (see section 5.3.4 below).

The full text of the Swedish law (in English translation) appears as Appendix 10.

5.3 Description of certain provisions

5.3.1 Primary agricultural products and game

Primary agricultural products and game are covered by the Swedish Product Liability Law, even if they have not undergone a processing of an industrial nature.

5.3.2 Development risk defence

Development risk defence based on the state of the art is allowed under the Swedish Product Liability Law. No liability will be incurred by any person or entity who shows that on the basis of scientific and technical knowledge at the time when he put the product into circulation, it was not possible to discover the defect.

5.3.3 Limits on total liability

No specific limits on total liability are given in the Swedish Product Liability Law, but the damages payable may be adjusted to the extent reasonable, if negligence on the part of the injured party has contributed to the injury or damage.

Furthermore, the provisions of the Tort Liability Law regarding the determination of damages also apply to compensation under the Product Liability Law.

5.3.4 Differences between national law and the Directive

There are some differences between Swedish national law on product liability, as laid down in the Swedish Product Liability Law, and the provisions of the Directive.

According to article 2 of the Directive the term 'product' includes electricity. This is not the case under the Swedish Product Liability Law, since Sweden has a specific law regarding electricity (*Elanläggningslagen*), implementing the Directive in this respect.

Article 3(3) of the Directive states that a supplier may be treated as the producer unless he '*within a reasonable time*' informs the injured party of the identity of the producer. The said time limit is set to 'one month' in the Swedish Product Liability Law.

Article 4 of the Directive regarding the proving of the damage, the defect and the causal relationship cannot be found in the Swedish Product Liability Law. As it may be very difficult or almost impossible in some cases to bring full evidence, general principles under Swedish law recognise that the burden of proof still rests with the claimant but that the Courts may decide what is actually needed as full evidence in each individual case. As a matter of fact, the Supreme Court in a case (NJA 1982, s 421) where the causal relationship could not be fully proven (it could be one of two substances that caused the injury) decided that the claimant only had to prove that the substance he claimed to be defective and causing the injury was *the most probable cause*.

Section 11 of the Swedish Law regarding right of recourse has no parallel in the Directive. This section 11 has been made part of the Swedish Product Liability Law in order to coordinate the specific product liability provisions in the Consumer Sale of Goods Act and the Consumer Service Act with the Product Liability Law.

As specified earlier in this chapter there are other Swedish laws and regulations, which also are applicable in matters of product liability. Thus, the Swedish Product Liability Law only covers a limited extent of the matter as a whole.

6 CRIMINAL LIABILITY FOR DEFECTIVE PRODUCTS ARISING FROM BOTH GENERAL SAFETY LAW AND THE IMPLEMENTATION OF EC DIRECTIVE 92/59 ON PRODUCT SAFETY IN SWEDEN

6.1 Introduction

In July 1989 the Swedish Product Safety Law (*Produktsäkerhetslagen*) entered into force. The purpose of the law is to prevent products and services from causing personal injury or property damage.

The Swedish Product Safety Law has thereafter been modified in order to implement EC Directive 92/59 (see section 6.2 below).

Furthermore, there are other Swedish laws and regulations promoting safety within certain areas of activities as well as regarding certain products.

Regarding criminal liability for defective products the following can be said in general.

The Swedish Product Safety Law does not contain specific provisions regarding criminal liability. However, under the Swedish Penal Code (*Brottsbalken*) negligence causing death or injury is a general criminal offence rendering up to two years of imprisonment (gross negligence up to six years). Also gross negligence endangering life or exposing somebody for the risk of severe injury may render up to two years of imprisonment.

In addition to the general liability under the Swedish Penal Code, many of the specific Swedish laws and regulations on product safety (see section 6.5 below) have certain provisions regarding criminal liability, eg:

(a) the Swedish Law regarding Foods (*Livsmedelslagen*) stating that violation, wilfully or by negligence, normally will lead to a fine or up to one year of imprisonment;

(b) the Swedish Law regarding Animal Feed (*Foderlagen*) stating that violation, wilfully or by negligence, normally will lead to a fine;

(c) the Swedish Pharmaceutical Act (*Läkemedelslagen*) stating that if a product is produced, imported or sold in violation of the provisions of the Act, the perpetrator can be fined or sentenced to up to two years' imprisonment;

(d) the Swedish Law on safety regarding Toys (*Lagen om leksakers säkerhet*) stating that violation, wilfully or by negligence, normally will lead to a fine or up to one year of imprisonment; and

(e) the Swedish Act regarding Chemical Products (*Lagen om kemiska produkter*) also stating that violation, wilfully or by negligence, normally will lead to a fine or up to one year of imprisonment.

6.2   Implementation of EC Directive 92/59 EC

Due to Sweden becoming a member of the EU on 1 January 1995, the EC Directive 92/59 on product safety was duly implemented into the Swedish Product Safety Law.

6.3   Anomolous provisions

The Swedish Product Safety Law contains stipulations extending the safety provisions further than the Directive. Thus, not only products but also *services* fall under the law. Also the risk of a product causing not only injury to persons but also *damage to property* has been taken into account. Finally, under the Swedish law, export of a dangerous product may also be prohibited.

6.4   Main provisions of the Swedish Product Safety Law

Under the law anyone conducting a business can be:

(a) ordered to give safety information regarding his products and services;
(b) prohibited from selling products and providing services;
(c) ordered to provide warnings regarding his products and services;
(d) ordered to withdraw his products and services;
(e) prohibited from exporting his products.

Products and services provided as a business activity fall under the Product Safety Law if the said products and services are or can be expected to be used

by consumers to a substantial extent (private use only).

The National Board for Consumer Policies (*Konsumentverket*) is the main supervising authority in respect of matters falling under the Product Safety Law. The Supervising Authority is supposed to take actions ex officio under this Act. Nevertheless, anybody may initiate such actions by raising the issue in a complaint to the National Board for Consumer Policies.

The Supervising Authority shall primarily negotiate with the supplier of the product or service in order to obtain a voluntary remedy. Failing this, the Supervising Authority may turn to the Consumer Ombudsman (*Konsumentombudsman*) who may ask the Market Court (*Marknadsdomstolen*) for a mandatory decision. In minor cases the Consumer Ombudsman may present his own decision to the supplier of the product or service but such a decision is only valid if it is accepted by the supplier within a certain period of time.

The decision of the Market Court shall normally be combined with a directive on penalty of a fine falling due if the decision by the court is not duly observed. The fine is normally set at SEK 100,000, but it can be varied.

6.5 Other product safety laws and regulations

The Pharmaceutical Act contains provisions regarding the production, import and distribution of pharmaceutical products. The Medical Products Agency (*Läkemedelsverket*) has the supervising responsibility regarding the observance of the act.

The Law regarding Foods contains stipulations regarding the handling and care of food. Various governmental bodies have supervising responsibilities regarding the law. As mentioned above, there is also a Law regarding Animal Feed.

The Act regarding Chemical Products concerns producers, importers and other providers of chemical products. The supervising responsibilities rest mainly with the National Inspection Board for Chemical Products (*Kemikalieinspektionen*) and with the National Board of Health and Welfare.

Other laws and regulations containing provisions to promote safety are the Working Environment Act (*Arbetsmiljölagen*), the Act regarding Transportation of Hazardous Goods (*Lagen om transport av farligt gods*), the Act regarding Explosives and Inflammable Goods (*Lagen om explosiva och brand farliga varor*) and the Radiation Safety Act (*Strålskyddslagen*).

Furthermore, in order to implement Directives regarding specific products, various laws and regulations have already been made or are being prepared in Sweden. Such specific products are pressure vessels (87/404/EEG), toys (88/378/EEG), building materials (89/106/EEG), electromagnetic interference products (89/336/EEG), machines (89/392/ EEG), personal safety equipment (89/686/EEG), non-automatic scales (90/384/EEG), active implantation products (90/385/EEG), gas equipment (90/396/EEG), tele terminal equipment (91/263/EEG), boilers (92/42/EEG), explosives (93/15/EEG), medical equipment (93/42/EEG), low tension equipment (73/23/EEG), products in explosive surroundings (94/9/EEG) and leisure boats (94/251/EEG).

7   CIVIL LIABILITY FOR DEFECTIVE PRODUCTS BROUGHT ABOUT BY BREACH OF STATUTORY REGULATION DESIGNED TO PROTECT CONSUMERS AND/OR TO PROMOTE SAFETY

7.1   Outline of nature of protective regulations

The specific safety laws and regulations referred to in section 6.5 above normally specify what must be observed regarding the products in question. If such regulations are not observed, criminal sanctions will normally follow in accordance with the provisions expressly laid down in the respective law or regulation. Due to general principles of law (see section 7.3 below), a liability to pay damages for any harm done may also follow.

The Product Safety Law expressly states what measures may be taken against unsafe products or services but does not state any damages or criminal sanctions. Nevertheless, as pointed out in section 6.1 above, criminal sanctions may follow under the Swedish Penal Code. A liability to pay damages might also be a consequence if any harm is done, namely – depending on the circumstanses – under the Tort Liability Act, the Product Liability Law, the Consumer Sales Act or the Consumer Service Act (see section 7.3.2 below).

7.2   Burden of proof

The burden of proof normally rests with the claimant. However, due to the fact that safety requirements often are subject to the specifications and interpretations of the supervising authorities, these authorities have an influence when the Court shall decide whether a statutory regulation on safety has been violated or not. It must be kept in mind that under general principles of Swedish law, ignorance of the actual content of the law is no excuse, even if the applicable regulation is difficult to interpret.

7.3   Nature of liability

7.3.1   *Criminal sanctions*

If Swedish statutory regulations designed to protect consumers and/or to promote safety are not met, such a breach might result in criminal sanctions as laid down in section 6.1 above.

7.3.2   *Damages*

According to the Tort Liability Act damages might follow for harm caused by a criminal offence.

If the breach of a statutory safety regulation results in the product causing personal injury or damage to property, damages might follow under the Product Liability Law irrespective of negligence.

Such a breach of statutory regulations would also – even if not made wilfully – at least be regarded as due to some degree of negligence. Under the Swedish Tort Liability Act personal injury or damage to property, caused wilfully or by negligence, may entitle the person injured/the owner of the property to damages.

Finally, the mandatory provisions of the Swedish Consumer Sale of Goods Act and the Swedish Consumer Service Act (see sections 3.3.2 and 3.3.3, above) expressly state that breach of safety provisions constitutes a defect in goods sold/services rendered and might therefore also involve damages.

CHAPTER XVII

United Kingdom

CHAPTER XVII

England and Wales

Michael Thornton

Laytons
325 Clifton Drive South
Lytham St Annes
Lancashire
FY8 1HN
England

Tel: ++ 1253 782808
Fax: ++ 1253 782153

CHAPTER XVII

England and Wales

1   INTRODUCTION

1.1   Introduction to the law of England and Wales

The United Kingdom of Great Britain and Northern Ireland is not one jurisdiction. The separate jurisdictions of the United Kingdom comprise England and Wales; Scotland; and Northern Ireland. The Isle of Man and the Channel Isles, although associated with the United Kingdom, are separate from it in most respects other than for defence and foreign policy matters. Although the Privy Council (the court which certain Crown colonies and former colonies of the United Kingdom have as an appellate body) is their ultimate Court of Appeal, they are each legally separate jurisdictions both from each other and from the United Kingdom. The body of this chapter deals with the law of England and Wales. The annexes to this Chapter deal with the variations to be found in Scotland and Northern Ireland. The Head of State of the United Kingdom is the Monarch. However, in practice, the political system of the country is that of a parliamentary democracy operated through a bicameral process. The two chambers are known as the House of Commons (lower, elected house) and the House of Lords (upper, non-elected house). The constitution is largely unwritten.

The English civil court system provides for the more important cases to be tried at first instance either in the High Court in London or at regional branches of that court known as district registries, while smaller cases are dealt with in the County courts which are found in most cities and towns. Appeals go to the Civil Division of the Court of Appeal and thereafter to the 'Law Lords' of the House of Lords. While the House of Lords acting as an appellant court sits in the same building as the upper house of the legislature, it comprises only a certain number of the latter who hold office by virtue of having followed a legal career and have then been appointed to the judiciary.

The legal system of England and Wales is based upon two concepts which have come to be interlinked, common law and statute law. The common law has its roots in the early middle ages when judges were despatched from the King's Court to sit in local courts. These judges became known as circuit judges and began the process of adopting the local laws and decisions and out of them creating the certainty of laws which were 'common' to the whole kingdom.

Alongside this common law has developed the legislation passed by monarchs, and later, governments. Today the courts of England and Wales consider both common and statute law as well as the new element of the law of the European Union.

Judges must now decide cases giving precedence to European law, then

statute law and finally decided cases or common law. The English court system is adversarial and relies heavily on oral rather than written evidence.

1.2   Overview of the law relating to defective products in England and Wales

At present in England and Wales there are four areas of law under which manufacturers of goods may have liability imposed on them in respect of producing defective goods. Liability may be imposed by virtue of:

(a) the law of contract and consumer guarantee;
(b) the law of tort;
(c) the law of product safety; and/or
(d) product liability law.

Each of these will be considered in greater detail during the course of this chapter. However, the following is a brief summary of the main principles involved.

1.2.1   Contract

In addition to the contractual terms on which a manufacturer or retailer of goods and the purchaser of such goods agree, legislation also imposes certain conditions (for example, as to quality of goods in consumer contracts) and restricts the ability of the manufacturer or retailer to exclude many such terms. However, the establishment of liability under contract may be difficult because of the doctrine of privity of contract which means that for a party to have either obligations or rights under a contract it is necessary for him to be a party to the contract. So, if a person is injured by defective goods, but does not have a contractual relationship with the manufacturer or retailer, he may find that he does not have a claim under contract law. Where a manufacturer chooses to give a consumer a commercial guarantee, the guarantee must not deprive the consumer of any of the rights he would otherwise have in law. Certain legal provisions relating to consumer guarantees are discussed later.

1.2.2   Tort

This is principally based on the tort of negligence. To establish liability for negligence in the manufacture of goods, the three following factors must be established:

(a) that the manufacturer owed the injured person a 'duty of care' when producing his goods (this is sometimes called in England the 'neighbour' principle);
(b) that the manufacturer failed in this duty of care; and
(c) that, as a result of this failure, the injured person suffered the injury of which he complains.

These three factors can cause an injured party considerable difficulties when seeking to establish a claim that a manufacturer was negligent. Can the injured party show that the manufacturer owed him a duty of care in the circumstances in which the injury occurred? If he can, can the manufacturer then exclude his liability? A further limitation upon the injured party's ability to claim is that damages for purely economic loss may not be recoverable at all. These topics are dealt with in greater detail later in this chapter.

1.2.3   Statute

Manufacturers and suppliers may also have liabilities in respect of defective products because of statute law and regulations made by government departments. Prior to the Consumer Protection Act 1987 which implements the Directive, a large body of safety law had been passed. This body of law makes the statutory provisions relating to defective products some of the most complex in Europe.

Breaches of this body of statute law can lead to claims for damages or criminal penalties. These will be dealt with in detail later in this chapter.

1.3   Definition and classification of terms

In this chapter the following definitions and abbreviations have been used:

CPA 1987	Consumer Protection Act 1967
MR 1967	Misrepresentation Act 1967
UCTA 1977	Unfair Contracts Terms Act 1977
SGA 1979	Sale of Goods Act 1979 (as amended)
QB	Queen's Bench Division
KB	King's Bench Division
AC	Appeal Cases
All ER	All England Law Reports
Build LR	Building Law Reports

2   PRE-CONTRACTUAL LIABILITY

2.1   Effect of pre-contractual matters on the interpretation and extent of the obligations of the parties to a contract

2.1.1   Liability

An agreement for the sale and purchase of goods is likely to arise after negotiations, advertisement or promotion of the goods in which various statements of intention or requirement will be made. Some of these statements may become express terms in the contract, others may not become a part of the contract but may nevertheless have contractual effect as a warranty collateral to the contract if the maker of the statement guarantees or promises that it is true; others still may not have any contractual effect at all but may induce a party to enter into an agreement.

> A representation ... is a statement of fact, express or implied, anterior to the contract, which is intended to and does induce the person to whom it was made to enter into the contract but is not at the time of its making intended as a promise, though it may later become incorporated as a term of the contract. Since a representation is not a promise as such, its falsity cannot constitute a breach of contract. If there is any remedy it must lie in tort or statute.[1]

Thus the legal effect of statements made prior to a contract on the interpretation and extent of the obligations of the parties to that contract depend on whether they were:

1   Roy Goode, '*Commercial Law*' 2nd edn, 1995, Penguin Books.

(a) mere opinions irrelevant to the contract or where there is no grounds to believe the opinion such as advertising slogans of little value or substance, such as 'probably the best beer in the world' which are known as 'mere puffs' or innocent misrepresentation. Such statements if false are not actionable;
(b) statements of fact intended and which do induce a person to whom they have been made, to enter into the contract. Such statements, if false, have their remedy in the tort of misrepresentation;
(c) statements of fact that are incorporated as terms of the contract or as warranties collateral to the contract. Such statements, if incorrect, have their remedy in breach of contract.

Actions based on misrepresentation fall under the headings of:

(a) fraudulent misrepresentation where the law of tort gives a remedy in 'deceit' for fraudulent statements;
(b) negligent misrepresentation where:
   (i) the law of tort gives a remedy in negligence as the mis-statement was given in circumstances where the Defendant owed a duty of care to the Plaintiff; or
   (ii) statute law gives a remedy with a tortious measure of damages under MR 1967, section 2(1) – here, the burden of proof is more favourable to the misled party.
(c) claims for rescission of a contract where the contract has been brought about on a false basis.

2.1.2   *Remedies for pre-contractual liability*

The doctrine of pre-contractual liability is not as well developed in the common law system as in many European civil law systems.

If a misrepresentation is contrary to MR 1967 then the contract is voidable at the option of the party misled, ie the misled party has the right to be restored to the pre-contractual position. This remedy, called rescission, is an equitable remedy which means that it is granted at the court's discretion and will not be granted if the parties cannot be restored to their original position. In addition, CPA 1987 confers upon the injured party the right to damages as well as rescission for fraudulent and negligent misrepresentations. Except in cases of fraud, the court has a discretion to award damages in lieu of rescission.

2.2   Extent that non-disclosure of facts during negotiations may lead to liability

Non-disclosure of facts may constitute a misrepresentation that is actionable in the manner described above either because:

(a) it varies or distorts some positive representation or,
(b) because the contract is one of a class that requires correct and accurate disclosure, as is the case with an insurance contract or where a fiduciary relationship exists between the parties.

Now that the Unfair Terms in Consumer Contracts Regulations 1994 have been implemented in English law, consumer contracts form a class of contract that contain an obligation of good faith on the part of the supplier. Provisions

of the contract excluding liability for non-disclosure or defects would permit the consumer to complain to the Office of Fair Trading and request it to take steps to render the term void. Alternatively, in view of the judgment of the European Court in *Brasserie du Pecheur*[2] it may be that the provisions of the Unfair Contracts Terms Directive have horizontal direct effect (see Chapter 1) and therefore consumers may be able to apply to the courts in England and Wales for declarations that such exclusion or limitation provisions are void as it would be open to competitors of a business imposing such terms to challenge them. Further the Regulations permit a party injured by a breach of the Regulations to bring an action for breach of statutory duty.

2.3 Does pre-contractual liability lie in contract or in tort?

As described in section 2.1 above, pre-contractual liability in English law arises in tort where the misrepresentation is not incorporated in the contract. Where the representation is incorporated in the contract then the liability will be contractual. Where the misrepresentation is one that affects the use to which the product could reasonably be expected to be put, this is relevant in determining whether the product is 'defective' under CPA 1987 in product liability law. Technically, such liability would be for breach of statutory duty but the measure of damages available in such an action is tortious.

2.4 Exclusion of pre-contractual liability

The extent to which a party may exclude or limit his liability for misrepresentation by a provision in a contract is substantially limited, particularly where the contract is with a consumer or in a standard form. Under the Unfair Contract Terms Act 1977, any such provision must satisfy the requirement of reasonableness. Additionally, any such provision in a consumer contract would be subject to the provisions of the Unfair Terms in Consumer Contracts Regulations 1994 implementing the Unfair Contracts Terms Directive. Finally, even in contracts between business people, the English courts have recently held that 'whole agreement' clauses in contracts where the parties confirm they have not been induced to enter into the contract through any representation may be invalid and unenforceable particularly where they exclude liability for fraudulent misrepresentation.[3]

3 LIABILITY IN CONTRACT

3.1 Contract law introduction

A contract for the sale of goods will contain various terms relating to the supply and delivery of the goods. Some will be essential to the contract, others less important. A term may be either expressed by the parties, or implied by statute or custom. In simple sales of consumer articles such as a television set, the express terms will usually relate to the physical characteristics of the goods,

2   (Cases C-46/93 and C-48/93) [1985] CMLR 000.
3   *Thomas Witter Ltd v TBP Industries* [1996] 2 All ER 573.

such as the type, its price, model, colour etc, while the implied terms will relate to the quality and fitness of the goods.

The legal consequences of breach of contractual terms in contracts for the sale of goods are discussed in greater detail below.

A condition is the most important type of term and relates to the main purpose of the contract. A breach of a condition gives rise to the right to treat the contract as at an end and to reject the goods.

A warranty is a less significant term than a condition. If a new motor car had a defective cigarette lighter this would be a breach of a warranty and would only give the buyer the right to claim damages (the cost of repair) and not the right to reject the motor car. However, if a new motor car was supplied without any wheels or an engine that would constitute a breach of condition.

Two interesting cases provide a good illustration as to how the courts categorise a term. In one[4] an actress was to play the leading role in an operetta. She was unable to take up her role until one week after its opening. It was held that her promise to perform was a condition. By contrast, in another case[5] a singer arrived three days late for rehearsals. The theatre company sought to terminate the contract. The court held that the rehearsal clause was subsidiary to the main purpose of the contract and, therefore, a warranty.

In recent years, a third classification, known as an intermediate or innominate term, has appeared. The legal remedies following a breach of an intermediate term will depend upon the consequences of the breach. If the damage suffered is relatively minor and capable of remedy the injured party's claim will be in damages alone. If, however, the damage is more serious the effect will be to treat the breach as a right for the innocent party to terminate the contract.

The disadvantage in English contract law that the ultimate consumer may not be the buyer may be overcome in some circumstances by the device known as 'the collateral contract'. This is what was decided in the case of *Shanklin Pier Ltd v Detel Products Ltd*,[6] the plaintiffs being the owners of an amusement pier at a place called Shanklin in Southern England. The defendants, who were paint manufacturers, assured the plaintiffs, who owned the pier, that their paint was suitable for the pier, so a clause was inserted in the contract for the repair of the pier stipulating that the defendant's paint had to be used. The paint proved unsuitable and the plaintiffs successfully sued the defendants for a breach of warranty in the collateral contract which the court decided existed between the pier company and the paint manufacturers.

3.2 Contractual warranties relating to quality of goods and safety of goods

English law, through various consumer protection statutes, implies into contracts for the sale and supply of goods (including contracts for hire, exchange, and hire purchase) terms relating to title, description, quality, fitness and sale by sample. So far as defective goods are concerned the most important of these will be the implied term of quality and fitness.

---

4   *Poussard v Spiers and Pond* [1876] 1 QBD 410.
5   *Bettini v Gye* [1876] 1 QBD 183.
6   *Shanklin Pier Ltd v Detel Productions Ltd* [1951] 2 KB 854.

3.2.1 Implied condition as to description

Section 13 of SGA 1979 states:

> Where there is a contract for the sale of goods by description there is an implied term that the goods will correspond with the description.

A sale by description takes place where the buyer identifies the goods by reference to their description. A buyer may identify a particular type of refrigerator he wishes to buy, perhaps, by reference to a particular model on display in the shop, or in a catalogue. It might be thought that a contract for specific goods can never be a sale by description as the buyer is purchasing a specific item and not relying upon its description. However, this is not always the case, as is illustrated by the following case.[7]

A buyer, after having inspected it, purchased a car described as a 'Herald convertible white 1961'. Unfortunately, only the back half of the car corresponded with the description as the front was a totally different car which had been welded on to it.

The main difficulty is to know which of the particular statements used to identify and describe the goods form part of the description. It is essentially a question of construction in each case although the courts have construed 'description' widely and, therefore, it may include not only the particular type of goods involved, but also the purpose and use to which the goods might be put as, for example, hair shampoo or baby food.

Once it has been established that there has been a sale by description and what the description attached to the goods is, it is necessary to consider whether the goods correspond with the description or not. As the courts have held:[8] 'if the written contract specifies conditions of weight measurement and the like, those conditions must be complied with. A tonne does not mean about a tonne or a yard about a yard.'

3.2.2 Implied terms as to quality or fitness

The implied terms as to quality and fitness are set out in SGA 1979, section 14 which was recently amended by the Sale and Supply of Goods Act 1994. Section 14(1) provides:

> ... except as provided by this section and section 15 below and subject to any other enactment, there is no implied term about the quality or fitness for any particular purpose of goods supplied under a contract for sale.

Section 14, as now amended, goes on to provide:

> (2)   Where the seller sells goods in the course of a business, there is an implied term that the goods supplied under the contract are of satisfactory quality.
> (2A)   For the purposes of this Act, goods are of satisfactory quality if they meet the standard that a reasonable person would regard as satisfactory, taking account of any description of the goods, the price (if relevant) and all the other relevant circumstances.
> (2B)   For the purposes of this Act, the quality of goods includes their state and condition and the following (among others) are in appropriate cases aspects of the quality of goods-
> (a) fitness for all the purposes for which goods of the kind in question are commonly supplied,

7   *Beale v Taylor* [1967] 1 WLR 1193.
8   *Arcos Ltd v E A Ronaasen & Son* [1933] AC 470.

(b) appearance and finish,
(c) freedom from minor defects,
(d) safety, and
(e) durability.

This section only applies to goods which are supplied 'in the course of a business'. A business is defined so as to include a profession and also the activities of any government department or local or public authority although the goods sold need not be of the type normally sold in that business. So, for instance, if a firm of architects sold some of its office equipment this would be a sale in the course of a business and the term of satisfactory quality would be implied.

SGA 1979 also extends to goods 'supplied under the contract' and therefore includes not only the goods themselves but their packaging, containers and instructions. So even if the goods are not defective the seller may still be in breach of the implied term of satisfactory quality if the packaging is faulty.

Illustrations of the principle are shown in a case[9] where a farmer bought a herbicide to kill wild oats. The instructions for use were misleading. Although on the particular facts of the case there was no breach of the implied condition, the court held that the instructions supplied with goods are one of the factors to be taken into account to determine whether or not there has been a breach of the implied term of quality.

The standard by which goods are assessed to be of satisfactory quality is an objective one, as it turns on what is acceptable to a 'reasonable person'. It is particularly important to note that durability of goods and their safety are factors to be borne in mind in determining the quality of goods supplied. However, the list of matters to be taken into account in determining the quality of the goods is non-exclusive and other features may in certain cases be relevant.

In the *St Albans* case[9a] the downloading of a software program was held not to be a supply of 'goods' within the statutory definition. The court decided, following Lord Pearson in *Trollope & Colls Ltd v North West Metropolitan Regional Hospital Board*[9b] that in the absence of any express term such a contract was subject to an implied term that the program would be reasonably capable of achieving its intended purpose.

3.2.3 *Description and price*

Other factors to be taken into account when determining satisfactory quality are their description and price which, when applied to goods, will have a significant effect on the standard of quality required. These factors take on particular significance when dealing with secondhand goods. Although the same principles will apply to secondhand goods as to new ones, a buyer can hardly expect secondhand goods to be in perfect condition but equally the buyer does not expect them to be useless.

A case illustrates this point.[10] It concerned the sale of a secondhand Mercedes motor car for the price of £14,850. After a few months defects appeared which required repairs at a cost of £635. The court accepted evidence that such faults were rare in a Mercedes car of that age and mileage but, nevertheless, came to the conclusion that the vehicle was merchantable.

9   *Wormell v RHM Agriculture (East)* [1987] 1 WLR 1091.
9a   *St Albans City and District Council v International Computers,* Times (Law Report) 14 August, 1996.
9b   [1973] 1 WLR 601, 609.
10   *Business Application Specialists Ltd v Nationwide Credit Corpn Ltd* (1988) Times, 27 April.

Quite often price can be an indication of the quality of goods expected. A consumer wishing to purchase, say, a television set will have a whole range to choose from – different types, sizes, functions, and so on – but, perhaps, the most important factor will be the price. The buyer expects better quality from the more expensive models and would, quite rightly, have more reason to complain if the picture was not in sharp focus or the sound distorted. Of course, one has to remember that we are all subject to the advertisers' skill to make us believe that because a product is more expensive than its rival it has to be better. This is reinforced by the consumer's own belief that 'you get what you pay for'.

Price may also be relevant to the question, for how long must goods remain of the correct quality. Clearly, goods must be of the correct standard at the time of delivery, but what about products, particularly electrical or household appliances, which initially work satisfactorily then, after a short time, break down? It was said by the House of Lords[11] that goods must remain fit for 'a reasonable time'. How long is 'reasonable' is a question of fact based on the circumstances of each case. Perhaps, as a rule of thumb, more expensive goods will have a greater life expectancy than the cheaper equivalent. Durability of goods is an express matter to be considered in determining if goods are of the correct standard.

3.2.4 Exceptions to the implied term of quality

There are, however, three exceptions to the implied terms of satisfactory quality which are set out in SGA 1979, section 14(2)c, namely:

(a) [as regards defects] specifically drawn to the buyer's attention before the contract is made; or
(b) [if] the buyer examines the goods before the contract is made, [as regards defects] which that examination ought to reveal; [or]
(c) in the case of a contract for sale by sample, which would have been apparent on a reasonable examination of the sample.

The first exception is a matter of common sense and one would not expect a buyer to be able to sue for defects brought to his attention. The use of the word 'specifically' would prevent a seller being able to escape the condition of quality by using such phrases as 'bought as seen'.

The second exception is not so straightforward. The test would appear to be subjective and relates to defects which that particular buyer with his knowledge and ability ought to have discovered, and not, in the case of a motor vehicle, a reasonable mechanic. It can be seen that the provision only relates to examinations carried out, and therefore, if the buyer does not carry out an examination at all the exception cannot apply.

The third exception is also a matter of commonsense.

3.2.5 Implied condition as to fitness for specified purpose

Section 14(3) of SGA 1979 provides:

Where the seller sells goods in the course of a business and the buyer, expressly or by implication, makes known
(a) to the seller, or
(b) where the purchase price or part of it is payable by instalments and the goods were previously sold by a credit-broker to the seller, to that credit broker
any particular purpose for which the goods are being bought, there is an implied

---

11 *Lambert v Lewis* [1982] AC 225.

term that the goods supplied under the contract are reasonably fit for that purpose, whether or not that is a purpose for which such goods are commonly supplied, except where the circumstances show that the buyer does not rely, or that it is unreasonable for him to rely, on the skill or judgment of the seller or credit-broker.'

In cases where the goods have only one purpose then the buyer will normally, by implication, make known the particular purpose to the seller. This is particularly true of consumer transactions where, for instance, a buyer wishing to buy a cooker hardly has to specify to the seller the particular purpose for which the cooker is being bought. Any breach by the seller in this type of case would give rise to a claim both under both section 14(2) and section 14(3) of SGA 1979.

Where, however, section 14(3) of SGA 1979 does become particularly important is where goods have more than one purpose and the buyer requires goods for a particular purpose which is different than, perhaps, the common purpose. An example of this is provided by the case of the lady who bought a tweed coat.[12] She had very sensitive skin and contracted dermatitis after wearing the coat. Unfortunately for the buyer, she did not tell the seller of her condition, and as the coat was fit to be worn by a person with normal skin, her claim failed. Of course, had she made known her condition and then been told it was fit to wear she would have succeeded in her claim.

Once the buyer has made known his particular purpose whether by implication or expressly, then the goods must be reasonably fit for that purpose. Although there is no statutory definition of 'reasonably fit' as there is for 'satisfactory quality', the courts have treated it in the same way, and therefore, for instance in cases concerning secondhand motor cars, the same factors, such as description, price and age would be considered.

As in section 14(2) of SGA 1979 there is an exception to the implied condition and that is where the buyer does not rely, or it is unreasonable for him to rely, upon the seller's judgment.

So if the goods are made to a specification provided by the buyer he can hardly complain if the goods are not fit for their purpose if the fault lies in the specification, but if the fault is due to some part of the specification left to the seller's skill and judgment, such as a manufacturing process, the buyer can complain about the goods' lack of fitness for purpose. In a case which involved two propellers to be made according to the specification of the buyer, certain matters, such as the thickness of the blades, were left to the seller's skill and judgment, which proved to be inadequate. The court found that the seller was in breach of the implied condition as to fitness.[13]

3.2.6 Implied condition as to sale by sample

SGA 1979, section 15 provides:

'(1)   A contract of sale is a contract for sale by sample where there is an express or implied term to that effect in the contract.
(2)   In the case of a contract for sale by sample there is an implied term:
(a)   that the bulk will correspond with the sample in quality;
(b)   that the goods will be free from any defect, making their quality unsatisfactory which would not be apparent on reasonable examination of the sample.

12   *Griffiths v Peter Conway Ltd* [1939] 1 All ER 685.
13   *Cammell Laird Co Ltd v Manganese Bronze & Glass Co Ltd* [1934] AC 402.

Sale by sample is relatively rare in consumer transactions, an example would be where one chooses a suit of clothing from a book of sample cloths or wallpaper from a book of sample wallpapers.

3.2.7   Conditions implied by custom of trade

Terms may be implied by a local custom or usage of a particular trade. Although this is a general principle which affects all contracts SGA 1979, section 14(4) gives it statutory recognition for contracts for sale by providing that: 'an implied condition or warranty about quality or fitness for a particular purpose may be annexed to a contract of sale by usage.

3.2.8   Commercial practice in giving consumer guarantees

While there is considerable variation in the practice of giving commercial guarantees by manufacturers, suppliers and retailers, the following broad description applies to the voluntary contractual guarantees as opposed to the legal guarantees that are given:

(a) manufacturers frequently give guarantees with their products. These appear on a card or the packaging. The manufacturer often guarantees to repair or replace the product if it is found to be defective within, say, twelve months;

(b) some retailers give similar guarantees to those described above as being given by manufacturers;

(c) so far as services are concerned, repairs to consumer products are frequently guaranteed against defects for twelve months, although longer guarantees are often given in respect of work done to domestic premises especially where they have undergone treatment for woodworm or have had a damp-proof course inserted;

(d) finally, consumers may be sold what are called 'extended guarantees' in relation to consumer durable goods whereby in return for what is quite a large fee, failures in the product will be repaired over, say, five years.

3.2.9   Legal provisions regulating the form and content of consumer guarantees

Where a commercial guarantee is given, it must specify that the rights given to the consumer by the guarantee do not limit or affect the consumer's legal rights. Criminal sanctions apply for non-compliance. Enforcement of the law is carried out by Local Trading Standards Departments.

3.3   Breach of contract for supply of defective products

3.3.1   Types of defect

Generally, the types of defect which will be held to infringe SGA 1979, section 14 are those which will render the goods supplied not to be of satisfactory quality as described above.

3.3.2   Buyer's rights: rejection

As we have already seen, a term may be classified as either a condition, a warranty or an intermediate term. A buyer's rights following a breach of contract depends upon which type of term has been breached.

Under SGA 1979 the implied terms as to quality and fitness are classified as conditions any breach of which enables the buyer to treat the breach as a repudiation which allows him to reject the goods; or, alternatively, he can affirm the contract, keep the goods and claim damages.

The right to reject the goods in the event of a breach of a condition is limited by section 11(4) of SGA 1979 which provides:

> Where a contract of sale is not severable, and the buyer has accepted the goods or part of them, the breach of any condition to be fulfilled by the seller can only be treated as a breach of warranty, and not as a ground for rejecting the goods and treating the contract as repudiated, unless there is an express or implied term of the contract to that effect.

It can be seen from this subsection that a buyer loses his right of rejection if he has accepted the goods.

The right to reject the goods is further restricted pursuant to section 15A of SGA 1979 where the buyer is not a consumer and the breach is so slight that it would be unreasonable for the buyer to do so.

If the contract is able to be split into smaller contracts, such as the delivery and payment of goods by instalments, then acceptance of one or more of the instalments will not stop a buyer from rejecting future instalments but if the contract cannot be severed in this way then acceptance of any part of the goods will stop the buyer from rejecting them. So, for example, if a buyer agrees to purchase a vehicle to be delivered in parts for assembly by the buyer, acceptance of some of the parts will prevent the buyer from rejecting the vehicle if some of the parts subsequently delivered are defective.

Acceptance is dealt with by section 35(1) of SGA 1979:

> The buyer is deemed to have accepted the goods (subject to subsection (2)) below:
>
> (a) when he intimates to the seller that he has accepted them; or
> (b) when the goods have been delivered to him and he does any act in relation to them which is inconsistent with the ownership of the seller.

There are three points that arise from the methods of acceptance:

i   Intimation of acceptance   It is uncertain exactly how a buyer can accept goods in this way. It may be that a buyer who signs a note on delivery which acknowledges that the goods conform with the contract intimates acceptance, although this is probably doubtful; or where a buyer returns faulty goods to the seller for repair. SGA 1979, section 35(2) now provides that:

> (2)   Where goods are delivered to the buyer, and he has not previously examined them, he is not deemed to have accepted them under subsection (1) above until he has had a reasonable opportunity of examining them for the purpose:
>
> (a) of ascertaining whether they are in conformity with the contract; and
> (b) in the case of a contract for a sale by sample, of comparing the bulk with the sample.

This means that an acceptance note can mean no more than that the goods have been delivered.

ii   An act inconsistent with the seller's ownership   This method of acceptance is subject to section 34 of SGA 1979:

> Unless otherwise agreed, when the seller tenders delivery of the goods to the buyer, he is bound, on request, to afford the buyer a reasonable opportunity of examining

the goods for the purpose of ascertaining whether they are in conformity with the contract and, in the case of a contract for sale by sample, of comparing the bulk with the sample.

A difficulty with SGA 1979, section 35 is that in the majority of cases ownership of the goods passes at the time the contract is made and, therefore, at the time of delivery the goods belong to the buyer and it is difficult to see how any act by the buyer can affect the seller's ownership. The only apparent explanation, and one which has some judicial support, is that the buyer loses his right to reject if he does any act which would affect the seller's ownership if those goods were revested in the seller.

iii Lapse of a reasonable time This method of acceptance has caused more disputes than any other method. Obviously, the difficulty is what is meant by a 'a reasonable time'. The SGA states that what is a reasonable time is a question of fact. After what is seen to be an unreasonable time the burden of proof shifts to the buyer to show that the delay was reasonable. Clearly, the longer the buyer keeps the goods the less likely he will be able to reject them. Goods such as fruit and vegetables will have a relatively short life span, and for a buyer to reject such goods he will have to act very quickly. Others, such as motor vehicles or electrical goods, have a much greater life expectancy and it is this type of case which has caused the most difficulty.

Does the word 'reasonable' in section 35 relate to the time to inspect the goods or to the time to discover the defect? The answer was provided in a case involving a motor car. The court held that the buyer had lost his right to reject having driven it for 140 miles since a 'reasonable time' meant sufficient time to give the vehicle a general try out. The court made the point that what is reasonable will depend upon the nature and function of the goods. The more complex the intended function of the goods is, the longer the buyer will have to reject the goods. What does seem clear is that in the majority of consumer transactions the buyer does not have a great deal of time in which to try out the goods and, if faulty, reject them.

3.3.3 Causation and damages

Before a buyer can succeed in a claim for damages arising out of a breach of contract he must show that the product was defective and that the defect was the cause of the damage suffered. There must be a direct link between the defect and the damage. This is known as the chain of causation and any break in the chain by, for example, an intervening event, will prevent a buyer from succeeding.

In the case of *Grant v Australian Knitting Mills Ltd*[14] a buyer purchased a pair of underpants and later contracted dermatitis after wearing them. It was discovered that an excess of a particular chemical had been allowed to remain in the garment. The seller argued that the attack of dermatitis was not caused by the wearing of the garment but was a pre-existing condition. The court found that the wearing of the garment was the cause of the dermatitis.

The longer the period between the sale of the goods and the damage occurring the harder it will be for the buyer to prove the damage was caused by a defect in the goods present at the time of delivery.

i Remoteness of damage Even if the buyer can prove a causal link between the damage caused and the defect in the goods the seller will not be liable for

14   *Grant v Australian Knitting Mills Ltd* [1936] AC 85.

all the loss which the buyer may suffer. A simple breach of contract may trigger off a series of events each linked with each other causing immense damage.

The general principle was laid down in the case of *Hadley v Baxendale*:[15]

Where two parties have made a contract which one of them has broken, the damages which the other party ought to receive in respect of such breach of contract would be calculated as such sum as may fairly and reasonably be considered either arising naturally, ie according to the usual course of things from such breach of contract itself, or such as may reasonably be supposed to have been in the contemplation of both parties, at the time they made the contract, as the probable result of the breach of it.

This has become known as the rule in *Hadley v Baxendale*. The rule has two parts to it:

(a) loss which flows naturally as a result of the breach; and
(b) loss which although it might not be a natural consequence of the breach was contemplated by the parties as likely in the event of a breach.

A look at some of the cases will illustrate the two parts of the rule.

In the *Hadley v Baxendale* case, the plaintiff claimed loss of profits following the late delivery of a crankshaft which meant the plaintiff's mill could not operate. The court had to decide whether to include loss of profits in awarding damages for breach of contract.

The court held that the loss of profit was not a consequence which was foreseeable at the time of the contract. The court found that the plaintiff could not rely upon the second limb of the rule as the special circumstance was not communicated to the defendant, so the loss was not in the contemplation of the parties at the time the contract was made.

ii Damage recoverable   The types of damage recoverable in practice are:

(a) Damage to property: this will include not only the cost of repair or replacement of the product itself but also damage caused to any other property.
(b) Personal injury to the buyer: If the goods cause personal injury to the buyer then he will be able to recover damages for the injuries caused by the goods.
(c) Economic loss not related to any physical damage to property or person, eg loss of profits.

3.4 Quantum of damages

A buyer may have an action against a seller for damages for non-delivery of the goods. With respect to delivered goods, which are defective, a buyer can either reject the goods, if that option is still open to him, or keep the goods and sue the seller for damages. On the other hand, a seller may have a claim against the buyer for non-acceptance.

The measure of damages in respect of non-delivery and non-acceptance of goods is laid down in ss 50 and 51 of SGA 1979 and is framed in similar terms. It is:

...the estimated loss directly and naturally resulting in the ordinary course of events ... from the buyer's breach of contract.

15   *Hadley v Baxendale* [1854] 9 Exch 341.

Take, for example, the case where a seller has agreed to sell and deliver to a buyer a box of soap at a contract price of £12 a box but fails to deliver the soap on the agreed date by which time the market price has risen to £15. The buyer can recover as damages for non-delivery the difference between the contract price and the market price, in this example £3 a box. If the market price falls below the contract price the buyer will still have a claim for damages for non-delivery but it will only be for nominal damages.

Where the seller is late in delivering goods bought for the buyer's own use, damages will be the additional costs incurred by the buyer as a result of the delay. Where the goods are bought to be resold the damage will be the difference between the market price when the goods ought to have been delivered and the market price when the goods were, in fact, delivered.

The seller's measure of damages for non-acceptance, although framed in the same terms as non-delivery, is given a different interpretation by the courts. In a case where[16] the buyers wrongfully refused to accept a motor vehicle from the sellers who were car dealers, the sellers were able to return the vehicle to the manufacturer but sued the buyer for their loss of profit on the sale. The buyer contended that as the market price, set by the manufacturer, was the same as the contract price, the seller was only entitled to nominal damages. The court held that the seller was entitled to his loss of profit on the transaction. This case can be contrasted with another[17] where the court came to the opposite view and only awarded the seller nominal damages. The rationale between the two decisions appears to be that in the first case supply of the particular vehicle exceeded demand whilst in the latter case there was an adequate supply of vehicles and no shortage of buyers.

The buyer's remedy for breach of warranty is set out in section 53 of SGA 1979.

> (1) Where there is a breach of warranty by the seller, or where the buyer elects (or is compelled) to treat any breach of a condition on the part of the seller as a breach of warranty, the buyer is not by reason only of such breach of warranty entitled to reject the goods; but he may:
>
> (a) set up against the seller the breach of warranty in diminution or extinction of the price; or
> (b) maintain an action against the seller for damages for the breach of warranty.
>
> (2) The measure of damages for breach of warranty is the estimated loss directly and naturally resulting, in the ordinary course of events, from the breach of warranty.
> (3) In the case of breach of warranty of quality such loss is prima facie the difference between the value of the goods at the time of delivery to the buyer and the value they would have had if they had fulfilled the warranty.

With respect to breaches of warranty of quality (which, confusingly, means breaches of condition of quality but where the buyer elects or is compelled to carry on with the contract) the measure of damages under SGA 1979, section 53 is the difference between the value of goods actually delivered and the value of the goods without the faults. In simple consumer sales the difference between the value of the goods delivered and the actual value of the goods will be an amount equal to the cost of putting the defect right.

16 *W L Thompson Ltd v Robinson (Gunmakers) Ltd* [1955] Ch 177.
17 *Charter v Sullivan* [1957] 2 QB 117.

In addition, the buyer is entitled to recover consequential loss, subject, as we have already seen, to the principle of remoteness. So, for instance, in the case of *Grant v Australian Knitting Mills* discussed above the buyer was able to recover damages for personal injury as a consequence of the underwear being of the wrong quality. The English courts are becoming more willing to award damages for inconvenience and disappointment although, in general, this will only be in consumer cases. As an example a buyer recovered damages for disappointment and general inconvenience for a ruined holiday caused by the continual breakdown of the buyer's new motor vehicle.[18]

In a commercial contract where the goods are brought for the purposes of making a profit and the goods fall below the warranted performance, the buyer must choose whether to claim damages for the difference in value between the goods supplied and goods conforming to the contract or loss of profit.

3.4.1　Mitigation

As a general rule the injured party must take reasonable steps to mitigate or lessen his loss. If he fails to do so then the defendant will only be liable for the loss the plaintiff would have suffered had he mitigated his loss. This was illustrated in a case[19] where an employee's contract of employment was terminated following a reorganisation. The employers offered him new employment on the same terms but the employee rejected their offer. The court held that he failed to mitigate his loss by unreasonably refusing to accept their offer of employment.

3.5　Burden of proof

As will be seen later, one of the principle advantages of bringing a claim for defective products in contract rather than tort, is that once it has been shown that the goods are not of the right quality or fitness he need not go on and show fault on the part of the seller. The seller's liability is strict: the seller has no defence to argue that it was not his fault.

3.6　Exclusion of liability

3.6.1　Position at common law

A seller may attempt to escape or limit liability by the insertion of an exclusion clause into the contract. Such a clause seeks to limit, exclude or modify a liability arising out of a breach of a contractual obligation.

To be valid an exclusion clause must be incorporated into the contract. Although this might seem an obvious point not all terms of a contract are contained in a single written document, and many of the cases involving exclusion clauses focus on whether the exclusion clause is incorporated into the contract. In one case[20] where the plaintiff stayed at the defendant's hotel, on the back of the door in his room was a notice which read:

> The proprietors will not hold themselves responsible for articles lost or stolen unless handed in to the manageress for safe custody.

18　*Jackson v Chrysler Acceptances Ltd, Minories Garages Ltd (Third Party)* [1978] RTR 474.
19　*Brace v Calder* [1895] 2 QB 253.
20　*Olley v Marlborough Court Ltd* [1949] 1 KB 532.

Owing to the negligence of the hotel staff the plaintiff's furs were stolen. The defendant sought to rely upon the exclusion clause to avoid liability contending that the clause was incorporated into the contract by notice. The court held that the contract was made at the reception desk, and as the clause had not been brought to the plaintiff's notice before or at the time that the contract was made, they could not rely upon it.

As notice may be given either before or at the time the contract was made, it is particularly important to know exactly when the contract is made. In *Thornton v Shoe Lane Parking Ltd*[1] the plaintiff drove his motor vehicle up to an automatic barrier at the entrance to a car park. The machine produced a ticket and the plaintiff drove in and parked his vehicle. Upon his return he was injured through the negligence of the owners of the car park. The defendants sought to rely upon a notice on the ticket which read: 'issued subject to conditions displayed on the premises'. Just inside the car park was a notice displaying lengthy conditions, one of which said the owners would not be responsible for injury to customers. The court concluded that notice of the conditions came after the contract was made.

One of the relevant factors in determining whether sufficient notice has been given is the type of document in which the exclusion clause appears.

For example, a cloakroom ticket would not normally have conditions printed on it and therefore any conditions printed on the reverse might not be sufficient.

This is illustrated by a case[2] where the plaintiff hired a deck chair and received a ticket in return. The ticket contained an exclusion clause which the defendant sought to rely upon to escape liability to the plaintiff for injury caused by the defendant's negligence. The court was of the view that the ticket was simply a receipt and not a contractual document where one would expect to find printed conditions.

Once the seller had overcome the hurdle of incorporation, he still has to face the court's strict interpretation of whether the clause covered the type of breach which the seller had committed and was seeking to avoid liability for. A clause excluding liability for implied terms will not cover express terms; a clause excluding liability for breach of warranty will not cover a breach of conditions. The courts have generally strained to construe exclusion clauses so as to prevent a seller from escaping liability.

3.6.2 Statutory controls

i UCTA 1977 The need for the court to safeguard the consumer from oppressive exclusion clauses has, to a large extent, been taken over by statute through the enactment of UCTA 1977 and later by the Unfair Terms in Consumer Contracts Regulations 1994, but it will still be necessary to have regard to the existing case law. A party seeking to rely upon an exclusion clause will first have to show the clause has been incorporated into the contract and, on a true construction, covers the breach which has occurred. Perhaps the only difference is that the court no longer needs to rely upon strained constructions to defeat an unreasonable exclusion clause because, once the clause has survived both common law tests, it then has to meet the requirements of UCTA 1977.

---

1   *Thornton v Shoe Lane Parking Ltd* [1971] 2 QB 163.
2   *Chapelbon v Barry Urban District Council* [1940] 1 KB 532.

UCTA 1977 was passed to control the effectiveness of exclusion clauses. In some cases liability cannot be excluded or restricted by reference to a term in the contract and in others it can only be excluded or restricted if it is 'reasonable' as defined in the Act. Certain contracts are specially excluded, such as international supply contracts, contracts of insurance and contracts of employment.

ii   Sale and hire purchase   So far as contracts for the sale of goods and hire purchase are concerned, section 6 of UCTA 1977 is the most important section. As against a 'Consumer', a seller cannot exclude or restrict liability for breach of the obligations arising from sections 12-15 of SGA 1979 dealing with implied conditions as to the vendor's right to sell, that the goods correspond with their description, are of 'merchantable quality' and fit for their intended purpose, and correspondence with any samples. As against a 'non-consumer' a seller cannot exclude or restrict his obligation under section 12 for having to have the right to sell and can only exclude or restrict his obligations under sections 13-15 dealing with the aforementioned if the clause is reasonable according to the standard laid down in UCTA 1977. A 'consumer' in UCTA 1977 is given an extended meaning by section 12(1):

> A party to a contract 'deals as consumer' in relation to another party if:
> (a) he neither makes the contract in the course of a business nor holds himself out as doing so; and
> (b) the other party does make the contract in the course of a business; and
> (c) in the case of a contract governed by the law of sale of goods . . . the goods passing under or in pursuance of the contract are of a type ordinarily supplied for private use or consumption.

Consider the following three examples:

(a) a firm of solicitors buys an ordinary domestic electric kettle for use in their staff kitchen;
(b) a car enthusiast buys a secondhand classic sports car from his neighbour;
(c) a private individual (keen on home improvements) buys a large quantity of materials from a builder's merchant to build an extension to his house.

Which of the above examples is a 'consumer' deal?

Certainly the first is a 'consumer' deal. Although it is a purchase by a business it is not in the course of business and the goods in question are of a type ordinarily supplied for private use. The courts have defined a purchase to be 'in the course of a business' if it was an 'integral part of the business'.

The second example above is not a consumer deal as neither party makes the contract in the course of business.

The third example is the most difficult to categorise. Clearly, the materials are sold 'in the course of business' but section 12(1)(c) of SGA 1979 would probably prevent it from being a 'consumer' deal as the goods are not of a type normally sold for private use. It is a question of degree; no doubt, the purchase of a handful of small nails from the same builder's merchant would be a 'consumer' deal.

iii   Liability arising in contract   Section 3 of UCTA 1977 controls liability in contract generally. It provides:

> (1)   . . . as between contracting parties where one of them deals as consumer or on the other's written standard terms of business.

(2)　　　　As against that party, the other cannot by reference to any contract term

(a)　when himself in breach of contract, exclude or restrict any liability of his in respect of the breach; or

(b)　claim to be entitled–

　　(i)　to render a contractual performance substantially different from that which was reasonably expected of him, or

　　(ii)　in respect of the whole or any part of his contractual obligation, to render no performance at all except in so far as ... the contract term satisfies the requirement of reasonableness.

This section applies, not only to contracts of sale and hire purchase, as does section 6 of UCTA 1977, but to all types of contracts (except those specifically excluded from the Act). Furthermore, it applies where one person deals as 'consumer' or on the other's written standard terms of business. It is, therefore, wide enough to include, not only a 'consumer' sale, but also a commercial transaction where the contract is based on one of the party's written standard terms.

The control imposed by section 3 of UCTA 1977 is twofold:

(a) a party cannot, by reference to a contract term, unless such term is reasonable, when in breach, exclude or restrict his liability; and

(b) claim to be entitled to render a performance substantially different from that which was expected, or, render no performance at all in respect of any part of his obligation.

It will be seen that the second part of sub-s 3(2)(b)(ii) of UCTA 1977 (above) does not require a party to be in breach of contract, but that a party claims to be able to perform the contract in a manner different than was agreed.

iv　The reasonableness test Where a contract term is required to satisfy the requirements of reasonableness, the test is laid down in section 11 of UCTA 1977.

In relation to a contract term generally section 11(1) of UCTA 1977 provides:

... the term shall have been a fair and reasonable one to be included having regard to the circumstances which were, or ought reasonably to have been, known to or in the contemplation of the parties when the contract was made.

In addition to the general test of section 11(1) of UCTA 1977, particular attention is to be paid to the matters referred to in Schedule 2 of UCTA 1977 when considering an exclusion clause in a contract for sale or supply; they are:

(a) the strength of the bargaining position of the parties relative to each other, taking into account (amongst other things) alternative means by which the customer's requirements could have been met;

(b) whether the customer received an inducement to agree to the term, or in accepting it had an opportunity of entering into a similar contract with other persons, but without having to accept a similar term;

(c) whether the customer knew or ought reasonably to have known of the existence and extent of the term (having regard, amongst other things, to any custom of the trade and any previous course of dealing between the parties);

(d) where the term excludes or restricts any relevant liability if some condition is not complied with, whether it was reasonable at the time of the contract to expect that compliance with that condition would be practicable:

(e) whether the goods were manufactured, processed or adapted to the special order of the customer.

The highest English Court of Appeal, the House of Lords, had the opportunity of considering the criteria in the case of *George Mitchell (Chesterhall) Ltd v Finney Lock Seeds Ltd*.[3] The facts were: a seed merchant agreed to sell to a farmer 30lbs of 'Finney Late Dutch special cabbage seed'. The seed supplied was, in fact, a variety of cabbage seeds and of poor quality. The farmer sued for damages and the sellers relied upon a clause of the contract restricting their liability to the price of the seed itself and contended that the clause was fair and reasonable. The court decided that the clause was unreasonable, making it quite clear that the relative strength of each party's bargaining position had played an important part in their decision.

If the court considers the clause to be unreasonable they will not substitute a reasonable clause in its place but will strike out the offending clause.

In the *St Albans* case[3a] a contract seeking to limit liability for damages arising from the supply of equipment, programs and services to £100,000, was held to be unresonable.

v   Unfair Terms in Consumer Contracts Regulations 1994   These regulations seek to implement the Unfair Contracts Terms Directive (93/13/EEC) that should have been implemented by 1 January 1995. The regulations, however, state that they only came into effect from 1 July 1995. It remains to be seen if any claims will arise against the British Government for delay in implementing the Directive under the principal of Vertical Direct Effect (see chapter 1, page 00).

Claims under the regulations by a consumer against a supplier for breach of the regulations would be for breach of statutory duty. It may be that from 1 January 1995 claims by consumers against manufacturers would also arise due to the principal of Horizontal Direct effect (see chapter 1, page 00) as set out in the decision of the European Court of Justice in *Brasserie du Pecheur*. The regulations also permit the Director General of Fair Trading to procure injunctions against persons using or recommending unfair terms on receipt of bona fide complaints from the public.

3.7   Limitation period

The right to bring an action for breach of contract does not last indefinitely. Statute imposes limitations: the principal statutes are the Limitation Act 1980 and the Latent Damage Act 1986.

For a contract which is not under seal or expressed to be by way of deed, an action must be brought within six years from the date the cause of action arose. On a contract under seal, or expressed to be by way of deed, this time is extended to twelve years from when the cause of action arose.

In an action based on contract the cause of action accrues when the breach occurs and not when the plaintiff suffers damage.

The courts have decided that where there is a continuing breach the latest date can be taken. Thus, in a case concerning a building contract,[4] engineers were engaged to design and supervise the construction of a building. The work was completed in 1978 and in 1982 the plaintiffs brought an action for faulty design. The engineers claimed that the action was statute-barred as the breach relating to the design occurred more than six years before the action was begun.

3   *George Mitchell (Chesterhall) Ltd v Finney Lock Seeds Ltd* [1983] 2 All ER 337.
3a   *St Albans City & District Council v International Computers*, Times (Law Report) 14 August, 1996.
4   *Chelmsford District Council v T J Evers* [1984] 25 Build LR 99.

The court held that the engineers' duties in respect of the design and supervision were a continuing contractual obligation and, therefore, the six years would not have started to run until 1978.

3.8   Liability for third parties

Generally, liability for third parties' acts cannot be excluded, although it is often sought to be excluded in respect of acts of employees or agents.

4   LIABILITY IN TORT

4.1   Introduction

From the section above dealing with English contract law it can be readily seen that only a party to a contract can sue upon that contract. Consequently, many people who suffer harm caused by a defective product do not have a remedy in contract. Take the following examples:

(a) A buys an electric toaster and gives it to B as a gift. The toaster blows up causing damage to B's property.
(b) A buys a bottle of lemonade and gives the bottle to B to drink it. Unknown to both, a decomposed snail had found its way into the bottle during the manufacturing process. B becomes violently ill.

In both examples B would not have a remedy in contract and unless he were able to sue under a manufacturer's guarantee, his only remedies would lie in tort and product liability.

4.2   Outline of tort law in England

4.2.1   Negligence

To meet the rising need for better consumer protection from defective and unsafe products in an age of increasing mechanisation and industrialisation there developed an area of law known as the tort of negligence. Surprisingly, it was not until 1932 that the House of Lords came to a landmark decision in a Scottish case to be applied in English law. In the case of *Donoghue v Stevenson*,[5] the tort of negligence was recognised in its own right as a separate tort. The importance of this decision lay in the fact that it was the first time that the courts had attempted to formulate a principle for universal application for liability in negligence which could be used in all situations and, at the same time, remain flexible to suit the changing needs of society. This principle became known as the 'neighbour principle'.

Mrs Donoghue was bought a bottle of ginger beer by a friend. She drank some of the contents and allegedly found the remains of a decomposed snail. It was held that:

> A manufacturer of products which he sells in such a form has to show that he intends them to reach the ultimate consumer in the form in which they left him with no reasonable possibility of intermediate examination, and with the knowledge

5   *Donoghue v Stephenson* [1932] AC 562.

that the absence of reasonable care in the preparation or putting up of the products will result in an injury to the consumer's life or property, owes a duty to the consumer to take reasonable care.

The breakthrough in the case was that the decision did not simply add manufacturer and consumer to the list of relationships which involved a duty to take care, but that it laid down a principle much wider than the facts of the case which could be used as a test in all cases to determine whether a duty of care exists or not:

> You must take reasonable care to avoid acts or omissions which you can reasonably foresee would be likely to injure your neighbour. Who, then, in law, is my neighbour? The answer seems to be – persons who are so closely and directly affected by my act that I ought reasonably to have them in contemplation as being so affected when I am directing my mind to the acts or omissions which are called in question.

In order to succeed in establishing liability in negligence, the plaintiff must show:

(a) the existence of a duty of care;
(b) breach of that duty; and
(c) consequential damage which is not too remote.

Once a duty of care has been established it is a question of fact whether the defendant has breached that duty by falling below the standard of care required. The legal standard is not that of the defendant himself but of a reasonable man using ordinary care and skill.

4.2.2   Warnings

In relation to the supply of goods, a manufacturer owes a duty to take reasonable care in their design and manufacture, and in providing adequate warnings so as not to cause injury to the buyer or his property provided the manufacturer has sold the goods in such a manner as to show that he intended them to reach the user in the form in which it left him without any reasonable prospect of an intermediate examination which would reveal any defects. A manufacturer may be in breach of his duty if a warning on the goods on how to use the product is misleading or, simply, inadequate. A good example of this is provided by the case[6] where the defendant sold ampoules of a chemical which were marked 'harmful vapour'. The chemical came into contact with water and an explosion occurred. The manufacturer was found to be in breach of his duty to take reasonable care as the ampoules should have been marked with a specific warning of the dangers of an explosion occurring. The warning given was clearly inadequate.

4.2.3   Product recall

A design defect may become apparent after the manufacturer has sold his product and, in some cases, it may affect hundreds of buyers as, for instance, where a new model of motor vehicle is recalled due to a design fault being discovered. Provided the design fault itself was not as a result of the manufacturer's failure to take reasonable care, whether he is in breach of duty or not will depend upon what steps he takes after becoming aware of the fault. In the case of *Walton v British Leyland*[7] a motor car manufacturer was found to be negligent for failing to properly warn all people who came into contact with their defective products. In that case

6   *Vacwell Engineering Co Ltd v BDH Chemicals* [1969] 3 All ER 1681.
7   Times, 12 July 1978.

the manufacturer was aware of a defect that caused the rear wheels of some of its cars to fall off. While they warned the dealers they didn't warn the drivers. The court found not only the manufacturer should have warned the public but they should have recalled the cars. Clearly both the greater the likelihood of the damage being caused by the defect and the greater the extent of the damage occurring if the defect does arise the greater the duty to warn and to withdraw the product or to take other steps to prevent harm from occurring by whatever steps are possible.

4.2.4 Exemplary damages

In cases of severe disregard for safety or recklessness claims for exemplary damages may lie against the reckless party.

4.3 Causation

4.3.1 'But for' test

It has to be shown that the product was defective when it was put into circulation, and the manufacturer's breach caused the damage suffered. In a large number of cases this is by far the most difficult problem faced by the buyer. It was said by the court in *Donoghue v Stevenson* that the manufacturer's responsibility ceases once he no longer has control over the product. The burden of proof, as will be seen later, is on the buyers to prove the manufacturer's action or omission caused, or contributed to, the damage. The legal test adopted by the courts is the 'but for' test; in other words: the damage would not have occurred 'but for' the manufacturer's breach of duty to take care.

In one case[8] an employee had been injured in an accident at work. His employers had been in breach of their duty in not providing a safety belt which could have prevented the accident. However, the action failed because he could not prove, on a balance of probabilities, that he would have worn the belt if it had been supplied.

The principle decided by the court is that the burden is on the plaintiff to prove that the defendant's actions or omissions caused the harm suffered, which means that causation will be the major stumbling block for a plaintiff trying to pursue a claim in negligence.

4.3.2 Nova causa interveniens

The chain of causation between breach of duty of care and damage caused may be broken by the wrongful act of another person.

An example of an act which breaks the chain of causation is found in a case[9] where the plaintiff sustained a leg injury due to the defendant's negligence. The plaintiff attempted to climb down stairs without assistance which was nearby. The court refused to hold the defendant liable for the plaintiff's further injury because his act intervened.

4.3.3 Contributory negligence

If the plaintiff has contributed in some way to the damage suffered his claim will not be defeated but any damages recoverable will be reduced according to his share of the blame.

---

8 *McWilliams v Arrol Ltd* [1962] 1 WLR 295.
9 *McKew v Holland & Hannen & Cubitts (Scotland) Ltd* [1969] 3 All ER 1621.

The plaintiff's negligence is so great it may be a *nova causa interveniens* if it is held to be very significant.

4.4   Remoteness of loss and damage

The basic principle of remoteness is to be found in the decision of the court in *The Wagon Mound*.[10] A defendant who is in breach of his duty to take care will be liable for the damage that was reasonably foreseeable as likely to happen at the time the breach occurred. It is not the exact damage which has to be foreseen, but the type of harm generally. The court in another case[11] put it this way: 'It is not necessary that the precise concatenation of circumstances should be envisaged. If the consequence was one within the general range which any reasonable person might foresee then it is within the rule that a person ... is liable for the consequences.'

In other words, what is needed then is to foresee the general type of harm as a result of a breach of duty to take care, but not, necessarily, the exact harm.

Whilst the principle, itself, may be clear, a look at the cases reveals a difficulty in applying the principle. In one case[12] a boy aged eight tripped over a paraffin lamp and fell into a hole left unattended by the defendant, and the boy suffered severe burns as a result of an explosion. Although it could not be foreseen that the lamp would explode, nevertheless the House of Lords held the defendant liable for the boy's injuries as they had created a foreseeable risk of injury by burning which was sufficiently similar in nature to the harm suffered.

4.5   Quantum of damage

Since the *Donoghue v Stevenson* decision it has been established that a manufacturer who puts into circulation a defective product will be liable in negligence for personal injury or damage to property which the product causes, but will not be liable in tort for any defect in the product itself.

The product is either capable of repair or it is worthless. In either case the loss is purely economic and is normally only recoverable in contract. 'Pure economic loss' is a term used to describe loss which occurs independently of any other physical damage either to the plaintiff or his property and is only recoverable in tort for negligent misstatement under the principles set out in the case of *Hedley Byrne v Heller*[13] or where there is a special relationship or proximity between the plaintiff and defendant.[14]

This principle that economic loss cannot be claimed in tort has been firmly established in a variety of recent cases.[15]

---

10   *The Wagon Mound* [1961] AC 388.
11   *Stewart v West African Terminals Ltd* [1964] 2 Lloyd's Rep 371, CA.
12   *Hughes v Lord Advocate* [1963] 2 WLR 779.
13   *Hedley Byrne v Heller* [1964] AC 465.
14   *Junior Books Ltd v Veitchi Co Ltd* [1983] AC 520.
15   *Muirhead v Industrial Tank Specialities Ltd* [1986] QB 507; *Murphy v Brentwood District Council* [1990] 3 WLR 414; *Department of the Environment v Thomas Bates & Son Ltd* [1990] 3 WLR 457.

4.6 Burden of proof

The burden of proof in an action for negligence rests primarily on the plaintiff which, in a claim for defective products, means that the plaintiff must show that a product was defective at the time it left the control of the manufacturer and that the defect in the product was the cause of the plaintiff's loss or damage. In *Donoghue v Stevenson* the manufacturer was treated as being in control of the ginger beer bottle until such time as it was opened by the customer. This difficulty increases for the plaintiff the longer the time between when the manufacturer puts the goods into circulation and the time the damage occurs, particularly in cases where there is an opportunity for interference with the goods.

There is, however, one very important exception to this basic rule: where the plaintiff proves damage in circumstances which can only be attributable to a breach of duty to take care on the part of the manufacturer. In this case the burden shifts to the manufacturer to prove that he has taken reasonable care.

This is known as the doctrine of '*res ipsa loquitor*' which literally means 'the thing speaks for itself'. Under this maxim the plaintiff establishes a prima facie case of negligence where it is not possible for him to know what caused the loss but it would not have happened had it not been for the negligence of the manufacturer. In other words, the plaintiff is able to treat the actual facts of the case as evidence of the negligence.

The rule has been used to establish a prima facie case of negligence in cases, for example, where objects have fallen from buildings and where motor vehicles have gone out of control and a stone was found in a cake.

If, of course, the manufacturer is able to offer an explanation which is consistent with having taken reasonable care, the manufacturer will not be liable.

4.7 Exclusion or limitation of liability

4.7.1 UCTA 1977

Before the passing of UCTA 1977 a manufacturer of a defective product could exclude or restrict liability for any damage caused by his product to the ultimate consumer provided he could show that the plaintiff was aware of the risk and had consented to an express exclusion of the manufacturer's duty. Normally such express exclusion would be by way of a notice or warning, and the manufacturer could rely upon this to set up the defence of '*volenti non fit injuria*', ie the plaintiff had consented to the risk of injury. However, in cases involving defective goods the fact that a warning or notice is given is more likely to be relevant to the manufacturer's duty to give adequate warnings to render the product safe than purporting to exclude liability. Since UCTA 1977 any notice purporting to exclude liability for negligence is subject to the provisions of the Act. As in contract the Act only relates to business liability.

Section 2 of UCTA 1977 provides:

(1)   A person cannot by reference to any other contract term or to a notice given to persons generally or to particular persons exclude or restrict his liability for death or injury resulting from negligence.

(2)   In the case of other loss or damage a person cannot exclude or restrict his liability for negligence except in so far as the term or notice satisfies the requirement of reasonableness.

(3)   Where a contract term or notice purports to exclude or restrict liability for negligence a person's agreement to or awareness of it is not of itself to be taken as indicating his voluntary acceptance of any risk.

The test to determine reasonableness in relation to a notice is that it should be fair and reasonable to allow reliance upon it, having regard to all the circumstances when the liability arose.

4.7.2   *Unfair Terms in Consumer Contracts Regulations 1994*

Additionally since the Unfair Terms in Consumer Contract Regulations come into effect as described in section 3.6.2 above, it is much harder for a manufacturer or supplier to exclude liability in negligence. The consumer may also claim against the supplier or manufacturer for breach of statutory duty where any such exclusion is unfair.

4.8   Limitation period

A claim will be statute barred unless it is brought within the statutory time limits. A plaintiff has six years from the date the cause of action accrued in which to bring a claim in negligence, although claims involving personal injury must be brought within three years. The time limits mean that a manufacturer is exposed to liability for a considerable time after the product was manufactured. In one case[16] a defective chisel splintered and caused injury to a mechanic seven years after the chisel was manufactured. The mechanic had three years after this to bring a claim which meant that in this particular case the manufacturer had an exposure to liability for ten years.

For actions involving latent defects the limitation period is either six years from the date when the cause of action arose or, if later, three years from the date when the plaintiff (or any person in whom the cause of action was vested before the plaintiff) had both knowledge of the damage and a right to bring the action. There is, however, an overriding time limit of 15 years from the date of the alleged negligent act or omission.

4.9   Liability for third parties

A manufacturer will be vicariously liable for the negligent acts or omissions of his employees during the course of their employment. Even if the manufacturer has taken all reasonable precautions and installed a safe system of work he will still be liable for the acts or omissions of his employees. In *Grant v Australian Knitting Mills* the court accepted that the manufacturer had a very good safety record with an allegedly foolproof system of production; nevertheless, he was still held liable as a result of the negligence of one of his operatives on the production line.

5   LIABILITY FOR DEFECTIVE PRODUCTS ARISING FROM NATIONAL LAW IN THE UK: IMPLEMENTATION OF EC DIRECTIVE 85/374 ON PRODUCT LIABILITY

5.1   Introduction

When CPA 1987 was brought into full effect in March 1988 it brought about an extension of the liability of manufacturers and suppliers to members of the

---

16   *Davie v New Merton Board Mills Ltd* [1959] AC 604.

public who are injured or suffer loss as a consequence of coming into contact with harmful or defective goods.

The liability upon manufacturers and suppliers under CPA 1987 is in addition to their responsibilities under the law of contract and tort and other existing statutory obligations such as the Health and Safety at Work Act 1974 and SGA 1979 described above.

A new liability arises under CPA 1987 from the fact of the supply of defective goods, whether or not the manufacturer/supplier can be said to be 'at fault' and whether or not there was a contractual relationship with the person using the goods.

CPA 1987 was introduced as a result of the Directive which required all EC countries to bring into effect product liability law based upon the detailed terms of that Directive. As a result of CPA 1987, a person who is injured or whose personal property is damaged by a product ('the claimant') will be able to claim against the manufacturer or supplier of that product and certain other parties if it can be shown that the product was defective.

The group of persons potentially liable is widely defined. It includes the producer of the finished product as well as of any material or component contained in it. Also any person who, by putting their name, trade mark, or other distinguishing feature on the product, represents himself as being the producer of the product, 'an own brander', may be liable. Anyone who first imports a product into the EU for re-sale, hire, leasing or any other form of distribution, is also to be treated as its producer.

If a producer of a product cannot be identified, each supplier will be treated as its producer. This is to protect the claimant from producers hiding behind chains of suppliers. However, provided a supplier informs the claimant within a reasonable time of the identity of the real producer of the product or of the person from whom the product was obtained, the liability is passed along the chain. Clearly complaints and claims must be handled by potential defendants speedily and accurately to avoid being treated as a producer by the courts when they have only acted as a supplier.

Consider Tom, Dick and Harry, a group of television set manufacturers, wholesalers and retailers. Tom manufactures the television set and Dick sells it wholesale to Harry who sells it retail to the claimant, who is injured when the set explodes. The claimant can claim against Harry unless he tells him that Dick supplied it, and can claim against Dick unless Dick tells him Tom manufactured it. Additionally, as we have seen, the claimant may have causes of action under common law in contract or tort against Harry as the supplier. However, if two or more persons are liable for the same damage then they are jointly and severally liable. This joint liability may occur, for example, where a defective component was also defectively installed in a product. Once liability has been established both the component producer and the installer would be equally liable but if one was unable to pay, the other could be made to pay all compensation under section 2(5) of CPA 1987.

5.1.1 *Defences to a claim for product liability*

A producer has six defences upon which to rely, namely:

(a) if he proves that he did not put the product into circulation; or
(b) having regard to all the circumstances, the product was not defective when he put it into circulation; or

(c) that the product was not produced for sale, hire, or any other distribution for commercial purposes, or that the producer has not produced and distributed the product within the course of his business activities; or

(d) the defect in the product is due to compliance of the product with mandatory public authority regulations; or

(e) if the product is a component, that the defect is attributable to the design of the product in which the component has been fitted and not to the component; or

(f) that the state of scientific and technical knowledge at the time when the product was put into circulation was not such as to enable the producer to know the existence of the defect or discover it ('the state of the art defence').

The state of the art defence, which was included largely due to the pharmaceutical industry's lobbying, will only be available to producers who can satisfy a court that the state of scientific and technical knowledge available in the world at the time the product was put on the market was insufficient to reveal the existence of the defect at that time. This places a high evidential burden on producers; to date, this defence has not been raised in any English reported case.

No proceedings may be commenced after ten years from the date when the producer brought into circulation the product which caused the damage. It is unclear whether the relevant commencement date is when the type of product was brought into circulation, or when the actual product was circulated. It is submitted that logically the latter must be the case, since otherwise it would be possible for the limitation period to have expired before the product reaches the consumer.

Although the Directive permits each EU country to impose a ceiling for liability for multiple design defects, no such ceiling has been provided under CPA 1987.

Liability under CPA 1987 is not retrospective and does not extend to products in circulation before the date upon which it came into force.

5.2 Description of special or anomalous provisions in respect of product liability law in the UK

Because of the existing framework of statute law certain products remain a risk business for the producer even if not specifically covered by CPA 1987. However, as has been demonstrated, most products, unless specifically excluded, are potentially caught by the Act.

5.2.1 Definition of 'product'

CPA 1987 defines 'product' as any 'goods or electricity' and also includes the term 'substances'. This raises the possibility that computer software will be caught by CPA 1987. Opinion is divided as to whether such claims will be successful but it is arguable that defective software provided on a tangible medium such as a computer disk can be treated as a product. If that defective software then causes injury or damage to property CPA 1987 would appear to apply. However, it is only likely that such software will be caught where it amounts to a defective component in a product. With the increasing control of high voltage/high risk technology by software care must be taken to ensure

that adequate safety checks and de-bugging have been carried out on the software being incorporated. The *St Albans* case dealt with a supply of software. It was held that this was only to be regarded as a sale of goods if the disk changes hands; where the software is transferred to a computer but the disk does not change hands the computer program would not be regarded as goods. If this case is followed in other cases the downloading of software would not be regarded as the supply of a product, whereas the supply of software on a disk or other tangible medium would be.[17]

It is quite likely that the 'state of the art' defence would be of help to producers of software provided they can demonstrate through documentation that full de-bugging and testing has been carried out.

The CPA 1987 follows the Directive and exempts primary agricultural products from its scope. However, food that has been processed will be within CPA 1987.

The building industry provides an example of how the Act produces surprising results. CPA 1987 has been drafted in such a way as to create a liability for defects in buildings which the Directive did not necessarily intend. Obviously components in buildings such as windows and doors are caught by CPA 1987. It would appear that the liability of a contract builder who builds for someone else on land that he does not own is different to the liability of a speculative builder who builds houses on land that he does own and subsequently sells or leases. It seems that the contract builder may only be liable as a supplier or producer in respect of defective products supplied or produced by him and incorporated into the building, whereas the speculative builder may be liable as a producer of the defective building as a whole, although exempted from liability as a supplier of any defective product comprised in the building.

5.2.2 Development risks defence

The CPA 1987 includes the 'state of the art' defence. However, the wording in section 4(i)(e) does not entirely mirror that of the Directive; it could be interpreted less strictly than article 7 of the Directive. The inclusion of the words 'might be expected to have discovered the defect' arguably detracts from the strictly objective test intended by the Directive, and introduces a concept of 'reasonableness'. It is submitted, however, that in view of section 1(1) of CPA 1987 which requires the Act to be construed in accordance with the Directive, that the English courts should be reluctant to apply the defence other than as it is written in the Directive.

5.2.3 Limits on total liability

The CPA 1987 places no ceiling upon liability. A *de minimis* provision applies to claims for property damage of £275 or less (including interest).

5.2.4 Differences between national law and the provisions of the Directive

The Directive clearly imposes a much stricter control upon the producer of a defective product than exists in contact or tort in English law. Once the claimant has shown that a product is defective and has caused damage then (subject to the defences above) he will obtain damages. The common law principles of privity of contract, foreseeability of damage and remoteness have been swept away.

17 Support for the view that software sold on disc is a product comes from the two recent cases, *Beta Computers (Europe) Ltd v Adobe Systems Europe Ltd* [1966] FSR 367 and *St Albans City & District Council v International Computers*, Times (Law Report), 14 August, 1996.

With the implementation of the Directive significant extensions have been introduced to the law relating to defective products. These extensions produce some fundamental differences in the way a claim relating to a product can be dealt with and the result of that claim.

i   Contract   In contract law SGA 1979 implies the term that goods will be of satisfactory quality and fit for their purpose; if they are not, the consumer will have remedies. However, under the Directive these are not the criteria upon which liability is based. The liability is much broader and more straightforward because it is based on the concept of 'defect'.

As has been seen earlier in this chapter, for a claim to succeed in contract law there must be privity of contract. However, under the Directive privity of contract plays no part. This means that the remedies under the Directive are available to an injured person whether or not that person has a contract with the manufacturer or supplier.

ii   Tort   The main difference between the English law of tort and the Directive is that the injured person no longer has to prove that the producer of the article owed a duty of care to the injured party. However, the injured person does still have to prove that damage has occurred (in excess of £275), that there is a defect, and that there is a causal relationship between the defect and the damage. Nevertheless, it is proving a duty of care which has been generally regarded as the most difficult element of such a claim in tort. In this respect the Directive considerably assists the claimant.

One area of comparison which will not become clear until cases under CPA 1987 have been determined by the courts in England is the concept of the 'safety which a person is entitled to expect' (CPA 1987 section 3(1)). If the courts adopt an objective test, that of the reasonable person in the circumstances, then the position will be analogous to that which already existed in tort. If the test is adopted subjectively, the law will have changed.

The Directive preserves the concept of contributory negligence dealt with earlier in this chapter. Under the Directive an injured person would be liable to have his claim reduced if he had contributed to his own injury by his misuse of the defective product.

6   CRIMINAL LIABILITY FOR DEFECTIVE PRODUCTS ARISING FROM BOTH GENERAL SAFETY LAW AND THE IMPLEMEN-TATON OF EC DIRECTIVE 92/59 EC ON PRODUCT SAFETY

6.1   Introduction

Apart from civil remedies when products fail it has long been recognised that a member state should be in a position to impose sanctions on producers and others involved in the chain of supply. If those national sanctions were to be truly effective they would have to be applied across the EU in a uniform manner. This philosophy led to the implementation of the Product Safety Directive.

6.2   Outline of implementation of Directive 92/59 EC

The Product Safety Directive was implemented in England and Wales by the General Product Safety Regulations 1994 which came into force on 3 October

1994. The principal effects of these Regulations are to require

(i) producers to place only safe products on the market, 'the general safety requirement' and
(ii) distributors not to supply 'products' which do not comply with the general safety requirement.

Failure to do so may result in steps being taken to rectify the fact that unsafe products are in circulation, including requiring the manufacturer to recall the product. In addition, the company found liable may be fined and certain individuals may be imprisoned. Although the Regulations do not expressly repeal section 10 of CPA 1987 (see section 5 above), they render the safety requirement contained in section 10 virtually redundant by disapplying that requirement in most usual circumstances of supply of products. Cotter's submission that section 10 will only continue to apply where products are excluded from Regulation 2 by virtue of the fact that they are 'used exclusively in the context of a commercial activity even if used for or by a consumer', such as a shopping trolley in a supermarket must be correct.[18]

6.3 Description of anomalous provisions on the implementation of Directive 92/59 EC

6.3.1 Defence of due diligence

A defence of due diligence may be available to a producer or distributor where it can be shown that 'he took all reasonable steps and exercised all due diligence to avoid committing the offence' (Regulation 14). This defence of due diligence is not found within the Product Safety Directive and is an extension of pre-existing defences available in England and Wales.

If it is alleged that the commission of the offence was due to 'the act or default of another' (Regulation 14 (a)) or 'reliance on information given by another' then notice of such defence must be served on the person bringing the proceedings not less than seven days before the hearing of the proceedings. Clearly such notice must sufficiently identify the other person to enable further enquiries to be made. It is possible to seek leave of the court to rely on such a defence even if the seven days limit is not adhered to but compelling reasons would have to be given for the application to succeed.

In any event for the defence to succeed it must be shown that the person charged with the offence acted reasonably in relying upon the information supplied to him having regard to

...the steps which he took and those which might reasonably have been taken, for the purpose of verifying the information; and ... whether he had any reason to disbelieve the information.

Where there has been a breach of Regulation 9(b) (the obligation of a distributor to pass on information on the product risks and cooperate in action taken to avoid those risks) the defence of due diligence is not available.

6.3.2 Individual liability

The GPSR 1994 provided that where a body corporate is guilty of an offence, then where it is established that the offence has been committed with the

---

18 Barry Cotter, *Defective and Unsafe Products – Law and Practice*, Butterworths, 1996.

consent, connivance (or by the neglect) of any director or other officer of the company, that person shall be liable to prosecution. The Product Safety Directive does not expressly provide for any such individual liability, leaving the question to be determined by the general provisions of company law of the relevant country.

6.3.3   *Capital goods*

The GPSR 1994 differ from the Directive and the view of the European Commission in that they specifically exclude capital goods used by consumers from their scope. This would mean, for example, that a shopping trolley would not be covered by the GPSR 1994. It would, however, be covered by section 10 of CPA 1987 (see section 6.2 above).

6.3.4   *'Professional'*

The GPSR include in the definition of 'producer' a literal translation of the word 'professional' which is used in the original text of the Directive. The word has several connotations in the English language and would not normally be applied to a manufacturer or distributor of consumer goods. It is submitted that it should be interpreted in its widest sense and not used to restrict the group of people who are involved in the supply chain, and therefore potentially liable.

6.3.5   *Preparatory acts*

Regulation 13 widens the scope of liability beyond that envisaged by the Directive to preparatory acts in the chain of supply.
It states:

... no producer or distributor shall:
(a) offer or agree to place on the market any dangerous product or expose or possess any such product for placing on the market; or
(b) offer or agree to supply any dangerous product or expose or possess any such product for supply.

6.4   Description of local optional provisions

Regulation 11 provides for enforcement of these Regulations by the Weights and Measures authority in Great Britain, save where the products are food or medicines in which case the relevant specific authority shall enforce the Regulations.

6.5   Other significant product safety law

Under English law a series of protective measures have been implemented in relation to specific products, including foodstuffs, drugs and chemicals, furniture and motor vehicles, to ensure that such products are safe. These regulations are now subsumed in CPA 1987 and are therefore subject to the legal principles discussed in section 5 above. However, there are certain categories of product for which it has been considered necessary to introduce special rules.

6.5.1 Nuclear power

Items relating to nuclear power installations are, as a matter of public policy, dealt with under a separate scheme. The Nuclear Installations Act 1965 is designed to deal with injury or damage which results from nuclear accidents. Under the scheme of the Nuclear Installations Act only a licence holder is permitted to operate a nuclear plant. The victims of emitted radiation have a claim against the licensee. The UK Atomic Energy Commission and government departments are also liable for emissions from sites operated by them.

If a duty imposed by the Act is breached the licence holder, UK Atomic Energy Commission, or government department incurs the liability in respect of that injury or disaster. This means that if a manufacturer supplies a faulty component to a nuclear installation, which is then shown to have caused the disaster, the licensee or operator of the installation is liable and is unable to claim an indemnity from the negligent manufacturer.

The sale of substances containing a radioactive chemical element are also controlled. The Ionising Radiation Regulations 1985 impose a duty to protect employees and other persons against ionising radiation arising from working with radioactive substances.

6.5.2 Foodstuffs

England has had food safety law since the thirteenth century when legislation was passed in relation to bread and ale. Apart from liabilities in contract or tort, foodstuffs are governed by the Food Safety Act 1990 and regulations made under it. These regulations control quality, composition, packaging and labelling of food. Such regulations are policed by local authorities through their environmental health and trading standards departments. Breach of such regulations can result in fines or prison sentences. The Food Safety Act 1990 makes it an offence to treat or process food so as to render it injurious to health, or to sell food which is not of the nature or of the substance or of the quality demanded by the purchaser, or which is unfit for human consumption.

6.5.3 Chemicals

There are also regulations to control the transport of dangerous chemicals, to impose a duty to report new dangerous chemicals to the Health and Safety Executive (an officially appointed body), to control the labelling and packaging of dangerous chemicals and to control any substance considered hazardous to health.

Similarly, there is a specific Act governing medicines, the Medicines Act 1968. Under the Medicines Act 1968 all dealings with medicinal products are controlled and the contravention of the major provisions of the Act is a criminal offence.

The Medicines Act imposes the duty that no person may, to the prejudice of the purchaser, sell any medicinal product which is not of the nature or quality demanded by the purchaser.

A system of licensing is in force for medicinal products and in general no such product may be manufactured or assembled without a licence. In addition, particular medicines may be prohibited from sale, supply or importation in the interests of public safety.

Reference to Her Majesty's Inspectorate of Pollution or the relevant local authority regarding 'relevant proscribed substances or processes' will need to be considered when the relevant regulations under the Environmental Protection Act 1990 are brought into force.

6.5.4   *Other products*

The extent to which England has implemented specific EU Directives relating to certain products is set out in Appendix 4.

7   CIVIL LIABILITY FOR DEFECTIVE PRODUCTS BROUGHT ABOUT BY BREACH OF STATUTORY REGULATION DESIGNED TO PROTECT CONSUMERS AND/OR TO PROMOTE SAFETY

7.1   Outline of nature of protective regulations

Apart from CPA 1987 English law has many Acts and regulations directed at product and consumer safety. For example, there are powers under the Health and Safety at Work Act 1974, the Food Safety Act 1990 and the Medicines Act 1968 which enable enforcing authorities to take action in relation to unsafe products or equipment.

CPA 1987 consolidated various previous legislation, as well as implementing the Directive. More importantly, in the area of product safety, CPA 1987 specifically adopted existing safety regulations. These regulations are made on the authority of the UK Government to impose safety requirements where it is considered necessary to reduce the risk of death or personal injury from products.

In particular, under CPA 1987 the Secretary of State can issue Prohibition Notices to prohibit a particular person or group of persons from supplying a particular product (section 13) or issue a Limited Duration Safety Regulation to prohibit the supply of a product or class of products which are considered unsafe (section 11).

The Limited Duration Safety Regulation replaces an existing power (the Prohibition Order) which was used to ban the supply of dangerous products such as children's pyjamas and nightdresses which had been treated with a carcinogenic flame-proofing material.

The Secretary of State is able to create regulations to cover dangerous, or potentially dangerous products. The present list of safety regulations covers a variety of products from asbestos, aircraft, bicycles, bunk beds and cosmetic products to snuff, toys, fireworks, radioactive material and many others.

7.2   Burden of proof

Because of the criminal nature of the enforcement of these provisions it is necessary for the government department or local authority bringing the prosecution to prove its case to the standard required in all criminal matters, namely, beyond reasonable doubt.

In a civil action for breach of statutory duty, it is necessary to prove the case on the balance of probabilities.

7.3 Nature of liability, damages or criminal sanctions

A person who contravenes a prohibition notice, a notice to warn, or a Limited Duration Safety Regulation, may be liable to criminal penalties. If the case is proved 'beyond reasonable doubt' then upon conviction that person would be liable to a fine and/or imprisonment. Similarly, where safety regulations prohibit a person from supplying or offering or agreeing to supply any product, any failure to comply with the prohibition may also result in a criminal penalty. The criminal penalty can range from a fine to a term of imprisonment.

Non-compliance with safety regulations may also give rise to a civil action for breach of statutory duty. Section 41(1) of CPA 1987 specifically provides that a breach of Safety Regulations made under the CPA 1987 gives rise to a civil claim for breach of statutory duty. However, this section does not relate to the general safety requirement of the CPA 1987 itself contained in section 10, nor the General Product Safety Regulations 1994. In order to determine whether a civil claim for breach of statutory duty will arise in relation to legislation in the absence of such civil claim being expressly provided, it is necessary to consider the common law position.

Whether a particular piece of legislation creates a liability and damage claims may result depends on its wording. If the legislation makes no provision for penalties or other means of enforcement the assumption is that an action may be brought for breach of it. If, on the other hand, the legislation provides sanctions for breach of it (as, for example, the General Product Safety Regulations 1994 and section 10 of CPA 1987 do), the assumption is that no action will apply. However, there are two exceptions to this general rule:

(i) where it is apparent that the obligation or prohibition was imposed for the benefit of a particular class of individual; or
(ii) when a statute creates a public right and an individual member of the public suffers particular direct and substantial damage different to that which is common to the rest of the public. English case law has generally shown a tendency to interpret a statute which is designed to protect a class of the public, and in particular their physical safety, as conferring a civil right of action, despite the existence of a penalty. It would therefore seem possible that an action for breach of statutory duty could be brought in relation to the General Product Safety Regulations 1994 or section 10 of CPA 1987.

Northern Ireland

David McFarland

Culbert & Martin
Scottish Provident Buildings
7 Donegall Square West
Belfast BT1 6JB
Ireland

Tel: ++ 01232 325508
Fax: ++ 01232 438669

1 INTRODUCTION TO THE LEGAL SYSTEM IN NORTHERN IRELAND

The Northern Ireland civil court system consists of the High Court in Belfast, with County Courts sitting in Belfast and in other provincial centres. The county Court has the jurisdiction to hear cases with a value of up to £15,000, and there is a Small Claims Court arbitration scheme contained within the County Court, having a jurisdiction up to £1,000. The High Court has jurisdiction to hear appeals (on all issues) from the County Court, and it will deal with cases in the first instance with a value in excess of £15,000. Appeals, on a point of law, can be made to the Northern Ireland Court of Appeal sitting in Belfast, with an ultimate appeal to the House of Lords in London.

2 OVERVIEW OF THE LAW RELATING TO DEFECTIVE PRODUCTS IN NORTHERN IRELAND

The law in Northern Ireland relating to defective products is identical to the law in England and Wales. Legislation in Northern Ireland is drawn from three sources – the Acts of the United Kingdom Parliament (if they are stated, in whole or in part, to apply to the Province), the Acts of the Northern Ireland Parliament before it was prorogued in 1973, and Orders in Council.

The principal legislation in this field, the SGA 1893, the CPA 1967, the MR 1967, the SG(IT)A 1973, the CCA 1974, the UCTA 1977, the SGA 1979 and the SGSA 1982 all apply to Northern Ireland. The Consumer Protection Act 1987 does not apply, but Part II of the Consumer Protection (Northern Ireland) Order 1987 enacts identical provisions.

Scotland

D Granger Brash

Alex Morison & Co WS, Solicitors
Erskine House,
68 Queen Street
Edinburgh
EH2 4NN,
Scotland

Tel: ++ 131 226 6541
Fax: ++ 131 226 3156

1   INTRODUCTION

Scots law is a legal system separate from English law, both in historic origin
and in much of modern practice. Standing as a bridge between civil law and
common law systems, the law of Scotland contains features of both.

While certain areas of Scots law and English law would call for entirely
separate treatment, the subject-matter of this book is not one of those areas.
Cross-border commercial activity has been going on for so long that England
and Scotland have inevitably influenced each other. Accordingly, this short
commentary on the Scots law of product liabilities takes the form of an
Addendum to the chapter covering England and Wales.[1] Space does not permit
a detailed exposition of the law of Scotland.

As will be seen, legislation passed by the United Kingdom Parliament does
not always extend to the whole of the United Kingdom; each piece of legislation
expressly states which of the English, Scottish and Northern Irish jurisdictions
are affected by it.

The Scottish civil courts system is quite different from that of England.
Throughout Scotland there are lower courts, known as Sheriff Courts, in cities
and many towns. It is usual for the more important cases to be heard in the
Court of Session, which sits only in Edinburgh. As in England, the courts system
is adversarial and relies mainly on oral evidence. Unlike the position governing
in some continental jurisdictions, a practising lawyer anywhere in Scotland may
raise proceedings on his client's behalf in any Sheriff Court, whether or not he
has a place of business, or normally practices law, in the relevant town.

---

1   For the sake of brevity, this Addendum refers to England, and to English law, meaning
England and Wales and the law applicable to those two countries.

A product liability case coming before a Scottish court may be decided – as in England – by reference to statute law or common law, the former taking precedence over the latter and, at least in certain respects, Community law being supreme over both.

2   PRE-CONTRACT LIABILITY

2.1   Effect of pre-contractual matters on the interpretation and extent of the obligations of the parties to a contract

The English chapter distinguishes three possible treatments of a statement made prior to the moment of contracting. Under English law, such a statement may:

(a) become a contractual term;
(b) constitute a collateral warranty; or
(c) induce a party to enter into a contract.

As regards (a), whether the Scottish court will consider a pre-contractual statement to form a term of the contract depends on the whole circumstances. Was the statement made only a short time before the contract was made? Was the statement something more than a mere expression of opinion? Was the maker of the statement in a better position than the party to whom it was made, to test its accuracy? Affirmative answers to questions such as these render it more likely that the statement will be held in Scotland to be a term of the contract.

As regards (b), the doctrine of collateral warranty, referred to in the English chapter, is not one with which Scots law is comfortable. The Scottish courts have occasionally acknowledged the existence of an agreement ancillary to the 'main' contract, but will generally be slow to recognise a collateral warranty which is not expressly contracted for. Where the contract is reduced to writing, a problem for the party arguing for the collateral warranty is the Scots law principle that written contracts are not generally to be added to by evidence of alleged oral agreement.

As regards (c), the misrepresentation provisions of the 1967 Act, referred to in the English chapter, do not extend to Scotland. The law of Scotland in relation to misrepresentation has grown up as an aspect of the law of error, detailed discussion of which is outwith the scope of this book. Under Scots law, if a misrepresentation which induces a contract amounts to an error so fundamental as to prevent *consensus in idem* – that is, a meeting of minds – there is no contract; though it is important to note that whether the parties are at cross-purposes will be determined by what they have said and done rather than by what they may have intended. If an error is not so substantial as to exclude consent, a contract induced by innocent misrepresentation is not void, but voidable. It may be reduced (a Scots law term for annulled) if *restitutio in integrum*, ie, restoration of the parties' pre-contract position, is possible. Because the passage of time makes restitution harder to achieve, the purchaser of an unsatisfactory product who wishes to have the contract reduced should not delay in seeking his remedy.

The entitlement to damages for misrepresentation depends on the kind of misrepresentation; a claim for damages is not permitted in cases of innocent

misrepresentation[2] but is permitted where the misrepresentation was fraudulent or, since 1985,[3] negligent.

2.2 Extent that non-disclosure of facts during negotiation may lead to liability

The position in Scotland is not unlike the position described in the English chapter. Generally, one party to a Scots law contract is under no duty voluntarily to reveal all matters relevant to the proposed contract. Subject to an obligation to answer questions honestly, he may remain silent.

There are, however, certain exceptions to that general principle. The English chapter refers to an insurance contract, this being the classic example of a contract described in Scotland as being one of *uberrimae fidei*, that is, of good faith; sometimes described as being of 'utmost' good faith. Space does not permit discussion of situations in which Scots law will impose a good faith duty of disclosure; for the purposes of this book, the important point is that a contract for the sale of goods is not generally such a situation.[4]

As observed in the English chapter, the position in consumer contracts is now amended by the Unfair Terms in Consumer Contracts Regulations 1994.

2.3 Does pre-contractual liability lie in contract or in delict?

The first question under this heading is whether the misrepresentation has become a term of the contract; if so, liability will be contractual. If the error is in such an essential aspect of the contract that the contract is void, there cannot be any contractual duty and thus there cannot be damages in contract for breach of any such duty. (Note that where the contract is voidable rather than void, the position is different, because the contract is valid until the party having the right to do so elects to rescind it.)

Where there is no contract but fraudulent or negligent misrepresentation gives a right to claim damages, such a claim will be delictual. Delict is discussed at section 4 below.

3 LIABILITY IN CONTRACT

3.1 Outline of Contract Law

The English chapter distinguishes a condition (breach of which entitles rescission), a warranty (breach of which entitles damages only), and an intermediate term. Scots law recognises no such classification.[5] That is why section 11(3) of SGA 1979, which sets out the available remedies for breaches of conditions and warranties, does not apply to Scotland.

When a Scottish contract is breached, the choice of remedies depends upon a single test: if the breach was 'material', the innocent party has a right to rescind but if the breach was not material, the right is to claim damages. Section 15B

---

2 *Manners v Whitehead* (1898) 1 F 171.
3 Law Reform (Miscellaneous Provisions) (Scotland) Act 1985, section 10(1).
4 *Shankland & Co v Robinson & Co* 1920 SC (HL) 103, at page 111.
5 This was recently confirmed in an interesting case: see *Fortune v Fraser* 1996 SLT 878.

of SGA 1979 applies only to Scotland; it was inserted into the 1979 Act by SSGA 1994 and now provides in sub-section (1):

> Where in a contract of sale the seller is in breach of any term of the contract (express or implied), the buyer shall be entitled -
> (a) to claim damages, and
> (b) if the breach is material, to reject any goods delivered under the contract and treat it as repudiated.

3.2   Contractual terms relating to quality of goods and safety of goods

i   Description   As regards sales by description, section 13(1) of SGA 1979, quoted in the English chapter, applies equally to Scotland. Generally, the position in Scotland is that description is a matter of identification, not touching upon issues of quality.[6]

ii   Quality and fitness   It is not necessary for a buyer, in making a claim for breach of the implied term of satisfactory quality under section 14 of SGA 1979, to show how or why the product failed. In *Coakley v John Lewis plc*,[7] the buyer of a set of aluminium steps succeeded in her claim by proving that one of the legs of the steps failed and that this failure was the cause of her injuries; the court held that she did not require to explain how the leg of the steps gave way.

The English chapter refers to section 14(2C) of SGA 1979 which provides that there is no implied term of satisfactory quality in respect of any matter specifically drawn to the buyer's attention before the contract is made. A Scottish case suggests that it may not be a straightforward matter for sellers to rely on this provision. In *Turnock v Fortune*,[8] the buyer of a car admitted having been told by the seller that the car had been in an accident, that a firm of car dealers had rejected it because of the extensive damage, and that the price was less than half of what would be asked for the vehicle if in good condition. However, it was held that this did not amount to a warning that the car was unroadworthy and the buyer succeeded in his claim under section 14.

The courts will be slow to accept a buyer's argument that a product is not of satisfactory quality, if the defects are minor blemishes in appearance or minor defects. Despite the buyer being disappointed by such flaws, he may still have difficulty in maintaining that the section 14 obligation of the seller has not been implemented. In *Millars of Falkirk Limited v Turpie*,[9] the buyer took delivery of a brand new car and, on discovering an oil leak, attempted to withhold payment on the basis of the then equivalent of section 14; the court held that the leak was very minor and could be fixed so easily that the seller succeeded in its action for payment of the price.

iii   Sale by sample   Section 15 of SGA 1979 provides that a sale is a sale by sample when the contract contains an express or implied term to that effect. It should be noted that the fact that the buyer has seen a sample of the goods does not necessarily mean that the sale was by sample; in *White v Dougherty*,[10]

---

6   *Border Harvesters Ltd v Edwards Engineering (Perth) Ltd* 1985 SLT 128.
7   1994 GWD 15-979.
8   1989 SLT (Sh Ct) 32.
9   1976 SLT (Notes) 66.
10   (1891) 18 R 972.

the buyer of apples at an auction had seen examples of the produce but failed in an argument that the contract was a sale by sample.

iv Wrong quantity SGA 1979 was amended in 1994, such that if the seller delivers the wrong quantity of goods (either too little or too much), the buyer may not reject the goods unless that shortfall or excess is material.[11]

3.3 Breach of contract for supply of defective products

3.3.1 Right of rejection

Section 15B of SGA 1979, which applies to Scotland only, provides that if the seller breaches any express or implied term of the contract, the buyer shall be entitled to claim damages and – but only if the breach is material – to reject the goods. The English chapter refers to section 11 and section 15A of SGA 1979, but neither of these sections applies to Scotland. It is however settled under Scots law that the buyer loses any right of rejection once the goods have been accepted. In *Mechans Ltd v Highland Marine Charters Ltd*,[12] the buyer of two vessels signed an acceptance certificate before discovering major defects; it was held that the express acceptance extinguished the right of rejection. The purchaser of products should bear in mind that rejection is inconsistent with further use of the goods; so where the buyer of boilers purported to reject them but continued using them for several weeks, it was held that the right of rejection was lost.[13]

3.3.2 Acceptance

i Intimation of acceptance SGA 1979 was amended in 1994 to remove doubt about the legal effect of the buyer asking the seller to repair goods. Section 35(6) now provides that: 'the buyer is not ... deemed to have accepted the goods merely because ... he asks for, or agrees to, their repair by or under an arrangement with the seller.'

ii Act inconsistent with seller's ownership In a recent Scottish case it was held that incorporating aluminium panels into a building is an act inconsistent with the seller's ownership.[14]

3.3.3 Causation and damages

As in England, the buyer of a defective product under Scots law will be awarded damages for breach of contract against the seller only if it can be shown that the product breached an express or implied term of the contract; but the buyer must also prove that the damage complained of was caused by the defect.

However, it may happen that damage occurs not only because of a defect in the product but also because of circumstances unrelated to the seller. In such cases, it is for the court to decide whether the seller's breach of contract materially contributed to the damage.

---

11 S 30(2D) SGA 1979, which applies to Scotland only. A similar provision was enacted for England but the English provision applies only where the buyer does not deal as a consumer.
12 1964 SLT 27.
13 *Croom & Arthur v Stewart* (1905) 7 F 563.
14 *Charles Henshaw & Sons Ltd v Antlerport Ltd* 1995 GWD 24-1315.

Sometimes the intervening event of a third party will exacerbate the buyer's position. So if a defective bottle merely cuts the finger of a buyer who then receives negligent medical attention and, as a result, loses the power of his arm, the seller will not be ordered to pay damages for the whole loss suffered.

Where the intervening event is occasioned by the buyer himself, the seller's liability will be restricted. So if a person buys a television set and continues to use it, even after repeated emission of smoke indicates an obvious defect, the buyer might be in some difficulty in recovering his whole loss in damages after his house burns down.

i   Remoteness of damage   The *Hadley v Baxendale* decision, though English, can be treated as a valid statement of the Scots law principle of remoteness of damage.

The English chapter refers to losses 'contemplated by the parties'. A seller of a product may *actually* know that certain consequences will follow from the product being defective but, in addition, the court will attribute to the seller the knowledge which a reasonable man would have – whether or not the seller in fact had that knowledge. There are, however, limits to the knowledge to be imputed, as is shown by the recent Scottish case of *Balfour Beatty v Scottish Power*,[15] decided by the House of Lords.[16] The construction of a road required a 'continuous pour' of concrete. The supply of electric power was, in breach of contract, interrupted with the result that substantial construction works had to be demolished and rebuilt. The court refused to impute to the power company the technical details of concrete construction; so the construction company failed to recover the costs of demolition and rebuilding.

ii   Damage recoverable   Whether or not the type of recoverable damage is, as in the English chapter, broken into three categories – property damage, personal injury and economic loss – the approach of the Scottish courts is to apply one basic test: what the defender ought reasonably to have foreseen. The case law includes instances where a certain kind of loss was (or should have been) foreseen, but in which an unforeseeable quantum of loss was in fact suffered. What is clear from the decisions of the courts is that each case will turn on its own particular facts.

One further head of possible recovery in a damages claim is that of solatium. Damages may be awarded for pain and suffering, injury to feelings, and gross inconvenience. Anecdotal evidence suggests that Scottish awards for solatium may be generally somewhat less than may be recovered in other (for example, USA) jurisdictions. The supplier of a defective camera might face a solatium claim if all photographs taken with it at a wedding were ruined, but it is not likely that the award of damages would be high.

3.4   Quantum of damages

The English chapter refers to the buyer's remedy for breach of warranty, set out in section 53 of SGA 1979. Until 1994 that section applied also to Scotland but, referring as it did to a breach of 'warranty', section 53 was never one with

---

15   1994 SLT (HL) 807.
16   Sitting, not as a legislative body, but as the highest Scottish civil appeals court.

which Scots law was comfortable. Accordingly, SSGA 1994 introduced a new section 53A into SGA 1979. This new section 53A applies only to Scotland and provides:

(1) The measure of damages for the seller's breach of contract is the estimated loss directly and naturally resulting, in the ordinary course of events, from the breach.

(2) Where the seller's breach consists of the delivery of goods which are not of the quality required by the contract and the buyer retains the goods, such loss as aforesaid is prima facie the difference between the value of the goods at the time of delivery to the buyer and the value they would have had if they had fulfilled the contract.

3.4.1 *Mitigation*

As in England, the aggrieved party must take all reasonable steps to minimise his loss; so where a supplier fails to deliver, the buyer will be expected to seek the product elsewhere. Where loss could have been avoided by reasonable inspection of a defective product, such loss may not be recoverable from the supplier – see, for example, *Carter v Campbell*[17] where a buyer contracted for 'oats, clear of barley' and failed to recover loss because the presence of barley in the delivered oats was readily detectable.

3.5 Burden of proof

The English chapter notes that the supplier of a defective product cannot avoid liability in contract by proving absence of fault on his part; the Scottish position is generally the same. It is, however, not uncommon for the contracting parties to agree expressly that the supplier of the product will have no liability for loss arising from *force majeure*.

The onus will generally be on the pursuer (English law: plaintiff) to prove that there was a contract with the defender (English law: defendant) and that the defender breached its express or implied terms; but the onus may shift to the defender in certain circumstances. For example, if the defender argues that the parties agreed there would be no remedy in respect of loss caused by the seller's negligence, the onus will be on the defender to prove that the exclusion clause was incorporated into the contract. Also, if the defender argues that the pursuer failed to minimise his loss, again the onus of proving that averment will fall on the defender.

3.6 Exclusion of liability

3.6.1 *Position at common law*

Exclusion clauses can be seen everywhere. 'All vehicles left in this car park are at the owner's risk' is typical of what members of the public experience daily. While such a clause is not necessarily unfair per se, the law of Scotland construes any ambiguity *contra proferentem*, ie, against the party seeking to rely on it.

Prior to the statutory regime set out in the Unfair Contract Terms Act 1977, Scottish courts developed various methods of restricting the intended effects

17   (1885) 12 R 1075.

of exclusion clauses. So in *Taylor v Glasgow Corpn*[18] the ticket given to a lady entering public baths (which contained words purporting to exclude liability) was held not to be a contractual document; and in *Henderson v Stevenson*[19] an exclusion clause on the back of a ferry ticket was held to be not sufficiently notified to the passenger because there was no mention of the clause on the front of the ticket.

3.6.2   Statutory controls

i   UCTA 1977   In the context of this book, it is important to note that UCTA 1977 does not apply to international supply contracts.[20] Most of what is stated in the English chapter does not relate to Scotland; Part I of UCTA 1977 (sections 1-14) applies only to England, while Part II (sections 15-25) applies only to Scotland. There are substantial differences – for instance, it is only since UCTA 1977 was amended in 1990 that its Scottish provisions have applied to non-contractual notices.[1]

Attempting to apply a foreign law to the contract will not generally evade the effect of UCTA 1977.[2] The various types of contract covered by UCTA 1977 include contracts to transfer ownership or possession of goods from one party to another. A very brief summary of the principal Scottish provisions of UCTA 1977, as applying to the situations with which this book primarily deals, is as follows:

(i)   a contractual term seeking to exclude or restrict liability, in the course of a business, for breach of a duty to take reasonable care or use reasonable skill is void where it relates to death or personal injury; and is of no effect in other cases unless it was fair and reasonable to incorporate that term into the contract.[3]

(ii)   in consumer contracts and standard form contracts, no term can exclude or restrict liability, and no term can seek to allow no performance or a performance substantially different from what the consumer or customer reasonably expected unless, in either case, its incorporation into the contract was fair and reasonable.[4]

(iii) a term of a consumer contract cannot make the consumer indemnify another person (whether a party to the contract or not) in respect of that other person's liability, incurred in the course of a business as a result of breach of duty or breach of contract, unless it was fair and reasonable to incorporate that term.[5]

(iv)   a guarantee of goods ordinarily supplied for private use (other than by one contracting party to the other, in a contract transferring ownership or possession of goods) is void where it seeks to exclude or restrict liability for loss or damage (including death or personal injury):

   (a)   arising from the goods proving defective when used for non-business purposes, and

---

18   1952 SC 440.
19   (1875) 2 R (HL) 71.
20   See s 26.
 1   Law Reform (Miscellaneous Provisions) (Scotland) Act 1990, s 68.
 2   Section 27(2).
 3   Section 16.
 4   Section 17.
 5   Section 18.

(b) resulting from breach of duty of a person manufacturing or distributing the goods.[6]

The definition of a consumer contract is broadly similar to that which applies in England.

The onus of proving that it was fair and reasonable to incorporate a term into a contract lies on the party so contending.[7]

The matters to be considered in applying the reasonableness test, set out in Schedule 2 of UCTA 1977 and in the English chapter, apply in certain instances to the Scottish provisions of the Act. In *Denholm Fishselling Ltd v Anderson*,[8] the purchaser of eleven boxes of cod refused to pay the price because the fish was unfit for human consumption. The seller's standard conditions excluded liability for breach of the implied term as to quality. The court held that it was fair and reasonable to incorporate that exclusion clause into the contract; it was further held that the fact that a seller will only deal on the basis of its own non-negotiable contractual terms does not necessarily mean that there is a preponderance of bargaining power in the seller's favour.

ii Unfair Terms in Consumer Contracts Regulations 1994   A few points of interest arise out of the new Regulations, which apply to Scotland as well as to England. First, a term of a contract to which the Regulations apply will be unfair if 'contrary to the requirement of good faith' the term causes a significant imbalance between the parties, to the consumer's detriment. Though perhaps the good faith requirement may turn out to be not substantially different from the concept of reasonableness, case law will be required before a clear picture emerges.

Second, the Regulations provide that it will be for the seller or supplier to discharge the burden of proving that a term of the contract was individually negotiated. If the contract was individually negotiated, the Regulations do not apply but even where there has been no such individual negotiation, it may be helpful to the seller if the consumer is given what the Regulations call a 'real opportunity of becoming acquainted' with the proposed terms before the contract is concluded.

Third, a couple of distinctions between the Regulations and UCTA 1977 may be mentioned. The Regulations protect only natural persons, whereas under UCTA 1977, a company can be a consumer; and while the Regulations only apply to standard contracts with consumers, UCTA 1977 can apply to business-to-business contracts.

3.7 Prescription and limitation

The distinction between prescription (which actually extinguishes the obligation) and limitation (which merely renders a right of action unenforceable) can be significant. Particularly when aspects of private international law arise, it may be important that prescription is a rule of substantive law, whereas limitation is a rule of procedural law. Where reference is here made to prescription of obligations or limitation of actions, the terminology is not interchangeable.

---

6   Section 19.
7   Section 24(4).
8   1991 SLT (Sh Ct) 24. See also *Knight Machinery (Holdings) Ltd v Rennie*, 1995 SLT 166.

The Limitation Act 1980 and the Latent Damage Act 1986, referred to in the English chapter, do not apply to Scotland. A claim for damages for breach of contract generally prescribes under Scots law in five years; see the Prescription and Limitation (Scotland) Act 1973, section 6. Leaving exceptional cases out of account, proceedings require to be commenced by the fifth anniversary of the date when the obligation to make reparation became enforceable, failing which that obligation will be extinguished. Loss, injury or damage occurring as a result of a continuing act, neglect or default is deemed to have occurred when the act, neglect or default ceased. Accordingly, as in England, the latest date can be taken.

However, where a contractual damages claim relates to personal injuries or to death following such injuries, the five-year prescription does not apply. Instead, such a claim is governed by a limitation period of three years (PLSA 1973, sections 17-18).

4   LIABILITY IN DELICT

4.1   Introduction

While the basic principle of liability in contract may be said to be the defender's breach of an obligation expressly or impliedly undertaken to the pursuer, liability in delict depends on breach of an obligation imposed by the law. The English law of torts and the Scots law of delict are by no means the same, Scottish principles having been influenced by Roman law remedies.[9]

4.2   Negligence

However, in the context of this book, the particular tort/delict under discussion is that of negligence and in that field the modern law has developed along similar lines in both countries. Where a product causes loss to a party who may have no remedy in contract, liability in negligence arises from a failure to take reasonable care to avoid damage to other persons, to their property, and in certain circumstances to their economic interests.

It has been said that, in terms of development of the law of negligence, the *Donoghue v Stevenson* decision about the snail, said to have been found in a ginger beer bottle in a cafe in the Scottish town of Paisley, has echoed round the English-speaking legal world. Though it would be wrong to say that *Donoghue v Stevenson* gave birth to liability for negligence in the law of Scotland, the duty of care test which it set out remains a cornerstone of this area of law. If the manufacturer of a product owed to the pursuer a duty to take reasonable care for the pursuer's safety, and if that duty was breached, and if as a result the pursuer suffered loss, the essentials of Scots law liability for negligence are in place.

The question of whether a duty is owed to this *particular* pursuer can be important. For example, a manufacturer of inflammable paint no doubt owes a common law duty to his employees to take reasonable steps to avoid the factory going on fire; if he fails in that duty, it is reasonably foreseeable that some

---

9   The *actio injuriarum* and the *actio legis aquiliae*. A historical analysis can be found in D M Walker's *The Law of Delict in Scotland*, 2nd edn, 1981.

workers may be killed or injured. Whether the same duty is owed to trespassers who gain entry by climbing a high, barbed-wire security fence which has 'Danger' notices affixed to it is, it is submitted, less clear.

In a well-known Scottish case decided by the House of Lords, a motorcyclist negligently collided with a car, and a passer-by suffered nervous shock from hearing the noise of the accident. The court had no difficulty in confirming that the infliction of mental shock can constitute an actionable wrong. However, it was held that the motor-cyclist may have owed a duty of care to the car driver, but not to the passer-by.[10]

The manufacturer of an unsafe product is unlikely to avoid liability on the grounds that the pursuer was specially sensitive. If a defective medicine would only give most people a temporary headache, but in the case of the particular pursuer caused permanent damage, the defender might seek to argue that his duty of care did not extend to the tiny minority who could suffer very badly. However, the so-called 'thin skull' rule has the effect that the manufacturer must take his product's consumers as he finds them; if it was reasonably foreseeable that the medicine would be taken by consumers in a specially sensitive minority, the duty to them is owed. In a case where a pursuer successfully sued in respect of an injury which caused an unusual reactivation of his tuberculosis, one of the judges stated:

> There is no ground for holding that a reasonable man would have assumed that the pursuer had a sound pair of lungs, and no justification for limiting an award in his favour to the amount which would have been due to another person with a stronger constitution.[11]

The English chapter refers to exemplary damages. Punitive awards are not made in Scotland, where damages are intended to put the pursuer in the same position – as far as money can ever do so – as if the breach of duty had not occurred. However, it is possible for damages to be aggravated where, for example, the pursuer is young and had excellent prospects.

4.3 Causation

4.3.1 'But for' test

As stated in the English chapter, the pursuer will not succeed unless he can prove that the defender's act or omission caused the damage. This hurdle may be a substantial one; in the *McWilliams v Arrol* case (a Scottish decision) quoted in the English chapter, the fact that a safety belt should have been provided and, if used, would have prevented the death, was not enough to let the widow succeed. One of the judges put it this way:

> If the accident would have happened in just the same way whether or not I fulfilled my duty, it is obvious that my failure to fulfil my duty cannot have caused or contributed to it.

Similarly, in *McKinlay v British Steel Corpn*,[12] serious consequences followed from a piece of metal entering a worker's eye. Finding that the worker never wore the safety goggles made available by his employer, the Scottish court rejected the claim.

10   *Bourhill v Young* 1942 SC (HL) 78.
11   *McKillen v Barclay Curle & Co Ltd* 1967 SLT 41, at page 44.
12   (1988) SLT 810.

A recent Scottish case, decided in the House of Lords, illustrates the possible extent of the pursuer's difficulty with causation. In *Kay's Tutor v Ayrshire & Arran Health Board*,[13] a two-year-old boy suffering from meningitis was given thirty times the correct dose of penicillin. On recovering from the meningitis, the boy turned out to be deaf. Despite the Health Board's admission of the doctor's negligence, the claim failed for lack of proof that the overdose was a *sine qua non* of the deafness.

4.3.2   *Nova causa interveniens and contributory negligence*

The principles described in the English chapter under these headings apply similarly in Scotland. The *nova causa* (or *novus actus*) *interveniens* (ie, the intervening event) may be the conduct of a third party, the conduct of the pursuer, or some other event entirely. The Scottish courts will be slow to decide that the pursuer's conduct broke the chain of causation, if that conduct – though perhaps aggravating the position – was a reasonable act intended, in an emergency, to avoid the damage being suffered. A degree of unwarranted carelessness on the pursuer's part will result in the court attributing fault between the parties in proportion to their share of responsibility for the damage suffered; but there can come a point at which the pursuer's own conduct – even if not harshly judged, because of the 'agony' of the situation – may amount to such unjustifiable negligence as will constitute a complete defence.

4.4   Remoteness of loss and damage

After (and only after) the pursuer has cleared the hurdles of satisfying the court that a duty of care was owed towards him, and that the duty was breached, a further hurdle remains. It was held in *Malcolm v Dickson* that: 'A wrongdoer is not held responsible for all the results which flow from his negligent act. Practical considerations dictate and the law accepts that there comes a point in the sequence of events when liability can no longer be enforced.'[14]

The test on remoteness of damage under Scots law is not precisely the same as the reasonable foreseeability test to which the English chapter refers. While the question of what could have been reasonably foreseen will always have a bearing on the issue, the Scottish cases require the court to assess whether the damages claimed by the pursuer arose naturally and directly out of the wrong done. In a case in which one ship collided with another on the River Clyde, one of the judges remarked that: 'the damage is recoverable ... if it is the natural and reasonable result of the negligent act and it will assume this character if it can be shown to be such a consequence as in the ordinary course of things would flow from the situation which the offending ship has created.'[15]

4.4   Quantum of damage

As in England, the recovery of damages in delict for purely economic loss is severely restricted under Scots law. The pursuer's difficulty is to bring himself within a few categories where the courts have recognised a sufficiently proximate

---

13   (1987) SLT 577.
14   1951 SLT 357, at page 359.
15   *Kelvin Shipping Co v Canadian Pacific Railway Co* 1928 SC(HL) 21, *per* Viscount Haldane.

relationship between pursuer and defender. Suppose the manufacturer of the *Donoghue v Stevenson* bottle of ginger beer faced a delictual claim for loss of profits (ie, purely economic loss) by the cafe proprietor who sold the bottle to the customer and subsequently contended that the incident had encouraged previously regular customers to go elsewhere; the manufacturer might be able to argue that, while there was of course a contractual relationship between him and the cafe proprietor, no special relationship existed, such as would have given rise to a duty of care in delict in respect of that particular pursuer's loss.

4.5 Burden of proof

As in England, it is for the pursuer to prove negligence. That negligence is to be demonstrated 'on the balance of probabilities'.

An example of *res ipsa loquitur* in a product liability context might be a situation in which most of the users of a new soap immediately developed an irritation of the skin; in the ordinary course of things, soap does not irritate the skin of most people so if the facts could not be ascertained, the pursuer might seek to argue that it is for the defender to provide a likely and reasonable explanation which does not involve fault on the defender's part.

It is important to appreciate that the *res ipsa loquitur* doctrine does not mean that it is generally open to the pursuer to challenge the defender to establish that he was not negligent. The pursuer must first satisfy the court that there is prima facie evidence of negligence on the defender's part; only then does the onus switch to the defender.

4.6 Exclusion or limitation of liability

4.6.1 UCTA 1977

The defence of *volenti non fit injuria* operates similarly in Scotland. It is important to recognise that the defence will only be available to a defender who can prove not just that the pursuer was willing to accept the risk of injury (or, more correctly, was willing to accept the defender's lack of reasonable care), but also that the pursuer really did appreciate the risk.

A summary of the main Scottish provisions of UCTA 1977, as regards contractual liability, has already been given. It should be understood that even if there is a contract between X and Y, that does not mean that X cannot also owe to Y a duty of care in delict.

Section 2 of UCTA 1977, quoted in the English chapter, has no application to Scotland but the ability of X to exclude or restrict his liability for breach of a duty owed to Y in delict is curbed in a similar manner. Section 16 provides, in relation to breach of duty in the course of any business, that a provision of a notice purporting to exclude or restrict liability shall be void as regards death or personal injury; and in any other case shall have no effect if it was not fair and reasonable in all the circumstances to allow the provision to be relied upon. Accordingly, what a supplier can achieve by warnings in, for example, a product's instruction manual is limited.

4.6.2 Unfair Terms in Consumer Contracts Regulations 1994

It is considered that the 1994 Regulations will generally affect Scots law and English law in a similar manner.

4.7   Prescription and limitation

A delictual obligation to make reparation, if not made the subject of proceedings commenced by the fifth anniversary of the date on which the obligation became enforceable, prescribes under Scots law when the five years expires. The obligation typically becomes enforceable when the loss, injury or damage occurs.

But a vitally important exception is in relation to cases of personal injuries or death resulting from such injuries. This type of action is subject to a limitation period of three years from the date when the injuries were sustained, subject to the court having power 'if it seems to it equitable to do so' (PLSA 1973, section 19A) to extend the period. In practice, this power is exercised sparingly.

Space does not permit discussion of cases in which the starting-date of the limitation period is later than the date of injury – such as, where the pursuer did not know and could not reasonably have discovered that the injuries were wholly or partly attributable to a negligent act or omission.

4.8   Liability for third parties

As stated in the English chapter, a manufacturer can be made vicariously liable for the negligent acts or omissions of his employees. A brief summary of the Scottish position is that there will be vicarious liability if (a) the manufacturer actually authorised the particular act or (b) the employee acted in a manner which the employer did not authorise and would not have authorised, but which was still within the scope of the employment for which the employee was appointed. Where the employee does something entirely outwith the scope of his employment, the employer is not generally liable in delict for the employee's negligent act.

5   LIABILITY FOR DEFECTIVE PRODUCTS ARISING FROM NATIONAL LAW IN THE UK: IMPLEMENTATION OF EC DIRECTIVE 85/324 ON PRODUCT LIABILITY

5.1   Introduction

Generally, CPA 1987 applies to Scotland as it does to England. It is not necessary here to discuss in detail a number of minor provisions of the Act which apply only to Scotland, mostly to deal with Scottish matters of procedure.

The English chapter points out that the liability of a supplier may be passed back up the chain by disclosure of the identity of the person from whom the product was obtained. So if A supplies to B who supplies to C (who suffers damage), B can avoid liability to C by identifying A. It should be noted that under section 2 of CPA 1987 it is *not* a condition of B's release from liability that C can in fact recover from A. A may be dead or insolvent or (if a corporation) even no longer in existence.

5.2   Description of special or anomalous provisions in respect of product liability law in the UK

5.2.1   *Definition of 'product'*

Under this heading the English chapter states that a speculative builder may be liable as a producer of a defective building as a whole, although exempted

from liability as a supplier of any defective product comprised in the building. No Scottish case has been reported yet on this point but it is submitted that the Scottish courts, in view of article 2 of the Directive and section 46(4) of CPA 1987, might not make the speculative builder liable as a producer of the defective building 'as a whole'.

5.2.2   *Differences between national law and the provisions of the Directive*

Under this heading the English chapter highlights the fact that nothing in CPA 1987 permits the producer of a defective product to avoid liability by reference to rules on privity of contract, foreseeability of damage or remoteness. Section 2(1) of the Act provides, in wide terms, for liability 'where any damage is caused wholly or partly by a defect in a product'. Although there is no reference to foreseeability or remoteness, the words quoted do refer to damage being 'caused', so the question of the chain of causation remains relevant.

Lawyers are familiar with imaginary situations such as where defective brakes in a motor car cause the car to skid into a lorry which takes avoiding action but collides with a bus whose inebriated driver crashes into a hospital which is destroyed in a massive explosion as a spark ignites gas leaking from a defective pipe. Reference has already been made to *nova causa interveniens* – the intervening act which breaks the chain of causation so as to restrict the liability of the producer of the defective brakes. Though foreseeability is not the test of liability under CPA 1987 it is nonetheless submitted that elements of what a reasonable man could or could not have foreseen, as a consequence of a certain act or omission, will arise whenever courts address the issue of causation by asking whether a particular act or omission caused a particular loss.

5.3   Product liability – prescription and limitation

As would be expected where the United Kingdom was required to implement an EC Directive, the ten-year period referred to in the English chapter applies to Scotland also. Strictly speaking, the obligation under Scots law arising from section 2 of the Consumer Protection Act prescribes (PLSA 1973, section 22A, as introduced by CPA 1987); whereas the English provision in the Limitation Act 1980 (an Act not applying to Scotland) operates to extinguish the right of action. As regards common law obligations to make reparation for product liability, no ten-year prescription applies.

Section 4(2) of CPA 1987, which basically provides for the ten years to commence on the date of supply of the defective product, applies to Scotland and England equally. The period will expire ten years after supply of the particular defective product – even if the producer continued to supply similarly defective products thereafter. The ten-year period cannot be extended at the court's discretion.

Quite separately, PLSA 1973 (as amended by CPA 1987) sets out a three-year limitation on an action to enforce an obligation under section 2 of CPA 1987. No such action is competent unless begun within three years from the earliest date on which the pursuer was, or could reasonably have been, aware (a) that there was a defect, (b) that the damage was caused or partly caused by the defect, (c) that the damage justified the bringing of an action, and (d) that the defender was a person liable under section 2 of CPA 1987 (PLSA 1973, section 22B). It should be noted that this particular limitation applies to property damage as well as to personal injuries.

A similar provision (PLSA 1973, section 22C) sets out a three-year limitation on proceedings following a death occasioned by 'section 2' liability.

The court may, if it thinks it equitable to do so, extend the three-year period except where the claim is for property damage alone.

Any period during which the pursuer was under legal disability caused by non-age or unsoundness of mind is discounted.

6   CRIMINAL LIABILITY FOR DEFECTIVE PRODUCTS ARISING FROM BOTH GENERAL SAFETY LAW AND THE IMPLEMENTATION OF EC DIRECTIVE 92/59 EC ON PRODUCT SAFETY

6.1   Introduction

As the General Product Safety Regulations 1994 are intended to implement a Directive, it is no surprise that they generally apply in Scotland as they do in England. Subject as mentioned below, the differences in application arise out of certain Scottish procedural matters which need not be discussed here.

6.2   Individual liability

Under this heading the English chapter points out that the GPSR 1994 provide for the personal liability of individual company directors and other officers, in certain circumstances, in addition to the liability of the body corporate itself. Such personal liability applies also to officers of Scottish companies but in addition the Regulations make special provision for Scottish partnerships. This is because (unlike in England) a partnership under Scots law has a legal personality of its own, ie, separate from that of the individual partners. Regulation 15(4) provides that where a Scottish partnership is guilty of an offence, a partner of the firm shall also be guilty 'in respect of any act or default ... committed with the consent or connivance of, or ... neglect on the part of' a partner.

6.3   'Professional'

It is submitted that, as in England, this word will be construed widely by the Scottish courts. Those who might be considered as professionals, and therefore producers, could in certain circumstances include packers, transporters and storers of products.

6.4   Specific products

Detailed comment on the Scottish position regarding nuclear power, foodstuffs and chemicals is not required. The English chapter refers to the Nuclear Installations Act 1965, the Food Safety Act 1990, the Medicines Act 1968 and the Environmental Protection Act 1990, all of which apply to Scotland.

In answer to a prosecution under the Food Safety Act 1990 it is a defence if the person charged can prove that he took all reasonable precautions and exercised all due diligence to avoid contravention.

7   CIVIL LIABILITY FOR DEFECTIVE PRODUCTS BROUGHT ABOUT BY BREACH OF STATUTORY REGULATION DESIGNED TO PROTECT CONSUMERS AND/OR TO PROMOTE SAFETY

The law on what, in the United Kingdom, is called 'breach of statutory duty' has developed similarly in Scotland and in England. When a statute expressly provides that there *shall be* liability under the civil law (such as in CPA 1987), no difficulty in interpretation arises. Equally, there is clarity when a statute expressly provides that there *shall not be* civil liability – such as under certain parts of the Health and Safety at Work etc Act 1974.

Less clear is the situation where the statute is silent on liability, whether civil or criminal. It has been judicially observed that if an Act of Parliament imposes a statutory duty but does not provide for a criminal sanction for breach of that duty, it can be assumed that civil liability exists – otherwise the statute would be pointless.

It is the statutes which impose criminal sanctions for breach of duty, while saying nothing about liability under the civil law, which require the closest interpretation. In such cases Scots law follows the English position, to the effect that one assumes there is no civil liability unless one of the two exceptions, as set out in the English chapter, applies.

CHAPTER XVIII

Jurisdiction, enforcement of judgments and conflicts of laws

Rebecca M Attree

Attree & Co
110 Cambridge Street
London
SW1V 4QF
England

Tel: ++ 44 71 630 6019
Fax: ++ 44 71 630 8681

CHAPTER XVIII

Jurisdiction, enforcement of judgments and conflicts of laws

Introduction

Many claims of product liability will be between victims and defendants from more than one country. The defective product itself may comprise components from different countries. It may, for example, have been made or assembled in Germany, exported to France, and then transported by a consumer to Italy, where it may cause harm. These situations raise questions of where and against whom a plaintiff may bring his claim and which law will govern the determination of such claim.

This chapter is divided into three sections. Section 1 will deal with the principal international conventions which may govern a product liability claim in Europe. Section 2 will deal largely with issues of when a court will have jurisdiction to hear a claim, and section 3 with which national law will be applied in determining the claim.

1 THE INTERNATIONAL CONVENTIONS

The law relating to jurisdiction and choice of law as between European member states is largely set out in a series of international Conventions. The adoption of the text of a treaty does not, by itself, create any obligations. A treaty does not come into being until two or more states consent to be bound by it, and the expression of such consent is usually by signature, exchange of instruments constituting a treaty, ratification, acceptance, approval or accession.

A treaty normally enters into force as soon as all the negotiating states have expressed their consent to be bound by it, but the negotiating states are always free to depart from this general rule by inserting an appropriate provision in the treaty itself. For example, a treaty may provide that it shall enter into force only when it has been ratified by a specified number of states.

Further, in some countries, there is a very clear difference between the effects of a treaty in international law and the effects of a treaty in domestic law. In the Netherlands, Portugal and France, a treaty becomes effective in domestic law following its publication. In the UK, Sweden and Denmark, a treaty becomes effective in international law when it is ratified, but it usually has no effect in national law until appropriate national legislation is passed. Indeed, the English House of Lords has held that UK ministers are not obliged to take the European Convention on Human Rights into consideration before issuing Directives, since to impose such an obligation 'would be to incorporate

the Convention into domestic law by the back door'.[1] In Austria, the effect of a treaty depends on its terms. If it contains no provisions to the contrary, it will be effective in national law upon signature or ratification. Otherwise, an Act of Parliament is required to give it effect.

International treaties require prior authorisation of the Spanish Parliament whenever they refer to political, military, financial or fundamental rights or territorial issues, or whenever they entail the amendment or superseding of an act or regulation or require the approval of legislation for its implementation. In any other case, a treaty may become effective in Spain by the signature of the representative, promulgation by the King and publication in the Official Gazette; no passing of national legislation is required. In these latter cases, Parliament should be immediately informed of the signature of the treaty.

Article 29 of the Constitution of Ireland, 1937 provides firstly that every International Agreement to which the State becomes a party is to be laid before Dail Eireann (the Irish Parliament). It is further provided in Article 29 that no International Agreement shall be part of the domestic law of Ireland save as may be determined by the Oireachtas (a term which incorporates the President, the Parliament and the Seanad).

A summary of the state of implementation of the International Conventions discussed below appears as Appendix 5.

1.1　Convention on Jurisdiction and the Enforcement of Judgments in Civil and Commercial Matters 1968 ('the Brussels Convention')

This Convention contains detailed rules on jurisdiction and defines which country will have jurisdiction over a particular action. Its aim is to reduce the possibility of 'forum shopping', that is, the multiplicity of jurisdictions in which a plaintiff may choose to commence proceedings. It also introduces an expeditious procedure for the recognition and enforcement of judgments of certain courts of member states throughout the EU.

The Convention was adopted by the six original members of the EC, namely Belgium, France, the Federal Republic of Germany, Italy, Luxembourg and the Netherlands and has since been acceded to by Denmark, the Irish Republic, the UK, Spain, Portugal and Greece. It has the force of law in each of these countries save Portugal.

When Spain and Portugal joined the EC in 1989, they were also required to accede to the Brussels Convention. They did so by way of the San Sebastian Convention, which also made some substantive amendments to the provisions of the Brussels Convention. The San Sebastian Convention is in force in all member states which acceded to the Brussels Convention before 1 January 1995, with the exception of Belgium and Denmark which have only signed the San Sebastian Convention and not yet ratified it.

The question of which version of the Brussels Convention will apply in any given case will depend upon the private international law of the relevant country. From an English viewpoint, it will depend upon whether the San Sebastian Convention was in force in both England and the country of domicile of the defendant on the date on which the proceedings are commenced. If it was not, but the relevant countries were parties to the Brussels Convention at such date, the Brussels Convention will apply.

1　*R v Secretary of State for the Home Department, ex p Brind* [1991] 1 AC 696.

As a result of Austria, Finland and Sweden becoming members of the EU on 1 January 1995, each of these states acceded to the Brussels Convention although they were already parties to the Parallel Convention (see section 1.2 below).

In European countries where the Brussels Convention is not in force, for example, Switzerland, existing national law and any relevant Conventions and bilateral agreements will continue to apply.

1.2   Parallel convention

On 16 September 1988 in Lugano the EFTA countries (Austria, Finland, Iceland, Norway, Sweden and Switzerland) entered into a Convention on Jurisdiction and the Enforcement of Judgments in Civil and Commercial matters with the member states of the EC ('the Lugano Convention'). The Lugano Convention contains materially the same provisions as those of the Brussels Convention and has largely been superseded by the latter. For practical purposes, the Lugano Convention is currently in force for Norway and Switzerland of the EFTA countries and also for France, Italy, Luxembourg, Netherlands, Portugal and the United Kingdom of the EU countries.

1.3   Hague Convention on the Law applicable to Product Liability 1973 ('the Product Liability Convention')

This Convention applies to international cases of product liability and designates the applicable law whether or not this is the law of the State party to the Convention. The Convention is currently in force in France, Luxembourg, the Netherlands, Norway and Spain.

The Product Liability Convention sets out a complex system of choice of law rules consisting of traditional conflict rules with certain refinements aiming to balance the interests of each party to a product liability case. It applies to claims brought by any legal person irrespective of whether or not they are a consumer. The provisions of the Product Liability Convention stand side by side with those of the Brussels Convention, the former dealing with choice of law and the latter dealing with jurisdiction and enforcement of judgments.

1.4   EC Convention on the Law Applicable to Contractual Obligations ('the Rome Convention')

This was adopted by the Council of the EC on 19 June 1980 in Rome. Its object is to provide in all member states of the EU uniform rules for the ascertainment of the law governing an international contract. The Rome Convention is in force in Belgium, Denmark, the Netherlands, France, Ireland, Italy, Luxembourg and the Federal Republic of Germany. It was introduced into UK law in April 1991 by the Contracts (Applicable Law) Act 1990. Greece acceded to the Rome Convention by way of the Luxembourg Convention. This has been ratified by all signatories to the Rome Convention with the exception of Italy.

The Convention regulates not only conflict situations between the laws of the member states but also cases in which the law of a member state conflicts with that of a non-member state. It establishes two principles:

(a) if the parties agree at the outset which country's law should apply, then that choice will be upheld;

(b) if no such choice has been made, the law of the country which is the most closely connected with the contract will apply. A set of principles has been established to assist the practical application of this rule.

1.5   The Hague Convention on the Law Applicable to International Sales of Goods 1955

This Convention, which is currently in force in Belgium, Denmark, Finland, France, Italy and Sweden within the EU and also Norway, Switzerland and Niger, seeks to ascertain the law applicable to international sales of goods. It applies to sales, based on documents, of goods (with certain exceptions, the most noteworthy being ships and aircraft). The Convention stipulates that such sales are to be governed by the domestic law of the country designated by the parties. If this is not clearly designated, the domestic law of the country in which the vendor is habitually resident at the time he receives the order will apply.

This Convention may be replaced by the Hague Convention on the law applicable to Contracts for the International Sale of Goods 1986 for states which are parties to both conventions. The latter convention is currently not in force; it needs five ratifications in order to become effective.

1.6   Relationship between the Rome Convention and the Hague Convention on the Law Applicable to International Sales of Goods 1955

The Rome Convention is expressly subordinated to both international conventions to which Contracting States are, or become, a party and also existing or subsequent acts of community institutions (articles 20 and 21). It follows that in principal the Hague Convention on the Law Applicable to the International Sales of Goods 1955 will apply as between Belgium, Denmark, France and Italy if there is an inconsistency with the Rome Convention. A logical difficulty will arise if other international conventions contain similar subordination articles as those contained in the Rome Convention as to which convention takes priority over another. The Vienna Convention on the Law of Treaties[2] expressly provides that in the event of incompatibility, the later treaty in time will prevail.

1.7   Unification of International Sales Law (the Hague International Sales Conventions and the Vienna Convention)

The Uniform Law on the International Sale of Goods (ULIS) and the Uniform Law on the Formation of Contracts for the International Sale of Goods (ULFC) were adopted at the Hague in 1964 (together referred to as 'the Hague International Sales Conventions'). The former seeks to unify the substantive law of international sales, in particular the obligations of the buyer and seller, and the passing of risk. The latter attempts to reconcile the differences of the

2   Art 30, paras 3 and 4A.

common and civil law on offer and acceptance leading to the conclusion of an international contract.

One of the defects of ULIS from an international conflicts of law standpoint is that article 17 provides that where the Convention does not expressly settle questions concerning matters it is intended to govern, the courts must decide them 'in conformity with the general principles on which the Convention is based'. With respect to private international law, article 2 prohibits the courts from applying this except under special circumstances. Since this Convention is not as comprehensive as other civil codes, and fails to lay down an explicit statement of the general principles upon which it is supposedly based, the courts have been unable to promulgate general principles which are essential for analogy to their particular systems of law.

The Hague International Sales Conventions are given effect in the UK by the Uniform Laws on International Sales Act 1967.[3] The number of countries which have ratified the Hague International Sales Conventions is disappointingly small.[4] The effect of these Conventions on international sales law has been very limited since they are only applicable if the parties so specify, and in practice very few parties do. As a result a further Convention, namely the United Nations Convention for the International Sale of Goods, was approved in Vienna in 1980 ('the Vienna Convention').

The Vienna Convention came into effect on 1 January 1988 between (inter alia) the USA, France and Italy, but, at the time of writing, has not been signed by the UK nor introduced into English law by way of an Act of Parliament. It has been acceded to or ratified in Europe by Austria, Denmark,[5] Finland, France, Germany, Italy, the Netherlands, Norway, Sweden (in part)[6] Spain (in part) and Switzerland. Certain other countries of the world have also acceded to or ratified the Treaty. It is intended to be the centrepiece of international harmonisation of trade laws, setting out to provide a unified system of law which attempts to meet the many demands of international commerce. In particular, it governs the formation of contracts for international sales, controls the transfer of goods, lays down the obligations of seller and buyer and addresses the issue of allocation of risk. Unlike the Hague International Sales Conventions, the Vienna Convention provides that national law is to be referred to wherever possible, but that it is to be supplemented, where necessary, by the rules of private international law.

The Vienna Convention deals principally with the sale of goods as between businesses. There is currently a draft Directive under discussion regarding the harmonisation of the law relating to guarantees for consumer goods and after sales service. If implemented, this Directive will operate for sales of consumer goods on parallel lines to sales of goods between businesses where the Vienna Convention applies.

---

3   Amended by the Sale and Supply of Goods Act 1994, Sch 2, para 3.
4   Notably Belgium, the Federal Republic of Germany, Italy, Luxembourg, the Netherlands and the UK.
5   The Vienna Convention was brought into force in Denmark on 1 March 1990, except for Part II which concerns formation of the contract. The Convention shall not, however, apply where both contracting parties have their places of business in Denmark, Finland, Iceland, Norway or Sweden.
6   Arts 1-13 and 25-88 apply as Swedish law from 1 January 1988, except in cases where both parties have their place of business within the Nordic countries.

1.8   UN Convention on the Limitation Period on the International Sale of Goods ('the Limitation Convention')

This Convention was signed on 14 June 1974 in New York. It was amended by a Protocol on 11 April 1980, the same day that the Vienna Convention was approved. The Protocol aligns the provisions of the Limitation Convention with those of the Vienna Convention. Of the European countries, only the Federal Republic of Germany and Norway have ratified or acceded to the Limitation Convention.

The Limitation Convention will replace in the countries which sign and enforce it a variety of conflicting national laws which provide limitation periods ranging from six months to 30 years. The basic aim of the Convention is to establish a uniform time limit that prevents the pressing of claims at such a late date that evidence has become unreliable.

The Convention limits to four years the period in which a buyer or seller may bring an action based on a contract for the International Sale of Goods. However, the Convention, as amended by the 1980 Protocol, does not apply to sales to which the Vienna Convention does not apply, which will continue to be governed by relevant national periods of limitation.

The Convention sets out when the limitation period begins and ceases, when it can be extended, how it can be modified by the parties, and how it is calculated. In the case of a breach of contract of sale, the limitation period begins on the date of the breach. When the buyer finds a defect in the goods supplied or discovers that they do not otherwise conform to the terms of the contract, the limitation period starts from the date of delivery or when he refused to accept delivery.

The Convention provides that the limitation period ceases to run when one party brings judicial proceedings against the other. When a party making a claim is prevented by circumstances beyond his control from starting legal proceedings, he may have a one-year extension from the time when those circumstances cease to exist. The overall limit for extensions of the limitation period is ten years from the date when the period began to run.

1.9   Summary of international Conventions

The practical result of the current state of play of enforcement of the above-mentioned Conventions is that most questions of jurisdiction, recognition and enforcement will be governed as between member states of the EU by the Brussels Convention as amended by the San Sebastian Convention and as between Norway and Switzerland by the Parallel Convention. The choice of law in tort will be governed by the private international law of the relevant country which may be a party to the Product Liability Convention. The 'proper law' of a contract is increasingly ascertained pursuant to the Rome Convention, as more states implement its provisions in their national law. It may, on occasions, be determined by the Hague Convention on the Law Applicable to International Sales 1955 or the Vienna Convention. If no private international law conventions are in force in the relevant countries, the 'proper law' of a contract will be determined in accordance with the private international rules of the countries in question. Many international sales contracts will be governed by the Vienna Convention and national laws relating to periods of limitation. Certain such contracts will be governed by the Hague International Sales Conventions and the Limitation Convention.

2 THE CONSIDERATIONS WHEN BRINGING AN INTERNATIONAL CLAIM

If a German plaintiff is injured by a defective product which has been, for example, manufactured in France and sold in Italy, there may be a choice of countries in which to claim.

Equally, a defendant put on notice of a potential claim may be faced with a selection of countries where it might be sued. Although it is generally the party suffering injury or loss which commences proceedings, on occasions a potential defendant may prefer to commence an action itself (for example, for substantive relief or negative declaration), and thereby seek to ensure that the proceedings are heard before a court of the jurisdiction which is most favourable to it.[7]

The four principal considerations which a party should bear in mind when deciding in which court an action should be heard are:

(a) Does the court in question have jurisdiction to hear the claim?
(b) Will that court accept jurisdiction (or will it grant a stay of those proceedings)?
(c) Will a judgment obtained from that court be enforceable elsewhere? and
(d) Which law will the court apply in deciding the claim?

A consideration of these questions will dictate the most appropriate forum in which the party should seek to have a dispute determined.

The first consideration is dealt with in section 2.2, below; the second is dealt with in section 2.4, below. The third question is dealt with in section 2.5, below and the fourth question is dealt with in section 3 of this chapter.

2.1 Choosing the forum in which to bring the claim

A choice of forum may be affected by various procedural and substantive factors, such as:

(a) whether the law is more favourable in one country rather than another;
(b) language;
(c) evidence; and
(d) time and money.

2.1.1 The law

Assuming that the courts will apply their own laws in determining the claim (although it is open for either party to plead the application of a foreign law[8]), a plaintiff should consider:

(a) Has the country in question implemented the Product Liability Directive by way of national law? If so,
  (i) when was the defective product put into circulation?
       The Directive does not apply to products put into circulation before the date on which the national implementing law came into force. Until that

---

7 The ECJ has confirmed that an action for negative declaratory relief may have the same cause of action as proceedings brought by a 'real' plaintiff for substantive relief. *The Tatry Case* 406/92 [1995] 1LPr 81 (ECJ).
8 See section 3 below.

date, existing national law will apply. As can be seen from the foregoing chapters, there are many differences between these laws. For example, in France, Luxembourg and Belgium, the producer is strictly liable for any defects in his product. In Ireland and the United Kingdom, the consumer must prove negligence. In Austria, Belgium, Denmark and West Germany, the burden of proof is reversed in the consumer's favour. In Danish law, the distributor of a product has a right of indemnity against its manufacturer, which cannot be excluded for product liability falling under the national legislation implementing the Directive. A distributor may therefore seek to insist on Danish law applying to the contract with the manufacturer, and the manufacturer on the other hand may wish to resist this.

(ii) Has the national implementing law derogated in one of the three ways permitted by the Product Liability Directive? (See Appendix 2 for details of derogation, if any, by the countries dealt with in this book.)

Namely, does the national law permit liability for primary agricultural produce and game, has provision been made for the 'development risks' defence and has a financial ceiling on damages payable for death or injury caused by the same defect been adopted?

(b) If the country in question has not implemented the Product Liability Directive by way of national law, what are the national laws relating to contract, tort and product liability?

For example, France has still to implement the Product Liability Directive.

(c) Have the Product Safety Directive and/or any other applicable EC Consumer Safety Directives been implemented in the relevant country?

(d) Which international conventions are in force in the country in question?

Appendix 5 reflects the current state of implementation of the most relevant conventions which are discussed in Section 1 of this chapter.

(e) If the defendant is a limited company in dissolution, can it be reconstituted in order for a claim to be brought against it or its insurers?

Appendix 3 reflects the current position in the countries dealt with in this book.

(f) Has the limitation period for bringing the claim expired in the country in question?

In Norway, the limitation period can be up to 20 years from the date when the product left the producer's control. In France, the designation of a court-appointed expert will often interrupt the limitation period.

(g) What are the private international laws of the country in question and, perhaps more importantly, is the court likely to consider at length whether it is the appropriate place to conduct the litigation?

(h) Do the courts of the country in question frequently apply 'public policy' when determining issues (ie adjudge a contract unenforceable on the grounds it is contrary to the public interest)?

For example, Austrian and French courts apply 'public policy' very rarely; English, Scottish and Spanish courts are slightly more willing to do so. In Denmark, public policy is probably frequently applied by the courts but is rarely expressly mentioned in judgments. In Ireland, the Irish Constitution 1937, which recognises the particular role of the Catholic religion, is a factor determining public policy. As a result, certain institutions regarded

as important to the Catholic religion, such as the family and marriage, are given particular protection.

(i) To what extent will it be possible to appeal against any decision made?

(j) Can a defendant in an existing action make a claim against another person and, if so, will the claim be dealt with as part of the main proceedings?

For example, in England, Belgium, Denmark, France, Ireland and Scotland this is possible. In Austria, a third party may be asked, but not compelled, to join as a co-defendant. In Spain, a defendant cannot generally claim against another person while the case is pending. In order to sue a third party, it is necessary for the claim to be rejected because the third party has not been sued, and for the plaintiff to then commence a new action against all relevant defendants.

(k) To what extent are claims for contribution and recourse allowed between co-defendants (other than as specified in the Product Liability Directive)?

In England, Denmark, France, Ireland, Scotland and Spain, defendants who have been made jointly and severally liable to a plaintiff can have their liability inter se decided by the court. However, this does not prevent the plaintiff from seeking a claim against each defendant jointly and severally.

In Austria, a defendant may bring a claim for contribution and recourse pursuant to section 1358, ABGB.

2.1.2 Language

Although the following points may seem obvious, they are often overlooked:

(a) To what extent do you speak the language of the country where you might bring a claim?

(b) Can you find a lawyer in that country who speaks your language?

(c) What language do your and the opposition's witnesses and experts speak?

(d) In what language are your evidential documents written?

(e) What will be the costs of interpretators and translators?

2.1.3 Evidence

Almost all cases are won or lost on evidence. Evidence is usually:

(a) oral;

(b) written; or

(c) expert.

i Oral evidence Certain jurisdictions have a greater tradition of giving oral evidence. For example, oral evidence plays a larger part in proceedings in the UK than in France.

It may be better where your opponent is to call witnesses for them to give oral evidence so that your lawyers have an opportunity to cross examine them on your behalf.

In certain jurisdictions, notably France and Germany, the judge assumes an inquisitorial function. This means that the character and ability of the judge becomes even more important than in an adversarial system. It is noteworthy that the career path of a judge in France, Germany and Italy is separate to that of a lawyer and, unlike in the UK, judges have rarely practised as lawyers.

ii   Written evidence   Not all jurisdictions permit or require parties to litigation to disclose their documents to the other side. The rules for this process known as 'discovery' vary from jurisdiction to jurisdiction.

(a)   What are the rules relating to obtaining information before commencing proceedings? ('Pre-Action Discovery')

In England, there are usually no opportunities to ask a court to order disclosure of information to see whether legal action may be worthwhile. A plaintiff must therefore generally risk initiating an action and subsequently finding his case to be very weak. However, in a product liability case brought before the English courts, an application can be made to the court for an order for inspection of property, which may become the subject of legal action. A potential plaintiff may also apply to the court for disclosure of documents, such as medical and hospital records, before the action starts.[9]

In Switzerland, the earliest moment a party can generally be forced to produce documents or disclose information is during evidence procedures, taking place after both parties have completely filed their written statements. Exceptions to this rule are where a contract relied on the disclosure of certain specific information, or if certain evidence is in danger of being lost.

In Germany, all documents to be relied upon in the action must be served with the Statement of Claim and Defence, although there is no obligation to serve documents which damage a party's case or advance that of the opponent.

(b)   What are the rules relating to obtaining information before and at the trial?

In product liability actions, discovery is a burden mainly on defendants. While it is useful to have details of a plaintiff's financial claims and his medical record, this task is small compared to the duty of, for example the manufacturer, who must disclose all documents relating to the development of a product over many years. The court will only order further discovery where it is necessary in the interests of justice or to save costs but a manufacturer's data will almost always be seen to be centrally relevant.

The common law jurisdictions in Europe in general allow for greater discovery than civil law jurisdictions. For example, a party to litigation in France must 'spontaneously' submit to the other parties all documents which he intends to use at a trial. Although there are rules whereby a judge may subpoena a party to produce a specific document and impose fines upon him if he fails to comply, in practice this procedure is rarely used. In Switzerland, subpoena orders are available against both the other party to the actions and third parties, although they must be very specific. A party's refusal to comply with such an order may be taken into account by the court when making judgment.

In English proceedings there is a positive duty on the parties to disclose all relevant documents unless they can plead there is a specific reason for not doing so. Further, in an English product liability claim, the court may order third parties who are not defendants to give discovery.[10] This contrasts with other English litigation where third parties can only be required by a subpoena to produce material, to bring to the trial. In Ireland, discovery may be ordered against the plaintiff, defendant or, in certain circumstances, third parties who are not defendants in the action.

---

9   Supreme Court Act 1981, s 33; RSC Ord 24, r 7A and Ord. 29, r 7A.
10   Supreme Court Act 1981, s 34.

> *In the German Civil Procedure law, no party has an affirmative duty to help inform the court or the other party of the objective facts of the case. There are a few statutory provisions which grant a right to obtain information explicitly, but none of these provisions is of importance with respect to product liability cases.*

iii   Expert evidence   What is the role of an expert?

In France and Germany, it is quite common for an expert to be appointed prior to the action on the merits, who will carry out an inquisitorial investigation, often involving all parties to the litigation and their legal advisers. The expert usually submits a written report to the court which, although not binding, normally carries considerable weight.

In England, an expert is called specifically on behalf of one of the parties in support of its claim. It is usual to seek the experts' agreement as between themselves on certain points in advance of the hearing.

2.1.4   Time and money: theirs or yours?

i   Time: theirs or yours?   *One practical, but very significant, factor is who will have to do the most travelling if you bring the claim in a country other than your own. Time has a cost both in terms of diverted management time and, particularly in jurisdictions where legal fees are calculated on the basis of an hourly rate, a monetary value. Travel costs may also form a material part of the cost of the litigation. Consider in particular the extent to which witnesses, lawyers, your opponent and yourself will have to travel.*

Also, if many of the documents to be adduced in evidence are in a foreign language it may take considerable time for them to be professionally translated.

ii   Time goes by   *The court procedure in certain jurisdictions may offer opportunities for quick remedies. In the Netherlands, the implementation of the Product Liability Convention may enable a plaintiff to recover interim damages within approximately one month of initiating the claim.*

Also, it may take longer in certain jurisdictions than others for your case to be heard. For example, in Belgium and Italy, the 'judicial overdue' has become critical and indeed for several months of 1995 Italian litigation lawyers were 'on strike'.

In certain countries, if a criminal trial is already being conducted against the defendant, the laws may allow you to intervene in certain circumstances to claim damages (see section 2.2.5 below). This procedure allows you to avoid taking time and paying the costs of mounting a separate civil court proceedings and to enjoy certain evidential benefits through the criminal and inquisitorial nature of the main action.

iii   Money: theirs or yours?

(a) In which jurisdiction are you likely to receive the largest sum of money and pay out the least if you win or lose?

Awards of damages, particularly for personal injury, tend to be low in Spain, Portugal, Italy, Switzerland and Belgium. Awards of damages from personal injury are higher in the United Kingdom and in the USA particularly where the awards are made by juries.

The Product Liability Directive provides in article 16 that member states may provide that a producer's total liability for damage resulting from identical

items with the same defect shall be limited to an amount not less than Ecu 70 m. Only Germany, Greece, Portugal and Spain have imposed such a limit. In Denmark and Finland, limits are imposed by other statutes.

(b) Can you get your lawyer to take all or part of the financial risk by agreeing to a conditional or contingency fee?

Unlike in the United States, the professional rules of most European countries expressly forbid lawyers from agreeing to be paid a proportion of the amount of damages recovered by the plaintiff. The exceptions are Finland, Norway, and Switzerland. In the UK and France, solicitors are permitted to uplift their fees by a sum equal to up to 20% of the damages awarded. In Scotland, contingency fees are not permitted but speculative actions are allowed. A speculative fee is where a solicitor agrees to receive no fee if the claim is unsuccessful, but to be entitled up to a maximum of twice his normal fees if the claim is successful.

(c) Can you get the other side to pay if you win?

In Austria, Denmark, England, Germany, Ireland, Scotland and Spain a proportion of the legal costs may be recoverable from the unsuccessful party.

In England and France, a plaintiff who is successful against a legally aided defendant will not recover any of his costs, and may therefore only achieve a 'Pyrrhic victory'. In Denmark, Ireland and Scotland, an award may be exceptionally made against the legal aid fund. In Spain, a legally aided defendant against whom a costs order is made must pay if 'his fortunes improve' within three years of the end of the proceedings. This is deemed to be the case if he earns twice the national minimum wage.

In France, the awards for legal costs are minimal and bear no real relationship to the actual fees paid to lawyers. Further, before French appellate courts, the parties must retain an 'avoué' in addition to an 'avocat'. Avoués are intermediaries having a monopoly as regards procedural aspects of the appellate proceedings. Avoués are by statute paid a percentage of the amount involved in the litigation and their costs are always borne by the losing party. A similar system applies in Spain, where the intermediary is called a 'procurador'.

In Switzerland, the practice of lawyers charging their clients is regulated by Cantonal law preventing lawyers from charging excessively. As a general principle, the losing party before a Swiss court will have to pay court costs and the winner's lawyer's fees.

(d) Can the state or some other third party pay or contribute to your costs?

Throughout the EU, (although rarely in Greece) a party may be eligible for a contribution towards their legal costs by way of legal aid. The contribution is generally made after the merits of the case have been considered and the financial position of the applicant assessed. In France, 15% to 20% of claimants are entitled to legal aid. In Spain, Consumer Associations bringing proceedings on behalf of consumers are entitled to legal aid.

The 1954 Hague Convention on Civil Procedure provides that the nationals of each of its contracting states shall in all other contracting states be entitled to free legal aid on the same basis as nationals of the latter states, provided they comply with the legislation of the state in which free legal aid is sought. The Convention has been ratified by Austria, Belgium, Denmark, Finland, France, Germany, Italy, Luxembourg, Netherlands, Norway, Portugal, Spain, Sweden and Switzerland.

In Switzerland, persons in financial difficulties can be relieved from paying court costs. In France, junior lawyers can be required to give free legal advice to people of low financial means.

Legal expenses insurance is generally available in Europe for actions brought by private individuals for damages. It is mainly confined to matters relating to motor vehicles in Austria, Scotland and Spain. Legal insurance for commercial litigants has only recently become available. Product Liability insurance will generally cover the legal costs incurred in defending a claim.

(e) Can you share your costs with others?

In Denmark, France and Ireland class actions are permitted. However, in France, procedural rules for class actions do not exist as such. It is noteworthy that authorised consumer groups, trade associations and trade unions may in certain circumstances bring an action on behalf of consumers or their members respectively. In Austria, England, Scotland and Switzerland, class actions cannot be brought to claim damages. In England and Scotland, a 'representative' plaintiff can act where numerous people 'have the same interest' on the basis that his claim is a specimen claim on a point of law. The limitation period in respect of the other claims may be extended until after the hearing of the specimen case. In Austria, all actions of claimants injured by the same accident may be passed on to one judge who determines all the cases.

Spanish law allows group actions to be brought. Two particularly important group actions have been brought. In 1978 a lorry carrying a dangerous substance caused 215 deaths and many injuries at a campsite. In 1981 a class action was brought as a result of the marketing for human consumption of oil manufactured for industrial use, which caused many deaths and injuries. Both cases were dealt with by the criminal courts.

These are the material factors to be borne in mind when considering where a dispute should be determined. Which is the determining factor will depend upon the nature of the claim, and the plaintiff's and the defendant's circumstances.

2.2 Jurisdiction

Since most of the countries dealt with in this book have adopted or acceded to the Brussels Convention as amended by the San Sebastian Convention, its provisions will be considered in some detail. The provisions of the Lugano Convention are broadly similar to those of the Brussels Convention. The jurisdiction of the courts of those countries which have not implemented the Brussels Convention or the Lugano Convention will be determined by the private international laws of the country in question.

The system for establishing jurisdiction provided by the Brussels Convention gives very little scope for judicial discretion, which previously played a significant role in common law jurisdictions. Thus, for example, if a plaintiff brings proceedings before an English court of competent jurisdiction, that court is not permitted to decline to hear the case on the grounds of *forum non conveniens* – ie that some other forum is more 'appropriate', in the sense of more suitable for the ends of justice. Incidentally, most continental European jurisdictions never accepted this doctrine, although Dutch appellate courts are obliged to apply it. The practical result is that where there may be two or more

courts with jurisdiction to try a particular case, and a prospective litigant has a view as to which court he would prefer, speed is essential in commencing proceedings.

2.2.1 Domicile

The cornerstone rule on jurisdiction contained in the Brussels Convention is that a defendant may be sued in the State where he is domiciled. The Convention does not provide any definition of domicile. The domicile of an individual and a company is broadly ascertained as follows:

i Individual   The question of whether an individual is domiciled in a particular country is determined by the national laws of that country. Since the laws relating to domicile have not been harmonised throughout Europe, a person could be held to be domiciled in two countries simultaneously according to each of the relevant laws.

In the UK and Ireland, a person will be domiciled there if they have been resident and the nature and circumstances of their residence indicate a substantial connection with the UK. Residence in the UK for a period of three months or more prior to the commencement of proceedings leads to a rebuttable presumption that a substantial connection with the UK exists.

In France, the domicile of a citizen is the place where he has his 'main establishment'.

In Belgium, the domicile of a citizen is separately defined for judicial purposes as the place where he is principally registered as resident in the local population register. Belgian law requires all persons resident in Belgium to be so registered, although the place where they are registered may not necessarily be the place where they are actually resident.

In Germany a person is domiciled in the city where he lives for most of the time. In practice, this is usually the city where the person is registered with the police, as required by law.

In Denmark, Norway and Sweden, a person is domiciled where his permanent home is situated (ie the place where his belongings are normally situated and where he usually lives).

In Austria, a person's domicile is the place where he has settled down with the proven intention, or the intention which results from his circumstances, of permanently residing.

ii Company   Article 53 of the Brussels Convention provides that the seat of a company shall be treated as its domicile. However, in order to determine that seat, the court shall apply rules of private international law. The seat of a company in English law and Irish law is defined in broad terms as being where it was incorporated and where it has its registered office, or where its central management and control are exercised. However, a corporation is not to be regarded as having its seat in a contracting state other than the UK if it is shown that the courts of that state would not regard it as having its seat there.[11]

In Denmark, the domicile of a company is where its main office is situated. If the domicile of a company has to be determined pursuant to the Brussels Convention, the Danish court will refer to the judicial system according to which the company was founded for the answer.

11   Civil Jurisdiction and Judgments Act 1982, s 42.

In Italy, France, Norway and Portugal, the mere fact of a company having its registered office (and conducting business) in the relevant country will mean it is considered domiciled there.

In Austria, a company is domiciled where it has its seat, which will normally be entered on the commercial register. If it is not so registered, the seat of a company is where its administration is located.

In Spain, a company is domiciled in the place stated in its byelaws. In the absence of such statement, it is domiciled in the place of its headquarters.

In Germany, a company is domiciled where it has its seat. If the company has a branch, then there is a choice between the place of the branch and the place of the seat, if the branch was involved in the claim.

In Norway, in addition to bringing claims based on domicile, it is possible to bring a claim against a person or company that owns any property in the country.

2.2.2 *Jurisdiction clauses*

Article 17 of the Brussels Convention permits the use of choice of jurisdiction clauses and sets out the formal requirements for their validity. The agreement of a specific jurisdiction must be in writing, or evidenced in writing, or agreed by way of commercial practice of which the parties are or ought to have been aware. The effect of this article is that a valid jurisdiction clause confers exclusive jurisdiction on the chosen court or courts, provided at least one of the parties is domiciled within the EU and exclusive jurisdiction is not provided for by article 16 (see section 2.2.3 below). Further, if the jurisdiction clause was for the benefit of only one of the parties then that party will have the right to bring proceedings in another member state's courts if it has jurisdiction by virtue of the Brussels Convention. Certain national laws preclude the exclusion of their own jurisdiction. For example, article 2 of the Italian *Codice di Procedura Civile* provides that jurisdiction can be excluded only for disputes between a non-national and a national non-resident.

In Portuguese law, the choice of jurisdiction must be expressed in writing, in the same form as is required of the contract it relates to (for example, since a contractual loan must be notarised, the choice of forum clause must also be notarised).

2.2.3 *Jurisdiction if no jurisdiction clause*

The Brussels Convention provides that, if there is no agreement as to jurisdiction, the courts may exercise:

(a) general direct jurisdiction;
(b) special jurisdiction;
(c) additional jurisdiction; or
(d) exclusive jurisdiction.

Since many claims in product liability are brought in tort, there will rarely be an agreement as to jurisdiction between the parties.

i General jurisdiction As stated above, the fundamental principle set out in the Brussels Convention is that, if a defendant is domiciled in the EU, the court of the country of his domicile will be the only one competent to entertain claims in civil and commercial matters. The rule of only one court being competent to entertain a claim is extended so that if proceedings involving the same cause

of action between the same parties are pending in the courts of one contracting state, any court in another contracting state shall decline jurisdiction over that case on its own motion. If 'related actions' are brought in the courts of different member states, the second court has a discretion to order a stay (see section 2.4, below). Actions are 'related' if there is a risk of irreconcilable judgments of the two courts concerned with the same matter.

A victim within the EU of a defective product manufactured outside the EU will always be able to bring an action in the EU provided the relevant country has implemented the Product Liability Directive and is a party to the Brussels Convention, as there will be an importer treated as a 'producer' for the purpose of the Directive. If the plaintiff cannot identify the importer, then the supplier becomes liable unless he in turn can identify the importer.

Plaintiffs outside the EU seeking to sue EU producers will have to look at their national rules and Conventions to establish whether they can bring those producers into their own jurisdiction. In the case of Norway and Switzerland, the Parallel Convention may be applicable. In Austria, the Act on Consumer Protection provides that the parties to a contract can agree upon the jurisdiction of a court only where the consumer either lives or works.[12] However, the consumer is free to choose any other forum which is provided for by private international law if he wishes to institute proceedings against a producer.

ii Special jurisdiction   Under article 5 of the Brussels Convention, in certain circumstances the plaintiff will have alternative fora available in which to bring his claim.

Since a product liability claim may be framed in contract and tort a plaintiff may have several options available.

In *contract*, the courts for the place of performance of the obligation in question will also have jurisdiction. The national court, using its own rules of private international law, must decide upon which is the primary obligation and where is its place of performance. In a product liability claim, this could be the place of sale or, if different, the place of delivery, depending on the conflicts of the *lex fori*.

In *tort*,[13] the courts for the place where the harmful event occurred will also have jurisdiction. The European court has interpreted 'harmful event' in the widest possible way[14] to refer both to the place where the damage occurred and the place of the event giving rise to it. Accordingly, it seems that where the act occurs in one member state and the damage occurs in another member state, the plaintiff has the option of suing the defendant in the courts of either state, as well as the state where the defendant was domiciled, if this happened to be different. For example, a Dutch court assumed jurisdiction on the basis of article 5(3) of the Brussels Convention in a product liability case over a German manufacturer who had shipped rolls of underfelt to a wholesaler in the Netherlands, where the goods caused damage to a Dutch business purchaser.[15]

---

12   Konsumentenschutzgesetz-KSchG, s 14.
13   Any claim which is not contractual will be considered to be in tort (*Kalfelis Schroder Case* 189/87 [1988] ECR 5565). However, in the UK, the Consumer Protection Act 1967, s 6(7) specifically provides that liability under Part 1 of the Act is tortious 'for the purposes of any enactment conferring jurisdiction'.
14   Case 21/76 *Bier v Mines Des Potasse, European Court* [1976] ECR 1735 (30 November 1976).
15   *Zwolle* 18 February 1976, (1976) 23 NILR 364.

iii   Additional jurisdiction   Additional fora are available in matters relating to insurance and to consumer transactions involving the grant of credit to the consumer.

iv   Exclusive jurisdiction   Certain cases in which the national courts of the contracting states to the Brussels Convention have exclusive jurisdiction, regardless of domicile, are listed in article 16 of the Convention. They include, among others, any proceedings concerning the enforcement of foreign judgments.

2.2.4   Consumer claims

Article 14 of the Brussels Convention makes a special provision for jurisdiction when a consumer (ie a person contracting outside his trade or profession) brings proceedings. The proceedings must be in respect of certain limited types of contracts, namely either (i) for the sale of goods on instalment credit terms, an instalment loan or other form of credit or (ii) for the supply of goods or services and in the state of the consumer's domicile the consumer was invited specifically to contract or advertising took place and the consumer took in that state the steps necessary to conclude the contract. In this case, a consumer may bring proceedings against the other party to a contract either in the courts of the contracting state in which the latter is domiciled or in the courts of the contracting state in which he is himself domiciled. So, for example, a Dutchman who buys an English manufactured toaster which causes a fire in his home could in certain circumstances bring proceedings in either the Netherlands or England against the manufacturer.

It follows that a component supplier may not even be aware of the destination of the final product, yet faces possible liability under less favourable laws than either in his own domicile or in that of the manufacturer of the finished product. For example, the 'development risk' defence may be ineffective when a victim uses the Convention rules to bring his case in a country such as Luxembourg, which has not adopted that defence.

2.2.5   Civil jurisdiction when criminal proceedings are brought against a defendant

Article 5(4) of the Brussels Convention provides that a defendant may be sued in a member state where it is not domiciled in respect of a civil claim for damages which is based on an act giving rise to criminal proceedings. This is allowed to the extent only that the court of such member state 'has jurisdiction under its own law to entertain civil proceedings'. Although these words in the English text of the Convention are ambiguous, it is clear from other contracting states' authentic language versions that all that is required is that the court seised should be procedurally competent to decide both the criminal and civil matters. It is irrelevant whether the court would otherwise have international or domestic jurisdiction to hear the civil claim.

This 'civil action' procedure exists in many European countries (most notably France, but also Austria, the Federal Republic of Germany, England and the Netherlands, where it seems to be of far less practical significance). It allows the plaintiff to avoid undergoing the procedural burdens of mounting separate civil proceedings, and to enjoy certain evidential benefits through the criminal and inquisitorial nature of the main action (the court eventually delivering judgment in the civil action at the same time as deciding on the

criminal cause). It is likely that this procedure will be invoked more frequently in view of the imposition of criminal liability by the General Product Safety Directive. It follows that, for example, English defendants prosecuted elsewhere within the EU, may find themselves doubly in jeopardy through civil proceedings being mounted on the back of criminal prosecutions brought by the State.

In the UK, victims of a crime who have sustained personal injury as a result of the crime may in certain circumstances be able to recover relatively small amounts of compensation.[16]

2.2.6   Interim jurisdiction

Article 24 of the Brussels Convention provides that a plaintiff may apply to the courts of the contracting State for provisional, including protective, measures even if, under the Convention, the courts of another contracting state have jurisdiction as to the substance of the matter. This means that courts of all contracting States possess jurisdiction to exercise their national law powers to grant protective measures – for example, Mareva injunctions – notwithstanding that jurisdiction to do so would otherwise be lacking on other Convention grounds. For example, if a Belgian takes certain medicines when on holiday in Portugal which have been manufactured in Spain by a Spanish company, he may choose to bring his main claim against the manufacturer in Spain. However, he may, pending the determination of the main action, seek an injunction in Portugal to prevent the distribution of the dangerous drug. The time, expense and ease with which such interim relief may be obtained varies considerably within the different EU jurisdictions. In view of the Product Safety Directive, it may be cheaper and more effective for a plaintiff to effect the withdrawal of an unsafe product from the market by reporting the matter to the national body set up by the Directive to intervene in such instances.

2.2.7   Branch/agency considerations

Article 5(5) of the Brussels Convention provides that a person domiciled in a contracting State may, in another contracting state, be sued as regards a dispute arising out of the operations of a branch, agency or other establishment, in the courts of the place in which the branch, agency or other establishment is situated. It is the location (and appearance of permanence) of the branch, agency or other establishment, and the fact that its operations gave rise to the claim, which form the connecting factors justifying the jurisdiction of the court for that place. For the courts to have jurisdiction, it is not necessary for the operations in question to be performed in the member state where the branch is situated.[17]

The words 'branch, agency or other establishment' have been held to imply an undertaking which must have the appearance of permanency, management and be 'materially equipped' to negotiate business with third parties so that

---

16   Such a claim is formally made to the Criminal Injury Compensation Board. If a victim has sustained other types of damage as a result of a crime, the prosecutor may ask the judge to make an award for damages against the defendant to compensate the victim. In view of the implementation in the UK of the General Product Safety Directive, which imposes criminal liability for the manufacture or supply of an unsafe product, it is expected that the occasions upon which a plaintiff might recover on this basis in the UK will increase.

17   *Lloyd's Register of Shipping v Société Campenon Bernard, Case* C-439/93 ECJ 6.4.1995.

they would not have to deal direct with head office.[18] An independent distributor or sales representative would not come within this definition.

2.2.8 Co-defendants and third party claims

Article 6 of the Brussels Convention provides that if there are ongoing proceedings in a State, a party domiciled in another contracting state may be made a joint defendant or third party to those proceedings. However, the third party proceedings cannot be used solely with the object of obtaining jurisdiction over a target defendant. Further, it is now clear that the national court has a discretion, under its own procedural rules, to decline to exercise jurisdiction over third parties.[19]

In a product liability claim, the manufacturer and original supplier of the product or its components might be joined as a defendant or third party in the same proceedings. Jurisdiction over the manufacturer or original supplier of products will be established by article 6 irrespective of whether the person or company in question is domiciled in that jurisdiction in accordance with the domestic law of that jurisdiction. For example, if an Italian buys a French car in Italy which is defective, he may choose to sue the Italian car dealer in Italy. It may not be clear before initiating proceedings whether the car was defective as a result of the Italian car dealer improperly servicing it before sale, or whether the fault lay with its original French manufacturer. The Italian plaintiff may in these circumstances consider suing both the Italian car dealer and the French manufacturer as potentially liable suppliers of the defective car. For such a combined action to lie, it is not necessary that each defendant be charged with a tort: the Italian could sue the car dealer on the contract in Italy and obtain jurisdiction in Italy in tort over the foreign manufacturer.

The outcome of the rule in Article 6 is that an inventive plaintiff may obtain a tactical advantage by foisting proceedings on an opponent in an unexpected European court.

The effects of articles 5 and 6 of the Brussels Convention are substantial, not only on jurisdiction but also through the private international laws of the forum, on choice of law. Further, these articles have a significant effect under the Convention's enforcement rules (see later), on enforcement of a judgment given, for example, in Belgium against an Irish manufacturer, in Ireland or, indeed, any other EU country.

It may often be the case that since in many product liability cases at least one prospective defendant is established within the EU country in which the plaintiff is domiciled, the Convention will permit litigation of the whole case in that country.

2.2.9 Insurance

Articles 7 to 12 of the Brussels Convention make specific provisions in relation to the insurance industry. Insurers domiciled in a contracting state may be sued in that state, or the courts of the contracting state where the policyholder is domiciled, or if he is a co-insurer, the courts of the contracting state in which proceedings are being brought against the leading insurer. When the insurer is the plaintiff, he may only bring proceedings in the courts of the contracting

---

18 *Somafer SA v Ferngas* [1978] ECR 2183.
19 *Kongress Agentur Hages GmbH v Zeehaghe BV* [1990] 1 ECR 1845.

State where the insured is domiciled. However, in the UK, Schedule 4 to the Civil Jurisdiction and Judgments Act 1982 contains no equivalent to these specific provisions. It follows that internal UK jurisdiction in direct insurance actions is governed by the same rules of Schedule 4 as apply to non-insurance proceedings brought under the Civil Jurisdiction and Judgments Act 1982.

2.2.10   Summary

The practical effect of the Product Liability Directive and the Brussels Convention is that parties may have a choice as to the court in which their claims are heard. Once judgment is obtained, it can be enforced in any other member state, even though no judgment could have been realistically anticipated against that defendant had the proceedings originally been brought in the country where the enforcement is to be undertaken. So, for example, a French plaintiff injured in Luxembourg by an exploding television manufactured in Germany, might choose to sue the German manufacturer in Luxembourg (as being the place where the harmful event occurred), since the 'developments risk' defence is not available there. If he were to obtain judgment, it could be enforced against the defendant in Germany, irrespective of whether the defendant could have avoided the claim by successfully pleading the 'developments risk' defence, had the claim originally been brought there.

2.3   Criminal Prosecutions

The implementing laws of the General Product Safety Directive of some countries impose criminal liability for certain acts and omissions in relation to the manufacture and supply of unsafe products. Criminal prosecutions are excluded from the scope of the Brussels Convention. The general rule is that the courts of one country have jurisdiction to prosecute crimes committed within their territory. Most courts refuse to apply foreign criminal law or to enforce penal judgments of foreign courts.

It is noteworthy that the implementing laws of the UK impose criminal liabilities on both corporate bodies and also their directors, managers, secretaries or other similar officers. Article 16(2) of the Brussels Convention provides that in proceedings which have as their object, inter alia, the decisions of a company's organs, the courts of the Contracting State in which the company has its seat shall have exclusive jurisdiction.

So, for example, say Company Z Limited is registered in England and manufacturing and selling consumer goods throughout Europe. Unsafe products are manufactured and sold in Belgium, causing injury. The Belgian manufacturing plant is supervised by a Belgian director of Company Z Limited. If criminal proceedings were to be brought against Company Z Limited, it is highly likely that they would be brought in Belgium in view of the crime being committed there. However, the question of whether the Belgian director would be individually responsible would be determined in accordance with English law in view of Company Z Limited being registered in England and Wales.

2.4   Restraint of proceedings

In most European cases, even where the Brussels Convention applies, the courts of more than one state may have jurisdiction in respect of one cause of action.

However, the Convention was designed to avoid such duplicity of proceedings and articles 21 to 23 contain specific rules relating to actions pending in different states. Article 21 provides that, in such circumstances, any court other than the court 'first seised' with the action must stay its proceedings until the jurisdiction of the court first seised is established. The question when a court is 'first seised' will depend upon the national law of the state in which the court is situated and different rules can apply.

In order for this rule to apply, the two sets of proceedings must involve the 'same cause of action' and involve 'the same parties'. It would appear that these phrases are not to be interpreted in accordance with national law criteria; they are to have an autonomous meaning, and to be interpreted broadly.[20] For example it is probably not necessary for the parties to be identical, nor does it matter if there are additional parties. The rule will apply only as between the parties who are involved in both actions. Article 21 applies whether or not a defendant is domiciled in a contracting state.

Article 22 of the Convention provides that the court of a contracting state may stay its proceedings where the courts of another state have been first seised of a related action which has not been the subject of a judgment. Further, the court may decline jurisdiction if the court seised first would have jurisdiction over the dispute brought before it and also will allow consolidation of related actions.

Actions are considered to be related when they are so closely connected that it is expedient to hear and determine them together to avoid the risk of irreconcilable judgments arising from separate proceedings.[1]

It is unclear whether a court of a contracting state which has jurisdiction under the Brussels Convention and in which proceedings have commenced may exercise a discretion to stay those proceedings. It is generally thought that where the Convention confers jurisdiction on a court, there is no question of a discretion to stay the proceedings in favour of the courts of another contracting state except pursuant to the specific rules relating to pending actions in the Convention.

2.5 Recognition and enforcement of judgments

Under the Brussels Convention, a judgment given in a contracting state shall in general be recognised in the other contracting states without any special procedure being required. However, a judgment shall not be recognised if such recognition is contrary to public policy in the state in which recognition is sought. The cases when a decision is considered to be contrary to public policy are rare in most contracting states (see section 2.1.1 above). Under no circumstances may the foreign judgment enforced pursuant to the Brussels Convention be reviewed as to its substance.

The Brussels Convention provides for a standard procedure by which a judgment given in one contracting state may be automatically enforced in another contracting state. This additional element of Convention regulation is as vital as that concerning jurisdiction discussed earlier, since the ability to proceed against foreign producers and importers under the Brussels Convention would be significantly reduced in impact, if it were not also possible to have a

---

20 *Gubisch v Palumbo* [1987] ECR 4861.
1 *The Tatry* [1995] 1LPr 81 (ECJ).

judgment obtained against them in the national courts enforced against their assets situated in other contracting states.

The Brussels Convention is very wide in its scope and is not limited to judgments of superior courts or to money judgments. It also appears that the Convention covers any judgment of a contracting state whether the defendant is domiciled inside or outside the contracting state. So, a judgment rendered by a French court against a German defendant could, if appropriate, be enforced against its assets in Spain.

In order to enforce a judgment, the plaintiff must apply to the court of competent jurisdiction. The procedure for obtaining enforcement in a particular country usually depends upon whether the Brussels Convention, some reciprocal enforcement Convention, or no Convention, applies.

Foreign judgments in Austria must be recognised before they may be executed. The party who wishes to enforce the judgment files an execution petition with a *res judicata* and execution clause. Certain international conventions require also an official copy of the court decision, stamped or sealed. A certified copy of the certificate of service must be provided as proof of service in due form of the originating summons. Documents must be submitted as originals in German, or as authorised translations. An Austrian person must be nominated and authorised to accept service when the petition is filed and the petition should specify the form in which the execution is to be effected.

In Denmark, foreign judgments are enforceable once their execution has been authorised. If a foreign judgment falls within the Brussels Convention, the judgment creditor applies in the first instance to the *Fogedret*. The documentation lodged with the application will often be accepted in English. Before the Brussels Convention came into force in Denmark, the only foreign judgments that were directly enforceable were those of other Nordic countries. Judgments of the courts of other countries were enforceable only by bringing a fresh action in the Danish courts. This is still the case for judgments not falling within the Brussels Convention. In such an action, the foreign judgment has only an evidential effect.

In England, an application for the enforcement of a judgment to which the Brussels Convention applies is made first to a procedural judge known as a Master on an ex parte basis. The application must be accompanied by an affidavit supporting the registration of the judgment, together with a copy of the judgment and proof that it can be enforced in the country in which it was made. Execution on a foreign judgment registered in the High Court in England may issue in the same way as on an English judgment. Where the foreign judgment is not enforceable under an international Convention or bilateral agreement, a fresh cause of action will be the foreign judgment itself. The position is broadly similar in Northern Ireland and the Republic of Ireland.

In Scotland, a judgment obtained under the Brussels Convention is enforceable once it has been registered in the Court of Session, following application to the Lord Ordinary. A judgment obtained otherwise than under the Brussels Convention may be enforced in a similar way under another relevant international convention. If no such convention applies, it is necessary to bring an action on the foreign judgment for a 'decree conform' and thereby obtain the authority to enforce from the Court of Session.

In Finland, provisions allowing the enforcement of certain types of foreign judgments are usually based on international conventions. Where conventions do not apply and the foreign judgment is not enforceable in Finland, a new

trial must be begun. Where the Nordic conventions apply, foreign judgments are recognisable and enforceable, subject to certain exceptions. Application is made to the Chief Executory Officer in a manner similar to that of the execution of domestic judgments. Where the bilateral convention between Finland and Austria applies, enforcement is sought again from the Chief Executory Officer. The application is accompanied by the original judgment or a certified copy, a certificate of legal force and a certificate of enforceability in Austria. Documents must be translated into Finnish or Swedish.

In France, foreign judgments are enforceable once their execution has been authorised by the endorsement of a *formule exécutoire*. If the Brussels Convention applies, the judgment creditor makes an application for an order that the judgment be endorsed. The application is made to the President of the *Tribunal de Grand Instance* for the district in which the defendant is domiciled or, if he is not domiciled in France, the district in which the assets to be seized are located. The original judgment or an authenticated copy of it must be produced together with proof that the judgment is enforceable in the country in which it was pronounced and that it has been served on the judgment debtor. The judgment and other documents need to be translated only if the judge so requires. If the Brussels Convention does not apply, nor any other bilateral or multilateral convention, a foreign judgment can only be enforced if an order for its enforcement is obtained from the *Tribunal de Grand Instance*. The other documents required are the original judgment, or an authenticated copy, evidence of service, and evidence that the judgment is enforceable in the country of origin. Certain conditions must be shown, including that the foreign court had jurisdiction in respect of the subject matter. Provided that these conditions are satisfied, there is no examination of the factual or legal merits of the foreign judgment.

In Germany, foreign judgments are enforceable by the same means as are available in respect of German judgments once their execution has been authorised by the endorsement of a *Vollstreckungsklausel*. If the Brussels Convention applies, the judgment creditor applies in writing for the judgment to be enforced. The application will usually be decided without an oral hearing by the presiding judge of the relevant Chamber of the *Landgericht*. The foreign judgment and supporting documentation must be accompanied by a German translation. If the Brussels Convention does not apply, the foreign judgment may be enforced after proceedings for an order for its enforcement have been brought in the *Amstgericht* or the *Landgericht* for the area of the defendant's domicile or where the assets are located. If there is no enforcement Convention with the country in which the judgment was given, the foreign court has jurisdiction according to German rules of private international law and if the judgment was final. The German court will authorise the judgment's enforcement if a German judgment would be enforced in that country. The court will also examine the judgment process both as to its form and its content, but will not reconsider the merits of the case.

Foreign judgments will be enforced in Greece when they are declared enforceable by the Single Member Court of First Instance. Written application is made to the Registry of the Court of the area where the judgment debtor has permanent residence, accompanied by an official copy of the foreign judgment, an attestation of enforceability in the state of its issue and an official translation. Execution takes place in a separate proceeding in which the respondent is served with a copy of the Court Order.

In Ireland, a foreign judgment to which the Brussels Convention applies is enforced by obtaining an order for its enforcement on an ex parte application to a procedural judge known as a Master of the High Court. The person against whom the judgment is given is then served with notice of enforcement together with a copy of the order. If the Brussels Convention does not apply, Irish law does not provide any special procedure for the enforcement of foreign judgments, and Ireland is not a party to any other Convention providing for the recognition or enforcement of foreign judgments in civil and commercial matters. The defences to an action for enforcement are limited, the most important of which is that the foreign court does not have jurisdiction.

Foreign judgments are enforceable in Italy by all means available in respect of Italian judgments once their execution has been authorised by the endorsement of a *formula esecutiva*. If the Brussels Convention applies, a certified copy of the foreign judgment is filed with the *corte d'appello* for the district of the defendant's domicile or, if he is not domiciled in Italy, the *corte d'appello* for the district where execution is to take place, together with certified copies of the other documents required by the Convention. A sworn translation of the judgment and other documents must be attached. In the absence of multilateral or bilateral Conventions, the recognition and enforcement of foreign judgments is governed by the provisions of the *Codice di Procedura Civile*, which lays down certain requirements, the most important of which is that the foreign judgment has been given by a court which had jurisdiction over the case according to the principles of Italian law and jurisdiction.

In Luxembourg, foreign judgments are enforceable by the same methods as are available in respect of Luxembourg judgments, once their execution has been authorised by the endorsement of a *formule executoire*. If the Brussels Convention applies, this can be obtained by means of a request to the President of the *Tribunal d'Arrondissement* of the area in which the debtor is domiciled. The judgment which is to be enforced and its accompanying documentation must be in French or German, or be accompanied by a translation into one of those languages. This procedure has been extended to the enforcement of judgments from any country with which Luxembourg has a bilateral Convention. If a judgment is not covered by the Convention, nor any other bilateral or multilateral Convention, proceedings for enforcement of a foreign judgment are brought in the *Tribunal d'Arrondissement* for the area in which the defendant is domiciled, by serving an assignation on the defendant, as in an ordinary action. Certain conditions apply for recognition. If these are satisfied, the court is precluded from considering the merits of the foreign judgment and will authorise its enforcement.

Foreign judgments are enforceable in the Netherlands by all the means available in respect of Dutch judgments, once their execution has been authorised by an order of the court (an *exequatur*). When the foreign judgment is covered by the Brussels Convention, the judgment creditor must apply for permission to enforce the judgment to the President of the *Arrondissement-srechtbank* for the place either of the debtor's domicile or, if the debtor has no domicile in the Netherlands, where the judgment is to be enforced. Once the judge has authorised enforcement, the creditor is given notice of the exequatur by means of a letter. The foreign judgment with the exequatur is then served on the judgment debtor. A foreign judgment cannot be enforced in the Netherlands unless it is covered by the terms of an appropriate enforcement Convention. If no such Convention applies, a fresh action must be brought in

respect of an original claim, but the foreign judgment may have evidential effect in that action.

In Norway, foreign judgments can be enforced, under the Lugano Convention, by application to the court of execution (*namsrett*) in the jurisdiction of which the Defendant has his principal establishment. Application is supported by a certified, authenticated copy of the judgment, and a certified translation of the same. Where bilateral conventions apply, the procedure is broadly similar.

Foreign judgments in Portugal must be reviewed and confirmed before they will take effect. The authenticity of the foreign judgment must be confirmed by its legalisation before a Portuguese consulate. A translation of the decision must be authenticated by a notary public or Portuguese consulate. The court of second instance (*Tribunal da Relacao*) will verify that the decision conforms to the conditions of authenticity and propriety, public policy and domestic private law. It then examines the decision with regard to finality of judgment, *lis pendens* and *res judicata*, and service of process. The applicant presents an initial *petition (Peticao Inicial)*, which is served on the respondent who has ten days to lodge a response (*Contestacao*). The *Tribunal da Relacao* having recognised the judgment, it can be enforced in accordance with the Portuguese Code of Civil Procedure.

In Spain, whenever there is no particular applicable Convention and no reciprocity with the country whose courts have issued the relevant judgment, an application for enforcement of a foreign judgment should be filed before the Supreme Court. This court reviews whether the relevant requirements are fulfilled and decides upon whether the judgment should be enforced. An application may take up to one year to be determined. In Belgium, foreign judgments are enforceable once their execution has been authorised by the endorsement of a *formule exécutoire*. An application to enforce a judgment to which the Brussels Convention applies must be made to the *Tribunal de Première Instance*. A copy of the foreign judgment must be produced, together with the translation into the language of the court. Once the judge has satisfied himself that the requirements of the Brussels Convention have been fulfilled, he will grant an order for enforcement in the form of a judgment of the Belgian court. If the Brussels Convention does not apply, the precise procedure to be followed will depend upon whether or not another convention applies and, if so, its terms. If there is no applicable enforcement convention, the Belgian court will re-examine the merits of the case and refuse to allow enforcement if the trial judge appears to have erred in fact or law.

In Sweden, application for enforcement of a foreign judgment must be made to a competent enforcement authority. The successful party applies to the *Svea Court of Appeal*, which is the competent court under the Lugano Convention, for exequatur, and then applies for enforcement. In an exequatur matter, the *Svea Court of Appeal* declares that the foreign judgment is enforceable in the same way as a domestic judgment. Judgment is enforced by filing a signed application with the appropriate enforcement authority. This must be accompanied by a certified copy of the exequator decision and a translation of the foreign judgment.

In Switzerland, whenever the Lugano Convention or other bilaterel conventions do not apply, enforcement of foreign judgments is governed by the Private International Law Statute. This requires the enforcing party to identify the competent cantonal authority, and make an application

accompanied by a certified original copy of the judgment, and confirmation that the judgment is final or that no ordinary appeal may be raised against it. Where bilateral conventions apply, enforcement procedures will not as a matter of course follow the Private International Law Statute rules.

The system of recognition and enforcement of judgments provided by the Brussels Convention has many advantages over national enforcement rules and those contained in bilateral enforcement Conventions. These can be summarised as follows:

(a) An application for enforcement is ex parte, which means that the other party is not summoned to appear. This preserves the element of surprise in favour of the applicant (article 34(1)).
(b) Courts of contracting states requested to recognise and enforce a judgment are not generally required, nor even entitled, to examine whether the judgment court properly exercised jurisdiction, nor to question the substantive correctness of the judgment requested to be enforced (articles 28(3), 29 and 34).
(c) The grounds upon which a court may refuse to recognise or enforce a judgment are limited. The list of grounds includes recognition being contrary to public policy, lack of proper service of process on the defendant and irreconcilability of judgments sought to be recognised (articles 27 and 28). The courts of most European countries, and in particular Germany, France and Norway, are reluctant to refuse to enforce a judgment on the grounds of public policy. Indeed, in France the courts will generally refuse to recognise a judgment only where the result of the application of the foreign law would be particularly unjust. The courts in Italy, by contrast, frequently invoke the doctrine of public policy, which is embodied in article 31 of the *Preleggi* to the Civil Code.
(d) The documents in support of an application for recognition and enforcement are specified, and where possible, reduced in number and simplified (articles 46 and 47).
(e) Possibilities of appeal against a decision in relation to enforcement are limited (articles 37, 40 and 41).

3 CONFLICT OF LAWS

Once a plaintiff has settled on a jurisdiction in which to bring a claim, the court seised with the action must then determine which law it will apply in determining the claim. The rules relating to choice of law will depend upon whether the claim is brought in contract, tort or product liability.

As a result of the implementation of the Product Liability Directive in Europe, with its near strict liability, it is likely that most claims brought by individuals for personal injury resulting from defective products will in the future be brought in product liability or tort, rather than in contract. However, in certain jurisdictions, the availability of an action in contract may preclude one in tort or product liability. In English law, a claim under Part 1 of the Consumer Protection Act 1987 is in tort (section 6(7)).

In English, Danish, Spanish and Swedish law, even if it is clear that a claim is governed by a foreign system of law, the judge or arbitrator has no obligation to ascertain the rules of that legal system. They regard foreign law as a question of fact which has to be proved to their satisfaction by expert witnesses or other admissible evidence. If a party fails to produce such evidence, national law will

be applied. Consequently, a party to proceedings brought in any of these countries will plead foreign law only if this is to his advantage; otherwise it is cheaper for him to have the issue decided in accordance with domestic law. This is unlike the position in many other European countries, such as, for example, Austria, the Netherlands and Portugal, where judges and arbitrators have to ascertain the foreign law, which in their view applies, *ex officio*.

3.1 The law governing product liability

The law applicable to a claim brought in respect of a defective product will be determined either by the rules set out in the Product Liability Convention (if the country in question has signed, acceded to or ratified the Convention) or by the rules of private international law in respect of tort of the relevant country.

3.1.1 The Product Liability Convention

As stated earlier, the Product Liability Convention sets out choice of law rules. The system of choice contained in the Product Liability Convention provides that a supplier's product liability is determined by the law of the country where certain pairs of connecting factors are located. These pairs are selected from among four connections, *viz* the place of injury, the victim's habitual residence, the place of business of the supplier and the place of acquisition of the product. If no relevant coincidence of factors is found, the law of the defendant's place of business applies, unless the claimant prefers the place where the harmful event occurred. The Convention provides that the place where the harmful event occurred shall be the place of injury, thereby excluding the possibility of interpreting this to mean the place where the defendant's action occurred which caused the harm. Unfortunately the meaning of the term 'place of injury' is left open. It may be that the place of the first impact of the act on the victim is regarded as material if subsequent elements of the tortious occurrence as a whole are located in different countries, although this is not conclusive.

A supplier may, however, challenge the applicability of either a place of injury combination or a habitual residence combination if he establishes that he could not reasonably have foreseen that the product would be marketed in the relevant state. The interpretation of this rather novel notion is entrusted by the Product Liability Convention to national courts. Furthermore, safety standards of the country of marketing may be taken into account.

The Convention applies whether the proceedings are brought in contract or in tort. However, the Product Liability Convention does not overcome the traditional tort/contract dichotomy whereby claims in tort and contract are treated differently. As a result, concurrent claims in contract and tort are regulated by different conflict rules even if both claims were to result from the same product damage and were to involve the same parties in the same proceedings. The other major defect of the Convention is it makes no provision for plurality of litigants. The procedural complications of the application of different laws in regard to different defendants in the same proceedings are obvious.

3.1.2 Specific product liability rules

The Swiss Private International Law Act expressly deals with the law governing a product liability claim, allowing the consumer the choice between the law of

the producer's domicile and the law of the place where the product was purchased.

3.1.3   *Product safety standards*

Another question which may be raised in an international product liability context is 'which country's product safety standard should apply?' For example, the State in which production takes place may completely prohibit the use of a certain chemical substance in a food product, whereas the State to which such food is exported may only require that a maximum content be observed. To the extent that there is a conflict of applicable standards, it may be resolved by considering the class of persons whom the statutory rule on its construction intends to protect, and giving only those persons the benefit of its safety standards. So, for example, the UK Health and Safety at Work, etc, Act 1974 is intended to protect those persons who use articles 'at work'; it seems that a reasonable construction would be to give effect to the statute wherever the incriminated article was so used or destined for such use, ie in England. For claims arising as a result of breach of statutory duty, see section 3.2.2 below.

3.2   Choice of law in tort, breach of statutory duty and unjustified enrichment

3.2.1   *Choice of law in tort*

There has to date been no harmonisation of the private international laws relating to choice of law in tort of EU member states. This is unfortunate since the various member states' rules are frequently complex and difficult to apply to a given set of facts. When an international tortious claim arises, the inter-relationship between these laws adds a further layer of complexity, which, when combined with the possible operation of renvoi, (see page 513), can give rise to uncertainty as to the applicable law and on occasions the appropriate forum. It is undesirable for both plaintiffs and defendants that such uncertainty and difficulty should predicate determining the substantive issues of claims and it is hoped that similar steps will be taken within the EU to harmonise the private international laws relating to tort as have already been taken in relation to contract.

European case law reflecting trends in general tort choice of law is somewhat sparse. The lack of international product liability cases reported in highly industrialised Western Europe suggests that the great part of such claims are settled out of court.

In the UK, legislation was implemented in 1996, which altered significantly the UK private international law relating to the choice of law in tort or delict, as it is referred to in Scotland.[2] The law introduced a new general rule that the applicable law of a claim in tort should be that of the place where the tort or delict occurred. Where the relevant events occur in two or more countries, the tort is to be taken to have occurred in the country where the plaintiff was injured, where property was damaged, or, in other cases, where the most significant elements in the sequence of events occurred. This general rule will be displaced in any case in which it appears to be 'substantially more appropriate' for another country's law to apply. Regretfully the legislation gives little guidance as to the

2   Private International Law (Miscellaneous Provisions) Act 1995.

circumstances in which the general rule should be displaced, and indeed the application of this exception may lead to different applicable laws for each case where there are multiple parties to an action. The exception will lead to flexibility as to the choice of law to govern a tort, but on the other hand a decree of uncertainty as to the law the courts may apply. It is noteworthy that the applicable law shall be the domestic law of a country, rather than its domestic and private international law (ie single renvoi applies – see section 3.5 below).

The new law is generally welcome since it abolishes the former rather parochial rule which required a wrongful act abroad to be both a tort in the law of the country where the act was done and in English law before it could be actionable in England ('the double actionability rule'). This rule, which also applied in Scotland and Northern Ireland, had been criticised in view of its assumption that the English domestic law of tort be predominantly applied irrespective of the foreign circumstances and the parties. The rule is almost unknown in the private international law of other European countries where generally the rule is that the act need only be a tort in the place in which the wrongful act was committed. Its abolition will facilitate more international product liability claims being brought in the UK, since it is no longer necessary for the wrong to be actionable in England, Scotland or Northern Ireland as appropriate for the case to be heard. This must logically be correct, since a judgment under a foreign tort law may well be enforceable in the UK in any event pursuant to the Brussels Convention.

In Norway, the Supreme Court decided a case involving a Norwegian woman who allegedly died through using a contraceptive pill made by a German pharmaceutical drugs manufacturer.[3] Lengthy discussions were devoted to the medical evidence and the claim ultimately failed for lack of a reasonable likelihood that the injury and death were caused by the use of the drug. Since no consideration appears to have been given to the choice of law issue, it must be assumed that Norwegian law was tacitly deemed applicable.

In Germany, a statutory rule applies if the plaintiff is a German national, namely that torts committed abroad between Germans are subject to German law.[4] The highest German court has upheld this rule in post war cases involving collisions between German ships outside German territorial waters.[5] It is disputed whether the rule is generally still valid, notably if the German parties involved do not, or one of them does not, habitually reside in Germany. If both do, then German law is deemed to apply. This rule is analogous to the one in English private international law established by *Boys v Chaplin* discussed earlier.

In Portugal, Italy, and usually in the Netherlands, an action brought in tort will be determined in accordance with the law of the place where the principal act which caused the damage occurred.[6]

The method by which this question is determined in Ireland has undergone somewhat of a change as a result of a decision of the Irish Supreme Court in the last ten years.[7] In that decision the Irish Supreme Court adopted a flexible approach for the determination of the choice of law in actions involving tort. The Court indicated that service out of the jurisdiction might be permitted if any significant element of the tort had occurred within the jurisdiction.

3   *Hoysterettsdom*, 14 November 1974, (1974) NRr 1160.
4   *Verordnung* of 7 December 1942, RGB1 1, 706.
5   BGH, 2 February 1961, 24 BGH 7 222.
6   Portuguese Code of Civil Procedure, art 45(1).
7   *Graham v Medical Incorporated and Valley Pines Associates* 1986 ILRM 627.

However, in deciding whether to do so, the Supreme Court indicated that the Court should be under a heavy burden to examine all the circumstances of each case.

In Belgium, the applicable law for a claim in tort is the law of the place where the defendant acted.

3.2.2   Breach of statutory duty

In addition to certain courts having civil jurisdiction when criminal proceedings are brought against a defendant (see section 2.2.5 above), in certain countries persons injured or suffering damage as the result of a person's failure to observe statutory provisions may have a claim against that person for breaching such statutory duty. The law relating to whether a particular act or regulation creates a liability and damage claims may result is far from settled.

In England, the question depends to some extent on the wording of the relevant legislation. If an Act makes no provision for penalties or other means of enforcement the assumption is that an action may be brought for breach of it. If on the other hand the Act provides sanctions for breach of it the assumption is that no action will apply. Where however the Act is plainly intended to protect an ascertainable class of persons where there are no common law rights upon which they may rely, it may be construed as creating a cause of action for breach of statutory duties. In relation to international claims, it is noteworthy that, for a cause of action for breach of statutory duty to arise, the breach by the defendant must be of a statutory rule of conduct of the *lex fori*. A breach by the defendant of a foreign statutory rule of conduct would merely at best constitute evidence of negligence.

3.2.3   Unjustified enrichment

The question of the governing law of a claim for unjustified enrichment (or restitution, as it is known in England), is a particularly difficult one. It may arise when one party seeks to be indemnified by another as a result of a claim being brought in product liability against the party, for which that other is also liable. First, it is not always clear within a particular domestic law whether such a claim is classified as being in tort, contract or *sui generis*. Second, in countries where it is considered as *sui generis* (such as, for example, England), the question of the applicable law will be determined by a further set of private international law rules, separate from those relating to tort or contract.

As with tort, no harmonisation of this aspect of private international law has taken place or is currently envisaged within the EU.

3.3   The law governing the contract

3.3.1   Introduction

Submission to the jurisdiction of the courts of a country does not necessarily mean that there is a submission to the particular legal system of that country.

The international Conventions mentioned earlier do not exclude the possibility of a conflict of national laws in the field of international commercial transactions. To solve such conflicts, the courts must turn to private international law. In the past, private international law differed from one EU country to another. The signature and ratification of the Rome Convention

has to a large extent harmonised the private international laws relating to choice of law in contract within the EU.

Although it is usual to talk of the proper law of the contract, it may be that one particular aspect of the contract is governed by one legal system and another aspect governed by another law. The proper law of the contract may thus be split by applying the laws of different countries to various aspects of the same contract.

3.3.2   The Rome Convention

This Convention, which is now in force in most EU member states, replaces the national rules of the signatory States on what is the 'proper law of the contract'. It applies to contractual obligations in any situation involving a choice between the laws of the contracting states (including, for example, conflicts between the laws of England and Scotland), and also to cases in which the law of a contracting state conflicts with that of a non-contracting state.

The Rome Convention does not apply to certain commercial transactions such as questions relating to bills of exchange, cheques and promissory notes, to agreements for arbitration or the choice of a court, to insurance contracts covering risks situated in an EU country, to the internal law of companies or to trusts. It also does not apply to the determination of certain legal questions, the most important of which for the purposes of this chapter is whether an agent is liable to bind a principal to a third party.

As stated earlier, two basic principles are adopted by the Rome Convention. The first is that the proper law of the contract shall be the law intended by the parties. The second is that, if the parties have failed to choose the proper law, it shall be the law with which the contract is most closely connected.

With regard to the first basic principle, it is of course advisable for parties to a contract to provide expressly which legal system they wish to be applied to their contract to avoid ambiguity. The parties may in general submit their contract to any legal system which they choose and, in particular, they are not limited to a legal system with which the circumstances surrounding their contract have an actual connnection. In certain civil law jurisdictions, such as Italy, any clause which purports to exclude Italian law or the jurisdiction of the Italian courts must be specifically agreed to in writing by the parties. In practice, words acknowledging specific agreement to the relevant clause are added at the end of the contract and the parties sign after these words of acknowledgment, in addition to signing the main contract.

However, the discretion of the parties to elect the law applicable to the contract is not entirely unlimited. The Rome Convention provides that the parties cannot contract out of the mandatory provisions of the law of a particular country if all the other elements at the time of the choice are connected with that country only.

Indeed, the national courts and laws of several EU member states operate to ensure that it is not possible to contract out of certain domestic laws. For example, although in theory parties to a contract in Italy may agree to any applicable law, in practice, particularly in the case of a contract between Italian nationals, the *Cassazione* has declared a foreign choice of law clause invalid for reasons of public policy. French law allows its nationals to contract out of applying domestic law, provided that the reason for their so doing is not to avoid the application of certain mandatory rules.

In the UK, the mandatory provisions of the Unfair Contract Terms Act

1977 and the Unfair Terms in Consumer Contracts Regulations 1994 cannot be contracted out by a choice of law clause adopting foreign law in certain circumstances. Also, in Denmark certain Acts, for example, in relation to maritime and transport law, cannot be contracted out of by the parties.

Incidentally, the English Court of Appeal has held (pre-implementation of the Rome Convention in the UK) that a provision that disputes arising under a contract should be referred to 'British' courts was an unequivocal reference to English courts, and inferred that the parties intended that the proper law of the contract should be English law.[8]

With regard to the ascertainment of the law of the closest connection, the Rome Convention establishes a rebuttable presumption that the law shall be the law of the 'characteristic performance'. This was a concept hitherto unknown in most common and civil law jurisdictions although it had been impliedly accepted in the Netherlands by certain decisions of the *Hoge Raad*. The law of characteristic performance is not the law where performance has to be carried out but is the law of the place where the party who has to effect the characteristic performance has his seat of business. For example, in a contract of sale, the characteristic performance is effected by the seller who has to deliver the goods, and not by the buyer who has to pay the price, and therefore the law of the seller's country will apply.

The Rome Convention does not enhance legal certainty, as was no doubt intended. For example, article 4(2) provides that if a contract, in which no choice of law is made by the parties, is to be performed by a branch office, the applicable law will be that of the country where the branch office is situated. This can lead to considerable uncertainty, particularly when dealing with multi-national companies who use contracts which leave it open to the multi-national to use any of its branch offices or subsidiaries for the performance of the contract.

Articles 5 and 6 of the Rome Convention provide special rules relating to certain consumer contracts and individual employment contracts. A consumer or an employee shall not be deprived by a choice of law of the parties of the protection afforded by the mandatory rules of the country in which he has his habitual residence. The Convention also provides that the application of a rule of foreign law, which by virtue of the Convention would generally apply, may be refused if such application is 'manifestly incompatible' with the public policy of the forum.

A controversial provision of the Rome Convention is article 7(1) which states that, when applying the law of the country, the judge may give effect to the mandatory rules of another country with which the situation has a close connection 'if and so far as, under the law of the latter country, those rules must be applied whatever the law applicable to the contract'. The extension of the effect of mandatory rules goes beyond the effect of those rules in the law of the country with the closest connection and might even admit the extra-territorial effect of mandatory rules of a third country. The justification for this is the 'public interest' of the domestic law. The far-reaching provisions of the US with regard to anti-trust embargoes, the freezing of assets and restrictions of resale to foreign countries may be given further effect.

The Convention allows contracting States to reserve the right not to apply this controversial article and the UK exercised the right of reservation when signing the Convention. The UK Contracts (Applicable Law) Act 1990 and

8   Komninos FT Law Reports, 16 January 1991.

the Luxembourg Law of 27 March 1986, which implement the Rome Convention in the respective national laws, exclude article 7(1).

Whatever law is applicable by choice of the parties or otherwise, consumers will remain protected by the mandatory rules of their country of residence in respect of purchases which were made at home from a foreign supplier's agent or on the strength of his local advertisement or direct offer, and even in respect of purchases made abroad if their shopping visit to another country was arranged by the seller.

3.3.3 Position where the Rome Convention does not apply

The Rome Convention specifically provides that the national implementing legislation shall apply only in respect of contracts made after its entry into force. It follows that the choice of law of certain slightly older contracts will still be determined in accordance with the private international laws which preceded the Rome Convention in the relevant country. These differ significantly, and it is not within the scope of this Chapter to deal in detail with those laws. Expert legal advice should be sought in the relevant jurisdiction.

3.4 Tort and contract

In some cases, the defendant may be liable for breach of contract as well as in tort. The Rome Convention, if applicable, will determine the law applicable to the contractual issues while the non-contractual issues will be determined independently of the Convention. It may be possible for the plaintiff to bypass the often difficult question of where the tort was committed by framing his claim in contract. For example, in England, a railway passenger who has paid for his ticket and is injured in a railway accident can sue the British Railways Board either in contract or in tort. The plaintiff cannot, of course, rely on a contract, for example, if at the time of a motor accident he was the driver's guest. In certain jurisdictions, such as France, a plaintiff cannot sue both in tort and in contract. If the plaintiff has a contractual link with the defendant his action must be founded solely in contract. In fact, even where the plaintiff is an end-user with no direct contractual link with the defendant producer, it is now settled case law that his claim will also lie in contract if brought in France.

3.5 Renvoi

When any of the above private international rules apply to the circumstances of a given case direct that the case be determined in accordance with the law, for example, of Scotland, this gives rise the difficult problem of renvoi. This is because the term 'Law of Scotland' may have one of three meanings. First, it could mean the domestic law of Scotland. That is, the matter will be determined in accordance with the domestic law of Scotland without reference to its conflicts rules and no further referrals to other laws will be made.

However, 'Law of Scotland' may sometimes mean any system of law which the Scottish courts would hold applicable to the particular case pursuant to the rules of Scottish private international law. No reference would be made to the Scottish rules of renvoi. In this case, the private international laws of Scotland may in turn refer the litigant back to the original law or even to the law of a third country. This is known as 'single renvoi'. It is accepted in Germany

and incorporated in its civil code, and has also been applied by certain judges in Europe. It is not generally applied by English courts.

The final interpretation is that 'Law of Scotland' requires reference not only to the private international rules of Scotland, but also to its rules relating to renvoi. This is known as 'double renvoi'. The result is that the court before which the issue is being heard will determine this issue in exactly the same way as the foreign court would determine it, including whether or not it would apply single or double renvoi. At worst, double renvoi can result in a 'stalemate' situation where two sets of private international laws refer to each other, thereby creating a '*circulus inextricabilis*' from which only the lawyers stand to benefit. Unfortunately it is currently applied in English law in a few specific cases.

There are in practice very few commercial cases on renvoi and it is rarely specifically pleaded in international cases. The Rome Convention specifically excludes renvoi, by stating that the application of the law of a country under the Convention means the domestic law, not the private international law of the country. Double renvoi is now excluded in UK private international law of tort as a result of the Private International Law (Miscellaneous Provisions) Act 1995, save in relation to defamation claims. Further, renvoi is expressly excluded by the Vienna Convention. However, Austrian courts are obliged by section 5 of the Austrian law on international private law (IPRG) to apply the doctrine of double renvoi.

4   SHOULD FORUM SHOPPING BE ALLOWED?

Disquiet has been expressed by English judges[9] as to the amount of litigation which the subject of forum shopping has created. It has been pointed out that parties to a dispute may choose to litigate in order to determine where they shall litigate.

Forum shopping has been defined as 'a plaintiff bypassing his natural forum and bringing his action in some alien forum which would give him relief or benefits which would not be available to him in his natural forum'. Unfortunately this definition raises as many questions as it answers. What is the natural forum? Is it the forum with which the dispute is most closely connected or the forum in which it can be resolved most conveniently? Is it necessarily objectionable to bring proceedings in an alien forum if that forum is one of the established centres for the resolution of disputes and offers specialised services or facilities not available in the natural forum? Is there any need to control forum shopping unless the plaintiff's principal object is to harrass the defendant or the alien forum is, in normal circumstances, highly inappropriate?

Outside the courts, two main arguments have been advanced for controlling forum shopping.

The first is that it may result in unfairness to the defendant. This implies that it is always the defendant who must be protected from abuse of the system by the plaintiff. This is not always the case. Defendants who try to put off the day of judgment, or drive the proceedings to a forum where they will have an advantage, are not unknown.

The second argument against forum shopping is based on public interest. It is said to be wasteful of the time of witnesses and others. It is also said to be

---

9   For example, Lord Templeman in *The Spiliada* [1985] 2 Lloyds Rep 116.

unfair to the interests of local inhabitants whose actions may be delayed as a result of the courts being clogged with foreign actions.

The advantage of forum shopping in the area of product liability is that it increases the protection of consumers and other plaintiffs by giving them a greater scope of recourse against defendants.

5   CONCLUSION

It has been seen that the Product Liability Directive imposes liability upon a number of parties, namely producers, own branders, importers from outside the EU and, in certain cases, suppliers. The national laws of most EU states implementing the Product Liability Directive provide that where two or more persons are liable for the same damage, their liability is joint and several. The availability of jurisdiction in respect of joint defendants, who may not otherwise be capable of being proceeded against, may therefore be of special importance in bringing claims for defective goods.

The relatively recent regulation of both product liability on the one hand and jurisdiction and recognition and enforcement of judgments in Europe on the other, form part of a broader process of improving and harmonising legal protection and recourse to remedies for consumers within the EU. This is of increasing importance to the economic success of the Single Market. In the area of private international law, the harmonisation of the laws determining the applicable law of a contract by way of the Rome Convention are welcome. It is hoped that similar measures will be adopted in relation to the applicable law in tort and product liability. This is particularly urgent in the context of international product liability claims, in view of the small number of signatories to the Product Liability Convention. Such measures would facilitate significantly the bringing of international claims for defective products.

I would like to thank each of the contributors to this book and Jocelyn Kellam of Clayton Utz, Sydney, Australia for their assistance in preparing this chapter.

CHAPTER XIX

Practical steps to be taken by producers and suppliers to manage product liability and safety risks

Patrick Kelly

Laytons
Carmelite
50 Victoria Embankment
Blackfriars, London
EC4Y 0LS
Tel: ++ 44 171 842 8000
Fax: ++ 44 171 842 8080

Rebecca Attree

Attree & Co
110 Cambridge Street
Pimlico
London
SW1V 4QF
Tel: ++ 44 171 630 6019
Fax: ++ 44 171 630 8681

CHAPTER XIX

Practical steps to be taken by producers and suppliers to manage product liability and safety risks

Introduction

While most of this book deals with purely legal issues, this chapter examines the effects of the law in practice. It examines a mixture of legal and practical matters dealing with assessing and managing product liability risk from a manufacturer's and supplier's viewpoint in the European Union countries and elsewhere,[1] as follows:

(a) Section 1 deals with legal issues in product liability risk management from a supplier's or manufacturer's viewpoint.
(b) Section 2 deals with administrative and general management issues of a quality control nature.
(c) Section 3 deals with advertising, warnings, instructions and manuals and provides a checklist of issues that need to be considered in drafting and preparing instructions.
(d) Section 4 discusses some of the issues that need to be dealt with in product recall.

While many people are injured or killed each year in the European Union through products being defective, more of these injuries or deaths are caused by defects in warnings, instructions or design rather than defects in manufacture. The people injured or killed clearly suffer enormous losses and costs as a result. Not unreasonably, the legal systems of each of the European Union countries seek to transfer those losses and costs to the manufacturers and suppliers of the defective products. Additionally, manufacturers and suppliers of products are subject to considerable regulation with criminal sanctions for failure to meet the regulatory requirements.

From the point of view of a manufacturer or supplier, it is easier in the long term to minimise the risk of producing defective products by investing more money in design, quality control and in the drafting of effective warnings

---

1 We would like to acknowledge the help that all the contributors to this book have made in providing information that has enabled this chapter to be written.

and instructions than it is to meet the costs of producing defective products. The reason for this is that not only in the long term are consumers unwilling to buy shoddy and defective products but also because the costs of producing defective products are very uncertain in their timing and amount whereas the costs of producing safe, quality products can be timed and controlled. With the implementation of the General Product Safety Directive into the law of each of the European Union countries, every manufacturer and supplier of a product within that market knows that it may be required, either by national enforcement authorities or by the EC Commission, to implement a product recall programme for defective products that it has put on the market. The costs of this may be very high and are better avoided as far as possible. To the extent they are not avoided, they should at least be managed, controlled and channelled by way of an effective product recall policy.

1 LEGAL ISSUES FOR SUPPLIERS AND MANUFACTURERS

1.1 Introduction

There are a number of legal issues which manufacturers and suppliers should ideally consider at the outset, before setting up a new business or a new division in relation to a new set of products. In practice, many people entering into a new field of activity are reluctant to spend a great deal of time and money in planning and setting up structures, preparing standard contracts, product recall policies etc, before the products have been successfully launched and profits made. A balance must be struck and it should always be borne in mind that the time and money spent at the outset on such matters are well invested, since defending claims or instigating product recalls which arise due to failure to consider the legal issues will be far more costly than the initial legal advice. The principal areas to be considered are:

(a) assessing the risks relating to the product;
(b) determining the functions to be performed by the organisation in relation to the product;
(c) how the risk might be managed by way of corporate structures;
(d) the effect of insolvency of the organisation on legal claims;
(e) how the risk might be managed by contractual provisions; and
(f) how any possible international claims might be best defended.

Each of these topics is discussed below.

1.2 Assessing the risks relating to the product

The manufacturer should consider, before launching a product, what are the likely risks associated with the product. Certain products are known to be inherently dangerous, such as a lawnmower or a rotor blade. Other products, such as, for example, shampoo, are not inherently dangerous but could be dangerous if they are misused. The extent and likelihood of damage or injury which may be caused by the product will dictate the extent to which a prudent manufacturer should take the steps outlined in this chapter. For example, if the risks associated with the product include severe personal injury or death, a high level of risk management should be adopted.

The following principles should be observed:

(a) Before the construction and design of a product is finally determined, prototypes should be submitted for extensive testing.

(b) Suppliers of raw materials and component parts must be selected on the basis of their suitability and reliability. For example, in the Netherlands there is a tendency in the industry to provide product components with a 'history' description. Exact specifications and requirements must be given for the raw materials and parts that are to be supplied. Their prototypes must also be scrutinised and the production process of the supplier must as far as possible be supervised and checked regularly.

(c) In assessing the safety of the product, a manufacturer should consider the extent to which the product needs to be made to comply with an EC or national standard. If they do so comply, products are *deemed* safe within the EU. An example of this is found in the The Product Safety Directive.[2] It is noteworthy, however, that the directive provides only a presumption of safety in this case and further that such presumption will not, of course, apply if the products find their way (either directly or indirectly) to non-EU countries. Although article 2(b) of the Product Safety Directive provides that the availability of other products presenting a lesser degree of risk shall not constitute grounds for considering a product to be 'unsafe' or 'dangerous', a manufacturer should bear in mind whether there are similar but safer products available, either in the countries where the product is to be sold or elsewhere.

(d) A system of quality control of the production line should be set up. This will be important to a producer if a claim is brought in product liability and it seeks to avail itself of the defence provided by Article 7b of the Product Liability Directive, namely that 'it is probable that the defect which caused the damage did not exist at the time when the product was put into circulation by him or that this defect came into being afterwards'.

(e) The nature and extent of such quality control will depend upon the product being manufactured.

The premises where manufacture takes place must be organised so that defects are recognised quickly and registered. Sophisticated product components that are difficult to examine once incorporated into a more complex structure must be examined before they are so incorporated. Ideally, samples of the product should be checked at each critical stage of production and records kept of the results of such tests. In particular, samples of each batch of the final product should be checked and records kept of to whom each batch of products is sent. This is obviously extremely important in the event of the manufacturer having to issue notices or warnings subsequent to the sale, or even recalling the product.

(f) Steps should be taken at the outset to ensure that the product is designed so that it is as safe as possible and that where appropriate safety devices such as tamper-proof or childproof packaging is used.

(g) The nature of any warnings, instructions or other details to be included on the product should be considered. These are discussed in more detail in section 3, below.

---

2   Article 4(1) of the Product Safety Directive.

1.3　The relationship of the organisation to the product

The role that the organisation plays in relation to the product will have a bearing on its potential liability in the event of a product liability claim. For example, if the organisation is a distributor or retailer, and a claim is made against it, it will usually be able to pass such claim to the party who supplied the product to it, provided it has done nothing more than sell the product to the claimant.

If, on the other hand, the organisation is the 'producer' under the Producer Liability Directive, it will be primarily liable and in general unable to pass liability to anyone else, save where the defective product is in fact a component part obtained from a third party. The term 'producer' includes not only the manufacturer but also any party who affixes its name, trade mark or other distinguishing feature on the product. Further, where a distributor or retailer has obtained the product from a party outside the European Union, it will be the 'first importer' and primarily liable under the Product Liability Directive. Where in those two instances a party could be primarily liable if a product is defective, it may wish to carry out its activities in relation to a potentially dangerous product by way of a separate entity set up purely for those purposes, with a limited share capital (see section 1.4, below). Alternatively, it may arrange for another party to be the 'producer' or first importer by either sub-contracting the manufacture under licence or arranging to obtain the goods from another party within the European Union rather than outside it if possible.

An organisation manufacturing a potentially dangerous product should decide at the outset the policy that it is to adopt in the event of it causing harm, and follow that policy both externally and internally. That is to say, if the company adopts a marketing strategy which promotes itself as being a 'consumer friendly' company, it should not on the other hand adopt terms and conditions which contain very strictly drafted exclusions and limitations of liability, or organise itself so that the company manufacturing or supplying the product has virtually no assets, thereby ensuring that any consumer claim would be likely either to fail in the first case or be a pyrrhic victory in the second. Clearly it is embarrassing if a consumer claim fails against a company which has particularly marketed itself as a 'consumer friendly' company.

Likewise, if a company adopts a pro-consumer image, it should ensure that it is indeed pro-consumer and, for example, has the correct procedures in place to recall a product in the event of it being defective.

1.4　Managing risk through corporate structures

As stated in section 1.3 above, it may be desirable for an organisation to carry out its activities in relation to a particularly dangerous product in a separate entity, which may be a limited liability company or a limited partnership. The general principle is that the shareholders of a limited liability company will be liable only to the extent of their paid up share capital. If the shareholders of a company wish to limit their exposure to a product liability claim, they should obviously keep the paid up share capital of the company to a minimum. In the case of a limited partnership, each of the general partners have unlimited liability, except for one partner which is corporate and has limited liability.

The general principle can be departed from, the most noteworthy exception being where the limited liability company is a member of a group of companies and it may be construed as acting as an agent or trustee for another company

within the group. In this case, if a claim were to be brought against one company, the court may 'pierce the corporate veil' and allow the claim to be brought against another company within the group. The courts may also 'pierce the corporate veil' on occasions and attribute liability to an individual where they hold all or most of the shares in the company. The extent to which the corporate veil may be 'pierced' will of course depend upon the relevant applicable national law. This law will usually be the law of country of incorporation of the company.

An alternative method to the one described above for reducing a company's risk of claims is to transfer the principal assets of the company engaged in the high risk activities to another company not engaged in such high risk activities. So, for example, one company may operate the production facilities which have, however, been leased (along with the premises and the equipment) from another company. The theory is that, if a claim were to be brought against the production company for manufacturing a defective product, the valuable assets, which are with another company, are protected. This is often referred to as 'company splitting'. If the transferee company is a member of the same group as the transferor company, again the possibility of the 'corporate veil being pierced' and insolvency law applying (see section 1.5 below) should be borne in mind.

In Germany the extent to which the 'corporate veil can be pierced' between two companies will depend upon the extent to which the shareholders and/or managers of the companies are the same and the extent to which the administrative and clerical work may be carried out by one company for the other.

In the Netherlands, where a parent company is closely involved in the policy of a subsidiary, or where the possibilities of redress against the subsidiary are reduced because of its actions (for example company splitting), the parent company can be held liable for the debts or shortcomings of the subsidiary. The extent of the parent company's liability as to damage will depend upon the extent of its influence on the policy of its subsidiary.

In Norway, section 15-1(2)(cf1) of the Companies Act provides that shareholders may be liable if they contribute either wilfully or negligently to a company causing damage. The provision is particularly important for groups of companies and means that the injured party may advance a claim for damages against the parent company. The prerequisite for this is that the parent company has acted wilfully or negligently. The provision applies to liablity vis-à-vis both the company itself and third parties. On the basis of this provision, a parent company – in instances where the necessary blame has been demonstrated on the part of the owners – can thus be held liable for the damage caused by a product manufactured or supplied by a subsidiary. The same applies for a physical person who, through his or her shareholding, has a decisive influence over a joint stock company. An example of where blame may attach to a parent company is where it exerts real control over a subsidiary and instructs the latter to start production of dangerous products without taking into account official production standards or any form of quality monitoring. Another example could be a subsidiary which is under-financed to the extent that it has insufficient funds to implement the product's supervision and measures, which such operations demand.

In Portugal, the Portuguese Companies' Code of 1986 introduced various innovative provisions on relationships between companies. The concept of 'total domination' and 'contracts of subordination' are relevant to the question of attributing liability to companies.

(a) Total domination (Companies' Code, articles 489 and 490) can occur either if a company is set up by another company which is its only shareholder (Companies' Code, article 488), or if more than 90% of a company's shares are acquired directly or indirectly by another company.
(b) Contracts of subordination (Companies' Code, articles 493 ff) are contracts concluded between companies under the terms of which one company (the subordinated company) subordinates its management to that of another (the directing company). This may occur irrespective of whether one company already has control over the other (through a majority shareholding or direct or indirect control of its management). Following the conclusion of such contract, the independent shareholders are permitted to choose between the sale of their shares or a guarantee of profits provided by the directing company.

In both of these situations, the Companies' Code provides that the dominant, or directing, company shall be liable for the obligations of the dominated, or subordinated, company for as long as the domination or subordination exists (article 501). An added liability is established at article 502, which states that the subordinated or dominated company may require its master company to compensate annual losses which cannot be covered by the former's reserves. In essence, therefore, a company may be held liable both by the creditors of its wholly-owned subsidiary and the company whose management it controls contractually, or it may be held liable by that company itself for its losses.

Apart from these situations, which are easily avoidable, in Portugese law a company or person with a controlling interest in another company cannot be held liable for the debts of the latter. Therefore, for businesses in high risk activities, incorporation and the use of shelf companies is a useful tool in Portuguese law, as long as total domination and contracts of subordination are avoided.

Similarly, in Sweden the corporate veil is not easily lifted. There are however certain decisions of the Supreme Court where shareholders were found to be liable. The reason, generally, was that the true business activities and interests lay with the shareholder and that the company was not a normally active company managing on its own behalf with its own financial resources. It seems that the minimum requirements for lifting the corporate veil in Sweden are:

(a) that the company's activities have been carried out in the interests of the parent company (or in the interests of other shareholders); and
(b) that the assets of the company have been clearly insufficient for the foreseeable risks and obligations.

In Ireland, the courts have been prepared in certain circumstances to 'lift the veil of incorporation' in limited circumstances, including the case of fraud. The ownership and control of the structure is an important factor in determining whether the court will lift the corporate veil. In a case where the manufacturing activity and assets of a group were split into two separate companies[3] it is stated that it is 'well established ... that a court may, if the justice of the case so requires, treat two or more related companies as a single entity so that the business notionally carried on by one will be regarded as the business of the group, or

---

3   *Power Supermarkets Ltd v Crumlin Investments Ltd* (1981, unreported), HC.

of another member of the group, if this conforms to the economic and commercial realities of the situation'.

The extent to which the corporate veil may be lifted between companies forming part of a multi-national group of companies raises interesting questions of private international law. In this case it is necessary in the first instance to ascertain which national law will apply to determine such a question.[4]

In addition to considering how a company may manage its risk through its corporate structure, it is also necessary to consider the effects of any reorganisation on the individuals involved with the various companies. For example, the national laws of some member states which implement the Product Safety Directive provide that the directors, officers and even employees responsible for the production or supply of the product may be personally liable in the event of it being unsafe. Such liability will result in a fine or even, on occasions, imprisonment. The transfer of the high risk activities to a separate company may therefore exonerate some individuals from such potential liability, while at the same time placing the potential burden on others. Also, in some instances, directors of a company may be liable in negligence for manufacturing or selling a defective product.

1.5 The effect of insolvency of the organisation on legal claims

The insolvency of an organisation will of course have an effect on legal claims brought against it. The three principal points to be borne in mind are as follows:

(a) The insolvency laws of many of the member states provide that a transfer carried out within a certain period of time of the insolvency can be set aside. For example, in England the Insolvency Act 1986 stipulates a period of two years. In Italy, article 2362 of the Civil Code states that in the case of insolvency of a company, when the corresponding liabilities arose during a period when there was only one shareholder, such shareholder shall bear unlimited liability for the obligations of the company. Although it is not clear whether such unlimited liability will arise in the case where the only shareholder is another company, still there is a sizeable risk that the courts will be inclined to 'pierce the corporate veil'. The relevant criterion seems to be whether or not the intention of the parties concerned was fraudulent – that is, if their only or main intention was to avoid liability. In this context it has been held that liability was not excluded by the fact that the only shareholder was a foreign company and/or the purchase of the shares of the subsidiary was made abroad. The Italian courts have not been consistent in applying article 2362 to cases where the shares of the subsidiary were held by more than one subject, although one clearly exercised actual control.[5]

(b) If the company which has become insolvent had a relevant insurance policy, the claimant may be able to bring a claim directly against the insurance

4 See Chapter XVIII.
5 It was held that, when the shares in a company were held by two persons and a minority holding was in turn wholly owned by the majority shareholder, there was unlimited liability on the part of the majority shareholder (Cass No 5413 of 1982). A similar case, however, was resolved in the opposite way, applying the fraudulent scope test (Cass 9 May 1985 No 2879 in *Le Società* 1985, 717).

company notwithstanding the insolvency of the company. The extent to which such claim can be brought will depend upon the relevant national applicable law. For example, in England, The Third Party's (Rights against Insurers) Act 1936 makes such provision.

(c) In some jurisdictions, the company may be reconstituted in order that it or its insurers may meet a claim and, indeed, its directors and/or shareholders may be liable. A summary of the position in the countries considered in the chapters of this book appears as Appendix 3.

1.6   Managing risk through contracts

There are a number of ways that a manufacturer or supplier may seek to reduce its risk of a claim being successfully brought against it by the contracts it enters into with others. The following points are listed by way of example only, and are by no means exhaustive:

(a) A party who sub-contracts the manufacture of a product or a component part should give detailed performance specifications, list the uses to which the product is likely to be put and place the onus on the sub-contractor to make a safe product or component part which will comply with those specifications and will be suitable for the specified use.

(b) A supplier should seek to obtain an indemnity from the party from whom it obtains the goods in the event of a claim being brought against it. This is because the Product Liability Directive merely allows for a claim in damages to be brought against the next party in the chain of supply. An indemnity will allow the supplier to recover a larger sum of money than a claim in damages since it entitles the plaintiff to recover a sum representing its entire loss and there is no duty implied for the plaintiff to mitigate their loss. It is noteworthy, however, that many insurance policies will not cover the contractual obligation of a party to pay sums of money pursuant to an indemnity.

(c) A manufacturer should contractually oblige its supplier to pass any warnings or instructions for use given with or on the product to the next party in the chain of supply. It should further require its supplier to enter into similar contractual provisions with the party to whom the supplier itself sells the product. This hopefully ensures that the warnings and instructions are brought to the attention of the consumer.

(d) The manufacturer should ensure that its supplier is familiar with and agrees with its product recall policy (in particular the provision relating to who bears the costs of recall), and that the supplier has in place a product recall policy which accords with that of the manufacturer. Again, similar obligations should be imposed on all subsequent suppliers.

(e) Insofar as is possible pursuant to the relevant national applicable law, exclusions and limitations of liability should be sought. It is not possible, pursuant to the Product Liability Directive, to exclude a claim in product liability. The implementation of the Unfair Contract Terms Directive in member states will harmonise the position to a large extent.

(f) The choice of the governing law of the contract needs to be considered carefully since it will have an impact on the potential liability of a manufacturer or supplier.

1.7 Defending international claims

A potential defendant may take certain steps to limit its liability where the anticipated claim is of an international nature. This is because where there is an international claim, it is likely that there will be a choice of jurisdictions where the plaintiff may seek redress. Certain jurisdictions may be more favourable to a defendant than others (see Chapter XVIII, section 2.1). Where one jurisdiction would be particularly more favourable to a potential defendant, it may wish to commence the action itself by seeking a negative declaration, thereby hopefully ensuring that the dispute will be determined in the jurisdiction of its choice (see Chapter XVIII, section 2, page 487).

2 ADMINISTRATIVE ISSUES

2.1 Documentation

Many claims are won or lost according to the amount of evidence available. This is particularly the case in many civil law jurisdictions where written documentary evidence is heavily relied upon in court proceedings. It is therefore vital that complete and accurate records are kept of the following:

(a) the contracts entered into by the company;
(b) the results of any tests carried out on the products during their manufacture pursuant to the company's quality control procedure. This is particularly important when defending a claim in product liability since documentation which proves that the goods were checked for absence of defects before they were put into circulation may be accepted as proof of the probability that the product was not defective at the time of distribution, ie that the defence in article 7(b) of the Directive is available. The records may include market tests, internal reports of defects of the product, quality control of component parts, raw materials and the final product, and even details of which employee worked at what place/machine at which time (especially if a safety measure of a product is installed or controlled). These may be recorded by photograph or even video, for example to show that warnings and instruction manuals have been attached to the product;
(c) details concerning the businesses from whom any component parts or raw materials were obtained and into which products the various components or raw materials were incorporated (this may be relevant where a claim in product liability can be passed up the chain of supply, in which case it is necessary to identify the earlier person in the chain);
(d) details of the person or business to whom the products are supplied (this should be kept by both the manufacturer and those in the chain of supply);
(e) the extent to which employees have been instructed and continuously educated in relation to the production of the product.
(f) when products are sold to countries where the 'state of the art' defence in the Product Liability Directive has been implemented into national law, detailed information should be kept on the state of the scientific and technical knowledge relating to the products at the time they are put into circulation.

If a company has attained a quality accreditation, such as ISO 9000 or BS 5750, it is likely that it will in any event have a number of the above procedures in place.

It is likely that the goods will be identified by way of batch number where they are of low value, fast moving consumer goods, or individual serial numbers where they are high value consumer goods. It is important that, so far as possible, batch and serial numbers will remain legible throughout the chain of supply and will not become erased or illegible. This raises an interesting question when goods are recycled since, at the point of recycling, it becomes important for any such identification numbers to be removed and for the recycled product to be re-numbered.

In view of the limitation period stated by the Product Liability Directive, it is advisable to keep the records referred to above for at least ten years. If the national law of the relevant country permits a longer period of limitation in contract or tort, the records should ideally be kept for such longer period. The use of computers to store information assists companies with the problem of how to retain the vast quantities of paperwork generated by this requirement. However, caution should be exercised before discarding original documents since the national laws in Europe vary as to the extent to which reproductions of original documents are admissible as evidence. Where documents or other relevant information are kept on computer disk or tape, it is very important to ensure that appropriate software and hardware are kept by the Company to view such documents and data many years after they are created.

2.2   Handling of claims

If a claim is threatened or made, it is important that any documentary evidence or samples of products which are relevant to the claim are retained.

In some countries in Europe, the system of 'product observation' is adopted. This allows user information and experience to be transmitted to the producer. It presupposes sufficient contact between the producer and the consumer, either directly, or indirectly via the distribution system. Defects that occur often must be reported by the distribution organisation to the producer. The same applies if the product is frequently used incorrectly.

Some manufacturers wish to take a proactive stance in relation to consumer complaints and even place a contact telephone number on their products encouraging customers to ring with their comments. If such a system is adopted, it is important that the relevant individuals within the organisation are selected to deal with such telephone calls and are appropriately trained.

2.3   Insurance

In addition to public liability insurance, manufacturers and suppliers may wish to consider purchasing insurance, to cover the costs of recalling a product. These issues are dealt with in further detail in Chapter XX. If any such policies are purchased, the correct amount of cover needs to be carefully considered in the light of the risk of damage and type of damage which may be caused by the product and in particular the jurisdictions where consumers are likely to use the products. For example, in the United States, product liability claims are frequently heard by juries who tend to make higher awards of damages and, further, are entitled to make awards of punitive damages. In view of the potential personal liability of directors, officers and managers in certain jurisdictions

pursuant to laws implementing the Product Safety Directive, a company may wish to consider taking out personal insurance for such individuals.

3 WARNINGS, INSTRUCTIONS AND MANUALS

3.1 The legal background

Liability for defective products may arise either as a result of a defect in the product itself, or as a result of a defect in its instructions, warnings and general presentation. This latter basis, which is known as the representational theory of product liability, has long been established in the United States and is fast developing in Australia. The concept is well summarised in 'A Representational Theory of Product Liability under Part V and Part VA of the Trade Practices Act 1974 (Cth)' Kellam and O'Keefe[6] as follows:

> A representational theory of product liability focuses on the expectation created in consumers by the way a manufacturer, supplier or retailer markets and presents its product. In each fact situation, a representational theory asks:
> (1) what was said (or not stated) about the product in sales and marketing, how was it packaged and so on?
> (2) given these express or implied representations or the absence of instructions, information or warnings, what should consumers have expected of this product?
> (3) did these pre-sale representations turn out to be true? That is, did the product live up to the expectations created by these representations?
> (4) did the consumer rely upon the representation and thereby suffer loss?'

It is vital therefore that manufacturers give adequate warnings, instructions for use or even instruction manuals with their products, since their existence can affect the extent to which a product is considered safe. Indeed, a safe product may be rendered unsafe simply by virtue of its warnings being inadequate. This was held in the famous Thalidomide case, by the Privy Council in England, sitting as an appeal court from New South Wales.[7] The appeal turned on whether the Supreme Court of New South Wales should have jurisdiction over the English manufacturers of a sedative containing Thalidomide. The facts assumed for the purposes of the appeal were broadly that Distillers Co (Biochemicals) Ltd was an English company carrying on business in Great Britain, one of whose products was a sedative and sleep-inducing tablet, the principal ingredient of which was thalidomide. The thalidomide had been obtained in bulk by Distillers from German manufacturers. The tablets were sold to an Australian distributor which marketed and sold them in Australia with the advertising matter and in the form supplied by Distillers. The accompanying printed matter described the drug as a sedative with no side effects.

The plaintiff was the infant daughter of a woman who had taken the drug; the child had been born with certain physical defects. The plaintiff claimed damages against Distillers and the Australian distributor.

Although the tablets, printed matter and the packaging were supplied as a unit by Distillers to the distributor in a form in which they were to reach the ultimate consumer, the Privy Council characterised the act of negligence as

---

6   Australian Trade Practices Law Journal, Vol 4, March 1996, p 4.
7   *Distillers Co (Biochemicals) Ltd v Thompson* [1997] AC 458.

the failure to give a warning that the tablets could be dangerous if taken by an expectant mother in the first three months of pregnancy. The tablets were unsafe because of the omission of this warning from the label. This lead the Privy Council to conclude on the jurisdictional issue that the failure to warn had taken place in both England and in New South Wales and therefore the plaintiff's cause of action arose within the jurisdiction of New South Wales. This case has since been applied by the Court of Appeal in England.[8]

Certain products, which are inherently dangerous, such as an electric knife, can be rendered safe by the provision of adequate warnings. The adjective 'adequate' is used advisedly; there are many considerations to be borne in mind when devising a warning, which are outlined in section 3.3 below.

The legal background in the EU to the above considerations is rather thin, and derives from:

(a) the definition of 'defect' in the Product Liability Directive;
(b) the definition of 'safe' in the General Product Safety Directive; and
(c) pre-contractual liability.

If the Draft Directive on Consumer Guarantees is implemented in its current form (November 1996) it will to some extent introduce the concept of representational theory of product liability into the courts of each member state, since article 2(2)b provides that in a contract of sale the goods must comply 'with the description given by the seller and that their quality and performance are satisfactory ... taking into account the public statements made about them by the seller, the producer or his representatives'

There have been to date very few cases in Europe where the representational theory of product liability has been considered. However, certain American and Australian legislation and jurisprudence provide a useful source of reference.[9]

The considerations set out in sections 3.2 and 3.3 below are merely those which good manufacturing practice, common practical sense and consumer awareness dictate, pending more detailed legal guidance from the national courts of the member states.

3.1.1   The Product Liability Directive

In the Product Liability Directive,[10] it is stated that:

(1) A product is defective when it does not provide the safety which a person is entitled to expect, taking all the circumstances into account, including:

(a) the presentation of the product;
(b) the use to which it could reasonably be expected that the product would be put; and
(c) the time when the product was put into circulation.

It is suggested that 'the presentation of the product' includes not only the packaging of the product, but also its marketing, design, warnings, safety instructions and manuals. The reference in the definition of 'defective' to the

8   *Castree v E R Sibb & Sons Ltd* [1980] 2 All ER 589, [1980] 1 WLR 1248.
9   Eg Part V and Part VA Australian Trade Practices Act 1974.
10 Article 6.

reasonable expectation of the use to which the product would be put is relevant to the drafting of warnings for two reasons: firstly, the manufacturer should consider the uses to which it could reasonably be expected that the product would be put and, where necessary, give guidance on the detail of such use. Secondly, the manufacturer should consider what might constitute 'misuse' and, on certain occasions, specifically state and warn against such misuses.

Further, article 8(2) of the Product Liability Directive provides a defence of contributory negligence to a manufacturer. If clear and adequate warnings given in relation to a product are ignored by a consumer, it is open for the manufacturer to plead that the damage has been caused partly or wholly as a result of the fault of the injured person and thereby avoid or reduce its liability. Indeed, some American companies now include in their list of contraindication for using a product the inability of the user to understand the instructions.

3.1.2 The Product Safety Directive

The Product Safety Directive goes a stage further and actually makes specific reference to instructions for use in its definition of a 'safe product'.[11] It provides that:

> safe product shall mean any product which *under normal or reasonably foreseeable conditions of use* ... does not present any risk ... taking into account the following points in particular:
>
> (a) the characteristics of the product, including its composition, packaging, *instructions for assembly and maintenance* – the presentation of the product, the labelling, *any instructions for its use and disposal* and any other indication or information provided by the producer;
> (b) the categories of consumers at serious risk when using the product, in particular children.

A safe product can therefore be rendered unsafe by virtue of its presentation (which could include any promotional or advertising campaign), labelling or instructions for use.

In addition to the general product liability and product safety law, it is noteworthy that certain products are subject to more specific rules on labelling and instructions pursuant to national or EU standards. For example, in Britain there are numerous British Standards which relate to specific products. Certain EU directives and regulations, such as those relating to toy safety and machinery, also stipulate requirements in relation to instructions. In certain jurisdictions, a breach of such regulations may give rise to a civil claim for breach of statutory duty.

3.1.3 Pre-contractual liability

The laws of most member states provide for a right against a manufacturer or seller for inaccurate or misleading statements or representations which induce the purchaser to enter into the contract of purchase of the goods. It is arguable that such statements or representations may be made not only by a sales representative orally at the time of sale, but also more generally by way of the product's promotional or advertising campaign.

---

11 Article 2(b).

For example, there has over the years grown a trend for car manufacturers to produce advertisements which show their cars being driven unconventionally such as on two wheels at high speed around hairpin bends. It is arguable that such an advertisement would suggest to the consumer that this would be a reasonable way to drive the car and, if anyone were to do so and it were to crash as a result of the car being unable to be driven on two wheels, the plaintiff could seek to bring a claim. Such a claimant would seek to prove that the car was unsafe on the basis that the advertisement led him or her to believe that this would be a reasonable way of driving the car.[12]

In contrast with a claim brought under the relevant law implementing the Product Liability or Product Safety Directives, it is not necessary for a claim in pre-contractual liability to succeed to prove that the product is defective or unsafe. It is sufficient that the representation is false, misleading or deceptive, has been relied upon, and damage or loss has ensued. A further difference is that many national laws envisage silence as a basis for liability, where it distorts a positive representation.

As stated in the other chapters of this book, the consequences of manufacturing and/or distributing an unsafe product include an exposure to a civil claim for product liability, contract or tort and/or a criminal prosecution which may result in imprisonment or a fine. It is therefore in every manufacturer and supplier's interest to take the necessary steps to ensure that the products with which they are associated are not rendered unsafe by virtue of their bearing no or inadequate warnings.

3.2   The 'get-up' of the product

For the reasons stated above, manufacturers and suppliers should exercise great care when devising any promotional or advertising campaigns in relation to products. The following points in particular should be borne in mind:

(i)   scientific claims such as that a product is 'healthy' or 'environmentally friendly' must be capable of substantiation;

(ii) the general compliance of a product with certain industry standards may be implied by specific statements. In the case of *Elconnex Pty Ltd v Gerard Industries Pty Ltd*,[13] a manufacturer stated that its conductors could be used in a plastic conduit to carry electrical wiring, when in fact they did not comply with the relevant standard. Although the producer made no express claim to comply with this standard, the court nonetheless held that the silence of the manufacturer created the impression that its product met all relevant standards. It will be interesting to see whether the courts of member states will adopt such a pro-consumer viewpoint;

(iii) a representation made about one aspect of safety may create expectations about another. For example, in Australia a pair of 'baseball sunglasses' were advertised as giving 'instant eye protection'. Although these words were aimed at giving protection from sunlight, a boy who lost an eye as a result of a baseball shattering the glasses recovered damages;[14]

---

12   Cf the US case of *Leichtamer v American Motors* 67 Ohio St 2d 456 (1981).
13   [1992] ATPR (Digest) 46-0833.
14   *Filler v Rayex Corpn* 435F 2d 336 (7th Cir 1970).

(iv) advertising should be realistic and not raise a consumer's expectations as to what may be done with this product (see the example in section 3.1.3 above relating to the performance of cars);

(v) any important technical limitations of the product should be brought to the attention of the user.

3.3 Warnings and instructions for use

Set out below is a checklist for the development of instructions. Before considering the matter in detail, it is necessary to answer the following basic questions:

(a) What kind of warning is intended to be given? For example, is there to be a brief warning on the product with a more detailed series of warnings on the packaging? Is there to be an instruction leaflet inserted in the packaging of the product? Is there to be a detailed instruction manual which accompanies the product? The answers to these questions may to some extent be driven by the size and/or design of the product.

(b) Are the warnings and instructions to be given largely in form, or are symbols and/or pictorial warnings and instructions to be given?

(c) To what extent can the warnings or instructions be simplified or shortened by the use of other safety precautions in the product? For example, can medicines be fitted with childproof caps and can a high voltage computer be fitted with a series of circuit breakers?

(d) Who are you likely to be warning? Although it is impossible for a manufacturer to guess exactly who the consumers of its product are to be, it can make a good general assumption as to the likely age, intelligence and nationality.

(e) Is the product likely to come into contact with other elements as water or heat, which may cause the warning to be erased or to become illegible?

Each of these factors will have an important impact on the drafting of the warnings. From a legal point of view, the following points are particularly noteworthy:

    (i) the language in which instruction is given. For example, in Switzerland instructions must be given in each of the three languages of the Swiss consumers, namely German, French and Italian. Care should be exercised in obtaining translations, which should always be carried out by a person whose mother tongue is the language into which the warning is being translated;

    (ii) whether a consumer will receive a product only under the supervision of an intermediary. An intermediary is someone who assumes responsibility in place of the ultimate user for selecting the product for use by that user, such as a doctor, teacher or hairdresser. In this case, it is necessary only that the instruction or warning reaches the attention and is understood by such intermediary.

(f) does the relevant national law contain any specific provisions as to the warnings to be given? For example, in Germany manuals and other instructions for use are required by law to contain, in particular, the following:

    (i) clear identification of dangers; however, dangers that are so obvious that every reasonable person is aware of them need not be mentioned

expressly;
(ii) handling instructions that also extend to combinations of accessories and other equipment that are commonly known to be used together with the products;
(iii) instructions concerning installation, assembly and fitting of spare parts. If such work should only be performed by trained personnel or experts, there must be notice to that effect;
(iv) instructions concerning care and maintenance, and safety measures to be observed in connection therewith.

The duty to warn and instruct does not end once the product has been placed on the market. It may be that certain facts will come to the knowledge of the manufacturer after the product has been placed on the market and that it is necessary for the manufacturer and others in the supply chain to inform purchasers of the product of such information.[15]

The nature of dissemination of such information will depend upon a number of factors, such as the ease with which purchasers can be traced, the urgency with which the information must be brought to the attention of the user and the risk of the information not reaching the attention of the user.

Indeed, in certain circumstances, a manufacturer may decide to take the more drastic step of recalling the product, which is considered in section 4. Since the instructions, warnings and advertisements are integral to a product, it is important that all the relevant specialist managers and consultants work together as a team in producing the final product. It is often difficult to determine to whom to assign the primary task of drafting the warnings and instructions. Possibilities include:

(a) the technical designer of the product – such person will obviously be well placed to write a technical instruction manual. However, he will probably be so familiar with the technical intricacies of the product that he may find difficulty in producing a very simple clear explanation for its use. It is therefore best that any such instructions be checked by a person who has no technical knowledge of the product.
(b) the marketing manager – his input is vital to ensure that the advertising and marketing campaign in relation to the product does not give consumers false expectations as to its use. He may be reluctant to include a series of warnings which state the adverse consequences of misusing a product, since he may view any such statement as casting a negative light on the product. Although this may be true from a strictly marketing point of view, it is important at all times to bear in mind the legal consequences of failing to do so.
(c) an ergonomist – a trained professional, experienced in drafting instructions, usually acting as an outside consultant. Any instructions drafted by an ergonomist should be checked by the technical designer or engineer of the product to ensure that they are technically correct.

Once the instructions have been drafted, it is recommended that they be 'tried out' on a cross-section of likely users to check that they are clear and adequate. Only once such tests have been carried out satisfactorily should the warnings then be printed.

15   Product Safety Directive Arts 3 and 6(e).

3.4   Checklist for the development of instructions[16]

3.4.1   Content

Define:	1. your users
	2. the purpose of the instructions.
Ensure they are:	3. complete
	4. accurate
	5. feasible
Include:	6. advice to keep the instructions
	7. explanations of actions
Check:	8. instructions apply to one model only
	9. the necessary sections are included and in the correct order:

        (a) product name and manufacturer
        (b) table of contents
        (c) introduction
        (d) safety information
        (e) components
        (f) handling information
        (g) installation/assembly
        (h) operating instructions
        (i) fault diagnosis
        (j) routine servicing and maintenance
        (k) professional overhauling and repair
        (l) disposal instructions
        (m) index

Decide whether you need:	10. a table of contents
	11. an index
	12. a reminder card or label

3.4.2   Safety information and special instructions

Remember:	13. to try to redesign your product to remove all possible hazards, or guard against them
Determine:	14. likely uses and misuses of your product
	15. the hazards
Ensure that you:	16. identify the level of each hazard
	17. keep safety information separate from general hints on use
	18. state that the safety instructions must be followed
	19. adequately describe the hazard
Clearly state:	20. the actions or uses which present the hazard
	21. what factors increase the level of risk
	22. how to avoid the hazard
	23. what to do if the hazard is encountered

16   We are grateful to Susan Cooper BSc and Magdalen Page BSc, MSc, SErgs of the Institute for Consumer Ergonomics for their permission to reproduce this checklist. For a detailed explanation of the checklist please see 'Instructions for Consumer Products' compiled by Susan Cooper and Magdalen Page for the Consumer Safety Unit of the Department of Trade and Industry, the United Kingdom.

24. what treatment to use on an injury
25. what *should   not* be done if the hazard is encountered
26. what must be done before re-using the product

The safety
information must
be:

27. definite, precise and unambiguous
28. realistic
29. placed at the beginning of the instructions if it is general
30. placed immediately before the instruction where it will be needed, if it is specific to a particular action
31. highlighted by means of the ! symbol, boxing, white space, underlining, type or colour
32. put on the product itself if the user should be constantly reminded of the hazard

3.4.3   Organisation and layout

Ensure you have:

33. a logical order for your sections
34. useful, informative headings
35. page numbers at the bottom outside edges
36. section numbers in the margin
37. illustrations and tables numbered sequentially

Place:

38. illustrations and tables below or next to their text

Use:

39. alternatives to prose where appropriate - pictures, tables, strip cartoons, etc
40. tables when you need to show several different states of conditions, or for numerical information
41. spacing between sections and paragraphs to show the layout of the text
42. a typographic reference grid to specify detailed layouts
43. a floating baseline at the bottom of the page
44. lists for actions and points, rather than continuous text

Choose:

45. the binding method before deciding on the layout as it affects the margin size
46. the number of columns

For multi-lingual
instructions ensure:

47. that when the instructions in one language are over 4 or 5 sides in length, there is, if possible a separate booklet for each language
48. each language can be easily distinguished
49. each illustration can be seen at the same time as its corresponding text in all the languages

3.4.4   Language and sentence construction

Consider:

50. your users' levels of knowledge

Check that:

51. there are no sentences of over 30 words
52. there is not too much information in a sentence
53. there are no ambiguities
54. translations are concise and comprehensible

Use:

55. simple, everyday words
56. verbs, not nouns formed from verbs

57. precise wording
58. phrases to describe proportions
59. concrete words and phrases
60. descriptive names for parts and actions
61. unbiased language
62. a glossary for unfamiliar words
63. the active voice
64. key words and connecting words
65. positive statements rather than negative
66. lists to indicate a sequence of actions

Avoid:
67. abbreviations and acronyms
68. foreign words and phrases
69. double negatives
70. symbols unless they are really needed

3.4.5   Illustrations

Check:
71. each illustration is relevant and necessary
72. each is referred to in the text

Position:
73. illustrations next to or immediately after their text

Choose:
74. photographs for realism
75. line drawings to show the appropriate amount of detail
76. exploded views for self-assembly products
77. cross-sections if this is the only way to show a detail or feature
78. concept diagrams only if your users will understand them

Check for:
79. clarity after reduction
80. necessary levels of detail
81. the correct angle of view
82. accuracy
83. realistic representations
84. labels in lower-case letters
85. labels not printed over the illustrations
86. reference letters or numbers and key used if more than about 5 labels are needed
87. consistency of labels between illustrations

Consider:
88. using colour to identify parts in illustrations (but do not rely on colour alone)

3.4.6   Physical elements

Consider:
89. alternatives to paper

Choose:
90. the correct paper size
91. the correct paper weight
92. paper which does not allow print to show through
93. plain, matt paper
94. the best orientation – landscape or portrait
95. the method of text origination
96. the method of printing or reproducing
97. either to fold or bind the instructions

Ensure:	98. instructions will be sufficiently durable
For 'on product' instructions:	99. use print which is large enough to be read easily
	100. put them in a prominent position
	101. ensure they will remain legible
	102. attach them permanently to the product

3.4.7   Typography

Choose:	103. a line length of 35-65 characters
	104. type with an x-height of 1.5mm (10-11 point)
	105. different type sizes (up to 3mm x height) for headings to emphasise their hierarchy
	106. a ragged righthand edge
	107. leading of one quarter of the type size
	108. a word space of one quarter of the type size
Use:	109. normal lower-case lettering with initial upper-case letters
	110. a typeface which will remain clear when copied
	111. black print on white paper
Avoid:	112. putting the first word of a sentence at the end of a line
	113. using a large variety of typefaces and sizes
	114. using upper-case, italics, bold-face or underlining over several sentences
Use colours	115. sparingly and consistently
	116. of sufficient contrast to be distinguished by those with colour-deficient vision
When printing on cardboard:	117. ensure the instructions will not be torn when the pack is opened

3.5   The law in practice

Since the concept of representational theory is as yet undeveloped in Europe, it is difficult for a manufacturer or seller to ascertain the extent to which the above considerations should be adhered to. Certainly, if the products are to be sold directly to, or are likely indirectly to be placed on the market in countries such as, America or Australia, great care should be exercised.

In any event, a manufacturer or seller cannot and should not be expected to warn against every risk associated with the product, nor should the effect of the law be that any advertising campaign that goes further than a bland representation of the product potentially exposes the manufacturer to a liability. The practice in Australia and America is that, where the potential injury is serious, it is warned against, even when the risk of it occurring is very low. Where, on the other hand, the potential injury is less serious, the duty to warn is lower. Kellam and O'Keefe compare two American cases as follows:[17]

> In *Davies v Wyeth Laboratories*, 399 F 2d 121 (1968), the plaintiff recovered damages for the defendant's failure to warn of an adverse physiological reaction to a vaccination, which was experienced by only 0.9 in 1 million recipients. On

17   Australian Trade Practices Law Journal, Vol 4, March 1996, p 4.

the other hand, in *Hafrier v Guerlain, Inc* 310 NYS 2d 141 (1970) the court denied recovery to a plaintiff who had suffered a serious skin allergy to a perfume where there had been 25 complaints out of 270,000 sales. The different verdict may reflect a difference in the seriousness of the harm suffered by the respective defendants..

4   PRODUCT RECALL

4.1   Introduction

The implementation of the Product Liability Directive throughout the EU has highlighted to manufacturers the importance of producing safe products. Previously, it was rare for manufacturers to take such obligations so seriously as to implement a policy of product recall, or to decide that recalling their products was necessary. As a result of the Product Safety Directive with its provisions which enable the relevant authorities of member states to require manufacturers to take steps to recall unsafe products as appropriate, more and more manufacturers are implementing product recall policies and realising that to be forewarned is to be forearmed. After all, the decision to recall a product is generally taken in an emergency situation where time is of the essence and it is vital that there is already a well thought out procedure put in place. Indeed, in Australia, where product safety law has been implemented for over twenty years, almost all companies, ranging from the very large to the very small, have in place a product recall policy.

4.2   Contents of a product recall policy

The nature of the product recall policy will vary depending on the product in question and the nature and structure of the organisation for whom it is prepared. However, the following features are likely to be present:

4.2.1   A system for assessing and categorising the risk

The question of whether or not to recall a product is a difficult one. From a legal point of view, when it becomes apparent that there is a serious risk of the product causing harm, the only sensible solution may be to recall it. However, from a public relations point of view, the fact of implementing a recall may cause a company's image to be tarnished in the eyes of the consumer unless it is implemented on the basis that the company is very caring and wishes to prevent injury taking place, rather than on the basis that the company has made grave mistakes in its production line in the first place.

4.2.2   Assessment of recall and decision of whether to recall

The extent to which it is practical to recall products needs to be assessed in each situation. For example, the manufacturer may be alerted to the defect before the particular batch of products has been sold to the consumer or even supplied to the retailer. In this case, recall is relatively easy, need not be public and cost is relatively low. If, on the other hand, the product has already reached the consumer, it is more difficult and expensive to implement a recall. However many factors there are to balance, it is important that a decision as to whether to recall or not is taken relatively quickly on the basis of the facts known at the

time of making the decision. This is particularly the case where the media has become aware of the issue since to delay will only lead to speculation by the media and cause confusion amongst the general public.

4.2.3   Recall action

The action to be taken in the event of a recall will depend upon a number of factors, including the nature of the risk and the number of persons likely to be affected by it. The possibilities include:

(a) notifying persons likely to be affected by the defect of the problem: this may be carried out in the press, on the television, or by writing to each of the consumers if there are a very few products in circulation;
(b) replacing the defective product with a new product;
(c) supplying and, possibly, fitting a replacement part; and
(d) carrying out certain modifications, either in situ or on a return basis.

4.2.4   Checking the supply chain

It is important that, once a recall has been put into operation, manufacturers keep a check on their suppliers and others in the supply chain to ensure that they are effectively carrying out the product recall plans and, so far as possible, to ensure that all the defective products are, indeed, recalled.

4.2.5   Public relations

It is important that the product recall is handled sensitively from a public relations point of view. Some companies issue a series of new advertisements following a major recall in the aim of restoring consumer confidence in their products. Any such advertisements need to be considered carefully since, if the product recall has not received high media attention, any advertisements which mention the problem will draw the attention of consumers to the recall and simply highlight the problem.

4.2.6   Contact details

Product recall policies should be relatively detailed and include information such as the contact details of key personnel, advisers and others who will work together in the event of a recall.

Once a recall policy has been adopted, it should not simply be put to one side and forgotten about. Ideally, it should be revisited annually to ensure that all those responsible for its implementation are familiar with it and understand and agree with its terms. Indeed, some companies who take their potential recall obligations seriously have a 'mock recall' from time to time, when they pretend that a product needs to be recalled and only the most senior managers know that it is in fact a practice run. Although such an exercise will take up valuable time and have a cost attached to it, it may prove invaluable in highlighting areas where the policy could be improved and ensure that, if a recall is necessary, it runs as smoothly as possible.

5   CONCLUSION

There are a number of steps that manufacturers and distributors should take in order first to reduce the risk of a claim for a defective product being brought

against them and, second, to ensure that they will have as good a defence as possible to any claims brought against them. In essence, manufacturers and distributors must ensure that the products with which they are involved are safe in all respects, including their packaging, advertising and accompanying literature. They should document the steps they take to ensure such safety and retain these records. There is, of course, a cost attached to taking such steps, which is ultimately partly borne by the consumer. To the extent that the cost is borne by the manufacturer or the distributor, it should be considered as a long-term investment. After all, the costs to a company in defending a claim for a defective product can be significant, unexpected and result in substantial loss of profits.

CHAPTER XX

Product liability insurance

D A Thomas Esq

Willis Corroon Limited
Willis Corroon House
Wood Street
Kingston-upon-Thames
Surrey KT1 1UG
England

Tel: ++ 44 81 787 6290
Fax: ++ 44 81 943 4297

CHAPTER XVIII

Product liability insurance

1 INTRODUCTION

Product liability law is complex and the responsibilities faced by those who introduce products to the marketplace are great.

Product liability insurance has a key role in risk management strategy in relation to the product liability exposure.

A clear understanding of the scope and limitations of product liability insurance is necessary if risk management planning is to achieve its objectives.

This chapter will outline the cover available from the insurance market and will explore some practical aspects of placing, underwriting and structuring a product liability insurance programme.

The viewpoint from which this is written is that of the London insurance market, which is still the most influential in Europe. There are differences in insurance practice within different countries in Europe. These are highlighted in the relevant country chapters. There are, however, many factors which are working to reduce or eliminate these differences. Product liability law is converging within the European Community. Many businesses operate across borders and wish to purchase insurance on the same basis in all territories. Many insurers do business in more than one country.

A product liability policy is a contractual promise made by an insurer in return for a premium payment to make good certain defined losses suffered by the insured.

In addition to the normal legal rules governing the making of contracts, there are some important principles which apply to insurance contracts including product liability insurance.

First, there must be an insurable interest, that is, the insured must be at risk of some financial loss in the event of the circumstances insured by the policy arising.

This does not usually cause problems in the case of liability policies as the establishment of a legal liability in respect of any event gives the insured an insurable interest in that event.

A liability insurance policy is a contract of indemnity. The insured may not recover more than his actual loss. This again does not cause difficulties as the measure of loss is an award or agreed settlement with a third party.

There is in connection with all insurance contracts a duty of disclosure. When asking an insurer to provide a quotation for product liability insurance all facts which are material to the risk must be disclosed. Information will be considered material if it can be demonstrated that it would have affected an insurer's acceptance of the risk or the terms and conditions of the quotation. Failure to disclose material information could allow the insurer to avoid the policy.

The duty of disclosure revives at each renewal of the policy. In addition there may be specific conditions within the policy requiring notification of certain changes of risk during the policy period.

The principle of subrogation applies and may often be significant in product liability insurance. Where an insured receives an indemnity from an insurer the insurer may then take over the insured's rights against any other parties that may be responsible for the loss. For example, the manufacturer or supplier of a defective product may be liable for an injury under the Consumer Protection Act and have to pay compensation. However, the defect in the product may have been the result of a defective component supplied by a sub-contractor. The insurer would then be subrogated to the insurer's rights and could endeavour to recover his outlay from the supplier.

2   THE PRODUCT LIABILITY POLICY

Product liability insurance normally forms part of a general liability policy covering public, product, and sometimes in the UK, employers' liability claims. The product liability insurance may be a separate section within the policy or the public and product liability insurance may be integrated.

For the purpose of examining the cover it will be more straightforward to treat the product liability insurance as if a separate policy had been issued. There is not, however, a standard product liability policy used by all insurers. Each insurer will have their own form and indeed many individual insured may have specially negotiated wordings. There are therefore many variations of cover to be found. Current practice also varies considerably in different European countries.

Whatever the detailed variations a product liability policy will tend to follow the same basic construction. A typical policy, an example of which is included in the appendix, will have:

(a) a schedule;
(b) a recital clause;
(c) an operative clause;
(d) policy definitions;
(e) policy exceptions;
(f) policy conditions.

Each of these will be examined in turn.

The recital clause in one form or another appears in all policies and usually makes reference to a proposal form. The wording of this clause makes the proposal the basis of the contract. In practice, particularly with large and complex risks, a proposal form may not be completed and the insurer will rely on detailed information supplied by the proposer or his broker. This is examined in more detail under the section dealing with practical aspects of placing and underwriting. The recital clause will also make reference to the payment of premium by the insured.

The operative clause defines the scope of the policy indemnity. There are two alternative forms of operative clause which affect the way in which the product liability cover operates. These are usually referred to as the occurrence form and the claims made form. The occurrence form of cover, which is the most common, will be examined first. The way in which the claims made form of cover operates and its impact will be examined in a later section.

The product liability policy is concerned with the insured's legal liability for injuries and property damage.

Financial losses suffered by a claimant which flow directly from such injury or damage will also be covered. For example, if a piece of equipment is supplied to a factory and because of a defect causes a fire, the product liability policy would provide an indemnity both for the direct property damage to the factory and the consequential losses suffered by the owner of the factory because production is brought to a halt. The policy would not cover a situation where the equipment caused no damage but due to a defect did not function resulting in consequential losses.

A product liability policy is applicable to insureds who may be involved at any point in the chain of supply and who may incur a liability.

The injury or damage for which indemnity is provided by the policy must happen during the period of insurance. The time when an injured third party brings a claim is not relevant, what matters is when the injury or damage complained of took place. Some types of injury and damage may take many years to become apparent and for third parties to realise that they have a cause of action. An example in the area of production liability would be asbestos-related diseases. Exposure to the substance may cause injury which remains latent for 20 or 30 years. Insurers may find themselves paying claims on policies which are many years old in relation to such exposures. The insured on the other hand knows that once he has effected a product liability policy on this 'occurrence' basis he has protection against injury or damage that may be caused during that policy period even if cover is subsequently cancelled or not renewed.

2.1   Legal costs

The policy also provides cover for legal and other costs incurred in defending any claim and the costs of a successful claimant. This is not the least important part of the cover as costs may be very substantial. Even where a claim is successfully defended it may not be possible to recover all costs from the plaintiff.

3   DEFINITIONS

A product liability policy will contain definitions of certain words and phrases. The significant definitions that may be found in a product liability policy and their effect are described below.

3.1   The product

The definition of product will usually include containers' instructions and advice given in connection with the supply. This is important as a product may be correctly designed and manufactured and not in itself defective but may be rendered defective by inadequate or inaccurate instructions or advice.

3.2   The insured

The Schedule of the policy will include the name of the insured. This definition may be extended to bring others under the protection of the policy. For

example, directors and employees of the insured. In some cases it may be necessary further to extend the definition by endorsement to include other categories of additional insured. For example, distributors of products may ask to be included as an insured.

3.3   Territorial limit

The territorial limit of the policy defines the geographical area within which injury or damage insured by the policy must occur. It is usual in the case of product liability for the territorial limit to be worldwide in respect of products manufactured or supplied by the insured businesses.

Occasionally insurers may seek to impose restrictions on the territorial limit. If this is the case the insured would have to consider carefully whether this is acceptable.

The geographical area most likely to be excluded is the USA. This is because of the particular problems associated with product liability in that jurisdiction. When assessing the impact of such an exclusion it is necessary to consider not only whether products are exported directly to any excluded territory by the insured but whether the insured's products could find their way to that area by some other route. The product may have been supplied to another manufacturer for incorporation into, for example, a motor vehicle. It may then be exported without the insured's knowledge. It is not unknown for companies to be involved in a product's liability action in the USA having never knowingly exported there.

3.4   Jurisdiction

The policy jurisdiction defines the geographical area within which the insurers will respond to legal actions. In most cases this will be the same as the territorial limits on the policy. It is possible, however, for the jurisdictional limit to be narrower.

It may be that injury or damage occurring anywhere in the world is covered but only if the legal action is commenced within the insured's domicile. This restriction would in some cases not provide adequate protection as a claimant may be able to bring a claim in particular circumstances in another jurisdiction (see Chapter 17).

It is more common for insurers to include a clause limiting the jurisdiction within which actions between the insured and the insurers may be heard in relation to disputes on policy cover.

3.5   The business

The business description is usually contained in the policy Schedule. The cover is limited to the described business and it is therefore vital that it is accurate and complete. The nature of the business undertaken is a major consideration in underwriting product liability insurance and any inaccuracy could result in insurers denying coverage. In many cases it is desirable to agree as general a business description as possible. For example, 'any activity undertaken by the insured'.

This does not, however, negate the duty of material disclosure. It is necessary to give insurers full information as to the business undertaken when cover is placed.

4 INDEMNITY LIMITS

There is usually in law no limit to the monetary amount of a claim that may be brought. A court award would reflect the legally recoverable losses of the claimant. A product liability policy, however, does have an indemnity limit which is the maximum sum the insurer will pay.

The product liability limit is usually expressed as being 'any one claim and in the aggregate during the period of insurance'. The indemnity limit is thus the maximum amount the insurer will pay during the policy period without regard to the number of claims. This is in contrast to public liability cover where the limit is usually expressed as 'each and every claim' with no limit on the number of claims. Insurers limit their exposure on product liability insurance because there could be many different claims arising from one defect which is reproduced in a product which is widely distributed. In the absence of an aggregate limit insurers are concerned that in these circumstances they could be liable for a multiple of the basic indemnity limit.

Legal costs incurred in defending claims are usually paid in addition to the limit of indemnity. On occasion, however, insurers may make the limit inclusive of costs, particularly where there is a North American exposure. This reflects the very high cost of litigation in that territory. In some circumstances the legal costs could equal or exceed the limit of indemnity being given under the policy.

The range of indemnities offered by one insurer may vary between £1m and £5m.

For many risks the indemnity limit offered by any one insurer may be insufficient.

Larger indemnities may be achieved by arranging for a number of insurers to accept part of the risk. This may be by co-insurance where each insurer writes a percentage of the whole limit or more usually by arranging excess layer policies.

Excess layer policies are separate insurance contracts that provide cover for claims which exceed the indemnity limit on the primary policy or on the total of the layers below. The excess layer policies should normally be arranged to follow the same terms and conditions as the underlying policies. Substantial limits may be built up with a series of excess layer policies; some insureds may buy limits exceeding £100m.

5 EXCLUSIONS

The limitations of cover or exclusions that appear in a product liability policy are of considerable importance in defining the cover provided by the underwriter. The insured has to demonstrate that a particular claim falls within the scope of the operative clause of the policy and it is for the insurer to prove the application of the exclusions.

Exclusions fall into three broad categories:

(a) those risks which underwriters consider are uninsurable or for which governments accept responsibility;

(b) those risks which are normally insured under separate policies by different segments of the insurance market;
(c) those risks which underwriters view as particularly hazardous. These exclusions may be negotiable on provision of additional information and possibly the payment of an additional premium.

The exclusions likely to be met in a product liability policy are described below. They are given in full in the specimen wording in the Appendix. The wordings can vary considerably from insurer to insurer with important differences in the effect of the exclusions.

5.1   War

This is the only exclusion which falls under the first category mentioned above. In the past this exclusion was not thought to be very relevant to Product Liability cover. Attempts by military personnel to recover damages for alleged health problems arising in recent conflicts call this view into question. It is conceivable that manufacturers of military products could be sued by servicemen alleging that defects gave rise to injury to users in war situations. The war exclusion means that in many such situations the Product Liability policy would not provide an indemnity.

There is not currently an easy answer to this problem. The attitude of the courts to such claims is not yet clear. Insurers as yet have not taken a view on amending the exclusion. Defence manufacturers should discuss the implications with their insurance advisers.

5.2   Radio-active contamination

If products are supplied to nuclear installations a liability could arise to the operators of the site. In most countries the site operator would be responsible for any injury or damage occurring off site. Product liability cover is available from nuclear pool arrangements in most European countries. In the UK the British Insurers Atomic Energy Committee issues such policies.

5.3   Contractual liability

The product liability policy is a legal liability policy. The phrase legal liability encompasses all forms of liability at law including tort, statute and liability accepted in contract. It is usual for insurers' standard policies to contain a contractual liability exclusion. This is because the range and scope of agreements entered into by the insured could be very wide, exposing the insurer to extensive additional liabilities. It is usually possible to negotiate the elimination of this exclusion if information is provided as to the type of contracts normally entered into. There may be an additional premium charged and in some cases insurers might wish to see each contract before providing cover.

5.4   Repair, replacement and recall

Insurers will not pay for the repair, replacement or recall of the product which gives rise to injury and damage. This exclusion can give rise to difficulties,

particularly where complex products which may consist of separate units are concerned. For example, a complete production line system may be supplied for a factory. An electrical failure in one small component could cause damage to the rest of the production line as well as the building in which it is installed. A dispute could arise with insurers as to whether it is only the defective component which is intended to be excluded or the complete production line. When placing cover it is important that the situation is addressed and agreement reached with insurers as to how such claims will be dealt with. One possible solution is to amend the exclusion so that the cost of damage to only that part of the product which gives rise to the claim is excluded.

This is not a complete answer as there are still problems of definition. An alternative approach is to limit the exclusion to products supplied under the same contract. There is a limited insurance market which is prepared to provide cover for the repair replacement or recall of products. This is often referred to as Products Guarantee and Recall Insurance. Both Products Guarantee and Recall may be purchased together or separately. The specialist Insurers that offer this cover seek quite detailed information in relation to the product, quality controls and failure rates. Excesses tend to be relatively high with limits up to £5m relatively easily available. Demand for such cover has in fact been relatively low although increased legislative attention to products, safety and increasing powers of Governments to order recalls has increased interest from industry.

5.5 Aviation products

Most product liability policies will have an exclusion of injury and damage caused by aviation products. This may be qualified by restricting its application to those products supplied knowingly by the insured for such purpose. Separate aviation product liability cover is needed where such products are involved.

The aviation insurance market has developed the special forms of cover and the capacity needed to deal with the extensive exposures presented by aviation products.

5.6 Advice, design and specification

Many policies will have an exclusion of legal liability arising out of the giving of advice, design work or specification for a fee where no product is supplied. This cover is normally available in a professional indemnity policy. The exclusion does not, however, apply where a product is actually supplied.

A manufacturer would need to scrutinise carefully his range of activities to ensure that this exclusion would not have an impact. It is increasingly the case that many contracts, particularly with Government organisations, fall into a number of stages. The potential manufacturer may at stage one have to submit design work for a new product and then at the second stage tender for the manufacture. It might be that the design is accepted but that the tender for manufacture goes elsewhere. If such an exposure does exist then a professional liability policy can be effected. It is however possible in some cases to negotiate with the product liability insurer to remove the exclusion and therefore provide the injury and damage element of the cover. There would still, of course, be no cover for pure financial losses which would still need to be insured in the professional indemnity market.

5.7 Other exclusions

There are a number of exclusions which appear in specific circumstances. For example, where there is an exposure in the USA or Canada punitive and exemplary damages may be excluded.

It would be usual where these territories are concerned to exclude all claims arising out of pollution. Where products are concerned it is sometimes possible to negotiate the retention of this cover.

Even where there is not a North American exposure insurers are becoming increasingly concerned about pollution exposures. Primarily this is in relation to public liability cover but certain products do represent a particular exposure. These may be potentially polluting chemicals or there may be equipment such as valves and tanks where failure could result in pollution damage. It is becoming increasingly common for coverage to be restricted to injury and damage caused by sudden and unintended pollution. This removes cover where there is a gradually operating cause.

There are circumstances in which insurers would apply exclusions of specific products. This arises where there is a known and substantial problem associated with that product and in effect insurers feel the exposure is uninsurable or is one that they in particular do not wish to underwrite. Many insurers would not be prepared to provide cover for claims arising from asbestos-related diseases. Certain pharmaceutical products with known problems are usually excluded.

Some types of product can cause injury and damage by remaining passive. A pharmaceutical product may fail to provide a cure. Equipment that is designed to provide a response in certain circumstances may not. Examples might be fire and burglar alarms and other warning equipment. In the case of pharmaceutical products it is extremely difficult, if not impossible, to obtain what is termed 'efficacy cover'. With other types of products there are insurers who are prepared to provide cover without an efficacy exclusion at additional premium.

6 POLICY CONDITIONS

Most, if not all, liability policies contain further clauses under the general heading of Conditions. Most conditions contained in the policy relate to particular circumstances in connection with claims and are therefore conditions precedent to liability and breach of the condition would not void the policy but enable insurers to avoid the particular claim. The most important conditions are as follows:

i Reasonable precautions This condition appears in most liability policies. Whilst it may appear out of place in a liability policy, which is designed to cover the insured's negligence, it could only be relied on by insurers in the case of reckless behaviour by the insured.

ii Notice of claims This condition is important since it requires that details of claims of circumstances which might result in a claim are reported quickly to insurers. It also stipulates that the insured should not admit liability or enter into negotiations in relation to the claim independently.

It makes it clear that the insurers are entitled to negotiate a settlement on behalf of the insured. A breach of this condition which would prejudice the insurer's position would be treated seriously. Late reporting of a claim could mean that important information becomes unavailable or witnesses are not traced and interviewed at an early stage.

The admission of liability and the negotiation of claims by the insured can result in settlements having to be made in circumstances where there might have been a defence if the claim had been handled properly from the beginning.

iii Cancellation This condition is rarely invoked. It would only be used in circumstances where perhaps insurers become aware of behaviour by the insured which may amount to a breach of one of the other conditions or a material non-disclosure and where they do not want to wait for a claim to arise before taking the point. It could, however, be invoked where the claims record deteriorates rapidly and unexpectedly and insurers simply want to avoid further involvement without waiting until expiry of the policy period. When negotiating policy cover it is a good idea if possible to extend the normal 30 days' notice to perhaps 60 or 90 days. This would give adequate time to try and secure a replacement cover in the event of notice of cancellation being given.

7 THE 'CLAIMS MADE' PRODUCT LIABILITY POLICY

The operative clause described above is the occurrence form. The alternative basis is referred to as 'claims made'. Insurers have become concerned with the exposure represented by some types of product particularly, but not exclusively, where there is exposure in the US. Some products may cause undetected or latent damage over a long period of time. This has led to claims being made under occurrence product liability policies many years after the policy was written.

The claims made form of policy is designed to enable insurers to control their exposure to latent claim more effectively. On this basis the policy provides an indemnity in respect of injury and damage for claims which are made by third parties during the currency of the policy.

The injury or damage does not have to have occurred during the policy period. The policy may be subject to a retroactive date. There would then be no cover for claims made in respect of an injury and damage occurring prior to the retroactive date. The major disadvantage of this form of cover is that in the event of insurers not renewing cover there would be no insurance for events which may have already occurred but have not yet come to light.

From the insured's point of view a claims made policy does mean that the current limit of indemnity applies to claims even when the damage which resulted in a claim occurred many years ago. With an occurrence form the limit of indemnity in force at that time may have been totally inadequate.

The use of the claims made form for products liability in the UK is still relatively rare except in the case of pharmaceutical products, chemical products and certain heavy exposures in North America. It is more common in some European countries.

It is likely that in the long term insurers will endeavour to make more use of the claims made form of cover and limit their exposure to the open-ended occurrence form.

With a claims made form the claims reporting additions are particularly critical. If the insured is aware of a claim and does not report it within the policy period cover could be lost.

8   PLACING AND UNDERWRITING THE PRODUCT LIABILITY RISK

It has already been said that product liability insurance normally forms part of a policy including the public liability risk.

It is true to say, however, that in many cases it is the product liability aspect of the risk which will be the focus of the insurer's attention when underwriting. It is still common with smaller risks for a proposal form to be completed by the insured giving the information required by the underwriter. With larger and more complex risks it is often the case that an underwriting submission is prepared by the insured's broker who will have carried out a thorough investigation of the insured's business and identified those areas which are of most interest to the underwriter.

The underwriter will be seeking to understand the nature of the business and to assess the premium he requires for future risks based on past experience of the proposed risk and his product liability account as a whole. Within Europe there is no marketwide statistical base which can assist the underwriter. Each insurer has to rely on the information he holds himself.

In forming a view of any particular risk there are a number of key areas of information which the underwriter needs. This information will form the basis of the contract and as has already been seen it must be accurate and complete.

The business description and details of the products manufactured or supplied is perhaps the most important information. The insurer will want to see product brochures and, in some cases, technical descriptions. The range of hazards that need to be assessed are considerable.

One proposer may be merely distributing a relatively low hazard product such as office furniture. He may have a liability for the products as he is in the chain of distribution but the main liability may well rest either with the manufacturer or the final seller. On the other hand, the proposer may be the manufacturer of hazardous chemicals which represents a quite different risk exposure.

The turnover of the proposer is important and should be supplied broken down between products. In some cases large companies may have subsidiaries manufacturing products ranging through the whole spectrum of potential hazards. It is also necessary to identify export turnover, in particular to North America, because of the high incidence of product liability claims and the higher awards in that territory.

The previous claims experience of the proposer is of obvious importance. Normally insurers would seek information for at least three previous years and in some cases five. They would want full details of any large claims. The claims experience gives a view of past costs which may be a guide to the future and in addition it can be helpful in identifying particular problems. It may show that there have been a large number of small claims involving a particular product. If these claims are continuing to happen insurers may form a view that sooner or later the particular product will be the cause of a much more substantial loss.

The contractual arrangements entered into by the proposer are important, particularly where it is desired to delete or modify the contractual liability exclusion which has been discussed earlier.

Insurers will wish to know the size of the indemnity limit required and what, if any, deductibles or self insurance the proposer is prepared to carry.

On the basis of this information the insurer will form a view as to whether the risk is acceptable. If the risk is acceptable a premium will be quoted together with any modification to the standard wording. When the insurer has arrived at a premium it would be normal to express this as a percentage rate of the turnover of the company. As indicated above, there may be differential rates for particular products and for exports to North America. Indeed, in some cases the rate for North America exports may be ten times that for identical products sold in other territories.

8.1   Risk control

It is by and large true to say that product liability underwriting has in the past been a desk exercise and very few insurers in the UK and Europe had become involved with physical risk assessment and control. This contrasts markedly with experience in the US where product liability insurance in many cases requires risk assessment surveys, both when risks are proposed and at continuing intervals. Insurers in the US have taken this path because of the particular circumstances there. Strict liability for injury and damage caused by products has a longer history. Americans are on the whole more willing to commence proceedings and juries inject a certain element of uncertainty into the outcome.

It is possible to see the beginnings of a more active approach to risk control by insurers in Europe. It is becoming rather more common for insurers to seek specialists' reports on particular high hazard product risks or risks where there have been past problems.

A number of large European insurers do employ specialist engineers and a number of specialist product liability risk assessment organisations do exist. In the future there will perhaps be more involvement by insurers in this respect. This would bring benefits both to the insurer who would have a much better view of the particular risk and to the insured, who would have the benefit of risk control advice in relation to his product exposure.

9   MULTI-NATIONAL POLICIES

Many companies who require product liability insurance have operations located in more than one country.

Such multi-national companies often wish to take a global view of the various insurable risks faced by the company and of the insurance protection required to meet those exposures.

The traditional approach of each subsidiary buying a product liability policy in its own territory on the basis of decisions made by local management may not meet group objectives.

The parent company may have a number of aims when considering the way in which product liability and indeed other types of insurance are arranged, such as:

(a) The protection of the group to a common standard. There may be a concern that individual arrangements made by subsidiary companies are inadequate, exposing them to potential insolvency in the event of uninsured claims. This impacts on the value of the group as a whole.

(b) Cost effectiveness. Focusing premium expenditure with one insurer may result in worthwhile discounts as against expenditure with large numbers of different insurers on an unco-ordinated basis.

(c) Large corporations operating in many territories with different subsidiaries may actually have a large degree of interdependence. Components may be supplied from one subsidiary to another for final manufacture.

Sales and marketing functions may be centralised or carried out in different parts of the group. In the event of product liability claims arising it may be difficult to identify which subsidiary is responsible. On a non-global basis it might be that the insurers of each subsidiary could be involved in legal action against each other establishing where the responsibility lies.

These objectives can be met by the issue of a global liability policy for all territories in which the insured operate. In theory this could be a single policy document for all territories. However, there are practical and legal difficulties with this approach. In many countries it is a requirement that insurance policies for local subsidiaries must be placed with locally regulated insurers.

Local subsidiaries may want a policy document in the local language and their customers may wish to see proof of insurance locally. It may be necessary to identify premia paid locally so that appropriate premium taxes are accounted for.

In practice there are number of insurers who themselves operate on a worldwide basis and have offices in many countries. These insurers issue multi-national policies with locally admitted documentation.

The approach is to issue a 'Master' policy to the parent company containing all the terms and conditions negotiated centrally. The insurers would then issue local policies, sometimes on a more restrictive basis, following local practice in each territory. The premium again will be agreed centrally but the insurer would collect a proportion of that figure for each of the insured subsidiaries.

There are a number of large insurance brokers who operate on a worldwide basis and would provide local broking services in parallel with the insurance protection provided by the insurer. They are also able to provide services in relation to the control of the programme and the flow of information to ensure that such arrangements operate smoothly across national boundaries.

Within the European Community regulatory barriers to purchasing insurance across borders are being removed in two stages. The first stage, which took place in July 1990, involves large companies. This means that at least within the European Community it is possible for an insurer to issue a single policy covering all the subsidiaries of a multi-national company. The second stage of implementation will extend this freedom to smaller companies.

It is likely that practical considerations will mean that local policy documentation in local language will still be required in some cases. This means that in the future a combination of approaches will be seen. At the very least the choice is available to the insured. Even where local policies are issued it would no longer be necessary for the insurer issuing the policy to be based in the territory concerned, although if local service, including claims handling, is required some local presence would be necessary.

10   THE EC PRODUCT LIABILITY DIRECTIVE AND PRODUCT LIABILITY INSURANCE

The legal effect of the implementation of the Product Liability Directive in each European Community country is discussed elsewhere.

The insurance industry has been concerned with assessing the likely impact of the Directive on the number and level of product liability claims in the future and the effect this will have on their underwriting.

It should perhaps be reiterated at this point that the product liability policy in common with other liability policies does not need to be endorsed or reworded to provide cover for claims brought under the new legislation. It responds to the insured's legal liability which includes liabilities introduced by statute. There has been no move at the time of writing by any product liability insurer to try and restrict cover because of the implementation of the Directive.

The intuitive view of the insurance industry is that the legislation will increase the number of smaller claims. The assessment is that where serious personal injuries have been suffered in the past claims have been brought notwithstanding the difficulties of proving negligence. People may have been more reluctant to try to pursue smaller claims. However, the effect of the legislation in terms of claims frequency and cost is going to be difficult to disentangle from other factors.

Potential claimants are becoming more aware of the rights and are more willing to bring claims.

There are still uncertainties within the legislation itself. The way in which the Consumer Protection Act 1987 in the UK has implemented the 'state of the art' defence arguably does not comply with the Directive. There are at the time of writing no authoritative court decisions in the United Kingdom dealing with any important aspect of the Act.

The liability insurance industry does not keep centralised statistics and each insurer has to rely on his own statistical base as a guide to development. Emerging trends will thus be more difficult to identify.

Some liability insurers believe that premium increases should be implemented in anticipation of rising claims costs in the future. Various percentages have been ascribed to the necessary increases but it is difficult to see from what base these have been calculated. In practice the insurance market throughout Europe is at the time of writing in a very competitive state and insurers find it difficult, if not impossible, to achieve premium increases.

The reality is likely to be that insurance costs will be affected if and when increased claims costs make their presence felt. Some seven years after the legislation came into force in the United Kingdom there has in fact been little or no visible impact on product liability claims.

Appendices

APPENDIX 1

Specimen product liability policy

SCHEDULE

Policy No:

The Insured:

Address:

| Period of Insurance: | From: To: | both days inclusive |

The Business:

| Indemnity Limit: | £ | in any one period of Insurance |

PRODUCT LIABILITY

The Insured having paid or agreed to pay the premiums specified in the Schedule the Underwriters agree to provide the Insurance set out below against liability incurred in the course of the Business.

Compensation 1. Subject to the Limit of Indemnity stated in the Schedule the Underwriters will indemnify the Insured for all sums (including claimants' costs and expenses) as the Insured shall become legally liable to pay in respect of or arising out of:
(a) Accidental personal injury to any person;
(b) Accidental loss of or damage to property other than:
(i) property belonging to the Insured;
(ii) property in the charge of or control of the Insured;

559

sustained within the Territorial Limits during the Period of Insurance in connection with the Business; caused by or arising out of the Products sold, supplied, manufactured, designed, repaired, altered, serviced, installed, treated or let on hire or handled in the course of the business or recommended by or on behalf of the Insured.

2.   And in addition the Underwriters will pay:
(a)   all costs and expenses (other than claimants' costs and expenses) incurred with their written consent;
(b)   the legal expenses incurred for representation of the Insured at any Coroner's inquest or fatal injury inquiry or in any Court of Summary jurisdiction in connection with liability described in Paragraph 1.

DEFINITIONS

Products   1.   The term Products shall include containers, labels, instructions for use and advice.

Insured   2.   The Insured shall also include:
(i)   the Insured's Executor or Administrator in the event of the death of the Insured but only in respect of liability incurred by the Insured;
(ii)   any principal in respect of the liability of such principal arising out of the performance by the Insured of any contract or agreement entered into by the Insured for the performance of work for such principal to the extent required by such contract or agreement;
(iii) (a)   any committee, officer, member or employee of the Insured's social sports welfare or theatrical organisations or clubs, first aid, fire or ambulance services in his respective capacity as such;
(b)   any director or employee of the Insured;
(c)   any director or senior executive of the Insured in respect of private work undertaken by the Insured's employees for such director or senior executive;
(d)   the repair or servicing of vehicles other than repair or servicing carried out in pursuance of the business of Motor Engineers and/or Repairers to the public;
(e)   the ownership, repair, maintenance, decoration, occupation and use of premises.

Personal Injury   3.   Personal Injury shall include but shall not be limited to death, illness, disease, bodily injury, false arrest, invasion of the right of privacy, dentention, false imprisonment, false eviction and discrimination.

Proposals   4.   Proposal shall mean any signed proposal form and

declaration and any information supplied by or on behalf of the Insured in addition thereto or in substitution therefor.

Territorial Limits 5. The Territorial Limits shall mean anywhere in the World.

EXCEPTIONS

Underwriters shall not be liable for:

Contractual Liability 1. Liability assumed by the Insured by agreement unless such liability would have attached notwithstanding such agreement.

Repair or Replacement 2. Loss of or damage to or the cost and expenses of repairing, recalling, removing, altering, treating or replacing goods which give rise to a claim.

Aviation Products 3. Personal Injury or loss or damage to property caused by Products incorporated in the structure of aircraft and which have been specifically supplied by the Insured for that purpose except where specifically stated to be included in the Business.

Radioactive Contamination 4. (a) loss or destruction of or damage to any property whatsoever or any loss or expense whatsoever resulting or arising therefrom or any consequential loss;
(b) any legal liability of whatsoever nature
directly or indirectly caused by or contributed to by or arising from:
(i) ionising radiations or contamination by radioactivity from any nucear fuel or from any nuclear waste from the combustion of nuclear fuel;
(ii) the radioactive, toxic, explosive or other hazardous properties of any nuclear assembly or nuclear component thereof.

War 5. Any consequence of war, invasion, act of foreign enemy, hostilities (whether war be declared or not), civil war, rebellion, revolution, insurrection or military or usurped power.

CONDITIONS

Cross Liability 1. Any claim made by any Insured against any other Insured shall be treated as though the party so claiming is not an Insured.

Material Facts 2. The truth of any statements and answers in any Proposal and the prompt notification by the Insured of any alteration in risk which materially affects this Insurance shall be conditions precedent to any liability of the Underwriters to make any payment under this policy.

Notification
Claims   3.   The Insured shall give to the Underwriters notice as soon as possible in writing with full particulars of the happening of any occurrence likely to give rise to a claim under this Insurance Policy or of the receipt by the Insured of notice of any claim and of the institution of any proceedings against the Insured.

The Insured shall not admit liability for or offer or agree to settle any claim without the written consent of the Underwriters who shall be entitled to take over and conduct in the name of the Insured the defence of any claim and to prosecute in the name of the Insured for Underwriters' benefit any claim for indemnity or damages or otherwise against any Third Party and shall have full discretion in the conduct of any negotiations and proceedings and the settlement of any claims. The Insured shall give to the Underwriters such information and assistance as the Underwriters may reasonably require.

The Underwriters may prior to or in the course of such proceedings or settlement in connection with any claim or series of claims pay to the Insured the appropriate Limit of Indemnity (after deducting therefrom any sum or sums already paid as compensation) and thereupon the Underwriters shall relinquish the conduct and control of and shall be under no further liability in connection with such claim or claims except for costs and expenses of litigation incurred prior to the date of such payment.

Contribution   4.   If at any time any claim is made under this Certificate there is any other existing insurance effected by or on behalf of any Insured covering the same liability the Underwriters shall not be liable to contribute more than its rateable proportion of any payment in respect of such claim.

Adjustment   5.   If the premiums are calculated on the statements and estimates furnished by the Insured then the Insured shall within three months after the expiry of each Period of Insurance furnish to the Underwriters such information as the Underwriters may require for such expired period and the premium for such period shall thereupon be adjusted by the Underwriters and the difference be paid by or allowed to the Insured as the case may be.

Cancellation   6.   This policy may be cancelled by or on behalf of the Underwriters by a recorded letter, sent to the Insured's last known address, giving not less than 30 (thirty) days' notice of the Underwriters' intention to cancel this Policy, such notice to run from midnight of the day following that upon which the letter is posted.

APPENDIX 2

Table comparing and contrasting the law on Product Liabilities in the European Union

ENGLAND AND WALES AND NORTHERN IRELAND

NOTE: Scottish Law has several detailed differences from that of England and Wales and Northern Ireland - see the Scottish section of the UK Chapter for details

REPUBLIC OF IRELAND

DATE LEGISLATION FOLLOWING EC DIRECTIVE 85/374 EEC CAME INTO FORCE

The Consumer Protection Act 1987 (CPA) came into effect on 1 March 1988

The Liability For Defective Products Act 1991 ("1991 Act") came into effect on 16 December 1991.

NATURE OF LIABILITY – CONTRACT

CPA does not affect the existing position in contract as between the actual parties to the contract e.g. seller and buyer. The Sale of Goods Act 1979 (as amended) does imply terms and conditions into contracts.

The 1980 Sale of Goods Act and Supply of Services Act ("1980 Act") does not affect the basic contractual relationship. It does however imply terms and conditions into contracts. The 1991 Act does not affect the existing position in contract as between the actual parties to the contract.

<u>Absolute liability</u> under Sale of Goods Act for failure to provide goods of merchantable quality and fit for the purpose for which they were bought

<u>Absolute liability</u> under the 1980 Act for goods not of merchantable quality and fit for the purpose for which they were bought

Quantum of Damage in Contract
All loss which is a likely consequence of the breach – would include loss on the purchase of the product itself, compensation for any illness, medical expenses,

Quantum of Damage in Contract
The loss which may be recovered is the loss which was at the time of the contract, a reasonably foreseeable consequence of the

damage to property and pure economic loss. Injured party is under a duty to mitigate his loss

Exclusion Clauses
Exclusion clauses in consumer contracts and otherwise in respect of death and personal injury are not enforceable but Exclusion Clauses in respect of commercial contracts involving persons other than Consumers are enforceable insofar as they are reasonable

Implementation of Directive 93/13/EEC on Unfair Terms
Implemented on 1 July 1995 by the Unfair Terms in Consumer Contracts Regulations 1994 in addition to Existing Law on Unfair Contract Terms
Implemented by the Unfair Contract Terms Regulations 1995 on 1 February 1995.

Limitation Periods in Contract Claims
Six year time limit from the date on which the cause of action occurred

breach. The injured party is under a duty to mitigate his loss

Exclusion Clauses
Where a purchaser of goods does not deal as a Consumer and where the exclusion is fair and reasonable certain implied warranties relating to the Sale of Goods may be excluded

Implementation of Directive 93/13/EEC on Unfair Terms
The Unfair Contract Terms Regulations apply to contracts concluded after 31 December 1994.

Limitation Periods in Contract Claims
Six year time limit from the date on which the cause of action occurred

NATURE OF LIABILITY - COMMERCIAL CONSUMER GUARANTEES

Commercial Consumer Guarantees may not limit a consumers rights in the law of Contract or Tort or otherwise against a manufacturer distributor or vendor. Persons giving commercial guarantees must give a certain minimum amount of information

The 1980 Act regulates Commercial guarantees given by manufacturers and distributors (other than the Retailer). The Person giving the Guarantee, whether the manufacturer, vendor, Persons giving commercial guarantees or Distributor is liable in Contract as if he were the

ENGLAND AND WALES AND NORTHERN IRELAND

REPUBLIC OF IRELAND

Seller of the Goods to the Consumer, Retailers may be liable for Guarantees given by third parties, normally by the distributor or manufacturer, unless the Retailer provides the Purchaser with a written undertaking that he will service, repair or otherwise deal with the goods following their purchase.

NATURE OF LIABILITY - TORT : NEGLIGENCE

Negligence Claims

A claim may lie in negligence against a manufacturer or supplier if fault can be proved

Negligence Claims

A claim may lie in negligence against a manufacturer or supplier if fault can be proved

Plaintiff must prove:

1.   That the defendant owed him a duty to take reasonable care

2.   A breach of that duty

3.   That he suffered loss

4.   A causal connection between that breach and the loss

Plaintiff must prove:

1.   That the defendant owed him a duty to take reasonable care

2.   A breach of that duty

3.   That he suffered loss

4.   A causal connection between that breach and the loss

Quantum of Damage in Negligence

The general principle is that the plaintiff should be placed in the same position as if the Tort had not occurred. Damages may be special or general. Nominal, Contemptuous or Exemplary damages may be awarded

Quantum of Damage in Negligence

The general principle is that the plaintiff should be placed in the same position as if the Tort had not occurred. Damages may be special or general. Nominal, Contemptuous or Exemplary damages may be awarded

Limitation Period in Negligence
Generally six years from the date of action accruing but three years from date of action accruing for personal injury

NATURE OF LIABILITY - TORT : PRODUCT LIABILITY

Strict liability under the Consumer Protection Act 1987 ("CPA 1987")
The producer of a product is liable to the claimant in respect of damage caused by a defect in his product.

Plaintiff must prove:
1. Defect
2. Damage
3. Causation

"Producer" includes
1. The manufacturer;
2. A person who puts his trade mark on a product;
3. Importer into the EC;
4. Supplier where the manufacturer cannot be traced.

"Product" excludes primary agricultural products unless they have undergone initial processing.

Limitation Period in Negligence
Generally six years from the date of action accruing but three years from date of action accruing for personal injury

Strict liability under the 1991 Act

The producer of a product is liable to the claimant in respect of damage caused by a defect in his product.

Plaintiff must prove:
1. Defect
2. Damage
3. Causation

"Producer" will include:
1. The manufacturer;
2. A person who puts his trade mark on a product;
3. Importer into the EC;
4. Supplier where the manufacturer cannot be traced.

"Product" excludes primary agricultural products unless they have undergone initial processing.

ENGLAND AND WALES AND NORTHERN IRELAND	REPUBLIC OF IRELAND

NATURE OF LIABILITY – TORT: PRODUCT LIABILITY (CONT)

ENGLAND AND WALES AND NORTHERN IRELAND	REPUBLIC OF IRELAND
"Defect" exists if the safety of the product is not such as persons generally are entitled to expect. In considering this, regard is had to marketing of the product, presentation and packaging, use of marks, instructions for use and warnings, and what might reasonably be expected to be done with and in relation to the product at the time the product was supplied by the producer. The fact that a later product may have higher safety standards is irrelevant (provided the producer took all due care to use the latest technology).	"Defect" similar to UK position

"Damage" means death or personal injury or loss of or damage to any property including land not damage to the product itself, and not purely financial loss.	"Damage" means:
	a) Death or personal injury, or
	b) loss of, damage to, or destruction of, any item of property other than the defective product itself, Provided that the item of property:
	  (i) is of a type ordinarily intended for private use or consumption, and
	  (ii) was used by the injured person mainly for his own private use or consumption

"Causation" Plaintiff must show the defect caused the damage. Defences: 1. Producer did not put Product into circulation 2. Defect attributable to compliance with statute or EC obligation 3. Supply of product was other than in the course of business.	"Causation" Plaintiff must show the defect caused the damage. Defences: 1. Producer did not put Product into circulation 2. Defect attributable to compliance with statute or EC obligation 3. Supply of product was other than in the course of business.

4. Defect did not exist at the relevant time.
5. The defect is in the final product of which the product is a component part.

6. <u>Development Risks Defence("State of the Art")</u>
That the state of scientific and technical knowledge at the relevant time was not such that a producer of products of the same description might be expected to have discovered the defect if it had existed in his products while they were under his control (note arguably wider than under the Directive).

<u>Quantum of Damages</u>
Minimum of £275. No maximum. All loss reasonably foreseeable. May be reduced by contributory negligence of the claimant.

<u>Limitation Period</u>
Three years from the date of knowledge of relevant facts eg damage, causation and identity of defendant, with a "cut off" point of ten years from the date the product was brought into circulation.

4. Defect did not exist at the relevant time.
5. In the case of the manufacturer of a component or the producer of a raw material, that the defect is attributable entirely to the design of the product in which the component has been fitted or the raw material incorporated or the instructions given by the manufacturer of the product.
6. <u>Development Risks Defence ("State of the Art")</u>
That the state of scientific and technical knowledge at the time when the product was put into circulation was not such as to enable the existence of the defect to be discovered.

<u>Quantum of Damages</u>
Minimum claim for damage to property is IR£350. No maximum.
May be reduced by contributory negligence of the claimant

<u>Limitation Period</u>
Three years from the date the cause of action accrued or the date (if later) on which the Claimant became aware, or should reasonably have become aware, of the damage, the defect and the identity of the producer.

ENGLAND AND WALES AND NORTHERN IRELAND   REPUBLIC OF IRELAND

SPECIFIC SAFETY LEGISLATION

General Product Safety Legislation
General Consumer Product Safety Regulations 1994
introduced with effect from 3 October 1994
following Directive 92/59 EEC

General Product Safety Legislation
Law as yet to be introduced on General Consumer Safety
to implement Directive 92/59 EEC

LUXEMBOURG	FRANCE	BELGIUM	GREECE

DATE LEGISLATION FOLLOWING EC DIRECTIVE 85/374/EEC CAME INTO FORCE

LUXEMBOURG	FRANCE	BELGIUM	GREECE
Directive implemented by law of 21 April 1989. Took effect on 2 May 1989.	A proposal presented on 23 May 1990 by the French government to incorporate EC Directive into French law failed to be adopted. A new proposal ("The Proposal") which integrates previous discussions in the Parliament was presented by a member of the Parliament 13 January 1993. The Proposal remains pending	1 April 1991	16 November 1994 by Law 2251/1994 that also implemented EC Directive 93/13 and 92/59.

NATURE OF LIABILITY - CONTRACT

LUXEMBOURG	FRANCE	BELGIUM	GREECE
			The object sold must be free *from* legal defects in title. Real defects must have the represented qualities

1. HIDDEN DEFECTS	1. HIDDEN DEFECTS	1. HIDDEN DEFECTS	1. REAL DEFECTS
A vendor warrants against hidden defects. Buyer may return the goods or claim a reduction in price, and if the vendor has acted in "bad faith" he must compensate the buyer for all losses.	Action against the seller and any prior seller in the chain (including the manufacturer) may be brought for hidden defects according to Article 1641 Civil Code (which is now also integrated in Article L. 211-1 of the *Code de la Consommation*)	A seller warrants against hidden defects. Buyer may return the goods or claim a reduction in price, and if the Seller has acted in "bad faith" he must compensate the buyer for all losses.	Article 534 Civil Code. The Seller warrants against real defects in the products unless these were known to the purchaser at the time of sale or the purchaser was unaware of them due to his gross negligence, unless the seller had fraudulently hidden it from the purchaser.
	The purchaser will have to prove that the defects were hidden and existed prior to or, at the latest, at the time of the purchase. The Proposal provides that any defect occurring within the period of a contractual warranty (or within a year from delivery when there is no warranty) is presumed to have existed at the time of		The Purchaser can demand: a) Cancellation of the sale or b) reduction in the price c) compensation for non performance instead of (a) or (b) if the seller knew or should have known of the defect.
Retailers practically as liable as manufacturers if they are specialists.		Under present law a retailer is practically as liable as a manufacturer if he is a specialist.	
Professional vendors are presumed to know the defects affecting the products they sell and are thus compelled to compensate all harm suffered by the Buyer.		Professional sellers are presumed to know the defects affecting the products they sell and are thus compelled to compensate all harm suffered by the Buyer.	

NATURE OF LIABILITY – TORT

LUXEMBOURG

Purchaser needs not to prove fault of vendor. Needs only to prove that at the time of the sale there was a hidden purchaser defect which was unknown to the Purchaser, which caused harm. The defect, however, will be considered to be apparent if it should have been discovered by a summary inspection

Quantum of Damages
Compensation includes all foreseeable losses.

FRANCE

the sale. Such a presumption will not be effective in a contract between professionals. For a non-professional purchaser, case law provides that the defect is hidden if it could not have been discovered through preliminary inspection. Professional purchasers are required to undertake a more thorough check of the product.

The seller is not liable for the defect when the purchaser shares the same area of expertise.

Quantum of Damages
Purchase price may be reduced or reimbursed. The proposal provides for repair or replacement of the product. A professional seller is presumed to know about the defect and is liable to pay damages which include all loss suffered as a direct consequence of the defect.

BELGIUM

Need not prove fault of seller, if at the time of sale there was a hidden defect, unknown to purchaser which caused harm. The defect, however will be considered to be apparent if it should have been discovered by a summary inspection.

Quantum of Damages
Compensation includes all direct and indirect losses.

GREECE

Quantum of Damages
Every loss and damage to the Purchaser (including loss or gains prevented) as an immediate and direct consequence of the real defect of the Product or of the absence of the represented quality or the non-performance of the Seller.

Limitation Period
Purchaser has to declare the hidden defect within a "short period" from the discovery of the defect. The purchaser loses his right to sue the vendor after expiry of a period of one year from the date of the declaration. The limitation period may be interrupted by negotiations, summary proceedings or by any other judicial means.

Exclusion Clauses
Disclaimers of liability are usually upheld if reasonable except for a "professional vendor". Disclosure of the defect may have a wider application than simply based on safety.

Limitation Period
The plaintiff must start proceedings within a short period of time from discovery of the defect. The Proposal provides that purchaser must inform the seller within one year from the date the defect is (or should have been) discovered.

Exclusion Clauses
Exclusion or limitation clauses are valid between professionals only.

Limitation Period
Proceedings must be brought within "a brief period". No specific limitation period.

Exclusion Clauses
Disclaimers of liability are usually upheld if reasonable except for a "Professional seller". However law of 14 July 1991 on Protection of Consumers provides that terms restricting preliminary consumer rights in respect of hidden defects are unfair and therefore void.

Limitation Period
Six months from date of delivery of movable products in respect of claims for real defects or claims for lack of represented quality. This is extended to twenty years where seller fraudulently conceals defects or lack of represented quality.

Exclusion Clauses
Exclusions or Limitations of Liability usually upheld in contracts between business people but in Consumer Transaction exclusion of liability must not be unfair within the meaning of Law 2251/1994 implementing EU Directive 13/93 on Unfair Terms

NATURE OF LIABILITY – TORT (CONT)

LUXEMBOURG	FRANCE	BELGIUM	GREECE
Implementation of Directive 13/93 on Unfair Terms Not yet implemented.	Implementation of Directive 13/93 on Unfair Terms Implemented by Statute No 95/96 of 1 February 1995 which amended Article L 132-1 of the *Code de la Consommation*	Implementation of Directive 13/93 on Unfair Terms Directive will largely be implemented by existing law. Draft implementing law under discussion.	Implementation of Directive 13/93 on Unfair Terms Directive implemented in full on 16 November 1994.

FRANCE

2. GENERAL SAFETY OBLIGATION

In the case of personal injury caused by the defective product, the courts decide that the seller is under an obligation to deliver products free of defect.

GREECE

2. LACK OF REPRESENTED QUALITY

Article 535 Civil Code. The Seller warrants the product will comply with any represented quality at the time of sale unless the purchaser was aware of the lack of qualities.

The Purchaser can demand:
a) cancellation of the sale or
b) reduction in the Price
c) compensation for non-performance instead of (a) or (b) if the Seller knew or should have known of the defect.

Quantum of Damage

The supply of a defective product is generally considered to constitute gross negligence. Damages directly caused by the defective product usually include compensation for personal injury, loss of profits and damage caused to other goods by the defective product. The manufacturer may be exonerated or his liability reduced if he proves that the injury is totally or partially due to an external cause.

Limitation period

Ten years starting from the day when the damage occurred when the plaintiff purchased the product for business purposes; thirty years for an action initiated by a plaintiff who purchased the product for private purposes.

Quantum of Damage

Every loss and damage to the Purchaser (including loss of gains prevented) as an immediate and direct consequence of the real defect of the Product or of the absence of the represented quality or the non-performance of the Seller.

Limitation period

Six months from date of delivery of movable products in respect of claims for real defects or claims from lack of a represented quality. This is extended to twenty years where Seller fraudulently conceals defects on lack of represented quality.

NATURE OF LIABILITY - COMMERCIAL CONSUMER GUARANTEES

LUXEMBOURG	FRANCE	BELGIUM	GREECE
No specific provisions regarding content of Guarantees. However a) All advertising concerning product guarantee by manufacturer distributor or vendor is an integral part of the sale contract. b) When the guarantee does not conform with the advertising the Purchaser may reject the contract or claim a price reduction.	Vendors giving contractual guarantees must state that they do not override the consumers other legal rights.	Advertising and contracts in general must comply with the Fair Commercial Practice Act of 14 July 1991.	Vendors must give consumers a written guarantee in the Greek language giving at least: a) Vendors name/business address b) The Beneficiary c) A Description of the Goods the subject of the guarantee d) Duration of the guarantee e) Date of Commencement The Guarantee must comply with the principle of good faith and not be overridden by any exclusion clauses. The duration of the Guarantee must be reasonable considering the possible life of the Product.

NATURE OF LIABILITY - TORT

1. ARTICLE 1382 OF THE CIVIL CODE
A Producer may be held liable for damages caused by a defective product where the defect was caused by the Producer's fault or negligence.

Breach includes situations where the manufacturer has failed to inform or warn the purchaser of the possible dangers of the product.

Fault or negligence may be interpreted widely so that a Producer may be held liable if it can be evidenced that his Product was defective.

1. ARTICLE 1382 OF THE CIVIL CODE
A manufacturer is liable for personal and property damage caused by a design or manufacturing defect in its product under Article 1382 of the Civil Code.

Breach also includes situations where the manufacturer has failed to inform or warn the purchaser of the possible dangers of the product.

1. ARTICLE 1382 OF THE CIVIL CODE
A manufacturer is liable in negligence if through "fault" he makes or designs a defective product although "fault" may be interpreted widely so that a manufacturer is at fault if he puts into circulation a product which becomes dangerous because of a defect or because of lack of information ie close to strict liability.

1. ARTICLE 1382 OF THE CIVIL CODE
A person who unlawfully and culpably causes damage to another is obliged to make reparation for the damage caused.

If a product is defective, and the Vendor refuses to repair or delays it excessively, the consumer has a right to demand a replacement or a reversion of the Sale.

NATURE OF LIABILITY – TORT (CONT)

LUXEMBOURG	FRANCE	BELGIUM	GREECE
		Manufacturers must: 1. Take care and diligence 2. Avoid producing products threatening to life, health or property 3. Be aware of technical and scientific progress 4. Comply with public safety regulations 5. Display appropriate warnings. There is a duty to inform of danger and advise on safety 6. Do everything to reduce risk of accident e.g. recall defective goods. Failure to do any of these is negligence. Defect and damage alone is not enough.	
Plaintiff must prove under Art. 1382 and 1383: a) a negligent act or omission; b) the damage suffered; c) a casual relationship between the negligence and the damage.	**Plaintiff must prove:** Plaintiff must prove that the product was defective.	**Plaintiff must prove:** a) failure to meet general duty of care; or b) breach of a legal obligation; c) damage; d) a causal link between the defect and the damage.	**Plaintiff must prove:** a) unlawful and harmful defect in the Product b) culpability c) damage d) a casual link between the defect and the damage.

Quantum of Damage

Damages which can be seen as an immediate and direct consequence of the non-performance of the contractual obligation.

Damages must be foreseeable as to possibility not as to amount.

Damage may be for material and immaterial losses and economic loss.

Limitation Period

Thirty years

Quantum of Damage

Damages directly caused by a tortious breach must be entirely repaired. The manufacturer may be exonerated or his liability reduced if he proves that the injury is totally or partially due to an external cause.

Exclusion Clauses

Clauses limiting or excluding the liability of the producer will be invalid in the case of an action based on tort. Exoneration of the manufacturer if he proves that the injury is due to an external cause.

Limitation Period

Ten years from when the damage occurred or from when the loss was further aggravated

Quantum of Damage

Compensation includes all direct and indirect losses but damage does not have to be foreseeable.

Limitation Period

Thirty years maximum from the day the injured party had knowledge of the damage and the identity of the person liable for the damage.

Quantum of Damage

Direct Damage and any further damage the consumer has suffered in risk to life, health and non material damage.

Limitation Period

Five years from the day the injured party had knowledge of the damage and the identity of the person liable for the damage, subject to a maxi-

NATURE OF LIABILITY – TORT (CONT)

LUXEMBOURG	FRANCE	BELGIUM	GREECE
2. ARTICLE 1384 PARAGRAPH 1 Liability under Article 1384 Paragraph 1 of the Civil Code in respect of injury caused by products which a person has in their custody ("garde"). The liability in this case is a strict Liability with a certain number of distinctions developed by the jurisprudence.	2. ARTICLE 1384 PARAGRAPH 5 OF THE CIVIL CODE Pursuant to Article 1384 paragraph 5 of the Civil Code, the manufacturer will also be liable for damages caused by his employees in the course of employment. 3. ARTICLE 1384 PARAGRAPH 1 Liability under Article 1384 paragraph 1 of the Civil Code in respect of injury caused by products which a person has in their custody ("garde"). Exoneration of the manufacturer if he proves that the damage was due to an external cause. His liability will be reduced if he shows that the victim has contributed to	2. ARTICLE 1384 PARAGRAPH 1 Liability under Article 1384 paragraph 1 of the Civil Code in respect of injury caused by products which a person has in their custody ("garde").	mum period of twenty years from commission of the Act in all cases.

the damage.
Case law concept of "custody of the structure" by which the manufacturer's liability continues after delivery since he is deemed to be able to control the internal structure of the product and check whether the product could be used without danger.

The victim will only have to show a causal relationship between the damage suffered and the product.

An Action based on Tort will often be dismissed if the Plaintiff and the Defendant were contracting parties.

Clauses limiting or excluding the liability of the producer are invalid.

Case law concept of "custody of the structure" by which the manu-facturer's liability continues after delivery since he is deemed to be able to control the internal structure of the product and check whether the product could be used without danger.

The victim will only have to show a causal relationship between the damage suffered and the product.

An Action based on Tort will often be dismissed if the Plaintiff and the Defendant were contracting parties.

Clauses limiting or excluding the liability of the producer are invalid.

LUXEMBOURG	FRANCE	BELGIUM	GREECE
Limitation Period Thirty years from the date the damage occurred.	Limitation Period Ten years from when the damage occurred or the loss was further aggravated.	Limitation Period Thirty years maximum.	

NATURE OF LIABILITY - TORT - PRODUCT LIABILITY

LUXEMBOURG	FRANCE	BELGIUM	GREECE
New Product Liability law.			
Directive has imposed strict liability on the "producer" for damage caused by defect in the Product.	No Product Liability law is yet in force under the Directive but the terms of the Directive are contained in the Proposal before the French Parliament.	New law implementing the Directive came into effect as of 1 April 1991 imposing strict liability on the Purchaser for damage caused by defect in the Product.	Strict liability under law 2251/1944 implementing EC Directive, whereby the Producer is liable for damage caused by the defects in his product as a consequence of having put it into circulation
Plaintiff must prove 1. Defect 2. Damage 3. Causation 4. Size of loss		Plaintiff must prove 1. Defect 2. Damage 3. Causation 4. Size of loss	Plaintiff must prove 1. Defect 2. Damage 3. Causation

"Producer" Includes: - a) The manufacturer of the final Product b) Producer of raw material or component c) A person affixing his name or trade mark to the Product	"Producer" Includes : - a) The manufacturer of the final Product b) Producers of parts included in the final Product c) Producer of a raw material d) Persons attaching their name or mark to the Product	"Producer" Includes: - a) The manufacturer of the finished Product b) Producers of components c) Producers of raw material d) Persons representing themselves as producers who apply trade marks etc e) Importers f) Suppliers
"Product" Widely defined as any movable product even if incorporated in any other immovable or movable Product. This includes primary agricultural products and game.	"Product" Includes all tangible movables but Excludes agricultural Products and game unless they have undergone initial processing.	"Product" Follows the definition in the directive but Excludes agricultural products and game.
"Defect" A product is defective if it does not provide the safety that could legitimately be expected with regard to all the circumstances.	"Defect" A product is defective when it does not provide the safety a person is entitled to taking all circumstances into account including; a) Presentation b) Normal or reasonably foreseeable use	"Defect" Definition is identical to the Directive.

NATURE OF LIABILITY - TORT - PRODUCT LIABILITY (CONT)

LUXEMBOURG	FRANCE	BELGIUM	GREECE
"Damage" The Damage is each and every type of Damage except damage:		c) The time the Product was put into circulation.	"Damage" Definition is identical to the Directive but the option for implementing a lower threshold for damage was not exercised when implementing the Directive.
a) from Nuclear Accidents b) to the Defective Product c) to property not used for private purposes on consumption.		"Damage" includes damage to persons including non material damages and damage to private property intended for private use or consumption other than the defective product which exceeds BEF22,500.	
"Causation" Causation must be proved.		"Causation" Causation must be proved on the basis of the "But for" test.	"Causation" Causation must be proved.
Defences 1. Producer did not put into circulation the product		Defences 1. Producer did not put Product into circulation	Defences 1. The Producer did not put the defective Product into circulation

2. Defect did not exist when product put into was circulation by producer

3. Product not been manufactured for sale or for means of distribution with an economic scope nor has been manufactured or distributed within the frame of producers professional activity

4. Defect due to the conformity of product to mandatory rules established by authorities

5. If the producer is the manufacturer of a component, a defect attributable to the conception of the final product or to the

2. Defect did not exist when Product put into circulation by Producer

3. Producer has not manufactured or distributed for an economic purpose or manufactured or distributed in the course of a Business

4. Defect due to the conformity of the Product to mandatory rules established by authorities

5. Development Risks Defence Scientific and Technical knowledge at the time did not permit the Product to be seen as defective

2. The defect did not exist at the time the Product put into circulation

3. The Product was not manufactured for sale or any form of Distribution

4. Development Risks Defence The state of scientific and technical knowledge at the time the product was put into circulation did not permit the product to be seen to be defective

5. If the producer is the manufacturer of a component, the defect was attributable to the overall design of the final product or the instructions given

GREECE

by the manufacturer of the final Product

Quantum of Damages
Damages for physical harm, death property damage, economic loss evaluated on a case by case basis

Limitation Period
Three years from the date the Plaintiff knew of the damage and the Producer's

BELGIUM

6. If the Producer is the Manufacturer of a component, the defect was attributable to the overall design of the final Product or to the instructions given by the manufacture of the final product

Quantum of Damages
There is no upper limit Threshold limit on damages BEF 22,500

Where two or more parties are responsible for the defect, joint and several liability exists

Limitation Period
Three years from the date when the Plaintiff became aware or should reasonably become

FRANCE

LUXEMBOURG

instructions given by manufacturer of the final product

The Development Risks Defence does not apply.

Quantum of Damages
Compensation without any restriction and compensation of the damage to property with deduction of an amount of approximately 22,500LUF

Where two or more parties responsible for defect, joint and several liability

Limitation Period
Three years from the date of discovery of the damage which must in any case be

no later than ten years from the date when the product was put into circulation

Certain regulations are in force for particular Products eg for Machinery under Directive (89/392 EEC)

General Product
Safety Legislation
Draft law under discussion to implement Directive 92/59 EEC

aware of the Damage the defect and the identity of the Producer which must be no later than ten years from the date the product was put into circulation

SPECIFIC SAFETY LEGISLATION

Certain regulations are in force for specific Products

Certain regulations are in force for specific Products

General Product
Safety Legislation
It is generally considered that existing French law is in conformity with Directive 92/59 Law No.83-660 of 21 July 1983 deals with certain issues of product safety

General Product
Safety Legislation
Law of 9 February 1994 implementing Directive 92/59 EEC and making a Commission for consumers' protection

identity subject to an overall maximum of ten years from the date the defective product was put into circulation

Certain regulations are in force for particular Products. Generally under Law2251/1994 the Ministry of Commerce may impose fines from Drachma 500,000 Drachma 20,000,000 for any infringement of the provisions of the Law by Suppliers.

General Product
Safety Legislation
EC Directive 92/59 implemented by Article 7 of the Law 2251/1994

DATE LEGISLATION FOLLOWING EC DIRECTIVE 85/374/EEC CAME INTO FORCE

SPAIN	PORTUGAL	ITALY
The Directive has been implemented by Act 22/1994 of 6 July 1994	Decree – Law 383/89 implemented on 6 November 1989	The Directive has been implemented through a presidential decree of 24 May 1988

NATURE OF LIABILITY - CONTRACT

SPAIN	PORTUGAL	ITALY
Vendor is liable to the purchaser for hidden defects or if the product is not fit for its purpose.	Vendor liable to the purchaser if the product does not function properly or is defective	Vendor is liable to the purchaser if defects make the product unfit for the intended use
Usually there is no contractual relationship between the purchaser and the manufacturer	Usually there is no contractual relationship between the purchaser and the manufacturer	Usually there is no contractual relationship between the purchaser and the manufacturer
Only parties to the contract can claim. Plaintiff must prove defect, damage and causation	Generally only the parties to the contract can claim. Plaintiff must prove defect, damage and causation	Only parties to the Contract can claim. Plaintiff must prove contractual obligation, defect and damage
Quantum of Damage in Contract If Vendor acted in good faith, buyer can claim for termination of contract, and reimbursement for losses or price reduction.	Quantum of Damage in Contract Vendor must repair damage that the purchaser probably would not have suffered if the product had not been defective.	Quantum of Damage in Contract Quantum of damage in contract is all loss suffered as a direct consequence of the breach, therefore including purely financial loss.

Not liable for disclosed defects or those discoverable on summary inspection.

If the Vendor acted in "bad faith" (i.e. the Vendor knew of hidden defects) plaintiff can claim damages including loss of income, medical costs etc.

All commercial contracts may have a liability for damages.

Limitation Period in Contractual Claims
Six months after delivery of product; except if contract is deemed commercial when the limitation period is four days

Exclusion Clauses
Exclusion clauses permitted.

Vendor not liable if purchaser mistaken in assessing the characteristics of the product and the Vendor, through no fault of his own was unaware of the defect.

Damages may be reduced or disallowed entirely if the damage has been caused or aggravated by the purchaser.

Limitation Period in Contractual Claims
Twenty years after the damage occurred

Exclusion Clauses
Exclusion clauses void. Certain limitation clauses permissible.

Limitation Period in Contractual Claims
One year after delivery provided that the seller is notified of the defect within eight days of discovery

Exclusion Clauses
Reasonable exclusion clauses may be upheld in certain cases

SPAIN

Implementation of Directive
93/13 EEC on Unfair Terms
Not yet implemented

PORTUGAL

Implementation of Directive
93/13 EEC on Unfair Terms
Implemented by Decree-Law 220/95
of 31 August Amending Decree-
Law 446/85 of 26 October

ITALY

Implementation of Directive
93/13 EEC on Unfair Terms
Implemented by amendment to Article
1469 into the Fourth book of the Civil
Code in February 1996

NATURE OF LIABILITY – COMMERCIAL CONSUMER GUARANTEES

SPAIN

There are mandatory commercial guarantees for certain durable goods. The General Act for the Defence of Consumers contains rules on the substance of these guarantees.

The consumers remedy is to have the product repaired free of charge or if this cannot be done the consumer may choose to have the Product replaced or be given a repayment of the Price

PORTUGAL

The Civil Code sets out rules for a guarantee of "Good Functioning" in addition to the Legal Guarantee. This guarantee is not mandatory but when provided it is usually valid for six months after delivery. The Purchaser must notify defects within 30 days of discovery. Onus of Proof of Defect is on Purchaser. The Purchasers remedy is repair or replacement

ITALY

The Civil Code provides for a guarantee of good functioning in addition to the Legal Guarantee. This guarantee is not mandatory but when provided it applies only to hidden defects for the period stipulated in the sale contract, defects must be notified within 30 days of coming to light and action must be commenced six months thereafter. The Purchasers remedy is replacement or repair

NATURE OF LIABILITY - TORT : NEGLIGENCE

SPAIN

Whoever causes damage to another person by an act or

PORTUGAL

Whoever, intentionally or through mere fault, illicitly violates the rights of

ITALY

Any event caused by fault, negligence or wilful misconduct binds its author to

omission and with negligence or fault is liable for the damage caused

Plaintiff Must Prove
1. Action or omission

2. Unlawfulness
3. Negligence (presumption of negligence in certain cases)
4. Damage not too remote
5. Causal link between the act or omission and the damage

Quantum of Damages in Tort
Damages in Tort to cover all damages directly caused, or deemed to have been caused by that act. They include replacing defective products, damage caused, damage to property and non-material or moral damage

Limitation Period
One year from when aware of damage

---

another person or breaches any rule of law designed to protect the interests of other persons shall be under an obligation to compensate the injured person for the damage arising from such violation or breach

Plaintiff must Prove
1. (a) Fault (unless it is presumed by law) or
(b) illicit violation of rights
2. Damage not too remote
3. Causation

Quantum of Damages in Tort
Plaintiff must pay damages to reconstitute the situation if the event which caused the damage had not occurred. Actual and potential damage is taken into account. Portuguese Courts are very conservative in their awards

Limitation Period
Three years from when aware of right to compensation.

---

indemnify any damage deriving therefrom.

Plaintiff must Prove
1. An act or omission on behalf of the Defendant

2. Its unlawfulness
3. Negligence

4. Damage
5. A causal link between the act or omission and the damage

Quantum of Damage in Tort
Damages should restore the aggrieved party to the position it was in before the tortious act occurred. Damages cover expenses losses and consequential losses. Moral loss cannot usually be claimed

Limitation Period
Five years from the day of the Tortious Action or the day the damage was done if earlier.

SPAIN

Fifteen years when criminal offences are involved.

Strict Liability
Strict Liability under the law of 6 July 1994

Manufacturers and Importers shall be liable for damage caused by the defects of the Products they manufactured or import respectively

Plaintiff must Prove:
1. Defect
2. Damage
3. Causation

"Producer"
Includes:

a) Manufacturer of a finished Product or a part thereof

PORTUGAL

Twenty years maximum limitation from when damage occurred

NATURE OF LIABILITY - PRODUCT LIABILITY

Strict Liability under decree 383/89 of 6 November 1989

The Producer is liable irrespective of intent or mere fault for damage caused by defects in his Product having put it into circulation

Plaintiff must Prove:
1. Defect
2. Damage
3. Causation

"Producer"
Includes:

a) The manufacturer of a finished product on a component part of

ITALY

If the Tortious Act is a crime the limitation period is the same as for the crime.

Strict Liability under the decree of 24 May 1988.

The Producer of a Product is liable for the damages caused by the defects of his product as a consequence of having put it into circulation

Plaintiff must Prove:
1. Defect
2. Damage
3. Causation

"Producer"
Is quite widely defined but may include a seller when the identity of the Producer is unknown or is outside the jurisdiction

b) Manufacturer of raw material	any new material; and b) any person who represents himself as a producer by placing his name, trade mark or other distinguishing feature on the product; and	
c) Persons representing themselves as producers and d) Importers of the Product into the European Union	c) The importer and supplier of the Product	
Strict Liability **"Product"** All movable goods including gas and electricity but excluding primary agricultural and stock farming products and game and fish that have not undergone initial Processing	**"Product"** Excludes primary agricultural products. No mention is made expressly to electricity but it is considered to be implied in the definition	**"Product"** Excludes primary agricultural products. A detailed definition of "primary agricultural products that have undergone initial processing" is included
"Defect" The definition follows the Directive in that a Product is defective when it does not provide the safety which a person is entitled to expect taking all the circumstances into account	**"Defect"** The definition follows the Directive in that a Product is defective when it does not provide the safety which a person is entitled to expect taking all the circumstances into account	**"Defect"** This differs from Directive. A Product is to be considered Defective when it does not provide the same degree of safety as that "normally offered by any other product of the same series"
"Damages" Damage is damage relating from Death or personal injury and	**"Damages"** Damage is damage resulting from death or personal injury and property	**"Damages"** See "Quantum of Damages" below

NATURE OF LIABILITY – PRODUCT LIABILITY (CONT)

SPAIN	PORTUGAL	ITALY
property damage other than for the defective product itself and as long as used or meant to be used for private use or consumption	damage other than to the defective Product itself Damage may be reduced by the extent to which it was caused by the injured person but not "any person for whom the injured person is responsible"	
Causation The Plaintiff must show the defect caused the damage	**Causation** The Plaintiff must show the defect caused the damage	**Causation** The Plaintiff must show the defect caused the damage
Defences 1. The Producer did not put the Product into circulation	**Defences** 1. The Producer did not put the Product into circulation	**Defences** 1. Defective product was not put into circulation i.e. on the market
2. The defect did not exist at the time the Product was put into circulation	2. The defect did not exist at the time the Product was put into circulation	2. The defect did not exist at the time the Product was put into circulation (Manufacturer has the burden of proof)
3. Defect is attributable to compliance with "Imperative rules in Force" and not "All Imperative rules issued by public powers"	3. Defect attributable to compliance with statute and mandatory regulations	3. Defect attributable to compliance with statute and mandatory regulations
4. The Product was not manufactured for sale or for any form of distribution	4. The Product was not manufactured for sale or for any form of distribution	4. The defect is in the final product of which the product is only a minor component

5. Development Risk Defence ie Scientific and technical knowledge at the time did not permit the Product to be seen as defective, except for manufacturers and Importers of Medical Products, food and food products for human consumption

6. If the Producer is the manufacturer of a component a defect is attributable to the conception of the Final Product or to the instructions given by the manufacturer of the Final Product

Quantum of Damages
Minimum of Ps 65,000

Maximum liability for death and personal injuries caused by identical items with the same defect shall be limited to Ps 10.500 million

5. Development Risk Defence ie Scientific and technical knowledge at the time did not permit the Product to be seen as defective

6. If the Producer is the manufacturer of a component a defect is attributable to the conception of the Final Product or to the instructions given by the manufacturer of the Final Product

Quantum of Damages
Minimum of PTE 70,000

Maximum of PTE 10,000,000,000

5. Development Risk Defence ie Scientific and technical knowledge at the time did not permit the Product to be seen as defective

6. If the Producer is the manufacturer of a component a defect is attributable to the conception of the Final Product or to the instructions given by the manufacturer of the Final Product

Quantum of Damages
Minimum of Lit 750,000

No maximum

Decree says Producer must repay damages due to death, damage to health and personal injury. Damages to goods must be paid if they are normally intended for private use or consumption and were used in this manner. Claims

SPAIN

PORTUGAL

ITALY

can also be made for non-material damages e.g. shock, mental distress, pain and suffering.

Other claims, including the value of the defective goods themselves, must be made using the general Italian law of tort based on negligence.

Damages are reduced if the injured person significantly participated in damages or denied if he did not try to avoid the damage occurring.

Limitation Period
Three years from date of knowledge of relevant facts.

Limitation Period
Three years

Limitation Period
Three years from damage occurring subject to maximum of Ten years from the Product being put into circulation

SPECIFIC SAFETY LEGISLATION

General Product Safety Legislation
Directive 92/59 EEC was implemented on 13 March 1996 by Decree 44/1996 of 19 January

General Product Safety Legislation
Directive 92/59 EEC was implemented by Decree Law 311/95 of 20 November

General Product Safety Legislation
Decree no 115 of 17 March 1995 implemented Directive 92/59 EEC

DATE LEGISLATION FOLLOWING EC DIRECTIVE 85/374/EEC CAME INTO FORCE

SWEDEN	DENMARK	NORWAY	FINLAND
Directive implemented with effect from 1 January 1993	Directive implemented with Act No 371 of 7 June 1989.	EC Directive has been the "Godfather" to Act No 104 of 23 December 1988.	The Product Liability Act came into effect on 1 September 1991.
	Took effect on 10 June 1989.	The Product Liability law came into effect on 1 January 1989 (Chapter 1 and 2) and on 1 July 1989 (Chapter 3)	The changes based on the Directive came into effect on 1 January 1994.

NATURE OF LIABILITY - CONTRACT

SWEDEN	DENMARK	NORWAY	FINLAND
From 1 January 1991 Sale of Goods Act For defects, Buyer of the Product is entitled to a price discount, or to cancel the contract, or a price reduction or the cancellation of the contract with compensation A defect exists if product lacks quality, quantity, character etc. agreed or if unsuitable for normal or intended use.	Product liability very rarely based on contract law. 1906 Sales of Goods Act does not govern the right to compensation for damage caused by the Product or to the Product.	Product liability very rarely based on contract law. Purchases Act 1988 governs sale of Goods law but not the right to compensation for personal injury caused by the Product. The Purchasers Act of 13 May 1988 This Act deals with claims for damage to and defects in the Product itself.	Product Liability very rarely based on Contract Law. According to the Commercial Code and the Consumer Protection Act the Buyer is entitled to rectification of the defect, replacement, repair, a price discount, or to cancel the contract and claim damages.

Consumer Sale of Goods Act

For defects, Consumer is entitled to repair, replacement, price reduction or cancellation with compensation

A defect exists if product lacks quality, quantity, character etc. agreed or if unsuitable for normal or intended use. Also if necessary instructions are missing or if use clearly endangers life or health

Quantum of Damage

Under the Sale of Goods Act Compensation for direct and indirect loss, however not for loss to other property than the product.

The Vendor of Products and manufacturers and those in the distribution chain have strict liability as against consumers for defects extending to direct losses only.

Damage for indirect losses can be claimed in certain circumstances.

Contractual claims can be made if the Goods do not possess expressly warranted characteristics.

Quantum of Damage

Assessed according to general principles of law.

Quantum of Damage in Contract

The injured party should be fully compensated for losses and expenses attributable to breach of contract which could have been reasonably foreseen.

Quantum of Damage in Contract

Compensation for the direct loss based on the Commercial Compensation Act is based on the Commercial Code and the Consumer Protection Act. Consequential loss will be compensated only in special cases

SWEDEN	DENMARK	NORWAY	FINLAND
Under the Consumer Sale of Goods Act Compensation for expenses, loss of income, difference in price etc. Compensation also for damage caused by the product to other property provided the property damage is intended for private use and belongs to the consumer or member of his household			
Exclusion Clauses Exclusion Clauses possible in non-consumer sales.	Exclusion Clauses Exclusion clauses possible in non-consumer sales.	Exclusion Clauses Businessmen supplying goods to customers cannot exclude liability.	Exclusion Clauses Exclusion clauses are basically valid so far as they are reasonable, but the Commercial Code and the Consumer Protection Act contain special provisions.
Implementation of Directive 13/93 on Unfair Terms Directive implemented by the Consumer Contract Terms Act on 1 January 1995	Implementation of Directive 13/93 on Unfair Terms Directive implemented by Act No 428 eg 1098 of 1994	Implementation of Directive 13/93 on Unfair Terms Directive effectively implemented by the Act on Marketing and Contract Terms and Conditions of 16 June 1972.	Implementation of Directive 13/93 on Unfair Terms Effectively implemented by the Consumer Protection Act of 20 January 1978.

Limitation Period in
Contract Claims
Within "reasonable time" from discovering defect; or within two years from receiving product unless longer guarantee period or gross negligence.

N.B. International Sale of Goods Sweden has adopted articles 1-13 and 25-88 of the UN Convention of 11 April 1980 on Contracts for the International Sale of Goods; except in cases where both Seller and Buyer have their place of business in Sweden, Denmark, Norway, Finland or Iceland.

Limitation Period in
Contract Claims
One year but this does not apply to produce liability claims.

Limitation Period in
Contract Claims
A claim must be brought within a reasonable period of time of it being discovered, and in any event within two years of the Goods being delivered.

Limitation Period
Based on the Compensation Act, within 10 years of the date of the wrongful event.

NATURE OF LIABILITY - COMMERCIAL CONSUMER GUARANTEES

Guarantees must make the beneficiary better off than he would be generally at Law. Non-binding recommendations on the form of Commercial Consumer Guarantees have been laid down by the Ombudsman

Guarantees are regulated under Section 40 of the Purchases Act.

Guarantees are frequently included in standard conditions of sale for moveable goods. If a seller assumes responsibility for the fitness for use of a product for a

SWEDEN	DENMARK	NORWAY	FINLAND
	and have a quasi regulatory status in determining whether a Guarantee is prohibited or not.		period of time and the product deteriorates within such time, it is deemed to be defective. The legal consequence of a guarantee depend entirely upon the contractual terms. A guarantee does not restrict the statutory liability for defects stipulated in the Consumer Protection Act.

NATURE OF LIABILITY – TORT: NEGLIGENCE

SWEDEN	DENMARK	NORWAY	FINLAND
<u>Negligence Claims</u> Claims founded in negligence under the Tort Liability Act. However, court practice requires little or even no negligence to have occurred.	<u>Negligence Claims</u> Liability for damage requires negligence of the Tort feasor. The low degree of fault approaches strict liability.	<u>Negligence Claims</u> Liability will arise where the manufacturer/vendor etc are at fault for the damage that has occurred or which could have been prevented by alternative action.	<u>Liability in Negligence</u> Claims founded in negligence under the Compensations Act.
Strict liability is provided in laws regarding certain dangerous activities eg. Nuclear Liability Law, Air		Strict liability exists for producers of products involving continuous risk that they will cause damage.	Strict liability is provided in specific laws for generally hazardous activities.

NATURE OF LIABILITY-TORT : NEGLIGENCE

Traffic Law and Electrical Power Plant Law.

Plaintiff must Prove:
1. Negligence (slight)

2. Causation

Quantum of Damage in Negligence
Compensation for the injured party's loss

Limitation Period in Negligence
Ten years from the date of the wrongful event

Plaintiff must Prove:
1. Negligence (slight)

2. Causation
3. Damage that is not too remote

Quantum of Damage in Negligence
Compensation awarded under basic tort law principles and excludes personal injury, and property damage and consequential damage.

Limitation Period in Negligence
Three years.

Plaintiff must Prove:
1. Negligence or Product involves continuous risk
2. Damage (must be foseeable)
3. Causation

Quantum of Damage in Negligence
Compensation for entire financial loss and damages for personal injury, pain and suffering together with consequential loss.

Limitation Period in Negligence
Claims must brought within three years from date of knowledge of possible claim but claims are statute Barred Ten Years from when the damage occurred. Claims under the Common law can't be brought more than twenty years from

---

Plaintiff must Prove:
1. Negligence

2. Causation.

Quantum of Damage in Negligence
Compensation for the injured party's loss, personal injury, pain and suffering etc.

Limitation Period
Ten years from the date of the wrongful event.

NATURE OF LIABILITY - TORT : PRODUCT LIABILITY

SWEDEN	DENMARK	NORWAY	FINLAND
Liability for personal damage caused by product and for property damage caused by a product on goods for private use.	The Directive has imposed strict liability on the 'producer' for damage caused by a defective product.	when the damaging Act occurred. The Product Liability Act has imposed strict liability on the 'producer' for damage caused by a defective product.	**Strict Liability** The Product Liability Act has imposed strict liability on the 'producer' for damage caused by a defective product.
Damage to the product itself is excluded.			
Liability includes manufacturer, importer, retailer or those who marketed product with own trade mark.			
Plaintiff must Prove:	Plaintiff must Prove:	Plaintiff must Prove:	Plaintiff must Prove:
1. Defect	1. Defect	1. Defect	1. The existence of damage.
2. Damage	2. Damage	2. Damage	2. The insufficient safety of the product.
3. Causation	3. Causation	3. Causation	3. Causation.
	4. Size of loss	4. Size of loss	4. Size of loss.

"Producer" includes:	"Producer" includes:	"Producer" includes:	"Producer" includes :
1. Manufacturer	1. Manufacturer	1. Manufacturer	1. Manufacturer
2. Importer	2. Importers	2. Importers	2. Importer
3. A Person who has sold the product as his own and sold it under his trade mark	3. Importers to the EC	3. Vendors	3. The supplier in some cases
4. Supplier when the manufacturer cannot be traced	4. Supplier when the manufacturer cannot be traced		4. A person who puts his trade mark on a product
"Product" All moveables (including Primary Agricultural Products and game) even though incorporated into another Product or moveable but does not include electricity.	**"Product"** Excludes Primary Agricultural Products unless they have undergone initial processing	**"Product"** Includes all items incorporated into other Products or real estate and waste products. Electricity is excluded. Agricultural Products are included.	**"Product"** Includes all items incorporated into other Products. Buildings on land are excluded. Agricultural Products are included.
"Defect" Exists if the Product when put into circulation was not as safe as could reasonably be expected at that time.	**"Defect"** Exists if the safety of the Product is not such as persons generally are entitled to expect.	**"Defect"** Exists if the Product does not have the degree of safety which a user or the general public would expect.	**"Defect"** Exists if the Product was not as safe as could reasonably be expected.

NATURE OF LIABILITY – TORTR: PRODUCT LIABILITY

SWEDEN	DENMARK	NORWAY	FINLAND
<u>"Damage"</u> Damage means compensatio for damage to property for personal use but not damage to the Product and damage for personal injury.	<u>"Damage"</u> Damage means death or personal injury or loss or damage to personal property and not damage to the Product.	<u>"Damage"</u> Damage means personal injury and damage to personal property. Damage to business property is excluded.	<u>"Damage"</u> Damage means death or personal injury or loss or damage to personal property and not damage to the Product.
<u>Causation</u> The Plaintiff must prove causation.	<u>Causation</u> The Plaintiff must prove causation.	<u>Causation</u> The Plaintiff must prove causation.	<u>Causation</u> The Plaintiff must prove causation.
<u>Defences</u> 1. Manufacturer did not put product into circulation under a business activity	<u>Defences</u> 1. Defect attributable to compliance with statute or EC obligation	<u>Defences</u> 1. Defect attributable to compliance with statute	<u>Defences</u> 1. Manufacturer did not put the Product into circulation under a business activity
2. Defect did not exist when put onto market	2. Defect did not exist at the relevant time	2. Defect did not exist at the relevant time	2. Defect did not exist at the relevant time
3. Supply of Product otherwise than in the course of business	3. Supply of Product otherwise than in the course of business	3. Supply of Product otherwise than in the course of business	3. The anticipated use of the Product is taken into consideration
4. Defect caused by compliance with the mandatory legislations	4. The Producer did not put the product into circulation	4. The Producer did not put product into circulation	4. Defect is in the final product of which the product is a component part

5. The Development Risks Defence does apply

6. Defect is attributable to the design of the Final Product on the instructions of the manufacturer of that product

Quantum of Damages: Minimum claim of 3,500 Skr. No maximum limit. BUT burden of proof in relation to damages with claimant.

5. Development Risks Defence

6. Manufacturer of a Component Part shall not be liable if he proves that the defect is caused by the design of a product of which the Component forms part or is caused by directions of the ultimate manufacturer

Quantum of Damages Minimum claim of 4,000K. No maximum.

If the loss is less than the minimum the Plaintiff must use existing jurisprudence based on negligence. The Defendant is liable for damages due to death, injury, harm to health and property (other than product itself) eg loss of income, loss of possibility to earn, medical expenses, compensation for invalidation, compensation for loss of breadwinner etc.

5. The Development Risk Defence does not apply

Quantum of Damages No minimum claim. No maximum.

Liability for damages due to death, injury, harm to health and property (other than product itself) eg loss of income, loss of possibility to earn, medical expenses, compensation for invalidation, compensation loss of breadwinner.

5. Development Risks

Quantum of Damage Minimum claim of 2.350 FIM. No maximum. Where two or more parties responsible for defect, shared liability

SWEDEN	DENMARK	NORWAY	FINLAND
	Existing jurisprudence provides for reclaiming value of product itself.		
	Where two or more parties responsible for defect, shared liability.	Where two or more parties responsible for defect, shared liability	
Limitation Period	Limitation Period	Limitation Period	Limitation Period
Three years from learning of the possibility of a claim; or	Three years from date of knowledge of a possible claim. Ten year cut off period has practically no effect.	Claims must be brought within three years from the date of knowledge of the possible claim but liability statute barred ten years from circulation of the Product.	Three years from the date of being informed of the damage, of the inadequate safety of the Product and of the party liable for compensation.
Maximum ten years from the day when product which caused the damage was put into Circulation.			Maximum ten years from the launch of the Product which caused the damage.

SPECIFIC SAFETY REGULATIONS

Under the 1989 Product Safety Law any business can be ordered to give safety information regarding its products and services, be prohibited from trading, be ordered to provide warnings or be ordered to withdraw products from the marketplace.

Also fine of SEK 100,000

Certain legislation for specific products and services eg Nuclear liability law etc.

General Product Safety
Legislation
Directive 92/59 EEC implemented on 1 January 1995 on Sweden becoming a member of the EU

Certain legislation for specific products eg Act on Damages, Act on Chemicals, Act on Foodstuffs, Machinery etc.

General Product Safety
Legislation
Directive 92/59 EEC implemented by Act on Product Safety No 364 which came into force on 15 June 1994.

Certain legislation for specific products e.g. Act on Drugs, Act on Nuclear, Energy, Act on Petroleum, Act on Product Supervision

General Product Safety
Legislation
Directive 92/59 EEC implemented by Law on Product Supervision of 11 June 1976.

Certain legislation for specific products e.g. the Food Stuffs Act, Act on Cosmetics, etc.

General Product Safety
Legislation
The Product Safety Act adopted in 1986 which took effect on 1 May 1987 was from the outset compatible with the currently valid Directive 92/59

	NETHERLANDS	GERMANY	AUSTRIA
DATE NEW LEGISLATION FOLLOWING EC DIRECTIVE 85/374/EEC COMES INTO FORCE	Directive came into effect on 1 November 1990, implemented by Article 185-193 and 197 of the Civil Code.	New Product Liability Act came into force on 1 January 1990.	The Federal Act of 21 January 1988 is based on the Directive which took effect on 1 July 1988. This Act has been revised by The Federal Act 1993/95 with effect from 1 January 1994 with regard to Austria joining the EEA. The law has been further amended in relation to genetically engineered products by Federal Act 1994/510.
NATURE OF LIABILITY - CONTRACT	Existing contract law remains unaffected. Applicable where there is a direct contract between the manufacturer / seller and the buyer. Any product must be fit for the purpose of the contract, and shall be free from any hidden defects, if not, then a claim for unsatisfactory performance arises.	Warranties relating to the product being free from defects may exist, remedies for breach are normally limited to repair or replacement. Damages can only be claimed where buyer wilfully deceived or if qualities are guaranteed.	The seller warrants that the Product has the stipulated or customary character, quality and is safe. Depending on the defect the buyer has the right for the defect to be corrected or to claim a price reduction or cancellation of the contract. The Buyer cannot claim damages based only on the provisions of a warranty.

Quantum of Damage in Contract
Quantum of damage in contract is all loss suffered as a direct and/or foreseeable consequence of the breach. Losses include loss of the possibility to purchase the product itself, compensation for any illness, medical expenses, damage to property and purely economic loss.

Injured party is under a duty to mitigate his loss.

Exclusion Clauses
Between professional traders, exclusion clauses are possible

Implementation of Directive 13/93 on Unfair Terms
Draft law under discussion to implement Directive 13/93 EEC

Where there is a positive violation of contractual duty there is a requirement to prove negligence.

Quantum of Damage in Contract
Quantum of damage in contract is all loss suffered as a direct consequence of the breach. Unlike tort, this includes purely financial loss.

Exclusion Clauses
In cases where the contract is not entered into or the Vendors standard terms exclusion clauses are permissible to some extent, however, in cases involving standard terms exclusion is limited.

Implementation of Directive 13/93 on Unfair Terms
Directive implemented on 1 January 1995

The chain of contract goes back to the producer. It is a breach of contract to supply defective goods whether due to design, insufficient instructions and warning or manufacturing errors.

Quantum of Damage in Contract
Claims are limited to damage caused by the unlawful Act that are not too remote Damages may include claims for loss of earnings and pain and suffering.

Exclusion Clauses
Exclusion clauses are possible to a limited extent.

Implementation of Directive 13/93 on Unfair Terms
Directive not yet implemented

<u>Limitation Period</u>
In case of "hidden defects" the buyer must notify the seller within two days after discovery.

<u>Limitation Period</u>
Where:
a) Wilfully deceived) 30 years
b) guarantee qualities do not)
exist or a positive violation) 6 Months
of contractual duties)

<u>Limitation Period</u>
Three years from time Claimant knew or ought to have known of the liability (both as to the damage and the person liable).

Thirty year shut-off period.

NATURE OF LIABILITY - COMMERCIAL CONSUMER GUARANTEES

Vendor's commercial guarantee may not limit consumers legal rights. Manufacturers commercial guarantee may limit its obligations subject to the Law on Unfair Contracts.

The Commercial Guarantee must supplement legal obligations to which the Purchaser is entitled.

Vendor's Commercial Guarantee may not limit consumer legal rights except that vendor is entitled to offer repair or replacement instead of reduction in price.

Manufacturers can limit their liabilities to the extent this is not an Unfair Term. Vendors cannot limit consumers legal rights.

Manufacturers Guarantee may have any scope, if in addition to vendor's Guarantee.

The Law on misleading advertising prohibits misleading advertising on the scope content and duration of the Guarantee.

The Code of Good Practice in advertising which is non binding contains specific provisions on advertising of commercial guarantees.

NATURE OF LIABILITY - TORT: NEGLIGENCE

<u>Liability in Negligence</u> Each unfair deed by which another has been damaged, being the person by whose fault the damage has been caused the obligation to make good the damage.	<u>Liability in Negligence</u> Anyone who wilfully or negligently and without justification infringes upon the life, body, health, liberty, property or other right of another person is obliged to compensate the other person for the damage resulting from such infringement.	<u>Liability in Negligence</u> If a party has breached an absolute right enforceable against everyone or a law a claim in tort will arise if fault can be proved.
<u>Plaintiff must Prove:</u> 1. Unfair deed or negligence 2. Causation 3. Damage not too remote	<u>Plaintiff must Prove:</u> 1. Infringement Right 2. Unlawful Conduct 3. Causation 4. Damage	<u>Plaintiff must Prove:</u> 1. Breach of an absolute right 2. Fault 3. Causation 4. Damage not too remote
<u>Quantum of Damage</u> The injured party should be put back into the position he would have been in had the damage not occurred.	<u>Quantum of Damage</u> Claimant must be put in the financial position that would have existed if the damaging event had not occurred.	<u>Quantum of Damage</u> Includes damage from physical harm, property damage and mental distress but pure financial loss can only be recovered if a protective law exists to prevent such damage.
<u>Limitation Period</u> Thirty years from the moment the damage occurs. From1 January 1991 this will become twenty years.	<u>Limitation Period</u> Three years from when claimant became aware of the damage.	<u>Limitation Period</u> Three years from the time the Plaintiff knew or ought to have known of the liability.

NATURE OF LIABILITY - TORT: PRODUCT LIABILITY

Strict Liability
A producer is liable for the damage caused by a defect in the product.

Plaintiff must Prove:
1. Defect
2. Damage
3. Causation

"Producer"
Includes:
1. Manufacturer
2. Importer to the EC

3. Person who applies his own trade mark to the Product

"Damage"
Means personal injury and personal private property damage.

"Defect"
A product is defective if it does not offer the safety that one might reasonably expect.

Strict Liability
A producer is liable for the damage caused by a defect in the product.

Plaintiff must Prove:
1. Defect
2. Damage
3. Causation

"Producer"
Includes:
1. Manufacturer
2. Importer from an EFTA State to the EC, or from the EC into an EFTA State, or from one EFTA State to another

3. Person who applies his own trade mark to the Product

"Damage"
Means personal injury and personal property damage.

"Defect"
A product is defective if it does not offer the safety that one might reasonably expect.

"Product"
Means any moveable property with the exception of Agricultural Products and Game that have no undergone initial processing.

"Causation"
The Plaintiff must prove causation.

Quantum of Damage
Minimum Dfl.1,263.85

No maximum.

Dutch courts tend to be conservative in their awards.

"Product"
Any moveable thing, including part of any moveable or immovable thing, including electricity. Excluding Primary Agricultural Products that have not undergone initial processing.

"Causation"
The Plaintiff must prove causation.

Quantum of Damage
Damages can be claimed for death, physical damage etc. but not for damage to the product itself or for pure financial loss.

Minimum liability: DM 1,125
Maximum liability: DM160,000,000

"Product"
Any moveable property, including energy but excluding Agricultural Products and Game that have not been initially processed together with genetically engineered Agricultural products.

"Causation"
The Plaintiff must prove causation.

Quantum of Damage
Min. 7,900 Austrian Shillings claim. If less Claimant must use old rules based on "negligence".

No maximum.

Defendant must pay damages due to death, injury, harm to health and property (other than the product itself).

Includes medical costs, loss of earnings and pain and suffering.

Where two or more parties are involved in causation of loss they share liability.

<u>Defences</u>

1. Defective product was not put into circulation by producer

2. The defect did not exist at the time the product was put into circulation

3. The product was not for sale nor had any commercial objective

4. Defect attributable to compliance with statute and mandatory regulations. Development Risk Defence ("State of the Art")

5. Scientific and technical knowledge at the time did not permit the product to be seen as defective

6. The defect is in the final product of which the product in question is only a component part

<u>Defences</u>

1. Not responsible for introducing the product onto the market

2. The defect did not exist when the product was brought onto the market

3. The Product has not been made for sale or any commercial purposes

4. The defect results from complying with legal requirements

5. Development Risk Defence ("State of the Art") The defect could not be ascertained according to scientific and technical knowledge available at the time of marketing the product

6. The defect is in the final product of which its product is a component part

<u>Defences</u>

1. The defect did not exist at the time the product was put into circulation by the Defendant

2. Defect attributable to compliance with statute

3. Development Risk Defence ("State of the Art")

4. Defendant did not distribute the product as a business person

5. A Defendant to a claim that a Genetically Engineered Agricultural Product is defective may show that he did not genetically engineer the Product himself

Limitation Period
Three years or later of knowledge of relevant facts and within ten years of the product being distributed

The Goods Act attaches duties to manufacturers, eg to include warnings, perform safety measures, give instructions etc.

Decrees, based on the Goods Act, provide various safety measures for toys, motorcycle helmets, cosmetics etc.

Law on Medical Supplies, Law on Serums and Vaccines, the Opium Law and the Law on Human Blood.

General Product Safety Legislation
Draft law on General Consumer Safety under discussion to Implement Directive 92/59 EEC

Limitation Period
Three years from the date of relevant knowledge

Ten years from the date of distribution (thirty years under existing laws)

SAFETY LEGISLATION

Specific safety regulations attach duties to manufacturers, eg to perform safety tests, to include warnings in sales literature/use instructions.

Officially approved standards and/or Protective Regulations exist for certain products.

Under the Equipment Safety Act 1968 all machines, work equipment, toys, etc imported into Germany must safeguard against risks to life and health.

General Product Safety Legislation
Law as yet to be introduced on General Consumer Safety to implement Directive 92/59EEC

Limitation Period
Three years from date of knowledge of relevant facts subject to a maximum Ten years from the date the product was put into circulation

Specific safety regulations attach duties to manufacturers(eg safety tests) and to importers and retailers (eg warnings in instructions).

Certain legislation for specific products e.g. Nuclear energy and heating systems with gas.

General Product Safety Legislation
The 1994 Product Safety Act implemented Directive 92/59 EEC

Product liabilities upon dissolution of a European company

	MINIMUM PERIOD REQUIRED TO DISSOLVE COMPANY	REVIVAL OF COMPANY TO RECOVER ASSETS OR INSURANCE	LIABILITY OF SHAREHOLDERS	LIABILITY OF DIRECTORS	LIABILITY OF LIQUIDATOR	LIABILITY OF PARENT IF 100% OWNER OF DISSOLVED COMPANY	PERIOD OF EXPOSURE TO CLAIMS FOLLOWING DISSOLUTION	INSURANCE
AUSTRIA	3 months for a GMbH but in practice 6 to 12 months	No, but so long as the company still has assets or the benefit of an insurance policy it does not cease to exist, although the company may have been deleted from the register	No, unless the company was undercapitalised from the beginning for its intended purpose	No, but see insurance coverage section	No	No	(a)Tort (b)Contract (c)Product Liability 10 years from date product last marketed or 3 years after plaintiff had knowledge of claim	Yes. Insurance must be maintained following dissolution to cover 10 year limitation period. Person(s) responsible for maintaining insurance may be personally liable if coverage prematurely lapsed.
BELGIUM	None. Could range from 1 month to 10 years depending on assets of company	Uncertain	Depends on type of company but on bankruptcy initial shareholders may be liable in tort in limited circumstances and directors have specific	Yes. May be sued by creditors for malpractice/negligence in carrying out the business of the company	Yes, may be sued in case of malpractice/negligence in carrying out dissolution	No, as a general rule, but exceptions exist	Liquidators usually insure against 5 year exposure	

			liabilities in respect of commercial companies					
DENMARK	Less than 1 year	No	Yes. Only if negligent or if dissolved company despite knowledge of existing claims	Possible	Possible	Possible	(a)Tort (b)Contract (c)Product Liability None	No
FINLAND	1 Year	No	Yes. For participation in breaching The Companies Act or the Articles of Association or for criminal offences	Yes. Liable for damages which he has caused to the company, its Shareholders or any other persons. Also criminal offences	Yes. May be sued for malpractice or negligence in carrying out dissolution	Yes. Based on shareholders liability	(a) and (b) 10 years (c) 3 years	No
FRANCE	Lengthy given certain employment laws protecting employees	No	Yes. Can be sued by Company's creditors for amounts received upon liquidation	Yes. Criminally if damage caused by non-compliance with French regulations. Civil if wrongdoing caused damage	Yes. Liable for negligence in dissolution for 3 years	No	(a)Tort (b)Contract (c)Product Liability 5 years	No

	MINIMUM PERIOD REQUIRED TO DISSOLVE COMPANY	REVIVAL OF COMPANY TO RECOVER ASSETS OR INSURANCE	LIABILITY OF SHAREHOLDERS	LIABILITY OF DIRECTORS	LIABILITY OF LIQUIDATOR	LIABILITY OF PARENT IF 100% OWNER OF DISSOLVED COMPANY	PERIOD OF EXPOSURE TO CLAIMS FOLLOWING DISSOLUTION	INSURANCE
GERMANY	1 Year	No	No	Yes, if the director is personally involved and/or in cases of mis-management	Yes, if he is personally involved and/or in cases of mis-management	In principle No but possible in cases of control agreements or in cases of so-called 'faktischer Konzern'	Depends on whether claims are known or unknown. Known claims during the whole limitation period. Unknown claims until the distribution of the assets of the Company	Until the cancellation or the registration of the Company
GREECE	Lengthy depending on the assets of the Company	Yes	Yes, if amounts were received upon dissolution	No	Yes	No	(a) Tort (b) Contract (c) Product Liability 10 years from date Product last marketed or 3 years after plaintiff had knowledge of claim	No

IRELAND	12 to 18 months approximately unless dissolution is as a result of the Company's failure to file annual returns. Period to dissolve Company depends upon complexity of Liquidation	Yes	Shareholders who have an outstanding liability in respect of unpaid shares can be called upon to honour their liabilities even though the Company has been dissolved	Directors who are guilty of breaches of their duties, or general breaches of Company Law, can be made liable even though the Company has been dissolved	A Liquidator of a Company may be made liable for breaches of his various duties to the Company	Not normally except in certain defined circumstances. It may be possible to find Parent Company liable on theories of Agency or Trust Law	A dissolved Company may be restored to the Companies' Register within 20 years of the date of its dissolution. The restoration does not affect the rights or liabilities of the Company with regard to any debt or obligation incurred by or on behalf of the Company between the date of its dissolution and the date of its restoration	There is no obligation for a dissolved Company to maintain insurance
ITALY	3 months, assuming assets of company are liquid and no contested creditors' claims	No, but shareholders on liquidation can claim back any assets which belong to the dissolved company	Yes. May be sued by creditors for amounts received upon dissolution	No, assuming no negligence in which case 5 years limitation period applies	Yes. May be sued by creditors for unpaid claims caused by liquidator's negligence	Yes.	(a)Tort–5 years (b)Contract–10 years (c)Product Liability 13 years	No

	MINIMUM PERIOD REQUIRED TO DISSOLVE COMPANY	REVIVAL OF COMPANY TO RECOVER ASSETS OR INSURANCE	LIABILITY OF SHAREHOLDERS	LIABILITY OF DIRECTORS	LIABILITY OF LIQUIDATOR	LIABILITY OF PARENT IF 100% OWNER OF DISSOLVED COMPANY	PERIOD OF EXPOSURE TO CLAIMS FOLLOWING DISSOLUTION	INSURANCE
LUXEMBOURG	None	Yes	Yes. May be sued by liquidator for payment of amounts due on shares subscribed	Yes, may be sued for wrongful acts or omissions in their duties prior to dissolution	Yes. May be sued by creditors for gross negligence in carrying out dissolution	No	(a) Tort (b) Contract (c) Product Liability 5 years from date of publication of liquidation	No
NETHERLANDS	At least three months	Yes	No	Yes, in specific circumstances and/or towards specific creditors	Yes. May be sued for failing to liquidate the company properly	Generally, No	(a) Tort: 5 years (b) Contract: 5 years Product Liability: 10 years	No obligation of liquidator to insure liability:
NORWAY	6 months	Yes	Yes, but limited to amounts received on dissolution	A dissolution board must be appointed. Such directors may be held liable unless they can prove they have been acting with due care to the	Similar to liability of the dissolution board	No	(a) Tort (b) Contract (c) Product Liability 3 years	No

PORT-UGAL	60 days to 3 years	No, but shareholders may bring actions in place of dissolved company	Yes if amounts are received liquidation	company and third parties in cases of fraud and mismanagement and to the State for tax and social security	Yes in cases of mismanagement	Possible	(a)Tort (b)Contract (c)Product Liability 10 years from date product was put into circulation, or 3 years after plaintiff had knowledge of claim	No
SPAIN	6 months	Yes. If dissolved company while litigation was pending	Yes, but only if dissolution tainted by fraud. Then, must return amounts received upon dissolution	Yes. If a claimant can prove serious negligence or fraud on the part of the Directors	Yes. If a plaintiff can prove serious negligence or fraud	No. Unless single shareholding has not been declared with Commercial Registry	(a)Tort (b)Contract (c)Product Liability 4 years	No

	MINIMUM PERIOD REQUIRED TO DISSOLVE COMPANY	REVIVAL OF COMPANY TO RECOVER ASSETS OR INSURANCE	LIABILITY OF SHAREHOLDERS	LIABILITY OF DIRECTORS	LIABILITY OF LIQUIDATOR	LIABILITY OF PARENT IF 100% OWNER OF DISSOLVED COMPANY	PERIOD OF EXPOSURE TO CLAIMS FOLLOWING DISSOLUTION	INSURANCE
SWEDEN	Approximately 12 months	Yes, the formal dissolution is only a statement that the liquidator has fulfilled his original assignment.	Normally no. They can only be forced to return amounts received upon dissolution if the liquidator did not keep enough funds to cover known debts, payable after the formal dissolution	Normally no, and only if not fulfilling their duties as directors	Normally no, and only if not fulfilling his duties as a liquidator	Normally no. If the two entities for an outside viewer appears to be an outside unit, or if the parent company takes part in producing/marketing the product, the parent company might be held liable as well	Product liability claims must be filed within 10 years from the time when the defective product was put into the market. However such claims will only be effective if there were, at the time of dissolution, substantial indications of possible future damages due to defective products	No, there is no obligation to keep the company insured after the formal dissolution.

SWITZ-ERLAND	1 year or less	No	No	No, unless fraud	No	Only if dissolved company entirely controlled by parent. Would be extremely difficult for plaintiff to recover	(a)Tort (b)Contract (c)Product Liability None	No
UNITED KINGDOM A ENGLAND	6 months	Yes	Yes. At least for amounts received upon dissolution	Yes. Must make statutory declaration upon dissolution which confirms contingencies on balance sheet if misstated criminal liability. Use accountants to counter risks	Yes. Personally liable if breach fiduciary or statutory duties	Perhaps. May be able to find parent company liable on theories of agency or trust law	(a)Tort (b)Contract (c)Product Liability 2 years for property damage. Effectively 3 years from injury or death claims provided the injured party has applied to restore the company to the register in that time	No

	MINIMUM PERIOD REQUIRED TO DISSOLVE COMPANY	REVIVAL OF COMPANY TO RECOVER ASSETS OR INSURANCE	LIABILITY OF SHAREHOLDERS	LIABILITY OF DIRECTORS	LIABILITY OF LIQUIDATOR	LIABILITY OF PARENT IF 100% OWNER OF DISSOLVED COMPANY	PERIOD OF EXPOSURE TO CLAIMS FOLLOWING DISSOLUTION	INSURANCE
B SCOTLAND	6 months	Yes	Yes. At least for amounts received upon dissolution	Yes. Must make statutory declaration upon dissolution which confirms contingencies on balance sheet if misstate criminal liability. Use accountants to counter risks	Yes. Personally liable if breach fiduciary, statutory duties	Perhaps. May be able to find parent company liable on theories of agency or trust law	(a) Delict (b) Contract (c) Product Liability 2 years for property damage. Effectively 3 years from injury or death, for personal injury or death claims, provided that the injured party has applied to restore the company to the register in that time	No

C **NORTHERN IRELAND**   The position is similar to that in England

Table relating to Product Safety Directives

Name of Directive	Date Directive due to be implemented	European Union Country in which Directive has been implemented as of 1 July 1995
GENERAL PRODUCT SAFETY		
Council Directive (EEC) 92/59 on General Product Safety	29.6.94	Belgium, Denmark, Spain, France, Netherlands, United Kingdom
DANGEROUS SUBSTANCES AND THEIR PACKAGING		
Council Directive (EEC) 67/548 of 27 June 1967 on the approximation of laws, regulations and administrative provision relating to the classification, packaging and labelling of dangerous substances	18.9.81	Largely implemented by all after multiple amendment by further Directives
Council Directive (EEC) 75/324 on the approximation of the laws of the Member States relating to aerosol dispensers	20.10.78	All
Council Directive (EEC) 88/379 on the approximation of laws, regulations and administrative provisions of the Member States relating to the classification. packaging and labelling of dangerous preparations	7.6.91	All except Luxembourg

Commission Directive (EEC) 90/35 defining in accordance with Article 6 of the Directive (EEC) 88/379 of the categories of preparations, the packaging of which must be fitted with child-resistant fastenings and/ or carry a tactile warning of danger	No specific regulations	All
Commission Directive (EEC) 91/155 defining and laying down the detailed arrangements for the system of specific information relating to dangerous preparations in implementation of Article 10 of Directive 88/379	Provisions on dangerous preparations are to be adopted by 30.5.91 at the latest and to take effect from 8.6.91. Implementing provisions for dangerous substances are to be adopted by 1.1.95	Belgium, Germany, Greece, Spain, France Ireland, Italy, Portugal, United Kingdom, Netherlands. (Member States which were sent an Article 169 letter in 1993 for failure to notify measures: Denmark)
Commission Directive (EEC) 91/442 on dangerous preparations the packaging of which must be fitted with child resistant fastenings	1.8.92	All
Council Directive(EEC) 76/769 on the approximation of these laws, regulations and administrative provisions of the Member States relating to restrictions on the marketing and use of certain dangerous substances and preparations	No single implementation date	All
Council Directive(EEC) 78/631 on the approximation of the laws of the Member States relating to the classification, packaging and labelling of dangerous preparations (pesticides)	1.1.81 postponed to 31.10.85	All
Council Directive(EEC) 91/157 on batteries and	Before 18.9.92 except where provided otherwise	Portugal, United Kingdom, Belgium,

accumulators containing certain dangerous substances		Spain, Ireland, Denmark, Luxembourg, Netherlands. (Member States sent an Article 169 letter in 1992 for failure to notify measures: Germany, Greece, Italy; and sent a reasoned opinion in 1993 for failure to notify measures: France)
Council Regulation (EEC) 2455/92 concerning the export and import of certain dangerous chemicals	29.11.92	All

TOYS

Council Directive (EEC) 88/378 on the approximation of the laws of the Member States concerning the safety of toys		All except Ireland

ELECTRICAL AND ELECTRONIC EQUIPMENT

Council Directive (EEC) 73/23 on the harmonisation of the laws of the Member States relating to electrical equipment designed for use within certain voltage limits	19.8.74 except Denmark until 19.2.78	All
Council Directive (EEC) 76/117 on the approximation of the laws of the Member States concerning electrical equipment for use in potentially explosive atmospheres. See also (EEC) 79/196, and 94/9		Directive prospectively repealed by Directive 94/9 from 1.7.2003
Council Directive (EEC) 89/336 EEC on the	1.7.91	All except Ireland and Netherlands

approximation of the
laws of the Member
States relating to
electromagnetic
compatibility

Council Directive
(EEC) 91/263 on the
approximation of the
laws of the Member
States concerning
telecommunications
terminal equipment,
including mutual
recognition of their
conformity

MEDICAL EQUIPMENT

Council Directive (EEC) 90/385 on the approximation of the laws of the Member States relating to active implantable medical devices	1.1.93	Germany, Denmark, Spain, France, Italy, Luxembourg, Netherlands, Portugal, Great Britain.
Council Directive (EEC) 93/42 concerning medical devices	1/1/95	Germany, Denmark, Italy, Great Britain

MECHANICAL EQUIPMENT

Council Directive (EEC) 73/361 on the approximation of the laws, regulations and administrative provisions of the Member States relating to the certification and marking of wire, ropes, chains and hooks	19.4.75	All
Council Directive (EEC) 76/767 on the approximation of laws of Member States relating to common provisions for pressure vessels and methods of inspecting them	27.1.78	All

Council Directive (EEC) 84/525 on the approximation of the laws of the Member States relating to seamless, steel gas cylinders	26.3.86	All
Council Directive (EEC) 84/526 on the approximation of the laws of the Member States relating to seamless unalloyed aluminium and aluminium alloy gas cylinders	26.3.86	All
Council Directive (EEC) 84/527 on the approximation of laws of the Member States relating to welded unalloyed steel gas cylinders	26.3.86	All
Council Directive (EEC) 87/357 on the approximation of the laws of Member States concerning products which, appearing to be other than they are, endanger the health or safety of consumers		All
Council Directive (EEC) 87/404 on the harmonisation of the laws of the Member States relating to simple pressure vessels	1.7.90	All except Netherlands
Council Directive (EEC) 89/106 on the approximation of laws, regulations and administrative provisions of the Member States relating to the construction products	27.6.91	All
Council Directive (EEC) 89/392 on the approximation of the laws of the Member States relating to machinery	31.12.92	All except Italy

Council Directive (EEC)   31.12.92
91/396 on the approxi-
mation of the laws of the
Member States relating
to appliances burning
gaseous fuels

European Parliament
and Council Directive
(EEC) 94/25 on the
approximation of laws,
regulations and
administrative provisions
of the Member States
relating to recreational
craft

MISCELLANEOUS MANUFACTURED GOODS

Council Directive (EEC)   All
73/404 on the approxi-
mation of the laws of the
Member States relating
to detergents

Council Directive (EEC).   1.7.92   All
89/686 on the approxi-
mation of the laws of
the Member States
relating to Personal
Protective Equipment

FOOD PACKAGING AND FOOD SAFETY

Council Directive (EEC)   21.12.91   All
89/109011 the approxi-
mation of the laws of the
Member States relating to
materials and articles
intended to come into
contact with foodstuffs

Council Directive (EEC)   17.10.87   All
84/500 on the approxi-
mation of the laws of the
Member States relating to
ceramic articles intended
to come into contact
with foodstuffs

Commission Directive   Originally by 31.12.90   All
(EEC) 90/128 relating   then 1.4.94

to plastics, materials and
articles intended to come
into contact with foodstuff

Commission Directive (EEC) 93/10 relating to materials and articles made of re-generated cellulose film intended to come into contact with foodstuffs	1.1.94	All except Greece
Council Directive (EEC) 88/146 prohibiting the use in livestock farming of certain substances having a hormonal action	1.1.98	All
Council Directive (EEC) 89/107 on the approximation of the laws of the Member States concerning food additives authorised for use in foodstuffs intended for human consumption	21.1.90	All
European Parliament and Council Directive (EEC) 94/35 on sweeteners for use in foodstuffs	31.12.95	All
Council Directive (EEC) 89/108 on the approximation of the laws of the Member States relating to quick-frozen foodstuffs for human consumption	21.6.90	All
Commission Regulation (EEC) 2251/92 on quality inspection of fresh fruit and vegetables	1.1.93	All
Council Directive (EEC) 93/77 relating to fruit juices and certain similar products		All
Council Directive (EEC) 89/437 on hygiene and	31.12.91	All

health problems affecting
the production and
placing on the market
of egg products

Council Directive (EEC) 93/43 on hygiene of foodstuffs	14.12.95	All

COSMETICS

Council Directive (EEC) 76/768 on the approximation of the laws of the Member States relating to cosmetic products	14.6.95	All
First Commission Directive (EEC) 80/1335 on the approximation of the laws of the Member States relating to methods of analysis necessary for checking the composition of cosmetic products	31.12.82 and amended provisions by 1.7.88	All
Second Commission Directive (EEC) 82/434 on the approximation of the laws of the Member States relating to methods of analysis necessary for checking the composition of cosmetic products	31.12.83 and amended provisions by 31.12.90	All
Third Commission Directive (EEC) 83/514 on the approximation of the laws of the Member States relating to the methods of analysis necessary for checking the composition of cosmetic products	31.12.84	All
Fourth Commission Directive (EEC) 85/490 on the approximation of the laws of the Member States relating to the methods of analysis	31.12.86	All

necessary for checking
the composition of
cosmetic products

Fifth Commission   30.9.94   All
Directive (EEC) 93/73
of the methods of analysis
necessary for checking the
composition of cosmetic
products

WATER

Council Directive (EEC)   15.7.95   All
80/778 relating to the
quality of water intended
for human consumption

Council Directive (EEC)   Dec 1977   All
76/160 concerning the
quality of bathing water

TOBACCO

Council Directive (EEC)   All
90/239 on the approxi-
mation of the laws,
regulations and
administrative provisions
of the Member States
concerning the
maximum tar yield for
cigarettes

Council Directive (EEC)   1.1.90 and in force by   All
89/622 on the approxi-   31.12.91. Amendments
mation of the laws   due for implementation
regulations and   by 1.7.92. No specific
administrative provisions dates set for the
of the Member States   applicability of various
concerning the labelling   amendments
of tobacco products

Implementation of relevant international conventions as at 5 July 1995

COUNTRY:	The Brussels Convention	The San Sebastian Convention	The Lugano Convention	The Product Liability Convention	The Rome Convention
Austria	/	/	S		
Belgium	/	/	S		/
Denmark	/	/	S		/
Finland	/	/	S		
France	/	/	/	/	/
Germany	/	/	S	/	/
Greece	/	/	S		*
Ireland	/	/	S		/
Italy	/	/	/		/
Luxembourg	/	/	/	/	/
Netherlands	/	/	/	/	/
Norway			/	/	
Portugal	(S)	/	/		
Spain	/	/	S		
Sweden	/	/	/	/	
Switzerland			/		
UK	/	/	/	/	/

/ = ratified
(S) = signatory but not yet ratified
* = Greece acceded by way of the Luxembourg Convention which has been ratified by all signatories to the Convention with the exception of Italy

641

COUNTRY:	The Hague Convention on the law applicable to Contracts for International Sale of Goods 1955	The Hague International Sales Conventions	The Vienna Convention	The Limitation Convention
Austria				
Belgium		–	–	
Denmark			/+	
Finland	–		–	
France	–		–	
Germany	–	–	–	–
Greece	–	–	–	
Ireland				
Italy	–	–	–	
Luxembourg	∽	–		
Netherlands	∽	–	–	
Norway	–			
Portugal				
Spain	∽			
Sweden	–		/+	–
Switzerland	–	–	–	
UK				

/+   =   ratified in part

Council Directive EC/85/374 on Liability for Defective Products

COUNCIL DIRECTIVE OF 25 JULY 1985 On the approximation of the laws, regulations and administrative provisions of the Member States concerning liability for defective products (No 85/374/EEC)

THE COUNCIL OF THE EUROPEAN COMMUNITIES,
Having regard to the Treaty establishing the European Economic Community, and in particular Article 100 thereof,
Having regard to the proposal from the Commission,
Having regard to the opinion of the European Parliament,
Having regard to the opinion of the Economic and Social Committee,

Whereas approximation of the laws of the Member States concerning the liability of the producer for damage caused by the defectiveness of his products is necessary because the existing divergencies may distort competition and affect the movement of goods within the common market and entail a differing degree of protection of the consumer against damage caused by a defective product to his health or property;

Whereas liability without fault on the part of the producer is the sole means of adequately solving the problem, peculiar to our age of increasing technicality, of a fair apportionment of the risks inherent in modern technological production;

Whereas liability without fault should apply only to movables which have been industrially produced; whereas, as a result, it is appropriate to exclude liability for agricultural products and game, except where they have undergone a processing of an industrial nature which could cause a defect in these products; whereas the liability provided for in this Directive should also apply to movables which are used in the construction of immovables or are installed in immovables;

Whereas protection of the consumer requires that all producers involved in the production process should be made liable, in so far as their finished product, component part or any raw material supplied by them was defective; whereas, for the same reason, liability should extend to importers of products into the Community and to persons who present themselves as producers by affixing their name, trade mark or other distinguishing feature or who supply a product the producer of which cannot be identified;

Whereas, in situations where several persons are liable for the same damage, the protection of the consumer requires that the injured person should be able to claim full compensation for the damage from any one of them;

Whereas, to protect the physical well-being and property of the consumer, the defectiveness of the product should be determined by reference not to its

fitness for use but to the lack of the safety which the public at large is entitled to expect; whereas the safety is assessed by excluding any misuse of the product not reasonable under the circumstances;

Whereas a fair apportionment of risk between the injured person and the producer implies that the producer should be able to free himself from liability if he furnishes proof as to the existence of certain exonerating circumstances;

Whereas the protection of the consumer requires that the liability of the producer remains unaffected by acts or omissions of other persons having contributed to cause the damage; whereas, however, the contributory negligence of the injured person may be taken into account to reduce or disallow such liability;

Whereas the protection of the consumer requires compensation for death and personal injury as well as compensation for damage to property; whereas the latter should nevertheless be limited to goods for private use or consumption and be subject to a deduction of a lower threshold of a fixed amount in order to avoid litigation in an excessive number of cases; whereas this Directive should not prejudice compensation for pain and suffering and other non-material damages payable, where appropriate, under the law applicable to the case;

Whereas a uniform period of limitation for the bringing of action for compensation is in the interests both of the injured person and of the producer; Whereas products age in the course of time, higher safety standards are developed and the state of science and technology progresses; whereas, therefore, it would not be reasonable to make the producer liable for an unlimited period for the defectiveness of his product; whereas, therefore, liability should expire after a reasonable length of time, without prejudice to claims pending at law;

Whereas, to achieve effective protection of consumers, no contractual derogation should be permitted as regards the liability of the producer in relation to the injured person;

Whereas under the legal systems of the Member States an injured party may have a claim for damages based on grounds of contractual liability or on grounds of non-contractual liability other than that provided for in this Directive; in so far as these provisions also serve to attain the objective of effective protection of consumers, they should remain unaffected by this Directive; whereas, in so far as effective protection of consumers in the sector of pharmaceutical products is already also attained in a Member State under a special liability system, claims based on this system should similarly remain possible;

Whereas, to the extent that liability for nuclear injury or damage is already covered in all Member States by adequate special rules, it has been possible to exclude damage of this type from the scope of this Directive;

Whereas, since the exclusion of primary agricultural products and game from the scope of this Directive may be felt, in certain Member States, in view of what is expected for the protection of consumers, to restrict unduly such protection, it should be possible for a Member State to extend liability to such products;

Whereas, for similar reasons, the possibility offered to a producer to free himself from liability if he proves that the state of scientific and technical knowledge at the time when he put the product into circulation was not such as to enable the existence of a defect to be discovered may be felt in certain Member States to restrict unduly the protection of the consumer; whereas it

should therefore be possible for a Member State to maintain in its legislation or to provide by new legislation that this exonerating circumstance is not admitted; whereas, in the case of new legislation, making use of this derogation should, however, be subject to a Community stand-still procedure, in order to raise, if possible, the level of protection in a uniform manner throughout the Community;

Whereas, taking into account the legal traditions in most of the Member States, it is inappropriate to set any financial ceiling on the producer's liability without fault; whereas, in so far as there are, however, differing traditions, it seems possible to admit that a Member State may derogate from the principle of unlimited liability by providing a limit for the total liability of the product for damage resulting from a death or personal injury and caused by identical items with the same defect, provided that this limit is established at a level sufficiently high to guarantee adequate protection of the consumer and the correct functioning of the common market;

Whereas the harmonisation resulting from this cannot be total at the present stage, but opens the way towards greater harmonisation; whereas it is therefore necessary that the Council receive at regular intervals, reports from the Commission on the application of this Directive, accompanied, as the case may be, by appropriate proposals.

Whereas it is particularly important in this respect that a re-examination be carried out of those parts of the Directive relating to the derogations open to the Member States, at the expiry of a period of sufficient length to gather practical experience on the effects of these derogations on the protection of consumers and on the functioning of the common market.

Article 1

The producer shall be liable for damage caused by a defect in his product.

Article 2

For the purpose of this Directive 'product' means all movables, with the exception of primary agricultural products and game, even though incorporated into another movable or into an immovable. 'Primary agricultural products' means the products of the soil, of stock-farming and of fisheries, excluding products which have undergone initial processing. 'Product' includes electricity.

Article 3

(1)   'Producer' means the manufacturer of a finished product, the producer of any raw material or the manufacturer of a component part and any person who, by putting his name, trade mark or other distinguishing feature on the product presents himself as its producer.

(2)   Without prejudice to the liability of the producer, any person who imports into the Community a product for sale, hire, leasing or any form of distribution in the course of his business shall be deemed to be a producer within the meaning of this Directive and shall be responsible as a producer.

(3)   Where the producer of the product cannot be identified, each supplier of the product shall be treated as its producer unless he informs the injured person, within a reasonable time, of the identity of the producer or of the person who supplied him with the product. The same shall apply, in the case of an imported product, if this product does not indicate the identity of the importer referred to in paragraph 2, even if the name of the producer is indicated.

Article 4

The injured person shall be required to prove the damage, the defect and the causal relationship between defect and damage.

Article 5

Where, as a result of the provision of this Directive, two or more persons are liable for the same damage, they shall be liable jointly and severally, without prejudice to the provisions of national law concerning the rights of contribution or recourse.

Article 6

(1)   A product is defective when it does not provide the safety which a person is entitled to expect, taking all circumstances into account, including:

(a) the presentation of the product;
(b) the use to which it could reasonably be expected that the product would be put;
(c) the time when the product was put into circulation.

(2)   A product shall not be considered defective for the sole reason that a better product is subsequently put into circulation.

Article 7

The producer shall not be liable as a result of this Directive if he proves:

(a) that he did not put the product into circulation; or
(b) that, having regard to the circumstances, it is probable that the defect which caused the damage did not exist at the time when the product was put into circulation by him or that this defect came into being afterwards; or
(c) that the product was neither manufactured by him for sale or any form of distribution for economic purpose nor manufactured or distributed by him in the course of his business; or
(d) that the defect is due to compliance of the product with mandatory regulations issued by the public authorities; or
(e) that the state of scientific and technical knowledge at the time when he put the product into circulation was not such as to enable the existence of the defect to be discovered; or
(f) in the case of a manufacturer of a component, that the defect is attributable to the design of the product in which the component has been fitted or to the instructions given by the manufacturer of the product.

Article 8

(1)   Without prejudice to the provisions of national law concerning the right of contribution or recourse, the liability of the producer shall not be reduced when the damage is caused both by a defect in product and by the act or omission of a third party.

(2)   The liability of the producer may be reduced or disallowed when, having regard to all the circumstances, the damage is caused both by a defect in the product and by the fault of the injured person or any person for whom the injured person is responsible.

Article 9

For the purpose of Article 1, 'damage' means:

(a) damage caused by death or by personal injuries;
(b) damage to, or destruction of, any item of property other than the defective product itself, with a lower threshold of Ecu 500, provided that the item of property:
  (i) is of a type ordinarily intended for private use or consumption, and
  (ii) was used by the injured person mainly for his own private use or consumption. This Article shall be without prejudice to national provisions relating to non-material damage.

Article 10

(1)   Member States shall provide in their legislation that a limitation period of three years shall apply to proceedings for the recovery of damages as provided for in this Directive. The limitation period shall begin to run from the day on which the plaintiff became aware, or should reasonably have become aware, of the damage, the defect and the identity of the producer.

(2)   The laws of Member States regulating suspension or interruption of the limitation period shall not be affected by this Directive.

Article 11

Member States shall provide in their legislation that the rights conferred upon the injured person pursuant to this Directive shall be extinguished upon the expiry of a period of 10 years from the date on which the producer put into circulation the actual product which caused the damage, unless the injured person has in the meantime instituted proceedings against the producer.

Article 12

The liability of the producer arising from this Directive may not, in relation to the injured person, be limited or excluded by a provision limiting his liability or exempting him from liability.

Article 13

This Directive shall not affect any rights which an injured person may have according to the rules of the law of contractual or non-contractual liability or a special liability system existing at the moment when this Directive is notified.

Article 14

This Directive shall not apply to injury or damage arising from nuclear accidents and covered by international conventions ratified by the Member States.

Article 15

(1)   Each Member State may:

(a) by way of derogation from Article 2, provide in its legislation that within the meaning of Article 1 of this Directive 'product' also means primary agricultural products and game;

(b) by way of derogation from Article 7(e), maintain or, subject to the procedure set out in paragraph 2 of this Article, provide in this legislation that the producer shall be liable even if he proves that the state of scientific and technical knowledge at the time when he put the product into circulation was not such as to enable the existence of a defect to be discovered.

(2)   A Member State wishing to introduce the measure specified in paragraph 1(b) shall communicate the text of the proposed measure to the Commission. The Commission shall inform the other Member States thereof. The Member State concerned shall hold the proposed measure in abeyance for nine months after the Commission is informed and provided that in the meantime the Commission has not submitted to the Council a proposal amending this Directive on the relevant matter. However, if within three months of receiving the said information, the Commission does not advise the Member State concerned that it intends submitting such a proposal to the Council, the Member State may take the proposed measure immediately. If the Commission does submit to the Council such a proposal amending this Directive within the aforementioned nine months, the Member State concerned shall hold the proposed measure in abeyance for a further period of 18 months from the date on which the proposal is submitted.

(3)   Ten years after the date of notification of this Directive, the Commission shall submit to the Council a report on the effect that rulings by the courts as to the application of Article 7(e) and of paragraph 1(b) of this Article have on consumer protection and the functioning of the common market. In the light of this report the Council, acting on a proposal from the Commission and pursuant to the terms of Article 100 of the Treaty, shall decide whether to repeal Article 7(e).

Article 16

(1)   Any Member State may provide that a producer's total liability for damage resulting from a death or personal injury and caused by identical items with the same defect shall be limited to an amount which may not be less than 70 million Ecu.

(2)   Ten years after the date of notification of this Directive, the Commission shall submit to the Council a report on the effect of consumer protection and the functioning of the common market of the implementation of the financial limit on liability by those Member States which have used the option provided for in paragraph 1. In the light of this report the Council, acting on a proposal from the Commission and pursuant to the terms of Article 100 of the Treaty, shall decide whether to repeal paragraph 1.

Article 17

This Directive shall not apply to products put into circulation before the date on which the provisions referred to in Article 19 enter into force.

Article 18

(1)   For the purposes of this Directive, the Ecu shall be that defined by Regulation (EEC) No 3180/78 as amended by Regulation (EEC) No 2626/84. The equivalent in national currency shall initially be calculated at the rate obtaining on the date of adoption of this Directive.
(2)   Every five years the Council, acting on a proposal from the Commission, shall examine and, if need be, revise the amounts in this Directive, in the light of economic and monetary trends in the Community.

Article 19

(1)   Member States shall bring into force, not later than three years from the date of notification of this Directive, the laws, regulations and administrative provisions necessary to comply with this Directive. They shall forthwith inform the Commission thereof.
(2)   The procedure set out in Article 15(2) shall apply from the date of notification of this Directive.

Article 20

Member States shall communicate to the Commission the texts of the main provisions of national law which they subsequently adopt in the field governed by this Directive.

Article 21

Every five years the Commission shall present a report to the Council on the application of this Directive and, if necessary, shall submit appropriate proposals to it.

Article 22

This Directive is addressed to the Member States.

Done at Brussels, 25 July 1985.

APPENDIX 7

Council Directive EC/92/59 of 29 June 1992 on general Product Safety

THE COUNCIL OF THE EUROPEAN COMMUNITIES,

Having regard to the Treaty establishing the European Economic Community, and in particular Article 100a thereof,

Having regard to the proposal from the Commission,[1]

In cooperation with the European Parliament,[2]

Having regard to the opinion of the Economic and Social Committee,[3]

Whereas it is important to adopt measures with the aim of progressively establishing the internal market over a period expiring on 31 December 1992; whereas the internal market is to comprise an area without internal frontiers in which the free movement of goods, persons, services and capital is ensured;

Whereas some Member States have adopted horizontal legislation on product safety, imposing, in particular, a general obligation on economic operators to market only safe products; whereas those legislations differ in the level of protection afforded to persons; whereas such disparities and the absence of horizontal legislation in other Member States are liable to create barriers to trade and distortions of competition within the internal market;

Whereas it is very difficult to adopt Community legislation for every product which exists or may be developed; whereas there is a need for a broadly-based, legislative framework of a horizontal nature to deal with those products, and also to cover lacunae in existing or forthcoming specific legislation, in particular with a view to ensuring a high level of protection of safety and health of persons, as required by Article 100(a)(3) of the Treaty;

Whereas, it is therefore necessary to establish on a Community level a general safety requirement for any product placed on the market that is intended for consumers or likely to be used by consumers; whereas certain second-hand goods should nevertheless be excluded by their nature;

Whereas production equipment, capital goods and other products used exclusively in the context of a trade or business are not covered by this Directive;

Whereas, in the absence of more specific safety provisions, within the framework of Community regulations, covering the products concerned, the provisions of this Directive are to apply;

1 OJ No C 156, 27.6.1990, p 8.
2 OJ No C 96, 17.4.1990, p 293 and Decision of 11 June 1992 (not yet published in the Official Journal).
3 OJ No C 75, 26.3.1990, p 1.

651

Whereas when there are specific rules of Community law, of the total harmonization type, and in particular rules adopted on the basis of the new approach, which lay down obligations regarding product safety, further obligations should not be imposed on economic operators as regards the placing on the market of products covered by such rules;

Whereas, when the provisions of specific Community regulations cover only certain aspects of safety or categories of risks in respect of the product concerned, the obligations of economic operators in respect of such aspects are determined solely by those provisions;

Whereas it is appropriate to supplement the duty to observe the general safety requirement by an obligation on economic operators to supply consumers with relevant information and adopt measures commensurate with the characteristics of the products, enabling them to be informed of the risks that these products might present;

Whereas in the absence of specific regulations, criteria should be defined whereby product safety can be assessed;

Whereas Member States must establish authorities responsible for monitoring product safety and with powers to take the appropriate measures;

Whereas it is necessary in particular for the appropriate measures to include the power for Member States to organize, immediately and efficiently, the withdrawal of dangerous products already placed on the market;

Whereas it is necessary for the preservation of the unity of the market to inform the Commission of any measure restricting the placing on the market of a product or requiring its withdrawal from the market except for those relating to an event which is local in effect and in any case limited to the territory of the Member State concerned; whereas such measures can be taken only in compliance with the provisions of the Treaty, and in particular Articles 30 to 36;

Whereas this Directive applies without prejudice to the notification procedures in Council Directive 83/189/EEC of 28 March 1983 laying down a procedure for the provision of information in the field of technical standards and regulations[4] and in Commission Decision 88/383/EEC of 24 February 1988 providing for the improvement of information on safety, hygiene and health at work;[5]

Whereas effective supervision of product safety requires the setting-up at national and Community levels of a system of rapid exchange of information in emergency situations in respect of the safety of a product and whereas the procedure laid down by Council Decision 89/45/EEC of 21 December 1988 on a Community system for the rapid exchange of information on dangers arising from the use of consumer products[6] should therefore be incorporated into this Directive and the above Decision should be repealed; whereas it is also advisable for this Directive to take over the detailed procedures adopted under the above Decision and to give the Commission, assisted by a committee, power to adapt them;

Whereas, moreover, equivalent notification procedures already exist for pharmaceuticals, which come under Directives 75/319/EEC[7] and 81/851/EEC,[8]

4   OJ No L 109, 26.4.1983, p 8.
5   OJ No L 183, 14.7.1988, p 34.
6   OJ No L 17, 21.1.1989, p 51.
7   OJ No L 147, 9.6.1975, p 13.
8   OJ No L 317, 6.11.1981, p 1.

concerning animal diseases referred to in Directive 82/894/EEC,[9] for products of animal origin covered by Directive 89/662/EEC,[10] and in the form of the system for the rapid exchange of information in radiological emergencies under Decision 87/600/Euratom;[11]

Whereas it is primarily for Member States, in compliance with the Treaty and in particular with Articles 30 to 36 thereof, to take appropriate measures with regard to dangerous products located within their territory;

Whereas in such a situation the decision taken on a particular product could differ from one Member State to another; whereas such a difference may entail unacceptable disparities in consumer protection and constitute a barrier to intra-Community trade;

Whereas it may be necessary to cope with serious product-safety problems which affect or could affect, in the immediate future, all or a large part of the Community and which, in view of the nature of the safety problem posed by the product cannot be dealt with effectively in a manner commensurate with the urgency of the problem under the procedures laid down in the specific rules of Community law applicable to the products or category of products in question;

Whereas it is therefore necessary to provide for an adequate mechanism allowing, in the last resort, for the adoption of measures applicable throughout the Community, in the form of a decision addressed to the Member States, in order to cope with emergency situations as mentioned above; whereas such a decision is not of direct application to economic operators and must be incorporated into a national instrument; whereas measures adopted under such a procedure can be no more than interim measures that have to be taken by the Commission assisted by a committee of representatives of the Member States; whereas, for reasons of cooperation with the Member States, it is appropriate to provide for a regulatory committee according to procedure III (b) of Decision 87/373/EEC;[12]

Whereas this Directive does not affect victims' rights within the meaning of Council Directive 85/374/EEC of 25 July 1985 on the approximation of the laws, regulations and administrative provisions of the Member States concerning liability for defective products;[13]

Whereas it is necessary that Member States provide for appropriate means of redress before the competent courts in respect of measures taken by the competent authorities which restrict the placing on the market of a product or require its withdrawal;

Whereas it is appropriate to consider, in the light of experience, possible adaptation of this directive, particularly as regards extension of its scope and provisions on emergency situations and intervention at Community level;

Whereas, in addition, the adoption of measures concerning imported products with a view to preventing risks to the safety and health of persons must comply with the Community's international obligations,

HAS ADOPTED THIS DIRECTIVE

9   OJ No L 378, 31.12.1982, p 58.
10   OJ No L 395, 30.12.1989, p 13.
11   OJ No L 371, 30.12.1987, p 76.
12   OJ No L 197, 18.7.1987, p 33.
13   OJ No L 210, 7.8.1985, p 29.

TITLE 1   OBJECTIVE – SCOPE – DEFINITIONS

Article 1

1.   The purpose of the provisions of this Directive is to ensure that products placed on the market are safe.

2.   The provisions of this Directive shall apply in so far as there are no specific provisions in rules of Community law governing the safety of the products concerned.

In particular, where specific rules of Community law contain provisions imposing safety requirements on the products which they govern, the provisions of Articles 2 to 4 of this Directive shall not, in any event, apply to those products.

Where specific rules of Community law contain provisions governing only certain aspects of product safety or categories of risks for the products concerned, those are the provisions which shall apply to the products concerned with regard to the relevant safety aspects or risks.

Article 2

For the purposes of this Directive:

(a) *product* shall mean any product intended for consumers or likely to be used by consumers, supplied whether for consideration or not in the course of a commercial activity and whether new, used or reconditioned.

However, this Directive shall not apply to second-hand products supplied as antiques or as products to be repaired or reconditioned prior to being used, provided that the supplier clearly informs the person to whom he supplies the product to that effect;

(b) *safe product* shall mean any product which, under normal or reasonably foreseeable conditions of use, including duration, does not present any risk or only the minimum risks compatible with the product's use, considered as acceptable and consistent with a high level of protection for the safety and health of persons, taking into account the following points in particular:
— the characteristics of the product, including its composition, packaging, instructions for assembly and maintenance,
— the effect on other products, where it is reasonably foreseeable that it will be used with other products,
— the presentation of the product, the labelling, any instructions for its use and disposal and any other indication or information provided by the producer,
— the categories of consumers at serious risk when using the product, in particular children.

The feasibility of obtaining higher levels of safety or the availability of other products presenting a lesser degree of risk shall not constitute grounds for considering a product to be 'unsafe' or 'dangerous';

(c) *dangerous product* shall mean any product which does not meet the definition of 'safe product' according to point (b) hereof;

(d) *producer* shall mean:
— the manufacturer of the product, when he is established in the Community, and any other person presenting himself as the

    manufacturer by affixing to the product his name, trade mark or other distinctive mark, or the person who reconditions the product,
— the manufacturer's representative, when the manufacturer is not established in the Community, or, if there is no representative established in the Community, the importer of the product,
— other professionals in the supply chain, in so far as their activities may affect the safety properties of a product placed on the market.

(e) *distributor* shall mean any professional in the supply chain whose activity does not affect the safety properties of a product.

TITLE II GENERAL SAFETY REQUIREMENT

Article 3

1.   Producers shall be obliged to place only safe products on the market.
2.   Within the limits of their respective activities, producers shall:
— provide consumers with the relevant information to enable them to assess the risks inherent in a product throughout the normal or reasonably foreseeable period of its use, where such risks are not immediately obvious without adequate warnings, and to take precautions against those risks.

    Provision of such warnings does not, however, exempt any person from compliance with the other requirements laid down in this Directive,
— adopt measures commensurate with the characteristics of the products which they supply, to enable them to be informed of risks which these products might present and to take appropriate action including, if necessary, withdrawing the product in question from the market to avoid these risks.

    The above measures shall for example include, whenever appropriate, marking of the products or product batches in such a way that they can be identified, sample testing of marketed products, investigating complaints made and keeping distributors informed of such monitoring.

3.   Distributors shall be required to act with due care in order to help to ensure compliance with the general safety requirement, in particular by not supplying products which they know or should have presumed, on the basis of the information in their possession and as professionals, do not comply with this requirement. In particular, within the limits of their respective activities, they shall participate in monitoring the safety of products placed on the market, especially by passing on information on product risks and cooperating in the action taken to avoid these risks.

Article 4

1.   Where there are no specific Community provisions governing the safety of the products in question, a product shall be deemed safe when it conforms to the specific rules of national law of the Member State in whose territory the product is in circulation, such rules being drawn up in conformity with the Treaty, and in particular Articles 30 and 36 thereof, and laying down the health and safety requirements which the product must satisfy in order to be marketed.
2.   In the absence of specific rules as referred to in paragraph 1, the conformity of a product to the general safety requirement shall be assessed having regard to voluntary national standards giving effect to a European

standard or, where they exist, to Community technical specifications or, failing these, to standards drawn up in the Member State in which the product is in circulation, or to the codes of good practice in respect of health and safety in the sector concerned or to the state of the art and technology and to the safety which consumers may reasonably expect.

3.   Conformity of a product with the provisions mentioned in paragraphs 1 or 2 shall not bar the competent authorities of the Member States from taking appropriate measures to impose restrictions on its being placed on the market or to require its withdrawal from the market where there is evidence that, despite such conformity, it is dangerous to the health and safety of consumers.

TITLE III   OBLIGATIONS AND POWERS OF THE MEMBER STATES

Article 5

Member States shall adopt the necessary laws, regulations and administrative provisions to make producers and distributors comply with their obligations under this Directive in such a way that products placed on the market are safe.

In particular, Member States shall establish or nominate authorities to monitor the compliance of products with the obligation to place only safe products on the market and arrange for such authorities to have the necessary powers to take the appropriate measures incumbent upon them under this Directive, including the possibility of imposing suitable penalties in the event of failure to comply with the obligations deriving from this Directive. They shall notify the Commission of the said authorities; the Commission shall pass on the information to the other Member States.

Article 6

1.   For the purposes of Article 5, Member States shall have the necessary powers, acting in accordance with the degree or risk and in conformity with the Treaty, and in particular Articles 30 and 36 thereof, to adopt appropriate measures with a view, inter alia, to:

(a) organizing appropriate checks on the safety properties of products, even after their being placed on the market as being safe, on an adequate scale, up to the final stage of use or consumption;
(b) requiring all necessary information from the parties concerned;
(c) taking samples of a product or a product line and subjecting them to safety checks;
(d) subjecting product marketing to prior conditions designed to ensure product safety and requiring that suitable warnings be affixed regarding the risks which the product may present;
(e) making arrangements to ensure that persons who might be exposed to a risk from a product are informed in good time and in a suitable manner of the said risk by, inter alia, the publication of special warnings;
(f) temporarily prohibiting, for the period required to carry out the various checks, anyone from supplying, offering to supply or exhibiting a product or product batch, whenever there are precise and consistent indications that they are dangerous;

(g) prohibiting the placing on the market of a product or product batch which has proved dangerous and establishing the accompanying measures needed to ensure that the ban is complied with;

(h) organizing the effective and immediate withdrawal of a dangerous product or product batch already on the market and, if necessary, its destruction under appropriate conditions.

2.   The measures to be taken by the competent authorities of the Member States under this Article shall be addressed, as appropriate, to:

(a) the producer;

(b) within the limits of their respective activities, distributors and in particular the party responsible for the first stage of distribution on the national market;

(c) any other person, where necessary, with regard to cooperation in action taken to avoid risks arising from a product.

TITLE IV   NOTIFICATION AND EXCHANGES OF INFORMATION

Article 7

1.   Where a Member State takes measures which restrict the placing of a product or a product batch on the market or require its withdrawal from the market, such as provided for in Article 6(1)(d) to (h), the Member State shall, to the extent that such notification is not required under any specific Community legislation, inform the Commission of the said measures, specifying its reasons for adopting them. This obligation shall not apply where the measures relate to an event which is local in effect and in any case limited to the territory of the Member State concerned.

2.   The Commission shall enter into consultations with the parties concerned as quickly as possible. Where the Commission concludes, after such consultations, that the measure is justified, it shall immediately inform the Member State which initiated the action and the other Member States. Where the Commission concludes, after such consultations, that the measures is [sic] not justified, it shall immediately inform the Member State which initiated the action.

TITLE V   EMERGENCY SITUATIONS AND ACTION AT COMMUNITY LEVEL

Article 8

1.   Where a Member State adopts or decides to adopt emergency measures to prevent, restrict or impose specific conditions on the possible marketing or use, within its own territory, of a product or product batch by reason of a serious and immediate risk presented by the said product or product batch to the health and safety of consumers, it shall forthwith inform the Commission thereof, unless provision is made for this obligation in procedures of a similar nature in the context of other Community instruments.

This obligation shall not apply if the effects of the risk do not, or cannot, go beyond the territory of the Member State concerned.

Without prejudice to the provisions of the first subparagraph, Member States may pass on to the Commission any information in their possession regarding the existence of a serious and immediate risk before deciding to adopt the measures in question.

2.   On receiving this information, the Commission shall check to see whether it complies with the provisions of this Directive and shall forward it to the other Member States, which, in turn, shall immediately inform the Commission of any measures adopted.

3.   Detailed procedures for the Community information system described in this Article are set out in the Annex. They shall be adapted by the Commission in accordance with the procedure laid down in Article 11.

Article 9

If the Commission becomes aware, through notification given by the Member States or through information provided by them, in particular under Article 7 or Article 8, of the existence of a serious and immediate risk from a product to the health and safety of consumers in various Member States and if:

(a) one or more Member States have adopted measures entailing restrictions on the marketing of the product or requiring its withdrawal from the market, such as those provided for in Article 6(1)(d) to (h);

(b) Member States differ on the adoption of measures to deal with the risk in question;

(c) the risk cannot be dealt with, in view of the nature of the safety issue posed by the product and in a manner compatible with the urgency of the case, under the other procedures laid down by the specific Community legislation applicable to the product or category of products concerned; and

(d) the risk can be eliminated effectively only by adopting appropriate measures applicable at Community level, in order to ensure the protection of the health and safety of consumers and the proper functioning of the common market,

the Commission, after consulting the Member States and at the request of at least one of them, may adopt a decision, in accordance with the procedure laid down in Article 11, requiring Member States to take temporary measures from among those listed in Article 6(1)(d) to (h).

Article 10

1.   The Commission shall be assisted by a Committee on Product Safety Emergencies, hereinafter referred to as 'the Committee', composed of the representatives of the Member States and chaired by a representative of the Commission.

2.   Without prejudice to Article 9(c), there shall be close cooperation between the Committee referred to in paragraph 1 and the other Committees established by specific rules of Community law to assist the Commission as regards the health and safety aspects of the product concerned.

Article 11

1.   The Commission representative shall submit to the Committee a draft of the measures to be taken. The Committee, having verified that the conditions listed in Article 9 are fulfilled, shall deliver its opinion on the draft within a time limit which the Chairman may lay down according to the urgency of the matter but what may not exceed one month. The opinion shall be delivered by the majority laid down in Article 148(2) of the Treaty for adoption of decisions by the Council on a proposal from the Commission. The votes of the representatives of the Member States within the Committee shall be weighted in the manner set out in that Article. The Chairman shall not vote.

The Commission shall adopt the measures in question, if they are in accordance with the opinion of the Committee. If the measures proposed are not in accordance with the Committee's opinion, or in the absence of an opinion, the Commission shall forthwith submit to the Council a proposal regarding the measures to be taken. The Council shall act by a qualified majority.

If the Council has not acted within 15 days of the date on which the proposal was submitted to it, the measures proposed shall be adopted by the Commission unless the Council has decided against them by a simple majority.

2.   Any measure adopted under this procedure shall be valid for no longer than three months. That period may be prolonged under the dame [sic] procedure.

3.   Member States shall take all necessary measures to implement the decisions adopted under this procedures [sic] within less than 10 days.

4.   The competent authorities of the Member States responsible for carrying out measures adopted under this procedures [sic] shall, within one month, give the parties concerned an opportunity to submit their views and shall inform the Commission accordingly.

Article 12

The Member States and the Commission shall take the steps necessary to ensure that their officials and agents are required not to disclose information obtained for the purposes of this Directive which, by its nature, is covered by professional secrecy, except for information relating to the safety properties of a given product which must be made public if circumstances so require, in order to protect the health and safety of persons.

TITLE VI   MISCELLANEOUS AND FINAL PROVISIONS

Article 13

This Directive shall be without prejudice to Directive 85/374/EEC.

Article 14

1.   Any decision adopted under this Directive and involving restrictions on the placing of a product on the market, or requiring its withdrawal from the

market, must state the appropriate reasons on which it is based. It shall be notified as soon as possible to the party concerned and shall indicate the remedies available under the provisions in force in the Member State in question and the time limits applying to such remedies.

The parties concerned shall, whenever feasible, be given an opportunity to submit their views before the adoption of the measure. If this has not been done in advance because of the urgency of the measures to be taken, such opportunity shall be given in due course after the measure has been implemented.

Measures requiring the withdrawal of a product from the market shall take into consideration the need to encourage distributors, users and consumers to contribute to the implementation of such measures.

2.   Member States shall ensure that any measure taken by the competent authorities involving restrictions on the placing of a product on the market or requiring its withdrawal from the market can be challenged before the competent courts.

3.   Any decision taken by virtue of this Directive and involving restrictions on the placing of a product on the market or requiring its withdrawal from the market shall be entirely without prejudice to assessment of the liability of the party concerned, in the light of the national criminal law applying in the case in question.

Article 15

Every two years following the date of adoption, the Commission shall submit a report on the implementation of this Directive to the European Parliament and the Council.

Article 16

Four years from the date referred to in Article 17(1), on the basis of a Commission report on the experience acquired, together with appropriate proposals, the Council shall decide whether to adjust this Directive, in particular with a view to extending its scope as laid down in Article 1(1) and Article 2(a), and whether the provisions of Title V should be amended.

Article 17

1.   Member States shall adopt the laws, regulations and administrative provisions necessary to comply with this Directive by 29 June 1994 at the latest. They shall forthwith inform the Commission thereof. The provisions adopted shall apply with effect from 29 June 1994.

2.   When these measures are adopted by the Member States, they shall contain a reference to this Directive or be accompanied by such a reference on the occasion of their official publication. The methods of making such a reference shall be laid down by the Member States.

3.   Member States shall communicate to the Commission the text of the provisions of national law which they adopt in the area covered by this Directive.

Article 18

Decision 89/45/EEC is hereby repealed on the date referred to in Article 17(1).

Article 19

This Directive is addressed to the Member States.

Done at Luxembourg, 29 June 1992.

For the Council
The President
Carlos Borrego

ANNEX   DETAILED PROCEDURES FOR THE APPLICATION OF
THE COMMUNITY SYSTEM FOR THE RAPID EXCHANGE OF
INFORMATION PROVIDED FOR IN ARTICLE 8

1.   The system covers products placed on the market as defined in Article
2(a) of this Directive. Pharmaceuticals, which come under Directive 75/319/
EEC and 81/851/EEC, and animals, to which Directive 82/894/EEC applies
and products of animal origin, as far as they are covered by Directive 89/662/
EEC, and the system for radiological emergencies which covers widespread
contamination of products (Decision 87/600/Euratom), are excluded, since they
are covered by equivalent notification procedures.
2.   The system is essentially aimed at a rapid exchange of information in
the event of a serious and immediate risk to the health and safety of consumers.
It is impossible to lay down specific criteria as to what, precisely, constitutes
an immediate and serious risk; in this regard, the national authorities will
therefore judge each individual case on its merits. It should be noted that, as
Article 8 of this Directive relates to immediate threats posed by a product to
consumers, products involving possible long-term risks, which call for a study
of possible technical changes by means of directives or standards are not
concerned.
3.   As soon as a serious and immediate risk is detected, the national authority
shall consult, in so far as possible and appropriate, the producer or distributor
of the product concerned. Their point of view and the details which they supply
may be useful both to the administrations of the Member States and to the
Commission in determining what action should be taken to ensure that the
consumer is protected with a minimum of commercial disruption. To these
ends the Member States should endeavour to obtain the maximum of
information on the products and the nature of the danger, without
compromising the need for rapidity.
4.   As soon as a Member State has detected a serious and immediate risk,
the effects of which extend or could extent beyond its territory, and measures
have been taken or decided on, it shall immediately inform the Commission.
The Member State shall indicate that it is notifying the Commission under
Article 8 of this Directive. All available details shall be given, in particular
on:

(a) information to identify the product;
(b) the danger involved, including the results of any test/analyses which are relevant to assessing the level of risk;
(c) the nature of the measures taken or decided on;
(d) information on supply chains where such information is possible.

Such information must be transmitted in writing, preferably by telex or fax, but may be preceded by a telephone call to the Commission. It should be remembered that the speed with which the information is communicated is crucial.

5.   Without prejudice to point 4, Member States may, where appropriate, pass information to the Commission at the stage preceding the decision on the measures to be taken. Immediate contact, as soon as a risk is discovered or suspected, can in fact facilitate preventive action.

6.   If the Member State considers certain information to be confidential, it should specify this and justify its request for confidentiality, bearing in mind that the need to take effective measures to protect consumers normally outweighs considerations of confidentiality. It should also be remembered that precautions are taken in all cases, both by the Commission and by the members of the network responsible in the various Member States, to avoid any unnecessary disclosure of information likely to harm the reputation of a product or series of products.

7.   The Commission shall verify the conformity of the information received with Article 8 of this Directive, contact the notifying country, if necessary, and forward the information immediately by telex or fax to the relevant authorities in the other Member States with a copy to each permanent representation; these authorities may, at the same time as the transmission of the telex, be contacted by telephone. The Commission may also contact the Member State presumed to be the country or origin of the product to carry out the necessary verifications.

8.   At the same time the Commission, when it considers it to be necessary, and in order to supplement the information received, can in exceptional circumstances institute an investigation of its own motion and/or convene the Committee on Emergencies provided for in Article 10(1) of this Directive. In the case of such an investigation Member States shall supply the Commission with the requested information to the best of their ability.

9.   The other Member States are requested, wherever possible, to inform the Commission without delay of the following:

(a) whether the product has been marketed in its territory;
(b) supplementary information it has obtained on the danger involved, including the results of any tests/analyses carried out to assess the level of risk,

and in any case they must inform the Commission as soon as possible of the following:

(c) the measures taken or decided on, of the type mentioned in Article 8(1) of this Directive;
(d) when the product mentioned in this information has been found within their territory but no measures have been taken or decided on and the reasons why no measures are to be taken.

10.   The Commission may, in the light of the evolution of a case and the information received from Member States under point 9 above, convene the above Committee on Emergencies in order to exchange views on the results

obtained and to evaluate the measures taken. The Committee on Emergencies may also be convened at the request of a representative of a Member State.

11. The Commission shall, by means of its internal coordination procedures, endeavour to:

(a) avoid unnecessary duplication in dealing with notifications;
(b) make full use of the expertise available within the Commission;
(c) keep the other services concerned fully informed;
(d) ensure that discussions in the various relevant committees are held in accordance with Article 10 of this Directive.

12. When a Member State intends, apart from any specific measures taken because of serious and immediate risks, to modify its legislation by adopting technical specifications, the latter must be notified to the Commission at the draft stage, in accordance with Directive 83/189/EEC, if necessary, quoting the urgent reasons set out in Article 9(3) of that Directive.

13. To allow it to have an overview of the situation, the Committee on Emergencies shall be periodically informed of all the notifications received and of the follow-up. With regard to points 8 and 10 above, and in those cases which fall within the scope of procedures and/or committees provided for by Community legislation governing specific products or product sectors, those committees shall be involved. In cases where the Committee on Emergencies is not involved and no provisions are made under 11(d), the contact points shall be informed of any exchange of views within other committees.

14. At present there are two networks of contact points: the food products network and the non-food products network. The list of contact points and officials responsible for the networks with telephone, telex and fax numbers and addresses is confidential and distributed to the members of the network only. This list enables contact to be established with the Commission and between Member States in order to facilitate clarification of points of detail. When such contacts between Member States give rise to new information of general interest, the Member States which initiated the bilateral contact shall inform the Commission. Only information received or confirmed through contact points in Member States may be considered as received through the rapid exchange of information procedure.

Every year the Commission shall carry out a review of the effectiveness of the network, of any necessary improvements and of the progress made in the communications technology between the authorities responsible for its operation.

Council Directive EC/93/13 of 5 April 1993 on unfair contract terms

THE COUNCIL OF THE EUROPEAN COMMUNITIES,

Having regard to the Treaty establishing the European Economic Community, and in particular Article 100 A thereof,

Having regard to the proposal from the Commission,[1]

In cooperation with the European Parliament,[2]

Having regard to the opinion of the Economic and Social Committee,[3]

Whereas it is necessary to adopt measures with the aim of progressively establishing the internal market before 31 December 1992; whereas the internal market comprises an area without internal frontiers in which goods, persons, services and capital move freely;

Whereas the laws of Member States relating to the terms of contract between the seller of goods or supplier of services, on the one hand, and the consumer of them, on the other hand, show many disparities, with the result that the national markets for the sale of goods and services to consumers differ from each other and that distortions of competition may arise amongst the sellers and suppliers, notably when they sell and supply in other Member States;

Whereas, in particular, the laws of Member States relating to unfair terms in consumer contracts show marked divergences;

Whereas it is the responsibility of the Member States to ensure that contracts concluded with consumers do not contain unfair terms;

Whereas, generally speaking, consumers do not know the rules of law which, in Member States other than their own, govern contracts for the sale of goods or services; whereas this lack of awareness may deter them from direct transactions for the purchase of goods or services in another Member State;

Whereas, in order to facilitate the establishment of the internal market and to safeguard the citizen in his role as consumer when acquiring goods and services under contracts which are governed by the laws of Member States other than his own, it is essential to remove unfair terms from those contracts;

Whereas sellers of goods and suppliers of services will thereby be helped in their task of selling goods and supplying services, both at home and throughout the internal market; whereas competition will thus be stimulated, so contributing to increased choice for Community citizens as consumers;

1   OJ No C73, 24.3.1992, p 7.
2   OJ No C326, 16.12.1991, p 108 and OJ No C 21, 25.1.1993.
3   OJ No C159, 17.6.1991, p 34.

Whereas the two Community programmes for a consumer protection and information policy[4] underlined the importance of safeguarding consumers in the matter of unfair terms of contract; whereas this protection ought to be provided by laws and regulations which are either harmonized at Community level or adopted directly at that level;

Whereas in accordance with the principle laid down under the heading 'Protection of the economic interests of the consumers', as stated in those programmes: 'acquirers of goods and services should be protected against the abuse of power by the seller or supplier, in particular against one-sided standard contracts and the unfair exclusion of essential rights in contracts';

Whereas more effective protection of the consumer can be achieved by adopting uniform rules of law in the matter of unfair terms; whereas those rules should apply to all contracts concluded between sellers or suppliers and consumers; whereas as a result inter alia contracts relating to employment, contracts relating to succession rights, contracts relating to rights under family law and contracts relating to the incorporation and organization of companies or partnership agreements must be excluded from this Directive;

Whereas the consumer must receive equal protection under contracts concluded by word of mouth and written contracts regardless, in the latter case, of whether the terms of the contract are contained in one or more documents;

Whereas, however, as they now stand, national laws allow only partial harmonization to be envisaged; whereas, in particular, only contractual terms which have not been individually negotiated are covered by this Directive; whereas Member States should have the option, with due regard for the Treaty, to afford consumers a higher level of protection through national provisions that are more stringent than those of this Directive;

Whereas the statutory or regulatory provisions of the Member States which directly or indirectly determine the terms of consumer contracts are presumed not to contain unfair terms; whereas, therefore, it does not appear to be necessary to subject the terms which reflect mandatory statutory or regulatory provisions and the principles or provisions of international conventions to which the Member States or the Community are party; whereas in that respect the wording 'mandatory statutory or regulatory provisions' in Article 1(2) also covers rules which, according to the law, shall apply between the contracting parties provided that no other arrangements have been established;

Whereas Member States must however ensure that unfair terms are not included, particularly because this Directive also applies to trades, business or professions of a public nature;

Whereas it is necessary to fix in a general way the criteria for assessing the unfair character of contract terms;

Whereas the assessment, according to the general criteria chosen, of the unfair character of terms, in particular in sale or supply activities of a public nature providing collective services which take account of solidarity among users, must be supplemented by a means of making an overall evaluation of the different interests involved; whereas this constitutes the requirement of good faith; whereas, in making an assessment of good faith, particular regard shall be had to the strength of the bargaining positions of the parties, whether the consumer had an inducement to agree to the term and whether the goods or services were sold or supplied to the special order of the consumer; whereas the requirement of good faith may be satisfied by the seller or supplier where

4   OJ No C92, 25.4.1975, p 1 and OJ No C 133, 3.6.1981, p 1.

he deals fairly and equitably with the other party whose legitimate interests he has to take into account;

Whereas, for the purposes of this Directive, the annexed list of terms can be of indicative value only and, because of the cause of the minimal character of the Directive, the scope of these terms may be the subject of amplification or more restrictive editing by the Member States in their national laws;

Whereas the nature of goods or services should have an influence on assessing the unfairness of contractual terms;

Whereas, for the purposes of this Directive, assessment of unfair character shall not be made of terms which describe the main subject matter of the contract nor the quality/price ratio of the goods or services supplied; whereas the main subject matter of the contract and the price/quality ratio may nevertheless be taken into account in assessing the fairness of other terms; whereas it follows, inter alia, that in insurance contracts, the terms which clearly define or circumscribe the insured risk and the insurer's liability shall not be subject to such assessment since these restrictions are taken into account in calculating the premium paid by the consumer;

Whereas contracts should be drafted in plain, intelligible language, the consumer should actually be given an opportunity to examine all the terms and, if in doubt, the interpretation most favourable to the consumer should prevail;

Whereas Member States should ensure that unfair terms are not used in contracts concluded with consumers by a seller or supplier and that if, nevertheless, such terms are so used, they will not bind the consumer, and the contract will continue to bind the parties upon those terms if it is capable of continuing in existence without the unfair provisions;

Whereas there is a risk that, in certain cases, the consumer may be deprived of protection under this Directive by designating the law of a non-Member country as the law applicable to the contract; whereas provisions should therefore be included in this Directive designed to avert this risk;

Whereas persons or organizations, if regarded under the law of a Member State as having a legitimate interest in the matter, must have facilities for initiating proceedings concerning terms of contract drawn up for general use in contracts concluded with consumers, and in particular unfair terms, either before a court or before an administrative authority competent to decide upon complaints or to initiate appropriate legal proceedings; whereas this possibility does not, however, entail prior verification of the general conditions obtaining in individual economic sectors;

Whereas the courts or administrative authorities of the Member States must have at their disposal adequate and effective means of preventing the continued application of unfair terms in consumer contracts,

HAS ADOPTED THIS DIRECTIVE

Article 1

1.   The purpose of this Directive is to approximate the laws, regulations and administrative provisions of the Member States relating to unfair terms in contracts concluded between a seller or supplier and a consumer.

2.   The contractual terms which reflect mandatory statutory or regulatory provisions and the provisions or principles of international conventions to which the Member States or the Community are party, particularly in the transport area, shall not be subject to the provisions of this Directive.

Article 2

For the purposes of this Directive:

(a) 'unfair terms' means the contractual terms defined in Article 3;
(b) 'consumer' means any natural person who, in contracts covered by this Directive, is acting for purposes which are outside his trade, business or profession;
(c) 'seller or supplier' means any natural or legal person who, in contracts covered by this Directive, is acting for purposes relating to his trade, business or profession, whether publicly owned or privately owned.

Article 3

1.   A contractual term which has not been individually negotiated shall be regarded as unfair if, contrary to the requirement of good faith, it causes a significant imbalance in the parties' rights and obligations arising under the contract, to the detriment of the consumer.
2.   A term shall always be regarded as not individually negotiated where it has been drafted in advance and the consumer has therefore not been able to influence the substance of the term, particularly in the context of a pre-formulated standard contract.

The fact that certain aspects of a term or one specific term have been individually negotiated shall not exclude the application of this Article to the rest of a contract if an overall assessment of the contract indicates that it is nevertheless a pre-formulated standard contract.

Where any seller or supplier claims that a standard term has been individually negotiated, the burden of proof in this respect shall be incumbent on him.
3.   The Annex shall contain an indicative and non-exhaustive list of the terms which may be regarded as unfair.

Article 4

1.   Without prejudice to Article 7, the unfairness of a contractual term shall be assessed, taking into account the nature of the goods or services for which the contract was concluded and by referring, at the time of conclusion of the contract, to all the circumstances attending the conclusion of the contract and to all the other terms of the contract or of another contract on which it is dependent.
2.   Assessment of the unfair nature of the terms shall relate neither to the definition of the main subject matter of the contract nor to the adequacy of the price and remuneration, on the one hand, as against the services or goods supplied in exchange, on the other, in so far as these terms are in plain intelligible language.

Article 5

In the case of contracts where all or certain terms offered to the consumer are in writing, these terms must always be drafted in plain, intelligible language. Where there is doubt about the meaning of a term, the interpretation most favourable to the consumer shall prevail. This rule on interpretation shall not apply in the context of the procedures laid down in Article 7(2).

Article 6

1.   Member States shall lay down that unfair terms used in a contract concluded with a consumer by a seller or supplier shall, as provided for under their national law, not be binding on the consumer and that the contract shall continue to bind the parties upon those terms if it is capable of continuing in existence without the unfair terms.

2.   Member States shall take the necessary measures to ensure that the consumer does not lose the protection granted by this Directive by virtue of the choice of the law of a non-Member country as the law applicable to the contract if the latter has a close connection with the territory of the Member States.

Article 7

1.   Member States shall ensure that, in the interests of consumers and of competitors, adequate and effective means exist to prevent the continued use of unfair terms in contracts concluded with consumers by sellers or suppliers.

2.   The means referred to in paragraph 1 shall include provisions whereby persons or organisations, having a legitimate interest under national law in protecting consumers, may take action according to the national law concerned before the courts or before competent administrative bodies for a decision as to whether contractual terms drawn up for general use are unfair, so that they can apply appropriate and effective means to prevent the continued use of such terms.

3.   With due regard for national laws, the legal remedies referred to in paragraph 2 may be directed separately or jointly against a number of sellers or suppliers from the same economic sector or their associations which use or recommend the use of the same general contractual terms or similar terms.

Article 8

Member States may adopt or retain the most stringent provisions compatible with the Treaty in the area covered by this Directive, to ensure a maximum degree of protection for the consumer.

Article 9

The Commission shall present a report to the European Parliament and to the Council concerning the application of this Directive five years at the latest after the date in Article 10(1).

Article 10

1.   Member States shall bring into force the laws, regulations and administrative provisions necessary to comply with this Directive no later than 31 December 1994. They shall forthwith inform the Commission thereof.

These provisions shall be applicable to all contracts concluded after 31 December 1994.

2.   When Member States adopt these measures, they shall contain a reference to this Directive or shall be accompanied by such reference on the occasion of their official publication. The methods of making such a reference shall be laid down by the Member States.

3.   Member States shall communicate the main provisions of national law which they adopt in the field covered by this Directive to the Commission.

Article 11

This Directive is addressed to the Member States.

Done at Luxembourg, 5 April 1993.

For the Council
The President
N. Helveg Petersen

ANNEX   TERMS REFERRED TO IN ARTICLE 3(3)

1. Terms which have the object or effect of:

(a) excluding or limiting the legal liability of a seller or supplier in the event of the death of a consumer or personal injury to the latter resulting from an act or omission of that seller or supplier;

(b) inappropriately excluding or limiting the legal rights of the consumer vis-à-vis the seller or supplier or another party in the event of total or partial non-performance or inadequate performance by the seller or supplier of any of the contractual obligations, including the option of offsetting a debt owed to the seller or supplier against any claim which the consumer may have against him;

(c) making an agreement binding on the consumer whereas provision of services by the seller or supplier is subject to a condition whose realization depends on his own will alone;

(d) permitting the seller or supplier to retain sums paid by the consumer where the latter decides not to conclude or perform the contract, without providing for the consumer to receive compensation of an equivalent amount from the seller or supplier where the latter is the party cancelling the contract;

(e) requiring any consumer who fails to fulfil his obligation to pay a disproportionately high sum in compensation;

(f) authorizing the seller or supplier to dissolve the contract on a discretionary basis where the same facility is not granted to the consumer, or permitting the seller or supplier to retain the sums paid for services not yet supplied

by him where it is the seller or supplier himself who dissolves the contract;

(g) enabling the seller or supplier to terminate a contract of indeterminate duration without reasonable notice except where there are serious grounds for doing so;

(h) automatically extending a contract of fixed duration where the consumer does not indicate otherwise, when the deadline fixed for the consumer to express this desire not to extend the contract is unreasonably early;

(i) irrevocably binding the consumer to terms with which he had no real opportunity of becoming acquainted before the conclusion of the contract;

(j) enabling the seller or supplier to alter the terms of the contract unilaterally without a valid reason which is specified in the contract;

(k) enabling the seller or supplier to alter unilaterally without a valid reason any characteristics of the product or service to be provided;

(l) providing for the price of goods to be determined at the time of delivery or allowing a seller of goods or supplier of services to increase their price without in both cases giving the consumer the corresponding right to cancel the contract if the final price is too high in relation to the price agreed when the contract was concluded;

(m) giving the seller or supplier the right to determine whether the goods or services supplied are in conformity with the contract, or giving him the exclusive right to interpret any terms of the contract;

(n) limiting the seller's or supplier's obligation to respect commitments undertaken by his agents or making his commitments subject to compliance with a particular formality;

(o) obliging the consumer to fulfil all his obligations where the seller or supplier does not perform his;

(p) giving the seller or supplier the possibility of transferring his rights and obligations under the contract, where this may serve to reduce the guarantees for the consumer, without the latter's agreement;

(q) excluding or hindering the consumer's right to take legal action or exercise any other legal remedy, particularly by requiring the consumer to take disputes exclusively to arbitration not covered by legal provisions, unduly restricting the evidence available to him or imposing on him a burden of proof which, according to the applicable law, should lie with another party to the contract.

2. Scope of subparagraphs (g), (j) and (l)

(a) Subparagraph (g) is without hindrance to terms by which a supplier of financial services reserves the right to terminate unilaterally a contract of indeterminate duration without notice where there is a valid reason, provided that the supplier is required to inform the other contracting party or parties thereof immediately.

(b) Subparagraph (j) is without hindrance to terms under which a supplier of financial services reserves the right to alter the rate of interest payable by the consumer or due to the latter, or the amount of other charges for financial services without notice where there is a valid reason, provided that the supplier is required to inform the other contracting party or parties thereof at the earliest opportunity and that the latter are free to dissolve the contract immediately.

Subparagraph (j) is also without hindrance to terms under which a seller or supplier reserves the right to alter unilaterally the conditions of a contract of indeterminate duration, provided that he is required to inform

the consumer with reasonable notice and that the consumer is free to dissolve the contract.

(c) Subparagraph (g), (j) and (l) do not apply to:
— transactions in transferable securities, financial instruments and other products or services where the price is linked to fluctuations in a stock exchange quotation or index or a financial market rate that the seller or supplier does not control;
— contracts for the purchase or sale of foreign currency, traveller's cheques or international money orders denominated in foreign currency;

(d) Subparagraph (l) is without hindrance to price-indexation clauses, where lawful, provided that the method by which prices vary is explicitly described.

Proposal for a Directive on the sale of consumer goods and associated guarantees (96/C 307/09)

COM(95) 520 final—96/0161(COD)

THE EUROPEAN PARLIAMENT AND THE COUNCIL OF THE EUROPEAN UNION,

Having regard to the Treaty establishing the European Community, and in particular Article 100a thereof,

Having regard to the proposal from the Commission,

Having regard to the opinion of the Economic and Social Committee,

Acting in accordance with the procedure referred to in Article 189b of the Treaty,

Whereas the internal market comprises an area without internal frontiers in which the free movement of goods, persons, services and capital is guaranteed; whereas free movement of goods concerns not only persons acting in the course of business but also private individuals; whereas it implies that consumers resident in one Member State should be free to purchase goods in the territory of another Member State on the basis of a minimum set of fair rules governing the purchase of consumer goods;

Whereas the laws of the Members States concerning the sale of consumer goods are quite disparate, with the result that national consumer goods markets differ from one another and that competition between sellers may be distorted;

Whereas consumers who are keen to benefit from the large market by purchasing goods in Member States other than their State of residence play a fundamental role in the completion of the internal market by preventing the artificial reconstruction of new frontiers and the compartmentalization of markets; whereas these opportunities have been greatly broadened by new communication technologies which allow ready access to distribution systems in other Member States or at international level; whereas in the absence of minimum harmonization of the rules governing the purchase of consumer goods, the development of the sale of goods through the medium of new distance communication technologies risks being impeded;

Whereas the creation of a common minimum corpus of consumer law, valid no matter where goods are purchased within the Community, will further

strengthen consumer confidence and enable consumers to make the most of the internal market;

Whereas the main difficulties encountered by consumers and the main source of disputes with sellers concern the non-conformity of goods with the contract; whereas it is therefore appropriate to approximate national legislation governing the sale of consumer goods in this respect, without however impinging on provisions and principles of national law relating to contractual and non-contractual liability;

Whereas the goods must, above all, conform with the contractual specifications; whereas the notion of conformity with the contract may be considered as common to the different national legal traditions; whereas the seller should be directly liable to the consumer for the conformity of the goods with the contract; whereas this is the traditional solution enshrined in the legal orders of the Member States; whereas, nevertheless, the seller should be free to pursue remedies against his own seller or the producer when the non-conformity is the result of an act of commission or omission on their part;

Whereas, in the case of non-conformity of the product with the contract, consumers should be entitled to request that the product be repaired or replaced, or to a reduction in the price paid by way of damages or cancellation of the contract of sale; whereas, however, exercise of these rights should be limited in time and time limits laid down during which these rights may be invoked against the seller;

Whereas, in the interest of a stable business environment and good faith in the relations between the Contracting Parties, it should be incumbent on the consumer to notify the seller of any non-conformity he detects within a short period; whereas in order to allow the parties to reach amicable settlements without immediately having to institute legal proceedings to safeguard their rights the limitation period should be interrupted once the consumer draws attention to the lack of conformity of the goods;

Whereas it is current practice, for certain categories of goods, for sellers and producers to offer guarantees on their products designed to insure consumers against any defect which becomes manifest within a certain period; whereas this practice can stimulate competition; whereas, however, these guarantees may be a simple publicity ploy and deceive the consumer; whereas to ensure market transparency certain common principles applicable to the guarantees offered by the economic operators should be laid down;

Whereas the rights granted to consumers should not be excludable by common consent between the parties since otherwise the legal protection afforded would be vitiated; whereas consumers should always be entitled to rely on the rights resulting from this Directive or any other applicable national provision, even if they accept the implementation of the guarantee; whereas consumer protection resulting from this Directive should not be reduced on the grounds that the law of a non-member country is applicable to the contract;

Whereas legislation and case law in this area in the various Member States show that there is growing concern to ensure a high level of consumer protection; whereas in the light of these trends and the experience acquired in implementing this Directive it may be necessary to envisage more far-reaching harmonization, notably by stipulating the producer's direct liability for defects for which he is responsible;

Whereas Member States must be allowed to adopt or maintain in force more stringent provisions, in the field covered by this Directive, to ensure a yet higher level of consumer protection,

HAVE ADOPTED THIS DIRECTIVE

Article 1 Scope and definitions

1.   The purpose of this Directive is the approximation of the laws, regulations and administrative provisions of the Member States on the sale of consumer goods and associated guarantees in order to ensure a uniform minimum level of consumer protection in the context of the internal market.
2.   For the purposes of this Directive,

(a) *Consumer* means any natural person who, in the contracts covered by this Directive, is acting for purposes which are not directly related to his trade, business or profession;
(b) *Consumer* goods means any goods, excluding buildings, normally intended for final use of consumption;
(c) *Seller* means any natural or legal person who sells consumer goods in the course of his trade, business of profession;
(d) *Guarantee* means any additional undertaking given by a seller or producer, over and above the legal rules governing the sale of consumer goods, to reimburse the price paid, to exchange, repair or handle a product in any way, in the case of non-conformity of the product with the contract.

Article 2 Conformity with the contract

1.   Consumer goods must be in conformity with the contract of sale.
2.   Goods shall be deemed to be in conformity with the contract if, at the moment of delivery to the consumer:

(a) they comply with the description given by the seller and possess the qualities of the goods which the seller has held out to the consumer as a sample or model;
(b) they are fit for the purposes for which goods of the same type are normally used;
(c) they are fit for any particular purpose for which the consumer requires them and which he had made known to the seller at the time of conclusion of the contract, except where the circumstances show that the buyer did not rely on the seller's explanations;
(d) their quality and performance are satisfactory given the nature of the goods and the price paid and taking into account the public statements made about them by the seller, the producer or his representative.

3.   Any lack of conformity resulting from incorrect installation of the goods shall be considered to be equivalent to lack of conformity of the goods with the contract, if the goods were installed by the seller or under his responsibility.

Article 3 Obligations of the seller

1.   The seller shall be liable to the consumer for any lack of conformity which exists when the goods are delivered to the consumer and which becomes manifest within a period of two years unless, at the moment of conclusion of

the contract of sale, the consumer knew or could not be unaware of the lack of conformity.

2.   When the goods are not in conformity with the public statements made by the producer or his representative, the seller shall not be liable if:

— the seller shows that he did not know and could not reasonably know the statement in question,
— the seller shows that at the time of sale he corrected the statement, or
— the seller shows that the decision to buy the goods could not have been influenced by the statement.

3.   Until proof of the contrary any lack of conformity which becomes manifest within six months of delivery shall be presumed to have existed at the time of delivery, unless this presumption is incompatible with the nature of the goods or the nature of the lack of conformity.

4.   When a lack of conformity is notified to the seller, pursuant to Article 4, the consumer shall be entitled to ask the seller either to repair the goods free of charge within a reasonable period, or to replace the goods, when this is possible, or to demand an appropriate price reduction or rescission of the contract. Exercise of the right of rescission or replacement of the goods is limited to one year.

Member States may provide that the scope of the rights referred to in the first subparagraph be limited in the case of a minor lack of conformity.

5.   When the final seller is liable to the consumer because of a lack of conformity resulting from an act of commission or omission by the producer, a previous seller in the same chain of contracts or any other intermediary, the final seller shall be entitled to pursue remedies against the responsible person, under the conditions laid down by national law.

Article 4   Obligations of the consumer

1.   In order to benefit from the rights referred to in Article 3(4) the consumer must notify the seller of any lack of conformity within a period of one month from the date on which he detected the lack of conformity or ought normally to have detected it.

2.   Notifications made pursuant to paragraph 1 shall interrupt the limitation period provided for in Article 3(4).

Article 5   Guarantees

1.   Any guarantee offered by a seller or producer shall legally bind the offerer under the conditions laid down in the guarantee document and the associated advertising and must place the beneficiary in a more advantageous position than that resulting from the rules governing the sale of consumer goods set out in the national provisions applicable.

2.   The guarantee must feature in a written document which must be freely available for consultation before purchase and must clearly set out the essential particulars necessary for making claims under the guarantee, notably the duration and territorial scope of the guarantee, as well as the name and address of the guarantor.

Article 6   Binding nature of the provisions

1.   Any contractual terms or agreements concluded with the seller before notification of the lack of conformity which waive or restrict the rights resulting from this Directive shall not be binding on the consumer.

2.   Member States shall take the necessary measures to ensure that, irrespective of the law applicable to the contract, and when the contract has a close connection with the territory of the Member States, consumers are not deprived of the protection afforded by this Directive.

Article 7   National law and minimum protection

1.   The rights resulting from this Directive shall be exercised without prejudice to other rights which the consumer may rely on under the national rules governing contractual or non-contractual liability.

2.   Member States may adopt or maintain in force more stringent provisions, compatible with the Treaty, in the field covered by this Directive, to ensure a higher level of consumer protection.

Article 8   Transposition

1.   Member States shall bring into force the laws, regulations and administrative provisions necessary to comply with this Directive not later than ...*. They shall immediately inform the Commission thereof.

When Member States adopt these provisions, these shall contain a reference to this Directive, or shall be accompanied by such reference at the time of their official publication. The procedure for such reference shall be adopted by Member States.

2.   Member States shall communicate to the Commission the provisions of national law which they adopt in the field covered by this Directive.

Article 9   Entry into force

This Directive shall enter into force on the 20th day following that of its publication in the *Official Journal of the European Communities*.

Article 10   Addresses

This Directive is addressed to the Member States.

---

*   Two years after its publication in the *Official Journal of the European Communities*.

The Swedish Product Liability Act (1992:18)

Conditions relating to the payment of damages

Section 1

Damages as laid down in this Act are payable for personal injury caused by a defect in a product.

Damages as laid down in this Act are also payable for damage caused by a defect in a product to property which is normally by virtue of its nature intended for private use, if, when the damage occurred, the injured party was using the product principally for such a purpose. Damage to the product itself will, however, not be compensated.

Section 2

For the purpose of this act, *product* refers to movables. A product which has been incorporated in or in some other way become a constituent of some other movable or immovable is still to be regarded as constituting a separate product within the meaning of this Act.

If injury or damage has arisen in consequence of a defect in a product which is a constituent of another product, both products are to be regarded as having caused the injury or damage.

Section 3

A product is defective, if it is not as safe as can be reasonably expected. Safety is to be assessed with regard to the uses to which the product could be expected to be put and the manner in which it was marketed, and also with regard to the instructions for its use, the time when it was put into circulation and other circumstances.

Section 4

This Act does not apply to injury or damage covered by the Nuclear Liability Act (1968:45).

Section 5

No contractual conditions which limit liability as laid down in this Act may be legally binding.

Liability

Section 6

Liability to pay damages in accordance with this Act rests with

(1) any person or entity that has manufactured, produced or assembled the product which caused injury or damage,
(2) any person or entity that has imported the product into the European Economic Area in order to put it into circulation there,
(3) any person or entity that, in order to put the product into circulation, has imported it from a state which is a member of the European Free Trade Asociation (EFTA) to the European Community, or from the European Community to an EFTA state, or from an EFTA state to another EFTA state, and
(4) any person or entity that has marketed the product as his own product by furnishing it with his name or trade-mark or some other distinguishing feature.

Sub-section 3 of the first paragraph above does not apply to imports between states which have ratified the Convention of 16 September, 1988 on the Jurisdiction and the Enforcement of Judgments in Civil and Commercial Matters, if a judgment in the importing state in favour of the injured party against any person or entity liable to pay damages in accordance with sub-sections 1, 2 or 4 of the first paragraph is enforceable under the terms of the Convention in the state in which the person liable for damages is domiciled (Act 1992:1137).

Section 7

If the person liable for damages in accordance with section 6 cannot be ascertained from a product manufactured, produced, or assembled in Sweden which has caused injury or damage, each supplier of the product is liable to pay damages as laid down in this Act, if he cannot, within the time stipulated in the third paragraph of this section, identify someone who has manufactured, produced or assembled the product, or marketed it as his own product, or supplied him with it.

If the identity of an importer as laid down in sub-sections 2 or 3 of the first paragraph of section 6 above cannot be ascertained from an imported product which has caused injury or damage, each supplier of the product is liable to pay damages as laid down in this Act, if he cannot, within the time stipulated in the third paragraph of this section, identify an importer as laid down in sub-sections 2 or 3 of the first paragraph of section 6 above, or the person who supplied him with the product.

Notification of identification as stipulated in the first and second paragraphs of this section must be submitted within one month of the date on which the injured party has presented a claim for compensation or requested such identification in some other manner (Act 1992:1137).

Section 8

No liability for damages in accordance with sections 6 or 7 above will be incurred by any person or entity who
(1) shows that he did not put the product into circulation by way of trade,
(2) shows that with all probability the defect did not exist when the product was put into circulation,

(3) shows that the defect is due to compliance with mandatory regulations issued by public authorities, or
(4) shows that on the basis of scientific and technical knowledge at the time when he put the product into circulation it was not possible to discover the defect.

Deductions for damage to property

Section 9

In determining compensation for damage to property in accordance with this Act, a sum of SEK 3,500 is to be deducted.

Contributory negligence of the injured party

Section 10

Damages payable according to this Act may be adjusted to the extent reasonable, if negligence on the part of the injured party has contributed to the injury or damage (Act 1992:1138).

Right of recourse

Section 11

Where and to the extent that a person is liable to pay compensation for damage under the terms of this Act, any person or entity that has paid compensation for damage in accordance with section 31 of The Consumer Sales Act (1990:932) or paragraph four of section 31 of The Consumer Services Act (1985:716), is entitled to restitution from this person of what he has paid.

Limitation period

Section 12

Anyone claiming damages in accordance with this Act is to bring his case within three years of the time at which he learnt, or should have learnt, that the claim could be made.

An action for damages must however be brought within ten years of the time at which the person who is alleged to be liable for damages put the product which gave rise to injury or damage into circulation.

Anyone failing to bring a case in time forfeits the right to compensation.

Interim provisions

1992:18

(1) This Act enters into force on 1 January 1993.
(2) This Act is not to be applied against any person or entity that has put the product which gives rise to injury or damage into circulation before the Act came into force.

1992:1137

(1) This Act enters into force, where sections 6 and 7 are concerned, on the date decided by the Cabinet, and otherwise on 1 January 1993 (in force 1 January 1994, 1993:1646). The Cabinet may bring sections 6 and 7 into force with regard to Liechtenstein and Switzerland at a later date than for the other EFTA countries.
(2) This Act is not to apply with regard to any person or entity that has put the product which gives rise to injury or damage into circulation before the Act came into force (1993:647).

APPENDIX 11

Swedish Sale of Goods Act

(Issued on 6 September 1990; Swedish Code of Statutes 1990:931)
In accordance with a decision of the Riksdag (Parliament), the following is hereby ordained.

Introductory provisions

Sphere of application

1.   This Act applies to the sale of all types of property other than real property. Where applicable this Act also applies to exchanges of all types of property other than real property.

This Act does not apply to transfer of site leaseholds.

In the case of the sale of a building constructed for permanent use, the provisions contained in Chapter 4, sections 11, 12 and 18-19d of the Real Property Code apply instead of the provisions in sections 3, 13, 17-21 and also 30-40 of this Act. If a transfer of a site leasehold in accordance with Chapter 13, section 5 of the Real Property Code has included transfer of a building, the said provisions in the Real Property Code do not apply if other provisions apply under Chapter 13, section 8 of the Real Property Code.

2.   This Act applies to orders for goods which are to be manufactured, except where the party ordering the goods undertakes to supply a substantial proportion of the materials. This Act does not apply to contracts for construction of buildings or other permanent construction on land or over water or under water.

This Act does not apply to contracts in which the party furnishing the goods shall also supply labour or other services, if the services comprise the predominant part of the obligations of this party.

Contractual freedom

3.   The provisions of this Act do not apply where other provisions result from the contract, by practices which the parties have established between themselves or by commercial usages or other customs which must be considered binding on the parties.

Consumer sales

4.   This Act does not apply in cases where the Consumer Sales Act (1990:932) is applicable.

683

International sales

5.   This Act does not apply in cases where the International Sale of Goods Act (1987:822) is applicable.

Delivery of goods

Collected goods

6.   The goods shall be kept at the buyer's disposal at the place where the seller had his place of business at the time of concluding the contract or, if he did not have a place of business which was connected with the sale, at his place of residence. If the parties knew, when the contract was concluded, that the goods or the consignment from which the goods were to be drawn were located elsewhere, the goods shall be kept at the buyer's disposal for collection at this location.

Goods have been delivered when they have been taken over by the buyer.

Carriage of goods sold

7.   If the goods are to be transported to the buyer within one and the same locality or within an area in which the seller usually arranges the carriage of similar goods, delivery takes place when the goods are handed over to the buyer. If the goods are to be transported to the buyer in other cases and where there are no obligations under the terms of delivery or otherwise under the contract, delivery takes place when the goods are handed over to the carrier who has undertaken to transport the goods from the place of dispatch. If the seller transports the goods himself, delivery does not take place until the goods are handed over to the buyer.

If the goods have been sold 'free', 'delivered' or 'free delivered' and a specific locality is specified, they are not considered to be delivered until they have arrived at this locality.

8.   If the seller is to arrange for carriage of the goods, he shall enter into such contracts as are necessary for carriage to the place of destination by means of appropriate transportation and in accordance with the customary conditions for such transportation.

Time of delivery

9.   If the goods are not to be delivered on demand or without delay, and if the time of delivery is not otherwise determined by the contract, the goods shall be delivered within a reasonable time after the conclusion of the contract.

If the goods are to be delivered within a specific period of time and it is not clear in the circumstances that the buyer is to determine the time for the delivery, the time for the delivery shall be determined by the seller.

If the goods are to be collected by the buyer and the seller is to decide the date of delivery, the seller shall inform the buyer in good time concerning when the goods will be at the buyer's disposal for collection.

The right to retain the goods

10.   If the seller has not allowed credit or an extension of time for payment, he is not obliged to hand over the goods or, by transfer of documents or in any other way, to relinquish the right of disposition of the goods until payment has been made.

If the seller is to send the goods from the place where they are to be delivered, he is not entitled by virtue of the preceding paragraph to fail to dispatch the goods. However, the seller may prevent the handing over of the goods or documents concerning the goods to the buyer before payment has been made.

Costs arising from the goods

11.   The seller is responsible for costs for the goods which arise prior to their delivery and which are not incurred by delay in the delivery of the goods as a result of circumstances attributable to the buyer.

Risk

What risk means

12.   If the buyer bears the risk for the goods, he is liable to pay for the goods even if they have been spoiled, lost, have deteriorated or are diminished through events which are not attributable to the seller.

Transfer of risk

13.   The risk passes to the buyer when the goods are delivered in accordance with the contract or in accordance with sections 6 or 7 of this Act.

If the goods are not delivered at the right time and this is attributable to the buyer or some circumstance attributable to the buyer, the risk passes to the buyer when the seller has fulfilled his obligations to enable delivery to take place.

If the buyer is to collect the goods from a place other than at the seller's place of business or residence, the risk passes to the buyer at the time delivery is due and when the buyer has been informed that the goods are at his disposal for collection.

14.   The risk never passes to the buyer until it has been made clear, whether by markings on the goods, by notation in the transportation documents or in some other way, that the goods are clearly intended for the buyer.

Goods in transit

15.   The risk in respect of goods sold in transit passes to the buyer at the time of sale, unless it is clear from the circumstances that the buyer has undertaken to bear the risk from the time the goods were handed over to the carrier who issued the transport documents. However, the seller always bears the risk for goods if, at the time of the sale, the seller knew or should have known that the goods had been spoiled, lost, had deteriorated or were diminished and did not inform the buyer of this.

Sale with option to return

16.   If sale with option to return has been agreed and the goods have been handed over, the buyer bears the risk until the goods have been returned.

Status of the goods

Conformity with the contract etc

17.   The goods must conform with what is implied by the contract as regards type, quantity, quality, other characteristics and also the packing or packaging.

Unless otherwise implied by the contract, the goods

(1) shall be fit for the purposes for which goods of the same description would ordinarily be used;

(2) shall be fit for the specific purposes for which the goods were intended to be used, if the seller at the time of the sale must have understood such specific purposes and the buyer had reasonable cause to rely on the seller's skill and judgment;

(3) shall possess the qualities of goods which the seller has referred to in providing samples or models; and

(4) shall be contained or packaged in a customary or otherwise adequate manner, if packaging is required to preserve or protect the goods.

If the goods do not comply with the provisions set out in the preceding paragraphs or do not conform in any other way with what the buyer can justifiably assume, it is to be considered that the goods do not conform with the contract.

18.   It shall also be considered that the goods do not conform with the contract if they do not comply with descriptions of the qualities (characteristics) or use of the goods provided by the seller in marketing the goods or in other contexts prior to the sale and which may be assumed to have influenced the sale.

It shall also be considered that the goods do not conform with the contract if they do not comply with descriptions of the qualities or use of the goods which a party other than the seller has given, at an earlier stage in the sales transaction or on behalf of the seller, in marketing the goods, and which can be assumed to have affected the sale. However, non-conformity does not apply if the seller neither was aware nor should have been aware of these descriptions.

The first and second paragraphs do not apply if the descriptions have been corrected in time and in a clear manner.

Goods sold in existing condition

19.   Notwithstanding the fact that the goods have been sold 'in their existing condition' or with any other similar general reservations, it shall be considered that they do not conform with the contract:

(1) if the goods do not conform with descriptions of their qualities or use which the seller has provided prior to the sale and which can be assumed to have influenced the contract;

(2) if, prior to the sale, the seller has failed to inform the buyer of a significant circumstance concerning the qualities or use of the goods which it must

be assumed he was aware of and which the buyer could with good reason expect to be informed of, on condition that the omission can be assumed to have affected the sale; or

(3) the goods are in a condition which is considerably inferior to that which the buyer had good reason to expect with regard to the price of the goods and other circumstances.

When second-hand goods have been sold by auction, they are considered to be sold 'in their existing condition'. Where sub-section 3 of the preceding paragraph applies, regard shall be paid to the price estimated or indicated by the auctioneer.

Examination of the goods prior to sale

20. The buyer may not claim lack of conformity if it may be assumed he must have been aware of the lack of conformity at the time of the sale.

If the buyer has examined the goods before the sale or without giving acceptable reason has failed to follow the seller's exhortation to examine the goods, he may not claim what he should have noticed upon examination as a lack of conformity, unless the seller has acted in breach of faith and honour.

The preceding paragraph also applies when the buyer has had an opportunity to examine a sample of the goods before the sale and the lack of conformity relates to qualities which would have been revealed in the sample.

Relevant time factors in judging whether there is a lack of conformity

21. When judging the question of whether there is lack of conformity, heed shall be paid to the condition of the goods at the time when the risk for the goods passes to the buyer. The seller is responsible for any failure to conform with the contract which existed at this time, even though such non-conformity does not appear until later.

If deterioration of the goods occurs after the risk has passed to the buyer, it shall be considered that the goods do not conform with the contract if the deterioration is a consequence of a breach of contract on the part of the seller. This also applies if the seller has undertaken by guarantee or a similar pledge to be responsible for the usefulness or other qualities of the goods during a certain period and the deterioration relates to a quality covered by such a pledge.

Remedies in the case of delay in delivering the goods

Remedies

22. If the goods are not delivered or if they are delivered too late and this is not attributable to the buyer or to circumstances which are attributable to the buyer, under sections 23-29, the buyer may claim performance by the seller or may declare the contract avoided (cancel the contract) and in addition claim damages. He may also withhold payment by virtue of section 42.

Performance

23. The buyer may adhere to the contract and demand performance by the seller. However, the seller is not liable to fulfil the contract if there is an

impediment to his performance which he cannot overcome or if performance would require sacrifices which are unreasonable in view of the buyer's interest in fulfilment of the contract by the seller.

However, if the above-mentioned circumstances cease within reasonable time, the buyer may require that the seller fulfil the contract.

The buyer loses the right to require that the seller fulfil the contract, if he waits for an unreasonably long time before presenting his claim.

24. If the seller asks the buyer whether, despite the delay, he will accept delivery within a specified period of time or if the seller notifies the buyer that he will fulfil the contract within a specified period of time, and if the buyer does not reply in reasonable time after receiving the inquiry or notification, the buyer may not declare the contract avoided if the seller fulfils his obligations within the time he has specified.

Declaring the contract avoided

25. The buyer may declare the contract avoided on grounds of the seller's delay, if the breach of contract is of substantial importance to the buyer and the seller was aware of this or should have been aware of this.

If the buyer has prescribed a specified additional period of time for delivery of the goods for the seller and if this period of time is not unreasonably short, the buyer may also declare the contract avoided if the goods are not handed over within the additional period of time.

During the additional period for delivery, the buyer may only declare the contract avoided if the seller declares that he will not fulfil the contract within the additional period.

26. If the sale refers to goods which are to be manufactured or acquired especially for the buyer in accordance with the buyer's instructions or wishes, and if the seller cannot make use of the goods in any other way without substantial losses, the buyer may only declare the contract avoided on grounds of delay if his purpose in signing the contract is essentially frustrated by the delay.

Damages

27. The buyer has the right to compensation for the damage he suffers as a result of the seller's delay, unless the seller proves that the delay is due to an impediment beyond his control and that he could not reasonably be expected to have taken the impediment into account at the time of the conclusion of the contract or to have avoided it or overcome it or its consequences.

If the delay is caused by a party the seller has engaged to wholly or partly fulfil the contract, the seller is only exempt from liability for damages if the party he has engaged is also exempt from liability for damages under the preceding paragraph. This also applies if the delay is caused by a supplier who has been engaged by the seller or by any other party at an earlier stage in the sales transaction.

In accordance with the preceding paragraphs, the indirect loss referred to in section 67, paragraph (2), is not compensated.

The buyer always has a right to compensation if delay or loss is due to negligence on the part of the seller.

28. If the seller is prevented from fulfilling the contract on time, he shall notify the buyer of the impediment and its effect on his performance. If the buyer does not receive such notification within reasonable time after the seller was aware of or should have been aware of the impediment, the buyer has a right to compensation for the loss which could have been avoided if he had been notified in time.

Notice of avoidance and damages

29. If the goods have been delivered too late, the buyer may not declare the contract avoided or make a claim for damages on grounds of the delay, unless he notifies the seller, within reasonable time after he has learnt that the delivery has taken place, that he is declaring the contract avoided or wishes to claim damages. However, if the buyer declares the contract avoided, he does not need to specially notify the seller that he wishes to claim damages.

Remedies in the case of goods which do not conform with the contract

Remedies

30. If the goods do not conform with the contract and this is not attributable to the buyer or to circumstances which are attributable to the buyer, under sections 31–40 the buyer may require the seller to remedy the lack of conformity by rectification, delivery of substitute goods, or price reduction, or to declare the contract avoided and in addition he may claim damages. The buyer may also withhold payment in accordance with section 42.

Examination of the goods after delivery

31. When the goods have been delivered, as soon as circumstances so permit, the buyer shall examine the goods in accordance with generally accepted business practices.

If it is apparent that the goods are to be transported from the place of delivery, the buyer may postpone the examination until the goods have arrived at their destination.

If the buyer changes the destination of the goods while they are in transit or sends on the goods without having had a reasonable opportunity to examine them and the seller was aware of or should have been aware of such redirection or forwarding when the contract was concluded, the examination may be postponed until the goods have arrived at their new destination.

Complaint

32. The buyer may not claim that the goods do not conform with the contract unless he has notified the seller of the lack of conformity within a reasonable time after he noticed or should have noticed the lack of conformity (complaint).

If the buyer does not complain about lack of conformity in the goods within

two years of having received them, he forfeits the right to do so unless other provisions are contained in a guarantee or similar pledge.

33. Notwithstanding sections 31 and 32, the buyer may claim that the goods do not conform with the contract, if the seller has acted with gross negligence or in breach of faith and honour.

Rectification and delivery of substitute goods

34. The buyer has the right to demand that the seller rectify lack of conformity free of charge if rectification can be carried out without unreasonable cost or inconvenience to the seller. Instead of rectifying the lack of conformity, the seller may deliver substitute goods in accordance with section 36.

The buyer has the right to demand delivery of substitute goods, if the breach of contract is of substantial importance to him and the seller was aware of this or should have been aware of this. However, the buyer does not have the right to demand delivery of substitute goods if the circumstances referred to in section 23 apply. Nor does the buyer have the right to demand delivery of substitute goods if it is a question of goods which were available at the time of the sale and which, in view of their qualities and what the parties must be presumed to have assumed, cannot be substituted by any other goods.

If the seller does not fulfil his obligations to rectify the lack of conformity, the buyer has the right to compensation for legitimate costs for rectification.

35. The buyer may not demand rectification of non-conformity or delivery of substitute goods if he does not notify the seller of his demand when he makes his complaint or within reasonable time thereafter. This does not apply, however, if the seller has acted with gross negligence or in breach of faith and honour.

36. Even though the buyer does not so demand, the seller has the right to rectify non-conformity at his own expense or deliver substitute goods if he can do so without substantial inconvenience to the buyer or without the risk that the buyer will not receive compensation for his own costs from the seller.

The seller may not claim that he was not given an opportunity to rectify non-conformity or deliver substitute goods if the buyer has rectified the non-conformity and, in view of the circumstances, the buyer could not reasonably be required to wait for rectification or delivery of substitute goods by the seller.

Price reduction and contractual avoidance

37. If the question of rectification of lack of conformity or delivery of substitute goods has not been raised or if rectification of lack of conformity or delivery of substitute goods does not take place within reasonable time after complaint, the buyer may demand a price reduction calculated in accordance with section 38 or may declare the contract avoided under section 39. However, the buyer is not entitled to a price reduction in the case of second-hand goods sold by auction.

38. If the buyer demands a price reduction, the price reduction shall be calculated in such a way that the relationship between the reduced price and the contractual price corresponds to the relationship at the time of delivery between the value of the goods in non-conforming and in contractual condition.

39. The buyer may declare the contract avoided on grounds of a lack of conformity if the breach of contract is of substantial importance to him and the seller was aware of this or should have been aware of this.

The buyer may not declare the contract avoided on grounds of lack of conformity, unless he notifies the seller within reasonable time after he noticed or should have noticed the lack of conformity, or after the time required to rectify the lack of conformity or deliver substitute goods under section 37, that he is declaring the contract avoided. However, this does not apply if the seller has acted with gross negligence or in breach of faith and honour.

Damages

40. The buyer is entitled to compensation for the damage he suffers because the goods lack conformity unless the seller proves that the lack of conformity is due to an impediment as described in paragraphs one and two of section 27. The provisions in section 28 regarding the seller's obligation to notify the buyer of impediments to fulfilling the contract on time apply correspondingly to impediments to delivering goods which conform with the contract.

In accordance with the preceding paragraph, no compensation may be claimed for the indirect losses referred to in paragraph two of section 67.

The buyer is always entitled to compensation if the lack of conformity or loss is the result of negligence on the part of the seller or if the goods did not conform with what the seller had especially pledged when the contract was concluded.

Remedies in the case of defective title to goods

41. If a third party has title to the goods or lien or any other similar right to them (defective title to goods) and the contract does not provide that the buyer shall take over the goods with the limitations due to the rights of third parties, the provisions on complaint in the first paragraph of section 32 and section 33, on rectification and delivery of substitute goods in sections 34-36, on price reduction and contractual avoidance in section 37-39, on damages in section 40 and on the buyer's right to withhold payment in section 42 shall apply.

The buyer is always entitled to compensation for the damage he suffers as a consequence of defective title to the goods which existed at the time of the conclusion of the contract, if he was neither aware of such defective title to the goods nor should have been aware of it.

Remedies for defective title to goods may also apply if a third party claims that he has the right described in the first paragraph above and there are probable grounds for the claim.

Common provisions concerning remedies for breach of contract by the seller

The right to withhold payment

42. If the buyer has the right to claim compensation on grounds of the seller's delay or of non-conforming goods, the buyer may withhold as much of the payment as corresponds to his claims.

Partial breach of contract

43.   If only part of the delivery is delayed or lacks conformity, the provisions concerning the breach of contract in question shall be applied in respect of this part. The buyer may declare the contract avoided in its entirety if the breach of contract is of substantial importance to him with regard to the total contract and the seller was aware of this or should have been aware of this.

If it can be assumed that the seller considers he has fulfilled the contract in its entirety despite the fact that not all the goods have been delivered, the provisions regarding lack of conformity apply.

Contractual avoidance in the case of successive delivery

44.   If delivery is to take place successively and if a part delivery is delayed or lacks conformity, the buyer may declare the contract avoided in respect of the part delivery in accordance with the provisions which otherwise apply for avoidance.

If the delay or lack of conformity gives reasons to assume that a breach of contract giving the right to avoidance will take place regarding any later part delivery, the buyer may on these grounds declare the contract avoided in respect of such later part deliveries, if he does so within reasonable time.

If the buyer declares the contract avoided regarding a part delivery, he may at the same time declare the contract avoided regarding earlier or later deliveries if, due to the interdependence of these deliveries, he would be caused considerable inconvenience by adhering to the contract regarding these deliveries.

The buyer's obligations

Determination of the price

45.   If the price is not implied or stated in the contract, the buyer shall pay what is reasonable with regard to the nature and condition of the goods, the current price at the time of the conclusion of the contract and other circumstances.

46.   If the price is to be calculated according to the number, dimensions or weight of the goods, the calculation shall be based on the quantity of the goods at the time when the risk for the goods passes to the buyer.

If the price is to be calculated according to the weight of the goods, the weight of packaging/packing shall be deducted first.

47.   If the buyer has received an invoice, he is bound by the price stated in the invoice. However, this does not apply if he notifies the seller within a reasonable time that he does not accept the price, if the contract implies a lower price or if the sum required is unreasonable.

Payment

48.   Payment shall be made at the seller's place of business or residence. However, if payment is to be made against the transfer of the goods or documents, payment shall be made at the place where such transfer occurs.

The obligation to pay also includes the obligation under the contract to accept bills of exchange and issue letters of credit, bank guarantees or other securities and to take other measures necessary to make payment possible.

49. If the time for payment is not implied or stated in the contract, the buyer shall pay when the seller requests payment. However, the buyer is not obliged to pay before the goods are made available or they have been placed at his disposal in accordance with the contract.

Before the buyer makes payment, he has the right to examine the goods in the manner which is customary, or which should be allowed in view of the circumstances, unless the form of delivery and payment which has been agreed is not compatible with such examination.

Notwithstanding the preceding paragraphs, if a bill of lading has been issued for transportation of the goods to their place of destination or if the goods are otherwise transported under conditions which prevent the seller from having disposal of the goods before payment has been made, payment may be required against the bill of lading or when the buyer has received the consignment note or other proof that the goods have been transported under such conditions.

Co-operation on the part of the buyer etc

50. The buyer shall

(1) co-operate in the sale in such a manner as may be reasonably expected of him if the seller is to fulfil the contract; and
(2) collect or receive the goods.

Remedies for breach of contract by the buyer

Remedies

51. If the buyer does not pay in time or does not co-operate in the sale in accordance with section 50, sub-section 1, and where this is not due to the seller or any circumstance attributable to the seller, in accordance with sections 52-59 the seller may require payment or other performance or may declare the contract avoided and may, in addition, claim damages. The seller may also withhold the goods in accordance with section 10 and demand interest in accordance with section 71.

If the buyer does not fulfil his obligation to collect or receive the goods and where this is not due to the seller or any circumstance attributable to the seller, section 55, section 57, paragraphs 2-4, and section 58 apply.

Demand for payment and other fulfilment of the contract

52. The seller may adhere to the contract and demand payment.

However, if the buyer cancels an order for goods which are to be manufactured or supplied especially for him, the seller may not adhere to the sale by completing the manufacture, making preparations for delivery and demanding payment. However, this does not apply if a cancellation would result in substantial difficulty for the seller or risk that the seller's loss as a result of

cancellation would not be reimbursed. Damages on the grounds of cancellation are estimated in accordance with sections 67-70.

If the goods have not yet been delivered, the seller forfeits the right to demand payment if he waits an unreasonably long time before demanding payment.

53.   The seller may adhere to the contract and require the buyer's co-operation in accordance with section 50, sub-section 1. However, the buyer is not obliged to co-operate in the sale if there is an impediment which he cannot overcome or if his co-operation would require unreasonable sacrifices with regard to the seller's interest in the buyer's co-operation.

However, if the circumstances mentioned above cease to apply within a reasonable time, the seller may require the buyer's co-operation.

The seller forfeits the right to require the buyer's co-operation if the seller waits an unreasonably long time before presenting such a requirement.

Contractual avoidance due to delay in payment

54.   The seller may declare the contract avoided on the grounds of delay in payment on the part of the buyer, if such delay constitutes a substantial breach of contract.

If the seller has specified a fixed additional period of time for payment and this period is not unreasonably brief, the contract may also be declared avoided if the buyer fails to make payment within the additional time allowed.

While the additional period applies, the seller may only declare the contract avoided if the buyer states that the payment will not be made within this period.

If the goods have come into the buyer's possession, the seller may only declare the contract avoided if he has reserved the right to avoidance or if the buyer has rejected the goods.

Contractual avoidance on the grounds of lack of co-operation

55.   The seller may declare the contract avoided if the buyer does not co-operate in the sale in accordance with section 50, sub-section 1, and if the breach of contract is not of substantial importance for the seller and the buyer had been aware of this or should have been aware of it. Similarly, the seller may declare the contract avoided if the buyer did not collect or receive the goods in time where it is stated or implied by the contract or the circumstances that the seller has a special interest in disposing of what he has sold.

Moreover, the seller may declare the contract avoided if, within a fixed additional time period which the seller specifies for the buyer and which is not unreasonably brief, the buyer fails to

(1) co-operate in the sale in accordance with section 50, sub-section 1; or
(2) collect or receive the goods in cases where it is stated or implied by the contract or the circumstances that the seller has a special interest in disposing of what he has sold.

While the additional period applies, the seller may only declare the contract avoided if the buyer states that he will not fulfil his obligations within this additional period.

Contractual avoidance in the case of successive deliveries

56.   If payment is to be made in stages, in special part payments, as deliveries take place, and if there is delay in payment for any delivery, the seller may declare the contract avoided as regards such a delivery in accordance with the provisions which otherwise apply for avoidance.

The seller may also declare the contract avoided as regards a subsequent delivery if there is reason to suppose that delay in making payment which would justify avoidance will be repeated.

Damages

57.   The seller has the right to compensation for the damage he suffers as a result of the buyer's delay in making payment, unless the buyer proves that the delay is due to the law, to a failure or breakdown in transport or communications' facilities or means of effecting payment or other similar hindrance which the buyer could not reasonably have been expected to take into account at the time of the conclusion of the contract and the results of which he could not have reasonably avoided or overcome.

The seller is also entitled to compensation for the damage he suffers if the buyer does not co-operate in accordance with section 50, sub-section 1, or if the buyer fails to collect the goods in time or receive the goods in cases where it is stated or implied by the contract or the circumstances that the seller has a particular interest in disposing of what he has sold. However, there is no right to compensation in such cases if the buyer proves that there has been an impediment of the type specified in section 27, paragraph 1 or 2, preventing him from co-operating or from collecting or receiving the goods.

In accordance with the second paragraph, indirect loss as covered by section 67, paragraph 2, is not compensated.

The seller always has a right to compensation if the breach of contract or the loss is due to negligence on the part of the buyer.

58.   If the buyer is prevented from fulfilling the contract in time, he shall notify the seller of the impediment and its effect on the possibilities of fulfilling the contract. If the seller does not receive such notification within a reasonable time after the buyer was aware of or should have been aware of the impediment, the seller has a right to compensation for the loss which could have been avoided if he had been notified in time.

Notice of avoidance and damages

59.   The seller may not declare the contract avoided on the grounds of the buyer's delay in paying, collecting or taking over the goods if he does not notify the buyer of his avoidance before fulfilment of the contract has taken place.

If the buyer has co-operated in accordance with section 50, sub-section 1, but such co-operation has occurred too late, the seller may not declare the contract avoided or claim damages on the grounds of delay if he fails to notify the buyer of his avoidance or that he wishes to claim damages within a reasonable time after he was aware that the buyer has co-operated. However, if the seller declares the contract avoided, he does not need to especially notify the buyer that he intends to claim damages.

Specifications

60.   If the buyer is to specify the form, dimensions or other qualities of the goods and if he fails to do so at the time agreed or within a reasonable period after the seller has requested such specification, the seller may draw up the specifications in accordance with what may be assumed to be the buyer's interest. However, this does not prevent the seller from applying other remedies. The seller shall notify the buyer of the specifications he draws up and prescribe for the buyer a reasonable time within which the buyer may change the specifications. If the buyer does not change the specifications within the prescribed period, the seller's specifications become binding.

Anticipated breach of contract

Right to stop performance under the contract

61.   If it appears after the conclusion of the contract that the actions or financial situation of one of the parties give every reason to anticipate that he will not fulfil a substantial proportion of his obligations, the other party may for his part suspend fulfilment of the contract and withhold his performance.

If the seller has already dispatched the goods and if it appears that circumstances such as those covered by the first paragraph exist in respect of the buyer, the seller may prevent the handing over of the goods to the buyer. This also applies where the buyer has received transport documents in respect of the goods.

The party suspending fulfilment of the contract or preventing the handing over of the goods shall immediately notify the other party to this effect. If he does not do so, the other party has the right to compensation for the damage he suffers because such notification has not been given in time.

The party who has suspended his fulfilment of the contract or prevented the handing over of the goods shall continue to implement the contract if the other party provides acceptable security for his fulfilment of the contract.

Contractual avoidance

62.   If it is clear that a breach of contract will occur which gives one party the right to declare the contract avoided, this party may declare the contract avoided prior to the time for performance. However, such avoidance is without effect if the other party immediately provides acceptable security for his fulfilment of the contract.

Bankruptcy etc

63.   If one party has been declared bankrupt, the estate of the bankrupt party may enter into the contract. The other party may require that, within a reasonable period, the estate notifies its entry into the contract.

If the estate of the bankrupt party enters into the contract and if the time for fulfilment of the contract by the other party is due, the other party may require that the estate complete its performance or, if an extension of time has been granted, that the estate provide acceptable security without unreasonable delay for the fulfilment of the contract. If the time for the fulfilment of the contract

by the other party is not yet due, the other party may require security if such security is necessary to protect this party against loss.

If the estate does not enter into the contract within a reasonable period of time after the other party has required entry into the contract in accordance with the first paragraph, or if the estate does not comply with the other party's requirement in accordance with the second paragraph, the other party may declare the contract avoided.

If the goods are handed over to the buyer or to his estate after the buyer has applied for the appointment of a trustee in accordance with the Composition with Creditors Act (1970:847) or has been declared bankrupt and payment has not been made, the seller may require that the goods are returned. However, it is not necessary for the goods to be returned if payment is made immediately or, where payment for the sale is not yet due, the buyer or the estate provides acceptable security for payment within a reasonable time after being required to return the goods.

If the estate has sold the goods or otherwise has utilised or disposed of them so that they cannot be returned in a substantially unchanged and undiminished state, the estate shall be considered to have entered into the contract.

Joint provisions regarding avoidance and delivery of substitute goods

The effects of avoidance and delivery of substitute goods

64.   If the contract is declared void, the seller's obligation to hand over the goods and the buyer's obligation to pay and to co-operate no longer apply.

To the extent that the contract has been fulfilled, either party may require the other party to return what he has received. In this connection, each party may retain what he has received until the other party supplies what he is to return and also makes payment or provides acceptable security for damages and interest for which he may be liable.

If the seller is to undertake delivery of substitute goods, the buyer may retain what he has received until delivery of substitute goods takes place.

65.   If the contract is declared void, the buyer shall pay for any gain from the goods and also pay reasonable compensation if he has had any other benefit from the goods.

If the seller is to return payment made, he shall pay interest from the day on which he received payment.

Lapse of the right to compensation and delivery of substitute goods

66.   The buyer may only declare the contract avoided or require delivery of substitute goods if he can return the goods substantially unchanged or undiminished.

However, the right to declare the contract avoided or require delivery of substitute goods is not forfeited if

(1) the goods have been spoiled, lost, impaired or diminished as a result of their nature or of any other circumstance which is not attributable to the buyer;

(2) the goods have been spoiled, impaired or diminished as a result of a measure which was required to investigate whether the goods were without fault; or

(3) the goods have been sold in part or in their entirety to a third party in a normal manner or have been used by the buyer for anticipated usage before he noticed or should have noticed the lack of conformity which gives him cause to declare the contract avoided or to require delivery of substitute goods.

Furthermore, the right to declare the contract avoided or to require delivery of substitute goods is not forfeited if the buyer compensates the seller for the loss in the value of the goods which is the result of the impairment or the diminution of the goods.

The extent of damages

General

67.   Damages on the grounds of breach of contract cover compensation for expenditure, price difference, loss of profits and other direct or indirect loss due to the breach of the contract. However, damages under this Act do not cover compensation for loss suffered by the buyer as a result of damage to anything other than the goods which have been sold.

Indirect loss is considered to comprise

(1) loss as a result of reduction or loss of production or turnover;

(2) other loss because the goods cannot be used in the manner intended;

(3) loss of profits as the result of the lapse of a contract with a third party or because such a contract has not been properly fulfilled; and

(4) other similar loss, if such loss was difficult to foresee.

However, a loss which the injured party has suffered in order to limit a loss of a kind which is not covered by the second paragraph is not to be considered an indirect loss in accordance with the second paragraph.

Difference in price

68.   If the contract has been declared avoided and the buyer has made a replacement purchase or the seller has again sold the goods (resale) and if such a measure has been taken with due consideration and within a reasonable time after the avoidance of the contract, the basis for calculating the price difference is the price under the terms of sale and the price for the replacement purchase or the resale of the goods.

69.   If the contract has been declared avoided and if there has been no replacement purchase or resale in accordance with section 68 and if there is an accepted and current price for such goods as are covered by the contract, the basis for calculation of the price difference is the price under the terms of contract and the accepted and current price at the time of avoidance.

Limitation of damage and reduction of damages

70. The injured party shall take reasonable measures to limit his damage. If he fails to take such measures, he must himself bear a corresponding proportion of the loss.

If the damages are unreasonable with regard to the opportunities of the person liable for damages to foresee and prevent the occurrence of damage, and with regard to other circumstances, the damages may be adjusted.

Interest

71. The Interest Act (1975:635) applies as regards the interest on the price and other claims which are not paid in time.

However, where the seller may require payment in exchange for supplying the goods, interest is payable in accordance with section 6 of the Act (1975:635) from the day when the seller makes such a demand, even if the due date of payment has not been determined in advance. This also applies where the seller may require payment against documents or verification which means that the seller may not have disposal of the goods when such documents or verifications have been handed over to the buyer.

However, the second paragraph does not apply if the seller supplies the goods, documents or verification despite failure to make payment.

Preservation of the goods

The seller's obligations

72. If the goods are not collected or received in time or if they are not handed over to the buyer as a result of some other circumstance attributable to the buyer, the seller shall, on behalf of the buyer, take reasonable measures as regards preservation of the goods if he has them in his possession or can otherwise take charge of them.

The buyer's obligations

73. If the buyer wishes to reject goods which he has received, he shall take reasonable measures on behalf of the seller as regards preservation of the goods. If the buyer wishes to reject goods which have been dispatched to him and kept available for him at the place of destination, he shall take charge of them on behalf of the seller if this can be achieved without payment taking place and without unreasonable cost or inconvenience. However, there is no such obligation if the seller or some other person who is acting on his behalf and who can take charge of the goods is at the place of destination.

Storage with a third party

74. If the party who is to preserve the goods has transferred the goods to a third party for storage on behalf of the other party and if the storer has been chosen with due care, the party responsible for preservation of the goods is not held responsible for the goods after the storer has received them.

Compensation for preservation

75. The party who is to preserve the goods on behalf of the other party is entitled to compensation for reasonable expenses and costs due to such preservation. He may retain the goods until compensation has been paid or acceptable security has been given for such compensation.

Resale of the goods

76. The party who is to preserve the goods may sell them if he cannot continue to preserve the goods without substantial costs of inconvenience or if the other party makes unreasonable delay in taking charge of the goods or in paying for the goods or in compensating the cost of preservation.

If the goods are subjected to rapid spoiling or deterioration or if preservation of the goods is unduly costly, they shall be sold if this is possible.

The goods shall be sold with due care. If possible, the other party shall be notified prior to such sale.

77. If a party has the right to sell the goods in accordance with section 76, but they cannot be sold or it is obvious that the price would not cover the costs of such a sale, this party may have disposal of the goods in some other reasonable manner. Before this occurs, the other party shall be notified, if this is possible.

78. The proceeds of such a sale and other benefit that a party has received from the goods, together with the costs incurred, shall be accounted for to the other party. Any surplus shall accrue to the other party.

Gain

79. Any gain yielded by the goods before the time agreed for delivery accrues to the seller unless there was good reason to consider that such gain would occur later. The gain which the goods yield after they are to be delivered accrues to the buyer unless there was good reason to consider that such gain would occur later.

80. The sale of shares includes dividends which are not yet due for payment prior to the conclusion of the contract and any such preferential rights for shareholders to participate in a share issue which it has been impossible to exercise prior to the conclusion of the contract.

81. The sale of an interest-bearing claim includes interest which has accrued but which is not yet due for payment at the agreed time for delivery of such a claim. In addition to the price to be paid for such a claim, the buyer shall pay the seller a sum corresponding to such interest unless the claim was sold as a doubtful claim.

Notifications

82. If a notification which the buyer shall make to the seller in accordance with sections 23, 24, 29, 32, 35, 39, 47 or 61 has been dispatched in an appropriate manner, the notification may be cited, even if it has been delayed, distorted or has not arrived.

This also applies to notification which the seller shall make to the buyer in accordance with sections 52, 53, 59 or 61.

★   ★   ★

This Act comes into force on 1 January 1991.

This Act revokes the Act relating to the Purchase and Exchange of Goods (1905:38 s 1) with the limitation that the references in the Act found in the Act on Commission, Commercial Agencies and Commercial Travellers continue to apply.

However, previous provisions apply as regards contracts entered into before this Act came into force.

On behalf of the Government

ODD ENGSTRÖM

LAILA FREIVALDS
(Ministry of Justice)

Index

Scotland–*contd*
  damage–*contd*
    recoverable, 464
    remoteness of–
      contract, where liability in, 464
      delict, where liability in, 470
  defective products–
    breach of contract for supply of. *See*
      breach of contract for
      supply of defective goods,
      above
    breach of statutory regulation, caused
      by, 475
    criminal liability, 474
    liability arising from national law. *See*
      product liability, below
    See also product liability, below;
      product safety, below
  delict, liability in–
    burden of proof, 471
    causation–
      'but for' test, 469-470
      contributory negligence, 470
      nova causa interveniens, 470
    exclusion of liability, 471
    generally, 468
    international claims, 506-507
    limitation of liability, 471-472
    negligence, 468-469
    prescription and limitation, 472
    remoteness of loss and damage, 470
    third parties, liability for, 472
  English law and, compared, 459-460
  exclusion of liability–
    contract, where liability in–
      common law position, 465-466
      reasonableness test, 467
      statutory controls, 466-467
    delict, where liability in, 447, 471
  General Product Safety Directive,
    implementation of, 474
  international claims–
    delict, choice of law in, 506-507
    recognition and enforcement of
      judgments, 500
  legal system, 459-460
  liability–
    contract, in. *See* contract, liability in,
      above
    criminal, 474
    delict, in. *See* delict, liability in, above
    individual, 474
    pre-contractual. *See* pre-contractual
      liability, below
    product. *See* product liability, below
    third parties, for, 472
  limitation–
    liability, of, where liability in delict,
      471-472
    prescription and, 467-468, 472, 473-
      474
  loss, remoteness of, 470
  negligence, 468-469, 470

Scotland–*contd*
  pre-contractual liability–
    contract or tort, whether liability lies
      in, 461
    non-disclosure during negotiations,
      effect, 461
    parties to contract, interpretation and
      extent of obligations, liability,
      460-461
  prescription, 467-468, 472, 473-474
  product–
    meaning, 472-473
    See also defective products, above
  product liability–
    anomalous provisions, 472-473
    differences between national law and
      Directive, 473
    generally, 472
    prescription and limitation, 473-474
    product, meaning, 472-473
    special provisions, 472-473
    See also PRODUCT LIABILITY DIRECTIVE;
      contract, liability in, above;
      delict, liability in, above
  Product Liability Directive,
    implementation of, 472-474
  product safety–
    generally, 474
    individual liability, 474
    professional, meaning, 474
    specific products, 474
    See also GENERAL PRODUCT SAFETY
      DIRECTIVE; consumer
      protection, above; defective
      products, above
  quantum of damage–
    contract, where liability in, 464-465
    delict, where liability in, 470-471
  safety. *See* product safety, above
  third parties, liability for, 472
Seller
  draft directive on Guarantees for
    Consumer Goods, in, 28-29
  liability of–
    Austria, in, 49, 53-54
    Belgium, in. *See* BELGIUM
    Germany, in. *See* GERMANY
    Greece, in, 204-205
    Ireland, in, 234
    Portugal, in, 350-351
    Spain, in, 378-380
  meaning, Unfair Terms in Consumer
    Contracts Directive, in, 25
Services
  consumer contracts for, in Finland, 117
  defective, in Sweden, 405
  guarantee concerning, in Belgium, 76-
    77
Spain
  agricultural products, 392
  air navigation, liability as to, 387
  breach of contract for supply of defective
    products, 379